MAINSTREAMII

HONG KON(

Mainstreaming Gender in Hong Kong Society

Edited by

Fanny M. Cheung and Eleanor Holroyd

The Chinese University Press

Mainstreaming Gender in Hong Kong Society
Edited by Fanny M. Cheung and Eleanor Holroyd

© **The Chinese University of Hong Kong**, 2009

ISBN 978–962–996–358–3

THE CHINESE UNIVERSITY PRESS
The Chinese University of Hong Kong
SHA TIN, N.T., HONG KONG
Fax: +852 2603 6692
    +852 2603 7355
E-mail: cup@cuhk.edu.hk
Web-site: www.chineseupress.com

Printed in Hong Kong

Contents

Contributors

Fanny M. CHEUNG is currently Professor of Psychology and Chairperson of the Department of Psychology, The Chinese University of Hong Kong. She pioneered the field of gender studies in Hong Kong and set up the Gender Research Centre at the Chinese University. Since the 1970s, Prof. Cheung has been active in promoting women's development. She spearheaded the War-on-Rape campaign and set up the first community women's centre in Hong Kong. She served as the founding Chairperson of the Equal Opportunities Commission from 1996–1999 and a member of the Women's Commission of the Hong Kong SAR Government from 2001 to 2006. Prof. Cheung is Fellow of the American Psychological Association and of the Association of Psychological Science, and a past President of the Hong Kong Psychological Society and of the Division of Clinical and Community Psychology of the International Association of Applied Psychology. Her research interests include cross-cultural personality assessment and gender equality.

Susanne Y. P. CHOI is an Associate Professor of Sociology at The Chinese University of Hong Kong. Her main research interests include gender-based violence, the social correlates of HIV risk behavior, health inequalities, and the health of migrants. Recent publications appear in *Social Science and Medicine, AIDS Care, Culture, Health & Sexuality, International Migration Review, Journal of Conflict Resolution, Human Rights Quarterly, and Journal of Health, Population and Nutrition.*

Priscilla Ching CHUNG is currently an Adjunct Associate Professor of History at The Chinese University of Hong Kong. She served as the Director (Gender) of the Hong Kong SAR Equal Opportunities Commission from 1998 to 2002 and was responsible for the investigation and legal support of the landmark case on Secondary Schools Places Allocation (SSPA) System.

While at the Commission, she also headed the study on Equal Pay for Work of Equal Value. Since returning to the field of History, her work is focused on women in imperial China and her book, *Palace Women in the Northern Sung*, published in 1981, is considered a pioneer work in the field of women in Chinese History. Dr. Chung received her doctorate in History from the University of Pennsylvania and has taught at the University of Pennsylvania, City University of New York, University of Hawaii, and Hong Kong University of Science and Technology.

Anne Marie FRANCESCO is a Professor in the Department of Management and Director of the Centre for Human Resources Strategy and Development at Hong Kong Baptist University. She received an M.A. and Ph.D. in industrial/organizational psychology from The Ohio State University and a B.A. in psychology from New York University. Previously, Prof. Francesco taught at Pace University, New York, the Hong Kong University of Science and Technology, the University of Alaska Fairbanks, The Chinese University of Hong Kong, and the University of Tennessee. She was also the managing director of A.M. Francesco & Associates Ltd., a Hong Kong–based human resource management consulting firm. Prof. Francesco is the co-author of the book *International Organizational Behavior*, and she has written numerous articles and conference papers. Her current research interests include cross-cultural management and organizational behavior, life balance, and culture and feedback processes.

Anthony Y. H. FUNG received his Ph.D. in communication at the University of Minnesota. He is now an Associate Professor in the School of Journalism and Communication at the Chinese University of Hong Kong. His research interests include political economy of popular culture, gender and youth identity, cultural studies, and new media technologies.

Suzanne C. HO is Professor of Community and Family Medicine. She also serves as Director of Postgraduate Programme in Epidemiology and Biostatistics, and Director of Centre of Research and Promotion of Women's Health of the School of Public Health of the Chinese University of Hong Kong. Her major research interests are in women's health, aging, nutritional epidemiology of chronic diseases, particularly osteoporosis, cardiovascular diseases, and the health effects of soy. Her publications have totaled 16 books and book chapters, and over 160 scientific publications in refereed journals.

Eleanor HOLROYD (R.N, Ph.D. Anthropology) is Professor of Asian and Gender Studies and Nursing, Division of Nursing and Midwifery, RMIT. She has formerly been an Associate Professor in the Nethersole School of Nursing, Faculty of Medicine, The Chinese University of Hong Kong. Her research background has focused on the intersection of gender, health, culture and community. Her grants and international publications encompass a number of ethnographic studies including women within a range of informal family caregiving options, health beliefs and cultural associations with Pap smears and mammography screening uptake, migrant women's mental health (Filipino domestic workers) and increasingly her focus has been marginalized women such as female sex workers in respect to health protection and promotion.

KAM Yip Lo Lucetta is an Assistant Professor at the Department of Journalism and Communication of the Chu Hai College of Higher Education. Her current research is on lesbian women and lala communities in China. Recent publications appear in *Lesbians in East Asia: Diversity, Identities, and Resistance* (Harrington Park Press, 2006) and *AsiaPacifiQueer: Rethinking Gender and Sexuality in the Asia-Pacific* (University of Illinois Press, 2008). She and James Welker are guest editors of "Of Queer Import(s): Sexualities, Genders, and Rights in Asia" for *Intersections: Gender, History and Culture in the Asian Context* (Issue 14, 2006). She is the editor and illustrator of *Yueliang de saodong — tata de chulian gushi: women de zishu* (Lunar Desires: Her first same-sex love in her own words) (2001), which includes 26 self-narratives of Chinese women in Hong Kong, Macau and overseas.

Gigi LAM is a Ph.D. candidate with concentration in demography at Hong Kong University of Science and Technology. She earned her undergraduate degree at HKUST with major in Marketing and M. Phil. in Social Science of HKUST. Her Ph.D. dissertation is focusing on the issue of gender development and fertility changes at HK.

Chung Man LEE is a former M.Phil. student in the Department of Economics at the Chinese University of HK.

Eliza W. Y. LEE (Ph.D. in Political Science, Syracuse University, 1993) is Associate Professor in the Department of Politics and Public Administration, The University of Hong Kong. Her current research interests are the politics of social policy development, civil society organizations, local governance, and gender, with particular focus on Hong Kong and its comparison with selected Asian states. Her articles have appeared in *Governance, Policy and Politics, Journal of Social Policy, Voluntas, Public Administration Review*, and *Asian Survey*. She is the editor of *Gender and Change in Hong Kong: Globalization, Postcolonialism, and Chinese Patriarchy* (Vancouver: University of British Columbia Press, 2003).

Hongbin LI is a Professor in the Department of Economics at the Chinese University of Hong Kong. He obtained his Ph.D. in economics in 2001 from Stanford University. His research is focused on two areas: 1) the incentives, behaviors and performance of governments, banks and enterprises in the context of economic transition, and 2) population issues and the development of labor market. His research mostly draws on data from China, and he has several major projects that involve collecting large scale first-hand datasets.

Micky LEE is an Assistant Professor of Media Studies at Suffolk University, Boston. She has previously taught at Ithaca College, New York and the University of Oregon where she obtained her Ph.D. in Communication and Society. Her research interests include international communication and the political economy of telecommunications, information and new information and communication technologies. She is currently working on a project on UN's conceptualisation of women and telecommunications. Her work has appeared in *Journal of Media and Cultural Politics, International Communication Gazette* and *Feminist Media Studies*.

LIONG Chan Ching Mario is currently Ph.D. Candidate in Gender Studies of the Chinese University of Hong Kong. He is now completing the dissertation on the social construction of masculinity in fatherhood in Hong Kong. His research interests include fatherhood and critical study on men and masculinities.

Vivian Wei-Qun LOU is currently an Assistant professor at the Department of Social Work, The Chinese University of Hong Kong. Dr. Lou received her BEd (Psychology) and MEd (Psychology) from the East China Normal University; and obtained her Master of Social Work and Ph.D. (Social Work) from The University of Hong Kong. Her research projects focus on the social adaptation and mental health of women and older adult. She has also a keen interest in practice research on factors that contribute to the enhancement of mental health status.

Grace C. L. MAK is a Principal Lecturer at the Department of Educational Policy and Administration, the Hong Kong Institute of Education, and was formerly an Associate Professor at the Chinese University of Hong Kong. She is also a short-term consultant to development education projects in Asia, the current one with a focus on rural girls' empowerment in China. Her research areas are women and development, basic education, and teacher education. She edited *Women, Education and Development in Asia* (Garland, 1996) and co-edited (with G. Postiglione) *Higher Education in Asia: An International Handbook and Reference Guide* (Greenwood, 1997).

NGO Hang-yue is a Professor at the Department of Management, The Chinese University of Hong Kong. He received his M.A. and Ph.D. degree in sociology from the University of Chicago. His current research interests include gender and employment, human resource management, and organization studies. He published more than 50 articles in academic journals on these areas. His recent works appear in *Sex Roles: A Journal of Research, Human Relations, Journal of World Business*, and *International Journal of Human Resource Management*.

PUN Ngai is Associate Professor of Hong Kong Polytechnic University. Her current researches are on global production, gender and labour in China. Representative publications include *Made in China: Subject, Factory Women Workers in a Global Workplace* (2005, Duke University Press); *Remaking Citizenship in Hong Kong: Community, nation and the global city* (co-editor, 2004, RoutledgeCurzon); "Opening a Minor Gene of Resistance in Reform China: Dream, Scream and Transgression in a Workplace" (Fall, 2000) in *Positions*; and "Subsumption or Consumption?: The Phantom of Consumer Revolution in Globalizing China" (Nov, 2003) in *Cultural Anthropology*.

Carole J. PETERSEN is currently the Interim Director of the Spark M. Matsunaga Institute for Peace and Visiting Professor at the William S. Richardson School of Law, University of Hawaii at Manoa, where she teaches Administrative Law, Legal Practice, and Human Rights. She previously taught law at the University of Hong Kong (1991–2006) and the City University of Hong (1989–91). She also served as the Director of the University of Hong Kong's Centre for Comparative and Public Law (2001–2004) and was an active member of its Women's Studies Research Centre.

Petersen holds a BA from the University of Chicago, a JD from Harvard Law School, and a Postgraduate Diploma in the Law of the People's Republic of China from the University of Hong Kong. Her recent books include: *Academic Freedom in Hong Kong* (co-authored with Jan Currie and Ka Ho Mok; Lexington Books, 2006) and *Human Rights in Asia* (co-edited with Randall Peerenboom and Albert Chen; Routledge 2006).

Margaret A. SHAFFER is the Richard C. Notebaert Distinguished Chair of International Business and Global Studies at the Sheldon B. Lubar School of Business, University of Wisconsin-Milwaukee. She was a professor with the Department of Management, Hong Kong Baptist University. She received a Ph.D. in organizational behavior and human resource management from the University of Texas at Arlington. Before joining HKBU in 2000, she taught at the Hong Kong Polytechnic University for 5 years. Dr. Shaffer is an active researcher in international management, with research streams in the areas of work-life balance and expatriation. She has published in leading management and international journals, and she has extensive business experience as a manager and consultant.

Siumi Maria TAM is Associate Professor in the Department of Anthropology, and co-chairs the Gender Studies Programme, the Chinese University of Hong Kong. She is a cultural anthropologist with research interests in issues of cultural identity in relation to gender, family, cross-border mobility, and social transformation. Her area focus is Hong Kong and mainland China. Her recent projects include a study of polygyny across the Hong Kong–China border, and transnational family networks among the Nepalese.

Catherine So-kum TANG obtained her Ph.D. in Clinical Psychology at the University of North Texas, USA. She has been at the Chinese University of Hong Kong for 19 years, as a Professor in the Department of Psychology and past Director of Graduate Studies in Clinical Psychology, Postgraduate Degree Programs in Trauma Psychology, Gender Research Program, and Gender Studies Program. Currently, she is a Professor, deputy head of the Department of Psychology, and Director of Clinical Psychology Program at the National University of Singapore. She is an active researcher with over 200 academic publications, book chapters, and conference presentations on violence against women, family violence, women's health, and psychotraumatology, etc.

Kwong-leung TANG is Chair and Professor of Social Work at the Department of Social Work, the Chinese University of Hong Kong. He received his doctorate in social welfare from the University of California at Berkeley. He is the author of "Social Welfare Development in East Asia" (Macmillan & St. Martin's Press, New York, 2000) and a co-editor of the two volume set entitled "What is Globalization? Critical Perspectives from North and South" and "What is Globalization? Critical Regional Perspectives" (Palgrave, New York, 2007). His academic interests include East Asian social welfare, law and social policy, and human rights and women's rights.

Kwok-fai TING is a Professor in the Department of Sociology at the Chinese University of Hong Kong. His areas of interest include life course studies, marriage and family, and statistical methods. Recent publications appear in *Marriage and Family* and *International Migration Review*. He is currently working on a diffusion model of global fertility decline.

Edward Jow Ching TU is Associate Professor of the Division of Social Science, Hong Kong University of Science and Technology. His specialty includes population aging, fertility and gender, mortality and aging, population transition in more and less developed countries. He received his graduate training in University of Tennessee and University of Pennsylvania.

WONG Pik-wan is a Lecturer at the General Education Centre, the Hong Kong Polytechnic University. She obtained her Ph.D. in Political Science from the University of California at Los Angeles. Her major teaching and research interests are in the fields of China/Hong Kong Studies, political studies, and gender studies, especially women and politics, women's movements, and women's history.

Wai-ching Angela WONG is an Associate Professor and Head of Graduate Division in Cultural Studies of the Department of Cultural and Religious Studies at the Chinese University of Hong Kong and an Honorary Professor of the Divinity School of Chung Chi College. She is the Acting Chairperson of Gender Studies Committee and an Executive member of the Gender Research Centre, Hong Kong Institute of Asia-Pacific Studies at CUHK. Her area of interests include: French Feminisms, Sexuality, Gender, Christianity and Postcolonial Hong Kong. She is currently a Trustee of the United Board for Christian Higher Education in Asia, and was formerly a member of the Presidium of Christian Conference of Asia. Her works include: *"The Poor Woman"*: *A Critical Analysis of Asian Theology and Contemporary Chinese Fiction by Women* (Peter Lang, 2002) and "Negotiating Gender Identity: Postcolonialism and Hong Kong Christian Women" in *Gender and Change in Hong Kong: Globalization, Postcolonialism, and Chinese Patriarchy* (UBC Press, 2003).

William C. W. WONG was Associate Professor in the Department of Community and Family Medicine, and Director of Men's Health Diploma, the Chinese University of Hong Kong. He is now Associate Professor and Director of General Practice and Primary Care Education at the University of Melbourne. His main research interests are sexual health, men's health and travel medicine. He works closely with social science disciplines applying both qualitative and quantitative research methodology in medicine. He has published nearly 70 papers on sex work, sexually transmitted infections, and homosexuality. The results of these researches were disseminated to the general public through 42 newspaper reports and, radio and TV interviews.

Hon Ming YIP is Professor in the Department of History, the Chinese University of Hong Kong. She published *Shehuishi yu Zhongguo funü yanjiu* (Social History and the Studies of Chinese Women) (1992), *Zhuti de zhuixun: Zhongguo funushi yanju xilun* (In Search of Subjectivities: Historical Studies of Chinese Women) (1999), and articles on women's/gender history, modern and contemporary Chinese socioeconomic history, local history of north and south China, Hong Kong–China relations and Chinese overseas networks. She is the co-editor of *Tung Chung before and after the New Airport: An Ethnographic and Historical Study of a Community in Hong Kong* (2005) and *Xingbiexue yu funü yanjiu, Huaren shehui de tansuo* (Gender and Women Studies in Chinese Societies) (1995) and the co-compiler of *Women in China: Bibliography of Available English Language Materials* (1996). Among her current research projects are "women's culture and the local culture of south China," "gender and colonialism," and "class, race, and gender in pictorial China."

Junsen ZHANG obtained his Ph.D. in Economics in 1990. Since 1993 he has been at the Chinese University of Hong Kong, where he is currently Professor of Economics in the Department of Economics. His research has focused on the economics of family behaviour, including crime, fertility, marriage, education, intergenerational transfers, marital transfers, gender bias, and old-age support (pensions). Using quantitative methods and many data sets from different countries (regions), either micro or macro, he has studied economic issues in Canada, USA, The Philippines, Taiwan, Hong Kong, as well as China. He is an Editor of the Journal of Population Economics, and President of the Hong Kong Economic Association.

CHAPTER 1

Introduction

Fanny M. Cheung

Promoting gender equality requires that we understand gender as a social construct cutting across the multifaceted political, economic and societal spheres. The social construction of gender is defined by the relationship between women and men, and the values associated with these gender roles. The gender lens that society adopts shapes women's experiences and the power structure underlying the relationship between the two sexes. Measures to promote gender equality need to be grounded on gender-based analyses of the social phenomena and sensitive deconstruction of the gender experience.

Gender Mainstreaming

While the women's movement in the late 20th century has succeeded in raising special attention to needs and concerns of women, isolating women without involving men in the process tends to sideline women from the mainstream of development. Empowerment of women through women-specific policies and programs has succeeded in raising the consciousness and competence of women. However, these changes would not be sustainable if only women are involved in the process, and if these concerns are considered just matters concerning women. To tackle the structural constraints to gender equality, the international community has initiated a mainstreaming strategy since the 1980s to integrate a gender equality perspective in social development and policy processes. Gender mainstreaming focuses on the policy processes and ensures that a gender equality perspective is incorporated in the organization, improvement, development and evaluation of these processes. The mainstreaming strategy would situate women-specific empowerment strategies in the context of the underlying social structure.

The Beijing Platform for Action adopted at the United Nations Fourth World Congress of Women (1995) in Beijing established gender mainstreaming as the main global strategy to address 12 critical areas of concern affecting gender equality. Over 160 governments endorsed the Beijing Declaration and Platform for Action (1995). The Platform for Action stipulated that gender mainstreaming could re-organize the common policy process to strengthen and sustain the goals of gender equality. As the first step, gender analysis could be used to evaluate the needs, responsibilities, contributions of women and men and the differential impact of the activities on them. Analysis of the situation with the collection of scientific data would help to correct biased assumptions and stereotypes in decision-making. This process would ensure that women and men have equitable access to, and benefit from, society's resources and opportunities.

The Council of Europe (1998) defined gender mainstreaming as "the (re)organisation, improvement, development and evaluation of policy processes, so that a gender equality perspective is incorporated in all policies at all levels and at all stages, by the actors normally involved in policy-making" (p. 15). The characteristics and prerequisites for effective implementation of gender mainstreaming include a political will, specific gender equality policy, sex-disaggregated statistics, knowledge of gender relations, knowledge of the administration, necessary funds and human resources, and participation of women in decision-making bodies (Council of Europe, 1998, p. 23).

The ECOSOC Agreed Conclusions 1997/2 (United Nations Economic and Social Council, June–July 1997) further outlined the gender mainstreaming strategy in the decision–making processes in the United Nations system. These conclusions delineate the design, budgeting, implementation, monitoring and evaluation of policies and programs using a gender-sensitive approach. The recommended tools for gender mainstreaming include systematic use of gender analysis, sex-disaggregated data, and gender surveys or studies.

Knowledge Base for Gender Mainstreaming

Gender mainstreaming presupposes that the necessary knowledge of gender relations is available for policy-makers. The mainstreaming strategy requires strong gender studies and analytic techniques. The Council of Europe (1998) outlined the methodology and good practices for gender mainstreaming in a specialist report. Examples of these tools included compilation of sex-disaggregated statistics and survey data, setting up of forecasts, calculation of cost-benefit analyses, development of checklists and guidelines for practice, and assessment of gender impact. The report also demonstrated that the systematic application of gender mainstreaming strategies would result in more effective and efficient policies.

Several frameworks have been developed by various national and inter-governmental agencies to assist policy makers in conducting gender analysis (e.g. Canadian International Development Agency, 1997; Status for Women Canada, 1998). Gender analysis collects information on the different conditions that women and men face in the economic, social and legal structures of the society. It highlights their differential needs, access to resources, patterns of involvement, and approaches to solutions, as well as the differential impact of these activities on sub-groups of women and men. It takes into account that gender intersects with other socio-economic variables such as class, age, and ethnicity. Sex-disaggregated data make visible the diversity ignored by gender-blind analysis that assumes scientific data to be neutral. Very different results and interpretation may be obtained when data are analyzed separately by sex across a life-span setting. Identifying between-gender and within-gender diversities enables more specific design of policies to suit specific needs, leading to more equitable and effective outcomes.

Meaningful employment of technical instruments requires users to be cognizant of gender concepts. To complement the technical tools, training and educational tools have been developed to sensitize practitioners and stakeholders on a gender equality perspective. Training workshops and manuals sustain the efforts to raise gender awareness and maintain commitment. Publicity and promotional activities engage the general public to share this commitment. To facilitate a broad-based participation of stakeholders in the planning, implementation and evaluation process, consultative and participatory techniques have to be in place to ensure the exchange of information, experience and knowledge. For example, directories of contacts and information database as well as public forums may be compiled to empower stakeholders to participate in the process (Council of Europe, 1998).

In addition to these practical tools, basic gender research informs policy makers by identifying current issues and problems in a given policy field, and explaining the basis of the gender differences. Gender research and women studies have grown rapidly since the 1970s. Gender scholars worldwide have contributed not only to the knowledge base but have often interfaced with the community to bring the knowledge into action.

The Gender Research Centre (GRC) at the Chinese University of Hong Kong was the pioneer in gender research in Hong Kong. *Engendering Hong Kong Society: A Gender Perspective of Women's Status* (Cheung, 1997) was the first academic treatise on gender analysis in Hong Kong aimed at providing scholars a gender perspective to study women's concerns. The GRC also spearheaded the reporting of sex-disaggregated data by publishing the first statistical profile of gender and society in Hong Kong (Westwood, Mehrain, & Cheung, 1995). Even though the Government's Census and Statistics Department has taken up the responsibility to publish annual statistics on women and men since 2001, there is still a need for multi-level analyses of gender statistics that takes into account the complexity of the gender dimension, in order to provide a sensitive assessment of women's status.

Gender Analyses of Gender Equality and Women's Status in Hong Kong

The concept of mainstreaming gender is complex. In the infancy stage of development of gender equality, the interpretation of equal opportunities prescribes equal treatment irrespective of one's gender. However, in some situations, we need to highlight gender differences in order to promote gender sensitive approaches to achieve equality of outcome. The "sameness vs. difference" or the "equal treatment vs. special treatment" debate in feminism highlights the apparent paradox that there are situations when men and women should be treated the same under "formal equality" where these appear to be the same circumstances. Yet, there are other situations that they should be treated differently under "substantive equality" where there are socially acknowledged differences (Williams, 2000). According to Williams, "to correctly apply the principle of treating men and women the same requires that formal equality be combined with an analysis of gender and power" (p. 207). Gender mainstreaming is a strategy to address the social structures, institutions, values and beliefs which create and perpetuate gender inequality.

According to UNDP (Menon-Sen, October 1998), gender mainstreaming "implies bringing the outcome of gendered socio-economic and policy analysis into all decision-making processes". The use of sex-disaggregated data and gender analyses provides an objective approach to address the concepts of "equality of opportunity", "equality of results" and "equality as transformation" (Fredman, 2003). Formalistic adherence to equality of opportunity that prescribes identical treatment for women and men without taking into account the disparity in the social structure and access to resources may inadvertently perpetuate gender inequality. An examination of the gender differences in key social domains will illustrate the relative status of women viz. that of men and the gaps in equality. Analyses of the relations among these differences help to identify the pervasive influence of gender and the underlying basis of the gender gaps.

Gender mainstreaming differs from specific gender equality policies. The former has its starting point in an already existing policy within a policy field whereas the latter starts from an identified gender inequality problem (Sterner & Biller, 2007). Gender mainstreaming is not only "a strategy for obtaining the objectives of gender equality policy, but it also becomes a way of *developing* the gender equality policy. That is a result of the fact that new objectives can be detected when a gender perspective is integrated into new policy areas" (p. 6). Gender mainstreaming concerns both women and men, and the responsibility is spread on all actors in policy-making.

Gender mainstreaming has been designated as one of the strategies and priorities of the work of the Women's Commission in Hong Kong. This book begins by examining the changes in women's status in Hong Kong and areas where women's status has improved or stagnated. We adopt the multidisciplinary approach to inform policy-making and to review policy implications. The chapters in the Gender Analyses Section present sex-disaggregated data to analyze the gender disparities and changing trends of women's situation relative to that of men. According to the UNDP Human Development Report (United Nations Development Program, 2006), the key indicators of the Gender-related Development Index (GDI) include life expectancy at birth, adult literacy rate, educational enrolment and earned income. The key indicators of the Gender Empowerment Measure (GEM) include relative proportion of women in legislature and in professional and technical positions, and gendered income differentials. Recent Human Development Reports also include analyses of gender inequality in economic activities, political participation, work burden and time allocation. In the 2006 Report, Hong Kong ranked 22nd among 136 ranked countries and regions on the Gender-related Index (GDI), and 22nd among 177 countries and regions on the overall Human Development Index (HDI). The 2006 Report did not have sufficient information on Hong Kong's performance on the Gender Empowerment Measure (GEM). Compared to other Asian countries at a high level of human development, Hong Kong fell behind Japan (7th on HDI, 13th on GDI, and 42nd on GEM) but slightly ahead of South Korea (26th on HDI, 25th on GDI, and 53rd on GEM) on the first two indicators. For Singapore where the GDI was not available, its HDI is ranked 25th and GEM is ranked 18th, which suggests that women's status is higher in Singapore than in Japan and South Korea. As a country at the medium level of human development, China ranked 81st on the HDI and 64th on the GDI (data on GEM not available).

Global comparison of statistics on a more comprehensive range of data related to gender issues, including demography, health, education, work, violence against women, poverty, decision making, and human rights, may be found in the *World's Report on Women 2005: Progress in Statistics* (United Nations, 2006), in which Hong Kong SAR is listed under China. The Report emphasizes the importance of collecting sex disaggregated data, especially at the more detailed level in which gender interacts with other social variables such as age, education and marital status.

Objective indicators such as those included in the UNDP HDI and GDI ride on the coattail of the overall socioeconomic development of the region or country. On the surface, the general public may hold an impression that women's overall status in Hong Kong is rather good. In a 2005 survey of the general public's attitude toward women's affairs, 85% of the male respondents and 77% of the female respondents believed that women's social status has improved over the past 10 years; 72.5% of the male respondents and 63% of the female respondents considered the status of women to be high or very high (Gender Research Centre, 2005). However, these impressions have not taken into account the diversity and complexity in women's backgrounds, and the interaction between gender and class and other social factors. Such complacency may mask the discrepancy among different groups of women, and the relative discrepancy between women and men.

The chapters in the first section of this book provide detailed analyses of the key dimensions that illustrate the relative status of specific groups of women and areas of inequality, including education, labour force participation, earnings differential, and political participation. The individual chapters provide more sensitive analyses of the objective indicators to reflect the complexity of gender inequality with implications for more gender-sensitive policy-making. Although some of the chapters may overlap in their coverage of similar topics, the different disciplinary perspectives they bring illustrate the multifaceted and interrelated nature of the issues and the strength of the interdisciplinary approach to gender analyses.

Although women's access to all levels of education has improved in the past two decades, Mak, in her chapter on "Girls' Education in Hong Kong: Incidental Gains and Postponed Inequality", contends that more sophisticated studies show that the gains are incidental products of haphazard policy and poorly coordinated social developments. These gains do not result in a "fundamental shift in women's subsequent life chances" and are not based on a strategic policy grounded in an ideology of gender equity. The improvement of women's educational enrolment paralleled the overall economic prosperity and social changes in the 1970s through 1990s with the result that gender inequality was only postponed to later life spheres of work, marriage and family. Mak raises questions about the simple comparison of numerical gender parity in school enrolment. She identifies an agenda for future research that requires a shift of attention from the structural to the personal to explain the gender gaps as well as the gender differences in school performances.

In their chapter on "Gender, Work and Employment in the Global Condition", Ngo and Pun review the long-term trends and recent changes in Hong Kong women's work and employment, given the social and economic impacts of globalization. They find that economic necessity has resulted in an increase in married women's participation in the paid labour force and the rise of dual-career families. At first glance, globalization seems to have a lesser impact on women who are unemployed. However Ngo and Pun's carefully conducted detailed analyses provide alternative explanations for this apparent trend. The trend of income and occupational polarization accompanying economic globalization has exacerbated the discrepancies among women in the labour force based on their age and educational attainment. The gendered pattern of unemployment rate is reduced and the duration of unemployment is lengthened for women over 30, showing the need for disaggregating statistics by gender and other social variables like age and education. Despite a rise in women's participation in professional and managerial positions, occupational sex segregation has in fact increased in the last decade. Gender gaps in earnings differentials have also widened especially in the low-income jobs, posing a risk of 'ghettoization' in low-paying service and elementary occupations that offer little advancement and job security. The disadvantages posed for marginalized groups of women, such as new immigrant women from Mainland China, are highlighted by their concentration in the low-skilled jobs marginal employment status and low income attainment.

Lee, Li, and Zhang provide more detailed economic analyses of occupational gender inequality in their chapter on "Gender Earnings Differentials in Hong Kong". The economic decomposition analysis illustrates a technical and scientific method that can be used to tease out underlying bases of gender earnings differentials. The overall narrowing of the gap in earnings differentials in the last decade of the 20th century is attributed to the increased educational achievement of women. By decomposing the earnings differentials between male and female workers into categories such as those due to differences in observable productivity characteristics and those differences due to unexplained factors including sex discrimination, the authors show that the earnings differentials and sex discrimination are more pronounced in lower-paid occupations. They also find that the earnings differentials are wider between married male and married female workers. Apart from the unexplained factors which point to explicit sex discrimination, the differences in observable productivity characteristics such as difference in average working experiences, may be partially informed by the gendered patterns of reproductive/fertility roles and family roles.

Other than economic empowerment, one of key indicators of women's status is their participation in decision-making positions. Wong and Lee's chapter on "Gender and Political Participation in Hong Kong: Formal Participation and Community Participation" shows that despite the increase in the proportion of women in the higher ranks of the civil service, gender gaps with regard to participation in the central and district level of governing institutions and the electoral process are remarkably resistant to change. Similarly, the proportion of women in the judiciary and the government-appointed advisory and statutory committees remains low. They trace the history of the development of community governance from the colonial era to the post-colonial administration. They attribute the exclusion of women from community participation to a localized leadership culture that is "conservative, paternalistic, patriarchal and hierarchical". By examining how political parties and the governing institutions in different countries have institutionalized mechanisms to strengthen women's political participation, Wong and Lee suggest new spheres for women's community participation through democratization of the political system and activism in NGOs and community advocacy causes.

Gender Neutral and Gender Sensitive Policies

The next four chapters on population and fertility, family relationships, social welfare system and reproductive health services demonstrate the need for gender-sensitive perspectives in policy-making. Public policies in these areas are generally made without reference to a gender perspective. As a result, the specific needs of stakeholders are neglected. These chapters illustrate that mainstreaming gender is not intended to just benefit women, but in fact, will generate more effective policies and services.

Tu and Lam's chapter on "Fertility and Gender Equity in Hong Kong" examines the patterns of Hong Kong fertility transition and its relationship to gender equity. Postponement of childbearing has played a great role in the emergence of Hong Kong as one of the lowest per capita fertility rates in the world, a trend they contend is attributable to socio-economic factors. They point out that despite women's higher educational attainment and labour force participation in the individual-oriented institutions, higher gender equity, lower equity in family-oriented institutions and in female reproductive roles have served to both delay childbirth and significantly reduce fertility rates. Tu and Lam adopted a Family Power Model to analyze the empirical relationship between indicators of gender equity and the fertility rate. Extracting data from three Knowledge, Attitude and Practice Surveys conducted by the Family Planning Association in 1992, 1997 and 2002, they showed that reproductive autonomy in different stages of childbearing, as indicated by the congruence between husbands' and wives' childbearing intention, the extent to which wives could reject husbands' sexual requests, and husbands' acceptance of responsibility for contraception, was inversely related to the mean number of children born. Understanding the interrelated social and cultural implications of gendered issues on fertility patterns is a prerequisite to developing a comprehensive and effective population policy in Hong Kong.

Choi and Ting's chapter on "A Gendered Perspective on Families in Hong Kong" provide corroborative evidence to support the centrality of gender equality in analyzing the family system. They review changes in gender relationships within the family in the past two decades. Studies on the division of domestic labour show that despite the smaller family size and women's increased labour force participation, women still shoulder the major responsibility for housework and childcare. They illustrate the perpetuation of gender inequality even with the employment of domestic helpers, contrary to popular beliefs which fail to recognize the invisible tasks of household management and the absence of husbands from the domestic sphere. Some explanations for the gender inequality within domestic spheres are attributed to the gendered-based "public/private, breadwinner/home-maker, and masculine/feminine divides operating at the housework level". Their review of empirical studies on the perception of marital relations, in terms of marital satisfaction, marital consensus, marital communication and marital intimacy, also reveal pronounced gender differences. These differences highlight the prevalence of traditional gender norms and patterns of marital interaction in Hong Kong families. They also identify new challenges to the family structure and relationships posed by globalization and Hong Kong's reunification to China. These empirical studies confirm the family as one of the strongholds resisting the advances in gender equity. The dialectics of a "harmonious family" should be carefully considered in the government's emphasis on the theme of social harmony in its social policies so that gender equity is not undermined.

Tang and Lou's chapter "Social Welfare and Women: The Dominant Approach and its Critique" examines Hong Kong's social welfare system and the associated services catering to women's needs, especially in terms of spousal abuse, childcare, single parenthood, and poverty. They review the "need paradigm" adopted by the colonial and post-colonial government, which bore a narrow focus on only areas with a clear need and public demand for action. Welfare policies have claimed to be gender neutral, and resources were channelled to the family as the primary unit without bringing direct benefits to women. The earlier chapter by Choi and Ting has already illustrated gender inequity embedded in the traditional family system. Where women's needs were identified in social welfare policies, they were identified as vulnerable groups. Tang and Lou critiqued the lack of gender sensitivity in social policies. They argue for a feminist analysis and the involvement of women's groups and NGOs in pioneering new social services that empower women to address their own needs, enhance women's economic security and rights, and improve the power relations within the family. Mainstreaming gender in social policy would provide a policy vision that leads to sustainable development and equal opportunities.

Holroyd, Ho, and Wong's chapter on "Improving Gender Equity in Hong Kong's Reproductive Health Services" illustrates how gender impacts health and health services. Using reproductive health as the focus, they explain how traditional gender norms pose barriers to accurate health information and prevention related to cervical cancer, sexuality and sexual health. Gender power differentials affect reproductive health risks and access to health services. These gendered vulnerabilities are not limited to female sex workers who are particularly exposed to abuse and sexually transmitted infections; these vulnerabilities also apply to young women and women in marital relationship who have limited ability to negotiate their rights to reproductive health. The lack of gender perspectives may unwittingly "create, maintain or reinforce gender roles and relations that may be damaging to health". The authors advocate the adoption of the World Health Organization guidelines on developing gender-sensitive health policies and reforms in Hong Kong.

Deconstruction of Gender Equity Issues

Gender analyses of existing policies have highlighted gendered bases for inequity that pose as barriers, create vulnerabilities, and limit access to equal opportunities. These specific gendered barriers illustrate the complexities of gender and how they contextualize the social milieu from which policies and services operate. Some of these barriers have traditionally been posed as women's problems. However, deconstructing these issues in a gender perspective will identify how both women and men are involved as actors as well victims of the system. Studies of these gender issues extend beyond simple disaggregation of data by sex, but also other empirical and qualitative approaches to cover the breadth and depth of gender issues in complex social contexts.

One of the critical areas of concern for Hong Kong women raised by the Beijing Platform for Action (1995) is violence against women. Tang's chapter on "Gender-based Violence in Hong Kong" reviews the relevant studies on the various forms of gender-based violence in Hong Kong, including the prevalence and the impact of rape, sexual violence, intimate partner abuse, sexual harassment and child sexual abuse. She identifies the gaps between prevalence rates and reported cases and critiques the current approaches to prevention and treatment. She situates gender-based violence in the wider structure of gender inequality and associated cultural myths. Citing international best practices, she advocates a gender mainstreaming strategy by adopting a more complex women-centred approach to examine gender-based violence within the context of the women's lives that involves local and international communities in a concerted effort to combat violence.

The analyses of gender differences in many social issues have focused on stereotypes and cultural ideologies as the underlying construction of gender. The Beijing Platform for Action (1995) has included women and the media as one of the critical areas of concern. In their chapter on "Media Ideologies of Gender in Hong Kong", Lee and Fung identify the ways that mass media perpetuates gender inequality in its representation of masculinity and femininity, as well as the commoditisation of the female body, especially through the contemporary attention given to the body slimming discourse. By adopting a gender lens to evaluate the media's portrayal of gender rather than just referring to quantitative measurement of male and female statistics, they deconstruct gender ideology in a historical, political and socio-economic context. They also call for attention to be paid to the representation of marginalized groups of women in the media.

Women's roles have undergone major changes in the 20th century. One of the challenges women in Hong Kong face as more women begin to take up senior positions at work is the interface between the traditional roles of the homemaker and the modern roles of women as professionals and managers. The identity of working women in senior positions in Hong Kong poses an interesting reflection on the conflict between the concept of a marginalized homemaker and that of an ideal worker (Williams, 2000), as well as on the dichotomy of masculinity vs. femininity in the image of professional women. Francesco and Shaffer's chapter "Working Women in Hong Kong: *Neuih Keuhng Yahn* or Oppressed Class?" reviews local studies that examine these issues. The availability of low cost domestic help provides the milieu that facilitates the career development of educated women while, at the same time, perpetuates gender role inequality within families where in the absence of negotiation of domestic roles, such work is passed on to other women from third world countries. Their pragmatic perception of their career success in terms of financial security for the family provides a possible interface between work and family for these women, although women still tend to experience more work-family conflict than their male counterparts. The ideal of retaining the feminine roles of wife and mother also makes the masculine image of a strong woman unattractive, which in turn, reinforces the acceptance of sexist stereotypes among women professionals. Studies that show the predominance of the family role among women professionals and the more permeable boundaries between work and family for Hong Kong Chinese suggest the need for more family-friendly policies in the workplace.

The campaign for gender mainstreaming has been framed in the context of improving women's status within the existing social structure, such as the family, marriage, and heterosexual relationships. Wai Ching Wong explores the emerging discourse on women's sexuality and feminists' agency in defining and controlling their bodies in her chapter "Our Bodies, Our Stories: Narrating Female Sexuality in Hong Kong". With little local research on female sexuality, Wong analyzes the stories available on the representation of Chinese female sexuality, especially on "unusual sexualities" based on accounts of lesbians, women bisexuals and sex workers in Hong Kong. Through the narratives of women with marginal experiences of sexuality, she paints a more informed picture to interpret regular surveys of sexual behaviors and attitudes conducted on the general public in Hong Kong. Her chapter provides a different voice on a marginalized subject matter — the minority sexualities, using the marginalized methodology of story telling and narratives. In sharp contrast to the previous chapters in which women's sexualities are presented as oppressed victims of violence or objects of exploitation in the media, the agency of women in expressing their sexual and human rights in this chapter raises provocative questions about gender equality, women's choices, and the creation of women's knowledge. It also demonstrates the tensions faced by the women's movement(s) today and broadens the discourse on the goals of gender mainstreaming.

With rapid and recent changes in the socioeconomic and political milieu, new gender issues have emerged. During the 1980s to 1990s, the fear of reunification with China by many Hong Kong residents and the subsequent flux of migration to western countries created the phenomenon of segregated families in which many male breadwinners remained to work in Hong Kong while their wives and children settled overseas. The reunification of Hong Kong to Mainland China in 1997 and the economic liberalization in China have created other forms of segregated families in which Hong Kong men have taken "second wives" across the border. Despite apparent gains in women's development, the new patriarchies have emerged within men's roles in the family that pose oppressive barriers to achieving equality in gender relations (Tam, 1996).

The fledging interest in rethinking manhood offers opportunities for scholars and practitioners to re-conceptualize gender roles and relations. With the major transformation of women's roles in the later part of the 20th century, there is a concomitant need to realign men's roles beyond that of an ideal worker in order to achieve balance in gender relations. Gender is a construct that examines the relative positions, roles and relations of women and men. The challenge for gender equality in the 21st century is not just to address women's issues amongst women themselves, but also to involve men in the joint effort to remove the unnecessary structural barriers posed by gender in restraining human potentials. Mainstreaming gender calls for the participation of men as equal partners in deconstructing gender.

In examining the emerging and responsive identities that men construct, and the set of related behaviour acted out by men as agents, Tam, Fung, Kam and Liong's chapter "Re-gendering Hong Kong Man in Social, Physical and Discursive Space" examines practices and representations of Hong Kong men in the new century, and provides an alternative look at masculinity by focusing on three groups of men, namely, infidel husbands, male consumers in the beauty industry, and metrosexuals. Their chapter sheds light on the heterogeneity of masculinity as ideology and as praxis, challenging the stereotypic idea of manhood which often renders masculinity invisible, and in turn informs the processes of gender identity formation and transformation as contextualized problematics rather than diametrical opposites of males and females. At the same time, the budding development of men's studies in Hong Kong offers the opportunity to involve more male students, scholars and practitioners to participate in the gender discourse.

Institutional Mechanisms and Responses

When we first published *Engendering Hong Kong Society: A Gender Perspective of Women's Status* (Cheung, 1997), we observed that women's voices were "murmurs on the fringe of Hong Kong society" (p. 1). In the decade that followed, many changes have taken place in Hong Kong since its re-unification with China in 1997. Some of the major legal instruments and institutional mechanisms that aim at promoting gender equality are now in place.

The Equal Opportunities Commission was set up in 1996 and the Sex Discrimination Ordinance has been implemented for close to a decade. CEDAW was extended to Hong Kong in 1996, and the Hong Kong SAR Government presented its first report to the United Nations in 1999 as part of the delegation from the People's Republic of China (Appendix 1).

Although the government initially resisted the idea of a Women's Commission, it relented and announced its intention to establish the Women's Commission in its report to the Beijing Plus Five review at the United Nations in 2000 (Appendix 1). The Women's Commission came into being in 2001. One of the first strategies adopted by the Commission to promote the status of women was gender mainstreaming. It has organized gender-related training to various government departments to complement its gender mainstreaming checklist. The government has also appointed gender focal points in all government bureaus and departments to coordinate the efforts. Although the strategy has yet to take root inside and outside the government, it provides a sustainable framework to pursue the goals. The second Hong Kong SAR CEDAW report was prepared and submitted to the Central Government in 2004 (Appendix 1) and presented at the United Nations in 2006.

Cheung and Chung's chapter on "Central Mechanisms" provides an overview of the development of these institutional mechanisms in Hong Kong, viz. the Equal Opportunities Commission and the Women's Commission. The historical account reveals the interplay among scholars, activists, politicians, and the government. The initial confusion about the roles of the Equal Opportunities Commission and what feminists have expected in their call for a central mechanism on women's affairs misdirected the advocacy efforts. Reference to the international instruments and processes has been influential in providing the framework as well as the impetus for changes, leading to the eventual establishment of the Women's Commission. The achievements, limitations and challenges of these two commissions are reviewed from the perspective of the authors who participated in the initial stages of these mechanisms.

The chapter "Stuck on Formalities? A Critique of Hong Kong's Legal Framework for Gender Equality" by Petersen reviews the international and domestic legal instruments that are in place, including CEDAW and the Sex Discrimination Ordinance. She critiques the strengths and weaknesses of the provisions, citing case laws as illustration. She also points to the usefulness of the international instruments in pushing forward the development of the equality movement in Hong Kong beyond an infancy stage to that of equality of opportunity (Fredman, 2003) in order to achieve substantive equality. The appendix at the end of this Introduction chapter lists the internet access to relevant government reports on CEDAW, Beijing Platform for Action, and gender-related policy reports in Hong Kong.

Two Decades of Gender Research in Hong Kong

Gender mainstreaming is based on evidence-based knowledge of gender equality. This knowledge base grounds the advocacy of stakeholders and decisions of policy makers on the basis of facts instead of rhetoric. In the European Union's recommendations on the implementation of gender mainstreaming, methods and tools are considered the indisputable cornerstones (Sterner & Biller, 2007) to "1. Ensure that statistics referred to individuals are disaggregated by sex; 2. Ensure that all materials that are the basis for decisions, legislation and programmes are gender analysed; 3. Integrate the gender perspective in other perspectives; 4. Train all involved in gender mainstreaming..." (p. 45). Academic institutions play a major role in providing the knowledge base and training.

In 1985, gender research was formally inaugurated in Hong Kong, Mainland China and Taiwan within the same year (Cheung, Yip, & Kwok, 1995). Initially set up as the Gender Research Programme under the Centre for Hong Kong Studies at the Chinese University of Hong Kong in 1985, the Gender Research Centre was subsequently re-structured under the Hong Kong Institute of Asia-Pacific Studies at the university. It initiated the compilation of bibliographies and gender statistics to support scholarly research on gender issues. It played a catalytic function in promoting gender-related research, course development and curriculum design, professional training as well as advocacy on public policies. For example, its first comprehensive report on sex-disaggregated statistics in 1995 (Westwood, Mehrain, & Cheung, 1995) served as the key reference for subsequent publication of official statistics on women and on men in Hong Kong (Census and Statistics Department (2001a; 2001b) since 2001. Members of the Gender Research Centre helped to establish the first undergraduate minor program and postgraduate research program in gender studies in Hong Kong in 1997 and 1998 respectively. The Centre also initiated training in gender analysis and gender awareness for policy makers and service providers, which has now become part of the gender mainstreaming strategy of the HKSAR government.

As the chapter by Tam and Yip shows, gender research and gender studies have taken root in Hong Kong in the past 20 years. Gender scholars and courses are found in a range of departments across the tertiary institutions in Hong Kong, contributing to the knowledge base as well as the pool of human resources. However, compared to conventional disciplines in established faculties, gender studies remain marginalized in local universities, with limited resources and inadequate infrastructure to support the interdisciplinary nature of the field that spans across faculties and departments. It remains a challenge to mainstream gender studies and a gender perspective within the academia.

One of the notable impacts of gender research lies in the interface between scholarship and action. Many gender scholars in Hong Kong have been active participants in the women's movement and in advocacy. They have joined forces with the community in bringing about some of the major developments affecting gender equality in Hong Kong. They have helped to inform the public and raise the gender sensitivity of policy makers and practitioners through gender-related training.

Conclusion

The chapters in this book demonstrate the importance of gender main-streaming in examining social issues and making decisions that affect women and men. They showcase the divergence of academic disciplines which converge to examine the underlying structure of gender equity. They also present a range of scientific methodologies and technical tools for gender analyses. Adopting a gender perspective and using sex-disaggregated quantitative and qualitative analyses provide a more sensitive understanding of these issues. Appreciating gender diversities allows us to address specific needs of sub-groups and leads to more effective policies and services. Gender analyses offer depth and breadth from which to examine women's status beyond the simplistic rhetoric of formal equality. The international and local studies reviewed in these chapters affirm the centrality of gender research which enrich our understanding of the social structures and trends within contemporary Hong Kong society. While women and men worldwide share common experiences, the case of Hong Kong society illustrates how gender issues can be deconstructed in the context of traditional culture as well as rapid social changes and political transitions in the past decades. The convergence of these global and local efforts in gender mainstreaming will in turn strengthen the study of international and indigenous feminism.

References

Beijing Declaration and Platform for Action (1995). Retrieved on 27 May 2007: http://www.un.org/womenwatch/daw/beijing/platform/index.html

Canadian International Development Agency (1997). *Guide to gender sensitive indicators*. Ottawa: CIDA Catalogue No. E94-266/1997. Retrieved on 27 May 2007: http://www.acdi-cida.gc.ca/cida_ind.nsf/8949395286e4d3a585256413 00568be1/7b5da002feaec07c8525695d0074a824?OpenDocument

Census and Statistics Department (2001a). *Thematic report — Women and men*. Hong Kong: 2001 Population Census Office, Census & Statistics Department, HKSAR.

Census and Statistics Department (2001b). *Women and men in Hong Kong: Key statistics*. Hong Kong: Technical Secretariat, Census & Statistics Department, HKSAR.

Cheung, F. M. (Ed.) (1997). *Engendering Hong Kong society: A gender perspective of women's status.* Hong Kong: The Chinese University Press.

Cheung, F. M., Yip, H. M., & Kwok, P. L. (Eds.) (1995). *Gender studies in Hong Kong, the People's Republic of China and Taiwan.* Hong Kong: The Chinese University Press (in Chinese).

Council of Europe, Directorate of Human Rights, Section on Equality between Women and Men (May, 1998). *Gender mainstreaming: Conceptual framework, methodology, and presentation of good practices.* Final report of Activities of the Group of Specialists on Mainstreaming (EG-S-MS). Retrieved on 27 May 2007: http://www.humanrights.coe.int/equality/Eng/WordDocs/EGSMS(98)%202 %20rev%20-%20Final%20report%20mainstreaming%20May%202000.doc

Family Planning Association of Hong Kong (1992, 1997, & 2002). *Family planning knowledge, attitude and practice survey in Hong Kong.* Hong Kong: The Association.

Fredman, S. (2003). Beyond the dichotomy of formal and substantive equality: Towards a new definition of equal rights. In I. Boerefijin et al. (Eds.), Temporary special measures: Accelerating de facto equality of women under Article 4(1) UN Convention on the Elimination of All Forms of Discrimination Against Women. Antwerpen: Intersentia.

Gender Research Centre (2005). *A survey of the opinions of the general public on women's issues in Hong Kong.* Hong Kong: Hong Kong Institute of Asia Pacific Studies, The Chinese University of Hong Kong. (In Chinese).

Menon-Sen, K. (October 1998). *Moving from policy to practice: A mainstreaming strategy for UNDP India.* UNDP: Retrieved on 3 July 2007: http://www.undp. org.in/Report/Gstrat/

Status for Women Canada (1998). Gender-based analysis: A guide for policy-making. Ottawa: Policy Analysis and Development Directorate, Status for Women Canada. Retrieved on 27 May 2007: http://www.swc-cfc.gc.ca/pubs/gbaguide/ gbaguide_e.html

Sterner, G., & Biller, H. (2007). *Gender mainstreaming in the EU member states: Progress, obstacles and experiences at governmental level.* Sweden: Ministry of Integration and Gender Equality.

Tam, S. M. (1996). Normalization of "second wives": Gender contestation in Hong Kong. *Asian Journal of Women Studies, 2,* 113–132.

United Nations (2006). *World's report on women 2005: Progress in statistics.* New York: UN Department of Economic and Social Affairs.

United Nations Development Program (2006). *Human development report 2006: Beyond scarcity: Power, poverty and the global water crisis.* Retrieved 17 April 2006: http://hdr.undp.org/hdr2006/report.cfm#

United Nations Development Program (2004) *Human development report 2004: Cultural liberty in today's diverse world.* Electronic version available from: http://hdr.undp.org/reports/global/2004/

United Nations Economic and Social Council (June–July 1997). ECOSOC conclusion on gender mainstreaming: Mainstreaming the gender perspective into all policies and programmes in the United Nations system. Retrieved on 27 May 2007: http://www.un.org/documents/ecosoc/docs/1997/e1997-66.htm

United Nations Fourth World Congress on Women (September 1995). Retrieved on 27 May 2007: http://www.un.org/womenwatch/daw/beijing/index.html

Westwood, R., Mehrain, T., & Cheung, F.M. (1995). *Gender and society in Hong Kong: A statistical profile*. HK Institute of Asia-Pacific Studies Research Monograph No. 23. Hong Kong: HKIAPS.

Williams, J. (2000). *Unbending gender: Why family and work conflict and what to do about it*. New York: Oxford University Press.

Appendix 1

Internet Editions of Relevant Gender-related Reports and Policy Statements in Hong Kong

CEDAW Reports

Hong Kong SAR Government (1998). *Initial Report on the Hong Kong Special Administrative Region under Article 18 of the Convention on the Elimination of All Forms of Discrimination against Women.* http://www.women.gov.hk/eng/document/govern/gov.html

Committee on the Elimination of Discrimination Against Women (1999). *Concluding Comments of the Committee on the Elimination of Discrimination against Women on the Initial Report on the HKSAR under the Convention on the Elimination of All Forms of Discrimination against Women.* (Extracted from the Committee's Report on its twentieth session, 19 January to 5 February 1999). http://www.women.gov.hk/eng/document/inter/inter.html

Hong Kong SAR Government (2000). *Follow-up on concluding comments of the United Nations Committee on the Elimination of Discrimination against Women on the Initial Report on the HKSAR under the Convention on the Elimination of All Forms of Discrimination against Women (CEDAW) (Discussion document for the Legislative Council Panel on Home Affairs Meeting held on 5 June 2000)* http://www.women.gov.hk/eng/document/govern/gov.html

Hong Kong SAR Government (2004). *Second Report under the UN Convention on the Elimination of All Forms of Discrimination Against Women (CEDAW)* http://www.women.gov.hk/eng/document/govern/gov.html

Discussion Paper at the Legislative Council Home Affairs Panel Meeting on 8 November 2002 on Second Report under the Convention on the Elimination of All Forms of Discrimination Against Women (CEDAW) http://www.women.gov.hk/eng/document/govern/gov.html

Hong Kong SAR Government (2006). *Response by the Government of the Hong Kong Special Administrative Region (HKSAR) to the list of issues*

and questions with regard to the consideration of periodic report of China (including the second report of HKSAR) under the Convention on the Elimination of All Forms of Discrimination against Women
http://www.women.gov.hk/eng/document/govern/gov.html

Beijing Platform for Action Reports

Hong Kong SAR Government (2000). *The Report of the Hong Kong Special Administrative Region Government on the Implementation of the Beijing Platform for Action.*
Available from http://www.women.gov.hk/eng/document/govern/gov.html

Hong Kong SAR Government (2005). *The Second Report of the Government of the Hong Kong Special Administrative Region on the Implementation of the Beijing Platform for Action*
Available from: http://www.women.gov.hk/eng/document/inter/inter.html

HKSAR Government Policy Statements on Women

The establishment of the Women's Commission in Hong Kong in 2001 is documented in the following policy papers:

2000 Policy Address: Policy Objectives of the Health and Welfare Bureau. "Promote the Well-being and Interests of Women."
http://www.policyaddress.gov.hk/pa00/epo/ewomen.pdf

2001 Policy Address: Policy Objective Booklet of the Health and Welfare Bureau. "Promote the Well-being and Interests of Women."
http://www.women.gov.hk/eng/document/govern/gov.html

Since 2001, the Hong Kong SAR Government's annual Policy Address, and the Policy Objectives of the Health, Welfare and Food Bureau in particular, include policies related to women:

The Government's Policy Address Archive is available from
http://www.policyaddress.gov.hk/06-07/eng/archives.html

PART I

Gender Analyses of Women's Status in Hong Kong

CHAPTER 2

Girls' Education in Hong Kong: Incidental Gains and Postponed Inequality

Grace C. L. Mak

In the last twenty years both girls' participation in education in Hong Kong and the study of it have seen an advancement, which at the same time underscores a continuing challenge to it as well. Girls have either caught up with or even surpassed boys in access to education and academic performance. Such progress is consistent and has been confirmed with systemic data from the Census and Statistics Department and the Education and Manpower Bureau over the years. At the same time, research on girls' education has branched out, though still on a limited scale, from a narrow focus before. Findings from studies employing different methodologies and theoretical perspectives have advanced our understanding of girls' and boys' performance in different areas of school knowledge. They serve to elaborate the systemic evidence. However, the focus of the new findings on the phenomena of measurable gains has paradoxically revealed conspicuously meagre attention on what has contributed to such phenomena. In other words, the field has advanced more in *what* than *why*. *Why* entails the complex dynamics between structural factors, such as policy and social trends, and the ways girls make use of them. Much has yet to be studied in two dimensions of the problem — girls' subjectivities in terms of their gendered identity formation and its interaction with the public policy and discourse on gender relations and educational provision, and the epistemological issues of gendering in knowledge acquisition and assessment.

This skew advancement in the study of girls' education reflects the dominance of the status attainment approach, which focuses on investigating the structural barriers that have kept women from a fair representation in the public spheres of education, economy and politics. Studies employing this approach in education concern the extent of the gap between males and females in educational participation, including enrollment and performance. This approach has an emphasis on comparable status for males and females and assumes the goal of attaining a status as unproblematic and probably desirable. It ignores the multiplicity and sometimes contradictory values different people attached to it. For example, in a status attainment perspective men and women aspire to gaining status; not getting there reflects only one's inability, hence deficit. It looks at outcome, not process, nor variation within a gender category. It fails to recognize that many women pursue a course of intrinsic gratification and steer away from positions of status by choice. Similarly, it ignores an important dimension of how girls respond to education and why, and why, despite their positive response to education, girls are rated somewhat negatively by society. Members of society attribute girls' success to their conformity and diligence, less admirable qualities than character and creativity that are commonly associated with boys. This ambiguity on girls' achievements underscores the nature of numerical equality as a necessary, but inadequate, condition to reach for a deeper sense of fairness and justice embedded in gender equity.

   In the first part of this chapter I examine girls' access to and performance in education in the typical status attainment approach in the context of policy and social development. I will argue that the gains in education have brought partial benefits, but not a fundamental shift, in women's subsequent life chances. The gains in education are an incidental product more of uncoordinated policy and social developments than an ideology of gender equity. Inequality perpetuates in the economy where male interests continue to be safeguarded. It is postponed but not eliminated. On the other hand, the discourse on girls' performance has drawn forth a fundamental contention between natural and social factors as a valid explanation for gender difference in education. Studies comparing gender difference in education tend to focus on enrollment figures and test scores in order to find out the extent to which girls are catching up with boys. A review of these studies raises questions on what is being compared, why, and whether numerical gender parity or a deeper sense of fairness is the ultimate objective of intellectual inquiry into the subject. In the last section of the chapter I will try to identify gaps in the research approach and topics — the two are closely related — and suggest future agendas for research in girls' education in Hong Kong. These gaps request a shift of attention from the structural to the personal, such as the gendered nature of values and identity formation of boys and girls which impact on their educational participation, and the ways in which they negotiate with the social constraints as well as potential on gender roles. Further efforts in the study of subjectivities and learning processes will be essential in the scaffolding of the field which thus far has rested on the status attainment approach.

Access to Education

This chapter starts by claiming that girls have caught up with or even surpassed boys in education, yet the educational profile of the female population as a whole only partially supports the claim. Table 1 shows that females relative to males have improved notably at upper secondary level and above, but have actually declined at the level of primary education and below. The inconsistency captures a point of social change between expansion for the younger generation and deprivation for the older one.

To better understand the paradox we need to single out each school-aged group. Since 1978 the provision of nine-year compulsory education has been enforced. The school attendance rates of children in the 6–11 and 12-16 age groups shown in Table 2 attest to this policy enforcement. The rates of boys and girls in the 6–11 age group are the same. Those in the 12–15 group would be near 100% due to the effect of compulsory education. The inclusion of age 16, typically Secondary 4 and post-compulsory, in the group has brought down the figures. The figures of girls of both 1991 and 2001 are higher than those for boys. Girls' school attendance rates have

Table 1. Percentage of Females Relative to Whole Population by Level of Educational Attainment, 1971–2001 (in %)

Educational attainment	1971	1981	1991	2001
No sch/kg	64	63	72	73
Primary	46	45	48	52
Lower secondary	40	41	40	43
Upper secondary	n.a.	46	51	52
Matriculation	40	38	49	54
Tertiary non-degree	n.a.	50	46	50
Degree	24	28	37	47

Sources: Census &Statistics Department (1988), Hong Kong Annual Digest of Statistics 1987, p. 199; and Census &Statistics Department (2002), 2001 Populations Census Main Report Vol. 1, p. 98.

Table 2. School Attendance Rates by Age Group and Sex, 1991 and 2001

Age Group	1991		2001	
	Male	Female	Male	Female
3–5	94.9	94.9	94.6	94.7
6–11	99.8	99.8	99.9	99.9
12–16	91.8	95.6	96.9	98.0
17–18	54.3	62.7	68.0	74.1
19–24	16.2	14.3	26.8	29.4
25+	0.2	0.2	0.4	0.3

Source: Census & Statistics Department (2002), *2001 Populations Census Main Report Vol. 1*, p. 100.

surpassed boys in the 17–18 age group since 1991 and in the 19–24 age group by 2001.

The compulsory education policy has expanded the base number of girls for transition to the next levels of schooling, which explains the improvement in post-compulsory education in Table 1. The affordability of post-compulsory education allows girls to continue to respond positively to educational provision. In 2003, they constituted 48 percent of enrollment in primary education and 49 percent in Secondary 1 to 5. They began to slightly exceed the number of boys at the age of 16 (32,980 girls and 32,047 boys) and constituted 55 percent of the enrollment in Secondary 6 and 7 (Census & Statistics Department, 2004, p. 270).

These high rates were reflected in higher numbers of female than male candidates who sat the public examination at the end of Secondary 5 and Secondary 7 respectively between 1996 and 2004. In 2004 girls represented 51 percent of the candidates who attempted the Hong Kong Certificate of Education Examination and 56 percent of those in the Hong Kong Advanced Level Examination for the first time in 2004 (Hong Kong Examination and Assessment Authority, 2004a: 20, 83; 2004b: 18, 75). The gains in girls' education are an outcome of the policy of mass education. However, little is known about how this has happened. An ethnographic study of the lad culture of resistance to schooling served to explain how working-class boys in England lost out in education (Willis, 1977). However, another study found that working-class girls employed a different, positive strategy toward schooling (McRobbie, 1978). A similar study of a secondary school in a humble district in Hong Kong found not only inter-gender, but also intra-gender differences in response to education. The students there were streamed into good and ordinary classes. The girls in the ordinary class expected to get married and become housewives, much like the prototype in their neighbourhood; those in the good class aspired to becoming upwardly mobile career women through success in education (Wong, 1995; Ch. 3). These findings suggest that boys and girls view education differently and girls tend to be more receptive to expansion in education and act accordingly. Anecdotal evidence suggests that the inferiority women of the older generation suffer is a constant reminder to girls of the importance of equipping themselves with education for economic independence. However, this plausibility has yet to be substantiated with empirical evidence.

The gender divide in subjects has remained but narrowed. Chinese, English and Mathematics as compulsory subjects conceal any gender divide in numbers. As Table 3 shows, Science subjects continued to attract more boys and Arts subjects more girls. The gender divide is more obvious when viewed in another perspective. Girls as a percentage of all candidates in the following subjects in 2004 were: Physics (40 percent), Additional Mathematics (41 percent), Chinese History (57 percent), Chinese Literature (67 percent), History (59 percent) (HKEAA, 2004a: 54–58).

Table 3. The 10 Most Popular Subjects for Male and Female Candidates
in the HKCEE, 2004

Subject	Male candidates N=31,445 As a % of total number of male candidates	Subject	Female candidates N=33,233 As a % of total number of female candidates
Mathematics	99.8	Mathematics	99.9
Chinese Language	99.6	Chinese Language	99.6
English Language (Syllabus B)	65.3	English Language (Syllabus B)	70.7
Physics	52.2	Economics	55.1
Chemistry	50.7	Geography	45.3
Biology	48.8	Chinese History	40.9
Economics	40.0	Biology	35.6
English Language (Syllabus A)	34.5	Chemistry	34.3
Additional Mathematics	32.6	Physics	33.9
Geography	31.2	History	30.0

Source: Hong Kong Examinations and Assessment Authority (2004). *Examination Report HKCEE 2004*, p. 36.

The pattern is similar at the Hong Kong Advanced Level Examination. Table 4 shows a continuation of the male identity of Physics and Mathematics, the latter no longer a compulsory subject for all students, and female identity of arts and social science subjects.

Again, the gender divide is more obvious when viewed by subject. Female candidates as a percentage of all candidates in the following subjects at Advanced Level in 2004 were: Applied Mathematics (22 percent), Physics (38 percent), Chinese History (65 percent), Chinese Literature (79 percent), History (65 percent) (HKEAA, 2004 (a): 54–58). These figures demonstrate an intensified divide in traditionally gendered subjects from Secondary 5 to Secondary 7.

In the past girls' high participation rates in primary and secondary schools dropped abruptly at tertiary level. In recent years they have sustained. Table 5 shows this steady increase. Women constituted 51 percent of the students by headcount of University Grants Committee supported programmes in 1997/98 and 55 percent in 2003/04. However, the conventional pattern of over-representation at the lower level of study and under-representation at

Table 4. The 10 Most Popular Subjects for Male and Female Candidates
in the HKALE, 2004

Subject	Male candidates N=16,549 As a % of total number of male candidates	Subject	Female candidates N=19,455 As a % of total number of female candidates
Use of English	95.8	Use of English	97.0
Chinese Language & Culture	90.2	Chinese Language & Culture	91.9
Physics	44.9	Economics	31.6
Chemistry	38.3	Chemistry	29.1
Pure Mathematics	33.8	Geography	24.3
Economics	21.5	Physics	21.7
Biology	20.1	Mathematics & Statistics	21.0
Mathematics & Statistics	16.1	Biology	20.3
Geography	13.5	Chinese History	16.2
Computer Applications	12.3	Principles of Accounts	15.8

Source: Hong Kong Examinations and Assessment Authority (2004). *Examination Report HKALE 2004*, p. 40.

Table 5. Women as a Percentage of Students Enrolled in UGC-funded Programmes by Level of Study, 1997/98 to 2003/04, selected years (in % of headcount)

Level of Study	1997/98 (%)	2000/01(%)	2003/04 (%)
Sub-degree	64	67	66
Undergraduate	50	53	54
Taught postgraduate	38	47	51
Research postgraduate	30	38	43
Total	51	55	55

Source: University Grants Committee, 2005.

the postgraduate level persists. In the latter the gap has been closing, with women reaching 51 percent of students enrolled in taught postgraduate programmes and 43% in research postgraduate programmes.

When it comes to distribution by field of study, women remain overwhelmingly represented in the traditionally 'feminine' fields, as shown in Table 6. They continue to be a minority in the sciences, engineering and technology.

Table 6. Women as a Percentage of Students Enrolled in UGC-funded Programmes by Broad Academic Programme Category, 1997/98 to 2003/04, selected years (in % of headcount)

Broad Academic Programme Category	1997/98 (%)	2000/01(%)	2003/04 (%)
Medicine, Dentistry &Health	56	60	64
Sciences	37	39	38
Engineering & Technology	16	23	28
Business & Management	60	62	62
Social Sciences	67	68	65
Arts & Humanities	79	79	76
Education	70	73	74
Total	51	55	55

Source: University Grants Committee, 2005.

The study of enrollment in Hong Kong tertiary education would be incomplete without parallel information on Hong Kong students abroad. Where family finance or students' academic ability allow, overseas education is a popular alternative. In the mid to late 1980s girls made up 27–29 percent, 34–40 percent, and 37–46 percent of Hong Kong students studying in British,

Table 7. Persons Aged 25 and Below Who Were Studying Outside
Hong Kong by Place of Study and Sex, 2002

Place of study	Male (%)	Female (%)	Total (N)
Canada	63	37	19,600
Australia	42	58	16,400
U.K.	55	45	16,100
U.S.A.	51	49	13,200
Chinese Mainland	73	27	3,000
Other places	60	40	5,800
Total	55	45	74,100

Source: Census and Statistics Department (2005), Survey on "Hong Kong students studying outside
Hong Kong" in 2002.

Canadian and Australian tertiary institutions respectively (Mak, 1991: 174). In 2002 the comparable figure had risen to 45 percent (Table 7). The 2002 statistics included tertiary level and below. These figures are indicative of parents' propensity of supporting sons' and daughters' education abroad. The figures concerning the most popular destinations of Hong Kong students which are also relatively expensive — Canada, Australia, United Kingdom, and United States — show an increase by country of girls' proportion from the 1980s. These figures indicate an increase in parents' willingness to invest in daughters' education.

These remarkable gains in girls' education can be directly attributed to educational policy and indirectly to demographic change. The introduction of six-year and nine-year compulsory education in 1971 and 1978 respectively had the effect of gender equality in access to basic education. Girls responded positively once the provision was available. A parallel factor was declining fertility rates. The total fertility rate (number of births per woman) in Hong Kong steadily dropped from 2.67 in 1975 to 0.93 in 2004 (Census and Statistics Department, 2005a). The latter is far below the replacement rate of 2 required for a stable population. According to another count the Total Fertility Rate reached an all-time low of 0.8 in 2001, the lowest in the world. Excluding births in Hong Kong by women from the Chinese Mainland, it had actually fallen to between 0.7 and 0.8 (Civic Exchange, 2005). These low rates can be attributed to late marriage, postponed childbearing and a growing number of women choosing not to marry, factors which were in part an outcome of women's rising educational attainment. Further educational expansion and declining number of children are then conducive to girls' participation. A family typically has one child to two children. Daughters and sons become equally valuable. The Confucian norm of daughters' low value is increasingly diluted by the scarcity of children in the family and increased opportunity in education. However, as will be posed later in this chapter, in arenas of competing interests society continues to be suspicious of girls' success and rewards it somewhat negatively. This begs the question of whether girls' gains in education derived from a gender equality ideology which entails conscious effort in changing values and behaviour, or the chance outcomes of education and demographic changes. The compulsory education policy rested on the rationale of need as a human right, need to protect children, need for economic development and need for employment (Education and Manpower Bureau, 1997: Ch. 3). The need originates from the population in general rather than a specific address to gender inequality; and the emphasis is more on education as a need than a right. The outcome in girls' participation in Hong Kong is incidental and not intended to be gender-conscious or progressive in nature.

Academic Performance

Girls' espousal of increased educational provision is also reflected in their academic performance. Studies in recent years have identified the same trend of girls outperforming boys in general. A study of underachievement among primary school children in Hong Kong in the early 1990s found that more boys were identified as underachievers than girls especially in Primary 5 and 6 (McCall, Beach and Lau, 2000). In 1993–1998 girls consistently performed better than boys in the Academic Aptitude Test which was administered to all Primary 6 students (Equal Opportunities Commission, 1999: Ch. 4). Another study comparing gender difference in academic performance found that just before this period, in 1992 boys as a group did better than girls at Primary 6. However, in the same cohort five years later, girls did better than boys in all areas of the school curriculum in the Hong Kong Certification of Education Examination (Wong, Lam & Ho, 2002).

The Secondary School Placement Allocation System was introduced in 1978 to select Primary 6 leavers for entry to secondary schools. An Academic Aptitude Test (AAT) was administered to Primary 6 students in December each year. The AAT scores of the students in each school were used to scale the internal assessment scores. They were not given to individual students. Students were then ranked in order of academic merit based on the scaled score. They were divided into five different bands, each band consisting of 20 percent of students in the rank order. The top 20 percent were placed in Band 1, the next 20 percent in Band 2, etc. In each co-educational school the allocation was in accordance with fixed numbers of boys and girls. Boys and girls were put into separate rank orders, resulting in different band cutting scores for each sex. In 1998 the banding of individual students was first made public. It was found that girls needed higher scaled scores to get into most Band 1 schools. There was concern about sex discrimination in the system. A computer simulation showed that if boys and girls were admitted solely according to academic merit, girls would constitute 59 percent of Secondary 1 students in Band 1, 48 percent in Band 2, and 38 percent in Band 3 schools, rather than the previous pattern of 50 percent in each band (Equal Opportunities Commission, 1999). This issue brought to public attention the significantly better performance of girls than boys and triggered a court case and heated public debates about gender difference in academic performance and assessment, which will be discussed later in this chapter.

The good performance of girls has led to a general perception that girls have surpassed boys. However, much more needs to be known about the relative strengths or weaknesses of girls and boys. It depends on the criteria in which boys' and girls' performance is examined. When the criterion is achieving grade E or above in at least five subjects in the Hong Kong Certificate of Education Examination, i.e., meeting the basic eligibility for promotion to post-secondary education, 67 percent of the girls and 58 percent of the boys reached this benchmark (HKEAA, 2004 (a), p. 23). Thus girls generally outperformed boys. However, when the criterion is shifted to each subject, the picture is less clear-cut. Table 8 shows that of the candidates who obtained A to C grades in the HKCEE in 2004, girls performed significantly better than boys in languages (Chinese and English), boys performed slightly better in Physics and Mathematics, and the two groups were rather close in Biology, Chemistry, Chinese History, Economics, and Geography. These figures suggest three trends. First, collectively girls did better than boys in the HKCEE. Second, however, except in the languages, the proportions of boys and girls that did well in the HKCEE are close. Third, the gender divide in the non-language subjects is blurring.

The data on the Hong Kong Advanced Level Examination, taken at the end of Secondary 7, pointed to a similar pattern. In 2004, 51.1 percent of female candidates and 48.7 percent of male candidates achieved at least grade E in Chinese and English as well as two other A-level subjects, which satisfied the general entrance requirements for first-degree courses in tertiary

Table 8. Percentage of Male and Female Candidates Who Obtained A-C grades in 10 Most Popular Subjects in the HKCEE, 2004

Subject	% of Male Candidates attaining A-C Grades	% of Female Candidates attaining A-C Grades
Biology	29.6	30.9
Chemistry	27.5	28.1
Chinese History	14.3	14.8
Chinese Language	10.4	21.7
Economics	18.9	20.8
English Language (Syllabus A)	10.2	17.8
English Language (Syllabus B)	7.3	12.7
Geography	19.7	22.5
Mathematics	30.9	27.2
Physics	27.1	23.0

Source: Hong Kong Examinations and Assessment Authority (2004). *Examination Report HKCEE 2004*, pp. 54–59.

institutions (HKEAA, 2004 (b), p. 26). Thus, collectively girls did slightly better than boys. However, the gender divide by subject has grown at this level of education. Table 9 shows that of the candidates who obtained A to C grades in the HKALE in 2004, girls performed significantly better than boys in languages (Chinese and English), and boys performed better in Pure Mathematics, Physics, and Chemistry. The two groups varied only slightly in Biology, Chinese History, Economics, Geography, and Principles of Accounts. The figures suggest that as the level of education goes up, the gender divide in some traditionally 'feminine' and 'masculine' subjects (the languages, mathematics and science) intensifies, but blurs in other subjects. These data have implication on when and what kind of intervention strategies are desirable.

It has been a popular perception that boys perform better in mathematics and science and girls in languages (Maccoby and Jacklin, 1974) and that this difference is natural. Later analyses have confirmed this pattern but with the amendment that the difference is narrowing (Willingham and Cole, 1997; Nowell and Hedges, 1998). This amendment is revealing of the shifting nature of gender difference in performance by type of knowledge. It begs the question of which factors have contributed to the shift. The true nature of the relationship between gender and mathematics is much more complex than people have been led to believe, and individual differences within gender are probably much larger than the differences between genders (Gilligan

Table 9. Percentage of Male and Female Candidates Who Obtained A-C grades in
10 Most Popular Subjects at A-level in the HKALE, 2004

Subject	% of Male Candidates attaining A-C Grades	% of Female Candidates attaining A-C Grades
Biology	16.0	17.8
Chemistry	25.7	19.6
Chinese History	19.7	15.9
Chinese Language & Culture	13.7	24.5
Economics	21.1	17.5
Geography	19.6	21.1
Physics	26.5	18.9
Principles of Accounts	20.0	18.4
Pure Mathematics	27.2	20.5
Use of English	9.4	16.2

Source: Hong Kong Examinations and Assessment Authority (2004). *Examination Report HKALE 2004*, pp. 54–59.

and Kaufman, 2005: 316). In recent years girls have consistently outperformed boys in Mathematics and later in Physics as well, notably in the General Certificate of Secondary Education and Advanced Level examinations in the U.K. Some scholars have identified gender difference in learning styles (Gipps, 1996) or a changing social context (Weiner, Arnot and David, 1997) as factors leading to the change. Both explanations challenge the assumption of natural difference between boys and girls in academic ability by subject. Notwithstanding the recent findings, this perception continues to be prevalent. In Hong Kong it is supported by the dominance of boys in the science stream and girls in the arts stream in upper secondary schooling. On the other hand, the blurring of the gender divide in girls' and boys' performance in numerous subjects in public examinations in Hong Kong argues that the gender identity of knowledge is socially oriented. Similarly, the difference in underachievement — a 2:1 ratio of boys to girls in the U.S. and a substantially lower one in Hong Kong — suggests the cultural, rather than biological, nature of gender difference in academic performance (McCall, Beach & Lau, 2000). What we know is that the pattern of gender difference has changed in the new educational context. What we do not know is the precise nature of the change. What are the elements of the new educational context that have encouraged girls' performance?

The studies comparing gender difference in performance in Hong Kong offered different explanations for girls' good performance. The organization of schooling seems to have an effect on performance. The Education Department data on student performance in the Academic Aptitude Test showed that Primary 6 students from single-sex schools performed better than those from co-educational schools, and that of the single-sex schools, girls' schools performed better than boys' schools (Equal Opportunities Commission, 1999). Wong et al. also found that girls from single-sex schools did better than those from co-educational schools whereas boys from co-educational schools did better than those from single-sex schools in the HKCEE (Wong, Lam and Ho, 2002). Unlike the controversies surrounding single-sex schools in the United States (Salomone, 2003), Hong Kong society's view on single-sex schooling is largely positive. The value of girls' schools in character and leadership building has long been cherished by the students and their parents (Walker, 2005). The recent findings on their academic performance would reinforce their value. However, one has to caution that single-sex schools in Hong Kong usually have a long history and good reputation. It is not known whether the variable of single-sex schooling or that of elitism associated with them is more predictive of student performance. If it is the former, policy makers would be caught in a dilemma if they followed the HKCEE evidence to re-formulate school organization by gender. More girls' secondary schools would optimize girls' performance, at least in theory, and more co-educational secondary schools would optimize boys' performance, but the two modes are mutually exclusive. If the variable of elitism is more predictive, then intervention would focus on school quality rather than school organization.

Another explanation for gender difference in academic performance was epistemological — whether certain components of school knowledge match boys or girls differentially. The study of underachievement by McCall et al. found that Hong Kong primary school girls did better in Chinese, English and general performance, whereas boys did better in mathematics (McCall, Beach & Lau, 2002: 793). The results of public examinations in Hong Kong also suggest a gender attribute of certain subjects. These data seem to confirm the gendered nature of components of school knowledge. However, the blurring of the gender divide in Mathematics at primary and secondary school argues against the assumption of gender difference as natural. Again, the shifting nature of the gender gap begs the question of where and how change occurs.

This shifting nature is best illustrated with an in-depth probe into how students perform within a subject. Two studies that focused on science and mathematics found mixed results. The Third International Mathematics and Science Study (TIMSS) conducted by the International Association for the Evaluation of Educational Achievement (IEA) found that eighth grade boys scored higher than girls in Hong Kong as well as in most of the participating countries in the study (Law, 1996). On the other hand, the Programme for International Student Assessment (PISA) of the Organization for Economic Cooperation and Development (OECD), which measures the scientific literacy of 15-year-old students, found no overall difference between boys' and girls' scores in 32 countries/regions, including Hong Kong. However, there was gender difference in specific test components, with boys scoring higher on tests with more earth and physical science items, understanding of scientific knowledge items, and closed items; and girls scoring higher on 'recognizing questions' and 'identifying evidence' items (Yip, Chiu and Ho, 2004). An explanation offered for the different findings from the TIMSS and PISA studies was the differential emphasis on content of the subject and assessment format. PISA placed more emphasis on life science, in which girls tend to do better, and TIMSS on physical science, in which boys do better. PISA also contained a higher proportion of open-response and contextual items, in which girls do better (Yip, Chiu & Ho, 2004: 6-8). The same explanation was identified in the HKCEE examination where the common format of open-ended essay-type questions is said to favour girls' (Wong, Lam & Ho, 2002: 840).

The above account suggests that both school organization and knowledge organization contribute to gender difference in student performance. These are external factors. A study has identified an internal factor underlying the difference. It found that the better performance of girls in the senior years of primary schooling could be attributed to their grasp of self-directed learning skills and greater motivation in studying (Ming Pao, 2005). Aptitude would be another internal factor. It is generally believed that girls have a greater aptitude to fit into the school regimens of self-discipline and diligence which might have contributed to their better performance proposed (Wong, Lam & Ho, 2002: 840). However, we do not have research-based evidence to substantiate this plausibility, or to tell whether these attributes as natural or social.

The above studies convey the message that girls do well because they treasure the new opportunities that have opened up to them. One of the arguments in this chapter is that gender difference in academic performance is socially oriented. If, in the current social context, girls respond positively to education, will they continue to do so in future? Do girls work hard because they realize that they have to seize the opportunities previously denied to their mothers' generation? In future, if and when the opportunities become taken for granted, will they treasure them less and work less hard? If so, girls' performance in education, like boys', may be a shifting rather than constant phenomenon. In fact the overall picture and stereotype of girls doing better conceals the many instances of girls that do not perform. Any secondary school teacher in Hong Kong can readily cite examples of girls who are disaffected from schooling, though such cases may be fewer than those of boys. The question emerges again regarding the origins of gender difference and when change occurs.

The Backlash on Girls' Achievements

The society as a whole is ambivalent about girls' achievements in education. This ambivalence is most revealing in the secondary school places allocation. Parents of the girls who would have qualified for allocation to a higher banding school but were not because of the gender quota filed complaints on sex discrimination to the Equal Opportunities Commission (EOC), which resulted in a court case of EOC vs the then Education Department. The case sparked public debates on the interpretation of equality. The view held by EOC and its proponents was that selection should be based on academic performance of each individual. The Education Department charged that since boys tend to be late bloomers, early selection would be unfair to them. Also, while girls performed better in school examinations, boys performed better in the public aptitude tests especially for the top 30 percent of students. The same score of a boy would be scaled downward in comparison with girls' scores in a co-educational primary school, but not in a boys' school where the gender factor is absent (Hau, 2001). Thus, the Education Department argued that separating girls and boys in rank order would ensure equality by sex as a group. The point of contention became whether allocation should be based on students as individuals or as a group, and student's demonstrated current performance or expected potential. Critics of the EOC report also argued that Chinese and English in the AAT combined to produce a heavy weighting on language abilities and, in comparison, a light weighing on Mathematics and thus favoured girls (Tsang, 1999). Interestingly, such a view had never been put forth in the earlier days when boys took the lead. In fact the Investigation Team for the EOC report found that the AAT might be biased in favour of boys in that both the verbal reasoning test and the numerical reasoning test had a high correlation with mathematical skills

(EOC, 1999: Ch. 4). The Education Department argued that boys developed later than girls intellectually. Be that the case, the gap between the scores for the subjects where girls did better than boys should narrow through the years. The Investigation Team's analyses followed the same cohort of students progressing from Primary 5 to Secondary 3 and found no narrowing of the gap over the years (Ibid.). The analysis of HKCEE results in 1997 by Wong et al. (2002, p. 833) found that boys did less well than girls in all aspects, including Mathematics. If so, the assumption of the relative strengths of boys and girls in mathematics and languages does not hold and strategies to raise boys' scores by increasing the weighting of Mathematics may be ineffective.

EOC won the case. From 2002 the gender variable was dropped and Secondary 1 girls outnumbered boys in many Band 1 schools. School personnel do not seem to espouse this long overdue fairness in education. It is not uncommon to hear school principals complaining about the disruption to time-honoured arrangements such as equal capacity in classes and number of toilets for boys and girls. The resentment that EOC has 'rocked the boat' comes not only from those working in co-educational schools, but from some principals of girls' schools as well, which were not affected by the court ruling. It has its roots not only in administrative consideration but a deeper ideological stance on the issue. Also, the legal verdict on the case was not conclusive of the controversy on whether gender difference in academic performance is natural and biological on the one hand or nurtured and social on the other.

Society's unease is shown in the way it accounts for gender difference in performance. A typical view is that girls do well only because they work hard, not because they are intelligent; and boys are naughty but intelligent, and do not achieve only because they so choose. This is a romanticized stereotype of boys' superiority and character. It reflects the ubiquitous essentialist account in Hong Kong of predetermined gendered properties in individuals, and ignores the fact that in reality many boys (and girls) simply do not fit the stereotype cast on them. More ironically, like other Chinese societies, Hong Kong society sings praises for those who work hard regardless of their level of intelligence. Indeed, few societies espouse workaholicism like Hong Kong. It is therefore strange that the same society casts a negative connotation on the virtue of diligence when it is associated with girls. Again, what is the subtext in discounting a culturally held virtue when it is associated with girls?

The same subtext is found not only in education. Reports on growing numbers of unmarried Hong Kong women tend to explain it with the remark "Hong Kong women are too brainy." Any good quality preceded by the word "too" carries a negative overtone. Parallel to this ambivalence is a new portrayal of boys and men as victims (Choi, 2003). The underlying rationale is a zero sum game in which girls and women succeed at the cost of boys and men. The unease shows that society has yet to come to terms with the enhancement of its female population.

Outcomes of Girls' Participation in Education

If an ideology of gender equality has been the drive behind the progress in girls' education, similar progress should have taken place in another public sphere, namely, employment. The trend in labour force participation rates of women does not reflect significant progress in their employment. Table 10 shows that between 1986 and 2001 women with little or no education were marginalized from the labour market, and those with an average or higher education managed to stay in it. The statistics have to be placed in the context of change from economic boom in the mid 1980s to downturn in the 1990s and a drop in overall labour force participation rates. What seems evident is that more education has some effect on keeping women in employment. However, we do not know the precise extent to which increased education has contributed to this effect.

The labour force participations rates are not an adequate indication of the benefits of education on women's employment. The earnings ratio, showing internal distribution, would be more relevant to our question. Data

Table 10. Labour Force Participation Rates of Women by Educational Attainment, 1986–2001 (in %)

Educational attainment	1986	1991	2001
No sch/kg	41	20	8
Primary	51	40	33
Lower secondary	54	50	60
Upper secondary	65	66	
Matriculation	66	68	
Tertiary non-degree	79	75	76
Degree	72	73	72
Total	56	49	51

Sources: 1986 and 1991 figures from Mak and Chung (1997), p. 23; 2001 figures from Census and Statistics Department (2005a).

Table 11. Earnings Ratios of Working Men and Women, 1991–2001 (Female/Male)

Educational attainment	1991	1996	2001
No sch/kg	0.686	0.675	0.575
Primary	0.640	0.686	0.579
Lower secondary	0.682	0.711	0.650
Upper secondary	0.833	0.850	0.833
Matriculation	0.750	0.800	0.607
Tertiary non-degree	0.789	0.781	0.765
Tertiary degree	0.607	0.666	0.686
Total	0.708	0.800	0.742

Sources: Calculated from C&S, *2001 Populations Census Main Report Vol. 1*, p. 139 (HK: C&S, 2002).

on the earnings ratios of working men and women in 1991, 1996 and 2001 show fluctuations in the two periods of 1991–1996 and 1996–2001. There was a slight rise in 1996, only to be followed by a slight fall in 2001. The tendency seems to be a growing gap at lower levels of educational attainment and a slightly reduced one at tertiary degree level. Overall, there is no significant mirroring of greater gender educational equality in female/male earnings ratios.

The above two tables show that while the time lag factor has to be taken into consideration, any improvement discernible at present in gender equality in employment is patchy and minor. Details of the gender ratios in teaching, an occupation most open to women, may explain why such improvement is sluggish.

Table 12 shows the extent of the feminization of teaching, with women comprising 78 percent of the primary and 56 percent of the secondary teaching force in 2003. It also shows the persistence of gender disparity, with women underrepresented at the high end and overrepresented the low end of the hierarchy. Thus, gains in girls' educational participation have not sustained in an occupation most receptive to women.

Agendas for Future Research

The analysis in this chapter of the recent developments in gender and education in Hong Kong points to new knowledge gained and, by implication, remaining gaps in research. The knowledge gained concerns mainly charting the changing pattern of gender gap in greater details. It is an elaboration of structural knowledge on the subject. In contrast, little is known about the

Table 12. Women as a Percentage of Primary and Secondary School Teachers, 2003

Primary School		Secondary School	
Rank	Women (%)	Rank	Women (%)
Government and Aided Schools		*Government, Aided and Caput Schools*	
Headmaster/Headmistress I	46	Principal I	31
Headmaster/Headmistress II	52	Principal II	13
Primary School Master/ Mistress	66	Principal Graduate Master/ Mistress	30
Assistant Primary School Master/Mistress	82	Senior Graduate Master/Mistress	42
Principal Assistant Master/ Mistress	47	Graduate Master/Mistress	59
Senior Assistant Master/ Mistress	34	Principal Assistant Master/ Mistress	34
Assistant Master/Mistress	68	Senior Assistant/Mistress	52
Certificate Master/Mistress	82	Assistant Master/Mistress	64
Other rank	77	Assistant Master/Mistress (Workshop teacher)	17
		Certificate Master/Mistress	69
		Certificate Master/Mistress (Workshop teacher)	19
		Other Rank	55
Private (incl Direct Subsidy Scheme) School		*Private (incl Direct Subsidy Scheme) School*	
Private School Head	70	Private School Head	20
Private School Teacher	85	Private School Teacher	53
Total	78	Total	56

Source: EMB, Statistics on Primary and Secondary School Teachers 2003, pp. 8, 45. (EMB: 2004)

perspectives of individuals as autonomous beings and how these inform their actions. We need insight into this dimension to complement and explain the structural knowledge that is already available. Thus advancement in research would require an expansion of attention from the structural to the personal, the latter mainly in the domains of epistemology and subjectivities.

Thus far the belief that boys perform well in mathematics and physical science and girls in language still has a strong currency. The notion of gendered knowledge assumes a natural, pre-determined association between gender and type of knowledge (Gellman and Taylor, 2000). However, the data on the closing gap between boys and girls in mathematics and some natural science subjects like chemistry and biology underscore the fluid relationship between gender and knowledge, and suggest that the relationship may be socially constructed. Scholars of comparative studies tend to attribute difference to culture, often cursorily. For example, the lower gender ratio in primary schoolchildren's underachievement in Hong Kong than the U.S. was attributed to the different cultures of the two societies (McCall, Beach & Lau, 2000). Few studies probe into what it is in a culture that causes the difference in achievement. Precisely how the social and cultural explanation overcomes the natural explanation is an important direction for future. In the same vein, a controversy related to gender difference is whether assessment formats are biased in favour of boys or girls. Assessment measures what students have learnt and is an extension of school curriculum. The views in Hong Kong on gender difference in assessment are typically informed by assumptions and need to be substantiated with research-based evidence. The conventional approach to studying gender difference in academic performance focuses on the demonstration of performance and treats the prior conditions leading to it as unproblematic. Is the difference caused by gendered ways of knowing and thinking? Is women's knowing built on the interaction of experience and thought and their mode of thinking contextual and narrative (Gilligan, 1982)? If so, does this perspective support the essentialist stance, which feminists of the post-modern school challenge, on the natural traits of women and men? The essentialist stance recognizes a collective voice of women, whereas the post-modern one recognizes diversity and a multitude of voices. The research in Hong Kong tends to set eye on girls as a group and ignores their individuality. This choice of perspective and unit of analysis exposes a grave omission of the important issue of underachieving girls. So far these girls are nonexistent in published works of educational research on Hong Kong, except for a brief account in Wong's study (Wong, 1995). How do they differ from the achieving girls and why? The variation in response to education among girls reveals that the structure of gender as a social category is shaped by the interaction of gender, class and other social factors. The interaction has no fixed essence and varies over time and across societies. The changing pattern of inter-gender difference in Hong Kong has been relatively well documented. That of intra-gender difference, if any, will well merit investigation.

The contributions of single-sex and co-educational schools to Hong Kong education constitutes another worthwhile area of research. Single-sex schools are a legacy of missionary sponsorship of schools in colonial Hong Kong. Students' and parents' faith in their long tradition of excellence eclipses the concerns about a lack of balanced gender relations in children's formative years. School quality and the specific role of school organization by sex overlap. While we have some knowledge of the history, mission and achievements of single-sex schools in Hong Kong, mostly in the forms of school histories or autobiographies of school principals, there is little published knowledge on how single-sex versus co-educational schools affect gendered learning.

Another important, but neglected, dimension in the field is the subjective meaning girls and women attach to their behaviour, which extends the Weberian interpretive sociology to the study of gender and education. This approach shifts the unit of analysis to individuals as autonomous beings in the construction of meaning in social life. It places the primacy of individuals over social systems. This approach has had a strong purchase in the last decade or two in educational research in the West in general, and to a lesser extent in gender difference in education. It would investigate into the process of gendered identity and value formation and ask why girls behave in one way or another. Findings from studies of Hong Kong employing this approach would explain the structural data presented earlier in this chapter and allude to the malleable nature of gender and education, as different from the deterministic subtext of structural knowledge. Wong's (1995) study of the construction of adolescent femininity in the schooling institution and Chan's (2001) study of the gendered constructions of primary teachers' identities in Hong Kong are good examples of studies in subjectivities. There is much room for studies in this category to cover the shifting nature of the lives of not only girls and women, but also boys and men. The approach also has potential for probing into the change that takes place in the transition from education to work. For example, the increase in women's enrollment in fields like engineering and technology has not been paralleled in these occupations. Are there contextual and subjective factors channeling women away from jobs in engineering and technology? Similarly, to what extent is the disproportionate representation of women in the hierarchy of the teaching force an outcome of patriarchy, a popular theory a few decades ago, or women's choice? We know that in reality quite many women choose to remain rank and file teachers in order to nurture students and decline opportunities for promotion to management positions. The concentration of women in middle and junior positions may derive from a celebration of the intrinsic values they pursue. To be sure, the glass-ceiling explanation is valid. The point is that multifaceted explorations into women's subjectivities will enable a fuller understanding of the reality. Studies in this direction will again complement our understanding of structural knowledge. Their findings on the complexity of the phenomenon will inform intervention strategies in education more effectively than those derived from monocausal perspectives.

Last but not least, if, as argued in this chapter, girls' gains in education are a chance outcome of uncoordinated social factors, will the gains stay? The data on women's employment do not suggest confirmed sustainable benefits of education on gender equality in the economy. A longitudinal perspective will have the merit over a cross-section of whether and how gender equality is sustainable.

References

Chan, A. K. W. (2001). *Gendering primary teachers: Discourses, practices and identities in Hong Kong*. Ph.D. thesis, University of Essex, U.K.

Choi, P. K. (2003). Education: Investigation in social context. In Association for the Advancement of Feminism (Ed.), *Archive on Hong Kong women*. Hong Kong: Association for the Advancement of Feminism.

Census and Statistics Department, Hong Kong Government (1988). *Hong Kong annual digest of statistics 1987*. Hong Kong: Hong Kong Government.

Census and Statistics Department, Hong Kong Special Administrative Region (2002). *2001 population census main report volume 1*. Hong Kong: Hong Kong Government.

Census and Statistics Department, Hong Kong Special Administrative Region (2004). *Hong Kong annual digest of statistics 2004*. Hong Kong: Hong Kong Government.

Census and Statistics Department, Hong Kong Special Administrative Region (2005a). http://www.info.gov.hk/censtatd/

Census and Statistics Department (2005b), Survey on "Hong Kong students studying outside Hong Kong" in 2002. (Private communication).

Civic Exchange, Hong Kong (2005). Hong Kong's challenge: Impact of population changes. http://www.civic-exchange.org

Education and Manpower Bureau, Hong Kong Special Administrative Region (1997). Report on review of 9-year compulsory education. Hong Kong: Hong Kong Government.

Education and Manpower Branch (2004). *Statistics on primary and secondary school teachers*. Hong Kong: Hong Kong Government.

Equal Opportunities Commission, Hong Kong. (1999). *Formal investigation report on secondary school places allocation (SSPA) system*. Hong Kong: Equal Opportunities Commission.

Gallagher, A. M. , & Kaufman, J. C. (2005). *Gender difference in mathematics*. Cambridge and New York: Cambridge University Press.

Gilligan, C. (1993). *In a different voice*. Cambridge, MA: Harvard University Press.

Gipps, C.V. (1996). Review and conclusions: A pedagogy or a range of pedagogic strategies? In P. F. Murphy & C. V. Gipps (Eds.), *Equity in the classroom: Towards effective pedagogy for girls and boys*. London: Falmer Press.

Hau, K. T. (2001, Autumn). Judicial review of sexual discrimination in Hong Kong secondary school place allocation: Legal, educational and psychometrical debates. *Hong Kong Journal of Social Sciences, 20,* 57–83. (In Chinese).

Hong Kong Examinations and Assessment Authority (2004). (a) *Examination Report HKCEE 2004*. Hong Kong: HKEAA.

Hong Kong Examinations and Assessment Authority (2004). (b) *Examination Report HKALE 2004*. Hong Kong: HKEAA.

Law, N. (1996). Science and mathematics achievements at the junior secondary level in Hong Kong. Hong Kong: TIMSS Hong Kong Study Centre.

Maccoby, E. E. & Jacklin, C. N. (1974). *The psychology of sex differences*. Stanford, CA: Stanford University Press.

Mak, G. C. L. (1991). The schooling of girls in Hong Kong: Progress and contradictions in the transition. In G. A. Postiglione (Ed.), *Education and society in Hong Kong* (pp. 167–180). Armonk, NY: M.E. Sharpe.

Mak, G. C. L, & Chung, Y. P. (1997). The education and labour force participation of women in Hong Kong. In F. M. Cheung (Ed.), *Engendering Hong Kong society*. Hong Kong: The Chinese University Press.

McCall, R. B., Beach, S. R., & Lau, S. (2000). The nature and correlates of underachievement among elementary schoolchildren in Hong Kong. *Child Development, 71*(3), 785–801.

McRobbie, A. (1978). Working class girls and the culture of femininity. In Centre for Contemporary Cultural Studies, University of Birmingham (Ed.), *Women take issue*.

Ming Pao (2005, 8 March). Girls have stronger self-directed learning ability than boys. *Ming Pao*, p. A11.

Nowell, A., & Hedges, L. V. (1998). Trends in gender differences in academic achievement from 1960–1994: An analysis of differences in mean, variance, and extreme scores. *Sex Roles, 39,* 21–43.

Salomone, R. C. (2003). *Same, different, equal: Rethinking single-sex schooling*. New Haven, CT: Yale University Press.

Tsang, W. K. (1999, 8 November). Systematic inequality and positive discrimination. *Ming Pao*, p. A24.

University Grants Committee (2005). www.ugc.edu.hk

Walker, A. (2005, 9 July). Sex and academic bottom line. *South China Morning Post*, p. E6.

Weiner, G., Arnot, M., & David, M. (1997). Is the future female: Female success, male disadvantage, and changing gender patterns in education. In A. H. Halsey, P. Brown, & H. Lauder (Eds.), *Education, economy, culture and society*. Oxford: Oxford University Press.

Willingham, W. W., Cole, N. S., Lewis, C., & Leung, S. W. (1997). Test performance. In W. W. Willingham & N. S. Cole (Eds.), *Gender and fair assessment*. Hillsdale, NJ: Lawrence Erlbaum.

Willis, P. (1977). *Learning to labor*. New York: Columbia University Press.

Wong, K. C., Lam, Y. R., & Ho, L. M. (2002). The effects of schooling on gender differences. *British Educational Research Journal, 28*(6), 827–843.

Wong, S. Y. (1995). The cultural construction of adolescent femininity: The case of Tuen Mun school girls. M. Phil. thesis, The Chinese University of Hong Kong.

Yip, D. Y., Chiu, M. M., & Ho, E. S. C. (2004). Hong Kong student achievement in OECD-PISA Study: Gender differences in Science content, literacy skills, and test item formats. *International Journal of Science & Math Education, 2*(1), 91–106.

CHAPTER 3

Gender, Work and Employment in the "Global Condition"

Ngo Hang-yue and Ngai Pun

Introduction

The post-1997 Hong Kong has been racing into a post-industrial city, and hence enters the "global condition", accompanied by a rapid relocation of capital into Mainland China and a serious challenge of economic downturn in the previous years. The new global age was accelerated by a number of ambitious "global" projects including Cyberport, Herbalport, and Disneyland to speed up the restructuring of the Hong Kong economy. This new initiative was advocated by the Hong Kong Special Administrative Region (SAR) government to create a policy framework that appeals to the imagination and aspiration of a global city. The recent change was striving to maintain Hong Kong's competitiveness and dominance as an Asia's World City in the twenty-one century. This "global condition" in accompany with rapid urban and economic restructuring in Hong Kong at the turn of the millennium creates substantial impacts on gender, work and employment.

In retrospect, the number of women entering the workforce has increased sharply since the 1960s, owing largely to the rapid growth of the manufacturing economy and hence a huge demand for labour when Hong Kong was rapidly incorporated into the world production. According to government statistics, the absolute increase of women who are economically active between 1961 and 2005 was from 324,000 to 1,607,900, or 4.96 times. Currently women constitute about 45% of the local labour force. The rise in female labour force participation has brought about some positive outcomes with regard to gender equality. For example, more women have become employers and self-employed, with greater economic power and resources than before. Young and better-educated women have also made substantial inroads into some occupations traditionally dominated by men, particularly managerial and professional jobs (Ngo, 2000). Additionally, the income disparity between the two genders declined substantially during the period of 1976 and 1996 (Tang, Au, Chung, & Ngo, 2000). The general trend has been a convergence of men's and women's employment pattern and outcomes. Nevertheless, subtle changes that deviated from the long-term trend have occurred over the past decade. Increasing gender differentiation and occupational polarization has been observed in the local labour market (Chiu & Lui, 2004; Ngo, 2000; Pun, 2001). In particular, the employment situations differed and diverged between young and middle-aged women. We attempt to understand these changes in the context of the urban and economic restructuring in Hong Kong as influenced by globalization in the post-1997 period.

In this chapter, we first provide a brief discussion of some major social and economic forces that have salient impacts on women's work and employment. These forces are related to the development of Hong Kong toward a global city, including the structural transformation of the local labour market and the expansion of higher education. Then, we examine the gender differences in the following aspects of employment: labour force participation, unemployment, status of employment, and occupational distribution and segregation. Our focus will be on both the long-term trend and the recent changes. Lastly, a supplementary analysis on gender and employment will also be provided for new immigrant workers from mainland China, who are a unique group in the local labour market. The increasing flow of labour, particularly skilled workers and young female workers, across national borders has been viewed as an important feature of globalization.

Economic Globalization

Globalization generally refers to the process whereby countries become more integrated via movements of goods, capital, labour, information, and ideas. Viewed as an advanced stage of capitalist development, it involves the strengthening of the global free trade regime, the fast flows of information and money, the emergence of multinational firms, and the transnational organization of production. Undoubtedly, the process of globalization has been accelerated in recent years. As a consequence of the advancement in technology and globalization, the basis of the world economy has been changing from industry to knowledge.

Globalization brings about tremendous impacts on various aspects of our social, cultural, and economic life (Gunter & Hoeven, 2004). Apart from the changes in cultures, communication, production and consumption patterns, there has been a general shift in economic activities toward the service sector and the development of global markets. New entrepreneurial and employment opportunities have been created as a consequence. Moreover, the growth of the service sector in developed countries and of low-cost manufacturing in developing countries has led to the rapid formation of a female labour force across the globe (Beneria, 2003; Meyer, 2003).

At the organizational level, firms have introduced new organizational structures and developed new business strategies in response to intensified competition associated with globalization. For example, systems of flexible production have been employed that enables the relocation of factories to developing countries with lower operation costs. New policies and practices have also been adopted by both indigenous and multinational firms in managing their workforce (Lui, Lau, & Ngo, 2004). Under the pressures of global competition, the following changes have occurred in the labour market.

(1) An increase in the relative demand for skilled labour in developed countries and unskilled labour in less developed countries. In advanced economies, workers with the skills needed to adjust to the new technologies and organizational structures benefit more in terms of employment opportunities and pay. However, some workers (such as women) have been excluded from the high-skilled works because of their lack of access to education and training and their domestic obligations (Meyer, 2003; Rama, 2003). This creates a widening income gap between the professional and technical workers and the less skilled and unskilled workers who are usually women.

(2) A shift of employment from "core" to "periphery" activities located in smaller firms and independent contractors. This is largely due to downsizing, outsourcing, and subcontracting of the large firms in response to global competition (Beneria, 2003). Unlike the large firms, these small firms tend to provide unstable employment for their employees.

(3) A growth of contingent work, including part-time, temporary, and

contract employment, owing to decentralized production systems and the pursuit of workplace flexibility. These jobs usually offer low pay, low employment security, and poor career prospects for the incumbents (Giele & Stebbins, 2003; Rai, 2002).

(4) A sharp increase in employment instability and in the number of workers experiencing the stressful consequences of unemployment. With the reduction in hierarchical levels and the establishment of self-managed teams in large firms, some middle managers suffered as their jobs have been eliminated. Low-skilled workers at the bottom of the labour hierarchy were also adversely affected by the restructuring of the economy and the transformation of employment structure (Beneria, 2003).

It has been argued that globalization and its resulting changes led to the deepening of social inequality, including gender inequality (Rupert, 2000). Because of globalization, a new international division of labour has been established, producing a "female proletariat" consigned to the lowest-paid and least secure jobs with the worst working conditions (Aguilar, 2004). New employment gaps have also been created between men and women. To be fair, globalization creates more job opportunities, yet the effects on male and female workers are different depending upon their gender roles and human capital (Carr & Chen, 2004; Meyer, 2003). In some countries, young women with more education are able to undertake the highly skilled works, and thus they gain a relatively advantageous position in the labour market. On the other hand, some older women had been displaced because of economic restructuring and the relocation of production to low-wage areas. They have been "marginalized" and can only take up the low-paid, flexible jobs at the bottom of occupational hierarchy (Afshar & Barrientos, 1998). Similar situation has also been found in Hong Kong, in which the effects of globalization on female workers are uneven. As the middle-aged women lack the educational qualifications and technical skills to compete in the labour market, their employment situation and income attainment have deteriorated in recent years. In contrast, young and better-educated women have more employment opportunities, and they received higher economic rewards as well (Ngo, 2002). Hence, a trend of economic polarization among female workers has set in.

Being a free and open economy with a long history of international trade, Hong Kong has integrated with other major economies of the world since its earlier days of economic development. The past two decades have witnessed the restructuring of the local economy from a low-cost manufacturing center into a regional financial and service center. Simultaneously, there has been a shift of employment from manufacturing to tertiary sector. Led by the global trend, in recent years Hong Kong has strived to become a knowledge-based economy. Globalization has led to severe competition from other Asian economies and major cities in China, and Hong Kong needs to reposition its economic role in the new millennium. More importantly, after 1997, Hong Kong has accelerated its economic integration with mainland China, in particular with the Pearl River Delta region. Cross-border economic activities have increased substantially. All these recent economic changes have profound impacts on the local labour market.

Changes in Hong Kong Labour Market

In Hong Kong, the growth of export-oriented industries before the 1980s has been associated with the growing participation of women in factory works. Since then, due to the emergence of low-cost competitors in the Asia-Pacific region and the erosion of Hong Kong's cost advantage, the growth of manufacturing industries in Hong Kong began to slacken. Along with the opening policy in China, a wave of outward investment began, leading to a process of "de-industrialization" and structural transformation in the local economy (Chui & Lee, 2003). The service sector started to grow and took up the prominent role in the local economy. In 2004, this sector accounted for 90% of GDP in Hong Kong and employed 85.7% of the work force. Significant changes have taken place in the labour market, which subtly affect men's and women's employment opportunities.

Table 1 shows the distribution of the working population in major occupational groups in 1991 and 2001. A number of changes in the occupational structure during the period deserve scrutiny. First of all, the expansion of professionals and associate professionals is remarkable, with the share of employment rising from 14% in 1991 to 20.8% in 2001. Part of this expansion is due to the growth of information technology (IT) industry over the period that absorbed thousands of highly-educated workers. According to the 2001 census, 33,055 workers are classified as "IT / computer professionals", representing 18.38% of all professionals in Hong Kong. Another 23,786 workers are classified as "IT / computer associate professionals". It is worthy to note that women have a low representation in these IT-related jobs (i.e., 19.89%). Second, there has been an expansion of

Table 1. Distribution of the Working Population in Major Occupational Groups, 1991 and 2001

Occupational group	1991		2001		1991–2001	
	Number	%	Number	%	Percentage change	Percentage point change
1. Managers and administrators	249,247	9.18	349,637	10.75	40.28	1.57
2. Professionals	99,331	3.66	179,825	5.53	81.04	1.87
3. Associate professionals	279,909	10.31	498,671	15.33	78.15	5.02
4. Clerks	431,651	15.90	529,992	16.29	22.78	0.39
5. Service workers and shop sales workers	359,319	13.23	488,961	15.03	36.08	1.80
6. Craft and related workers	397,992	14.66	321,000	9.87	−19.35	−4.79
7. Plant and machine operators and assemblers	365,826	13.47	238,666	7.34	−34.76	−6.13
8. Elementary occupations	503,832	18.55	635,393	19.53	26.11	0.98
9. Others	27,996	1.03	10,561	1.32	−62.28	−0.71
Total	2,715,103	100.00	3,252,706	100.00	19.80	–

Source: Census and Statistics Department, 1992 and 2002

white-collar occupations (e.g., administrative, clerical, service, and sales jobs) and a contraction of blue-collar occupations. To a large extent, this reflects the structural transformation of the local economy that began in the 1980s when some manufacturing firms moved from Hong Kong to Mainland China. This trend has accelerated during the 1990s with the further liberalization of the Chinese economy, and thus the employment share of "craft and related workers" and "plant and machine operators and assemblers" has declined sharply. During the period, a large proportion of the labour force has moved into the growing service sector. Third, over the past decade, more workers have been employed in "elementary occupations" that include such low-status, low-paid jobs as watchmen, messengers, domestic helpers, and cleaners. Some of the incumbents are the "displaced workers" from the manufacturing sector, who often suffered income reduction by filling these job positions.

As pointed out by some local researchers (e.g., Chiu & Lui, 2004; Ngo,

2000), Hong Kong has undergone a process of "occupational polarization", which is characterized by an increased share of both administrative, professional, and semi-professional occupations (at the top of occupational hierarchy) and low-level service and elementary occupations (at the bottom of occupational hierarchy). Similar to other advanced economies, the growth of the service sector in Hong Kong has generated new demand for both high-skill and low-skill workers. As the labour market becomes differentiated, some young and better-educated women are able to take up the high-status administrative and professional posts, and thus they fare well in terms of income attainment and career prospects. On the other hand, many middle-aged women were confined to the low-end jobs, owing to their disadvantages with respect to age, education qualifications, and work skills (Ngo, 2000). Their job choice becomes rather limited as they were "trapped" into the periphery of the labour market. The employers offer them low salary as they have little bargaining power (Pun, 2001).

Another major change in the labour market is the growth of contingent employment. After the Asian financial crisis in 1997, many local firms have implemented downsizing and restructuring, and adopted a cautious attitude toward staffing. Labour casualization has become a trend in some industries such as retail and personal services where employers continuously used more contingent workers (e.g., part-time and contact workers) to replace the full-time permanent staff. They did so not only to avoid paying some of the employee benefits such as paid leave, medical insurance, and provident fund contributions, but also to increase the numerical flexibility of firms (Ngo, 2002). Owing to limited job choice, more women have been engaged in part-time employment, particularly in the retail and personal services industries. As compared with their full-time colleagues, these part-time workers received lower income and few fringe benefits, and excluded from training and promotion opportunities. Their job security was also lower as well.

Expansion of Higher Education

One salient factor contributing to a gendered labour market is education as it expands in the age of globalization. To improve the quality of human resources and to compete in the global market, most countries have invested heavily in education, especially in technical and higher education (Bloom, 2004; Gunter & Hoeven, 2004). There is no exception for Hong Kong. In fact, one of the main government's policy objectives in education is to enable

60% of the upper secondary school leavers to have access to tertiary education by 2010. The recent expansion in higher education (including both undergraduate, post-graduate and sub-degree programs) is seen as essential to the development of Hong Kong as a knowledge-based economy.

Education has long been viewed as an important mechanism of social stratification in contemporary societies, since it facilitates upward social mobility. Higher education, in particular, imparts knowledge and skills that enable individuals to contribute more to work, to take up more prestige job positions, and to earn more (Tang *et al.*, 2000). For that reason, the improvement in women's education is considered as a crucial step toward gender equality. Given the highly competitive labour market in Hong Kong, women's educational qualifications (and hence their stock of human capital) are likely to translate into labour market gains, and thus reduce the gender gaps in employment.

In Hong Kong, women's access to formal education, both in terms of the decrease in the rate of illiteracy and in years of schooling attended, has been improving continuously over time. With the introduction of nine-year compulsory education in 1978, the educational attainment of women has risen significantly. For example, in 2005, the proportion of women having attended secondary and above education was 70.6%, which is comparable to that of men (i.e., 78.2%). The 1990s has witnessed a decade of marked expansion of higher education in Hong Kong. The total number of students enrolled in higher education funded by the University Grant Committee (UGC) rose from 47,404 in 1986 to 78,780 in 2004 (Census and Statistics Department, 2006a). Women seem to be the main beneficiaries of this policy, as more female students have been admitted to local universities (Leung & Bryant, 2000). In fact, the percentage share of female students enrolled in the UGC-funded programmes increased from 32.9% in 1986 to 55.2% in 2004 (Census and Statistics Department, 2006a). Hence, the traditionally male advantage in higher education has gradually disappeared.

The increasing educational attainment of women has important implications for their employment and work lives. With greater desire and better preparation for paid employment, highly educated women usually have a strong labour force attachment. Their educational qualifications have also facilitated their entry into high-paying managerial and professional occupations that have been dominated by men. As a consequence, the degree of occupational sex segregation and the gender pay gap in the labour market are likely to reduce. As young women are continuing their education and attaining higher levels of education than in the past, the disparity in educational attainment between different generations of women has enlarged. Compared with the younger generation with high qualifications, older generation women had limited access to education when they were young. The training provided by the government and the employers is inadequate for upgrading their work skills. Their deficiency in human capital makes them difficult to compete in the new economy.

Labour Force Participation

The labour force participation rate is often viewed as the first indicator of the overall level of labour market activity. It generally refers to the proportion of the economically active population among all persons aged 15 and over. In every country for which information is available, women have a lower rate of labour force participation than men. Another related indicator is *inactivity rate*, which represents the proportion of the working-age population (i.e., those aged 25 to 54 years) not in the labour force (Elder & Johnson, 1999). In general, a low inactivity rate is associated with a high labour force participation rate.

Table 2 displays the labour force participation rates and inactivity rates for men and women in Hong Kong over the past four decades. The female labour force participation rate increased rapidly during the 1960s and 1970s, along with labour-intensive industrialization. Since then, it has been stabilized around 50%. In 2001, the highest rate of 51.56 was recorded. As the rate for

Table 2. Labour Force Participation Rates and Inactivity Rates by Sex, 1961–2001

Year	Labour Force Participation Rate			Inactivity Rate		
	Male	Female	Difference	Male	Female	Difference
1961	90.37	36.83	53.54	2.25	62.66	60.41
1966	86.05	40.98	45.07	1.58	58.92	57.34
1971	84.68	42.83	41.85	2.09	60.97	58.88
1976	80.55	43.62	36.94	6.69	57.25	50.56
1981	82.49	49.54	32.95	2.24	46.87	44.63
1986	80.86	51.20	29.65	3.21	40.67	37.46
1991	78.73	49.54	29.19	4.08	38.99	34.91
1996	76.64	49.22	27.42	4.01	36.71	32.70
2001	71.89	51.56	20.33	7.20	32.97	25.77

Source: Census report of various years, Census and Statistics Department

men has dropped steadily (i.e., from 90.37 in 1961 to 71.89 in 2001), the gap between men and women in labour force participation has narrowed over time. The inactivity rates also show a similar trend. For men, consistent with the decline in their labour force participation, their inactivity rate has risen slightly from 2.25 in 1961 to 7.20 in 2001. In contrast, the rate for women has dipped sharply since the 1970s, indicating that more women in the age group of 25–54 have entered into the labour market. In 2001, the inactivity rate for women was 32.97, implying only 1 out 3 women in that age group was economically inactive.

The continuous influx of women into the labour market can be attributed to many factors. The growth of the service sector and hence a large demand for female workers is definitely a main reason behind. For example, in 2005, 93.23% of the female labour force was absorbed in that sector. This percentage is relatively high by international standard. Additionally, the rising real wages has attracted more women to enter into the job market. Some supply-side factors have also contributed to the feminization of the labour force, including women's improved educational attainment, shifts in marriage and fertility patterns, the attitudinal changes towards gender role, and legislation on equal employment opportunities (Ngo, 2001; Tang *et al.*, 2000). Since domestic maids have been widely used in the local families, household responsibilities become less a constraint for married women to work outside.

It is well known that the economic participation of women is profoundly affected by the family life cycle. In general, young and unmarried women have the highest rate of labour force participation. Figure 1 presents the age-specific pattern of female labour force participation in Hong Kong in selected years. The general trend is a move from a double-peaked (or a M-shape pattern) to a single-peaked pattern over time[1]. Several factors contribute to this trend. First, the higher education participation enrollment rate has contributed to a decline in the labour force participation rate by those aged 15–24. Second, there has been a higher economic activity rate of women at the childbearing and childrearing ages (i.e., 25–39), due to delayed marriage and declined fertility[2] and thus less household and child care demands for them. The higher educational attainment of young women is also conducive to their paid employment, since more career opportunities are now open for them. Third, there has been a drop in labour force participation among older women who are less educated. As a consequence of economic restructuring, some of these women had been displaced and reluctantly left the labour market.

Figure 1. Age Specific Female Labour Force Participation Rates,
1986, 1996 and 2003

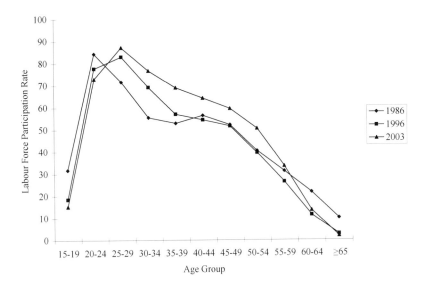

Source: Census and Statistics Department, 1997 and 2002.

Although the overall female labour force participation rate remains rather steady during the past decade, increasing number of married women have been drawn into the workforce. The rate for married women has risen from 38.3% in 1991 to 44.9% in 2005, while the rate for never-married has dropped slightly from 70.1% to 68.4% during the same period (Census and Statistics Department, 2006a). As a result, the gap in economic activity between never-married and married women has diminished. Because of economic necessity, more dual-earners families emerge in Hong Kong. With the extensive use of domestic maids, household responsibilities were no longer a main constraint for married women to work outside. It seems that marriage becomes a less inhibiting factor for women to seek gainful employment.

Table 3 reveals the labour force participation rate of ever-married women by age group and educational attainment in 2001. The impact of educational attainment is obvious — the more education a woman has had, the greater her attachment to the labour force. As expected, the family life cycle also plays a salient role — the highest rate is in the age group of 25–29 and then

Table 3. Labour Force Participation Rate of Ever-Married Women by
Age Group and Educational Attainment, 2001

Age Group	No Schooling/ Kinder- garten	Primary	Lower Second- ary	Upper Second- ary	Matricula- tions	Tertiary: Non- degree	Tertiary: Degree	Total
	Educational Attainment							
15–19	51.72	87.5	28.97	30.38	38.50	50.00	71.43	34.10
20–24	61.78	60.6	52.31	68.97	76.07	81.89	69.57	64.74
25–29	43.81	53.71	50.36	76.61	82.61	87.84	83.64	71.48
30–34	37.06	42.23	44.00	72.27	78.10	84.16	82.83	66.46
35–39	34.69	40.41	44.05	65.85	74.67	79.25	79.01	59.38
40–44	43.92	46.33	50.34	61.53	71.18	76.18	76.53	56.26
45–49	45.66	48.95	53.99	61.20	68.15	70.19	73.26	54.98
50–54	35.72	41.53	45.61	49.39	57.02	65.28	67.59	45.37
55–59	24.21	28.92	29.55	33.19	42.19	50.77	47.61	30.99
60–64	11.27	12.35	14.00	15.37	18.48	17.14	26.49	13.44
65+	1.80	2.66	3.86	4.43	4.08	5.71	11.70	2.41
Total	9.93	31.85	43.54	62.64	67.75	70.98	73.30	43.37

Source: Census and Statistics Department, 2002

the rate declines steadily for the older age groups. An overall single-peak pattern of labour force participation is observed for married women in Hong Kong. Nevertheless, if we compare the patterns for those who received less education (i.e., lower secondary or below) with those who have more education (i.e., upper secondary or above), a shape contrast can be found. The former shows a double-peak pattern (i.e., the rate reaches its peak in early 20s, starts to fall after 25, and increases again after 40) while the latter follows a typical single-peak pattern. This suggests a complex relationship among educational attainment, family life cycle, and labour supply of married women in Hong Kong. Arguably, education not only has a direct positive effect on women's economic participation, it also affects their life course that has significant impacts on their decision to reenter the labour market at midlife.

Unemployment

The economic restructuring of Hong Kong in recent years not only affects the labour force participation in general, but also shapes unemployment in the context of globalization. Unemployment became a serious social issue since the Asian Financial Crisis and the subsequent economic downturn period. It is generally indicated by unemployment rate, which refers to the proportion of unemployed persons in the labour force[3]. Since 2000, there has been a continuous rise in the numbers and rates of unemployment. In 2003, a historic high rate of 7.9% was recorded, with 254,200 persons being jobless. A number of factors may account for this economic phenomenon, including job mismatch in the local labour market under economic restructuring, economic recessions, widespread downsizing and layoffs of large firms, and the relocation of local jobs to other lower cost areas. These changes, to a certain extent, are triggered by economic globalization.

In some Western countries, women generally had a higher unemployment rate than men (Elder & Johnson, 1999). The gender differential follows a cyclical pattern, such that the gender difference in unemployment rates has been smallest during recessions and largest during prosperous times (Blau & Ferber, 1992). However, the situation is different in Hong Kong. Table 4 shows the employment rates for the two genders during the period of 1991–2005. In 2005, the number of unemployed persons and unemployment rate for women were 71,200 and 4.4% respectively, while the corresponding figures for men were 129,500 and 6.5% respectively (Census and Statistics Department, 2006a). At first glance, unemployment among female workers appeared to be less serious than that among male workers. However, as argued by Chiu and Lee (2003), in Hong Kong unemployment figures report as unemployed only those who say that they are "actively seeking" a job. Women may be out of work for a variety of reasons that are often misinterpreted as "not actively seeking" and hence not classified as unemployed. Thus, women's unemployment rate may not truly reflect their employment situation. According to the official definition, for people who "might consider entering the labour force only if they 'encounter' jobs with terms favourable to their own situations (such as remuneration meeting their own expectation, working hours with adequate flexibility or workplace near work)" belong to *economically inactive persons* (Census and Statistics Department, 2004a). As compared with men, women (particularly married women with young children) more are likely to fall into this category, since their employment decision is more constrained by factors like gender role, household responsibilities, and time availability. They may have some desire for work, and occasionally search for employment opportunity. Yet these women may not actively seek a job because they encounter several barriers, or they believe that jobs matching

Mainstreaming Gender in Hong Kong Society

Table 4. Number of Unemployed Persons and Unemployment Rates by Sex,
1991–2005

Year	Number of Unemployed		Unemployment Rate		
	Male	Female	Male	Female	Total
1991	33,800	16,600	1.9	1.6	1.8
1996	58,700	28,700	3.1	2.3	2.8
1998	101,200	52,900	5.2	4.0	4.7
1999	140,600	66,900	7.2	4.9	6.2
2000	109,600	57,300	5.6	4.1	4.9
2001	118,300	56,500	6.0	3.9	5.1
2002	164,800	90,700	8.4	6.0	7.3
2003	181,400	95,900	9.3	6.2	7.9
2004	153,900	88,600	7.8	5.6	6.8
2005	129,500	71,200	6.5	4.4	5.6

Source: Census and Statistics Department, 2006a

their specific needs are hardly available under the current economic conditions. Based on the official definition, these women are excluded from the calculation of unemployment rate.

Another possible explanation of why men had a higher unemployment rate than women in Hong Kong is that they are more concentrated in the manufacturing and construction industries. These industries were badly hit by recent economic recessions and thus more unemployed men came from these industries. For example, in 2003, the unemployment rates in the manufacturing and construction industries were 7.6% and 19.0% respectively. In contrast, the unemployment problem was less serious in the service sector in which women were concentrated. The unemployment rate in the "community, social, and personal services industries" was 3.5% in 2003, much lower than the overall rate (Census and Statistics Department, 2004a).

It is obvious that the unemployment rates vary by age group. Youth and old people generally have a high rate of unemployment. According to government statistics, in Hong Kong, men have higher unemployment rates than women across all age groups. Such a gap, however, is greater for the young workers (i.e., those aged below 30). For the age group of 15–19, the unemployment rates for men and women were 24.4% and 18.8% respectively in 2005. This indicates that young men have greater difficulty to find a job than young women. Such a gender differential was much smaller for workers in the age groups of 30–39 and 40–49 (Census and Statistics Department, 2006a).

Another gender difference is the median duration of unemployment for workers who lost their jobs. Unemployed workers with different demographic characteristics (e.g., gender, age group, and educational level) are likely to spend different time spells to find a new job. In recent years, because of the slowdown in the local economy, it took more time for an unemployed worker to search for another job. For example, in 1991 the median duration of unemployment was 54 days and the figure rose to 97 days in 2004 (Census and Statistics Department, 2006a). Table 5 shows the median duration of unemployment by age group and sex from 1991 to 2004. Overall speaking, unemployed men need more time than unemployed women to find a new job[4]. However, if we examine such a gender difference among various age groups, it is interesting to note that young women (i.e., those aged below 30) generally have a shorter duration of unemployment than young men. This is consistent with the fact that the unemployment rates for young women were lower than young men, probably because more job opportunities are available for them in the service sector. However, for women aged 40 and above, a reverse pattern is observed such that they spent more time in an unemployment spell than their male counterparts. This reflects the difficulty middle-aged women faced under the slack labour market conditions.

Table 5. Median Duration of Unemployment by Age Group and Sex (in Days), 1991–2004

Age Group	Sex	1991	1996	1998	2000	2001	2002	2003	2004
15–19	Male	54	64	71	69	73	74	81	72
	Female	50	71	65	64	67	74	76	58
20–29	Male	53	65	68	66	68	77	81	75
	Female	45	63	67	66	66	77	76	65
30–39	Male	52	70	71	78	74	84	88	97
	Female	53	75	77	88	71	97	93	91
40–49	Male	58	84	77	81	78	88	84	106
	Female	51	91	86	8	93	100	90	116
50–59	Male	70	93	89	98	92	118	125	155
	Female	137	88	87	90	97	132	145	168
60+	Male	78	148	89	102	87	164	180	203
	Female	46	67	56	66	126	176	85	152
Overall	Male	56	73	74	77	76	86	89	99
	Female	49	71	72	75	74	89	88	93

Source: Census and Statistics Department, 2006a

Flexible Employment

In addition to the unemployment problem seriously attacked the post-handover Hong Kong society, flexible employment became another trend to survive the global competition and the race to bottom production strategies. The growth of non-standard work arrangements, such as part-time work, temporary employment and contract work, has been a major trend in the labour markets of most industrial economies (Kalleberg, 2000). Since these forms of employment enable workers to combine family and work roles, married women are more likely to be engaged in them. In Hong Kong, although these forms of employment are not as popular as other Western industrial countries, there has been a growth of the total number of *part-time employees*[5], especially in the past few years.

Table 6 reveals the number of part-time employees by sex over the past two decades. The overall rate of participation in part-time employment (i.e., the proportion of part-time workers in the whole working population) has increased from 2.2% in 1982 to 5.2% in 2005. After the Asian financial crisis, more local firms replace the full-time workers by the part-time workers in order to save the labour cost and to increase employment flexibility (Ngo, 2002). Part-time positions were mostly found in the following industries: wholesale, retail and trades, restaurants and hotels, community, social and personal services. Although women outnumbered men in this form of employment, the proportion of men has been high (e.g., 37.31% in 2005). Unlike female part-timers who were concentrated in the service sector, a substantial number of male part-timers were employed in the construction

Table 6. Number of Part-time Employees by Sex, 1982–2005

Year	Number of Part-time Employees			Percent Female
	Male	Female	Total	
1982	20,100	33,700	53,800	62.64
1988	12,100	41,700	53,800	77.51
1994	25,800	42,000	67,800	61.95
1997	24,400	57,600	82,000	70.24
1999	51,000	65,200	116,200	56.11
2000	52,300	69,700	122,000	57.13
2002	53,100	77,800	130,900	59.43
2003	64,700	78,500	143,100	54.86
2005	56,300	94,600	150,900	62.69

Source: General household survey of various years, Census and Statistics Department

industry. Moreover, it has been reported that women are more likely to take up a part-time job because of voluntary reasons such as taking care of housework and family members, while most men did so because of involuntary reasons such as unable to find a full-time job and slack work in company (Ngo, 2002). Among the female part-time workers, most of them were married, in their middle age, and less-educated. Given their domestic constraints and labour market disadvantages, these women earned much less than their full-time sisters (Ngo, 2002).

Unlike part-time workers, the total number of casual workers has decreased in recent years. The number of male and female casual employees employed in the labour market during the period of 1999 and 2005 are reported in Table 7. Surprisingly, women constitute a low proportion of casual employees, with only 14.91% (or 10,300 in total number) in 2005. Most of the female causal workers were in their middle age and employed in service industries (68.9%). When asking about the main reason for participating in casual work, 39.6% of women suggested that they "could not find a permanent job", and another 29.2% of them said that they had to take care of household and family members. For men, the majority of them (82%) were employed in the construction industry. "The custom of trade/ norm of company/ business arrangement of the company" had been given as the major reason (41.6%) for these men to work as casual employees (Census and Statistics Department, 2006b).

It has been suggested that the organization of work in Asian countries is remarkably different from their Western counterparts (Brinton, 2001). A greater variety of employment statuses can be found there. Apart from employers, self-employed, and wage employees, a significant proportion of the local labour force is working as outworkers and unpaid workers in family

Table 7. Number of Casual Employees by Sex, 1999–2005

Year	Number of Casual Employees			Percent Female
	Male	Female	Total	
1999	86,000	16,500	102,500	16.10
2000	102,200	20,700	122,900	16.84
2001	77,000	16,800	93,800	17.91
2002	67,800	12,900	80,700	15.99
2003	63,300	8,800	72,100	12.21
2005	58,800	10,300	69,100	14.91

Source: General household survey of various years, Census and Statistics Department

enterprises. These forms of family-based employment are characterized by greater flexibility in terms of time schedule, location, and autonomy of work. Thus, in the past women had a high representation in them (Ngo, 1992). However, as pointed out by Westwood, Ngo, and Leung (1997), the proportion of workers employed in these types of employment has gradually declined in Hong Kong since the 1970s. Currently less than 1% of working population was engaged in outworking and unpaid work in family business, compared to 6.3% in 1976. Similar to other advanced economies, "salaried employees" has been the prominent form of employment in the local labour market. As shown in Table 8, 83.18 % and 93.30% of male and female labour force were employed in this category in 2005.

It is worthy to note that the number of self-employed women has surged dramatically from 19,300 in 1991 to 53,900 in 2005, or 2.79 times. Hence, the proportion of self-employment in the female labour force rose from 1.87% to 3.51% during the period (please refer to Table 8). Although there are still more self-employed men in the labour market, the growth rate for self-employed women has been higher than for men. Compared with their male counterparts, self-employed women tend to be younger, single, better education, and more concentrated in service industries such as retail and personal services (Census and Statistics Department, 2004b). Self-employment becomes an attractive option for women probably owing to the following three reasons. First, similar to part-time work, self- employment can provide time flexibility that can make it easier for women to juggle work and family life. In fact, "better self-control on working hours" was given as the main reason for women to become self-employed (Census and

Table 8. Distribution of Employed Persons Among Various Employment Status by Sex, 1991–2005

Employment Status	Sex	1991	1996	2001	2005	Change in percentage, 1991–2003
Employees	Male	84.65	85.44	83.40	83.18	−1.47
	Female	94.08	95.01	94.31	93.30	−0.78
Employers	Male	7.95	7.94	7.44	6.79	−1.16
	Female	1.52	1.77	1.91	1.79	+0.27
Self-employed	Male	7.23	6.51	9.01	9.83	+2.60
	Female	1.87	1.82	2.58	3.51	+1.64
Unpaid family Workers	Male	0.15	0.11	0.14	0.20	+0.05
	Female	2.53	1.38	1.20	1.39	−1.14

Source: Census and Statistics Department, 1992 and 2006a

Statistics Department, 2004b). Second, the rapid expansion of the service sector provides a vast of opportunities for women to set up their own businesses in retail, trades, and personal services that require less start-up capital. As indicated by government statistics, in 2003, 98.1% of self-employed women were concentrated in the service sector. Third, for some women, self-employment is viewed as a means to escape barriers in paid employment such as glass ceiling that restricts their career advancement. Highly educated women, in particular, have a strong motive to start their own business, after accumulating some work experience and establishing business networks. As more women become entrepreneurs, the gender gap in self-employment has narrowed over the past decade. Another related trend is the increasing share of women being employers, which rose from 1.52% in 1991 to 1.79% in 2005. The corresponding rate for men has declined from 7.95% to 6.79% over the same period.

Occupational Sex Segregation

Despite massive entry of women in the labour force, the introduction of new technologies, and economic restructuring over the past few decades, employers continued to assign men and women to different occupations, resulting in an obvious occupational sex segregation (Padavic & Reskin, 2002). Occupational sex segregation refers to the different distributions of men and women across different occupations. It has been considered as a pervasive and persistent labour market phenomenon in industrial economies. Occupational sex segregation not only affects women's job opportunities and pay, it also leads to the devaluation of women's work. Throughout the world, women are over-represented in clerical, sales, and services work, while men are predominant in production and managerial occupations. There is no exception in Hong Kong.

Table 9 examines the changes in the gender composition of occupations between 1991 and 2001. Several points need to be noted. First of all, there has been an increase in women's representation in managerial, administrative, and professional occupations. As discussed before, higher education enables young women to enter into these better-paid, high-status jobs that used to be dominated by men. Based on the argument of Reskin and Roos (1990), the job growth in these occupations raised labour demand beyond the number of qualified men available, and thus the employers allow the highly educated women to fill the vacancies left. Second, women have also increased their share in associate professionals, clerical, service, and sales occupations. In

Table 9. Working Population by Occupational Group and Sex, 1991 and 2001

Occupational Group	1991			2001			Change in
	Male	Female	Percent female	Male	Female	Percent female	percent female 1991–2001
1. Managers and administrators	198,857	50,390	20.22	257,023	92,614	26.49	+6.27
2. Professionals	68,516	30,815	31.02	114,340	65,485	36.42	+5.40
3. Associate professionals	164,121	115,788	41.37	265,829	232,842	46.69	+5.32
4. Clerks	135,665	295,986	68.57	148,646	381,346	71.95	+3.38
5. Service workers and shop sales workers	230,823	128,496	35.76	264,466	224,495	45.91	+10.15
6. Craft and related workers	352,264	45,728	11.49	294,036	26,964	8.40	−3.09
7. Plant and machine operators and assemblers	234,929	130,897	35.78	207,001	31,665	13.27	−22.51
8. Elementary occupations	280,434	223,398	44.34	260,337	375,056	59.03	+14.69
9. Others	20,757	7,239	25.86	7,725	2,836	26.85	+0.99
Total	1686,366	1028,737	37.89	1,819,403	1,433,303	44.06	+6.17

Source: Census and Statistics Department, 1992 and 2002

2001, these occupational categories together employed 58.51% of the female labour force, compared to 52.52% a decade ago. Young women have been recruited in such female-typical jobs as health care workers, teachers of primary school and kindergarten, public relations officers, clerks, receptionists, bank tellers, and shop assistants. Third, the proportion of women employed as "craft and related workers" and "plant and machine operators and assemblers" fell rapidly between 1991 and 2001. With the shrinkage of blue-collar employment, women have left these occupations faster than men. Thus, these occupations have become more male-dominated than before. Lastly, a large number of women have entered into elementary occupations, and worked as cleaners, domestic helpers, and hand-packers. Many of them were factory workers who had lost their jobs in the process of economic restructuring. Without high educational qualifications and marketable skills, they were crowded into these low-status, low-paying jobs at the bottom of occupational hierarchy. Hence, the percentage of women in this occupational category has risen sharply from 44.34% in 1991 to 59.03% in 2001. These elementary occupations thus display a tendency of feminization. In view of the above, it seems that the temporal changes in gender composition of occupations have altered the pattern of sex segregation in the local labour market.

Occupational sex segregation is commonly measured by two indexes. The first is the index of dissimilarity (D), which is defined as follows:

$$S = 1/2 \, \Sigma \mid m_i - f_i \mid * 100$$

where m_i and f_i are the percentage of the male and female labour force employed in occupation i respectively. The range of the index is between 0 and 100, where 0 implies perfect gender integration and 100 implies complete segregation. A straight-forward interpretation is that the index value indicates the proportion of men (or women) that would have to change their occupations if women were to be distributed in the same manner as men. In general, a more detailed occupational classification scheme tends to yield a higher index value.

The dissimilarity index measures only one major dimension of segregation — *unevenness*. It indicates the degree to which two groups (e.g., men and women) are unevenly distributed over a set of occupational categories. Another key dimension of segregation is *concentration* and is represented by the concentration index (C). This index indicates the proportion of a particular group of workers who would have to change occupations to be evenly distributed across all occupations. It compares the actual distribution of women (or men) to an equal distribution, instead of comparing the distribution of women to that of men. We can calculate the concentration index for male workers (MC) and for female workers (FC). A measure of relative concentration (RC) can be also obtained, showing the extent to which women are more concentrated across occupations than men. The mathematical definitions of FC, MC, and RC are as follows:

$$FC = 1/2 \, \Sigma \mid f_i - (1/n) \mid * 100$$
$$MC = 1/2 \, \Sigma \mid m_i - (1/n) \mid * 100$$
$$RC = 1/2 \, \Sigma \mid f_i - (1/n) \mid - \mid m_i - (1/n) \mid * 100$$

where n is the total number of occupational categories and f_i and m_i are the percentage of women and men in the labour force employed in occupation i.

Table 10 reports the various indexes of segregation for the years of 1991, 1996, and 2001. The calculation is based on 29 occupational categories[6]. The value of the dissimilarity index rose slightly from 39.41 in 1991 to 40.10 in 2001. This suggests that the labour market has become more sex segregated than a decade ago. Along with the growth of the service

Table 10. Occupational Segregation Indexes in Hong Kong, 1991–2001

	1991	1996	2001	Change, 1991–2001
Index of Dissimilarity	39.41	39.80	40.10	+0.69
Male Concentration Index	41.36	42.33	43.81	+2.45
Female Concentration Index	52.26	51.45	55.62	+3.36
Relative Concentration Index	10.90	9.12	11.81	+0.91

sector, there has been an expansion of typically female jobs such as health care workers, receptionists, beauticians, cashiers, and shop assistants. Some women have moved into these occupations from the production occupations that have been declining since the 1980s. These expanding occupations have also absorbed a substantial number of young women who left the school. On the other hand, only few women have filled the newly created positions in the IT industry, as they lack the relevant knowledge and training. Men have been dominated in this industry. In addition, men have become more represented in the manufacturing sector than before. Lastly, many middle-aged women have been crowded into the low-paid, low-status elementary occupations. All these changes in gender composition of occupations contribute to an increase in the level of occupational sex segregation.

Furthermore, during the period of 1991–2001, both the male and female concentration index showed an upward trend. The value of female concentration index was 55.62 in 2001, much higher than the corresponding index for men (43.81). In other words, women were more concentrated than men in the occupational structure, especially in clerical and elementary occupations. In fact, 52.77% of women were employed in these two occupational categories in 2001. Due to a higher level of women's occupational concentration, the value of relative concentration index has also increased slightly from 10.90 in 1991 to 11.81 in 2001. In sum, all the indicators point to a higher degree of occupational sex segregation in Hong Kong than a decade before.

Immigrant Women and Employment

Hong Kong has been an immigrant society since it early history of incorporating into world economy. According to the 2001 census, slightly less than 60% of Hong Kong population is indigenous. Approximately 2.2 million of 32.7% of its current population have emigrated from mainland

Table 11. Employment Characteristics of New Immigrants from Mainland China

Employment Characteristics	Male (%)	Female (%)
Overall labour force participation rate	57.7	38.7
Age-specific labour force participation rate		
20–29	70.0	48.0
30–39	74.2	32.0
40–49	88.9	45.5
50 and above	53.1	28.3
Occupational group		
Managerial, professional, and associate professional	19.5	5.1
Clerks	6.3	12.8
Service workers and shop sales workers	16.7	35.8
Craft and blue-collar workers	40.7	5.6
Elementary occupations	16.8	40.2
Others	0.0	0.5

Source: Census and Statistics Department, 2000

China over the years, largely from the adjacent Guangdong province. Among them, 1,119,170 (i.e., 51.02%) are female, and 338,154 (i.e., 15.42%) are recent immigrants who have less than 7 years of residence in Hong Kong. It is worthy to note that the majority of these recent immigrants are women who came to Hong Kong for family reunion. Official statistics indicate that, for those holding one-way permit entering Hong Kong from mainland China during the period of 1997–2003, women constitute about 70%. These recent immigrant women were younger and had a lower educational attainment than their local sisters. In the process of economic assimilation in the host country, the employment pattern and labour market experiences of female immigrants are unique and deserve close examination (Ngo, 1994). Below we provide an analysis of the differences in work and employment between male and female immigrants who come from mainland China after 1997.

Table 11 provides information about the main differences between male and female immigrants in the labour market. The data come from the General Household Survey conducted by the Census and Statistics Department in 1999 (Census and Statistics Department, 2000). First of all, the level of economic participation of recent immigrants was much lower than that for the entire population. To be specific, the labour force participation rates for male immigrants, female immigrants, and whole population were 57.7%, 38.7%, and 62.0%, respectively in 1999. Recent immigrants have several disadvantages that adversely affect their work opportunities, including their poor qualifications, a lack of location-specific human capital, weak social networks, the language barriers, and employment discrimination (Chiu & Lui, 2004; Lee, 2002; Ngo, 1994).

Recent immigrant women had a particularly weak labour force attachment. In the workplace, they are likely to suffer from double disadvantages of being an immigrant and a woman at the same time. They are often the victims of employment discrimination. According to the above-mentioned survey, 81.1% of these recent immigrant women were married, and thus domestic responsibilities would be a constraint for them to work outside. Worse still, the lack of childcare support further inhibits them from seeking gainful employment (Lee, 2002). This can be reflected by their age-specific pattern of labour force participation. The rate for recent immigrant women aged between 30–39 (i.e., a period of child bearing and rearing) was 32%, much lower than the corresponding rate for the whole population (i.e., 67%). Such a gap in labour force participation can also be noted for other age groups, albeit smaller.

It is difficult for immigrant women to compete a job with local women who generally have higher educational attainment and more local work experience. Even when they are employed, they tend to become marginal workers and fill the low-paid unskilled jobs at the bottom of occupational hierarchy. As shown in Table 11, 35.8% of them were "service workers and shop sales workers" and another 40.2% were employed in "elementary occupations". As for male immigrants, a high percentage of them (i.e., 40.7%) were employed in the blue-collar occupations. Compared with female

Table 12. Distribution of Monthly Employment Earnings among
Various Groups, 2001

Monthly earnings (HK$)	Recent Immigrants from Mainland		Overall Population	
	Male	Female	Male	Female
Below 4,000	8.3	15.8	14.4	19.0
4,000 – 5,999	13.7	35.8	4.9	10.9
6,000 – 7,999	25.2	29.0	11.3	13.6
8,000 – 9,999	18.9	9.8	14.4	11.9
10,000 – 19,999	27.0	7.8	39.4	26.9
20,000 and above	6.8	1.9	27.1	17.8
Total	100.0	100.0	100.0	100.0
Median income	8,000.0	5,800.0	12,000.0	8,500.0

Source: Census and Statistics Department, 2002 and 2004a

immigrants, they were more represented in other occupations (such as managerial, craft and blue-collar jobs) and were less concentrated in a small number of occupations.

Because of their occupational placement, recent immigrants on average earned less than the local people. In 1999, their median income was about 60% of that of the whole population. Table 12 compares the income distribution of recent immigrants with that of the entire working population for the year of 2001. Among the four groups of workers, it is the female immigrants who had the lowest income attainment. On average, they earned about $5,800 from their main employment, which was 72.5% of that of male immigrants and 68.2% of that of female working population in Hong Kong. Moreover, about 80% of these immigrant women earned less than $8,000 in a month, reflecting that they were highly concentrated in low-paying jobs. In comparing with other groups, their income distribution was skewed toward the low end.

Conclusions

The post-handover Hong Kong is marked by its decision to actively engage in the process of globalization and informational economy, though the Hong Kong economy, at its early entrèpot stage, had already been deeply incorporated into the world market. With further emphasis upon building Hong Kong as a global city, however, the SAR government rendered unprecedented importance to information technologies and related trends of socio-economic development. Under these circumstances, we witness that this global restructuring is shaping new gendered work and employment patterns and creating disadvantaged actors who in Hong Kong are mainly working class people, middle-aged women, and the new immigrant women with low human and social capital. This is particularly true for the current generation of middle-aged lower-class women, who would be further excluded from this new mode of social and economic development. The difference in ability of access to the power of information technology in a global city will become a critical source of gender inequality in work and employment.

In Hong Kong, the past few decades has witnessed a steady and significant increase in women working outside the home. Women currently account for 45% of the local labour force. There has been a tendency to convergence of male and female labour force participation patterns. More women have become self-employed or employers with greater control over their work lives, while fewer women were engaged in unpaid family work. Women have also achieved more representation in prestigious occupations such as managerial and professional jobs. The income disparity between men and women has narrowed since the 1970s. In view of the above, one may conclude that a higher degree of gender equality has been achieved in Hong Kong.

Nevertheless, not all employed women were equally benefited in the process of economic development in the global age. It is true that young women have taken advantage of better assess to employment opportunities in the expanding industries. Their rising educational attainment enables them to compete successfully with men in the workplace. Hence, on average they earned as much as the male colleagues, and were much better off than other women. On the other hand, the less-educated and older women have been marginalized in the labour market owing to their disadvantages and domestic constraints. In the new global era with severe job competition, some of them have become unemployed, while others were drawn into the low-paid and low-skilled jobs. As such, there has been increasing differentiation among female workers in terms of employment situations and work outcomes. The overall pattern of gender inequality has also been subtly affected by this change. For example, a higher level of occupational sex segregation has been observed in Hong Kong in recent years.

In this paper, we argue that the trend of occupational and income polarization among employed women is accompanied with the advent of economic globalization in recent years. Globalization not only increased the demand for female labour, it also brought about several salient changes in the labour market with various impacts on the work lives of women. More importantly, the impacts of globalization appear to be uneven among them. As such, some women have made significant gains while others have suffered substantially (Carr & Chen, 2004). During the past two decades, the expansion and contraction of jobs have altered the employment structure in Hong Kong. In the process of "de-industrialization", many female factory workers had been displaced. Middle-aged and older women who had low educational qualifications and marketable skills were most vulnerable to job loss. They became the losers in the labour market, and experienced great difficulties in adjusting to the new economy.

Another impact of globalization is the rapid growth of the service sector, which becomes the main source of employment for women. Some of the jobs generated in the service sector require high-skilled workers, yet more require low-skilled workers. Men and women were unevenly drawn into the newly created positions. A large number of women have taken up those low-status and low-paid jobs (e.g., caring and cleaning jobs), because these jobs were considered as well suited for them based on gender stereotypes. In contrast, men tend to fill the professional, managerial, and IT-related jobs that offer high income. Unlike men, only a few women with high educational qualifications have overcome the barriers raised by employers and entered into these high-paying positions. Hence, the growth of the service sector brings about growing income disparity between the sexes and among women as well.

According to dual labour market theory, globalization and the new division of labour are associated with increasing differentiation and segmentation of the local labour market. In particular, there has been a polarization of jobs into the primary and secondary labour market. Highly-educated women in the primary labour market have taken advantage of their increased human capital and occupied jobs that offer good pay and career prospects. On the other hand, within the secondary labour market, low-skilled women have been crowded in a small number of low-paying service and elementary occupations that offer little advancement and job security (Aguilar, 2004). With an abundant supply of female labour, a process of 'ghettoization' has taken place in that sector (Ngo, 2000). The earnings of women employed in these jobs have remained low over time.

Furthermore, globalization also leads to the casualization of the employment relations in the form of rising job insecurity and part-time jobs (Chui & Lui, 2004; Pun, 2001). More flexible works have been available and reserved for women (especially those with heavy domestic responsibilities in their family life cycle). Since these flexible works generally offer low income, the overall pay gap has been widened between men and women as well as between young and middle-aged women.

To conclude with, western literature suggests that integration into the global economy significantly expands opportunities for women in the labour market, but does not remove barriers to women's advancement or ameliorate the predominance of low-paying inferior jobs held by them (Meyer, 2003). Thus, globalization results in the occupational polarization and deepening of gender inequality (Carr & Chen, 2004; Rupert, 2003). Similar to other industrialized countries, we observe these phenomena in the Hong Kong labour market in recent years. Another salient outcome of globalization is the increasing inequality among employed women in terms of job opportunities and income attainment. It seems that a new pattern of gender and age stratification has emerged in Hong Kong in the twenty-one century.

In this chapter, we provide some initial discussion on this topic. The intersection of gender and age on work outcomes in the global era should be further explored in future studies. More policy research should also be conducted to examine issues related to gender gap in education and employment in Hong Kong.

References

Afshar, H., & Barrientos, S. (1998). Introduction: Women, globalization and fragmentation. In H. Afshar & S. Barrientos (Eds.), *Women, globalization and fragmentation in the developing world* (pp. 1–17). New York: St. Martin's Press.

Aguilar, D. D. (2004). Introduction. In D. D. Aguilar & A. E. Lacsamana (Eds.), *Women and globalization* (pp. 11–24). New York: Humanity Books.

Beneria, L. (2003). *Gender, development, and globalization: Economics as if all people mattered*. New York: Routledge.

Blau, F., & Ferber, M. A. (1992). *The economics of women, men, and work*. Second Edition. New Jersey: Prentice Hall.

Blau, F., Ferber, M. A., & Winkler, A. E. (2002). *The economics of women, men, and work*. Fourth Edition. New Jersey: Prentice Hall.

Bloom, D.E. (2004). Globalization and education: An economic perspective. In M. M. Suarex-Orozco & D. B. Qin-Hilliard (Eds.), *Globalization: Culture and education in the new millennium* (pp. 56–77). Berkeley, CA: University of California Press.

Bodkin, R.G., & El-Helou, M. (2001). Gender differences in the Canadian economy, with some comparisons to the United States (Part I: Labour force characteristics). *Gender Issues 19*(2), 3–21.

Brinton, M. C. (2001). Married women's labor in East Asian economies. In M. C. Brinton (Ed.), *Women's working lives in East Asia* (pp. 1–37). Stanford: Stanford University Press.

Carr, M. & Chen, M. (2004). Globalization, social exclusion and gender. *International Labour Review*, 143, 129–160.

Census and Statistics Department. Various years. *Hong Kong annual digest of statistics*, Hong Kong: Government Printer.

Census and Statistics Department. (1992). *Hong Kong 1991 population census: Main tables*. Hong Kong: Government Printer.

Census and Statistics Department. (1997). *1996 population by-census: Main tables*. Hong Kong: Government Printer.

Census and Statistics Department. (2000). *Social data collected via the general household survey: Special topics report No. 25*. Hong Kong: Government Printer.

Census and Statistics Department. (2002). *2001 population census: Main tables*. Hong Kong: Government Printer.

Census and Statistics Department. (2004a). The movement of the unemployment rate in 2003. In *Hong Kong monthly digest of statistics, April 2004*. Hong Kong: Government Printer.

Census and Statistics Department. (2004b). *Social data collected via the general household survey: Special topics report No. 36*. Hong Kong: Government Printer.

Census and Statistics Department. (2006a). *Women and Men in Hong Kong: Key Statistics*. Hong Kong: Government Printer.

Census and Statistics Department. (2006b). *Social data collected via the general household survey: Special topics report No. 43*. Hong Kong: Government Printer.

Chiu, S. W. K., & Lee, C. K. (2003). Withering away of the Hong Kong dream? Women workers under economic restructuring. In E. Lee (Ed.) *Gender and change in Hong Kong: Globalization, postcolonialism, and Chinese patriarchy* (pp. 97–132). Hong Kong: Hong Kong University Press.

Chiu, S. W. K., & Lui, T. L. (2004). *Global city, dual city? Globalization and social polarization in Hong Kong since the 1990s*. Occasional paper no. 144. Hong Kong: Hong Kong Institute of Asia-Pacific Studies.

Elder, S., & Johnson, L. J. (1999). Sex-specific labour market indicators: What they show. *International Labour Review, 138*, 447–464.

Giele, J. Z., & Stebbins, L. F. (2003). *Women and equality in the workplace*. Santa Barbara, CA: ABC-CLIO, Inc.

Gunter, B. G., & Hoeven, R. (2004). The social dimension or globalization: A review of the literature. *International Labour Review, 143*, 7–43.

Kalleberg, A. L. (2000). Nonstandard employment relations: Part-time, temporary and contract work. *Annual review of sociology, 26*, 341–365.

Kaur, A. (2004). Economic globalization, trade liberalization, and labour-intensive export manufactures: An Asian perspective. In A. Kaur (Ed.), *Women workers in industrialising Asia: Costed, not valued* (pp. 37–58). New York: Palgrave.

Lee, W. K. M. (2002). The experience of recent mainland Chinese immigrant women in Hong Kong: An examination of paid and unpaid work. *Asia Journal of Women's Studies, 8*(4), 27–57.

Leung, C. B., & Bryant, S. L. (2000). Gender equity in the context of education in Hong Kong. *Educational Research Journal, 15*(1), 95–112.

Lui, S. S., Lau, C. M., & Ngo, H. Y. (2004). Global convergence, human resources best practices, and firm performance: A paradox. *Management International Review, 44* (Special Issue 2), 67–86.

Mak G. C. L., & Chung Y.P. (1997). Education and labour force participation of women in Hong Kong. In F. M. Cheung (Ed.), *Engendering Hong Kong society* (pp. 13–39). Hong Kong: The Chinese University Press.

Meyer, L. B. (2003). Economic globalization and women's status in the labor market: A cross-national investigation of occupational sex segregation and inequality. *Sociological Quarterly, 44*(3), 351–383.

Ngo, H. Y. (1992). Employment status of married women in Hong Kong. *Sociological Perspectives, 35*(3), 475–488.

Ngo, H. Y. (1994). The economic role of immigrant wives in Hong Kong. *International Migration, 32*(3), 403–423.

Ngo, H. Y. (2000). Trends in occupational sex segregation in Hong Kong. *International Journal of Human Resource Management, 11*(2), 251–263.

Ngo, H. Y. (2001). Perceptions of gender inequality at work in Hong Kong. *Asian Journal of Women's Studies, 7*(1), 111–132.

Ngo, H. Y. (2002). Part-time employment in Hong Kong: A gendered phenomenon? *International Journal of Human Resource Management, 13*(2), 361–377.

Padavic, I., & Reskin, B. (2002). *Women and men at work.* 2nd edition. Thousand Oaks, CA: Pine Force Press.

Pun, N. (2001). Gendered space and labour in the age of globalization. In Chan, K. W., Wong, K. M., & Leung, L. C. (Eds.), *Difference and equality: New challenges for the women's movement in Hong Kong* (pp. 201–209). Hong Kong: The Association for the Advancement of Feminism.

Pun, N., & Wu, K. M. (2004). Lived citizenship and lower-class Chinese migrant women: A global city without its people. In A. S. Ku and N. Pun (Eds.), *Remaking Citizenship in Hong Kong: Community, nation and the global city* (pp. 139–154). London and New York: RoutledgeCurzon.

Rai, S. M. (2002). *Gender and the political economy of development: From nationalism to globalization.* Cambridge: Polity.

Rama, M. (2003). Globalization and the labor market. *The World Bank Research Observer, 18*(2), 159–186.

Reskin, B. F., & Roos, P. A. (1990). *Job queues, gender queues: Explaining women's inroads into male occupations.* Philadelphia: Temple University Press.

Rupert, M. (2000). *Ideologies of globalization: contending visions of a new world order.* New York: Routledge.

Tang, C., Au, W. T., Chung, Y. P., & Ngo, H. Y. (2000). Breaking the patriarchal paradigm: Chinese women in Hong Kong. In L. Edwards & M. Roces (Eds.), *Women in Asia: Tradition, modernity, and globalization* (pp. 188–207). Australia: Allen Unwin.

Westwood, R. I., Ngo, H. Y., & Leung, S. M. (1997). The politics of opportunity: Gender and women in Hong Kong. Part I: The gendered segmentation of the labour market. In F. M. Cheung (Ed.), *Engendering Hong Kong society* (pp. 41–99). Hong Kong: The Chinese University Press.

Notes

1. For example, in 2001, the female labour force participation rate increased from a low level at the age group of 15–19, peaked at the age group of 25–29, and it

then decreased gradually with increasing age. It constitutes a typical single-peaked pattern.

2. The age-specific fertility rates for women in the age groups of 25–29, 30–34, and 35–39 declined sharply from 153.0, 97.3, and 34.4 respectively in 1981 to 62.0, 64.4, and 29.6 respectively in 2005 (Census and Statistics Department, 2006a). The crude birth rate in Hong Kong was 7.2 in 2004, which is also low by international standard.

3. According to official definition, a person is classified as *unemployed* if he or she (1) not have has a job and performed any work for pay or profit during the seven days before enumeration; (2) have been available for work profit during the seven days before enumeration; and (3) have sought work during the thirty days before enumeration. Unemployment rate is then calculated by dividing the number of unemployed persons by the size of the labour force and multiplying the quotient by 100% (Census and Statistics Department, 2004a).

4. It has been argued that the longer duration of unemployment for men than for women may reflect a greater tendency of female long-term unemployment to drop out of the labour force (Bodkin & El-Helou, 2001). The term "discouraged workers" is used to describe workers who leave the labour market or postpone their entry into it until economic conditions improve.

5. According to official definition, *part-time employees* refer to employees aged 15 or above who usually work (1) less than five days per week, or (2) less than six hours per day, or (3) less than thirty hours per week in their main employment. This definition includes both voluntary and involuntary part-timers. *Casual employees* refer to employees who were employed by an employer on a day-to-day basis or for a fixed period of less than 60 days. In other words, they are temporary workers or short-term contract workers.

6. Since the reported occupational categories (i.e., sub-major group) in the three censuses are not perfectly compatible, some standardization procedures have been used to correct for discrepancies. We collapsed some categories in the original classification scheme for the years of 1991 and 2001 and developed a new scheme of 29 occupations.

CHAPTER 4

Gender Earnings Differentials in Hong Kong

Chung Man Lee, Hongbin Li, and Junsen Zhang

Introduction

Gradual changes in social norms and culture have altered the role of women in Hong Kong. In the traditional society, men were the principal breadwinners in a family. Women were the homemakers, and they seldom entered the labour market. However, the trend has been changing in recent years. Nowadays, in Hong Kong, women are not only homemakers, they also contribute to the family income. Moreover, women today receive better education, are more career-minded, and are also welcomed by the labour market.

In terms of income, however, women may not be receiving equal treatment with men. Empirical findings show that female workers on average earn less than male workers. Using early data, Mak and Chung (1997) find the earnings of female workers are 35% less than those of male workers in 1976. Although the gender earnings differential decreased between 1976 and 1986, it increased again by 1991. Westwood et al. (1997) find a similar pattern for that period. According to Chung (1996) and Sung et al. (2001), the 1991 Hong Kong Census data showed female workers earning 30% less than male workers on average, and the 1996 Hong Kong By-Census data showed female workers earning 16% less than male workers. Lui and Suen (1993) and Suen (1995) obtain similar results using the same data sets. This indicates that a gender earnings differential still existed in Hong Kong in the 1990s. On the other hand, previous empirical studies have found that the gender earnings differential in Hong Kong has been diminishing in the

Junsen Zhang thanks the Hong Kong Research Grants Council (CUHK 4006-PPR-2) for financial support.

past two and a half decades. It narrowed from 40% to 31% during the period 1976-1986, remained unchanged during the period 1986–1991, and narrowed again from 30% to 16% during the period 1991–1996 (Lui and Suen 1993, Suen 1995, Chung 1996, and Sung et al. 2001).

The existence of gender earnings differentials may affect family decisions regarding the division of labour and resource allocation, and may reduce the incentive of females to work. Social problems may result from this. In the interests of stability, therefore, the HKSAR Government should be more concerned about the issue of gender earnings differentials. Most existing analyses have used data prior to 1995, thus, it is unknown what has happened to the gender earnings differentials since 1995, when the Sex Discrimination Ordinance was implemented.

This chapter analyzes gender earnings differentials using data from the 1991 Hong Kong Population Census, the 1996 Hong Kong Population By-Census, and the 2001 Hong Kong Population Census. We find that the female-male earnings ratio in Hong Kong increased significantly from 0.77 in 1991 to 0.82 in 1996, but by 2001 it had fallen back slightly to 0.81. That is to say, surprisingly, the gender earnings differential widened slightly even after the implementation of the Sex Discrimination Ordinance in 1995. Notwithstanding this slight widening from 1996 to 2001, the gender earnings differential still narrowed significantly over the whole decade from 1991 to 2001. The narrowing of the earnings differential between male and female workers from 1991 to 2001 is partly due to the rise of female educational achievement during that period. Indeed, a higher percentage of females than males had university degrees in 2001. In addition, the rate of return to education is also higher for females than males in all sampled years.

In examining the causes of existing gender earnings differentials, we employ the Blinder-Oaxaca method to decompose the earnings differentials between male and female workers into a part due to differences in observable gender productivity characteristics, such as education and work experience, and a part due to unexplained factors such as gender discrimination. Using several decomposition approaches, we find that over 90% of the earnings differentials in 1991, 1996 and 2001 are due to unexplained factors which may be caused by gender discrimination. Most of the decomposition approaches find a largest unexplained portion in 1996 and a smallest one in 2001. The decomposition analysis suggests that the wider gender earnings differential found in 2001 is caused by larger differences in productivity characteristics between male and female workers rather than by discrimination. In fact, the degree of discrimination is at its lowest level in

2001. Thus, this analysis suggests that the Sex Discrimination Ordinance may indeed have been successful in reducing discrimination.

Different age, educational level and occupation groups may face different sizes of gender earnings differential and different levels of gender earnings discrimination. For instance, Chung (1996) finds that the female-male earning ratio falls with age, and Lui and Suen (1993) find that a rise in female education level narrows the gender earnings differential. By dividing our samples into groups by age, education level and occupation, we find that both the size of the gender earnings differential and the level of discrimination vary among the groups. The gender earnings differential widens with age but the unexplained portion of the earnings differential becomes smaller as age increases. When looking at the earnings differentials at different education levels, we find that the gender earnings differential narrows up to a certain education level and it slightly widens after that level. By contrast, the unexplained portion of the differential rises up to a certain education level and it drops after that level. Lastly, our data suggest that both the gender earnings differentials and the unexplained portions are more pronounced in the lower-paid occupations.

The remainder of the chapter is organized as follows: Next section briefly reviews the literature on the gender earnings differential; the following section describes the data; another section describes the gender earnings differential in Hong Kong; the final section decomposes the differential by various methods. Section 6 concludes.

Literature Review

Generally speaking, a study of gender earnings differentials involves two steps: the estimation of the earnings equation for both men and women and the decomposition of the gender earnings differential using coefficients estimated from the earnings equation. Before moving to the empirical analysis, we first discuss the methods and empirical issues involved in the two steps, and then review findings on gender earnings differentials in Hong Kong.

The Determinants of the Earnings Equation

The most widely used earnings function for examining gender earnings differentials is in the form:

$$\log(\text{earnings}) = \alpha + \beta_1 \text{ education} + \beta_2 \text{ experience} + \beta_3 \text{ experience}^2 + \beta_4 \text{ sex} + \mu$$

where α and β are coefficients to be estimated and μ is the random error term.

As data are rarely available for the actual number of years of work experience, most studies follow Mincer (1974) and use the potential experience, defined as age — years of education — 6, as a proxy for actual experience. Mincer's potential experience measure is a reasonable proxy for actual experience for male workers because males on average exhibit a strong attachment to the labour force (Oaxaca 1973). However, Mincer's potential experience proxy is problematic for females, as females may leave the labour force for periods due to their household and childbearing activities, and hence the actual years of work experience of females may be overstated.

To proxy for females' potential years of lost labour market experience, Oaxaca (1973), for example, adds the "number of children" variable in his earnings equation of females. Using the 1967 Survey of Economic Opportunity, he finds that the presence of children reduces the earnings of white females at a rate of 2–3% for each child born. However, other studies such as Kidd and Shannon (1994) and Meng (1998b) find that the "number of children" variable is not significant. This may be because some children are not under the direct care of their parents, so that their mothers do not need to leave the labour market on account of having them.

Another variable that may affect a worker's earnings is his/her marital status. Although the simple earnings equation does not include the "marital status" variable, marital status may change one's productivity and work history and thus affect one's earnings. To account for the effect of marital status on the gender earnings differential, Hill (1979) investigates the validity of using marital status as a proxy for individual differences in labour force attachment. He finds evidence of a strong positive earnings effect of marriage among men, but no significant earnings effect of marriage among women. Similarly, Kidd and Shannon (1994) find a positive earnings effect for married men but there is no significant effect of marriage on women's earnings.

Besides the number of children and marital status, some other variables may also be included in the earnings equation to fully control for one's experience. These include occupation (Blau and Kahn 1997), total days of training (Liu et al. 2000), job tenure (Liu et al. 2000), grade point average (GPA) (Weinberger 1998), health (Oaxaca 1973), the veteran dummy variable

(Borjas 1983 and Cotton 1988), and regional variables (Oaxaca 1973 and Meng 1998a). All these variables may influence the earnings received by workers and thus alter the gender earnings differential.

Decomposition of Gender Earnings Differentials

It is commonly found that male workers earn substantially more than female workers. However, we cannot simply attribute all the earnings differentials to gender discrimination. There are at least two reasons for the gender earnings differential. The first is the difference between males and females in endowment, or productivity characteristics such as their education and work experience. It is reasonable to assume that a better endowed individual earns more. Therefore, if the average productivity characteristics of males are better than those of females, a gender earnings differential will arise. However, if females, on average, are better endowed than males, but males still receive higher earnings than females, this may be due to discrimination against women — a likely result of culture and social norms. In examining the components of the gender earnings differential, we use the method developed by Blinder (1973) and Oaxaca (1973) to decompose the earnings differential into a portion of the differential attributable to different endowments and a portion of the differential attributable to different coefficients (which may be due to discrimination). See details of the method in the appendix.

Empirical Findings on Gender Earnings Differentials

Previous studies examining the gender earnings differential in Hong Kong include Lui and Suen (1993, 1994), Suen (1995), Chung (1996) and Sung et al. (2001). These studies find that a gender earnings differential exists in Hong Kong, but the differential diminishes over time. For example, Chung (1996) and Sung et al. (2001) show that the overall female-male earnings ratio in Hong Kong increased from 0.60 in 1976 to 0.84 in 1996, using the Hong Kong Population Census data.[1] Lui and Suen (1993) and Chung (1996) find that the rises in female schooling and female labour participation are the main reasons for the narrowing gender earnings differential.

Among the different decompositions, the Blinder-Oaxaca decomposition is the most widely used in the literature. When examining the earnings differential in Hong Kong, both Lui and Suen (1994) and Chung (1996) decompose the gender earnings differential by the Blinder-Oaxaca method.

Lui and Suen (1994) use the Blinder-Oaxaca male-weighted and female-weighted decomposition to decompose the gender earnings differential in 1986, and find that the differences in productivity characteristics between male and female workers account for only about 24% (male-weighted) and 17% (female-weighted) of the overall earnings differential. Chung (1996) uses the males' earnings structure and females' earnings structure to examine the dynamics of the gender earnings differential fluctuations from 1976 to 1991. He finds that the major reason for the decreasing gender earnings differential in Hong Kong is the improvement of females' personal characteristics, particularly in regard to human capital.

Data Description

The data used in this study come from the 1% random sample of the 1991 Hong Kong Population Census, the 1% random sample of the 1996 Hong Kong Population By-Census, and the 1/14 random sample of the 2001 Hong Kong Population Census. This chapter primarily focuses on the gender earnings differential in 2001. The results of 1991 and 1996 are mainly used for comparison. All individuals selected were aged between 15 and 64 and worked for pay as employees in the government or the private sector with positive earnings. We observe that in recent years a large number of highly educated but low paid female overseas domestic workers have been present in the Hong Kong labour market. As this could significantly affect the estimate of the returns to tertiary education for females, we focus on local workers, who were born in Hong Kong or Mainland China. The resulting data set for 2001 contains a total of 177,081 observations, with 99,394 males and 77,687 females. The 1991 and 1996 samples contain 20,551 (12,637 males and 7,914 females) and 23,811 (14,313 males and 9,498 females) respectively. Table 1 reports the mean values of the characteristics for the three years by gender.

In this chapter, we define earnings as the monthly income from main employment. For employers or self-employed persons, this is the amount earned excluding expenses incurred in running their main business. For employees, this is the total amount earned from their main employment including salary or earnings, bonus, commission, overtime, housing allowance, tips and other cash allowances. New Year bonus and double pay are excluded. The amount recorded refers to the income for February of 1991, 1996 or 2001.

From 1991 to 2001, the educational attainment of both males and females increased to similar extents. The average years of schooling for males amounted to 9.10 in 1991, 9.90 in 1996, and 10.35 in 2001. The average years of schooling for females amounted to 9.38 in 1991, 10.33 in 1996 and 10.62 in 2001. According to Sung et al. (2001), females were less educated than males in 1981 and 1986 but they were, on average, more educated than males in 1991 and 1996. Consistent with the rising trend, our results show that females on average had higher education than males in 1991, 1996 and 2001 (Figure 1).

The increase in the levels of education among females can be explained as follows. In the traditional society, females had responsibility for most household production. They stayed at home, taking care of children and doing the housework. In addition, females were discriminated against by the labour market. However, as technology improved, household production became more efficient, and females no longer needed to spend as much time at home, leaving them free to take advantage of their opportunities in the labour market. As a result, the incentive for females to raise their human capital level has increased. Moreover, the government policy of free and compulsory education has also raised the educational and employment opportunities for women.

As well as showing the pattern of education attainment of males and females, Table 1 indicates that the average potential years of work experience for males was significantly higher than for females in 1991, 1996 and 2001. Since the data sets do not have information on individuals' hours of work and years of experience, we employ the Mincer (1974) measure (experience = age − years of schooling − 6) as a proxy for potential experience. This

Figure 1. Average Years of Education

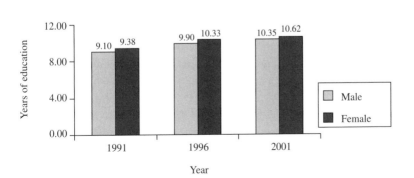

Table 1. The mean characteristics of the workforce

	1991		1996		2001	
	Male	Female	Male	Female	Male	Female
Age	35.987	32.857	37.131	34.168	38.125	35.959
Education	9.099	9.384	9.898	10.326	10.348	10.620
Experience	20.894	17.485	21.239	17.858	21.779	19.341
Experience^2	620.847	478.253	616.351	468.721	635.722	526.099
Married	0.5994	0.5298	0.6287	0.5606	0.6280	0.5488
China	0.3859	0.2909	0.3450	0.2787	0.3036	0.2697
Earning	7615.062	5873.224	13788.640	11327.310	16876.010	13650.240
Log Earning	8.715	8.463	9.277	9.096	9.455	9.240

experience measure is consistently larger for males than females. This may be mainly due to the fact that the average male was significantly older than the average female in all three years.

To facilitate later analysis of gender earnings differentials by age, we divide the sample for each year into three age cohorts: the young cohort (aged 15 to 29), the middle cohort (aged 30 to 44) and the old cohort (aged 45 to 64). As expected, the average education level of both male and female workers is highest for the young cohort and lowest for the old cohort. Table 2 reports the numbers of observations in each age group in 1991, 1996 and 2001.

We also divide the samples by education level. In this chapter, we have seven education levels:[2] no schooling, primary, lower secondary (F.1 – F.3), upper secondary (F.4 – F.5), matriculated (F.6 – F.7), craft and technical, and degree or above. Table 3 shows the number of observations and the corresponding percentage for each education level group in each year. Among the seven education levels, in all years, the highest percentage of people completed upper secondary education. The education levels of males and females increased significantly from 1991 to 2001. At the same time, the percentage with no education dropped from 4.43% to 1.40% for males and from 6.44% to 2.38% for females. Moreover, the percentage of people with degree level or above education increased from 6.76% to 14.74% for males and from 5.05% to 14.89% for females. This shows that from 1991 to 2001, the percentage of males who completed degree or above education nearly doubled, while that of females nearly tripled. This is consistent with our earlier finding that the average years of schooling of males and females increased through 1991 to 2001.

Table 2. Age structure of males and females in the workforce

Age Cohort	1991		1996		2001	
	Male	Female	Male	Female	Male	Female
Young (15–29)	4341	3718	3971	3531	25611	23991
	(34.352%)	(46.980%)	(27.744%)	(37.176%)	(25.767%)	(30.882%)
Middle (30–44)	5376	3001	6648	4373	44755	36523
	(42.542%)	(37.920%)	(46.447%)	(46.041%)	(45.028%)	(47.013%)
Old (45–64)	2920	1195	3694	1594	29028	17173
	(23.107%)	(15.100%)	(25.809%)	(16.782%)	(29.205%)	(22.105%)
Total	12637	7914	14313	9498	99394	77687

Figures in parentheses indicate percentages.

Table 3. Educational structure of males and females in the workforce

Education Level:	1991		1996		2001	
	Male	Female	Male	Female	Male	Female
No schooling	549	489	269	288	1380	1807
	(4.430%)	(6.444%)	(1.930%)	(3.182%)	(1.404%)	(2.376%)
Primary	3084	1581	2779	1510	15974	11346
	(24.887%)	(20.836%)	(19.943%)	(16.681%)	(16.250%)	(14.921%)
Lower secondary	3165	1200	3694	1367	24235	11380
	(25.541%)	(15.814%)	(26.509%)	(15.102%)	(24.654%)	(14.966%)
Upper secondary	3399	3082	4085	3751	29071	29076
	(27.429%)	(40.617%)	(29.315%)	(41.438%)	(29.573%)	(38.238%)
Matriculated	653	513	780	700	7058	6599
	(5.270%)	(6.761%)	(5.597%)	(7.733%)	(7.180%)	(8.678%)
Craft and techical	704	340	636	422	6091	4513
	(5.681%)	(4.481%)	(4.564%)	(4.662%)	(6.196%)	(5.935%)
Degree or above	838	383	1692	1014	14493	11319
	(6.762%)	(5.047%)	(12.142%)	(11.202%)	(14.743%)	(14.886%)
Total	12392	7588	13935	9052	98302	76040

Figures in parentheses indicate percentages.

Finally, we divide the samples by occupation. As we need a sufficient number of observations in all the groups, we group occupations under eight broad categories: (1) managers and administrators, (2) professionals, (3) associate professionals, (4) clerks, (5) service workers and shop sales workers, (6) craft and related workers, (7) plant and machine operators and assemblers, and (8) elementary occupations. The occupational distributions of males and females are given in Table 4. Broadly, the percentages of males and females working as managers and administrators, professionals, associate professionals, and service workers and shop sales workers increased over the years. Nevertheless, the percentages of males and females working as craft and related workers, plant and machine operators and assemblers, and in elementary occupations, decreased over time. The numbers of male professionals were at their lowest percentages in 1991, 1996, and 2001. The numbers of males in the crafts and related fields were at their highest

Table 4. Occupational distribution of males and females in the workforce

Occupation	1991		1996		2001	
	Male	Female	Male	Female	Male	Female
Managers and Administrators	654 (5.393%)	212 (2.748%)	1205 (8.711%)	506 (5.447%)	8375 (8.850%)	4297 (5.420%)
Professionals	510 (4.205%)	278 (3.603%)	755 (5.458%)	430 (4.629%)	4119 (4.353%)	6604 (8.329%)
Associate Professionals	1413 (11.652%)	1067 (13.828%)	1818 (13.142%)	1512 (16.277%)	16095 (17.009%)	14785 (18.648%)
Clerks	1228 (10.126%)	2673 (34.642%)	1423 (10.287%)	3435 (36.979%)	9546 (10.088%)	25491 (32.151%)
Service Workers and Shop Sales Workers	1848 (15.239%)	963 (12.481%)	2248 (16.251%)	1405 (15.125%)	15735 (16.628%)	13246 (16.707%)
Craft and Related Workers	2429 (20.030%)	138 (1.788%)	2475 (17.892%)	196 (2.110%)	15069 (15.924%)	796 (1.004%)
Plant and Machine Operators and Assemblers	1832 (15.107%)	1158 (15.008%)	1749 (12.644%)	424 (4.565%)	10636 (11.240%)	1968 (2.482%)
Elementary Occupations	2213 (18.249%)	1227 (15.902%)	2160 (15.615%)	1381 (14.867%)	15054 (15.908%)	12099 (15.260%)
Total	12127	7716	13833	9289	94629	79286

Figures in parentheses indicate percentages.

percentages in 1991 and 1996. However, by 2001, the pattern had changed; in that year most males worked as associate professionals. The numbers of females in the "craft and related workers" category were at their lowest percentages in 1991, 1996 and 2001. The number of females working as "clerks" was at their highest percentages in the same years. Among the eight occupations, fewer males than females worked as professionals and clerks. To the extent that the number of female clerks far exceeds that of male clerks, it seems that clerical work is, to a certain extent, a female-dominated field.

The above analysis only gives us a brief summary of the mean characteristics of males and females by age, education, and occupation. To more systematically examine the gender earnings differential, we will employ the econometric and earnings decomposition methods detailed in the following sections.

The Gender Earnings Differential in Hong Kong

Although there have been several studies of the gender earnings differential in Hong Kong, such as Lui and Suen (1993 and 1994), Suen (1995) and Sung et al. (2001), they all use data for the year 1996 or before. With the 2001 census data available, we can carry out further analysis of the gender earnings differential for the early 2000s and can carry out a more thorough study of the whole of the 1990s.

Table 5 shows a generally decreasing gender earnings differential from 1991 to 2001. In 1991, the average earnings of males was $7,615 and that of females was $5,873, implying a female-male earnings ratio of 0.77. The female-male earnings ratio increased to 0.82 in 1996 and decreased slightly to 0.81 in 2001. Despite the later small decrease in the earnings ratio, over the whole decade from 1991 to 2001 the gender earnings differential decreased by 0.04, or four percentage points.

The gender earnings differential differs for different age cohorts. Taking 2001 as an example, the gender earnings differential was not serious for young workers, with a female-male earnings ratio of 98% (Table 6). Moving to the middle and old cohorts (Tables 7 and 8), the gender earnings differential widens to 82% and 67% respectively. The narrow differential for the young cohort may be due to improved education levels of young females relative to young males. The trend over time also differs across age cohorts. For the young cohort, although the differential decreases from 1991 to 1996, it widens from 1996 to 2001. However, for the middle cohort, the differential

Table 5. Average earnings and the wage differentials

Year	Average Monthly Earnings		Female-Male Earnings Ratio	Average Monthly Log Earnings		Log Differential
	Men	Women		Men	Women	
1991	7615.062	5873.224	0.7713	8.715	8.463	0.2519
1996	13788.640	11327.310	0.8215	9.277	9.096	0.1816
2001	16876.010	13650.240	0.8089	9.455	9.240	0.2156

Table 6. Average earnings and the wage differentials for young cohort

Year	Average Monthly Earnings		Female-Male Earnings Ratio	Average Monthly Log Earnings		Log Differential
	Men	Women		Men	Women	
1991	6061.209	5467.405	0.9317	8.575	8.513	0.0627
1996	10375.120	10551.510	1.0170	9.096	9.126	−0.0299
2001	11590.300	11330.540	0.9776	9.198	9.181	0.0167

Table 7. Average earnings and the wage differentials for middle cohort

Year	Average Monthly Earnings		Female-Male Earnings Ratio	Average Monthly Log Earnings		Log Differential
	Men	Women		Men	Women	
1991	9266.787	6676.408	0.7205	8.895	8.529	0.3667
1996	15963.080	12824.890	0.8034	9.429	9.179	0.2506
2001	19740.950	16165.930	0.8189	9.630	9.398	0.2321

Table 8. Average earnings and the wage differentials for old cohort

Year	Average Monthly Earnings		Female-Male Earnings Ratio	Average Monthly Log Earnings		Log Differential
	Men	Women		Men	Women	
1991	6884.102	4558.778	0.6622	8.591	8.144	0.4464
1996	13544.830	8937.384	0.6598	9.198	8.801	0.3976
2001	17122.390	11540.610	0.6740	9.413	8.984	0.4282

has a monotonic decreasing trend. Finally, for the old cohort, the differential has almost no change over years.

We next analyze the gender earnings differential for different education levels. Earnings increased with education for both males and females in 2001. However, the gender earnings differential may have a non-linear relationship with education levels. As expected, the gender differential is largest among persons with no schooling; the differential decreases and reaches the smallest level among the upper secondary group; and it widens again among groups with higher education. The gender earnings differential narrows most rapidly from lower secondary education to upper secondary education. By contrast, surprisingly, the differential widens most from the matriculated to degree holders. The gender earnings differential for 1991 and 1996 has a similar pattern across education levels, except that there is an even smaller gender earnings differential among illiterates than among people with primary school education.

Although gender earnings differentials can arise from the differences in occupational distributions of males and females, Table 9 shows that in 2001, even within the same occupation, males and females were paid differently. Associate professionals, followed by clerks, have the narrowest gender earnings differential among the eight occupations. However, in the lower-paid occupations such as service workers, shop sales workers, craft and related workers, plant and machine operators and assemblers, and in elementary occupations, the earnings differentials between male and female workers were larger. The gender earnings differential was largest for plant and machine operators and assemblers.

To show the trend over time of the differentials for each occupation, the gender earnings differentials for differential occupational sectors in 1996 and 1991 are reported in Tables 10 and 11. We can see that among high-skilled workers such as managers, administrators, professionals, associate professionals, and clerks there is a decreasing gender earnings differential from 1991 to 2001. However, among lower-skilled workers, the differential narrows from 1991 to 1996 but widens from 1996 to 2001.

Some argue that the gender earnings differential exists because of occupational segregation: female workers are discriminated against when they seek to enter the high-paid occupations and are therefore most likely to work in the lower-paid occupations. However, Section 3, Table 4 shows that a higher percentage of males than females work in the lower-paid occupations. This suggests that occupational segregation may not be a principal cause of higher average earnings among males. Indeed, Sung et

Table 9. Average earnings and the wage differentials of different occupations in 2001

Occupation	Average Monthly Earnings		Female-Male Earnings Ratio	Average Monthly Log Earnings		Log Differential
	Men	Women		Men	Women	
Managers and administrators	40166.430	34368.850	0.8557	10.370	10.247	0.1228
Professionals	38086.150	32411.690	0.8510	10.300	10.195	0.1048
Associate Professionals	20546.500	19198.290	0.9344	9.755	9.701	0.0535
Clerks	11796.930	11006.680	0.9330	9.261	9.196	0.0653
Service Workers and Shop Sales Workers	13150.240	8542.778	0.6496	9.340	8.899	0.4414
Craft and Related Workers	11076.440	8597.367	0.7762	9.203	8.932	0.2712
Plant/Machines Operators and Assemblers	11280.960	6523.936	0.5783	9.247	8.637	0.6102
Elementary Occupations	8431.889	6209.456	0.7364	8.939	8.609	0.3298

Table 10. Average earnings and the wage differentials of different occupations in 1996

Occupation	Average Monthly Earnings		Female-Male Earnings Ratio	Average Monthly Log Earnings		Log Differential
	Men	Women		Men	Women	
Managers and administrators	31326.450	26496.410	0.8458	10.092	9.958	0.1334
Professionals	32399.190	26787.290	0.8268	10.157	10.003	0.1533
Associate Professionals	18268.330	16279.700	0.8911	9.625	9.526	0.0994
Clerks	10703.870	9734.857	0.9095	9.182	9.102	0.0806
Service Workers and Shop Sales Workers	11083.730	8005.640	0.7223	9.192	8.852	0.3398
Craft and Related Workers	9533.013	7582.796	0.7954	9.047	8.809	0.2377
Plant/Machines Operators and Assemblers	10009.610	5830.649	0.5825	9.123	8.510	0.6127
Elementary Occupations	7499.088	5661.386	0.7549	8.824	8.537	0.2874

Table 11. Average earnings and the wage differentials of different occupations in 1991

Occupation	Average Monthly Earnings		Female-Male Earnings Ratio	Average Monthly Log Earnings		Log Differential
	Men	Women		Men	Women	
Managers and administrators	19347.250	15589.230	0.8058	9.603	9.422	0.1806
Professionals	19815.230	15596.700	0.7871	9.662	9.502	0.1604
Associate Professionals	10704.150	9220.790	0.8614	9.095	8.972	0.1234
Clerks	6495.160	5717.447	0.8803	8.680	8.571	0.1091
Service Workers and Shop Sales Workers	6805.670	4708.445	0.6918	8.704	8.338	0.3661
Craft and Related Workers	5947.369	3817.696	0.6419	8.573	8.143	0.4303
Plant/Machines Operators and Assemblers	5732.386	3307.582	0.5770	8.579	8.006	0.5728
Elementary Occupations	4553.954	3293.545	0.7232	8.338	8.000	0.3379

al. (2001) also find that gender earnings differentials are most likely to occur within occupations, rather than between broad occupational categories.

Decomposition of the Gender Earnings Differential

We have illustrated that a gender earnings differential exists in Hong Kong. Moreover, the difference in the average endowments of males and females shown earlier provides a simple explanation for the existence of the gender earnings differential. However, the factors that really cause the differential remain unanalyzed. For instance, the earnings differential may be a result of discrimination, or it may reflect differences in productivity characteristics. In this section we perform various widely adopted decomposition analyses in an attempt at a more in-depth investigation of the components of the gender earnings differential.

Decomposition for the Overall Samples

Using the Blinder-Oaxaca male-weighted decomposition, of the 0.2156 log earnings differential in 2001, only 7.56% can be explained by differences in personal characteristics; the remaining 92.44% is unexplained (Table 12).

As we can see from the data, the difference in average working experience of males and females contributes most to the explained portion of the gender earnings differential. Indeed, males on average have 2.44 years more work experience than females.

The 92.44% unexplained portion is caused by differences in coefficients estimated from the male and female earnings equations, and in particular from the estimated coefficients on the constant, the marriage dummy, and experience. As shown in Table 12, most of the differences in coefficients arise from the differences in the estimated intercepts. The intercept of the male earnings equation is much larger than that of the female equation, which suggests that, ceteris paribus, a male worker earns substantially more than does a female. This difference is caused by either discrimination or other variables omitted in our regression model. As well as the huge unexplained part from the intercept, a large unexplained portion arises from the different reward to marriage. Marriage increases the earnings of a male worker by 25.12%, but of a female worker by only 3.21%, which suggests that the gender earnings differential is much wider for married workers than for single ones. Marital status is thus a possible source of discrimination. The discrimination may be caused by the disincentive for companies to invest in training of married female workers who may temporarily quit the labour market for childbearing. The difference in return to work experience (4.28% for males and 3.71% for females), measured by the coefficients on

Table 12. The male-weighted Blinder-Oaxaca decomposition

	1991		1996		2001	
	Explained	Unexplained	Explained	Unexplained	Explained	Unexplained
Constant	0.0000	0.2481	0.0000	0.1492	0.0000	0.2788
Education	−0.0253	−0.2220	−0.0421	−0.1670	−0.0305	−0.2361
Experience	0.1292	0.2540	0.1185	0.2106	0.1043	0.1101
Experience^2	−0.0823	−0.1677	−0.0769	−0.1175	−0.0701	−0.0835
Married	0.0158	0.1184	0.0137	0.0919	0.0199	0.1202
China	−0.0210	0.0047	−0.0128	0.0140	−0.0073	0.0098
Mean log earnings differential	0.2519		0.1816		0.2156	
Explained	0.0164		0.0004		0.0163	
% of explained	6.500%		0.233%		7.559%	
Unexplained		0.2355		0.1812		0.1993
% of unexplained		93.500%		99.767%		92.441%

the experience variables in the earnings equation, also increases the portion of unexplained earnings differential, but the effect is smaller than that caused by the intercept or the marriage dummy.

For 1996, the unexplained portion is even larger. Nearly 100% of the gender earnings differential is unexplained and may be due to discrimination. The explained portion due to productivity differences between males and females is only a very small part of the overall differential (0.23%). For 1991, there is a larger explained part (6.50%). As we can see from Table 12, most of the unexplained parts in 1991 and 1996 arise from the different reward to work experience. For instance, in 1991, one more year of work experience increases the earning of a male worker by 3.79%, but of a female worker by only 2.34%. If an additional year of work experience increases the productivity of a male worker by the same amount as a female worker, then the difference in the return to work experience is most likely the result of sex discrimination in the labour market.

To conclude, the unexplained portion of the overall gender earnings differential due to coefficient differences increased from 1991 to 1996 and fell back again in 2001. Therefore, sex discrimination, in terms of the percentage of the unexplained factor in the overall gender earnings differential, is believed to have been most serious in 1996. The pattern of the unexplained portions over the ten years given by the other decompositions is similar to that obtained from the male-weighted decomposition (Figure 2).

Figure 2. The unexplained portion given by the decompositions

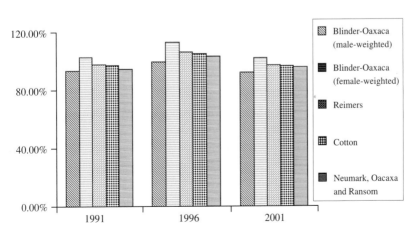

Decomposition by Groups

In this part, we divide the samples into groups and decompose the gender earning differentials for each group by the five decompositions specified in the Appendix. To save space, decomposition results are not reported; we just discuss the results.

Decomposition by Age Cohort

The explained portion of the overall earnings differential for the young cohort is negative in all three years, indicating that young females exceed young males in productivity characteristics. Despite their higher productivity characteristics, female workers earned more than males only in one of the three years, 1996. In 1996, the mean log earnings differential is negative. However, even in that year, gender discrimination still existed, with a positive unexplained part of the earnings differential.

For the middle cohort, the explained portion found from the male-weighted decomposition is very small in all three years. Nearly all the earnings differential between males and females is unexplained and may be due to sex discrimination. A large component of the unexplained part comes from the large difference in reward to marriage. For 2001, marriage increases the earnings of a male worker by 24.47%, but of a female worker by only 1.60%. The explained part in 2001 and 1991 is positive, indicating that the males were better in productive characteristics in these two years, and is negative in 1996, indicating that females exceeded males in productivity characteristics in that year.

In the old cohort, a larger portion of the earnings differential is explained by the male-weighted decomposition, 17.28%, 12.49% and 18.60% in 1991, 1996 and 2001, respectively. In all sampled years for this cohort, the average years of schooling for males exceed those of females, which explains part of the earning differentials. Most of the unexplained gender earning differentials of the old cohort comes from the differences in the intercepts between males' and females' earnings equations, which suggests that discrimination may be the underlying reason.

In summary, the explained portion of the earning differential between male and female workers is largest for the old cohort, becomes smaller for the middle cohort, and becomes negative for the young cohort. This trend suggests that the improvement of female human capital over time tends to reduce the gender earnings differential. However, surprisingly, the more educated cohorts (young and middle) have larger unexplained parts in percentage terms. Our results are robust, as we use different decomposition methods. The sizes of the unexplained portions given by other decompositions lie between those given by the male-weighted and the female-weighted decompositions (see Figure 3).

Decomposition by Education Level

In 2001, the unexplained portion of the earnings differential between male and female workers is largest for the lower secondary group (103.25%), and smallest for the group with degree or above (37.81%). The explained parts even become negative for the primary and lower secondary groups. The unexplained part for the matriculates and degree holders mainly comes from the difference in the return to education between male and female workers. Indeed, an additional year of schooling increases the earnings of matriculated (degree holding) males by 16.34% (29.67%), but of females in the same group by only 13.20% (25.70%). On the other hand, the unexplained parts for the people with no schooling, primary or lower secondary education are mainly caused by gender differences in the return to work experience, while the unexplained parts for the upper secondary, craft and technical groups are mostly due to the gender differences in reward to marriage.

The result for 1996 is similar to that for 2001, but the result for 1991 differs a little. In 1991, the unexplained part of the gender earnings differential is largest for the group with primary education, and smallest for the

Figure 3. The unexplained portion given by the decompositions
for each age cohort, 2001

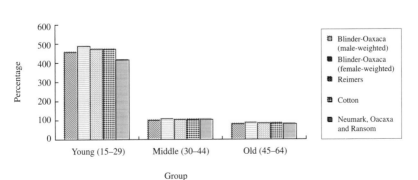

matriculated group. It is also worth noting the trends of the unexplained portions for the primary and "craft and technical" groups. The percentage of unexplained earnings differential for the primary group generally decreases over the years, from 108.51% in 1991 to 105.36% in 1996 and finally 101.05% in 2001. Therefore, the degree of discrimination might decrease over time for this group. However, although the unexplained portion for the craft and technical workers is quite low, it increases slightly over the years, from 39.79% to 45.72% and 46.11% in 1991, 1996 and 2001 respectively. Therefore, the degree of discrimination for this group seems to increase over time. As expected, the percentages of unexplained components in most groups given by the other three decompositions fall between those found from the male-weighted and female-weighted decompositions (Figure 4).

Decomposition by Occupation

For 2001, the two groups, "managers and administrators" and "professionals," face a low degree of discrimination with more than 50% of the gender earning differentials explained. In contrast, the three groups, "clerks," "craft and related workers," and "elementary occupations," face a high degree of discrimination with the unexplained portions exceeding 100%. As with previous findings, the coefficient differences of most groups come from the intercept terms and the differences between male and female workers in the

Figure 4. The unexplained portion given by the decompositions
for each education level, 2001

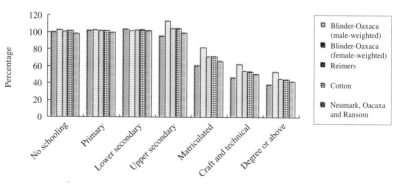

reward to additional years of work experience. For instance, the return to work experience is 2.43% for male plant and machine operators and assemblers, but it is only 0.27% for the female workers in that occupation. For professionals, on the other hand, the return to schooling accounts for most of the coefficient difference and thus the unexplained part. An additional year of education increases the earning of a male professional by 15.16%, but of a female professional by only 12.38%.

The results for 1996 by the male-weighted decomposition are a little different from the results for 2001. As for professionals, managers and administrators, the explained part for associate professionals also exceeds 50%. The unexplained portion exceeds 100% only for craft and related workers and the elementary occupations. As with the result for 2001, the group with the smallest unexplained part is "managers and administrators" (33.47%). The group with the largest unexplained portion is craft and related workers (clerks in 2001). Again, the coefficient differences in most groups come from the "work experience" variable.

In 1991, the unexplained portion is smallest for professionals, and largest for craft and related workers. However, for all occupations the unexplained part is less than 100%. In addition, the explained part for professionals and clerks is more than 50%. As for 1996 and 2001, the coefficients of the "work experience" variable contribute largely to the unexplained portion in most groups.

The differences in productivity characteristics between male and female professionals explain more than 50% of the overall gender earnings differentials in all three sampled years. Nevertheless, the unexplained portion for clerks jumps dramatically from less than 50% in 1991, to 92.55% in 1996 and finally to 113.19% in 2001. Furthermore, the unexplained part of the overall gender earnings differential for craft and related workers and elementary occupations increases slightly from below 100% in 1991 to more than 100% in 2001. Again, the sizes of the unexplained portions given by the three other decompositions lie between those given by the male-weighted and female-weighted decompositions (Figure 5).

Conclusion

This chapter analyzes gender earnings differentials in Hong Kong from 1991 to 2001. Using data from the 1991 Hong Kong Population Census, the 1996 Hong Kong Population By-Census, and the 2001 Hong Kong Population Census, we find that the female-male earnings ratio in Hong Kong increased

Figure 5. The unexplained portion given by the decompositions
for each occupation, 2001

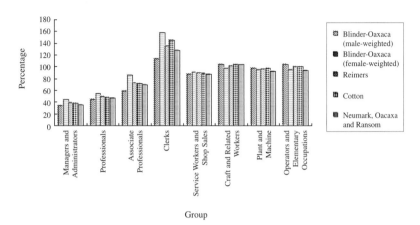

significantly from 0.77 in 1991 to 0.82 in 1996, but it decreased slightly to
0.81 in 2001. That is to say, surprisingly, the gender earnings differential
widened slightly even after the implementation of the Sex Discrimination
Ordinance in 1996. However, after carrying out a deeper investigation of
the gender earnings differential in 2001, we find that the wider gender
earnings differential was caused by the larger productivity characteristics
differences between male and female workers. The degree of discrimination
is found to have been lower in 2001. This may indicate the success of the
Sex Discrimination Ordinance. The narrowing of the earnings differential
between male and female workers from 1991 to 2001 is partly due to the
rise in female education achievement during that period. A higher percentage
of females than males entered universities in 2001. In addition, the rate of
return to education for females is higher than the return for males in all
sampled years.

     To examine the causes of the existing gender earnings differentials, we
decomposed the earnings differentials between male and female workers
into a part due to differences in observable productivity characteristics and
a part due to unexplained factors such as sex discrimination. Five
decomposition approaches of the Blinder/Oaxaca type, which only differ
in defining the non-discriminatory earnings structure, were used. The
decomposition method can help to examining the underlying basis of earnings

differentials that could be attributable to discrimination. Most of the decomposition approaches find a largest unexplained portion in 1996 and a smallest one in 2001. In other words, the unexplained portion of the overall gender earnings differential due to coefficient differences increased from 1991 to 1996 and then decreased to a smallest size in 2001. The decompositions show that over 90% of the earnings differentials in these three years were due to unexplained factors which may be caused by discrimination or the omitted variables in our regression model. The results from the five decompositions only differ very slightly (2% to 10%). The Blinder-Oaxaca male-weighted decomposition always serves as a lower bound for the estimates of the unexplained portions, while the female-weighted approach most likely serves as an upper bound for the estimates.

After dividing our samples into groups by age, education level and occupation, we find that not only the size of the gender earnings differential, but also the level of discrimination varies across groups. It is found that the gender earnings differential widens with age but the unexplained portion of the earnings differential gets smaller as age increases. When looking at the earnings differentials in different education levels, we find that the gender earnings differential narrows up to a certain education level and then widens slightly after that level. By contrast, the unexplained portion of the differential rises up to a certain education level and drops after that level. Finally, our data suggest that both the gender earnings differentials and the unexplained portions are more pronounced in lower-paid occupations.

References

Blau, F. D., & Kahn, L. M. (1997). Swimming upstream: Trends in the gender earnings differential in the 1980's. *Journal of Labour Economics, 15,* 1–42.

Blinder, A. S. (1973). Earnings discrimination: Reduced form and structural estimates. *Journal of Human Resources, 8,* 436–455.

Borjas, G. J. (1983). The measurement of race and gender earnings differentials: Evidence from the federal sector. *Industrial and Labour Relations Review, 37*(1), 79–91.

Chung, Y. P. (1996). Gender earnings differentials in Hong Kong: The effect of the state, education, and employment. *Economics of Education Review 15*(3), 231–243.

Cotton, J. (1988). On the decomposition of earnings differentials. *The Review of Economics and Statistics, 70*(2), 236–243.

Fan, C., & Lui, H. K. (2003). Structure change and the narrowing gender gap in earnings: Theory and evidence from Hong Kong. *Labour Economics*, *10*(5), 609–626.

Hill, M. S. (1979). The earnings effects of marital status and children. *The Journal of Human Resources*, *14*, 579–594.

Hinks, T. (2002). Gender earnings differentials and discrimination in the New South Africa. *Applied Economics*, *34*, 2043–2052.

Kidd, M. P., & Shannon, M. (1994). An update and extension of the canadian evidence on gender earnings differentials. *Canadian Journal of Economics*, *27*, 918–938.

Liu, P. W., Meng, X., & Zhang, J. (2000). Sectoral gender earnings differentials and discrimination in the transitional Chinese economy. *Journal of Population Economics*, *13*, 331–352.

Lui, H. K., & Suen, W. (1993). The narrowing gender gap in Hong Kong: 1976–1986. *Asian Economic Journal*, *7*(2), 167–180.

Lui, H. K., & Suen, W. (1994). The structure of the female earnings gap in Hong Kong. *Hong Kong Economic Papers*, *23*, 15–29.

Mak, C. L., & Chung Y. P. (1997). Education and labour force participation of women in Hong Kong. In F. Cheung (Eds.), engendering Hong Kong society (pp. 13–40). Hong Kong: The Chinese University Press.

Meng, X. (1998a). Male-female earnings determination and gender earnings discrimination in China's rural industrial sector. *Labour Economics*, *5*, 67–89.

Meng, X. (1998b). Gender occupational segregation and its impact on the gender earnings differential among rural-urban migrants: A Chinese case study. *Applied Economics*, *30*, 741–752.

Mincer, J. (1974). Schooling, experience and earnings. *National Bureau of Economic Research*, New York.

Neumark, D. (1988). Employers discriminatory behavior and the estimation of earnings discrimination. *Journal of Human Resources*, *23*, 279–295.

Oaxaca, R. L. (1973). Male-female earnings differentials in urban labour markets. *International Economic Review*, *14*, 693–709.

Oaxaca, R. L., & Ransom, M. R. (1994). On discrimination and the decomposition of earnings differentials. *Journal of Econometrics*, *61*, 5–21.

Reimers, C. W. (1983). Labour market discrimination against hispanic and black men. *Review of Economics and Statistics*, *65*, 570–579.

Suen, W. (1995). Gender gap in Hong Kong: An update. *Asian Economic Journal*, *9*(3), 311–319.

Sung, Y. W., Zhang, J., & Chan, C. S. (2001). Gender earnings differentials and occupational segregation in Hong Kong, 1981–1996. *Pacific Economic Review*, *6*, 345–359.

Weinberger, C. J. (1998). Race and gender earnings gaps in the market for recent college graduates. *Industrial Relations*, *37*(1), 67–84.

Westwood, R. I., Ngo, H. Y., & Leung S. M. (1997). The politics of opportunity:

Gender and work in Hong Kong. In F. Cheung (Eds.), *Engendering Hong Kong society* (pp. 41–100). Hong Kong: The Chinese University Press.

Appendix: Decomposition Method

The difference (Δ) of logarithmic average earnings between males and females can be decomposed into:

$$\Delta = (\overline{X_m} - \overline{X_f})\,\beta_m + \overline{X_f}\,(\beta_m - \beta_f)$$

where $\overline{X}$ is a vector of average characteristics, the subscript m indicates the male group, the subscript f represents the female group, and β, the coefficients estimated from the log(earnings) equation, represents a non-discriminatory earnings structure. On the right hand side of the equation, the first term reflects the part of the earnings differential attributable to differing endowments while the second term is the unexplained part of the differential attributable to differing coefficients, which may reflect discrimination and unmeasured skills. In other words, the first term is an explained part measured by the differences in average endowment between male and female workers, and the second term represents the unexplained part measured by differences in parameters that are estimated from the earnings equations of males and females separately.

However, it is well known that the Blinder-Oaxaca decomposition of the gender earnings differential is not unique. The above equation is referred to as a male-weighted decomposition, which uses the estimated coefficients from the male's earnings equation to calculate the gender earnings differentials. Similarly, we could also have a female-weighted decomposition. Moreover, there are also three alternative decomposition methods including that by (Reimers, 1983), one by Cotton (1988) and one by Neumark (1988) and Oaxaca and Ransom (1994). In our empirical work, we will focus on the Blinder-Oaxaca method, but will also report results from other decomposition methods as comparison.

Among the five decompositions, the Blinder-Oaxaca decomposition is the most widely used in the literature examining the earnings differential. This chapter focuses on the decomposition results from the Blinder-Oaxaca (1973) male-weighted decomposition. The Blinder-Oaxaca (1973) female-weighted, Reimers (1983), Cotton (1988), and Neumark (1988) and Oaxaca and Ransom (1994) decompositions are also reported for comparison.

Before the decomposition analysis, we first estimate the earnings equations for males and females. The following Mincer (1974) human capital earnings equation is estimated separately for males and females:[3]

$$\log(\text{earnings}) = \beta_0 + \beta_1 (\text{Education}) + \beta_2 (\text{Experience})$$
$$+ \beta_3 (\text{Experience})^2 + \beta_4 (\text{Married}) + \beta_5 (\text{China}) + \varepsilon$$

where 'Education' is the number of years of education of the person, and 'Experience' is the potential years of work experience of an individual. This chapter applies the Mincer measure of actual experience, which is defined as (experience = age – years of education – 6). The square of experience is added in the earnings equation to capture the nonlinear effect of work experience on earnings. 'Married' is a dummy variable which reflects the marital status of the individual. It is equal to one if the person is married and is equal to zero otherwise. The dummy variable 'China' represents people who were born in Mainland China. It is equal to one if the person was born in Mainland China and is equal to zero otherwise.

Notes

1. Indeed, both Lui and Suen (1993) and Chung (1996) point out that the gender earnings gap in Hong Kong narrows during the period 1976–1986. Suen (1995) further finds that the gender earnings gap in Hong Kong remains virtually unchanged between 1986 and 1991.
2. The groups indicate the highest education level completed by the individuals.
3. Occupation and industry may be important for the determination of the gender earnings gap. An in-depth analysis can be found in Fan and Lui (2003).

CHAPTER 5

Gender and Political Participation in Hong Kong: Colonial Legacies and Postcolonial Development

Wong Pik-wan and Eliza W. Y. Lee

In recent decades, equality in gender representation has emerged worldwide as a major feature of "good governance." It is stressed that democratic governance should include equal participation and representation of women in politics and decision-making. Accordingly, the global community has been trying to increase women's political participation through various means. On 22 December 2003, the U.S.-sponsored resolution on women and political participation was adopted by the full General Assembly of the United Nations. The United States, joined by 110 co-sponsors, succeeded in passing the much-needed resolution, giving a resounding United Nations endorsement to women across the globe becoming active participants in the political life of their countries. The resolution reaffirms basic principles on women's participation in the political process, such as the right of women to vote in all elections and to run for and hold office. Governments are urged to ensure equal access to education and to eliminate laws and regulations that discriminate against women. The resolution also urges political parties to seek qualified female candidates and provide them with the training and support that would help to expand the political, management, and leadership skills of women (U.S. Department of State, 2003).

As of 31 March 2007, on average, global female representation in both Houses of all parliaments constitutes only 17%. The Nordic countries score 41.7%, the highest among all countries and regions. The overall extent of female representation in parliaments in Asia remains lower than in the Nordic countries and most European countries. Within Asia, mainland China,

Taiwan, and Hong Kong fare better than many other Asian countries such as Philippines, South Korea, Indonesia, Thailand, India and Japan (Table 1).

In 1995, the Hong Kong government participated in the United Nations Fourth World Conference on Women held in Beijing at which the Beijing Platform for Action was endorsed. The Platform for Action sets out strategic objectives to empower women through promoting their advancement and removing all the obstacles to their active participation in all spheres of public and private life. Governments, the international community, and civil society, including non-governmental organizations and the private sector, were called upon to take measures to ensure that women have equal access to and fully

Table 1. Representation of Women in Parliament, Regional Averages as of 31 March 2007

	Lower or Single House	Upper House or Senate
Nordic countries	41.7%	–
Americas	20.0%	19.3%
Europe: OSCE member countries (including Nordic countries)	19.8%	17.5%
Europe: OSCE member countries (excluding Nordic countries)	17.7%	17.5%
Asia	16.5%	15.7%
Mainland China	20.3%	–
Taiwan[1]	20.9%	–
Hong Kong[2]	18.3%	–
Singapore	24.5%	–
Philippines	15.3%	16.7%
South Korea	13.4%	–
Indonesia	11.3%	–
Thailand	8.7%	–
India	8.3%	10.7%
Japan	9.4%	14.5%
Sub-Saharan Africa	16.8%	18.0%
Pacific	12.4%	32.1%
Arab States	9.5%	6.3%

Note: 1. Situation as of 2004. See Table 6 of Sun (2005).
2. Information based on Table 2. Information from the by-election in December 2007 is not included.

Source: Information mainly drawn from the Inter-Parliamentary Union (http:// www.ipu.org/wmn-e/classif.htm, retrieved on 4 May 2007).

participate in power structures and decision-making at all levels; and to increase the capacity of women to participate in decision-making and leadership.[1] On 14 October 1996, the United Nations Convention on the Elimination of All Forms of Discrimination against Women (CEDAW) was extended to Hong Kong. Article 7 of the CEDAW states that "States Parties shall take all appropriate measures to eliminate discrimination against women in the political and public life of the country and, in particular, shall ensure to women, on equal terms with men, the right: (a) To vote in all elections and public referenda and to be eligible for election to all publicly elected bodies; (b) To participate in the formulation of government policy and the implementation thereof and to hold public office and perform all public functions at all levels of government; (c) To participate in non-governmental organizations and associations concerned with the public and political life of the country."[2]

This chapter will provide a historical overview on gender and political participation in Hong Kong, covering the colonial period and postcolonial development. We focus on three different aspects of gender and political participation. The first section analyzes gender participation in the formal governing institutions and in the administration of the Hong Kong Special Administrative Region (HKSAR) government. The second section focuses on gender participation in the electoral processes. The participation of women as voters and as candidates in the electoral processes will be scrutinized. We seek to understand whether a gender gap exists in political participation, and to explore whether the recent partial democratization process has affected the representation of women in the District Council (DC) and in the Legislative Council (LegCo). The last section explores gender and community participation in Hong Kong

Formal Participation

Gender and Participation in the Governing Institutions and Administration

Legally speaking, not only do women in Hong Kong have the same rights as men to vote and to stand for elections, the HKSAR Government has also adopted a policy of equal opportunities in recruiting and promoting civil servants. Nevertheless, the Government has failed to implement affirmative action or special measures to enable and realize the right of women to participate in all areas of public life and particularly at high levels of the political decision-making process. This section provides an overview of the relative status of both sexes in the central and district levels of governing institutions, in the civil service, in the judiciary system, and in government advisory and statutory bodies.

Representation of Women in Governing Institutions

In 2007, women were both under-represented at both the central and local levels of governing institutions. As shown in Table 2, women now occupy 13.8%-18.3% of all positions in formal governing institutions in Hong Kong. The government of the HKSAR is led by the Chief Executive and the Executive Council. The Executive Council, the highest governing institution, assists the Chief Executive in policy-making and all its members are nominated by the Chief Executive. In May 2007, women held only 4 of the 29 seats (13.8%) in the Executive Council.[3] As for the legislature, all of its members are elected, with half of the seats directly elected through geographical constituencies, and the other half elected by functional constituencies. In the LegCo election held in September 2004, 26 out of 159 candidates were women. Of the 26 female LegCo candidates, half had participated in elections in geographical constituencies, and half had competed for the seats elected by functional constituencies. In May 2007, women hold only 11 of the 60 seats (18.3%) in LegCo. Anson Chan won the by-election and joined the LegCo since 3 December 2007. Of the present 12 female legislators, 7 were elected by geographical constituencies; the remaining 5 were elected by functional constituencies. In the DC election held in 2003, of the 502 elected and appointed members, only 90 (17.9 %) were women.

Table 2. Percentage of female councillors at the central and local levels of governing institutions, May 2007

		Total number	Number of women	Percentage of women
Central level	Executive Council	29	4	13.8%
	Legislative Council[1]	60	11	18.3%
District Level	District Councils[1]	502[2]	90	17.9%

Notes: 1. By-elections figures are not included.
2. 27 ex-officio members are not included.
Source: Census and Statistics Department (2006:99–100)

Representation of Women in the Civil Service

In 2007 women held about a third of civil service posts. In general, women remain less well represented in the top tiers of the administrative and judicial systems. As shown in Table 3, in May 2007, in the top level of government administration, only 3 of 19 principal officials and officials at the rank of directors of bureau were women. Of the 35 officials of directorate grade 6 rank and above (and equivalent), only 8 were women. It is only in the post of permanent secretary that female civil servants had a relatively high degree of representation (42.1%).

In recent decades, the growth of representation of women in the civil service has been better than that in other governing institutions. The representation of women in directorate-level positions has risen from 4.9% in 1981 to 24.6% in 2003 (Burns 2004:44–45, 202–203).[4] The gender composition of the Administrative Officer grade has changed dramatically over the past two decades. In 1983, women made up less than 18% of the grade as a whole. By 2003, women were holding nearly 52% of all positions in the administrative Service. The trend towards gender equality in the administrative service is remarkable. Burns (2004:110–111, 202–203) has argued that this may have been caused by an increase since 1996 in the participation of female students in programmes funded by the University Grants Committee. Consequently, many more qualified female graduates than male graduates have been competing for government jobs. Female university graduates have also been performing at a better than average level in civil service recruitment examinations that "place a premium on verbal skills and communication ability, which may favor business, arts, and social science graduates. Women now dominate these subjects in Hong Kong's universities."

Table 3. Percentage of women in government administration, May 2007

Posts	Total number	Number of women	Percentage of women
Principal officials and officials at the rank of directors of bureau	19	3	15.8%
Permanent secretaries	19	8	42.1%
Officials of directorate grade 6 rank and above (and equivalent)	35	8	22.9%

Source: Civil and Miscellaneous Lists (http://www.info.gov.hk/cml/, retrieved on 4 May 2007)

Representation of Women in the Judiciary System

In the judiciary system, Table 4 shows that all four of the judges of the Court of Final Appeal are men. However, the percentage of female judges in the High Court has increased from 0% in 1991 to 19.4% in May 2007, while in the same period in the District Courts the percentage of female judges increased from 14.7% to 35.7%. As in the administrative service, the increase in the representation of women in the High Court and District Courts can be explained by a rise in the number of female undergraduate students admitted to law schools. Since the early 1980s, females have out-numbered males in the law programme of the University of Hong Kong (Choi, 2003: 47). Consequently, women have been able to enter the judiciary, improving the balance of its gender composition in the last decade or so.

Representation of Women in Government Advisory and Statutory Bodies

Although political powers are highly centralized within the executive-led government, a network of government advisory and statutory bodies (ASBs) has been established. The government seeks to obtain, through consultation with interest groups and individuals in the community, the best possible advice on which to base decisions or to perform statutory functions. The existing 501 ASBs are divided among those that are advisory in nature and those that are executive bodies performing public functions on a wide range of matters affecting the lives of residents in Hong Kong. The proportion of women in ASBs has remained relatively low. This issue has captured the

Table 4. Percentage of women in the judiciary, 1991 and 2007

Posts	Total number		Number of women		Percentage of women	
Year	1991	2007	1991	2007	1991	2007
Judges of the Supreme Court (prior to 1997)	10	–	0	–	0 %	–
Judges of the Court of Final Appeal (after 1997)	–	4	–	0	–	0%
Judges of the High Court	22	31	0	6	0%	19.4%
Judges of the District Court	34	28	5	10	14.7%	35.7%

Sources: Civil and Miscellaneous Lists (http://www.info.gov.hk/cml/, retrieved on 4 May 2007); data of 1991 adapted from Lui (1995:141).

attention of the Women's Commission, who discussed the matter with the Home Affairs Bureau in March 2001. The Women's Commission (2004: 42–43) suggested that positive measures be taken to enhance the participation of women. Currently, the HKSAR government is adopting a modest gender benchmark, with each sex having a minimum representation in such bodies of 25%. With this gender benchmark, we observe that the representation of women in ASBs has gradually improved. As shown in Table 5, as at 31 October 2006, the total number of female non-official members appointed to ASBs was 1,294 (or 25.8%), while 3,727 members (or 74.2%) were men.

Notwithstanding the conscious effort by the government, the representation of women in ASBs has demonstrated an increase of only 6. 5% since 2001 (from 19.3% in 2001 to 25.8% in 2006). As reported by the Secretary of Home Affairs, Dr. Patrick Ho, in 2006, there were 369 ASBs with appointed non-official members, the remaining 132 ASBs did not have appointed non-official member. Of these 369 ASBs, 180, or nearly half, have reached the benchmark of 25%, while 189, or more than half of the ASBs, have failed to do so (Home Affairs Bureau, 2006). The latest Home Affairs Bureau figures showed that 37 comprised between 20–25% of female members, 77 had fewer than 10% of women, while in 66 ASBs, women comprised 10 to 20% of members (Lam 2007). To ensure that the voices of women are heard at different stages of policy formulation and decision-making, the government will have to constantly review and raise the gender benchmark to be in line with the international standards.

Summing up so far, we can say that the expansion of the higher education sector since the 1990s has increased the proportion of women entering universities and other institutions of higher education. This, in turn, has led

Table 5. Percentage of women non-official members serving on pubic sector ASBs, 2001–2006

Year	Number of persons	Number of women	Percentage of women
2001	5,939	1,147	19.3%
2002	5,981	1,208	20.2%
2003	5,319	1,190	22.4%
2004	8,638	1,971	22.8%
2005	4,115	935	22.7%
31 Oct.2006	5,021	1,294	25.8%

Source: Census and Statistics Department (2006:103); Home Affairs Bureau (2006).

to the participation of more women in both the higher ranks of the civil service and the lower ranks of the judiciary. However, women are still under-represented, especially in the top tiers of the administrative, governing, and judiciary institutions. Nor is the situation any better in the ASBs. Here, despite the government's recent adoption of a modest gender benchmark, the representation of women has only marginally improved and more than half of the ASBs failed to reach the benchmark. In the following section, we will examine women's participation in the electoral processes and see if there has been any significant improvement over the past two decades.

Gender Participation in the Electoral Process

As there are different levels of participation, rather than making the general claim that women participate less than men, a distinction should be made according to specific forms of political participation. This section examines gender participation in the electoral process and seeks to understand if any gender difference exists. We will first examine the participation of women as electors who cast their votes in the central and district elections; and second, look at women who participated as candidates and ran for public office.

Gender and Voter Participation

At the first level of political participation, the conventional understanding that "women don't care about politics" can no longer be substantiated in Hong Kong. Table 6 shows that, in recent years, there has not been a significant gender gap in registered voters and voter turnout rates. In the DC election held in 2003, there were over 2.97 million registered electors, and close to half of them (48.8%) were women.[5] In the 2004 LegCo election, there were over 3.2 million registered electors, and again almost half of them (48.9%) were women. Similarly, in the two recent LegCo elections, there was no significant gender gap in terms of voter turnout rates. In fact, in 1998, slightly more women than men turned out to vote. In the two recent DC elections held in 1999 and 2003, the gender gap (though a minor one) in voter turnout was also reversed, with women voting more often than men.

Gender and Participation as Candidates

If there is no significant gender gap in voter turnout rates, is there any gender

Table 6. Registered electors and voter turnout in DC and LegCo elections,
1998–2004

	DC Election		LegCo Election		
	1999	2003	1998	2000	2004
Registered electors (gender percentage)					
Females	1,359,507 (48.0%)	1,450,339 (48.8%)	1,334,792 (47.8%)	1,477,334 (48.4%)	1,568,594 (48.9%)
Males	1,473,017 (52.0%)	1,523,273 (51.2%)	1,460,579 (52.3%)	1,578,044 (51.7%)	1,638,633 (51.1%)
Total	2,832,524	2,973,612	2,795,371	3,055,378	3,207,227
Voter turnout (turnout rate)					
Females	396,859 (29.2%)	522,998 (36.1%)	716,639 (53.7%)	643,766 (43.6%)	868,387 (55.4%)
Males	419,644 (28.5%)	543,375 (35.7%)	773,066 (52.9%)	687,314 (43.6%)	916,019 (55.9%)
Total	816,503	1,066,373	148,9705	1,331,080	1,784,406 (55.6%)

Sources: Census and Statistics Department (2002:83, 2006:101).

difference in participation as candidates in elections? In this section, we will examine gender participation as candidates at both the district level and the central level. We will identify whether women have made any progress in this form of participation over the past two decades.

To elect women to public office you need to ensure two things: women who are willing and able to stand as candidates, and voters who are willing to vote for them. In Hong Kong, voters in general do not have strong bias against female candidates or politicians. Two recent surveys on the popularity of legislators show that the three most popular legislators, namely Rita Fan, Audrey Eu, and Selina Chow, are all female.[6] Indeed, the success rate of female candidates is, in general, slightly higher than that of their male counterparts. Unfortunately, for the past four Chief Executive elections conducted from 1996 to 2007, all candidates contested for the post were male. Women were more enthusiastic in joining the DC and LegCo elections though the proportion of women candidates remains low in both elections. As there has been little work that focusing on female candidates, this section also analyzes their profiles and seeks to understand their party identities.

DC Elections

The 18 DCs came into being on 1 January 2000 by virtue of the District Councils Ordinance. The DCs have a wider role than the former District Boards (DBs). The Councils advise the HKSAR government on district affairs and promote recreational and cultural activities, and environmental improvement within their respective districts. In 1994, as part of the political reforms of the last Governor Chris Patten, all appointed DB seats were abolished. Following Hong Kong's return to Chinese sovereignty, the first Chief Executive of the new HKSAR government, Tung Chee-hwa, reverted to the pre-1994 practice, that is, he reinstated 102 appointed seats in the DCs. The DCs comprise both elected members and appointed members.

As shown in Table 7, the percentage of female candidates in DC elections has increased gradually from 5.0% in 1982 to 17.4% in 2003. In the first DBs elections held in 1982, there were only 20 women among 403 candidates (Tong, 2003:198). The number of female candidates rose to 146 among 837 in 2003. In 1982, only 10.1% of District Councillors were female; by 2003, the representation of women in the DC had increased to 17.9%.

Over the last two decades, there has been a huge gap between the two sexes in terms of participation as candidates in the DC elections. Table 8

Table 7. Percentage of female candidates in district-level elections, 1982–2003

Year of DB/ DC election	1982	1985	1988	1991	1994	1999	2003
Candidates							
Number of women	20	30	52	48	97	129	146
	(5.0%)	(6.0%)	(10.6%)	(10.3%)	(12.8%)	(16.2%)	(17.4%)
Total Number	403	501	493	467	757	798	837
Councillors							
Number of women	24	23	29	43	36	72	90
	(10.1%)	(8.0%)	(9.1%)	(9.8%)	(10.4%)	(14.6%)	(17.9%)
Total number	237	289	320	441	346	492	502

Note: By-election figures are not included.
Sources: Data partially adapted from Tong (2003:198); Westwood, Mehrain & Cheung (1995: 148); and Census and Statistics Department (2006:100).

Table 8. Gender analysis of the candidates participating in the 2003 DC elections

	Males	Females	Total
Number of candidates	691 (82.6%)	146 (17.4%)	837
Number of elected councillors	264 (81.0%)	62 (19.0%)	326
Number of uncontested councillors	65 (87.8%)	9 (12.2%)	74
No. of appointed councillors	83 (81.4%)	19 (18.6%)	102
Total number of district councillors	412 (82.1%)	90 (17.9%)	502

Sources: Based upon information posted on the Electoral Affairs Commission's website (http://www.eac.gov.hk/en/distco/2003dc_elect.htm) and Census and Statistics Department (2006:100)

shows that 82.6% of the candidates who ran for office at the district level were men, while women accounted for only 17.4%. Table 8 also shows that while 102 district councillors were appointed in 2003, women constituted only 18.6% of the appointed seats. The continuation of the appointment system has always been a matter of debate, as many democrats have argued that it violates the principles of democracy and political equality. The principles governing the appointment system have also not been disclosed. The government, on the other hand, has insisted that democracy has more than one definition, and that no political system worth the name of democracy should ignore the minority voices that may be marginalized and ignored in a simple majority voting system. Seen in this light, the point of maintaining the appointment system is to balance the different voices and interests within the wider society. Be that as it may, from a gender perspective there is no obvious sign that the government has used the appointment system as a way of promoting gender parity in the DCs.

Since political parties have played an important role in recruiting female candidates over the previous DC elections, it is worth taking a closer look at their performance. We have chosen the two largest political parties, the Democratic Party (DP) and the Democratic Alliance for Betterment and Progress of Hong Kong (DAB) for in-depth analysis. Table 9 shows that in the 2003 DC elections, women constituted only 18.5% of the DP candidates.

Table 9. Political party and gender participation in the 2003 DC elections

		DP		DAB
Total number of candidates	Overall	124	Overall	205
	Male	101 (81.5%)	Male	173 (84.4%)
	Female	23 (18.5%)	Female	32 (15.6%)
Number of elected candidates	Overall	93[1]	Overall	61
	Male	75 (80.6%)	Male	50 (82.0%)
	Female	18 (19.4%)	Female	11 (18.0%)
Success Rate (%)	Overall	75.0%	Overall	29.8%
	Male	74.3%	Male	28.9%
	Female	78.3%	Female	34.4%

Note: 1. In October 2006, the number of DC members of the Democratic Party has dropped to 78 as 15 elected members left the DP after the election.

Sources: Suen (2003) and the Electoral Affairs Commission's website (http://www.eac.gov.hk/en/distco/2003dc_elect.htm)

Of the 93 DP district councillors, only 18 were female (19.4%). A similar gender gap was apparent for DAB, where more of the candidates and councillors were male than female. In the DC elections held in 2003, women constituted only 15.6% of the DAB candidates. Of the 61 DAB district councillors, only 11 were female (18.0%).

Table 9 shows that the under-representation of women in the recruitment and nomination of female candidates is a problem for both political parties. If the representation of women in the DCs is to increase, it is important that the political parties follow a more progressive strategy to increase their female party membership and to nominate more female candidates, and provide them with training, support, and necessary resources. Since the election success rate for female candidates of both parties is higher than that of male candidates, political parties should change their election strategies in future so that women's interests have a fair and equal representation in the DCs.

LegCo Elections

As for the central level, prior to 1985 all members of the LegCo were appointed by the Governor. LegCo began to introduce indirect elections in 1985, and direct elections in 1991. The gradual process of democratization has created new room for women to participate in formal politics. Table 10 shows that the number of female candidates running for office increased from 4 in 1985 to 26 in 2004. However, the number of female candidates seems to have reached a ceiling of 24 to 28 in the past three LegCo elections. Despite the fact that women make up half of the electorate, relatively few women reach this central level of political participation and, as yet, female representation in LegCo has not broken the 19.3% barrier.

Comparative studies on gender and democratization in other countries have shown that democratization alone is not a sufficient factor to determine the degree of improvement in the social and political status of women. The general public has demonstrated a strong desire to have a democratically elected legislature, as seen from the mass rallies on 1 July 2003 and 2004. However, we should be aware that the process of increasing democratization and the emergence of party politics since the 1990s have not automatically brought more female legislators into the LegCo. The first direct election conducted in 1991 was for 18 seats that were directly elected through geographical constituencies; six women participated but only one (Emily Lau) was able to win a seat.[7] If we compare the figures of LegCo elections held in 1988 and those in 2004, the representation of women has dropped

Table 10. Number of female candidates in the LegCo elections, 1985–2004

Year of LegCo elections	1985	1988	1991	1995	1998	2000	2004
Number of female candidates							
Functional constituencies	1	3	1	7	6	10	13
Election Committee	3	2	0	0	4	1	–
Geographical constituencies	–	–	6	8	14	17	13
Total	4	5	7	15	24	28	26
Number of elected female councillors							
Functional constituencies	0	0	1	4	4	5	5
Election Committee	0	2	0	0	2	1	–
Geographical constituencies	–	–	1	3	4	5	6
Total	0	2	2	7	10	11	11
Number of appointed female councillors (including ex-officio members)	7	9	5	0	0	0	0
Total number of female councillors	7*	11*	7*	7	10	11	11
	(12.3%)	(19.3%)	(11.7%)	(11.7%)	(16.7%)	(18.3%)	(18.3%)
Total number of councillors	57	57	60	60	60	60	60

Note: * Including ex-official members, appointed members, and elected members.
Sources: PA Professional Consultants Ltd. (1993); Tong (2003:197); and information posted on the LegCo website
            (http://www.legco.gov.hk).

slightly after the gradual political opening of the legislature. Women entered LegCo as appointed members prior to 1995, but after 1995 all appointed seats in the legislature were cancelled and women have had to take part in elections (in which candidates are elected through an Election Committee, functional constituencies, or geographical constituencies). The growth in the representation of women in LegCo has been rather disappointing.

Geographical Constituency Elections

Table 11 shows that of the 13 female candidates who ran in the LegCo elections in 2004, the majority were members of a party or were affiliated with a political group or trade union. Seven of the 13 were incumbent legislators seeking re-election. All seven were re-elected except for Cyd Ho. The other six "new bloods" all failed to win election. Their failure can probably be explained by the Proportional Representation System adopted by the HKSAR government after the handover, and by the way the political parties handled their party lists. Many female candidates were placed lower down the party list, and this consequently lowered their chances of success in the election. Most of the major political parties (including the DP and the

Table 11. List of women candidates of the 2004 LegCo geographical
constituency elections

Candidate	Ranking on the voting list	Party identity/Political affiliation
Hong Kong Island		
CHOY So Yuk*	2nd on a list of 6 candidates	DAB
FAN HSU, Lai Tai Rita*	1st on a list of only 1 candidate	Independent
EU Yuet Mee, Audrey*	1st on a list of 2 candidates	Basic Law Article 45 Concern Group (Civic Party, in 2007)
HO Sau Lan, Cyd	2nd on a list of 2 candidates	The Frontier, Civic Act-up
Kowloon West		
LEE Wai King, Stary	3rd on a list of 3 candidates	DAB
LEUNG Suet Fong	2nd on a list of 2 candidates	union
Kowloon East		
CHAN Yuen Han*	1st on a list of 3 candidates	Hong Kong Federation of Trade Unions/ DAB
New Territories West		
KONG Fung Yi	2nd on a list of 4 candidates	Hong Kong Association for Democracy and People's Livelihood
AU YEUNG Po Chun	4th on a list of 8 candidates	DAB
CHOW LIANG Shuk Yee, Selina*	1st on a list of 2 candidates	Liberal Party
New Territories East		
LAU Wai Hing, Emily*	2nd on a list of 7 candidates	The Frontier
HO Suk Ping, Shirley	6th on a list of 7 candidates	DP
WONG Pik Kiu	6th on a list of 7 candidates	DAB

Note: * Denotes candidate who won the election.

Source: 2004 Legislative Council Election (http://www.elections.gov.hk/elections/legco2004/english/results/
rs_gc_overall.html)

DAB) handled their party lists in this way, showing that party leaders were
not keen to send more women into LegCo.

Functional Constituency Elections

In 2004, there were 13 female candidates who participated in the functional
constituency elections. Only five of them had a party identity or political
affiliation; most of them ran for office as independent candidates. Of the
five candidates who won seats, four were incumbent legislators, with only
one "new blood" (Tam Heung Man) able to win a seat (Table 12).

Factors Constraining the Formal Participation of Women

The persistence of the gender gap cannot be attributed to one single factor,

Table 12. List of women candidates of the 2004 LegCo functional
constituency elections

Functional constituencies	Candidate	Party identity/ Political affiliation
Transport	LAU Kin Yee, Miriam*	Liberal Party
Legal	NG Ngoi Yee, Margaret*	Basic Law Article 45 Concern Group (Civic Party, in 2007)
	KWONG Ka Yin	Independent
	TONG Kei Yuk, Judy	Independent
Accountancy	TAM Heung Man*	Independent (Civic Party, in 2007)
Social Welfare	FANG Meng Sang, Christine	Independent
Health Services	PONG Oi Lan, Scarlett	Independent
	SIU Kwai Fung	Independent
Labour	LI Fung Ying*	The Federation of Hong Kong and Kowloon Labour Unions
Textiles and Garment	LEUNG LAU Yau Fun, Sophie*	Liberal Party
Information Technology	LEUNG Mun Yee, Miriam	Independent
Catering	WONG Sin Yin, Lillian	Independent
	CHAN Shu Ying, Josephine	Democratic Party

Note: * Denotes candidate who won the election.
Source: 2004 Legislative Council Election (http://www.elections.gov.hk/elections/legco2004/english/results/ rs_gc_overall.html)

but rather should be seen as the result of a subtle interplay of various elements, involving gender roles, family and child-rearing responsibilities, differences in socioeconomic resources because of job inequality, institutional factors, and biased media attention (Hooghe and Stolle, 2004). Since the 1970s, feminist scholars have stressed that inequalities in the private sphere (with regard to the division of labour and power in the household) have inhibited women from participating politically in formal political institutions. The sexual division of labour in production and reproduction make it much more difficult for women to fully exercise their citizenship. Feminist theorists have also argued that any evaluation of the democratization process must take into consideration not only the level of representation of women in political institutions, but also their general position within the family and the society. A political system that excludes women from participating fully and equally in political life should not be considered "democratic" (Pateman, 1988, 1989:210; Phillips, 1992:71–75; Rai, 1994:210).

Recent research in Hong Kong has pinpointed the various contextual factors that have inhibited the formal participation of women in Hong Kong.

The constitutional arrangement of the Basic Law allows for only partial democracy and a slow pace of democratic transition (Tong 2003), and acts as a hindrance to both the healthy development of party politics and the nurturance of politicians. A female councillor stressed that:

> "There is no prospect in politics in Hong Kong, both in terms of personal career and in terms of monetary reward. It is difficult to entice elites to go into politics." (Hong Kong Polling and Business Research Co., 2003:55)

This constitutional setting and partial democratization, however, affects both sexes. In themselves, they cannot explain why there is a gender gap in formal participation. The gender gap could be explained by other internal (or situational) factors facing women, and by institutional factors of our political system. In a survey report, it was found that traditional thinking on gender roles and self-perception, and family responsibilities such as household duties and child care responsibilities still contributed to the low level of political representation of women in formal political institutions. A female councillor maintained that:

> "Participation in politics is very time-consuming and resource-taxing. Women from the grassroots social strata can ill afford it." (Hong Kong Polling and Business Research Co., 2003:55)

In addition to these internal factors, the institutional setting of our political system and electoral law are also hampering formal participation by women. With regard to the 2004 LegCo election, Tables 11 and 12 show that only six women gained seats through the geographical constituencies, and only five through the functional constituencies. Both election methods are unfavourable for the participation of women; yet the reasons for this differ.

The functional constituency elections pose certain barriers to the political participation of women (Tong, 2003). Of the existing 28 functional constituencies that are responsible for the election of 30 legislators, most are male-dominated sectors such as commerce and finance, real estate and construction, engineering, transport, catering, and DC (Constitutional Development Task Force, 2004:20–21). As the current institutional arrangement has not taken into consideration the reality of gender segregation in employment, and the low labour force participation rate of women, the participation of women in functional constituency elections is unequal. Feminist movement organizations have criticized the unequal electoral arrangements for women and called for the abolition of functional constituency elections, with the entire legislature to be directly elected through geographical constituencies. If this cannot be achieved in 2008, the government needs to reform the current classification of functional constituencies to ensure that women have a fair chance to take part in the functional constituency elections.

Legally speaking, there has been no direct discrimination against women in the geographical constituency elections. Women enjoy the same legal right as their male counterparts to run for public office. Nevertheless, as mentioned earlier, there are other institutional and non-institutional factors hindering women from participating in politics, resulting in their marginalization in both local political parties and governing institutions. The under-representation of women in governing institutions has been a worldwide phenomenon, except for the Nordic countries. To help increase the representation of women in politics and decision-making, many governments have adopted various effective measures including affirmative action to encourage the participation of women. The Hong Kong SAR government, however, has ignored the unfavourable factors affecting women and has not adopted any particular measures to address the issue of gender imbalance in political representation. Neither the government nor most political parties in Hong Kong consider this issue to be a problem that needs to be addressed, nor do they have the strong political will or desire to increase the representation of women in the legislature. In Table 11, we can see that many female candidates were unable to win seats because they were not placed in a winnable position by their political parties.

Institutional Design and Strengthening the Participation of Women

There are numerous ways of strengthening the participation of women in political parties and governing institutions. First, a government may adopt specific measures such as quota systems and/or reserved seats where women must make up at least a minimum proportion of the elected representatives. Political parties in a number of countries have adopted quota systems for women (Argentina, Venezuela, Denmark, Norway, Sweden, Austria, Belgium, France, Germany, Greece, Iceland, Italy, Netherlands, Spain, and Israel). These quotas were designed to ensure that a minimum percentage of women (varying from 20% to 50%) were members of various political bodies, including their leadership and/or lists of candidates for elections. Such quotas are usually perceived as a transitional mechanism to lay the foundation for a broader acceptance of female representation. For example,

Sweden, which was the first country to introduce a quota system for women in 1972, has now achieved gender parity in political representation (United Nations, 1995:216). Second, the electoral law can require parties to field a certain number of women candidates; this is the case in the proportional representation systems (list voting) of Belgium and Namibia. Third, political parties may adopt their own informal quotas for women as parliamentary candidates. This is the most common mechanism used to promote the participation of women in political life, and has been used with varying degrees of success all over the world. For example, in Sweden, the Social Democratic Party has an internal quota of a minimum of 40% women, combined with a "zipper" system (alternation of male and female candidates on the party list) (International Institute for Democracy and Electoral Assistance, 2003: 69). Reserved seats have also been set aside for women in Taiwan and other countries. Again, as with all reserved seats, these mechanisms help guarantee that women make it into elected positions of office. Recent discussions on the quota system in Taiwan suggest that "gender ratio" for both sexes should be introduced in the place of the existing "women quota" system (Huang, 2003).

There are also other considerations that can be applied in the proportional representation System. In addition to Sweden's "zipper" system, political parties can consider setting "closed lists" to include women in winnable positions, or allocating a percentage of head of lists to women; or giving priority to women in the allocation of electoral remainders (Corrin, 1999:182).

The HKSAR government has not adopted any measures or enabling devices to increase the proportion of women in the legislature and in the DCs. In the foreseeable future, significant improvement is unlikely unless more institutional encouragement is introduced to enable equal participation for both sexes in the formal governing institutions. The government should adopt the principle of "gender mainstreaming" in its political recruitment and its project of political reform. In the reform of the future Election Committee, the possible reorganization of functional constituencies, and District Councils, the HKSAR government should consider the gender impact of political reform, and ensure equal participation of both sexes (P. Wong, 2005).

As required by the Beijing Platform for Action and the CEDAW, the HKSAR government should seek to realize the right of women to participate in all areas of public life and particularly at high levels of the decision-making process. The United Nations Committee on CEDAW has recommended that the HKSAR government study the experiences of other countries in using women/gender quotas, reserved seats, and timetables; and consider introducing suitable affirmative action and temporary special measures in its institutional design (United Nations, 1999:paragraph 322). In Hong Kong, since most political parties are male-dominated and do not have strong gender sensitivity or political will to close the gender gap, it is the role of the HKSAR government and the civil society to launch public discussion and to seek new insights as to how to achieve gender equity in formal political participation.

Pressure for the implementation of quotas or adoption of affirmative action in reforming Hong Kong's political institutions should come not only from above but also from below. The feminist movement organizations should consider launching a campaign to achieve gender balance in politics and to decide what kinds of measures should be adopted, and in what ways the election law and political party laws should be drafted. They can also seek active participation by sending and supporting more women with gender consciousness to run for the DCs election in November 2007 and the LegCo election in 2008.

Community Participation

Community, in Chaskin et al.'s (2001:8) sense, refers to "a geographical area that is recognizable by a set of attributes tied to its physical location or appearance, such as natural boundaries, a recognized history, demographic patterns, or the presence and work within it of particular industries or organizations." The term can be used interchangeably with neighborhood. Community participation can thus be understood as the engagement of citizens, as members of a community, in activities related to a wide range of associations, from neighborhood associations, civic clubs, neighborhood-level business associations, community development centres, neighborhood-based service organizations, schools, churches, universities, hospitals, and coalitions (umbrella organizations and other collaborative arrangements among local associations that operate on behalf of clusters of neighborhoods). The mode of participation is also diverse, ranging from membership in organizations and their executive committees, activism in organizing community activities and attending group meetings, to volunteer work. While such activities may be of a primarily political or nonpolitical nature, quite often nonpolitical activities can be translated into political influence. Worldwide, community participation is increasingly viewed as important action that will bring about empowerment and better public service.

Inclusiveness and diversity are regarded as important values of community participation (Reid, 2000). On the other hand, all over the world, women are still often excluded from meaningful participation in public life. Factors commonly recognized as hindering their participation are the process of gender socialization, the differential access and utilization of channels for participation, differences in resources such as time and money, the patriarchal nature of social organizations, and social attitudes at large (Lee, 2000).

Such factors seem to have held Hong Kong women back from community participation. For instance, Lee (2000) found that as a whole, there was a low level of community participation in Hong Kong in terms of organizational membership. Where women participated, they tended to concentrate on organizations such as women's centers, community service centers, and religious organizations, where they were probably receiving service. There is definite evidence to show that women are under-represented as community leaders. Women currently constitute 17.9% of District Councillors. They have been found to be much less likely to hold executive positions in social organizations and hence tend to be less influential in community affairs (Lee, 2000). Social attitude is also less favorable towards female leaders as compared with male leaders (Tam, 1993; Tang, 1993; Lee, 2000). Women tend to be confined by their gender role as caretakers of the family (Tam 1993; Tang 1993). Other studies have also shown that women have fewer resources to participate, especially in terms of time. Women assume a heavier burden of housework and have less free time than men (Census and Statistics Department, 2004).

Apart from these general reasons, the public participation of women is often structured by institutions. In the case of Hong Kong, Fischler's (2003) study has shown how the colonial institution and the history of political development have structured the public participation of women. Put briefly, there was a strategic alliance between the colonial state and the Chinese male traditional and merchant elites. The colonial state offered the Chinese male elites status and honour and preservation of the patriarchal social system in return for their partnership in governance. Following this line of argument that colonial domination relied on Chinese patriarchy as part of its institutional setup, we contend that women were disadvantaged in community participation as a result of the institution of local governance constructed by the colonial state. Such colonial institutions have been inherited by the postcolonial government, which continues to utilize them as institutions of social control. The HKSAR government has inherited the local administrative system of its colonial predecessors, which had used local institutions as administrative tools for top-down control, cooptation, and political surveillance. Such state control of participatory space has been particularly detrimental to the participation of women. As will be shown later, state dominance in local governance has resulted in a highly patriarchal participatory culture, which leads to the marginalization of women.

History of Development of Community-Based Governance

The relationship between the state and community groups has been very much shaped by the history of colonialism. In the history of British rule, civic associations have been subjected to selective intervention by the colonial authority, ranging from passive tolerance, cooptation, and administrative control to political suppression. The early history of the development of civil society testified to such selective interventions. Colonial Hong Kong was largely a migrant society; the early settlers, mostly from mainland China, developed a robust system of communal self-governance through temples, clans organizations, merchant guilds, and so on. Among the neighborhood-based associations were the District Watch Committees and the *kaifong*, a form of neighborhood association that had long existed in South China (Tsai, 1993). Many of these communal organizations were led by male merchant elites who naturally excluded women, and the colonial government generally tolerated their existence. On the other hand, the state intervened in the running of civic organisations such as the Tung Wah Hospital and the Po Leung Kuk, which were found to be threatening to the state as a result of their immense power and social influence (Sinn, 1989).

By the 1950s, an administrative system of surveillance was developed under the Secretariat for Chinese Affairs, with the aim of guarding against the infiltration of civic groups by "subversive elements" (Wong, 1972:106). Among the communal associations to be watched closely were the *kaifongs. Kaifongs* were revived by the colonial government after WWII as a way to provide charity, relief, schooling, medical services and recreational facilities to residents. Liaison Officers from the Secretariat for Chinese Affairs would try to establish personal ties and to cultivate good relations with the *kaifong* leaders, and reward those who were subservient by granting them honors and other public positions. The position thus tended to attract traditionalists who were seeking social status and business advantages through making proper social and political connections. Such community groups thus became, in the eyes of the government, important pro-establishment forces (Lee, 2005).

This method of managing state-society relations was extended to the system of local administration established in the late 1960s. The City District Office (CDO) scheme was established in 1968 after the social riots in 1966 and 1967. District Offices were first established in the New Territories in the early days of colonial rule as a way of indirect rule. With the CDO Scheme, the urban area was divided into ten areas, each managed by a CDO and headed by a District Officer. Officially, these CDOs were to function as a link, if not a channel of communication, between the government and the people. In actuality, the CDOs became the "antennae" of the colonial government, detecting any potential dissatisfaction at an early stage, and also acted as its appendages for penetrating society. Each CDO oversees a City District Committee, an Area Committee (AC), and, from the early 1980s, a DB (renamed DC in 2000), mutual aid committees, and other local organizations set up by the Home Affairs Department and other government units for various purposes, e.g. the District Fight Crime Committee and the Junior Police Call. A CDO liaises with community organizations such as the *kaifongs*, local business associations, neighborhood-based organizations, women's organizations, NGOs and their local service centers, ethnic associations, recreational clubs, and so on.

The Gender Consequence of the Current System of Local Governance

The major political goal of the system of district administration was for the colonial government to nurture local leaders that were pro-establishment. Local committees, councils, and community-based organizations were not sites for the articulation of popular opinion or for the genuine participation of residents in deciding on issues that were really concerned about. Rather they were sites for political control.

The mechanisms of control are multiple. First, the state controls the appointment of personnel to the Area Committees and to many local boards and committees. One of the District Officer's jobs is to observe the behavior of local leaders in organizations such as the mutual aid committees and the *kaifongs*. Those people who have consistently demonstrated a subservient and pro-establishment attitude will then be recruited to the Area Committees and local boards and committees. Such a system of reward tends to attract conservative figures, often small businessman, that are looking for status and honors.

Second, a system such as this results in the development of extensive patron-client relationships not only between the state and local leaders, but also between the leaders and their followers. In a patron-client relationship, the client is supposed to show obedience and respect to the patron, who in return is obligated to sponsor the client. Essentially, people who are interested in serving the community through established channels would have to get into the network, as the local leaders would hold the power to "refer" suitable candidates to the state. Likewise, outsiders would have to establish a relationship with the immediate followers of the leaders in order to get into the inner circle. In such a system, women often find it hard to get into the network. They may serve as low-level volunteers but cannot become leaders. Occasionally, where there are women leaders, more often than not they adopt the same style of leadership that is entrenched in the dominant system. The woman leader will often behave like a "godmother", recruiting and rewarding followers who are loyal to her while she offers her support to the state.

Thirdly, the formation of networks is often complicated by other social organizations. One such category is ethnic groups. Far from the popular image of a fully integrated migrant society with a homogenous identity, ethnic politics is alive and well in some areas. For instance, local business may be dominated by an ethnic group, as seen in the dominance of Chiuchowese in the dried seafood business in the Central and Western districts of the Island. In such situations, community leaders may form a rather closed circle making it difficult for outsiders to get in. Women, being traditionally excluded from such groups, will have a slim chance of rising to power through such channels.

Fourth, state control over the recruitment of local leaders is also fostered through state control over funding for local associations. The District Office provides a small sum of money to associations for organizing community functions. Associations holding recreational and cultural functions, activities that are traditionally considered "appropriate" by the District Office, will receive funding. Thus, state funding serves as a form of control over associational life, as associations that hold activities considered contentious by the state will not be sponsored. Such funding mechanisms serve to perpetuate the existing patriarchal networks of power.

New Space for Community Participation and Its Gender Implication

Despite the imposition of top-down control by the state apparatus, developments in the past two to three decades have changed the societal landscape. The question is whether this new societal landscape offers more room for community participation from the bottom up and, if so, whether women benefit from it.

One such change has been the democratization of the political system, including the development of political parties. At the local level, many of the district councilors now have a political party background. The fielding of candidates for elections is decided by the political parties. As discussed in the previous sections, political parties have not been particularly conducive to opening up opportunities for women to become public leaders. This has been largely attributed to the lack of executive power. In the DCs, the modest annual budget was often divided up among the councilors to fund their own constituency works, which often entailed organizing recreational activities that serve only parochial interests. Such a practice has the effect of reinforcing the advantage of incumbents and their followers. Individuals with the aspiration to make a difference to the status quo will find little space to do so. This situation is not conducive to the participation of women who want to make a difference. Despite this, in the past few years, in some districts more progressive candidates, among them a couple of women, have managed to get elected through producing campaign platforms that offer alternatives to the status quo.

Second, NGOs, through their social service and community building work, have been a major source of grassroots empowerment. Many NGOs operate service and community centers under state funding, while others receive most of their funding from private donors. In past decades, through their community-building activities, NGOs have empowered the grassroots population in fighting for their social rights, and have helped nurture community leaders. NGOs that are financially independent from the government have been found to be more able to carve out their own space. In recent years, collaboration between NGOs and progressive local politicians has not been uncommon.

Third, various social groups largely excluded from official channels of participation are increasingly organizing themselves to fight for their interests. This is evident, for instance, in some cases of urban redevelopment. Women are involved in these instances of activism and have emerged as community leaders. Such locally based activism can spill over into other territory-wide issues, as activists, upon participating in local affairs, are mobilized to participate in collective actions related to other issues. An example of one such case is the redevelopment of the Hopewell Center into a "MegaTower" (a hotel project) in Wanchai. A group of middle-class women organized themselves to protest against the redevelopment project for the reason that it would have a detrimental effect on the value of their real estate property. Some of these women leaders later became participants in social campaigns related to the reclamation of the Victoria Harbor and the West Kowloon Cultural District project. There is also evidence that these women activists are collaborating with the more progressive women district councillors in fighting for their interests.

Conclusion

The conventional understanding on women and political participation assumes that gender differences in political participation will gradually disappear as the process of modernization accelerates, and women become able to catch up with men in the fields of education, professional careers, and income. This chapter shows that this assumption is only partly correct. In the first section of this chapter, we observed certain improvements in gender representation among the ranks of Permanent Secretaries of the Civil Service, and in the judges of District Courts. These improvements can be seen as a product of the increasing educational opportunities for women in higher education. However, gender differences with regard to participation in governing institutions and participation as candidates in the electoral process have proven to be remarkably persistent. Moreover, even where the gender gap has decreased, it has done so at a very slow pace. This chapter shows that the representation of women in the DCs increased from 10.1% in 1982 to 17.9% in 2006, while there has been no improvement in the representation of women in LegCo when compared with 1988 and on a high of 19.3%.

As to community participation, the long history of state penetration into the local community through the district administrative apparatus has resulted in a community leadership culture that is conservative, paternalistic, patriarchal, and hierarchical. Such a community culture contributes to the exclusion of women from leadership positions. The postcolonial state has largely inherited such administrative apparatus and has little incentive to reform it. One major reason is that, lacking in popular legitimacy, the postcolonial authoritarian state relies on pro-establishment forces as a source of support. Conversely, such control over the recruitment of formal leaders also ensures that anti-government forces will not have access to formal positions of power. The persistence of such a structure of power, however, largely goes against the societal changes toward more pluralistic interests and a heightened democratic consciousness, which necessitate the opening up of channels for popular participation.

In Hong Kong, popular elections at all three levels (the election of the Chief Executive, LegCo, and DC) remain an objective to be achieved. Given this state of affairs, it is understandable that much of the attention and energy of the pro-democracy movement of the past two decades has focused on the expansion of elected seats in LegCo and in the DCs, as well as on the popular election of the Chief Executive. This laudable aim, however, has resulted in a relative neglect of other important issues, not the least among which is the gender gap in the governing institutions, the electoral process, and participation at the community level. We have demonstrated that, despite the opening up of the administrative structure and political processes, this gender gap has proved to be rather stubborn and deep-rooted.

Acknowledgments

Wong Pik-wan is grateful for a research grant (G-T584) from the General Education Centre of the Hong Kong Polytechnic University. For the part on community participation, Eliza W. Y. Lee has benefited tremendously from an interview conducted in 2005 with Ms. Ada Wong (then the chairwoman of the Wanchai District Council) and Ms. Mary Ann King (then a Wanchai District Councilor). Lee would like to express her gratitude to Ms. Wong and Ms. King for generously sharing with her their personal experience as community leaders. The responsibility for the contents and the opinions expressed in this chapter rests solely with the authors.

Notes

1. See "Platform for Action," (http://www.un.org/womenwatch/daw/beijing/ platform/decision.html, retrieved on 4 June 2005).
2. See "CEDAW,"(http://www.ohchr.org/english/law/cedaw.htm#part2, retrieved on 2 May 2007).
3. The four female members of the Executive Council are: Sarah Liao Sau-tung, Denise Yue Chung-yee, Selina Chow Liang Shuk-yee, and Laura M. Cha. In April 2008, 5 out of 30 members are women. With the departure of Sarah Liao Sau-tung, two other women (Carrie Lam Cheng Yuet-ngor and Eva Cheng) were appointed into the Executive Council.

4. See also Census and Statistics Department (2004:104).
5. See also Appendix 1 "2003 Final Register Geographical Constituencies: Age and Sex Profile," of the *Report on the 2003 District Council Election* (Electoral Affairs Commission, 2004).
6. See *Sing Pao Daily News*, 18 May 2005, p.A05, and "Legislators' Ratings Take a Hammering," *South China Morning Post*, 23 February 2005.
7. The six female candidates were: Emily Lau (elected), Leung Wai-tung, Chow Kit-bing, Cheung Wai-sun,Chan Yuen-han, and Yeung Lai-yin.

References

Burns, John P. 2004. *Government Capacity and the Hong Kong Civil Service*. Oxford: Oxford University Press.

Census and Statistics Department. 2002. *Women and Men in Hong Kong: Key Statistics* (2002 Edition). Hong Kong: Printing Department.

———. 2004. *Women and Men in Hong Kong: Key Statistics* (2004 Edition). Hong Kong: Government Logistics Department.

———. 2006. *Women and Men in Hong Kong: Key Statistics* (2006 Edition). Hong Kong: Government Logistics Department.

Chaskin, Robert J., Prudence Brown, Sudhir Venkatesh and Avis Vidal. 2001. *Building Community Capacity*. New York: Walter de Gruyter, Inc.

Choi, Po-king. 2003. "Education," In Hung Suet-lin and Fung Kwok-kin (eds.), *Hong Kong Women's File: 2003 Revised Edition*. Hong Kong: Association for the Advancement in Feminism, pp. 41–66. (In Chinese)

Constitutional Development Task Force. 2004. *The Third Report of the Constitutional Development Task Force* (http://www.cab.gov.hk/cd/eng/report3/index.htm, retrieved on 29 July 2005).

Corrin, Chris. 1999. "Political Participation, Representation, and Resistance," in *Feminist Perspectives on Politics*. London: Longman, pp. 173–92.

Fischler, Lisa. 2003. "Women's Activism during Hong Kong's Political Transition," in *Gender and Change in Hong Kong: Globalization, Postcolonialism, and Chinese Patriarchy*, edited by Eliza W.Y. Lee. Vancouver: University of British Columbia Press, pp. 49–77.

Health, Welfare and Food Bureau. 2005. *The Second Report of the Government of the Hong Kong Special Administrative Region on the Implementation of the Beijing Platform for Action*. Hong Kong: Health, Welfare and Food Bureau.

Home Affairs Bureau. 2006. "LCQ 9: Promotion of Women's Participation in Advisory Bodies" (6 December). (http://www.info.gov.hk/gia/general/200612/06/P200612060136.htm, retrieved on 4 May 2007).

Hong Kong Polling and Business Research Co. 2003. *A Survey on Women's Views on Women's Political Participation and Discourse*. Hong Kong: Hong Kong Women Development Association. (In Chinese, with English Summary)

Hooghe, Marc & Dietlind Stolle. 2004. "Good Girls Go to the Polling Booth, Bad Boys Go Everywhere: Gender Differences in Anticipated Political Participation Among American Fourteen-year-olds." *Women and Politics*, Vol. 26 (3/4):1–24.

Huang, Chang-ling. 2003. "From Women Quotas to Gender Ratio Principle: Institutional Design for Women's Political Participation," *Alumni's Bi-monthly Journal of the National Taiwan University*, 30 (http://www.alum. ntu.edu.tw/read.php?num=30&sn=616, retrieved on 24 July 2005). (In Chinese)

International Institute for Democracy and Electoral Assistance. 2003. *The Implementation of Quotas: Asian Experiences* (http://www.idea.int/publications/ quotas_asian/index.cfm, retrieved on 29 July 2005).

Lam, Anita. 2007. "Fewer women in top advisory bodies." *South China Morning Post* (8 March).

Lee, Eliza W.Y. 2000. "Gender and Political Participation in Hong Kong," *Asian Journal of Women's Studies*, 6(3):93–114.

———. 2005. "Nonprofit Development in Hong Kong: The Case of a Statist-Corporatist Regime," *Voluntas*, 16(1):51–68.

Lui, Terry T. 1995. "Political Participation," in Veronica Pearson and Benjamin K.P. Leung (eds.), *Women in Hong Kong*. Hong Kong: Oxford University Press, pp. 133–66.

PA Professional Consultants Ltd. (ed.). 1993. "Appendix II: Members of Executive and Legislative Council 1980–92," in *Read Their Lips (1): A Dossier of Political Leaders in Hong Kong*. Hong Kong: Pace Publishing Ltd.

Pateman, Carole. 1988. *The Sexual Contract*. Stanford: Stanford University Press.

———.1989. *The Disorder of Women: Democracy, Feminism and Political Theory*. Stanford: Stanford University Press.

Phillips, Anne. 1992. "Must Feminists Give Up on Liberal Democracy?" *Political Studies*, XL (Special Issue):68–82.

Rai, Shirin M. 1994. "Gender and Democratization: or what does democracy mean for women in the third world." *Democratization*, 1(2):209–28.

Reid, J. Norman. 2000. "Community Participation: How People Power Brings Sustainable Benefits to Community," USDA Rural Development Office of Community Development (http://www.ezec.gov/Pubs/commparticrept.pdf, retrieved on 29 July 2005).

Sinn, Elizabeth. 1989. *Power and Charity: the Early History of the Tung Wah Hospital, Hong Kong*. Hong Kong: Oxford University Press.

Suen, Kar-yin. 2003. "Information on Democratic Party's Candidates for the DC election 2003" (Internal document, Democratic Party.)

Sun, Tsai-wei. 2005. "Gender Representation in Politics and Public Administration: Taiwan and Asian Countries," *Asia-Pacific Forum* (Taipei), 28:148–184.

Squires, Judith. 1996. "Quotas for Women: Fair Representation?" In Joni Lovenduski and Pippa Norris (eds.), *Women in Politics*. Oxford: Oxford University Press, pp. 73–90.

Tam, Siumi Maria (ed.). 1993. *Community Participation by Women in Shatin: A Research Report*. Hong Kong: Committee on Community Development, Shatin District Board. (In Chinese)

Tang, Catherine (ed.). 1993. Community Participation by Women: 1993 Annual Gender Role Worksop Proceedings. Hong Kong: Gender Research Programme, Hong Kong Institute of Asia-Pacific Studies, The Chinese University of Hong Kong. (In Chinese)

Tong, Irene L.K. 2003. "Women's Political Participation," In Hung Suet-lin and Fung Kwok-kin (eds.), Hong Kong Women's File: 2003 Revised Edition. Hong Kong: Association for the Advancement of Feminism, pp. 190–215. (In Chinese)

Tsai, Jung-fang. 1993. *Hong Kong in Chinese History: Community and Social Unrest in The British Colony, 1842–1913*. New York: Columbia University Press.

Westwood, Robert, Toni Mehrain, & Fanny Cheung. 1995. *Gender and Society in Hong Kong: A Statistical Profile*. Hong Kong: Hong Kong Institute of Asia-Pacific Studies, The Chinese University of Hong Kong.

Women's Commission. 2004. *Women's Commission Report 2001–2003*. (http:www. women.gov.hk/report2003/eng/content.htm, retrieved on 29 July 2005).

Wong, Aline 1972. *The Kaifong Associations and the Society of Hong Kong*. Taipei: The Orient Cultural Service.

Wong, Pik-wan. 2005. "Political Development and Equal Participation by the Two Sexes," *Ming Pao Daily News*, 5 March. (In Chinese)

United Nations, Committee on the Elimination of Discrimination against Women. 1999. "Concluding Comments of the Committee on the Elimination of Discrimination against Women on the Initial Report on the HKSAR under the Convention on the Elimination of All Forms of Discrimination against Women" [extracted from the report of the Committee on the Twentieth Session (19 January-5 February)] (http://www.hwfb.gov.hk/en/press_and_publications/otherinfo/CEDAW2.HTM,retrieved on 29 July 2005).

United Nations, Secretary-General. 1995. *From Nairobi to Beijing: Second Review and Appraisal of the implementation of the Nairobi Forward-Looking Strategies for the Advancement of Women*. New York: United Nations.

U.S. Department of State. 2003. "UN General Assembly Adopts U.S.-Sponsored Resolution on Women and Political Participation" (http://www.state.gov/g/wi/rls/rep/28497.htm, retrieved on 18 September 2006).

PART II

Gender Neutral and Gender Sensitive Policies

CHAPTER 6

Fertility and Gender Equity in Hong Kong

Edward Jow Ching Tu and Gigi Lam

The authorship is in alphabetical order. Both made equal contribution to the research project.

Introduction

The secular reductions in fertility are now well-established feature of the demography around the globe. Hong Kong has followed suit to experience population aging because of its rapidly declining fertility and increasingly long expected longevity. In a comparison of total fertility rate (TFR)[1] over a total of 177 countries by the United Nations in 2006, an alarming picture has already been manifested in Hong Kong in which TFR is found to be the lowest among all 177 countries (Table 1). The doldrums of Hong Kong is further exacerbated by its exceedingly long life expectancy. According to 2006 Population By-census, the proportion of people aged 65 or over is projected to account for 27% by 2030s (Census and Statistics Department, 2007). Old age dependency ratio[2] also rose from 0.159 in 2002 to 0.168 in 2006 (Census and Statistics Department, 2007). The high old age dependency ratio warrants public attention about how to provide old-age security to the elderly when there is a change of people's expectation about children's role in providing financial and emotional support at their old age, especially feminization of poverty among elderly women caused by asymmetry distortion between women's concentration in the realm of unpaid housework and the only avenue to entitle to Manual Provident Fund via full-time employment (Cheung, 2002).

Due to its far-reaching consequences on solvency of public pension system, studies of low fertility remain its supremacy. A growing number of studies has addressed the determinants of low fertility in contemporary world (Kohler, Billari & Ortega, 2002; Caldwell and Schindlmayr, 2003); a debate on convergence of demographic trends (Wilson, 2001; Coleman, 2002; Billari & Wilson, 2001); unique low fertility theories pertaining to particular countries (Macura, 2000; Kohler & Kohler, 2002; Witte & Wagner, 1995) and the effects of increasing age at childbearing on period fertility (Lesthaeghe and Willems, 1999; Bongaarts, 2002; Lutz, O'Neill and Scherbov, 2003; Sobotka, 2004). Relatively scant attention, however, has been paid to disentangle how the emerging trend of gender equity affects fertility.

A recent attempt to study the relationship between gender equity and fertility is initiated by the United Nations in 2005. The UN survey asked respondents whether they agreed with the statement that "a man's job is to earn money; a woman's job is to take care of the home and family." It found

Table 1. World comparison of total fertility rate

Country	TFR	Ranking
Africa		
Niger	7.9	1
Central Europe		
France	1.9	162
Germany	1.3	168
Northern Europe		
Norway	1.8	163
Finland	1.7	164
Sweden	1.6	165
Oceania		
New Zealand	2	164
Australia	1.7	164
Southern Europe		
Italy	1.3	168
Spain	1.3	168
Asia		
China	1.7	164
Japan	1.3	168
South Korea	1.2	175
Singapore	1.4	167
Hong Kong	0.9	177
World average	2.59	

Source: The United Nations. Human Development Report 2006.

that the Nordic countries, the US and Canada showed strongly or moderately favorable attitudes toward gender equity but the birth rate is comparatively higher or rising than the other category of countries such as Germany, Japan, Italy and Spain with much less favorable attitudes towards gender equality (OECD, 2005). It runs contrary to a common assertion that the accelerating growth of individual self-realization and a growing need of satisfaction of personal preferences in modern societies act as a mere confrontation to time-consuming childbearing. Chesnais (1996, 1998) even coined this unexpected phenomenon of gender equity associated with higher fertility as the present feminist paradox or future feminist paradox. McDonald (2000) solved this paradox by distinguishing two forms of gender equity: gender equity in family- oriented institutions (industrial relations, family services, tax system, social security and the family) and gender equity in individual-oriented institutions (market employment and educational opportunities for females). Role conflict across these two institutions poses stumbling blocks over childbearing decisions. While numerous studies have investigated the repercussions of the gendered division of labor on male and female wages (Noonan, 2001); marital satisfaction (Cooke, 2004); psychological well-being (Lennon & Rosenfield, 1994), none has explored extensively how gender equity at home affects the family outcomes of fertility. Much of our attention is therefore devoted to how gender equity at home affects fertility in this chapter.

This chapter is organized into four sections. The first section will focus primarily on the trend of gender equity in Hong Kong. It will then be followed by an overview of conceptual framework of relation between gender equity and fertility. Data description used for this chapter will be described in the following section. Major findings will be summarized in next section. It will be concluded with some policy implications.

Trends of Gender Equity in Hong Kong

According to McDonald (2000), full gender equity at home is achieved as gender is no longer to be a determinant of which member of the couple undertook the three forms of housework: income generation, caring and nurturing and household maintenance.

To capture McDonald's definition of gender equity, both the family income management and housework division will be used to indicate the trend of gender equity at home in Hong Kong from 1960 to 2000.

a) Family income management

Figure 1. Family income management pattern

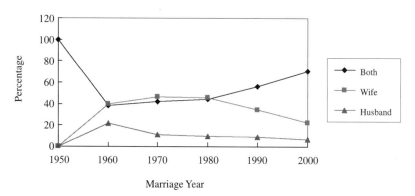

Marriage Year

Source: Compiled from 1992, 1997 and 2002 KAP survey data of Family Planning Association of
          Hong Kong

A synopsis of trend of gender equity at home can be captured from Figures 1 and 2. Figure 1 shows a trend of family income management pattern from 1950 to 2000. It reveals an overlapping of the wife to be the sole decision-maker with both husbands and wives jointly managing the family income between 1960 and 1980. A diverging pattern is displayed from 1990 onwards with a majority of 56% of husbands and wives together to make decisions on the use of family income. Further improvement in the decision- making process is revealed from 2000 onwards that husbands are more willing to share an equal burden with their wives in deciding how to use family income.

Figure 2 provides the snapshot of the trend of contraceptive responsibility among couples. Initially, wives shoulder similar extent of responsibility of using contraception as the husbands but there is declining propensity for wives to be the only one to use contraceptive. From 1970 onwards, an increasing proportionate share is found for both husbands and wives to practice contraception. Practicing contraception is no longer the sole responsibility of wives. It is rather the joint responsibility of husbands and wives. This change is accompanied with a rising proportion of husbands to practice contraceptive as well although the percentage is comparatively smaller than the joint responsibility.

Figure 2. Major bearer of contraceptive use

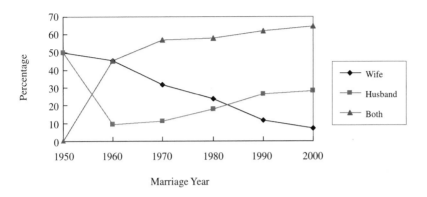

Source: Compiled from 1992, 1997 and 2002 KAP survey data of Family Planning Association of Hong Kong

Figure 3. International comparison of family income management

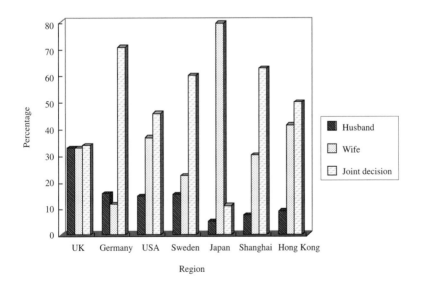

Source: 徐安琪 (Xu Anqi) (1992)

Although a compromising picture of family status is observed for women across time, it is still in a pale comparison with other Western countries. Figure 3 indicates that the joint management of family income in Hong Kong is relatively better than in Japan, the United Kingdom and the United States but in a much less advantaged position than German, Sweden and Shanghai family. Hong Kong wives need to bear the brunt of larger share of making family economic decision. It is in a stark contrast to Germany, Sweden and Shanghai that the family adopts the joint decision- making pattern in commonplace.

Speculation is raised as well over the wives who have participated in making family economic decision may probably mean they have more family power and enjoy a higher family status. It may, however, need to decompose the indicators of family economic decision into several categories include the trivial household decision and significant family decision. The survey about housework division conducted by YWCA in 2005 reveals that only 34% of women make significant family decision whereas a relatively larger percentage of husbands make much more important family decision.

b) Housework division

Figure 4. Housework division, 2005

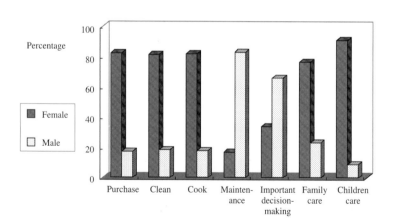

Housework Categories

Source: YWCA (2005)

Apart from family income management, another clear picture can be revealed from housework division. Summarized from the survey result of YWCA in 2005, wives are found to do most of household chores in various aspects such as purchase, cleaning, cooking, family care and children care except the maintenance work and decision-making (Figure 4). Proportionate larger share of housework borne by females regardless of their employment status really poses barrier over the capabilities of females to parallel both housework and childbearing.

Overview of Conceptual Models

Renewed interest pointing to the recognition of intricate linkage between fertility and empowerment has emerged since the heated debate over gender equality and female reproduction health in 1994 Cairo International Population Conference. A plethora of empirical studies concerning the linkage between female empowerment and reproduction can be divided into two camps. The first school of thought can be simply categorized as family power model. According to this model, an increase of family status of females is found to be a significant determinant of fertility decline. In this model, gender equity and empowerment is always used interchangeable. Gender equity is fully achieved when females achieve the same family status as males by two routes either via mass education or employment. Family status can be mirrored as the place along the hierarchy while power implies the relation between couples within this hierarchy. Different studies provide consistent evidence to family power model (Larsen & Hollos, 2003; DeRose, 2003; Mason & Smith, 2000). Result showed that women who have larger autonomy in making family decision are usually the one to have greater say in reproductive decision. Women with higher status are found to have better communication with husband about the timing and number of birth. They also feel free to discuss with their husbands over how to use contraceptive. In contrast, gender stratification poses stumbling block over open discussion with husbands pertaining to contraceptives. Contraceptive prevalence hence is found to be lower in highly gender stratified setting across five different Asian countries (Mason & Smith, 2000).

Despite the confirmative studies, some may argue all the above studies are conducted in developing countries such as Larsen & Hollos's (2003) study in Northern Tanazia; DeRose's (2003) study in Ghana; Mason's (2003) study in five Asian developing countries and hence questions the credibility and applicability to developed countries. Chesnais (1996, 1998) proposed a model of bifurcation of family power as a distinct phenomenon across developed and developing countries. According to this model, gender equity is negatively related to fertility only in developing countries while gender equity is positively related to fertility in developed countries. Chesnais coined this disparate situation as present feminist paradox. It gives rise to another school of thought that the conflict between housework and childbearing may refer to developed countries particularly.

In this second school of thought, McDonald (2000) divided gender equity into those falling in family-oriented institutions and in individual-oriented institutions. As women enjoyed increasingly high gender equity in individual-oriented institutions such as formal education and market employment while the change of family-oriented institutions remains slow, the conflict or inconsistency between high gender equity in individual- oriented institutions and low gender equity in family- oriented institutions results in very low fertility. Consequently, many women will eschew the family role so as not to have children. Persistence of very low fertility will continue unless gender equity within family-oriented institutions rises to a higher level.

The applicability of the bifurcation of family power model and McDonald's hypothesized incompatibility of gender equity across family and employment varies across different stages of fertility transition[3]. In the onset of fertility transition, improving gender equity within families is a necessary condition, especially the rights to determine the number of children by women even in the absence of major changes in women's lives outside the family. Therefore, family power model is more appropriate for developing countries. At a later stage of fertility transition, McDonald's model is more suitable to explain current lowest-low fertility in developed countries.

This simplified dichotomy is superficially logical and may be valid to explain fertility changes across different stages of fertility transition. However, the family power model can also link with the incompatibility of gender equity hypothesis to explain low fertility in developed countries. We will show this linkage with the following bivariate analysis of 2002 Knowledge, Attitude and Practice (KAP) Survey data in next section.

KAP Survey Data

The Knowledge, Attitude and Practice (KAP) Survey conducted by the Family Planning Association of Hong Kong in 2002 is uniquely suited to an empirical test of the relationship between gender equity and fertility. KAP Survey is the longest standing survey in Hong Kong. The first one was conducted in 1967 and it has been carried out once every five years since then. From 1997 onwards, KAP Survey started to include a survey on the husbands of 1,511 female respondents as well. This Survey kept up with its effort and successfully interviewed 1,607 women and 1,147 men respectively in 2002. KAP Survey enjoys an advantage over other surveys in Hong Kong as it has taken the initiative to interview the husbands of the respondents for the purpose of making wife- husband comparison.

Our present analysis of relationship between gender equity and fertility will focus primarily on family power model. Reproductive autonomy will be used as the main indicator and is further divided into three stages of childbearing. The first stage pertaining to reproductive autonomy refers to childbearing intention. The second stage refers to wives' abilities to refuse husbands' sexual request. The final stage refers to fertility outcome with particular emphasis on the couples' responsibility of using contraceptive. The major reason to choose these three stages is mainly because gender equity displayed in each stage has a direct impact on childbearing outcome.

Result of the Family Power Model

a) Childbearing intention

A bivariate relation between childbearing intention and number of children is shown in Figure 5. Childbearing intention is first calculated by subtracting actual fertility from ideal fertility of husbands and wives respectively. Fertility surplus exists when actual fertility is larger than ideal fertility while fertility shortage refers to actual fertility being less than ideal fertility. Comparison is made over the differential of fertility surplus or shortage between husbands and wives. Fertility differential is made across three levels. Wives who share equal fertility surplus/ shortage with the husbands belongs to the first group. The second level refers to the extent to which fertility surplus/ shortage of wives is larger than husbands and the third refers to the extent to which fertility surplus/ shortage of husbands is larger than wives.

The mean number of children is shown to be the smallest when the fertility surplus/ shortage of wives is equal to their husbands. Mean number of children starts rising as the fertility surplus/ shortage of wives is larger than their husbands, indicating the family status of wives is lower than their husbands. In contrast, when fertility surplus/ shortage of wives is smaller than their husbands, fertility drops again. An inverted U-shape curve is identified between childbearing intention and number of children.

Figure 5. Number of children by childbearing intention

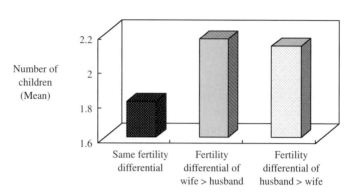

Childbearing intention

b) Wives' ability to reject husbands' sexual request

Wives' ability to reject husbands' sexual request is measured across three levels. The first level refers to the wives who can definitely refuse husbands' sexual request while the wives who definitely cannot reject husbands' sexual request is the second group. Wives who can refuse in principle but have difficulty to put into practice is the third group.

A similar negative relation between gender equity and fertility is also found when the ability to reject sexual request is used instead in Figure 6. Inverted U- shape curve starts from the trough in which the wives definitely can reject husbands' sexual request, indicating the family status of women is relatively higher than their counterparts. Inverted U-shape curve reaches its highest point when the wives definitely cannot reject their husbands' sexual request. It drops when the wives may reject but have difficulty to put this into practice. Their mean number of children is slightly higher than their counterparts who can definitely refuse husbands' sexual request.

c) Contraception responsibility

Contraceptive usage has been divided into three categories. The first category includes those husbands who are the only ones responsible for contraception. In comparison to the first group, the wives who are the only ones to practice contraceptive are categorized as the second group. And both husbands and wives sharing responsibility in contraception are categorized as the third group.

Figure 6. Number of children by wives' abilities to reject husbands' sexual request

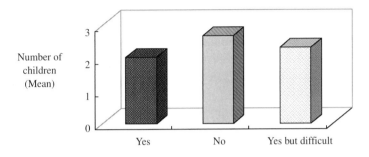

Wives' abilities to reject husbands' sexual request

Figure 7 confirms the relation by the contraception responsibility. The highest fertility is found for the wives who bear the whole responsibility of practicing contraceptive. Conversely, fertility drops when both husbands and wives share the joint responsibility of practicing contraceptive and even drops further when only husbands are responsible for practicing contraceptive, indicating family status of wives is relatively higher than their spouse.

Results of the analyses from Figures 5 to 7 support the hypothesis generated from family power model: the propensity to have children is negatively related to the wife's status achieved in the family relative to their husbands across all stages of childbearing decision.

Figure 7. Number of children by contraceptive responsibility

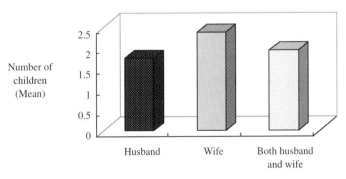

Contraceptive responsibility

Explanation of Current Phenomenon

Empirical results of the bivariate relation elucidate that fertility is negatively related to gender equity at home in Hong Kong. The results are consistent with most of demographic studies that lower fertility is commonly associated with women's higher reproductive autonomy (Larsen & Hollos, 2003), and contradict McDonald's (2000) assertion.

In order to understand why the Hong Kong data do not fit McDonald's (2000) hypothesis of incompatibility of gender equity across work and family, it is necessary to trace the major determinants of women's subordinate family position. Following Blood and Wolfe's (1960) resource theory of family power, comparative resources of husband and wife in terms of education, income and occupation exert influence on marital decision making. Based on social exchange theory (Blood and Wolfe, 1960), housework division is the result of frequent negotiation between spouses over inputs (earnings) and outcomes (housework) in the household. When women have lower inputs in terms of lower wages and work status relative to their husbands, the expectation of an equal share of housework is then countervailed by fewer economic resources and limited alternatives to marriage. Women have to bear an asymmetric housework division and perceive it as an appropriate situation.

According to Blood and Wolfe's (1960) resource power theory, females with higher status tend to do less housework. Their high status is achieved by higher education and better employment opportunities. All these exert fertility-depressive impact because education increases the opportunity costs of childbearing for women as education opens up new occupational opportunities and provides a vehicle for social mobility. Moreover, women's employment in the labor market tends to lower fertility because of the difficulty to play the role as mother and worker, according to the role incompatibility hypothesis (Buvini, 1994). As employment and childrearing occur concurrently in different locations, women's employment and childrearing tend to compete against women's time and energy. Further research, however, should compare two contradictory results: fertility-depressive effect associated with higher family status and fertility-enhancing effect with higher willingness of husbands to share housework.

Policy Implications

In light of low fertility, Hong Kong government has attempted to encourage citizens to consider having three children each family. The slogan indicates that "Three children are the best". Without a consolidated population policy, this call to raise fertility level will not bring any particular effect. In contrast to other low fertility countries such as Japan and Singapore, Hong Kong is still staggering in the desert of population policy. Singapore and Japan are strikingly enthusiastic to implement population policy such as dating arrangement for university graduates in Singapore and providing free prenatal examination to pregnant females in Japan. On the other hand, Hong Kong government's attempt to propose an effective population policy to raise fertility level has been feeble. The only concrete measure was a proposal in the 2007 Financial Budget plan (Financial Services & Treasury Bureau, 2007) to introduce tax exemptions up to $50000 regardless of which parity of the birth.

In reality, tax exemptions granted to parents offer not much incentive because the major reasons behind low fertility have less to do with the costs of children per se. Rather, low fertility is related to the intricate linkage of high employment status enjoyed in individual-oriented institutions and asymmetrical housework responsibility borne by women in family.

Moreover, solely relying on direct financial subsidies may work well when female labor force participation rate is low or female income is negligible. When their wage fall short of the cash subsidies for children, women opt for staying at home to take care of their children. However, female labor force participation rate is around 51% in Hong Kong and 40% of women work in professional sector now (Census & Statistics Department, 2006). Therefore, the opportunity cost of childbearing rises when women give up their jobs and earn the direct cash subsidies. On the other hand, direct costs of children are less responsive to rising income except for a positive relation between income and expenditure on children. Women are more willing to combine both their jobs and childcare instead of staying home and rely on direct cash subsidies because their earned incomes are much higher than cash subsidies. This situation can be exemplified by the failure of direct financial incentives in Singapore. After many years of attempt, the total fertility rate (TFR) in Singapore, especially among the Chinese population, still stays in a trough of 1.3 (McDonald, 2002).

Overall, countries with moderately low fertility tend to have implemented major programs to reduce the opportunity costs of childbearing. Effective policies suggested by McDonald (2002) include

a) availability of part-time work,
b) access to long- duration parental leave and the level of maternity leave payments which is sufficient to meet income needs,
c) access to affordable and high quality childcare,
d) guaranteed return to work with an option of reduced and flexible hours,
e) family-friendly workplace and encouragement of higher levels of gender equity at home such as training husbands to share the housework

Among all these five aspects, fertility policy in Hong Kong policy still lags behind most developed countries, particularly with respect to maternity leave. A pregnant employee in Hong Kong is entitled to have 10 weeks of maternity leave with maternity pay equivalent to four-fifths of her normal wages. This particular maternity pay falls short of the international standard. Starting from April 2007, all female pregnant employees in the United Kingdom are entitled to have 52 weeks of paid maternity leave. Generous parental leave is exemplified in Sweden, where all working parents are entitled to have 18 months' paid leave per child. As a rebuttal to the criticism of short maternity leave in Hong Kong, the Economic Development and Labor Bureau replied to a question raised in the Legislative Council: "Despite relatively short duration of maternity leave in Hong Kong, the maternity pay in Hong Kong amounts to 80% which is higher than other countries (around 60% of normal wages)" (Legislative Council, 2006). However, in other developed economies, a pregnant female employee in the United Kingdom can earn 90% of average weekly income for the first six weeks, then up to £108.85 a week for the remaining 33 weeks. Similarly, pregnant women in Sweden can earn 80% of their wage for the first 390 days and the maternity pay remains at a flat rate for the remaining 90 days.

At the same time, the HKSAR government has not made any attempt to introduce legislation to grant employees paid parental leave. Male employees are not entitled to have any paid leave in order to share the responsibility of taking care of the newborn babies. Many developed countries have already provided parental leave to husbands. For example, fathers in the United Kingdom can apply for 2 weeks of paid parental leave for bringing up the child. Fathers in Sweden can apply for up to 3 months of parental leave to encourage fathers' participation in taking care of both the mother and the new born baby. Swedish legislators even argue for an equal division of parental leave between mother and father because the effectiveness of father's uptake of parental leave on continued childbearing has been confirmed by a longitudinal study on all intact unions in Sweden (Duvander and Anderson, 2005). In that study, Duvander and Anderson (2005) found a positive effect of a father's moderately long parental leave on the couples' second and third child intensities because father's uptake of parental leave not only signals a commitment to share the duties of childbearing with mother but also an interest in children and childrearing which is reflected by positive childbearing intentions. This result supports the findings of Bulanda's study (2004) that demonstrated how egalitarian United States fathers were also more likely than traditional fathers to be involved with their children. Due to their childbearing intention, Hyde, Essex & Horton (1993) found that egalitarian fathers were more likely to take relatively longer parental leave than their traditional counterparts.

Since maternity and parental leave have effectiveness on fertility rate, we summarize the details of maternity and parental leave in different countries in Table 2.

In contrast to the enthusiasm devoted to encourage fathers to participate in childrearing by many countries, Hong Kong still stays in the very preliminary stage. The Economic Development and Labor Bureau still argued against introducing parental leave, citing reasons such as the small size of

Table 2. Parental leave rights in different countries around the world

Country	Paid maternity leave	Paid paternity leave
Europe		
Italy	22 weeks	13 weeks
Denmark	18 weeks with 100% pay	14 days
Norway	38 weeks with 100% pay	6 weeks
Sweden	15 months	3 months
United kingdom	52 weeks	2 weeks
Asia		
China	12 weeks with 100% pay	—
Japan	14 weeks with 60% pay	—
Korea	8 weeks with 100% pay	—
Malaysia	8 weeks with 100% pay	—
Philippines	8 weeks with 100% pay	7 days
Singapore	8 weeks with 100% pay	—
Hong Kong	10 weeks with 80% pay	—

Source: Wikipedia, the free encyclopedia (2007)

Hong Kong firms which are less flexible in staff management. Two possible side effects are, however, totally neglected by most Hong Kong officials. Firstly, it generates another type of gender inequity in employment that only women are granted maternity leave whereas men do not deserve to have any parental leave. Secondly, it internalizes and reinforces gender inequity at home. Without granting any parental leave to men, it implicitly reinforces the notion that women should be the main bearer of household chores and child care while men are not expected to assist the childrearing work. Sexual division of labor at home is internalized by such disparity in parental leave practice. Lack of parental leave will throttle the husbands' intention to lessen the childrearing burden of the wives. This practice contradicts the central tenet of cherishing the family and creating family-friendly work environment advocated by the Chief Executive, Donald Tsang, in his Policy Address in October 2005.

Some may criticize that direct comparison of Hong Kong situation with other developed countries is inappropriate as the social, economic and cultural background are different. While this argument seems reasonable, we can learn many lessons from other countries. A package of supportive policies needs to be in place in order to raise the fertility level. Unfortunately, there is a lack of coordination among various policy bureaus of the HKSAR Government. For instance, the Education and Manpower Bureau introduced the kindergarten coupon to ease the financial burden of parents. Introduction of such a coupon may be helpful but it would not be effective in addressing the issue of low fertility without the cooperation and coordination of other policies across different policy bureaus.

Conclusion

As a review of the literature, this chapter examines the contentious debate concerning how gender equity affects fertility. Unfortunately, little empirical research of good quality is available. The United Nations has endeavored to conduct some meaningful empirical studies. In this chapter, we have attempted to fill the gap by using wives' abilities to reject husbands' sexual request, contraceptive responsibility and the differential between ideal and actual fertility across couple as the major indicators of gender equity to provide more insight into the relationship between gender equity and fertility. As expected from the family power model, fertility was found to be associated negatively with all three aspects of gender equity.

On the basis of the results of our analyses and the literature review, we proposed a comprehensive policy package including introduction of part-time work, longer duration of paid maternity leave, paid parental leave, affordable and high quality childcare, guaranteed return to work with an option of reduced hours and family-friendly workplace. The short maternity leave and the lack of paid parental leave in Hong Kong lag behind other developed countries. These gaps highlight the difficult task of proposing a comprehensive population policy which involves not only demographic issues but also issues of gender equity. It requires the coordination across different government bureaus and departments. Further research is needed to illuminate the determinants of the complex phenomenon of fertility. Quality research and gender-based analyses are essential to the formulation of an effective population policy in Hong Kong.

References

Billari, F. C., & Wilson, C. (2001). Convergence towards diversity? Cohort dynamics in the transition to adulthood in contemporary western Europe, MPIDR Working paper WP 2001-39. Max Planck Institute for Demographic Research, Rostock.

Blood, R. O., & Wolfe, D. (1960). *Husbands and wives.* New York: Free Press.

Bongaarts, J. (2002). The end of the fertility transition in the developed world. *Population and Development Review, 28*(3), 419–443.

Bulanda, R. E. (2004). Paternal involvement with children: The influence of gender ideologies. *Journal of Marriage and Family, 66*, 40–45.

Buvini, M. (1994). Population policy and family planning programmes: Contributions from a focus on women, in F. G. Smith (Ed.), *Population—The complex reality* (pp. 211–228). London: The Royal Society.

Caldwell, J. C., & Schindlmayr, T. (2003). Explanations of the fertility crisis in modern societies: A search for commonalities. *Population Studies, 57*(3), 241–264.

Census and Statistics Department (2006). *Women and men in Hong Kong: Key statistics.* HKSAR: The Author.

Census and Statistics Department (2007).Life vital events. Retrieved on 30 April2007: http://www.censtatd.gov.hk/hong_kong_statistics/statistical/index.jsp?charsetID=1&subjectID=1&ID=004

Census and Statistics Department (2007). HK's ageing population trend continues. Retrieved on 30 April2007: http://www.news.gov.hk/en/category/administration/070222/html/070222en01005.htm

Cheung, F. (2002). Ageing population and gender issues. In Y. M. Yeung (Ed.) *New challenges for development and modernization: Hong Kong and the Asia-Pacific Region in the new millennium* (pp. 207–223). Hong Kong: The Chinese University Press.

Chesnais, J-C. (1996). Fertility, family, and social policy in contemporary Western Europe. *Population and Development Review, 22*(4), 729–739.

Chesnais, J-C. (1998). Below-replacement fertility in the European Union (EU-15): Facts and policies, 1960–1997. *Review of Population and Social Policy, 7,* 83–101.

Coleman, D. A.(2002). Populations of the industrial world—A convergent demographic community? *International Journal of Population Geography, 8,* 319–344.

Cooke, L. P. (2004). The gendered division of labor and family outcomes in Germany. *Journal of Marriage and Family, 66,* 1249–1259.

DeRose, L. F. (2003). Marriage, lineage, relative spousal power and fertility decline in Ghana.

Duvander, A-Z & Andersson, G. (2005). Gender equality and fertility in Sweden: A study on the impact of the father's uptake of parental leave on continued childbearing. Max Planck Institute for Demographic Research Working Paper WP 2005-013.

Family Planning Association of Hong Kong (1992). *Family planning knowledge, attitude and practice survey in Hong Kong.* Hong Kong: The Association.

Family Planning Association of Hong Kong (1997). *Family planning knowledge, attitude and practice survey in Hong Kong.* Hong Kong: The Association.

Family Planning Association of Hong Kong (2002). *Family planning knowledge, attitude and practice survey in Hong Kong.* Hong Kong: The Association.

Financial Services & Treasury Bureau (2007). The 2007–08 budget. Website: http://www.budget.gov.hk/2007/eng/speech.htm.

Hong Kong Special Administrative Region (2003). Report of the task force on population policy. Hong Kong Special Administrative Region Task Force on Population Policy, Hong Kong.

Hyde, J. S., Essex, M., & F. Horton. (1993). Fathers and parental leave: Attitudes and experiences. *Journal of Family Issues, 14,* 616–641.

Kohler, H. P., & Kohler I. (2002). Fertility decline in Russia in the early and mid-1990s: The Role of economic uncertainty and labour market crises. *European Journal of Population, 18*(3), 233–262.

Kohler, H. P, Billari, F., & Ortega. J. A. (2002). The Emergence of lowest-low fertility in Europe during the 1990s. *Population and Development Review, 28*(4), 641–680.

Larsen, U., & Hollos, M. (2003). Women's empowerment and fertility decline among the pare of Kilimanjaro region, northern Tanzania. *Social Science & Medicine,* (57), 1099–1115.

Legislative council. (2006). LCQ20: Paid maternity leave. 11 January 2006.

Lennon, M., & Rosenfield, S. (1994). Relative fairness and the division of housework: The importance of options. *American journal of sociology, 100*(2), 506–531.

Lesthaeghe, R., & Willems P.. (1999). Is low fertility a temporary phenomenon in the European Union? *Population and Development Review 25*(2), 211–228.

Lutz, W., O'Neill, B. C., & S. Scherbov (2003). Europe's population at a turning point. *Science 299* (5615), 1991–1992.

Macura, M. (2000). Fertility decline in the transition economies, 1989–1998: Economic and social factors revisited. In *Economic Survey in Europe, 2000/1*. Geneva: United Nations, Economic Commission for Europe, pp. 189–207.

Mason, K. O., & Smith, H. (2000). Husbands' versus wives' fertility goals and contraceptive use: The influence of gender context in five Asian countries. *Demography* 37, 299–311.

McDonald, P. (2000). Gender equality in theories of fertility transition. *Population and Development Review, 26*, 427–439.

McDonald, P. (2002). Below replacement fertility in Asia: Determinants and consequences. Paper presented at an International Workshop on Fertility Decline, Below Replacement Fertility and the Family in Asia: Prospects, Consequences and Policies, 10–12 April 2002, National University of Singapore, Singapore.

Noonan, M. (2001). The impact of domestic work on men's and women's wages. *Journal of Marriage and Family, 63*, 1134–1145.

OECD. (2005). Does gender equality spur growth? *Observer, 250*, 14–16.

The United Nations (2006). *Human development report 2006.* Website: http://hdr. undp.org/hdr2006/statistics/indicators/48.html

Sobotka, T. (2004). Is lowest-low fertility in Europe explained by the postponement of childbearing? *Population and Development Review, 30*(2), 195–200.

Wilson, C. (2001). On the scale of global demographic convergence 1950–2000. *Population and Development Review, 27*(1), 155–171.

Witte, J. C. and Wagner, G. G. (1995). Declining fertility in East Germany after unification: A demographic response to socio-economic change. *Population and Development Review, 21*(2), 387–397.

Wikipedia (2007). Encyclopedia. Website: http://en.wikipedia.org/wiki/Parental_ leave#_note-1

YWCA. 2005. *Survey of gender identity and housework division in Hong Kong.* Retrieved on 30 April 2007: http://www.ywca.org.hk/research/200512a/

Xu, A. (1992). Zhongwai funü jiating diwei de bijiao (International comparison of family status). *Xiehui* (Society), 1, 12–14. (In Chinese).

Notes

1. Total fertility rate (TFR) measures the average number of children that women would bear in lifetime if they were subject to age-specific fertility rates of that period.
2. Old age dependency ratio refers to the number of persons aged 65 and over per 1 000 persons aged between 15 and 64.
3. The decline from high level of fertility to low level is termed as fertility transition.

CHAPTER 7

A Gender Perspective on Families in Hong Kong

Susanne Y. P. Choi and K. F. Ting

Gender is a pivotal aspect of family relationships. It positions men and women differently within the family, where gender relationships are systematically created and reproduced. As a social institution, the family, through its distribution of resources, division of labour, and perceptions about gender, reinforces a hierarchical relationship between men and women in which men are privileged (Ferree, 1990). On the one hand, the family is important as an interactive arena for examining how people produce and do gender, and how gender strategies are created in everyday life (Berk, 1985, West & Zimmerman, 1987). On the other hand, gender is a tool for dissecting the structure of family, its processes, and the outcomes of interactions between its members.

Over the past twenty years, feminist research has advanced our understanding of the interrelationship between gender and the family. Firstly, it has demonstrated that gender underpins every domain of family life, including the marital relationship, the division between paid and unpaid work, parenthood, and kinship (Thompson & Walker, 1989; Walker, 1999). Secondly, it has rejected the notion that there is a division between the public and private domain as far as the family is concerned. It argues that the family is not part of the private domain and therefore separate from society. It contends that what takes place inside a family is related to what takes place in broader society (Ferree, 1990). Societal changes transform gender relationships, which in turn act as catalysts for change within the family. These changes, particularly changes in the structural composition and pattern of interactions between family members, generate novel issues to which society, the economy, and the state are obliged to respond (Tang & Lou, this volume). Thirdly, feminist research has questioned the notion that the family is a unitary whole. It highlights the divergent and even conflicting interests that exist among family members (Ferree, 1990, Tang, this volume). These research findings about gender and the family constitute both the premises and the framework for this review article.

Families in Hong Kong have undergone dramatic changes in size and, to a lesser extent, structure since the onset of industrialization in the post war era. The proportion of nuclear families has risen from 60% in 1976 to 66% in 2001, whereas median household size has dropped from 5.1 persons in 1961 to 3.1 persons in 2001. The latter change can largely be attributed to declining fertility rates and an increase in the age at which people enter into marriage. Fertility rates have dropped from 35 births per 1000 population in 1961 to 11 births per 1000 population in 2001 (Tu & Zhang, this volume), while the median age of entrance into marriage for men has increased from 28 in 1961 to 32 in 2001. The increase in the median age at marriage entrance for women has been even more marked, from 23 in 1961 to 31 in 2001 (Census and Statistics Department, 1962, 2001).

Researchers have been particularly interested in the impact of these changes on the relationship between spouses and the status of women in the family. Wong (1981), for instance, has argued that maternal employment has enabled women to enjoy relatively equal status with men within the family, and that this has inevitably transformed spousal relationships from dominance-submission partnerships to partnerships involving mutual collaboration. Yet a study of twenty-eight working daughters by Salaff (1995) in the early 1970s painted a more complex picture of the relationship between industrialization and women's status in the family. While wage employment did indeed provide women with the resources to negotiate for more personal freedom in leisure and the choice of intimate partners, the interest of the larger family in most cases continued to prevail over the interests of individual women, who often sacrificed their own individual interests to advance the welfare of the family as a whole. Other studies have also revealed the persistence of gender inequality in the domestic division of labor (Choi & Lee, 1997; Lee, 1998; Lee, 2002). Ng (1989, 1994) has argued that the claim that industrialization will increase the status of women and eventually give rise to more egalitarian gender relationships in families is too simplistic, and overlooks the possibility that men will continue to defend their supremacy in most areas of family life.

This paper reviews changes in gender relationships within families in

Hong Kong since the 1980s. We focus on two areas: domestic division of unpaid work and marital relations. The division of domestic labor reflects the unequal distribution of resources and power among family members, and also embodies culturally and historically specific notions of masculinity, femininity, wifehood and motherhood. The quality of domestic work performed by a woman is often used to evaluate her competence in fulfilling her role as mother and wife (Berk, 1985; Ferree, 1990; Hochschild & Machung, 2003). Domestic division of labor thus provides a window for examining existing norms about gender roles, the pattern of gender division of labor, and consequently the respective contribution and burden of women and men in families and the reinforcement of their status. A marital relation, on the other hand, is more concerned with the subjective evaluation of the marital life of two individuals. Bernard (1982) has argued that there are two marriages in every marriage—his and hers, suggesting that husbands and wives experience and interpret their marriages very differently. However intimate and unique a marital relationship may be, gender governs the way in which husbands and wives negotiate their way through day-to-day routines. Marital relationships involve power dynamics, exchange of resources, division of labor and communication of love and affection between two individuals whose behavior tends to vary according to their gender.

Domestic Division of Labor

Gender is one of the most powerful predictors of how domestic labor will be divided among family members. Berk (1985) has argued that the family simultaneously produces goods and gender. Domestic division of labor provides a means for "doing gender" (West & Zimmerman, 1987). It is through the division of domestic labor, the carrying out of 'male' and 'female' tasks, and the way in which men and women perform those tasks, that family members construct and reaffirm their identity as men, women, wives, husbands, mothers or fathers. This symbolic dimension of the division of domestic work challenges the validity of economic models that explain gender division of housework either in terms of utility maximization and relative marketability (Becker, 1993) or in terms of resource allocation and dependency (Blood & Wolfe, 1960). It explains the persistence of a seemingly unequal and irrational distribution of housework between a husband and wife in dual earner households (Hochschild & Machung, 2003). The view of family as a site for "doing gender" also explains why a husband who relies on his wife for economic support is likely to do less housework as his dependency increases. By refusing to do housework, an economically dependent husband reaffirms his masculinity (Brines, 1994).

In Hong Kong there is a lack of rigorous data for analyzing the patterns of domestic division of labor and the effect they have on gender equality. Such data that is available comes from four main sources: (a) the special module on family life added to Social Indicators Surveys since 1987 (Chan & Chu, 1996); (b) the Social Change and Economic Life Survey conducted by the Department of Sociology, the Chinese University of Hong Kong between 1994 and 1996; (c) a survey conducted by the Equal Opportunities Commission in 1996 and 1997; and (d) a thematic household survey conducted by the Census and Statistics Department in 2001. However, each of these studies measured different items of housework and used different response categories. For example, the 1995 Social Indicators Survey enquired how eleven major items of housework (buying food and preparing meals, dish washing, house cleaning, bills recording, baby-sitting, getting children up in the morning and to bed at night, supervising children's homework, taking care of sick children, meeting with school authorities, maintaining and repairing household apparatus, and car washing) were shared. In contrast, the survey conducted by the Equal Opportunities Commission in 1996 and 1997 only measured nine items of housework (shopping for food, preparing meals, dish washing, repairing of household apparatus, supervising children's homework, meeting children's teachers, taking care of elderly family members, organizing activities with kinsmen, and taking care of sick family members). More importantly, the response categories of the two surveys also differed. While the first survey had four categories (husband alone, wife alone, husband or wife, other people), the second survey had ten categories (husband alone, wife alone, husband or wife, husband and wife together, parents of husband or wife, sons, daughters, the whole family, maids, other people) (Chu, 1995; Equal Opportunities Commission, 1997). These differences hinder comparison across studies over time.

Another drawback of survey data of this kind is that they seldom reveal the less visible tasks, such as assigning chores, planning dinner, setting cleanliness standards, making grocery lists, making doctor's appointments, and getting ready for the next day (Walker, 1999). Furthermore, surveys rarely address the manner in which specific tasks are performed by family members. As far as middle-class families are concerned, they do not address the work these families do to maintain family status, such as making a careful choice of clothing, entertaining colleagues, and bringing up children in an appropriate manner (Thompson and& Walker, 1989). The surveys also do not investigate the emotional work that members of families do to meet the psychological needs of other family members (Walker, 1999). Since women are often responsible for the less visible tasks, family status production, and emotional work, and because they tend to have a higher standard of housework, the omission of these less tangible, more invisible aspects of housework in surveys are likely to underestimate the contribution of women in housework.

The Trend of Gender Division of Domestic Labor in Hong Kong since the 1980s

Overall, research on the domestic division of labor in Hong Kong between 1987 and 1996 reveals similar patterns: the domestic division of labor has remained stable and is biased against women. Women have shouldered most of the regular housework, including meal preparation (over 60% was done by wives alone), and dish washing (around 50% was done by wives alone). Women also do most of the work associated with child rearing, including supervising children's homework (around 60% was done by wives alone, and only around 10% was done by husbands alone) and meeting with the school authorities (nearly 70% was done by wives alone and less than 10% by husbands alone) (Chu, 1998).

The pattern of domestic division of labor found in 1995 reflected this broad pattern (Chu, 1995). In respect of the eleven items of housework surveyed, women alone did most of the regular housework, including buying food and preparing meals (60.1%), washing dishes (48.0%), housekeeping (44.8%), and keeping records of bills (49.2%). Women alone also did most of the child care, including baby-sitting (58.5%), urging children to go to bed/get up (54.8%), supervising children's homework (46.8%), taking care of sick children (55.2%), and meeting with the school authorities (56.5%). Men (alone), on the other hand, did most of the irregular housework, including maintaining and repairing household appliances (60.1%) and car washing (31.9%).

It is likely that these data under-estimated the contribution women made to domestic work because women might be actually doing more when respondents chose the response category 'husband or wife'. Moreover, these data are likely to under-estimate women's share of housework in society as a whole. The category "the couple's parents" might often mean the mothers of the husband or wife. The category 'other people' might often refer to 'domestic helpers', the majority of whom were (and are) women.

Although men with employed wives did more regular housework, the division of labor in dual earner households was far from equal. Employed women alone still did most of the regular housework, including buying food and preparing meals (57.3%), washing dishes (48.1%), house cleaning (39.7%), and keeping track of household bills (50%). They also did most of the child care. Around sixty per cent of employed women (alone) shouldered most child care, including baby-sitting (63.6%), urging children to go to bed/get up (63.1%), supervising children's homework (57.8%), taking care of children when they were sick (51.3%), and meeting with the school authorities (57.7%) (Chu, 1995).

If we include maintaining relationships with relatives, which is another important aspect of family life in Chinese society and which requires much work because of the energy and time it demands, the pattern of the domestic division of labor is even more skewed. According to a survey conducted by the Equal Opportunities Commission between 1996 and 1997, 30% of women on their own took care of parents /parents-in-law, 36% maintained contact with relatives and friends, and nearly 50% took care of family members when they were sick. The comparative figures for husbands taking care of these tasks on their own were 10%, 14% and 5% respectively (Equal Opportunities Commission, 1997).

The process of de-industrialization, economic restructuring, and economic recession that has taken place in the past few decades, despite its influence on individual life opportunities and labor market positions (Chiu & Lee, 1997), has not impacted greatly on the pattern of the domestic division of labor. According to a survey conducted between 2001 and 2002, 40% of women (as compared with 9% of men) were responsible for over 60% of the housework. Moreover, while around 70% of men did less than 20% of housework, the corresponding figure for women was 36%. Although the disparity between men and women's share of domestic work was slightly smaller among the economically active population, it was still substantial. Over 70% of employed men did less than 20% of housework, as compared with 46% of employed women. Only 6% of employed men were responsible for over 80% of housework, as compared with 13% of women (Census and Statistics Department, 2003).

Education, Social Class, and Domestic Help

If the employment status of women has had little effect on the pattern of gender division of domestic labor, other contextual factors such as education and social class have also had a marginal effect. It is often hypothesized that providing more opportunities for education will reduce gender inequality in the domestic division of labor, because more educated people are likely to hold more liberal views. Empirical data suggest that this hypothesis is only partially true. In absolute terms, men with an elementary education were responsible for more housework than men with a tertiary education. Twelve per cent of men with an elementary education were responsible for over 80% of housework, as opposed to only 6% of men with a tertiary education. On the other hand, 55% of men with an elementary education were responsible for less than 20% of housework, as opposed to 72% of men with a tertiary education. Relative to the amount of housework performed by their female partners, educated men may be doing more than their less educated counterparts. Assuming that married people have similar levels of education, the disparity in the domestic division of labor between educated men and women was smaller than that between less educated men and women. Although 72% of men with a tertiary education were responsible for less than 20% of housework, the comparative figure for women with a tertiary education was 62%, a 10% difference. On the other hand, while 55% of men with an elementary education were responsible for less than 20% of housework, the comparative figure for women with an elementary education was 17%, a 38% gender difference (Census and Statistics Department, 2003).

Education is often closely associated with social class, and the reason why both educated men and women do less housework may be because educated women are more likely to hold a full time job after marriage (Ting, 2000) and to employ domestic helpers (Chan, 2000). Data from the household surveys provide some preliminary evidence to support this hypothesis. Only 2% of men in households with a monthly income of more than 40,000 were responsible for more than 80% of housework, compared to 20% of men in households with a monthly income of less than 10,000. Around 13% of women in households with a monthly income of more than 40,000 were responsible for more than 80% of housework, compared to 40% of women in households with a monthly income of less than 10,000. The difference between women and men in high income households (>40,000) who performed more than 80% of housework was 9%, but that between women and men in households with a monthly income of less than 10,000 was 20% (Census and Statistics Department, 2003). No men in families with domestic helpers were responsible for more than 60% of housework, as opposed to 10% of men in families without domestic helpers. One per cent of women in families with domestic helpers did more than 60% of housework, as opposed to 41% of women in families without domestic helpers (Census and Statistics Department, 2003). Since around 10% of Hong Kong households employed domestic helpers (Census and Statistics Department, 2001), the impact of domestic helpers on gender equalities in the division of domestic labor in middle class families is not a trivial issue.

In sum, these data suggest that, although education and social class have a bearing on the gender division of housework among marriage partners with a tertiary education, in households with a monthly income of more than 40,000 and in families with domestic helpers, the division of housework is far from equal. Women in these groups are still doing more than their male partners. Yet the data also suggest that education seems to increase gender equality, albeit only slightly. Social class, as indicated by household income, also seems to increase gender equality in the division of housework, although the measurements used in the survey may exaggerate its impact. Domestic help may relieve women of regular housework such as food shopping, preparation of meals, dish washing, house cleaning, laundry, and baby-sitting, but it also creates other tasks, mainly work involving the management, training, and supervision of domestic helpers. Domestic help is also rarely able to relieve women of the work of planning and child care, such as supervising children's homework, going through their lessons, preparing for tests and examinations, and meeting children's teachers. On the other hand, husbands often withdraw totally from housework and even child rearing when domestic help is available (Lee, 2002). The impact of domestic help on the gender division of housework is therefore contradictory. At best it perpetuates existing gender inequalities in the domestic division of labor. It is more likely that it may actually increase gender inequalities in these families, and produce the illusion of gender equality. The tasks that female employers allocate to domestic helpers are often more visible than those that they keep for themselves and the tasks that arise as a result of the employment of domestic helpers. It is more obvious who does the cooking, cleaning, and baby-sitting than who plans, allocates, and supervises.

Explanations of Gender Division of Domestic Labor

With few exceptions, most studies on the division of housework in Hong Kong have been descriptive. Studies have suggested that the position of both men and women in the labor market will affect their share of domestic work. Women with time-consuming and better-paid jobs do less housework.

On the other hand, full time employment and a stable job reduce the contribution that men make to housework. Yet market positions only explain around 16% of the variance in the domestic division of labor (Ting, 2000). Lee (2002) has reported that traditional gender ideology and a patriarchal familiar structure have influenced the allocation of housework and childcare. These are duties that women, regardless of their employment and class status, are expected to carry out (see also Francesco & Shaffer, 2008). Choi & Lee (1997) have argued that housework has been allocated within an entrenched framework of a breadwinner (husband) versus homemaker (wife) dichotomy. The career of the husband has received priority over that of the wife, and the wife has shouldered most housework in order to make time for the husband to pursue his career. Negotiation of housework, even if it has occurred, has been within this arch framework. Choi & Lee (1997) have thus argued that it is the household rather than the individual that should be taken into account. This diverges from traditional analysis that ignores the role of women in the allocation of household work. Instead of constructing women as passive victims who take up work allocated to them reluctantly, Choi & Lee (1997) have examined the active role of women in the allocation and justification of the domestic division of labor as members of the household. Given the breadwinner/home-maker gender discourse that endorses the public and private division of labor between men and women, and the skewed labor market structure that generally disadvantages women, in order to maximize the interests of the household, it is not difficult to understand why many women consider it 'natural' to reduce the loads of their husbands in domestic work to enable them to concentrate on their careers. This also helps to explain why the obviously unequal division of domestic work between the genders has not been fundamentally challenged and remains so resistant to change.

Summary

As in most Western societies, the domestic division of labor in Hong Kong families is gendered (Thompson & Walker, 1989; Ferree, 1990; Walker, 1999). Despite the increase in women's education and labor market participation and the changes in family structures, women still shoulder the bulk of housework and child care. Women's full time employment, education, and middle class status have increased men's share of housework and to some extent reduced the burden borne by women. Yet these changes have not yet become substantial enough to reverse the unequal pattern of women doing more housework than men. The reasons for the persistence of gender inequalities in this area still require exploration. The few studies that have dealt with the reasons for gender inequalities in domestic work seem to suggest that the public/private, breadwinner/home-maker, and masculine/ feminine divides operating at the household level explain the current situation. We also know very little about the consequences of this inequality on the life chances of men and women. Future studies could profitably explore the impact of inequality on the time husbands and wives spend on other activities, their career development, and the stress, burden, and guilt women experience if they have other professional commitments.

Marital Relations

The previous section documented the patterns and dynamics of the gender division of domestic labor and its evolution in Hong Kong since the 1980s. Against this background, this section will review the subjective evaluations of couples about the quality of their marital life, including marital satisfaction, consensus, communication, and intimacy. Gender not only shapes the distribution of power and the division of labor at home, but also underlies the subjective perceptions of couples about their marital relationships. Studies in the United States have shown that men and women have different subjective perceptions of their marital life because of divergent needs, experiences, attitudes, and values. This may be even truer among Chinese whose cultural heritage places great emphasis on gender role differentiation, making marital interaction between the two genders a more polarized experience (Shek, 1995, 1996).

Early studies on husband-wife relationships in Hong Kong treated marital partners as consensual units who reacted to marital norms in similar ways (Podmore & Chaney, 1974). Since the mid-1990s, local studies have begun to examine marital relationships with a greater recognition of gender differences (City University of Hong Kong & Hong Kong Catholic Marriage Advisory Council, 2001; Kam & Man, 1993; Shek, 1995; Young, 1995). Common to all these studies, however, have been their heavy reliance on the survey methodology and the use of measurement instruments developed for use in Western societies.

Four instruments are particularly popular in Hong Kong. The Dyadic Adjustment Scale (DAS) which captures relationship adjustment in four different domains (dyadic satisfaction, relating to issues such as considering divorce, regretting marrying, quarreling, confiding in mate, kissing, degree of happiness, and commitment; dyadic consensus, which addresses spousal agreement on issues such as dealing with finances, recreation, religion, friends and relatives, philosophy of life and household tasks; dyadic cohesion, which concerns the sharing of emotions, ideas and activities; and emotional expressions, which include the showing of love and affection and interest in the sexual relationship) (Spanier, 1976). The Kansas Marital Satisfaction Scale (KMS) assesses satisfaction with the marital relationship. It asks how satisfied respondents are with their marriages, with their spouse and with their spousal relationship (Schumm et al., 1986). The Evaluating Nurturing Relationship Issues Communication and Happiness (ENRICH) scale provides a comprehensive measure of marital life in areas including communication, conflict resolution, roles, financial concerns, leisure time, sexual relationship, parenting, family and friends, and religion (Olson, Fournier & Druckman,1983). The Marital Comparison Level Index (MCLI) examines interdependence and reciprocity between marital partners in the four domains of expectation, equity, commitment, and constraints to dissolution. The measurement emphasizes that respondents evaluate their marital experience by comparing them against prior expectations (Sabatelli, 1984).

Based on questionnaire surveys, these instruments provide a useful tool for researchers to quantify the feelings of couples on different aspects of their relationships. Although the instruments are well established in terms of validity and reliability and have been modified to suit the Chinese context, the numeric values recorded in variable format hardly give us a full picture of how marital relationships evolve. Ethnographic studies to supplement survey methodology in the field are curiously absent and we were left with no narrative accounts to show how marital relationships are constructed and maintained separately by men and women. Thus, our current understanding of marital relationships in Hong Kong is skeletal.

Marital Satisfaction

Among the various indicators of marital relations, marital satisfaction seems to be the best global measure summarizing perceptual differences between marital partners. In one of the earliest attempts at quantifying marital experiences in Hong Kong, Shek (1995) found that women in Hong Kong were less pleased with their marital relationships than men in terms of satisfaction, consensus, cohesion and affection expression on the Chinese DAS scale. Similarly, women were less satisfied than men with their marriage, spouse, and marital relationship on the KMS scale. Comparatively speaking, marital satisfaction seems to be a key aspect for identifying gender differences. Shek (1995) also notes that the gender difference in marital satisfaction in Hong Kong was bigger than that found in the United States, suggesting some cultural conditioning of marital interaction. The same gender difference in marital satisfaction also appears in the studies conducted by Young (1995) and the City University of Hong Kong and Hong Kong Catholic Marriage Advisory Council (2001). More recently, a survey in 2002 found that 73.4% of women (compared with 83.8% of men) were satisfied with their marital life, indicating that this gender gap has persisted (The Family Planning Association of Hong Kong 2004).

Although all survey results point to the same gender gap in marital satisfaction, the problem of data comparability and the short period covered by these studies makes it difficult for us to be certain whether the gap has been widening or narrowing. There have also been no systematic efforts to link structural causes, such as family power and female employment, to the gender difference in marital satisfaction, leaving much room for post hoc speculation. For instance, men might be more satisfied with their marriages because they enjoy greater privileges within the family, such as avoiding household work, whereas women's marital life might be burdened by role overload in combining family with work. These highly plausible theses should be submitted to empirical tests. Besides elucidating the mechanisms of gender differences in marital relationships, superimposing the divergent perceptions against their structural context would also help us to project future marital development in line with social changes.

Marital Consensus

If a person perceives fewer conflicts and feels greater consensus in a relationship, he or she is naturally likely to consider such a relationship more satisfactory. This seems to be the case in marital relationships. By combining exploratory interviews and questionnaire surveys, Young (1995) observed that, in addition to higher marital satisfaction, men were more idealistic about their marriage. Contrary to conventional wisdom; they considered marriage more permanent and felt less regretful about it than women. Men also experienced their relationships as more harmonious than their wives and tended to trivialize marital problems. Men typically characterized their marital relationships as fair, while their spouses often felt that their husbands had taken advantage of them. As a result, men reported a lower degree of marital conflict and a higher level of consensus in spousal interactions, whereas women reported more quarrelling and arguments on a wide range of family issues. The inclination among men to ignore marital problems and disputes might be rooted in Chinese culture which treasures family harmony and suppresses individual differences. Husbands as heads of their families are responsible for appearing to live up to these cultural ideals.

There seems to be some support to women's account that marital consensus was much lower than their husbands imagined. Studies have shown that husbands and wives disagree on just about everything. Differences of opinion on marital roles is certainly an important area of disagreement, and such differences begin before marriage. For example, in a sample of premarital couples who had registered their first marriage in 1991, 68.8% of the grooms-to-be felt that supporting the family was their responsibility, but only 43.6% of the brides-to-be agreed (most of them actually thought that it was a joint responsibility). Regarding the issue of family power, 25.0% of grooms-to-be felt that they should have the final say on family finances, whereas only 9.7% of brides-to-be felt the same way (Kam & Man, 1993). A study in 1997 comparing the fertility preferences of husbands and wives also revealed a lack of consensus on this important family matter. Only 32.4% of couples agreed on whether to have more children. In most cases (59.3%), the husbands wanted more children while the wives did not, and in a small proportion of cases (8.3%) the reverse was true (The Family Planning Association in Hong Kong, 1999).

While gender differences in role expectations were quite remarkable, there were indications that differences in some areas have been narrowing. For example, an initial survey in 1997 showed that more men than women rejected the possibility of married persons having close friends of the opposite sex, and of refusing a spouse's sexual request. Men seemed to define marital relationships more restrictively — that personal space should be sacrificed to maintain a marital relationship. As shown in Table 1, these gender differences almost disappeared in a subsequent survey in 2002 (The Family Planning Association of Hong Kong, 2004). Although these changes suggest greater consensus in marital life, it may also suggest adjustments in selected domains rather than a general trend in this direction.

Marital Communication

Whether greater consensus can be achieved in marital life depends on the

Table 1. Attitudes toward sex roles in a marriage

Sex role statements	1997		2002	
	Husband	Wife	Husband	Wife
1 A woman's career achievement can be higher than her husband's	77.8	78.8	74.5	75.0
2 A woman need not give birth to a son in order to gain respect from friends/relatives	85.9	85.5	87.6	86.5
3 A woman can have close friends of the opposite sex after marriage	47.0	67.7	68.0	72.5
4 A man can have close friends of the opposite sex after marriage	50.4	61.6	69.9	66.1
5 A wife can reject her husband's sexual request	66.8	75.4	90.9	89.0
6 A husband can reject his wife's sexual request	64.9	77.3	89.8	88.7
N	1,681	1,511	1,147	1,607

Source: The Family Planning Association of Hong Kong. 2004. *Family Planning Knowledge, Attitude and Practice in Hong Kong Survey 2002.* http://www.famplan.org.hk/fpahk/common/pdf/ar-02-03/KAPSurvey2002.pdf

quality of communication between both partners in a marriage. It is not clear to what extent men and women actually understand and communicate their differences regarding their expectations of each other's roles in marriage. Research findings suggest that men were less ready than women to communicate with their spouses. Among premarital couples, 72.6% of women versus only 34.3% of men reported that they were able to express their feelings and emotions to their future spouses openly, and 70.1% of women versus 40.4% of men believed that they were able to talk about anything with their future spouse (Kam and Man, 1993). This pattern may relate to the social practice that encourages women to express feelings but restrains men from doing the same. Structural factors, however, may play a role too. Men's dominant role in family means that they may not be able to open themselves up and reveal their weaknesses. Sexual needs seem to be the only exception, with more men than women, or 77.8% versus 56.4%, being eager to honestly express themselves.

Marital Intimacy

Intimacy is another dimension that captures gender difference in marital relationships. A recent survey in 2002 showed that more men than women were interested in sexual life and felt satisfied with it (The Family Planning

Association of Hong Kong, 2004). This may reflect a tendency that men were more willing than women to communicate their sexual needs. Besides sexual intimacy, men also reported a higher level of spousal intimacy in other aspects and felt more satisfied than women did (City University of Hong Kong and Hong Kong Catholic Marriage Advisory Council, 2001). More specifically, gender differences were found in four domains, namely, intellectual, emotional, sexual, and recreational intimacy. Men tended to agree more on such items as "your partner can help clarify your thoughts," "your partner shares his/her worries with you," "you and your partner express affection to each other frequently," and "you enjoy your sexual life with your partner." Given these results, it was somewhat surprising that more men than women agreed with the statement that "there is an emotional gap between you and your partner." Women, on the other hand, felt more strongly about the statement "you and your partner share common interests." It is important to note that the men and women covered in this survey agreed on the intimacy assessment items more often than not, but the disparity shown above does point to specific gender issues that matter in the development of marital relationships.

Explanations of Gender Differences

The asymmetrical perception of marital life between husbands and wives is puzzling given that marital interaction is naturally intimate and continuous over a long period. Recent studies in Hong Kong have revealed various domains of gender differences in marital life, but have stopped short of linking them to the basic fabric of family life. Shek (1995), based on a comparison between Hong Kong with the United States, suggests that Chinese culture may have an important influence on marital relationships. He argues that "Chinese people's emphasis on familism, dominance of the husbands, and submissiveness of the wives and the greater reliance of females on marriage in defining their identities and the stressful nature of the female marital roles under the Chinese culture … might intensify gender differences in marital quality" (p. 702). The Family Planning Association in Hong Kong (2004) recently began to design survey questions parallel to those of mainland studies for cross border comparison. A comparative perspective on cultural variations is useful, but culture does not seem to be a crucial explanation for the gender differences in marital experiences, bearing in mind that these differences are not unique to Chinese societies but have also appeared in other parts of the world (Bernard, 1982). Culture may play a role in the extent of gender differences and their expressions, but it does not completely change the landscape of marital life.

Gender socialization, a slight modification of the cultural thesis, is another popular explanation which stresses differential role training and expectations. Because of differences in role socialization, men emphasize instrumental behavior more whereas women focus more on affectionate behavior. Thus, each sex uses different criteria for evaluating its own performance in marital interactions and their associated outcomes. Young (1995), for example, argues that "[Chinese] women are inclined to derive their senses of satisfaction with marriage and with themselves from their appraisal of the adequacy of emotional sharing which they have engendered. ... men are socialized to be achievement oriented, outward looking, independent, unemotional, and to hide their vulnerability. They are inclined to use instrumental means assessing marital and family well-being" (p.101-102). While the socialization explanations seem to make sense, little work has been done to examine the specific mechanisms that cause gender differences and test their empirical derivations.

The socialization thesis may have exaggerated the extent to which people internalize the gender norms regarding marital roles. In a series of studies conducted on three birth cohorts of school students, working youth and premarital couples, the marital norms perceived by these cohorts were not consistent with the trends of less gender stereotyped socialization in this highly modern, urban society (Yeung Chan & Kwong , 1995, 1996, 1997). Instead of espousing a more egalitarian ideology on gender roles, school students (the youngest cohort) held traditional views on gender norms in almost every item in Table 2. They believed that women should prioritize family over work, take primary responsibility for child care, provide a comfortable home, and listen to the husband. Men, on the other hand, should shoulder the provider role, making sacrifices in the interests of their wives and families. The older cohorts, in contrast, held more egalitarian and more realistic attitudes. Premarital couples, in particular, realized that it was not possible for men to be the sole family providers, and believed that men were equally responsible for child development.

It is entirely possible that gender role socialization may give way to the emerging needs of the situation. Role performance and expectation in a marriage may be situational, which calls for greater attention to the structural properties of marriage in order to reveal how marital relationships are constructed and maintained. Marital power is one example of structural force in a marriage. It has been suggested that working women have greater power

Table 2. Attitudes toward Marital Relationship in Three Birth Cohorts

Domains of Marital Relationship	Premarital couples (age 21 to 46)		Working youth (age 17 to 30)		School students (age 15 to 18)	
	Male	Female	Male	Female	Male	Female
Family-work priorities						
1. Wife should accommodate her work role to family needs	59.7	60.7	58.3	44.8	73.2	64.7
2. Family is more important to women whilst work is more important to men	42.3	49.7	39.8	34.8	45.4	31.1
3. Men may take overtime work if their job requires, but women should try to avoid overtime work as far as possible	43.1	25.0	44.0	19.8	49.0	25.7
Provider role						
4. The primary responsibility of a man to his family is to work hard and earn a good living for his wife and children	66.9	64.8	75.0	69.8	84.7	77.2
5. The husband is expected to be primarily responsible for meeting the financial needs of the family	66.4	73.8	59.8	68.1	74.7	76.8
6. The two partners should bear equal responsibilities for earning a living for the family	90.6	91.7	90.8	94.8	74.6	84.5
Homecare role						
7. The primary responsibility of a woman is to give care to children and make a comfortable home for her husband	66.7	70.1	68.5	61.2	84.7	73.4
8. The mother has a far more important and active role to play than the father in child development	36.2	17.4	39.4	20.7	43.8	36.9
9. Housework should be equally shared by both husband and wife if they are both working	96.4	97.2	94.5	99.1	96.2	97.6
Family dominance						
10. A working wife should give up her job whenever her husband so wishes	37.4	27.6	44.0	24.1	50.2	30.1
11. The husband should be the head of the family and has greater say in family decision-making than the wife	38.8	19.4	30.3	19.8	35.1	13.6
Marriage maintenance						
12. A wife should be accommodative and avoid conflicts with her husband	64.5	34.7	60.6	37.1	65.9	50.4
13. A husband should be willing to make sacrifice for the interest of the wife and the needs of the family	97.1	88.8	87.2	91.3	92.5	85.6
14. Couple should have space for individual pursuit after marriage, and respect the private life of one's spouse	89.9	88.3	80.7	89.6	74.1	76.8
15. A wife should be subservient to her husband since he is the head of the family	51.1	36.4	56.5	22.4	55.0	27.7
16. Couples should have share interests and joint social activities after marriage	91.4	94.5	81.7	83.6	69.1	70.2
17. A wife should be willing to make sacrifice for the interest of the husband and the needs of the family	86.3	84.0	75.2	76.7	75.9	72.7
N	139	145	109	116	451	501

Source: Yeung Chan, S.T. & Kwong, W.M. 1995. *Attitudes toward Marriage in a Time of Change: A Survey Study of the Attitudes of Secondary School Students toward Marriage in Hong Kong*. Hong Kong: Dept. of Applied Social Studies, City University of Hong Kong. Yeung Chan, S.T. & Kwong, W.M. 1996. *Attitudes toward Marriage in a Time of Change: A Survey Study of the Attitudes of Working Youth toward Marriage in Hong Kong*. Hong Kong: Dept. of Applied Social Studies, City University of Hong Kong. Yeung Chan, S.T. & Kwong, W.M. 1997. *Attitudes toward Marriage in a Time of Change: A Survey Study of the Attitudes of Pre-marital Couples toward Marriage in Hong Kong*. Hong Kong: Dept. of Applied Social Studies, City University of Hong Kong.

on matters such as family planning (Mitchell, 1972), family resources (Rosen, 1978), and family decision making (Podmore & Chaney, 1974; Wong, 1972a, 1972b), all of which may subsequently affect the quality of spousal interaction. The division of domestic labor and patrilocal residence are other structural features that may have different consequences for the way in which partners interact with each other and perceive marital quality within the family.

Conclusion

By focusing on the gender division of domestic labor and marital relations, this review highlights the persistence of gender inequalities in the family. Women across all classes and working statuses in Hong Kong have continued to shoulder most of the burden of domestic work. The employment of domestic helpers by middle class families may have relieved women in these families of some household tasks and child care, but has simultaneously created invisible tasks for women and enabled the almost complete withdrawal of husbands from domestic work. The invisibility of these tasks gives the impression of increased gender equality, but in reality it may perpetuate and even widen existing inequalities. Marital relations, indicated by marital satisfaction, marital consensus, marital communication and marital intimacy, have also shown clear patterns of gender differences in Hong Kong. Men on average are more satisfied with married life than women. They also perceive a higher level of spousal consensus than women do. On the other hand, men are less able to communicate frankly their opinions and needs (except their sexual needs) than women. Sexuality remains a taboo for many women in marriage. All in all, these findings seem to suggest the prevalence of traditional gender norms and patterns of spousal interaction in families in Hong Kong despite major societal changes that have transformed the structural locations of women and men in education and the labor market since WWII (see for example, Francesco & Shaffer, this volume; Tang, this volume; Tang & Lou, this volume; Tu & Zhang, this volume).

References

Becker, G. S. (1993). *A treatise on the family*, 4th edition. Cambridge, MA: Harvard University Press.

Berk, Sarah F. (1985). *The gender factory: The apportionment of work in American households*. New York: Plenum Press.

Bernard, J. (1982). *The future of marriage*. Yale University Press.

Blood, R., & Wolfe D. (1960). *Husbands and wives: The dynamics of married living*. Glencoe, Ill: Free Press.

Brines, J. (1994). Economic dependency, gender and the division of labor at home. *American Journal of Sociology, 100*, 652–688.

Census and Statistics Department. HKSAR. (1962). *Census 1961: Main report*. Hong Kong: Census and Statistics Department.

Census and Statistics Department. HKSAR. (2001). *Thematic household survey report no. 5*. Hong Kong: Census and Statistics Department.

Census and Statistics Department, HKSAR. (2003). *Thematic household survey report no. 14*. Hong Kong: Census and Statistics Department.

Chan W. S., & Chu W. C. (1996). Assessing gender issues in local family study: a lesson to learn for social indicators research? In Lau Siu-kai et al. (Eds.), *New frontiers of social indicators research in Chinese societies* (pp. 605–630). Hong Kong Institute of Asia-Pacific Studies.

Chan, H. N. (2000). "Jiawu yu nvxing jiuye: xianggang youguan haiwai jiating gugong zhengce dui xingbie fenceng zhi yingxiang" (Domestic work and female employment: The impact of policy on the employment of foreign domestic helpers on social stratification). In Z. J. Liu, B. S. Wen, M. K. Li, & S. L. Huang (Eds.), *Shichang, jieji yu zhengzhi: bianqian zhong de huaren shehui*. (pp. 251–271). Xianggang zhongwen daxue yatai yanjiusuo.

Chiu, W. K., & Lee, C. K. (1997). After the miracle: Women workers under industrial restructuring in Hong Kong. *Asian Survey, 37* 752–770.

Choi, P. K., & Lee, C. K. (1997). The hidden abode of domestic labor: the case of Hong Kong,. In F. Cheung (Ed.), *Engendering Hong Kong society: A gender perspective of women's status* (pp. 157–200). Hong Kong: The Chinese University Press..

Chu, Wai-chi. (1995). Who is doing what? The implication behind housework sharing. In Lau Siu-kai et al. (Eds.), *Indicators and social development: Hong Kong 1995* (pp. 203–232). Hong Kong: Hong Kong Institute of Asia-Pacific Studies.

Chu, Wai-chi.(1998). Xianggang jiating xingbie yanjiu he qu he cong (Which direction should research on gender and family in Hong Kong go). In Z. J. Liu, B. S. Wen, M. K. Li, & S. L. Huang (Eds.), *Huaren shehui de bianmao: shehui zhibiao de fenxi* (pp. 469–500). Xianggang zhongwen daxue yatai yanjiusuo.

City University of Hong Kong and Hong Kong Catholic Marriage Advisory Council. (2001). Marital intimacy and satisfaction among Chinese couples in Hong Kong.

Equal Opportunities Commission. (1997). *A Baseline survey of equal opportunities on the basis of gender in hong kong*. Hong Kong: Equal Opportunities Commission.

Ferree, M. M. (1990). Beyond separate spheres: Feminism and family research. *Journal of Marriage and the Family, 52*, 866–884.

Francesco, A. M., & Shaffer, M. A. (2008). Working women in Hong Kong: *Neuih keuhng yahn* or oppressed class?

Hochschild A. R., & Machung A. (2003). *The second shift*. New York: Penguin Books.

Kam, P. K., & Man, K. Y. (1993). *Preparation for marriage: A study of premarital people in Hong Kong*. Hong Kong: City Polytechnic of Hong Kong.

Lee, C. K. (1998). *Gender and the South China miracle: Two worlds of factory women*. Berkeley: University of California Press.

Lee, W. (2002). Gender ideology and the domestic division of labor in middle-class Chinese families in Hong Kong.

Mitchell, R. E. (1972). Husband-wife relations and family planning practices in urban Hong Kong. *Journal of Marriage and the Family, 34*, 139–145.

Ng, C. H. (January 1989). "Jiating weiji, shui de weiji? — Gongyehua yu xianggang jiating bianqian de tansuo" (Family crises? Whose's crises? Industrialization and family change in Hong Kong), *Mingbao yuekan*, 3–10.

Ng, C. H. (1994). Power, identity, and economic change — 25 years of family studies in Hong Kong. In B. Leung & T. Y. C. Wong (Eds.), *25 years of social and economic development in Hong Kong*. Hong Kong: Oxford University Press.

Olson, D. H., Fournier, D. G., & Druckman, J. M. (1983). *PREPARE/ENRICH Counselor's Manual*. PREPARE/ENRICH, Inc.

Podmore, D., & Chaney, D. (1974). Family norms in a rapidly industrializing society: Hong Kong. *Journal of Marriage and the Family, 36*, 400–407.

Rosen, S. (1978). Sibling and in-law relationships in Hong Kong: The emergent role of Chinese wives. *Journal of Marriage and Family, 40*, 621–628.

Sabatelli, R. M. (1984). The marital comparison level index: A measure for assessing outcomes relative to expectations. *Journal of Marriage and the Family, 46*, 651–661.

Salaff, J. (1995). *Working daughters of Hong Kong: Filial piety or power in the family?* 2nd Edition. New York: Columbia University Press.

Schumm, W. R., Paff-Bergen, L. A., Hatch, R. C., Obiorah, F. C., Copeland, J. M., Meens, L. D., & Bugaihis, M. A. (1986). Concurrent and discriminant validity of the Kansas Marital Satisfaction Scale. *Journal of Marriage and the Family, 48*, 381–387.

Shek, D. (1995). Gender differences in marital quality and well-being in Chinese married adults. *Sex Roles, 32*, 699–715.

Shek, D. (1996). Marital quality and psychological well-being of married adults in a Chinese context. *Journal of Genetic Psychology, 156*, 45–56.

Spanier, G. B. (1976). Measuring dyadic adjustment: New scales for assessing the quality of marriage and similar dyads. *Journal of Marriage and the Family, 38*, 15–28.

Tang, S. K. (this volume). Gender-based violence in Hong Kong. social welfare and women: The dominant approach and its critique.

The Family Planning Association of Hong Kong. (1999). *Family planning knowledge, attitude and practice in Hong Kong survey 1997*. Hong Kong: The Family Planning Association of Hong Kong.

The Family Planning Association of Hong Kong. (2004). *Family planning knowledge, attitude and practice in Hong Kong survey 2002*. http://www. famplan.org.hk/fpahk/common/pdf/ar-02-03/KAPSurvey2002.pdf, accessed on October 18, 2004.

Thompson L., & Walker A. J. (1989). Gender in families: Women and men in marriage, work, and parenthood. *Journal of Marriage and the Family, 51*, 845–871.

Ting, K. F. (2000). "Cong jieji fenxi kan xianggang de jiating fengong" (A class perspective on domestic division of labor). In Z. J. Liu, B. S. Wen, M. K. Li, & S. L. Huang (Eds.), Shichang, jieji yu zhengzhi: bianqian zhong de huaren shehui (pp. 231–250). Xianggang zhongwen daxue yatai yanjiusuo.

Tu, E., & Zhang, X. (n.a.). Fertility transition and gender equity in Hong Kong.

Wong, F. M. (1972a). Maternal employment and family task-power differentiation among low income Chinese families. Research Series. Hong Kong: Social Research Center of Chinese University of Hong Kong

Wong, F. M. (1972b). Modern ideology, industrialization and conjugalism: The Hong Kong case. *International Journal of Sociology of the Family, 2*, 139–150.

Wong, F. M. (1981). Effects of the employment of mothers on marital role and power differentiation in Hong Kong. In A. Y. C. King & R. P. L. Lee (Eds.), *Social Life and Development in Hong Kong* (pp. 217–234). Hong Kong: Chinese University Press.

Yeung Chan, S. T., & Kwong, W. M. (1995). Attitudes toward marriage in a time of change: a survey study of the attitudes of secondary school students toward marriage in Hong Kong. Hong Kong: Dept. of Applied Social Studies, City University of Hong Kong.

Yeung Chan, S. T., & Kwong, W. M. (1996). Attitudes toward marriage in a time of change: A survey study of the attitudes of working youth toward marriage in Hong Kong. Hong Kong: Dept. of Applied Social Studies, City University of Hong Kong.

Yeung Chan, S. T., & Kwong, W. M. (1997). Attitudes toward marriage in a time of change: A survey study of the attitudes of pre-marital couples toward marriage in Hong Kong. Hong Kong: Dept. of Applied Social Studies, City University of Hong Kong.

Young, K. P. H. (1995). *Understanding marriage: A Hong Kong case study*. Hong Kong: Hong Kong University Press.

Walker, A. J. (1999). Gender and family relationships. In M. Sussman, S. K. Steinmetz, & G. W. Peterson. (Eds.), *Handbook of marriage and the family*, 2nd edition. (pp. 439–474). New York: Plenum Press,

West, C., & Zimmerman, D. H. (1987). Doing gender. *Gender and Society, 1*, 125–151.

CHAPTER 8

Social Welfare and Women: The Dominant Approach and Its Critique

Kwong-leung Tang and Vivian W. Q. Lou

In any review of the historical development of social welfare services for women in Hong Kong, two strands emerge as dominant: the prevalence of a needs paradigm and the feminist critique. Social amelioration remains a central concern in the delivery of social welfare in Hong Kong, and social welfare as an institution is based on the principle of need (Mishra, 1981; Titmuss, 1976). Since 1971, while there has been constant and significant expansion in social welfare, most of the social welfare services have been need-driven. During the final decades of colonial rule, a high proportion of the social welfare services were directed toward meeting the needs of women. According to the Clientele Information System of the Hong Kong Council of Social Service (HKCSS), the majority of clients in family and children services, elderly services, people receiving welfare and specialized services (new arrivals and single parents) are women (Association for the Advancement of the Feminism, 2003). Up until recently, however, women have been treated no differently from any other client group by the welfare system.

In the late 1980s, feminists developed a critique of Hong Kong society, attacking its patriarchalism and its attitudes and practices in such areas as sex-role stereotyping, women's subordination, inequality, oppression, and discrimination. In some cases, this critique led to action and resulted in some changes, particularly in the sphere of women's rights. Social welfare also came under scrutiny and was found wanting. Feminist analysis contended that the colonial state had made some progress when it expanded social welfare services in the 1970s (AAF, 2003). However, it lacked a gender perspective in the provision of social welfare and the "unintended consequences of many of these policies exact a heavy toll on women" (Kwok et. al., 1997: 251). Further, social policy in Hong Kong failed to "socialize the privatized labor of women under patriarchal relationship in the household" (Ibid). Importantly, they were critical of the colonial government's disposition to treat social policy as a gender-free or gender-neutral zone, and to ignore the gender impacts of policy choices. They further observed that all social policy outcomes in terms of social protection, equality, and poverty had implications for gender equality or for lessening gender inequality. All in all, the feminists contended that the colonial social policy was problematic and needed to be replaced by a policy that respected and implemented feminist principles of equality (i.e. the adoption of a feminist or women-centered approach in social policy). Specifically, finding that household responsibilities and familial ideology had hampered Hong Kong women's participation in public affairs, some feminists argued that the government had an important role to play in alleviating the burden of housewives by providing more welfare services (Chan, 2002; Chan et al., 1985). Though some limited headway has been made in actual practice, the major achievement of the feminist critique has been to expose the inadequacies of the current welfare system.

In light of these two strands in its history, this paper assesses the development of social welfare services for women in Hong Kong. We argue that the colonial state espoused a residual model of welfare, relying mainly on familial support, occupational welfare, and individual effort. Even after the rapid expansion of welfare in the 1970s, the colonial state did not single out women as a special client group. Though the post-colonial government has recently declared its intention to maintain a gender perspective in public policy, this has been followed through with only limited advances in social policy. As Hong Kong moved into an "era of (fiscal) constraint" in the wake of the Asian financial crisis (1997) and the huge fiscal deficits that followed (Chau & Wong, 2002), it has become increasingly difficult for some women to find services to meet their needs. The services provided and the policies adopted by the Hong Kong Special Administrative Region (HKSAR) government, non-government organizations (NGOs) and the women groups will be discussed in this paper. The paper will emphasize the feminist approach to service and the advocacy of the women's groups.

There is an implicit conviction in this paper that the intricate relationships between women and social welfare ought to be viewed under the lens of a colonial/post-colonial framework. There are a number of merits for using this approach. First, a purely descriptive or even analytical approach of women's welfare in Hong Kong is deemed inadequate, at least without a concurrent look at the colonial intervention and its underlying philosophy. In both the pre- and post-1997 periods (that is, as a colony and as a special administrative region), Hong Kong has produced much literature on women and social welfare. Furthermore, we believe that the use of such a framework will show that the supposedly gender-neutral approach undertaken by the colonial government fuelled an open polemic. Toward the end of colonial rule, the feminist critics of colonial policy successfully reminded the public (as they still do today) of the importance of a woman-centred approach in social policy. Finally, the use of such a framework highlights the question of whether changing political contexts promote women's welfare or entrench relationships of dependency.

Colonial Social Policy and Feminist Critique

In social welfare policy, the colonial leaders wanted to maintain a minimal state in Hong Kong. They preferred to rely mainly on family networks, individual effort and occupational benefits to meet social needs (Tang, 1998). Social intervention to assist the needy was to be meagre. In its first White Paper on Social Welfare (Hong Kong Government, 1965), the colonial government defended its position by placing the responsibility on the family and the voluntary sector. A few points were regularly made in justification of this non-action. The colonial government argued that social welfare was not common even in other countries, and it believed that Chinese families felt a duty to look after members who were in trouble. Further, the population in Hong Kong had been transient immediately before and after the Second World War, rendering programs to aid the poor useless and even incurring the risk of attracting people from China in very large numbers.

This residual model of social non-interventionism had been in use by the colonial government since 1842. It was not until the early 1970s that social welfare made a "great leap forward" and the government, under the leadership of Governor MacLehose, began providing social welfare services to the needy on a much larger scale. The key factor leading up to this was the massive Riots in 1966–67, which posed the most serious challenge thus far to the legitimacy of the colonial government and forced it to respond to the territory's massive social needs (Tang, 1998). Governor MacLehose's plan for social reform gave center stage to housing, education, medical and health, and social welfare. He opined that these four areas would be the pillars to support the future well-being of the community. In the area of social welfare, public assistance and social allowances for the disabled and the elderly were introduced in the early 1970s. The key policy paper, the "Social Welfare in Hong Kong: The Way Ahead," was published in 1973 (Social Welfare Department, 1973). A number of other policy documents were also produced (White Papers on Youth, the Elderly, and Rehabilitation). A new social welfare planning machinery was introduced: the Five Year Plan setting out the policy objectives governing the provision and future development of social welfare services, the specific targets of expansion for each service area and alternative measures to alleviate shortfalls in the provision of services. New social welfare services programs were later put in place in 1977: school social work, outreach youth services, special services for the disabled and the elderly as well as the expansion of social and recreational facilities. Scholars called the decade of the 1970s the "golden era" in the development of social security and social welfare services in Hong Kong (Chow, 1984).

The thinking underlying these rapid developments was the need paradigm which the colonial government had adopted. The approach in this paradigm was to begin with a narrow focus, concentrating on areas where there was a clear need and public demand for action. The British government at the time went for the "systematic examination of discrete social problems and their solutions by way of piecemeal reforms" (Mishra, 1981:3). This approach has a number of merits: social relevance, commitment to humanitarian values, and practicality. However, critics in Hong Kong contended that this need-based perspective was constrained by the belief that piecemeal social engineering is the key to social change. They argued that social policy carried out from this perspective proceeded in the absence of social goals (Hodge, 1980). In all the policy documents on social welfare, one cannot find any social goals articulated which could be translated into policies and programs. This absence of goals is matched by a similar absence of social research on social programs (Tang, 1998).

In the last two decades of colonial rule, the government did not incorporate a gender perspective in its social welfare policy. The comment that some scholars have made about the policy assumption behind British social policy is equally valid in the case of Hong Kong: "The assumptions that governments have made about female dependency have historically been simple and in accordance with the male breadwinner model: that adult married women will be dependent on men." (Lewis, 2003: 111). True, the services provided under family welfare, nursery and crèche places and family casework, have mostly assisted mothers. Services for special needs children have helped mothers enhance their life quality. Programs for autistic children, resource centers for parents of children with disability and respite services have also helped mothers (Hong Kong Government, 1989, 1991). These subsidies and provisions have basically reinforced women's role as mothers and caregivers in families. They have been premised on the government's neglect of the fact that women have individual needs and specific roles to perform in society.

The end of the 1980s saw the emergence of the feminist critique of colonial social policy. This was fully articulated in the text "Women and Welfare Policies in Hong Kong" published by the Association for the Advancement of Feminism (AAF) (1990), a body made up of professionals, social workers, teachers, and university professors. The colonial state was painted in this book as upholding a residual view of welfare, thus ensuring that welfare provision was not adequate, particularly in terms of the needs of women. The book contended that, despite the phenomenal expansion of social welfare since 1971, the colonial state failed to develop a gender perspective in social welfare and many of its policies therefore placed a heavy toll on women. One undesirable effect was that the welfare system reinforced the traditional sexual division of labor in society. The welfare system was faulted since it espoused a traditional view of the roles of men and women within the family. Limitations in social welfare services, the lack of sufficient childcare services and the absence of a positive discrimination policy in favor of women in the colony also put them in the very difficult situation of having to shoulder all the responsibilities in the family while reinforcing their role as carers (AAF, 1990). Further, social policy tools did little to elevate women to substantive equality, as feminists argued that public assistance and housing policy served only to channel resources to the family, where it frequently did not bring direct benefits to the women. They argued that it was not enough for welfare policies to be gender neutral; social policy ought to take account of the special needs of women. The book underscored the importance of a feminist social policy.

Despite the feminist critique, the colonial government stood by its existing policy. In fact, after the great leap of the early 1970s, it pursued an incremental social policy: it did not cut back on its social welfare services but neither did it formulate any comprehensive and rational planning to meet the new social needs. The approach was characterized by small adjustments and readjustments. Social policy was continually being improved upon in response to social needs. This approach of piecemeal social engineering was grounded in the planning philosophy of disjointed incrementalism in public policy (Tang, 1998).

In the 1980s, some NGOs and women's groups took the lead in providing needed and pioneering services for women. A case in point was the Hong Kong Council of Women that campaigned for women's rights in the area of marriage, abortion, inheritance and sexual violence. Emphasizing women's development, the Council started the Women's Centre (Cheung, 1989), which was funded entirely by overseas church bodies. Opened in 1985, the Centre pioneered in providing various services such as provision of information, networking women, and organizing women's forum (Cheung, 1989). Additionally, the Council of Women together with Family Welfare Society and other social workers initiated to establish the first refuge (Harmony House) that offered much-needed sheltered services for battered women. In face of massive demands for refuge, there was a perennial shortage. For instance, during the year 1993–94, 100 women and 114 children were admitted. The average daily attendance rate in refuge was 84.7%. The number of rejected cases due to a full house increased by 100%, from 66 in 1992–93 to 140 in 1993–94 (Harmony House, 1994).

In the mid 1990s, an intensified version of the need-based perspective emerged, supported in part by the buoyant economy. Besides traditional childcare and family casework services, extra resources were allocated to several needy groups newly identified – women suffering from domestic violence, single parent families, and families with new immigrants from Mainland China. Moreover, a new administrative mechanism, the Working Group on Battered Spouses, was formed in 1995, and a new refuge for battered women was set up in 1996. Supplemental funding was allocated to single parent families (in the form of a cash supplement for those on welfare) and there was liaison with NGOs in the planning of post-migration services for the new arrivals from the Mainland (Hong Kong Government 1994, 1995). These groups of women were identified mainly because they were considered the most vulnerable, needing formal social services. Single parents centers and new arrival centers were set up by the government to cater for their special needs.

Working women encountered many challenges. Since the 1980s, working women in manufacturing industry, in particular, have fallen victim to the structural changes that have taken place in Hong Kong's economy. Some experienced poverty when the plants they were working in were relocated from Hong Kong to Mainland China. Middle-aged women became the most vulnerable because of historical factors (low level of education), their socially constructed role (women being expected to take care of family issues rather than earning a living), and discrimination (both gender and age). However, these middle-aged women's needs for employment and skills training were dealt with in a remedial and ad hoc manner by the colonial government through the establishment of the Employees Retraining Board, which provided retraining courses for them (Tang, 2000). In addition, the existing training programs demonstrated a lack of sensitivity to women's needs in relations to motivation, schedule, contents and training mode. For example, it was a great challenge for women who had been working in manufacturing industry for twenty years to learn new skills such as computer operation. Meanwhile, some women reported that a lack of childcare services and age discrimination limited their ability to participate in these programs.

Post-colonial Social Policy and Women

In the three decades prior to the 1997 transition, Hong Kong had enjoyed a sustained and impressive period of economic development. The adoption of an export-led, industrialization approach to economic development produced rapid rates of growth and significant increases in per capita income. GDP per capita rose in Hong Kong from around US$2,400 in 1965 to US$12,000 in the early 1990s. Despite the high rate of growth, social welfare development lagged behind economic development. Compared to other advanced industrialized nations, state-led social welfare services in Hong Kong have had a relatively short history of some forty years.

Up to 1997, strong economic growth, coupled with a strong occupational and indigenous welfare system, reduced the need for comprehensive government social welfare programs. The situation changed dramatically, however, with the onset of the Asian financial crisis in 1997. Hong Kong's economy, with a GNP per capita close to that of Japan, recorded a decline in GNP through 1998 and 1999. Its economy expanded modestly in 2000, but slipped back into recession in the latter half of 2001. In 2002, Hong Kong's fiscal deficit reached a record level. Unemployment reached 6.7% in March 2002, rose to 8% in mid-2003 after the SARS outbreak, and eased back to 6.7% in late 2004. Although there has been a modest rebound since late 2003[1], many more people have applied for Comprehensive Social Security Assistance (CSSA). The Asian crisis has had a serious impact on most people in Hong Kong, dogged as it has been by the intractable problems of unemployment, poverty, and homelessness. Income disparities have worsened. Believing that the economy would soon achieve a quick turnaround of its own accord and that the benefits would trickle down to the less well off, the SAR government only intervened selectively at different times to assist specially targeted groups (such as unemployed youth, the middle class, small businessmen, etc.).

It needs to be emphasized that the colonial government neither formulated coherent social policies nor created comprehensive social welfare programs. This policy legacy was not abandoned when the first HKSAR Chief Executive, Tung Chee-hwa, took up the leadership of the post-colonial government. Social welfare continued to expand incrementally. Its share of total recurrent government spending rose from 9.4% in 1995–96 to 16.2% in 2005–06 when it stood at $34 billion (Hong Kong SAR Government, 2006). A policy of incrementalism was the direction chosen, with government spending on various sectors of social welfare on an upward trend in the last decade of colonial rule.

The post-colonial government, however, was confronted with continuing economic downturn, an aging society, widening income disparities, increasing unemployment and escalating social expenditures. Tung's government paid much attention to fiscal soundness, making it clear that it aimed for a balanced budget by the year 2008 (*SCMP*, October 23, 2003). A stringent policy of financial retrenchment has been adopted, and there has been heavy emphasis on efficiency, savings, contracting out, service performance and cutting back on public expenditures as the key goals of Tung's government.

A comprehensive study of social development in Hong Kong commissioned by the Hong Kong Council of Social Service (HKCSS) in the aftermath of the Asian financial crisis, noted a gap between economic and social development (Estes, 2002). The study used a total of 47 social, economic and political indicators to empirically measure the social development of Hong Kong between 1981 and 1998. While confirming that substantial social progress occurred in those two decades, the study also found that Hong Kong's low-income population doubled between 1986 and 1998 (Estes, 2002). They included many children, women, elderly and others with serious physical and emotional disabilities, all left out of Hong Kong's explosion in economic prosperity. Some of the study's findings in relation to vulnerable groups were particularly distressing: the percentage of children aged 1–14 years living in low income households increased by 75% from 13% to 23% in the twelve years under investigation; the percentage of women living in low income households increased by 61% from 10% to 17%; and the percentage of the elderly living in low income households increased by 50% from 22% to 34% (Estes, 2002).

Estes' study noted that despite some gains on the employment front, social progress for many women in Hong Kong is "far from secure" (Estes, 2002: 344), because one of their traditional sources of strength, the extended family system, is in decline. Furthermore, Estes (2002: 342), the lead researcher for the study, highlighted the loss in family solidarity:

> *The very severe decline in Hong Kong's performance on this subindex is associated with (1) sharp deceases in the marriage rate ... (2) even sharper increases in Hong Kong's divorce rate ... and (3) rapidly increasing rates of reported family violence — including between spouses, between adults and children, and in the case of the elderly, between adult children and their aging parents.*

Growing numbers of vulnerable groups and the decline in family solidarity are evidence of distorted development. This occurs when "economic development has not been accompanied by an attendant degree of social progress" (Midgley, 1995: 3–4), when sections of the population are excluded from full participation in development. The impact of the Asian financial crisis on poor women has been particularly severe as household real incomes declined due to job losses. Poor women have been pressured to seek other sources of income. The cutbacks in social welfare services have further increased the pressure on women as responsibility for nurturing (e.g. care of the sick) still rests on them. Analysts argue that it is imperative that the government devise means to extend the benefits of rapid economic development to all women.

Vulnerable Women

Several vulnerable groups at present receive attention from the government and the professionals: single parents, victims of abuse and new arrivals.

Single parents: Women head the majority of the single parent families in Hong Kong. From 1991 to 2001, the number of women single parent families almost tripled from 11,210 to 33,554, while men single parent families only increased slightly from 7,490 to 10,870. At the same time, the proportion of new migrant women single parent families increased about five times between 1991 to 2001 (from 16.9 to 77.2 out of 100,000 population aged 20 or above), which complicates the needs and difficulties faced by women single parent families (HKCSS, 2004). According to a recent study, these women face much discrimination despite the fact that divorce is socially accepted. Migrant women from China experience a double jeopardy, being stigmatized both as new arrivals and as divorcees (Kung, Hung & Chan, 2004). Generally, women single parent families which have resulted from divorce or separation have diverse needs: complex feelings regarding their ability to serve as confident and competent mothers; unsatisfactory parent-child relationships; and worries about their childcare and disciplining abilities (Young, 1985; Law & Hong Kong Family Welfare Society, 1991). On the other hand, female single parent families in poverty share similar difficulties with all families in poverty, such as being forced to live in a crowded environment, lack of resources for basic living, lack of recreational facilities, and limited social interactions with others. More importantly, women single families fall into poverty because their dual role as caregiver and breadwinner for the family places an impossible burden on them, especially when they have dependent children.

Recently, the number of CSSA cases based on single parent families reached more than 38,500, almost 7 times the number in 1993 (Social Welfare Department, 2006a). Current policies pertaining to single women on CSSA only reinforce the negative stereotypes commonly adopted towards them and ought to be reviewed. Even the government is critical of its own policy, admitting that it fails to prepare them to get back to work. A review report on the CSSA Scheme (Social Welfare Department, 1998) stated: "The existing policy of giving single parents the choice not to work until their youngest has reached 15 is considered excessively generous by emerging international practice which aims to get single parents back into the workforce." In May, 2005, the government intended to tighten this generous policy on CSSA single parents, stipulating single parents on CSSA with children above the age of twelve must go out and find work (Ming Pao, May 2 2005). This proposal drew immediate and fierce criticism from some women's groups and social workers. They argued that unskilled women, particularly if they were over 35 year of age, would have great difficulty in finding work (Ming Pao, May 4, 2005). In early July, the government revised its original proposal, asking single parents with the youngest child aged 12 to 14 to seek part-time employment (eight hours a week) (Women's Commission, 2005).

Abused Women: The numbers of reported cases on domestic violence have increased rapidly and reached over 3,000 in 2003. After child abuse cases, women again topped the list of victims in spousal abuse cases. In the first half year of 2006, 85.9% of the new reported spousal violence cases were case of wife abuse or female partner abuse (1176 verses 292 reported cases) (Social Welfare Department, 2006b). Among the various kinds of abuse, physical abuse dominated the reported cases (some 80%). The incidence of psychological abuse also seems to have increased recently, reaching 11% among the cases reported in 2002. Due to the socially constructed role of women and for other reasons, wife abuse has occurred more frequently than is acknowledged by official statistics (Tang, 1994, 1999). According to a study carried out in 1999 based on a randomly selected community-wide sample, about 65% of women had experienced verbal abuse while about 10% had experienced physical abuse (Tang, 1999).

Many difficulties are encountered by abused women (see Tang's chapter on Gender-based violence in Hong Kong). In line with their socially constructed role, women often tend to be submissive to their husbands. This factor, and the personality characteristics of men, are identified as the factors most frequently leading to wife abuse. The experience of being abused physically or psychologically is usually related to women's feelings of fear and guilt and the erosion of their confidence and self-esteem. Family conflicts are also associated with financial difficulties, suspected extra-marital affairs and the burden of childcare, demonstrating that women frequently come under tremendous pressure in various aspects of life. Abused women thus often feel helpless. As women are the main care-givers in families, they are strongly impacted by episodes of spousal violence against children. The higher probability of children who have experienced spousal violence at home suffering from emotional and behavioral problems creates great difficulties for women in child-care and parent-child relationships as well as in spousal relationships. Finally, abused women face a critical life decision on whether they should remain in the marriage or seek alternative solutions. Financial sustainability, housing arrangements, low self-esteem and the related sense of lack of security, concern for children, and possible social discrimination toward divorced women and single parent families have all become major barriers for women faced with such decisions. Considering that many of the female victims of family violence did not speak about what was happening and continued living in violent families for 5 or even 10 years, there is an urgent need for early identification and intervention so that the long-term impact of family violence on women and children can be prevented (Christian Family Service Centre & Chan, 2000; Tang, 1997).

In face of these rapidly rising new needs, the policy emphasis of the HKSAR government has remained unchanged. It stresses the integrity of the family and the need for family solidarity, though it must be admitted that mechanisms have been set up to deal with the immediate social problems faced by women as previously discussed. Additionally, battered women could rely on the Domestic Violence Ordinance (1987), which allowed them to seek a 3-month injunction against their husbands. The government also funded programs such as family life education counseling, a hot line service, temporary housing, legal aid, and child protective services; it also had initiated public education and media programs.

New arrivals: In recent decades, the composition of Chinese immigrants in the territory has altered dramatically. Before the 1970s, the majority of those who entered Hong Kong from China were illegal immigrants, most of them single men in their twenties. In recent years, however, most Chinese immigrants are legitimate. They are predominantly dependents, mainly wives and children of Hong Kong residents who have entered the territory to reunite with their families (Table 1). For some time, workers from Hong Kong have crossed into the mainland in search of spouses because they believe that women in Mainland China demand less in financial terms than those in Hong Kong (So, 2003). Hong Kong's restrictive immigration policies result in these Mainland wives and children having to wait for ten years or more before they can migrate to Hong Kong.

Table 1. Distribution of Chinese legal immigrants entering Hong Kong for family reunion

Year	Number of legal immigrants (rounded off to the nearest hundred)	Entering for family reunion			Percentages of those entering for family reunion
		Wives	Children	Husbands	
1987	27300	9559	13292	998	87.4
1988	28000	10009	13400	952	87.0
1989	27300	9565	13216	937	86.9
1990	28000	10302	13259	1042	87.9
1991	26800	10113	12513	1020	88.2
1992	28400	11128	12457	1082	86.9
1993	32900	13250	14504	1370	88.5
1994	38200	16774	17220	1423	92.7
1995	45986	18274	23033	1572	93.2
1996	61179	24780	31774	1649	95.1
1997	50287	25088	21758	1304	95.6

Source: Hong Kong Annual Reports, 1988 –1997 (Census and Statistics Department). Notes: Only figures on the total number of immigrants were available in the annual reports of 1998 through 2000 although the reports had stated that most of the immigrations are for family reunion. Total numbers of immigrants for the years 1998 to 2005 were around 55000 – 56000.

Studies on the new arrivals have shown that the process of migration leads to certain difficulties (Lou, 2000; Wong, 2001). First, among these are the needs arising from their settling in a new physical and psychological environment, language difficulties and lack of knowledge of social services in Hong Kong such as child care, education, housing, financial support, and the labor market. Second, financial needs for emergency or long-term support arise due to the economic disadvantages faced by these families. The 2001 Population Census showed that the median monthly domestic household income of persons from the Mainland who have resided in Hong Kong for less than 7 years is HK$12,050, significantly lower than that of the whole population in Hong Kong (HK$18,705). Third, there are needs for social support. Research has found that husbands of the new migrant women might not be able to provide sufficient support due to their own constraints such as long working hours and the lack of financial resources. Fourth, they are not able to claim their rights when confronted with the unfriendly reality and the social discrimination towards new arrivals (Chan, 2001, 2003; Christian Family Service Centre, 2000; Hong Kong Federation of Women's Centres, 1999; Hong Kong Young Women's Christian Association, 1998; Lai, 1997; Lam & Mok, 2002; Lou & Law, 2004). Often, when they arrive in Hong Kong, they are discriminated against and condemned as the cause of Hong Kong's social and economic problems.

Most recently, some NGOs like Caritas and the HKCSS have paid attention to the needs of the cross-border families. According to the official statistics (Census and Statistics Department, 2005), the number of Hong Kong residents who work across the border increased from 52,300 in 1988 to 237,500 in 2004, a rate increase from 1.9% to 7.2% among the average working population (Census and Statistics Department, 2005). Most of these are middle-aged males. The massive relocation of industrial activities from Hong Kong to Mainland China since the late 1970s has given rise to different sets of cross-border familial relations (So, 2003). Recently, middle-class managers and technicians from Hong Kong have taken "second wives" during their stay in southern China. With the 2003 Agreement on Closer Partnership in the Economic Relationship (CEPA) between Hong Kong and Mainland China, it is expected that closer Hong Kong-Mainland economic exchanges will become more frequent in the next decade. Strengthening families to develop resilience to routine separations and identifying effective ways to assist them poses a new challenge to social services in Hong Kong (Tang, Fung & Lau, 2006; Tam et al., 2004). Currently, some NGOs offer limited specialized counseling services and educational programs for these families. Existing services are rather remedial and reactive. Their main focus is on the problem of extra-marital relationships. Inadequate attention is given to the other adjustment issues, as well as to the successful coping strategies already achieved by some families.

Policy Responses

In response to these needs, the interdisciplinary Working Group on Battered Spouses (replaced by the Working Group on Combating Violence in 2001) has coordinated efforts to tackle domestic violence, and knowledge and research on new immigrants has been improved. The Family and Child Protective Services Unit was created in 2000 to deal with child abuse and battered spouse cases. Earlier, in 1998, a mediation service was introduced to help divorcing and separating couples resolve disputes over child custody and access.

Despite these positive steps, feminists have remained critical, arguing that these services for poor women, single parents, new arrivals, and unemployed women have reinforced women's inequality and vulnerability in the society. They note that services for these needy groups have been placed under the family and children programs. Clearly, the HKSAR government still believes that women can and should be supported by their families. This family-oriented and gender-neutral approach has meant that women do not have rights and an identity of their own in the government's eyes.

Although Tung's efforts have focused almost exclusively on economic revival measures after the Asian crisis in 1997, there have been some positive developments in women's rights in recent years. Prior to the transfer of sovereignty from Britain to China, the feminist movement had already had an impact on the public policy arena in Hong Kong. After the Second World War, while most Hong Kong people were concerned with their basic needs for food and shelter, the Hong Kong Council of Women started raising consciousness and status of women by campaigning for the abolition of the legally sanctioned polygamous system (Lai, Au & Cheung, 1997). Consisted mainly of expatriate women and Chinese women who had studied abroad, it was formed in 1947 to campaign for rights in areas such as marriage, abortion, inheritance and sexual violence. Soon afterwards, the Family Planning Association was revived in 1950 to provide family planning, education, clinics and other services. Family planning was able to give women a degree of control over reproduction (Wu, 2001; Cheung, 1989).

After a protracted struggle with the women's groups, the colonial government finally decided to ratify the United Nations Convention Against All Forms of Discrimination Against Women on behalf of the colony. Women's groups firmly believed that the adoption of this Convention would have a positive impact on the conditions of women in the society. Parallel to this development, women's groups strived for the establishment of an institutional mechanism within the government for the advancement of women. Such machinery ensures that the government would take up its responsibility to implement international obligations and its own commitment to promote the status of women (See Cheung and Chung's chapter on Central Mechanisms). Seen in this light, the setting up of the Equal Opportunity Commission (EOC) in 1996 represented another landmark development in women's rights, which could be regarded as a partial response to the 1995 Platform for Action as endorsed by the United Nations (1995). Since its inception, the Commission has been championing women's rights. It assists women who suffer unlawful discrimination in their pursuit of justice through conciliation and by assisting them to take the perpetrator to court for damages (EOC, 2005).

In 2000, following pressure from the United Nations and feminist groups and the increasing attention to women's conditions, promoting the well-being and interests of women in Hong Kong became a significant goal in the HKSAR government's policy address. In January 2001, the Women's Commission was set up, which could be regarded as a milestone in the government's efforts to coordinate policy advocacy, multi-sector coordination and service provision for the advancement of women in Hong Kong. In the same year, the goal to "incorporate women's perspective in the process of policy making" was added, which could be regarded as a "belated" response to the United Nations Committee's Concluding Comments on the Government initial report under the Convention on the Elimination of All Forms of Discrimination against Women (CEDAW). It could also be seen as a step toward fulfilling the Beijing Platform for Action in 1995 (Hong Kong SAR Government, 2000, 2001a, 2002a, 2002b). Since its establishment, the Women's Commission have organized various activities in these three areas, including a publicity campaign, drafting the Gender Mainstreaming Checklist for policy makers, arranging forums, conferences and training, drafting a collaborative framework with NGOs, women's groups and others interested in working on women's issues in Hong Kong, and launching a Capacity Building Mileage Programme for the development of women's potential.

While the HKSAR government has recognized that gender inequality and imbalances of power exist in Hong Kong, and while it has had the intention of bringing about equal opportunities for women in policy making and service assessment, the HKSAR government has failed to ensure that women's rights are enforced in all policies and services. A case in point can be seen in the "Integrated Family Service Center" (IFSC). In 2003, the HKSAR government started this new service delivery model to integrate family welfare services and community-based services. This restructuring was based on an evaluation report done by a local university (HKUSWSA, 2001). This family service review report argued that the existing 8 programs of family services (the Family Casework Service in Family Service Centers, Senior Social Work Practitioners, Family Life Education and Family Life Education Resource Center, Family Activity and Resource Centers, Family Aid Service, Family Care Demonstration and Resource Center cum Carers' Support Center, Family Education, Support Services for the Family like post-migration Centers and Single Parent Centers) vary in provision and operation, often overlapping and proceeding in a reactive, remedial and casework-dominated fashion. They did not proactively plan for emerging family issues, nor did they show sensitivity to the hard-to-reach families with real needs.

A new IFSC model was proposed. It aims at promoting accessibility to users with minimum physical, psychological and administrative barriers. It stresses early identification of needs and intervention before further deterioration of problems; deeper integration of services cutting across program boundaries; and partnership between service providers to achieve efficient and effective use of scarce resources. Adopting a "child-centred, family-focused and community-based" approach, it is designed to provide a continuum of preventive, supportive and remedial services meeting the needs of families in a holistic and cost-effective manner. Structurally, the IFSCs are to be formed by the transformation of conventional family services centers or the merging of conventional family services centers with community-based units. Each center is to have three main units (counseling unit; support unit; and resource unit), stressing the development of the preventive and developmental functions of social work practice. Hence, family needs will be proactively identified and intervened by a multi-skilled team, in a framework in which case referrals and case management can be easily implemented.

Thus far, fifteen pilot projects have been evaluated to see whether this new model would work to meet the needs of families in the community, whether it is capable of setting a benchmark level for future IFSC development, and whether it can achieve the goal of cost-effectiveness. The HKSAR government seems committed to this new model. In April 2004, the Social Welfare Department proposed a four-phase development plan, which aims to establish 61 IFSCs by the first quarter of 2005, covering all geographical areas of Hong Kong. Each IFSC, which will serve a population of 100,000 to 150,000, is to be staffed by a minimum of 12-14 social workers, broken down into 1 supervisor, 4-6 counselors in a family counseling unit, six group workers and brief counselors in a family support unit, and 2 community and group workers in a family resource unit.

Despite the government's optimism, critics have their concerns about this new model. Many contend that it would fail if the government fails to provide adequate resources. Others are skeptical about its effectiveness, insisting that the formation of the IFSC should be separated from the issue of efficiency and savings (HKCSS, 2003; HKUSWSA, 2003). Critics further question whether this model is a cure-all, as some service gaps are inevitable. Importantly, as the IFSC took off, the HKSAR government decided to shut down five specialized centers in 2004, contending their main functions could now be subsumed under the IFSC framework. These centers were set up three years ago to assist single parents to overcome their difficulties, develop supportive and self-help networks, and to enhance their ability for self-reliance. Each specialized center received HK$1.56 million a year and handled 1,200 cases. Critics argue that it would be naive to assume that services for single parents, originally provided by these specialized centers, can now be provided by the newly formed IFSCs (Tung Hah Group of Hospitals, 2000; Lam & Mok, 2002).

Despite the adoption of an integrative model, a gender-sensitive perspective is generally absent in the planning and implementation of the IFSCs. For some time, Social Welfare Department, NGOs and the HKCSS have met regularly in the Task Group on Implementation of Integrated Family Service Centers to discuss and work out a common Funding and Service Agreement, service polices and common practice guidelines. Notably, the guiding principle for the IFSC is to promote the welfare and interests of clients, rather than women's welfare. It is thus not optimistic that the IFSC would respond to the specific needs of women. In all likelihood, the IFSC would reinforce the traditional construction of women in terms of their family roles.

The above discussion rests on the understanding that traditional family welfare services direct resources in such a way as to reinforce family unity and to preserve the family harmony. Women's needs and rights are sacrificed for the sake of family unity. This family-oriented ideology not only influences family and child services but also affects workfare and unemployment-support services. Except for maternity welfare, all working conditions and benefits regarding leave and constraints on overtime work in Hong Kong are not gender-sensitive.

There is mounting evidence that women's rights are not fully respected in the territory. Firstly, working women receive less pay than men for the same job. Eight years after the enactment of the Sex Discrimination Ordinance, the pay discrepancies between male and female are 29% on average and 48% in non-professional occupations (Hong Kong SAR Government, 2001b). Secondly, more and more women have fallen into poverty. About half of all low-income earners are middle-aged women. Some 80% of employees whose monthly income is below US$350 are women (Hong Kong SAR Government, 2001b; Wong & Lee, 2000). Thirdly, women's indirect contributions to the labor market have not been recognized and reflected in current policy and services, including women's provision of voluntary services, their services of caring in the family and the community, and their dual responsibilities where they are career women.

When it comes to retirement protection, women remain vulnerable to poverty despite the introduction of the Mandatory Provident Fund (MPF) in December 2000. Studies done in the West highlight the fact that formal social security systems often target male workers and disadvantaged women. The MPF is principally employment-related and contributory (coming from employees and employers), benefiting those who have a long work record. Thus, the MPF excludes half of the women population (homemakers and part-timers) from its protection as well as lower income groups, represented disproportionately by women in the case of Hong Kong. Twenty to thirty years from now, when Hong Kong's aging population reaches about one-fourth of the total population, this will be one of the key issues for the society (Census and Statistics Department, 2004). The possible scenario is that by that time, while the majority of the male population will be over 60 years old and will be partially supported by their contributions to the MPF, a far smaller proportion of the female older population will get this kind of support due to a different life-cycle by aged women (Cheung, 2002). Such a worry is empirically grounded. Lee (2003), based on a telephone survey of 1,078 respondents, examined middle-aged adult's retirement planning activities and found that men are more likely to be involved in financial planning. Women are more likely to take part in planning for health, living arrangements, and psychological well-being. Because they live longer and because of their lack of financial retirement planning, they are prime candidates for poverty.

Policy Advocacy: NGOs and Women's Groups

The NGOs in the territory who deliver services to women in need are mainly subsidized by the government and work within the need paradigm. However, the Hong Kong Council of Social Service (HKCSS), an association of NGOs, in response to the colonial government's lack of a gender perspective in policy-making, took the lead in collecting information about women's services and needs. In 1984, they promoted a women-centered approach by setting up a Working Group on Women's Services under the Community Development Division. This working group conducted a number of surveys on service needs and delivery for women in 1985, 1990 and 1996, which provided a profile of the women's services run by NGOs (HKCSS, 1990; 1996; 1997). As discussed above, both the Women's Centre and Harmony House, opened in 1985, became a positive force in mobilizing and supporting the HKCSS in the direction of advocating for a women-centered approach for the government. The HKCSS also fostered networking among women's organizations, promoting a women-centered approach in service provision and advocating for the establishment of the Women's Commission.

According to the HKCSS's report, in mid 80s women's services were provided by various NGOs and projects such as the Neighborhood Level Community Development Project, Community Centres, Children and Youth Centres, Family Life Education, and other projects that were not supported by government funding. These were considered part of the social welfare services, regardless of the fact that women, who were the major target groups, were also the major resources for service units to promote their services and recruit members. However, given the lack of a gender perspective in social welfare policy, the diverse nature of the NGOs made it impossible to reach a consensus regarding the purposes of service provision for women. In view of this, in the early 1990s the HKCSS reiterated a women-centered approach to service provision, which stressed gender-sensitive, individual rights and personal development of women (HKCSS, 1990).

Years of advocacy by the HKCSS and women's groups have yielded some changes. Besides traditional services promoting family relationships, parenting skills, utilizing leisure time, recreational activities and community participation, new service contents gradually emerged such as self-understanding, and identifying personal needs and potential areas for development (HKCSS, 1996). After NGOs started to introduce new programs for women, feminist ideas of empowerment caught up quickly in some centers. For instance, Kwok (1995) documented the setting up of an empowerment networking group for women in a family service center dealing with problems associated with extramarital affairs, which was inspired by feminist thinking. Through the collective sharing of their experiences and the causes of their emotional problems, women gave expression to their own difficulties and concerns. Unfortunately, notwithstanding these occasional developments, it has been found that services focusing on family relationships and parenting skills are perceived to be more popular than services aimed at promoting gender equality (HKCSS, 1996).

Regrettably, according to a later report, the traditional ideology in which women are perceived as caregivers and wives has not changed much. It is still dominant in service delivery (HKCSS, 2004). The HKCSS's failure to promote the women-centered approach among various service providers needs to be highlighted. Among the reasons for the underdevelopment of women-centered services are: women have no time to avail of the services due to work or household duties; a lack of resources; and a lack of experienced social workers (HKCSS, 1997). A further reason is that the Working Group on Women's Services itself did not take a strong stand to influence service agencies. The disbandment of the Working Group in 2001 showed how little headway this kind of advocacy had made.

Currently, social workers in the voluntary sector continue to engage in a number of areas of services for women: individual development and growth, education, health, employment, human rights, and crisis. NGOs have always played a significant role as policy advocate as well as service provider in the area of women. They are regarded as partners of the government. Being strongly influenced by the dominant family ideology, most of the social services provided by the NGOs such as integrated family services, services for battered women, single parent services, and family support services have not been purposefully designed to take account of women's perspectives, even though the majority of the service recipients at family and child service centers are women and their children.

Nevertheless, some NGOs could serve as vehicles for progressive social change. In the present context of economic globalization and free trade, efforts to fight unemployment among women are focused at the community level. In times of adversity, social workers had a unique opportunity to develop innovative approaches to meet women's needs. Some of them advocated for community development as a strategy to help communities become more stable and achieve greater control over their resources. In the past decade, various NGOs used the "Community Economic Development" (CED) strategy to assist unemployed and underemployed women to gain better access to jobs that pay a living wage and achieve individual empowerment. These activities include the launching of a housecleaning cooperative taking its workers from the ranks of unemployed women. According to Shragge (1994), CED is a process by which a community organizes economic activity in ways that benefit the community as a whole, aiming to achieve community and personal empowerment through strategies which encourage cooperation and interdependence and which seek to equalize resources among its rich and poor populations.

In addition to the NGOs, various women's groups emerged to promote women's rights and empowerment. As noted above, the Hong Kong Council of Women pioneered the first community-based Women's Centre and popularized the community approach to the development of women. At the same time, it took into consideration indigenous characteristics of Chinese women, while enhancing women's empowerment. The Centre shied away from the radical feminist approach that promoted "power to women through a battle between two sexes" (Cheung, 1989: 104). In sum, the Women's Centre (later renamed Hong Kong Federation of Women's Centres after becoming independent of the Hong Kong Council of Women) successfully promoted women's rights through enhancing women's competence and elevated the status of Chinese women in the society.

On the other hand, the setting up of the Association for the Advancement of Feminism (AAF) and to some extent, the Hong Kong Federation of Women's Centres, can be regarded as an important outcome of the feminist critique of social welfare in Hong Kong. Since the mid-1980s, the AAF has engaged in policy advocacy for gender equality, eliminating gender discrimination, women's participation in politics and public policy, and pursuing equality. To achieve these ends, it undertook various activities: monitoring of the government's policy-making process; providing resource backup for women's groups; raising women's consciousness; conducting women's studies; and providing legal consultation for needy women. Several books and reports published by the AFF became major reference sources for people interested in the relationship between social welfare and feminism (AAF, 1990, 2001, 2003).

From the late 1980s onwards, the development of women's associations was marked by a unity springing from their shared concerns. First, there was the development of geographically located women's associations in new towns such as Tin Shui Wai, which were populated by newly arrived women and single parents. A family tragedy in Tin Shui Wai in April 2004, in which three members (a mother and 2 young children) of a family receiving CSSA were killed by the husband, triggered protests from these organizations against the lack of resources for needy women and the inadequacies of the current social services. The murdered mother was a new arrival from the Mainland and had sought help from social workers, a shelter for women, and the police immediately before the tragedy (Review Panel on Family Services in Tin Shui Wai, 2004). Believing this tragedy could have been averted, these organizations were critical of the underlying assumption of "family integrity" adopted by social workers and policemen and the insufficient resources being devoted to women's services. Some groups argued that the government should treat domestic violence as a criminal offence.

Another trend was the development of women's associations focusing on specific issues confronting needy women, such as the Association Concerning Sexual Violence Against Women and Action for Reach Out (showing concern for sex workers). These associations provided various kinds of assistance and services for women and their family members. Professional association, such as the Hong Kong Professionals and Entrepreneurs Association has also been established. The work of women's organizations has certainly improved the general welfare of women in Hong Kong. At the same time, there has been significant development of women's groups that are devoted to eliminating gender discrimination and raising women's consciousness.

Conclusions

In this contribution, we argue that two potent forces have emerged as important determinants of the services made available to women in Hong Kong: the need paradigm adopted by the colonial and post-colonial governments and the feminist critique. The feminist perspective is important as it furnishes the society with a perceptive critique of the reality, but there are still comparatively few feminists and their influence remains circumscribed in the area of social welfare. Hence, their impact on policy development is not strong. Advocating women's rights and challenging the traditional family ideology is still an uphill task (AAF, 2003; Tam & Yeung,

1994). After years of advocacy, the lack of a feminist social policy and the prevalence of a need-based perspective testify to the fact that the feminist perspective has not had a major influence.

Admittedly, the need-based paradigm adopted by the government has made some contributions in promoting women's well-being and meeting some of their immediate needs. However, many women, such as battered wives, new arrivals and middle-aged unemployed women, continue to face special barriers to enhancing their well-being because their gender-specific needs have been neglected. Thus the problems linger. Social isolation and marginalisation still beset such women. Newly arrived women are not allowed access to CSSA on their own; women in a family cannot apply for social security assistance as individuals; unemployed middle-aged women are marginalized by social discrimination; and victims of family violence are vulnerable due to a lack of recourse to help and outreaching services for the prevention of family tragedy.

Hong Kong has a long history of a gender-neutral social policy geared to supporting family solidarity. Even after the establishment of the Women's Commission, Gender Mainstreaming Checklists have not been widely established at various levels of policy-making and service provision. There is an implicit assumption that such a policy is based on the fundamental formal equality of the individuals in the community and that women's needs can be fulfilled within the "family integrity" (i.e. "family as a unit") framework (Chan, 2003). In sum, the HKSAR government treats women's work as welfare work that is meant to maintain social stability. However, the above discussion indicates that women are treated unequally and women's rights are made subservient to the needs of the family. This observation is consistent with the analysis of the development of social policy in the advanced western countries where women are still treated unfairly after the introduction of a social policy that adopts a gender-free approach (Brown, 1984; International Labour Organisation, 1984). Such an approach would only address women's needs and concerns to the extent to which they conform to male norms (Bakker, 1998). By contrast, a gender-sensitive approach would promote gender awareness among social policy makers and practitioners so that women's needs and interests are addressed in the planning and implementation process. Overseas, feminist analysis puts its emphasis on the complex relationship between welfare systems and women and the significance of gender in the analysis of social policies (Lewis, 2003). Locally, feminist organizations like the AAF (2003) advocate for some necessary changes to the study of women's welfare. These include: collection of comprehensive data on women; continuous studies of women's needs and problems; heightened sensitivity to existing policies that might promote a particular sexual division of labor; and increased exchanges of social workers that serve needy women.

Globally, feminist analysis criticizes the traditional assumptions regarding female dependence on men and the ignoring of women's contributions to welfare (both formal and informal) (Lewis, 2003). Women act as unpaid providers of welfare when they withdraw from the labor force in order to care for children or dependent adults. Feminists further argue that women's economic security and rights means more than helping women find jobs. It means improving the power relations in a woman's home, in her community and in the market so that she can take advantage of growing international markets (UNIFEM, 2004). Similar criticisms of the welfare system have been made in Hong Kong. If the HKSAR government is to implement fully the Beijing Platform for Action (1995), strong commitment is needed. Paragraph 286 of the Platform states: "To ensure effective implementation of the Platform for Action and to enhance the work for the advancement of women at the national, subregional/regional and international levels, Governments, the United Nations system and all other relevant organizations should promote an active and visible policy of mainstreaming a gender perspective, inter alia, in the monitoring and evaluation of all policies and programmes." The post-colonial government ought to take a strong lead by establishing mechanisms at various levels so as to bring about adequate mobilization of existing resources as well as the allocation of additional resources to addressing these issues. Considering that the goals of the empowerment and the well-being of women in Hong Kong were set more than a decade ago, we have achieved very slow progress and considerable barriers remain.

Up until now, the key stakeholders, such as clients and social work professionals, have not been satisfied with these governmental responses. This is not to deny that both the colonial and the HKSAR governments have expended considerable resources on family and children's care and created many new programs. In most cases, however, these services have evolved incrementally and ad hoc; they have been rather limited in coverage and provision has been inadequate and poorly coordinated (Tang & Midgley, 2002). There is also a serious lack of policy vision, and a corresponding dearth of policy statements, in the key areas of social services (e.g., the poor and immigrants). Above all, the "social welfare reforms" introduced in the past few years by the government have led to the redefinition of the working relationship between the government and the NGOs, while at the same time resulting in the capping of the financial commitments of the government (Tang, Fung & Lau, 2006). In particular, the post-colonial government has been hamstrung by a number of factors in its delivery of social care: continuous economic downturn, rising budget deficits, the policy legacy and the impact of the New Managerialism. As a consequence, the HKSAR government is not in a position to pioneer new directions for the social services. This means that the call to address women's needs and rights remains something of a voice in the wilderness. There is still a long way to go before the government, NGOs and women's groups work together for a sustainable and just Hong Kong society, a society in which women and men can equally enjoy the opportunities arising from the society's achievements.

References

Association for the Advancement of Feminism (AAF) (1990). *Women and Welfare Policies in Hong Kong* (2nd ed.). Hong Kong: The Author. (In Chinese)

Association for the Advancement of Feminism (AAF) (2001). *Difference and equality: New challenges for the women's movement in Hong Kong*. Hong Kong: The Author. (In Chinese)

Association for the Advancement of Feminism (AAF) (2003). *Chronicle on women issues*. Hong Kong: The Author. (In Chinese)

Bakker, I. (1998). *Unpaid work and macroeconomics: New discussions, new tools for action*. Canada, Ottawa: Status of Women.

Brown, M. B. (1984). *Models in political economy*. Penguin Books: Harmonds Worth.

Census and Statistics Department (2004). *Hong Kong population projections, 2004–2033*. Hong Kong: The Author.

Census and Statistics Department (2005). Social data collected via the general household survey special topics report No. 42. *Hong Kong residents working in the mailand of China*. Hong Kong: The Author.

Chan, M. C. (2001). *A study on the cross-cultural impression and acceptance between local people and new arrivals*. Hong Kong: Hong Kong Council of Social Service. (In Chinese)

Chan, M. C. (2003). *Study on the cross-cultural impression and acceptance between local people and new arrivals*. Hong Kong: Hong Kong Council of Social Science. (In Chinese)

Chan, S. H. (2003). *Traditional value/family dynamics*. Paper presented at the 5th East Asian Women Forum, 19–22 December, Hong Kong.

Chan, S. H. (2002). Interfacing feminism and cultural studies in Hong Kong: A case of everyday life politics. *Cultural Studies, 16*(5), 704–734.

Chan, S. H., Cheng, K. F., Nip, Y. M., Siu, M. W., Chan, P.K., & Chan, S. S. (1985). *Survey report on women's participation in public affairs in Hong Kong.* Hong Kong: Association of the Advancement for the Feminism.

Chau, K., & Wong, C. K. (2002). The social welfare reform: A way to reduce public burden? In S. K. Lau (Ed.), *The first Tung Chee-hwa administration* (pp. 201–236). Hong Kong: Chinese University Press.

Cheung, F. M. (1989). The women's center: A community approach to feminism in Hong Kong. *American Journal of Community Psychology, 17*(1), 99–107.

Cheung, F. M. (2002). Ageing population and gender issues. In Y. M. Yeung (Ed.), *New challenges for development and modernization: Hong Kong and the Asia-Pacific region in the new millennium* (pp 207–223). Hong Kong: The Chinese University Press.

Chow, N. W. S. (1984). *A critical study of Hong Kong welfare policy.* Hong Kong: Cosmos Press. (In Chinese)

Christian Family Service Centre, Division on community development service (2000). *Self-identify and coping strategies among new female arrivals.* Hong Kong: Christian Family Service Centre. (In Chinese)

Christian Family Service Centre, & Chan, K. L. (2000). *A study of the impact of family violence on battered women and their children.* Hong Kong: Christian Family Service & Department of Social Work & Social Administration, The University of Hong Kong.

Department of Social Work and Social Administration, HK (HKUSWSA) (2001). *Meeting the challenge: Strengthening families — Report on the review of family services in Hong Kong.* Hong Kong: The University of Hong Kong.

Department of Social Work and Social Administration, HKU (HKUSWSA) (2003). *Interim report on the implementation of family service review.* Hong Kong: The University of Hong Kong.

Equal Opportunity Commission (EOC) (2005). Home website. Retrieved on 29 March 2005: http://www.eoc.org.hk/CC/case/index.htm.

Estes, R. J. (2002). Toward a social development index for Hong Kong: The process of community engagement. *Social Indicators Research, 58*, 313–347.

Harmony House (1994). *Harmony House annual report 1993–1994.* Hong Kong: The Author.

Hodge, P. (1980). Social planning models and their application in Hong Kong. In N. Chow (Ed.), *Social welfare in Hong Kong* (pp. 1–22). Hong Kong: Hong Kong Council of Social Service (HKCSS).

Hong Kong Council of Social Service (HKCSS) (1990). *Community development and women services: A survey report.* Hong Kong: The Author. (In Chinese)

Hong Kong Council of Social Service (HKCSS) (1996). *The development of women services in Hong Kong: A survey.* Hong Kong: The Author.

Hong Kong Council of Social Service (HKCSS) (2003). *NGOs' view on the interim report of the implementation of family services review.* Hong Kong: The Author.

Hong Kong Council of Social Service (HKCSS) (2004). *Social development index 2004*. Hong Kong: The Author.

Hong Kong Council of Social Service Community Development Division (HKCSS) (1997). *Paper on the future development of women service in Hong Kong*. Hong Kong: The Author.

Hong Kong Federation of Women's Centres (1999). *A study on mental health of married women who are newly arrived Hong Kong*. Hong Kong: The Author. (In Chinese)

Hong Kong Government (1965). *Aims and policy for social welfare in Hong Kong*. Hong Kong: The Author.

Hong Kong Government (1989). *Address by the Governor, Sir David Wilson, KCMG, at the opening of the 1989/90 session of the Legislative Council on 11 October 1989*. Hong Kong: Government Printer.

Hong Kong Government (1991). *Address by the Governor, Sir David Wilson, GCMG, at the opening of the 1991/92 session of the Legislative Council on 9 October 1991*. Hong Kong: Government Printer.

Hong Kong Government (1994). *Policy commitment: The 1994 policy address*. Hong Kong: The Author.

Hong Kong Government (1995). *Policy commitment: The 1995 policy address*. Hong Kong: The Author.

Hong Kong SAR Government (2000). *Hong Kong budget 2000*. Hong Kong: The Author.

Hong Kong SAR Government (2001a). *The 2001 policy address*. Hong Kong: The Author.

Hong Kong SAR Government (2001b). *Women and men in Hong Kong key statistics*. Hong Kong: The Author. (In Chinese)

Hong Kong SAR Government (2002a). *The 2002 policy address*. Hong Kong: The Author.

Hong Kong SAR Government (2002b). *Second report under the convention on the elimination of all forms of discrimination against women*. Hong Kong: The Author.

Hong Kong SAR Government (2006). *The 2006–07 budget*. Hong Kong: The Author.

Hong Kong Young Women's Christian Association (1998). *A study on life adaptation and needs among married women who are newly arrive Hong Kong*. Hong Kong: The Author. (In Chinese)

International Labor Organization (1984). *The development of social security*. Geneva: International Labor Organization.

Kung, W. W., Hung, S. L., & Chan, C. L. W. (2004). How the socio-cultural context shapes women's divorce experience in Hong Kong. *Journal of Comparative Family Studies, 35*(1), 33–50.

Kwok, P. C. Y. (1995). Empowerment networking groups for women whose spouses are having extramarital affairs. *Hong Kong Journal of Social Work, 29*(1), 60–64.

Kwok, P. L., Chow, G., Lee, C. K., & Wu, R. (1997). Women and the state in Hong Kong. In F. M. Cheung (Ed.), *Engendering Hong Kong society: A gender perspective of women's status* (pp. 237–266). Hong Kong: Chinese University Press.

Lai, B. L. L., Au, K. C., & Cheung, F. M. (1997). Women's concern groups in Hong Kong. In F. M. Cheung (Ed.), *Engendering Hong Kong society: A gender perspective of women's status* (pp. 267–305). Hong Kong: The Chinese University Press.

Lai, P. C. Y. (1997). An exploratory study on Chinese immigrant women in Hong Kong. In D. T. L. Shek, M. C. Lam., & C. F. Au. (Eds.), *Social work in Hong Kong: Reflections and challenges.* Hong Kong: Chinese University Press.

Lam, C. M., & Mok, B. H. (2002.) *Family life planning among new arrivals: A report on service evaluation.* Hong Kong: Hong Kong Boy's and Girl's Club Association & Department of Social Work, The Chinese University of Hong Kong. (In Chinese)

Law, C. K., & Hong Kong Family Welfare Society (1991). *Needs of single parent families: A comparative study.* Hong Kong: Hong Kong Family Welfare Society.

Lee, W. K. M. (2003). Women and retirement planning: Towards the "feminization of poverty" in an Aging Hong Kong. *Journal of Women and Aging, 15*(1), 31–53.

Lewis, J. (2003). Feminist perspectives. In P. Alcock et al. (Eds.), *The student's companion to social policy* (pp. 107–12). Oxford: Blackwell.

Lou, V. W. Q. (2000). *Identity formation and coping of new immigrant women from mainland China.* Hong Kong: Hong Kong Christian Service — Family Service Centre.

Lou, V. W. Q., & Law, L. L. (2004). Women from split families: The case of Mainland Chinese wives, Hong Kong husbands. In L. L. Thang & W. H. Yu (Eds.), *Old challenges, new strategies: Women, work and family in contemporary Asia* (pp. 233–248). Leiden: Brill.

Midgley, J. (1995). *Social development: The developmental perspective in social welfare.* London: Sage Publications.

Ming Pao (2005, 2 May). *The government proposed that single parents need to get back to work earlier — the youngest child above 12 would be the new policy.* Retrieved on 24 June 2005: http://hk.news.yahoo.com/050501/12/1c3au.html (In Chinese)

Ming Pao (2005, 4 May). *Reform has urgent needs, long time depend on CSSA will lose touch with the social development.* Rretrieved on June 24, 2005: http://hk.news.yahoo.com/050503/12/1c5et.html (In Chinese)

Mishra, R. (1981). *Society and social policy.* London: Macmillan.

Review Panel on Family Services in Tin Shui Wai (2004). *Report of review panel on family services in Tin Shui Wai*. Hong Kong: Social Welfare Department.

Shragge, E. (1994). *Community economic development*. Toronto: University of Toronto Press.

So, Y. C. (2003, December). Cross-border families in Hong Kong. *Critical Asian Studies*, *35*(4), 515–534.

Social Welfare Department (1973). *Social welfare in Hong Kong: The way ahead*. Hong Kong: The Author.

Social Welfare Department (1998). *Support for self-reliance: Report on review of the Comprehensive Social Assistance Scheme*. Hong Kong: The Author.

Social Welfare Department (2006a). *Statistics and figures on social security*. Retrieved on 28 December 2006: http://www.swd.gov.hk/en/index/site_pubsvc/ page_socsecu/sub_statistics/index.html.

Social Welfare Department (2006b). *Statistics on child abuse, battered spouse and sexual abuse cases*. Retrieved on 28 December 2006: http://www.swd.gov.hk/ vs/english/stat.html.

South China Morning Post (SCMP) (2003, 23 October). *Balanced budget deadline is delayed*.

Tam, M., Cheung, F. M. C., Choi, M. C., Lau, Y. K., Zhang, J. S., & Wong, K. Y. (2004). *The Impact of Split Households on Gender Relations*. Hong Kong: Hong Kong Institute of Asia-Pacific Studies.

Tam, T. S. K., & Yeung, S. (1994). Community perception of social welfare and its relations to familism, political alienation, and individual rights: The case of Hong Kong. *International Social Work*, *37*, 47–60.

Tang, C. S. K. (1994). Prevalence of spousal aggression in HK. *Journal of Family Violence*, *9*(4), 347–356.

Tang, C. S. K. (1997). Psychological impact of wife abuse: Experience of Chinese women and their children. *Journal of Interpersonal Violence*, *12*(3), 466–478.

Tang, C. S. K. (1999). Wife abuse in HK Chinese families: A community survey. *Journal of Family Violence*, *14*(2), 173–191.

Tang, K. L. (1998). *Colonial state and social policy*. Lanham: University Press of America.

Tang, K. L. (2000). Ageism and sexism at work: The middle-aged women of Hong Kong. *Gender, Technology and Development*, *4*(2), 225–253.

Tang, K. L., Fung, H. L., & Lau, Y. K. (2006). Social care in Hong Kong: Challenges and responses. In N. T. Tan & S. Vasoo (Eds.), *Social care in Asia*. Singapore: Marshall Cavendish Academic.

Tang, K. L., & Midgley, J. (2002). Social policy after the East Asian crisis: Forging a normative basis for welfare. *Journal of Asian Comparative Development*, *1*(2), 301–318.

Titmuss, R. (1976). *Essays on the welfare state*. London: George & Unwin.

Tung Wah Group of Hospitals (2000). *A report on integrated support service for families with new arrivals*. Hong Kong: Tung Wah Group of Hospitals, Social Service Sector. (In Chinese)

UNIFEM (2004). Website retrieved on 2 December 2004: http://www.unifem.org

United Nations. (1995). *Platform for action — Fourth world conference on women*. Retrieved on 2 December 2004: http://www.un.org/womenwatch/daw/beijing/ platform/plat1.htm

Women's Commission (2005). *Revised proposals for single parent recipients under the Comprehensive Social Security Assistance (CSSA) Scheme*. Retrieved on 1 August 2008: http://www.women.gov.hk/download/woc_19-05_revised_ proposal_of_cssa-e.pdf.

Wong, D. F. K. (2001). Differential functions and sources of social support of mainland Chinese immigrants during resettlement in Hong Kong: A qualitative analysis. *Journal of Social Work Research, 2*(2), 319–332.

Wong, H., & Lee, K. M. (2000). *Marginal workers in Hong Kong: New development*. Hong Kong: Oxfarm. (In Chinese)

Wu, A. (2001, 10 May). *Women in Hong Kong*. Paper delivered at the 2001 Fortune Global Forum.

Young, K. (1985). *Report on single parent families in Hong Kong*. Hong Kong: Department of Social Work & Social Administration, The University of Hong Kong.

Note

1. The number of total CSSA recipients has been decreased a little bit, though the number on low earnings and single-parent has increased.

CHAPTER 9

Improving Gender Equity in Hong Kong's Reproductive Health Services

Eleanor Holroyd, Suzanne C. Ho, William C. W. Wong

Introduction

Sex — the biological fact of being male and female — and gender — the cultural norms that determine masculinity and femininity — have a profound impact on health. It is increasingly well recognized that there are gender differences in the factors determining health and the burden of ill-health (World Health Organization, 2002).

Society prescribes to women and men different roles in different social contexts. There are differences in the opportunities and resources available to women and men, and in their ability to make decisions and exercise their rights, including those related to protecting health and seeking care in the case of ill health. Gender roles and unequal gender relations interact with other social and economic variables, resulting in different and sometimes inequitable patterns of exposure to health risks, and in differential utilization of health information, care and services. Gender roles resulting from power differentials serve to direct, promote and constrain health beliefs and health behaviors for women and for men.

In less developed societies there tends to be large gaps in gender roles associated with a more traditional division of labor and correspondingly a lower health status for women. Thus, the 'feminisation' of poverty reflects women's unequal situation in the health arena due to the lower value placed on their labor, their unequal status in the household, their absence or subsistence within existing welfare systems serving to further marginalize women (Ussher, 1989). This inequality is most obvious in the distribution of income and wealth. Around the world, women make up about 70% of those who are poor (United Nations Development Program (UNDP, 1995). The World Health Organization (WHO) stresses the importance that gender equality and equity concerns be mainstreamed into all policies, programs and projects. The integration of gender policy ensures a common understanding and coherent approach. The specific objectives of WHO's gender policy are; to ensure that programmes promote equality between men and women and do not create, maintain or reinforce gender roles and relations that may be damaging to health. The overall aim is to increase coverage of programmes by tailoring interventions to the specific needs of men and women.

An increasing number of developmental agencies and other organizations are now adopting 'gender and development' as an appropriate methodology for tackling the massive inequalities that continue to limit the potential of so many women around the world (Moser, 1993; UNDP, 1995).

In Asia and in particular Hong Kong, rapid and recent urbanization has accelerated the social changes in women's roles in both the public and private spheres having a differential impact on health. Historically gender roles have been associated with obedience for Chinese women, and the Confucius teaching of "the three obedience's and four virtues" (san cong si de), with the "virtuous wife and a good mother" (xian qi liang mu) placing women in a subservient role basis.

Conversely, men are perceived as strong masculine figures. Traditional Chinese sayings such as "a man prefers blood to tears" (nan er liu xue bu liu lei); "men have to be self independent" (nan er dang zi qiang); "men have no fear" (nan er wu wei) depict a man must have qualities of being a leader and decision maker while being able to hide weaknesses and unpleasant feelings. The predominate socio-cultural expectations about the role of adult males limits their sense of shared responsibility when dealing with failures. This in turn causes them to experience more social isolation to the point of self-fragmentation, and thus heightened vulnerability such schizophrenia (Yip, 2003). This results in Chinese males being less likely to report depression to their families or to health professionals when compared with women.

The following chapter will, from a research base, examine the impact of imbalance in power relationships in respect to gender and reproductive health risks. The outline for the chapter will include gender policy and norms, issues of equity of access to health services and prevention programs underscored by power, inequality and underlying social and cultural determinates.

Developments in gender policy

Internationally in the past decade, gender policy development and education has sought to increase health professionals' awareness of the role of gender norms, values, and inequality in perpetuating disease, disability, and death. The Beijing Declaration and Platform for Action in 1995 agreed on mainstreaming a gender perspective into all policies. Recent programs of the United Nations have given further support to this approach.

In Hong Kong, a specific focus has been to promote a societal change with a view to eliminating gender inequality as a barrier to health. From 2001 onwards, there has been a marked shift from an exclusive focus on women to a focus on gender, that is, the socially constructed differences and the power relations between women and men, as a determinant of health.

The influence of traditional gender norms on reproductive health risk

Women are much more likely than men to suffer health problems connected with their reproductive systems. For example, screening for cancer of the cervix and breast cancer is a female concern. Another example is provided in the introduction of HPV vaccine which prevents cervical cancer in women and while risk factors include the number of and sexual behaviors of the male partners, the vaccine remains unlicensed for male use. The implications being that all responsibility and fault lie with women solely. Women's vulnerability is exacerbated during their childbearing years with their capacity to conceive and bear children bringing them into the arena of the health care system more so than that of men.

Traditional gender norms of masculinity and femininity contribute to related silences, denial, stigma, and discrimination against women. These norms affect access to accurate prevention and information. Such unequal relations, in turn, are often further reinforced by larger social, economic, and legal inequalities. The result is that inequalities in power between women and men limit women's ability to control whether, when, and how to engage in reproductive health screening, sexual relationships and contraceptive use (Gupta, et al., 2002). Further manifestations are found in women and girls' lack of access to reproductive resources so reducing their ability to negotiate condom use or leave abusive relationships. In some instances, lack of educational and economic opportunities may cause some women to exchange sex for material goods.

Cervical cancer

An important strategy in the prevention of cervical cancer is the uptake of cervical screening. Cancer of the cervix as the seventh cause of cancer deaths in Chinese women with a rate of 12.7 per 100,000 women with Hong Kong having the fourth highest worldwide age standardized incidence rate for cervical cancer (Hong Kong Cancer Registry, 1999).

Chinese beliefs about cancer are influenced by culturally associated ideas about the body, family systems (patriarchy), ideas surrounding interactions with lay and professionals of the opposite gender, availability, health information, and the influence of family and friends. The research to date on Chinese women's beliefs regarding cancer causation has drawn almost exclusively on populations of migrant Chinese women residing in the USA. Mo (1992) has reported a fatalistic view of reproductive cancer in Chinese-American populations. The belief that cancer is determined by one's fate and women's beliefs about their susceptibility to cancer, has been reported as high among Chinese populations residing in Asia (Lu, 1995; Seow et al., 1995).

Cultural barriers to screening behaviors amongst Hong Kong Chinese include avoidance of social assertiveness and the association of reproductive screening procedures with immodesty and sexually inappropriate behaviors (Marin & Marin 1991). In addition, Chinese women residing both in Hong Kong and the USA have been found to associate the up-take of preventive health behavior with increasing age, marriage and the expectation of procreativity (Hoeman et al., 1996; Twinn et al, 1999). The assumption being that the intention to bring up and look after children signals a readiness to engage in protective behaviours according to which medical professionals can legitimately offer a woman a Pap smear.

In Hong Kong, Twinn et al (2001) found in groups of non- attendee and attendees for Pap smears an association between promiscuity and perceived risk of the disease indicating that women may not be willing to acknowledge their greatest risk factors. A lack of social assertiveness in respect to information seeking, particularly in regard to reproductive health matters has also been documented to be another cultural barrier to health screening behaviours in Chinese women (Louie, 1985).

A Hong Kong based survey of approximately 2000 women aged between 45–55 years recruited through random telephone dialing revealed that older women were less likely to have had a Pap smear within the past year (Chan et al., 2002) than younger women and than international cohorts of older women. Another Hong Kong study undertaken with a population of female clerical staff at a tertiary institution found that 68.2% of women associated a Pap smear with pain and 78.6% with embarrassment, in particular older women. Qualitative data portrayed women interviewed providing graphic descriptions of a Pap smear being associated with "vulnerablity"and "immodesty" (Holroyd et al., 2004).

Chinese traditional norms of femininity inhibit women's knowledge and assertiveness, and decrease their ability to negotiate cervical screening. These gender norms for femininity include sexual innocence, passivity, virginity, and motherhood. Yet also apparent are the choices and agency in that women do make micro-decisions such as not going for Pap smears as a form of resistance against a dominant health structure. This could be argued to be a form of political authoritarianism, which discourages public participation and restricts public debate on the issue of health services, costs health rights and policies. Historically in Hong Kong, health professionals, especially doctors, have not placed health on the public agenda and tended to medicalise health systems and policy making. Thus, preventive approaches based on rights and social determinants have seldom been at the forefront of health policy changes In Hong Kong, men have tended to dominate health policy making, management, and medical services thus devaluing women's health, in particular reproductive health.

Female vulnerability, sexually transmitted infections and sex as work

In general, Chinese cultural norms dictate that women and girls are not supposed to be knowledgeable about sex and generally have more limited access to relevant information and services. They often, therefore, remain poorly informed about sexuality, and reproduction and are less able to discuss these issues with their sexual partners. Norms of masculinity inhibit sexual health knowledge and support for shared decision making, and promote sexual aggression and risk-taking. Gender norms for masculinity may often dictate that men and boys should be knowledgeable, experienced, and capable of taking the lead in sexual relationships.

A Hong Kong study undertaken using diagnoses and drug data obtained from the logbooks of 50–100 successive medical consultations, documented all patients with a diagnosis of a sexually transmitted infections (STIs) or a symptom that was likely to be caused by it and drugs that were used as treatment (Wong et al., 2004). These patients accounted for 1.1% of the family practitioners workload, a proportion that matches that of dyspepsia or low back pain encountered in Hong Kong's primary care settings (Lee et al., 1995). This study, demonstrates that men were more likely than women to engage in high-risk sexual behaviors. Men tended to have more sexual partners than did women (Hong Kong Family Planning Association, HKFPA, 2001) and twice as many young men than women reported rarely using condoms during pre-marital sex (HKFPA, 2000).

Men also outnumbered women significantly in reported STI cases at the government's Social Hygiene Service (Ho, 2002). Diagnoses in terms of genitourinary symptoms were commonly seen in women whereas a more definite diagnosis of STI was given in male patients. In addition, female doctors were more likely to diagnose genital syndromes for their female patients when compared to their male colleagues. Doctors were more likely to diagnose STIs or genitourinary complaints to patients of the same sex reflecting the unequal power relations. The norms surrounding men's sexual initiation and multiple partners are barriers to effective HIV/ STI prevention. Use of alcohol and drugs are also associated with traditional norms of strength and masculinity, and both limit the ability to negotiate male sex and increase the likelihood of violence (Barker, 2000).

A series of surveillance surveys of all new STI clinic attendees conducted between 1996 and 2002 in Hong Kong (Chan, Ho, & Lo, 2002; Chow, 1999; Department of Health, 2002) reported on the type of sex partner, place of contact, and condom use with regular and casual sex partners. A slight increase was noted in male clients not using condoms consistently during casual sexual encounters, ranging from 40.5% to 70.4%. On the other hand, 34.3% female sex workers (FSWs) reported not using condoms consistently during commercial sex. The findings of these surveys also indicated differences reported in condom use between male clients and female sex workers.

While social and economic inequalities tend to increase women's vulnerability to STIs including HIV, gender patterns in employment also impact on men's vulnerability. When access to employment and income is limited, men sometimes leave their communities to seek economic opportunities. Men who migrate for work or have mobile jobs that take them away from their families (e.g., truck drivers) are in environments that increase their vulnerability to HIV through unprotected sex with sex workers. In China, many young women are increasingly migrating for employment and may not have the skills needed in formal work sectors, hence may be more likely to turn to sex work for income; other young women may face vulnerabilities related to being away from traditional support structures (Rivers & Aggleton, 2001).

Taking the example of commercial sex work in Hong Kong, it was estimated that there were at least 200,000 FSWs in 2002 and the total population involved as sex workers, supporting staff and male clients exceeded half a million in a city of 6.8 million people. A study of 89 female street sex workers (Wong et al. 2005) indicated that most of these women surveyed who had crossed the Chinese border to work in Hong Kong had dependents and they worked to support their families back in China.

Many sex workers were exposed to abuse while at work. Overall, the women surveyed scored significantly lower in physical, psychological and environmental health when compared to non-sex workers of the same age group and sex in Hong Kong.

By virtue of their occupation, FSWs, both within Asia and internationally, engage in high-risk sexual behaviors due to multiple sexual partners and unprotected penetrative sex. They are regarded as a core vector in the spread of STIs (Wong, et al., 1994). More seriously, STIs facilitate HIV transmission and so weaken the social and financial fabric of the society (Grosskurth et al., 1995). STIs cause many harmful, and costly reproductive health complications, including fetal and perinatal health problems, pelvic inflammatory diseases, long term disability and death (Matthews, 2001). The fact that the incidence of STIs is much higher among FSWs than in the general population is cause for considerable concern.

While these FSWs' perception of personal health was good, a considerable proportion suffered from a number of illnesses but the consultation rate was only a third of the mean rate of the general population in Hong Kong (Wong et al., 2006a, b). Many mainland Chinese street workers experienced difficulty in utilising health service in Hong Kong but even when they did, it was mainly for acute problems. Since April 2003, non-Hong Kong residents have been subject to a fee seven times higher than which locals are paying when ubilising of medical services in Hong Kong. Affordable access to public health services is in effect excluded and many women found private services unaffordable due to the high prices charged by the doctors. It was common for these women to self-medicate, delay in seeking medical help, or travel back to China for treatment. It is possible in this analysis that power was not a coherent or coercive force merely exercised through class or status position; instead originated from an external force (Foucault, 1976), such as through the government, realized and passed to individuals as a means that systematically denied these women their fundamental human rights to health care.

In comparison, two recent studies examined condom use in FSWs in Mainland China and found a relatively high percentage of condom use (61% and 71% respectively) (Rogers, et al., 2002; Zhang et al., 2000). Respondents in both studies, 82% and 87.1% respectively claimed condoms were used to prevent disease. However, 37% and 13% respectively stated it was difficult to access a condom when needed or at work. In general, relatively more male clients reported having casual or commercial sex without the use of condom on did female sex workers.

The tenant of this argument is that gender norms are fundamental to shaping men's and women's sexual relationships and their ability to gain access to health information and services that can help prevent STI transmission. A public health discourse that focuses on the decisions that sex-workers make in their daily lives and the reasons behind these decisions can help advance a more humane public health system.

Amongst disadvantaged women, the tendency to speak of women's 'powerlessness' fails to account for the range of coping strategies and social support networks that women have constructed to deal with their day-to-day life challenges.

Strategies for improving gender equity in reproductive health services

Policies that aim to decrease the gender gap in education, improve women's access to economic and health resources, increase women's political participation, and protect women are essential for women's empowerment (Gupta, 2000). Furthermore, lack of awareness by researchers, policy-makers and planners has frequently resulted in gender biases. This is often unconscious, with 'gender blindness' leading both individuals and organizations to ignore the realities of gender as a key determinant of social inequality. This problem can only be resolved through the development of 'gender-sensitive' policies that acknowledge both the reality and also the undesirability of the inequalities between women and men, including the unequal division of labor and power.

Improving men's support for women's reproductive health, discussions about sexuality and safer sex practices, and women's decision making and rights are fundamental to change. It is important to ensure that male involvement in programs is carefully evaluated in respect to gender relations and the impact of such involvement so these strategies do not cause unintended harm (e.g., reinforce men's control over decision making). Thus developing responses that address norms of masculinity across the range of prevention, testing, care, and support programs is a key aspect of comprehensive public health policies aimed at sharing the burden of care. It becomes important to promote, develop and strengthening positive masculine gender norms that support health-promoting behaviors and gender equity.

One approach is to build gender equity into reproductive screening services strategies that emphasise male sexual dominance through health promotion slogans advocating that men be involved in their female partners' health care services. In some cases, accommodating inequitable gender norms may provide benefits more quickly than do approaches that seek to change gender systems. An example of promoting inequitable gender norms to gain a positive health outcome would be to emphasisze family health, men's influence in women's decision making, and Chinese women's modesty in campaigns that promote cervical screening. This would serve to provide legitimate protection for women while at the same time preserve certain cultural beliefs about women's roles in Chinese society

Furthermore, there needs to be efforts made to reduce stigma and discrimination, including community and police harassment of marginalized groups that create barriers to accessing health services. Health services programs are important allies in advocacy efforts to change the policy environment to reduce stigma and discrimination and promote human rights — and these changes are central to a program's ability to reach and serve clients from vulnerable groups. Of crucial importance is to increase coverage, effectiveness and efficiency of interventions; promote equality between women and men, throughout the life course, and ensure that interventions do not promote inequitable gender roles.

Fundamental to such initiatives is the importance of building capacity with providers and clients to address gender, sexuality, and power dynamics, including assessing how power issues affect sexual health protection choices, and how to help client's critically assess their prevention needs. In particular, tailoring recommendations to known needs. Addressing gender inequality through examining power dynamics is important in identifying the types of counseling and sessions that best foster skills building.

As well as changing basic conditions, new health policies must also challenge existing gender roles and stereotypes, transforming women's situation with respect to men. To take an example, a reproductive health service that simply gave women the technical means to control their fertility would fall short of addressing the context of their lives. Thus services need to enable women to choose between a range of contraceptive methods, to understand the functioning of their own bodies, to make women aware of their rights and the risks in relation to childbearing, and to identify the various strategies needed to promote their own well-being.

While it is important that women's health needs are met through appropriate service provision, improving women's educational opportunities and making it easier for a woman to get a job, for instance, may simply increase her overall health burden if there is no associated change in who performs family care giving or who does domestic labour. Thus, mainstreaming gender and health concerns through policies designed to meet men's and women's practical needs must also take their circumstances and strategic interests into account if they are to be of lasting benefit.

For Hong Kong to follow WHO guidelines on developing gender-sensitive health policies and programs, this should be built explicitly into existing health and welfare objectives. This will require a preliminary analysis of the context in which health policies will be operating and a clear understanding of the gender issues involved. Local and regional (South East Asian) data bases are needed with sex aggregated statistics collected in a way that can usefully be incorporated into subsequent monitoring and evaluating the gender impacts of healthcare.

In respect to the provision of specific women's and men's health services in Hong Kong, the HKFPA represents the largest non-governmental organization (NGO). In 1990, in response to the increasing number of breast and cervical cancers, the Tung Wah Board of hospitals initiated the first well women's clinic to detect reproductive cancer at an early stage. The first men's' health clinic was established in 2001 and a few private men's health clinics' have recently sprung up in private hospitals. By placing gender at the forefront of service delivery for women and men's health services, gender sensitivity and equity where the addressed through structural changes in the service provider's roles and orientation. At the same time gender equity was reinforced in the public arena by way of publicity on gender-specific and gender-sensitive heath services.

Advocating and enacting gender-sensitivity will increase the coverage and effectiveness of health programs. Making health-empowering interventions more appropriate to the specific needs of men and women will ensure that these programs and projects do not unknowingly create, maintain or reinforce gender roles and relations that may be damaging to health. In addition, protecting gender-specific health and social needs through legislation will improve health in a more equitable manner for both women and men. Examples could include using women's and men's health care experiences as the basis for change, NGO's pressuring for reproductive health policy and planning, mainstreaming responsibility for gender issues into all health services and including training in gender awareness and equal opportunities for all health professionals. This approach would serve to promote public understanding of the centrality of gender and equity in the delivery of reproductive health services.

Summary

By highlighting reproductive health risks, the lack of information and understanding on the impact of health sector reform becomes evident. Gender must be placed alongside other determinants of health and health care, such as social class, education and ethnicity to effectively assess and intervene in the health of the Hong Kong population and in the planning of health services. Thus emphasizing gender sensitivity and health policy reform will require an understanding of some of the key concepts that have emerged from the wider literature on gender and development (United Nations/INSTRAW, 1993; Moser, 1993).

If gender-sensitive health plans are to be put into place, the importance of educating health professionals and policy-makers on gender sensitivity cannot be underestimated. Sensitivity and capacity-building programs must be designed for both women and men and need to focus not just on 'women's issues' but on the wider question of gender itself. They may include broadly-based 'gender awareness' courses for the public and NGOs, and also more detailed briefings on gender and health related topics not generally included in the curriculum's of health professionals.

In summary, it is important to develop a strategy for making women's as well as men's health concerns and experiences an integral dimension in the design, implementation, monitoring and evaluation of policies and programs in all political, economic and social spheres, such that inequality between men and women is not perpetuated. The ultimate goal being to achieve gender equality. In conclusion, mainstreaming gender is both a technical and a political process which requires shifts in organizational cultures and ways of thinking, as well as in the goals, structures and resource allocations in order to redress power imbalances.

References

Barker, G. (2000). What about boys? *A literature review on the health and development of adolescent boys.* World Health Organization

Chan, C., Ho, S. C., Chan, S. G., Yip, Y. B., Wong, F. C., & Cheng, F. (2002). Factors affecting uptake of cervical and breast cancer screening in perimenopausal Hong Kong women. *Hong Kong Medical Journal, 30*(8), 334–341.

Chan, M. K. T., Ho, K. M., & Lo, K. K. (2002). A behavior surveillance for female sex workers in the social hygiene service in Hong Kong (1999–2000). *International Journal of Sexually Transmitted Infections and AIDS, 13,* 815–820.

Chow, K. Y. (1999). STD control: A sentinel surveillance of the STD clinic attendees. *Hong Kong Dermatology and Venereology Bulletin, 7,* 52–58.

Family Planning Association (2000). *Youth sexuality study: out-of-school survey, 1996.* Hong Kong SAR.

Family Planning Association (2001). *Men's health survey (2001).* Retrieved on 30 April 2007: http://www.famplan.org.hk

Foucault, M. (1977). *Discipline and punish: The birth of the prison,* trans. Alan Sheridan. London: Penguin Books.

Grosskurth, H., Mosha, F., Todd, J., Mwijarubi, E., Klokke, A., Senkoro, K., & Mayaud, P. (1995). Impact of improved treatment of sexually transmitted diseases on HIV infection in rural Tanzania: Randomised controlled trial. *The Lancet, 346*(8974), 530–536.

Gupta, G. R. (2002). How men's power over women fuels the HIV epidemic. *British Medical Journal, 324*(7331), 183–184

Ho, R. (2002). Sexually transmitted diseases reporting at government social hygiene services. *Hong Kong STD/AIDS Update, 8*(2), 24–33.

Hoeman, S. P., Ku, Y. L., & Roth Ohl, D. (1996). Health beliefs and early detection among Chinese women. *Western Journal of Nursing Research, 18,* 518–533.

Holroyd, E., Twinn, S., & Adab, P. (2004). Socio-cultural influences on Chinese women's attendance for cervical screening. *Journal of Advanced Nursing, 46*(1), 42–52.

Hong Kong Cancer Registry (1999). *Cancer incidence and mortality in Hong Kong 1998–1999.* Hong Kong: Hospital Authority.

Louie, K. B. (1985) Providing health care to Chinese clients. *Topics in Clinical Nursing, 7*(3), 18–25.

Lee, A., Chan, K. K. C., Wun, Y. T., Ma, P. L., Li, L., & Siu, P. C. (1995). A morbidity survey in Hong Kong, 1994. *Hong Kong Practice, 17*(6), 246–255.

Lu, Z. J. (1995). Variables associated with breast self-examination among Chinese women. *Cancer Nursing, 18*(1), 29–34.

Marin, G., & Marin, B. V. (1991). *Research with hispanic populations.* Newbury Park, CA: Sage Publications.

Mo, B. (1992). Modesty sexuality and breast health in Chinese American women. *Western Journal of Medicine, 157*(3), 260–264.

Moser, C. (1993). *Gender planning and development: theory, practice and training.* London, Routledge.

Rivers, K., & Aggleton, P. (2001). Working with young men to promote sexual and reproductive health. Safe Passages to Aulthood Programme, Faculty of Social Sciences, University of Southampton, Southampton.

Rogers, S. J., Ying, L., Xin , Y. T., Fung, K., & Kaufman J. (2002). Reaching and identifying the STD/HIV risk of sex workers in Beijing. *AIDS Educ Prev, 14*(3), 217–227

Seow, A., Wong, M. L., Smith, W. C. S., & Lee, H. P. (1995). Beliefs and attitudes as determinants of cervical cancer screening: a community-based study in Singapore. *Preventive Medicine, 24*, 134–141.

Twinn, S., Holroyd, E., & Shiu, A. (1999). An investigation of the extent to which service provision for the screening of cervical cancer meets the needs of Hong Kong women. Unpublished Departmental Report. The Chinese University of Hong Kong.

United Nations Development Program-Gender and Human Development (1995). Human development report 1995. UNDP, New York, USA.

United Nations/INSTRAW (1993). The development of thought on gender and women in development (WID): Towards a new paradigm. In R. Blumberg & B. Knudson (Eds.), *Gender training portfolio.* Santa Domingo: UN.

Ussher, J. (1989). *The psychology of the female body.* London: Routledge.

Wong, W. C. W., Chan, C. S. Y., & Dicksinson, J. A. (2004). The prevalence of STD infection and standard of treatment in primary care in Hong Kong. Manuscript submitted for publication (*Hong Kong Medical Journal*).

Wong, W. C. W., Chan C. S. Y., & Dickinson J. A. (2005). The prevalence of STI infections and standard of treatment in primary care in Hong Kong. *Hong Kong Medical Journal, 11*(4), 273–280.

Wong, W. C. W, Lee, W. K., & Lau B. S. T. (2006). Are Chinese men really less susceptible to anxiety and depression? A community-based cross-sectional survey from Hong Kong. *Journal of Men's Health and Gender, 3*(2), 152–159.

Wong, W. C. W., Gray, A., Ling D. C., & Holroyd E. (2006a). Patterns of health care utilization and health behaviors among street sex workers in Hong Kong. *Health Policy, 77*(2), 140–148.

Wong, W. C.W., Holroyd, E., Gray, A., & Ling, D. C. (2006b). Female street sex workers in Hong Kong: Moving beyond sexual health. *Journal of Women's Health, 15*(4), 390–399.

Wong, K. H., Lee, S. S., Lo, Y. C., & Lo, K. K. (1994). Condom use among female commercial sex workers and male clients in Hong Kong. *Int J STD AIDS, 5*(4), 287–289.

World Health Organization. (2002). *Integrating gender perspectives in the work of WHO — WHO gender policy*. Geneva: World Health Organization

Yip, K. S. (2003). Gender differences in mental illness in Hong Kong. *Administration and Policy in Mental Health*, *30*, 361–368.

Zhang, S., Zhang, S., Abdullah, A. S. M., Jiang, L., Tian, H., Zhang, X., Li, X., & Shen, M. (2000). Evaluation on condom use among the underground prostitutes and clients in Shenzhen, *Journal for China AIDS/STD Prevention and Control*, *6*, 9–11.

PART III

Deconstruction of Gender Equity Issues

CHAPTER 10

Gender-based Violence in Hong Kong

Catherine So-kum Tang

Introduction

Gender-based violence (GBV) is violence directed at individuals on the basis of their gender. It cuts across status, class, religion, race, economic, and geographic barriers. Boys and men are also targets of violence, but the majority of victims are girls and women (Heise, Ellsberg, & Gottemoeller, 1999; World Health Organization (WHO), 2002a). In addition to being defined as a social and criminal justice problem, GBV is often viewed as a public health threat because of its high prevalence across women's life span and of its multiple and severe health consequences (Briere & Jordan, 2004; Heise, Pitanguy, & Germain, 1994; WHO, 2002a). GBV is also viewed as a human right issue because it violates a number of absolute human rights: Right to life, right to freedom from fear and torture, right to safety and security, and right to freedom of movement (Astbury, 2003).

GBV evolves from unequal gender power relations, whereby women are more likely to be disadvantaged relative to men (United Nations Population Fund (UNFPA), 2005). The 1995 Fourth World Conference on Women (Beijing) and subsequent United Nations conferences recognized the elimination of GBV as central to the equality, empowerment, and development of women. A gender mainstreaming approach to combat GBV involves integrating both men's and women's needs and experiences into the design, implementation, monitoring, and evaluation of programs and policies (UNFPA, 2005). This will necessitate a careful scrutiny of available knowledge base of the phenomenon (Cheung, in this volume).

The bulk of the available literature on GBV was collected from developed countries in North America and Europe, very little is known about the magnitude and nature of this problem in developing countries in Asia and Africa. Multi-country prevention/intervention programs and research on GBV have typically failed to include contemporary Chinese societies (Heise, Ellsberg, & Gottemoeller, 1999; WHO, 2000, 2002a, 2002b; Yodanis, 2004), where GBV remains a marginalized discourse in the academic, social, legal, and political arena (Chow, Zhang, & Wang 2004; Jaschok, 2003; Milwertz, 2003; Tang, Wong, Cheung, & Lee, 2000; Xu, Campbell, & Zhu, 2001).

This chapter aims to document available information on GBV in a contemporary Chinese society – Hong Kong. In subsequent sections, various theoretical perspectives that facilitate the understanding of occurrences of GBV in Hong Kong will first be reviewed. Issues relating to the definition, determination of the scope, and assessment of the outcome and costs of GBV will be discussed. Current strategies to combat GBV by formal and informal sectors in Hong Kong will also be examined. Finally, future directions in gender mainstreaming local GBV prevention and intervention efforts will be proposed. Notwithstanding there are many forms of GBV, this chapter focuses primarily on rape and sexual violence, intimate partner or spouse abuse (IPV), sexual harassment, and child sexual abuse.

Social Construction of Gender and Violence

Gender and violence is a complex problem rooted in the interplay of multiple factors. In recent years, feminist scholarship and activism has led a paradigmatic shift away from the notion of women as temptresses of innocent men toward the examination of the role of men and society in the perpetration and maintenance of GBV (Berns, 2001; Bohan, 1997; Gelles, 1993; Gilbert, 2002). According to feminist theorists, GBV is a not only a manifestation of inherent unequal power relations between men and women in the society, but also serves to maintain this gender inequality to prevent the full advancement of women (Bograd, 1988; Brownmiller, 1975; Dobash & Dobash, 1992). Studies have indeed shown that the prevalence of GBV is closely tied to the inferior status of women in the family (Coleman & Straus, 1986; Straus, 1994; Tang, 1999a) and in the society (Yodanis, 2004). In societies where men dominate family, political, economic, and other social institutions both in number and in power, policies and practices of these institutions are more likely to embody and legitimatize men's domination (violence) over women. In addition to actual acts of violence, men can also secure their superior status over women by creating a culture of fear (Brownmiller, 1975; Stanko, 1995). It is through this fear of violence, especially sexual violence, that men are able to control women's behaviors by keeping women out of the public sphere or by confining women's participation in domestic affairs.

Gender ideologies and cultural myths have also led both men and women to construct women as legitimate victims of GBV. In most societies, women are typically charged with the responsibility of maintaining family integrity and ensuring social stability. Policies that design to keep the family intact also function to keep a significant proportion of women expose to unknown risks of IPV and marital rape. The need to protect the family from shame often leads victims and family members of child sexual abuse being reluctant to report or support victims. Employed women have to tolerate sexual harassment at work in silence to avoid being labeled as "men-haters" or trouble-makers. Explanatory models of GBV such as psychoanalytic and victimological approaches have also helped to "degender the problem and gender the blame" (Berns, 2001; Tang, Wong, & Cheung, 2002) by perpetuating myths and victim-blaming interpretations that proclaim women's experiences of victimization as attributable to qualities within them. These explanations perpetuate the cycle of GBV, serve as "evidences" that women are the weaker and inferior gender, and thus reinforce men's superiority in the society. A number of studies have documented that individuals, especially men, who believe in traditional gender roles and accept rape myths are more likely to engage in aggressive activities toward women than those who do not adhere to these beliefs (Allison & Wrightsman, 1993; Brownmiller, 1975; Burt, 1980; Pollard, 1992; Sanday, 1981; Whatley, 1996).

GBV has been a problem in Chinese societies for many centuries, as Chinese culture embraces rigid gender norms and emphasizes patriarchy values, familism, and social order that are conducive to the exploitation of women (Choi & Ting, this volume; Croll, 1995; Jaschok, 2003; Luo, 2000; Xu, et al., 2001). The inferior status of Chinese women as well as patriarchal cultural attitudes and practices often place Chinese women in vulnerable positions within the family and in the society, thereby making them suffer repeated victimizations in silence and expose to unknown risks of future violence. For example, child sexual abuse and incest may be condoned as legitimate treatment of girls as filial daughters should defer to their fathers (Okamura, Heras, & Wong-Kerberg, 1995; Rhind, Leung, & Choi, 1999).

Marital rape or IPV is an acceptable means to discipline women when they are perceived as failing to meet the prescribed cultural and social standard of obedient wives (Tang, Wong, et al., 2002). In ancient Chinese societies, rape was often employed by men to acquire sexual access to desired women as a socially acceptable precedent to marriage. Even nowadays, a woman who survived acquaintance rape is still encouraged to marry her rapist to preserve her chastity and to avoid social disgrace to her family (Chou, 1995; Luo, 2000). A recent focus group study conducted in three contemporary Chinese societies, namely Hong Kong, People's Republic of China, and Taiwan, have found that Chinese still use psychiatric explanations in their discussions of GBV (Tang, Wong, et al., 2002). They believe that men who commit violence are usually sick and often blame women for provoking men to violence. However, younger and relatively well-educated Chinese tend to reject various cultural myths about GBV, oppose victim-blaming explanations, and challenge pro-violence beliefs (Ng & Wong, 2002; Tang, Wong, et al., 2002).

In Hong Kong, many traditional patriarchal attitudes still persist despite British colonial influences for almost one-and-a-half centuries (Tang, Wong et al., 2002; Tang, Wong, & Lee, 2001). While there is a current trend toward expanding roles of women with increased educational opportunities (Mak, in this volume) and labor force participation (Ngo & Pun, in this volume), people generally have ambivalent attitudes toward gender equality. Gender stereotypes and conservative attitudes toward family roles are still endorsed by primary and secondary school students (Equal Opportunities Commission, 2000), university students (Tang, Yik, Cheung, Choi, & Au, 1995), the general public (Equal Opportunities Commission, 1997, 1999; Tang, Wong et al., 2002; Women's Commission, 2001), as well as human service professionals (Tang, Pun, & Cheung, 2002). While Hong Kong people are less rigid about women's roles and status relative to men in educational, occupational, and social domains, many still believe that women's proper place should be in the home where they are primarily responsible for household chores and childcare. Choi and Ting (in this volume) note that married women in Hong Kong across all classes and working status have continued to shoulder most of the burden of domestic work, while their husbands remain dominant over marital communication and sexual intimacy. A great majority of people in Hong Kong, including the general public, university students, as well as human service and law enforcement personnel, endorse victim-blaming attitudes and accept myths in relation to rape (Lee & Cheung, 1991; Ng & Wong, 2002), IPV (Tam & Tang, 2005; Tang, Pun, et al., 2002), child sexual abuse (Tang & Yan, 2004), and sexual harassment (Tang, Yik, et al; 1995). Chinese men who espouse traditional attitudes toward women and victim-blaming explanations are more likely to report engaging in violent acts against their intimate partners (Chan, 2004; Tang, 1999a) or sexually harassing behaviors against their peers (Tang, Yik, Cheung, Choi, & Au, 1996). Wife batterers are also found to adhere rigidly to traditional gender role expectations of men (Chan, 2004). They believe that men can bleed but not cry, and only immature and incompetent men express their emotions before others.

Definition and Scope of GBV

Despite the fact that GBV exists in almost every corner of the world, there is still little agreement on behaviors that constitute GBV. However, the way in which GBV is defined and measured has great impacts on the determination of its scope, public perception of its seriousness, mobilization of resources, and formulation of social policies to eliminate its occurrence. There are three major approaches in defining GBV, including that of the criminal law, public health system, and feminist movement. The criminal justice approach adopts criminal codes of violent crimes in defining GBV and typically includes violent crimes of murder, sexual offences, and rape (Hanmer & Saunders, 1993; Rantala, 2000). The public health approach describes GBV as a subset of interpersonal violence that includes physical, sexual, psychological, and sexual violence as well as deprivation or neglect directed at women of various ages in the family or in community settings (WHO, 2002a). The feminist approach to GBV is the broadest, and includes a wide range of abusive or aggressive behaviors that adversely affect women (Koss, Goodman, & Browne, 1994). In essence, the criminal justice and public health approaches focus on intentionality of perpetrators, while the feminist perspective emphasizes women's experiences as the defining criteria of GBV.

In Hong Kong, the understanding of GBV is also plagued with definitional and measurement issues similar to those observed in Western countries (Kilpatrick, 2004; Saltzman, Fanslow, McMahon, & Shelley, 2002; Tjaden, 2004). The term GBV or violence against women is relatively new to Hong Kong and other Chinese societies, and there is not yet a widely recognized or agreed upon Chinese translation of this term (Tang, Cheung, Chen, & Sun, 2002; Tang et al., 2000). The majority of Hong Kong people, especially men, typically adopt the criminal justice approach that emphasizes physical harm and intentionality in defining GBV (Tang, 1998, 2002; Tang et. al., 2000; Tang, Yik, et al., 1995; Tang & Yan, 2004). In general, Hong Kong people have the greatest agreement in defining rape, unwanted physical touch, IPV, and sexual harassment as GBV; followed by child sexual abuse, controlling and trafficking of prostitutes, and obscene phone calls; and foul language, pornography, and sexual discrimination at work are the least likely to be perceived as GBV. Individuals who hold conservative attitudes toward women's roles and undermine women's rights are more likely to endorse narrow definitions of GBV (Tang, Pun, et al., 2002). As compared to human service professionals such as psychologists, social workers, and nurses, law enforcement and legal professionals tend to use narrower and more rigid criteria in determining the scope of GBV (Tang, Pun, et al., 2002; Tang & Cheung, 1997).

Researchers and feminist activists have long argued against narrow, legalistic definitions of GBV (DeKeseredy, 2000; Kilpatrick, 2004; Tang et al., 2000). Such definitions not only disregard many women's subjective experiences, they can also exacerbate the problem of under-reporting and reluctance in seeking assistance from social services. When frontline professionals adopt legalistic approach in defining GBV, their effectiveness may be compromised because they may fail to detect, prevent, or handle various forms of GBV that fall outside the legal definition of criminal behaviors. They may treat victims of GBV with insensitivity as well as delay or refuse to make appropriate referral for further services. Narrow definitions of GBV also contribute to low estimates of incidence and prevalence rates, with which policy makers are unlikely to allocate resources for prevention and intervention programs. In Hong Kong, feminist groups and service organizations also recommend using broad definitions of GBV. For example, it is argued that wife abuse should not only include physical violence, but also psychological abuse, stalking behaviors, marital rape, and sexual violence (Women's Commission, 2006). Recently, a growing number of researchers and civil society organizations in North America have proposed a multi-definitional and multi-dimensional approach to GBV (Kilpatrick, 2004; Saltzma et al., 2002; Tjaden, 2004), given that many women live on a "continuum of violent actions" and some women also simultaneously experience different types of violence. It is argued that these broad and women-centered approaches to GBV will enable women feel more at ease in talking and discussing their life experiences. Indeed, in various focus group studies conducted in Hong Kong, People's Republic of China, and Taiwan (Tang et al., 2000; Tang, Wong, et al., 2002), Chinese women who were encouraged to use a variety of local idioms and terms to describe women's distressing interpersonal experiences were more able to articulate and to focus not only on physical violence but also on sexually and verbally violent acts than when they were simply asked to define GBV or violence against women.

Prevalence and Magnitude of GBV

Similar to many countries, it is difficult to assess the extent of GBV in Hong Kong because it occurs mostly behind closed doors as in cases of IPV and sexual harassment, with which social service or law enforcement personnel are reluctant to intervene (Tam & Tang, 2005; Tang, 2003). GBV is typically under-reported given shame and stigma attached to sexual victimizations as in incidents of rape (Lee & Cheung, 1991; Ng & Wong, 2002) and child sexual abuse (Rhind, et al., 1999; Tang, 2002; Tang & Lee, 1999). Furthermore, many investigators in Hong Kong use the Conflicts Tactics Scales (Straus, 1979; Straus, Hamby, Boney-McCoy, & Sugarman, 1996) to collect information on women's victimization experiences of physical and psychological abuse, especially those committed by intimate and dating partners. These scales were developed in the United States and have been heavily criticized for their lack of attention to contextual and cultural factors (Kilpatrick, 2004; Straus, 1992). Violent acts specific to local settings are rarely identified, assessed, and reported. Recently, attempts have been made to delineate locally relevant behavioral parameters of intimate partner psychological abuse (Tang, 1998), sexual harassment (Tang, Yik, et al., 1995), and child sexual abuse (Tang, 2002) to enable a more detailed understanding of the nature and magnitude of GBV within the local context.

Other barriers in determining the extent of GBV in Hong Kong include when, how, and with whom the information should be collected. In addition to having information about recent incidents or past victimization experiences occurring within a specific period of women's life span (e.g., childhood, adolescence, adulthood, or during pregnancy), it is also important to gather data on GBV throughout the entire life span of women given the pervasiveness of its occurrences and persistence of its impacts (Kilpatrick, 2004; Tjaden, 2004; WHO, 2002a, 2004a). In other countries, there are already debates about whether history of GBV perpetration and victimization should be collected from one gender or from both genders as in IPV, from children/adolescents or from adults as in child sexual abuse, and from crime victimization surveys or from statistics collected by service settings of criminal justice agencies, crisis centers, women shelters, and health clinics etc. In fact, each of these sources provides invaluable information on GBV, but different sources can greatly influence estimates of incidence and prevalence rates (Kimmel, 2002).

In Hong Kong, prevalence rates of GBV are typically estimated from survivors' recall of lifetime victimization experiences (e.g., Tang, 2002) or incidents in a given year (e.g., Tang, 1998), from victimization surveys (e. g., Chan, 2004; Tang, 1999b), as well as from reports of various government (e.g., annual reports of the Police and Social Welfare Departments) and non-government organizations. Gender scholars, service organizations, and feminist activists each produce their own estimates of GBV that are often based on small-scale surveys on one specific form of GBV. Official statistics on GBV are mainly captured by the annual crime report of the Police Department as well as the Child Protection Registry (CPR) and the Central Information System on Battered Spouse Cases and Sexual Violence Cases (CISBSSV) of the Social Welfare Department.

Among various forms of GBV, rape is the most feared by women across countries. Yet, it is also an "invisible" crime that is the least recognized, reported, or prosecuted. It is predominately directed against women, often perpetrated by intimate partners, and frequently used as a weapon during war and armed conflicts (UNFPA, 2005; WHO, 2002a). The lifetime prevalence of rape and attempted rape among college-aged women in developed countries is estimated to range from 21% to 28% (Heise et al., 1999; Koss, Heise, & Russo, 1994). In developing countries, rape prevalence estimates are not systematically collected, but are thought to be about 43%–90%. In Hong Kong, very little is known about the prevalence of rape given the immense stigma attached to sexual victimization. Studies on sexual aggression showed that 2–5% of surveyed young adult women (Tang, Critelli, & Porter, 1995) and 4% of surveyed teenage girls (Chiu & Ng, 2001) reported being raped by their male dating partners. In the educational setting, about 5% of surveyed female university students reported being forced to engage in sexual intercourse by either their teachers or fellow students (Tang, 2007a; Tang et al., 1996). Coercive sexual activities perpetrated by classmates were also reported by 1–2% of surveyed female high school students (Tang, 2004). In the work setting, 1–4% of surveyed female secretaries admitted to being coerced or bribed to sexual activities by either their supervisors or co-workers (Chan, Tang, & Chan, 1999). In a large community-wide survey, about 8% of adult respondents reported knowing someone who had been raped by either strangers or acquaintances (Ng & Wong, 2002). Similar to other countries, official statistics on rape in Hong Kong as captured by annual crime reports and the Central Information System of various governmental departments are poor estimates of the problem. Nevertheless, these statistics show that rape and sexual assault do not confine to young women, but threaten practically women of all ages.

The most common form of GBV is that perpetrated by a husband or intimate male partner. In more than 50 population-based surveys from around the world (Heise et al. 1999; WHO, 2002a), 10–69% of women reported being physically and about 25% being sexually assaulted by an intimate male partner at some point in their lives, while 30–52% experienced intimate male partner physical violence in the previous year. Among pregnant women around the world, GBV by a spouse or intimate sexual partner is about 3–13%. Given that a majority of IPV occurred behind closed doors, 20–70% of abused women never tell another person about the violence until they are interviewed by researchers. In Hong Kong, a telephone survey of a large community sample showed that 10% of surveyed married women reported physical violence and 67% verbal violence perpetrated by their husbands over the past twelve months (Tang, 1999b). Similar prevalence rates were also obtained from university students' report on paternal violent behaviors toward mothers (Tang, 1994). In a sample of pregnant women attending their first antenatal clinic (Leung, Leung, Lam, & Ho, 1998), about 16% reported being physically and 10% sexually abused by their husbands in the past year, with 4% of the physical violence occurring during their current pregnancy. Within a nine-month period in a large regional hospital, 72 women were identified by the medical staff of the emergency and accident department as victims of intimate partner physical violence, i.e., 7 per 10,000 attendances (Wong et al., 1998). Among these abused pregnant women, 87% presented with blunt soft tissue injuries and 5% sustained fractures or open wounds, while one woman with head injury was admitted to the hospital for observation. In recent years, Official statistics from the Central Information System of the Social Welfare Department have shown a threefold increase of spouse battering cases from 1,009 in 1998 to 3,298 in 2003, with 92% of victims being women. In general, risk markers for IPV are: Young couples, large age disparity between couples, conflicts or dissatisfaction with the relationship, and male dominance in the relationship (Chan, 2004; Tang, 1999b).

Another review of studies from 20 countries showed that rates of childhood sexual abuse were 7–36% for girls and 3–29% for boys, with most studies reporting 1.5 to 3 times more sexual violence against girls than boys (Finkelhor, 1994). Across countries, up to one-third of girls had forced sexual initiation (WHO, 2002a). There are two studies in Hong Kong on adult recall of childhood sexual abuse experiences. In a large scale survey on university students (Tang, 2002), the overall prevalence rate of childhood experience of sexual abuse was 6%, with females being twice more likely than males to be sexually victimized. In particular, about 1% also reported being coerced to engage in vaginal and/or anal sexual activities. Another survey showed that 58% of adult clients receiving services in a local family center reported various forms of childhood sexual victimization (Caritas Family Service, 1996). Rates of active cases of child sexual abuse on the centralized Child Protection Registry have increased from 4% in 1979 to 18% in 1995, and to 31% in 2003. As documented by research reports and the Child Protection Registry, the mean age of the onset of the sexual abuse was 11–14 years, but 6–10% of the sexual abuse incidents occurred among children under 5 years old. Over 60% of perpetrators were victims' father or step-father. However, it should be noted that intra-familial child sexual abuse may be over-represented in official statistics and victimization surveys, as this form of child sexual abuse is viewed as a more serious violation of Chinese moral codes and as having greater threat to the well-being of child victims.

Compared to other forms of GBV, sexual harassment is a relatively new concept with only a few decades of public discourse and legal history. It is widespread, occurs mostly in educational and work settings, usually targets at women, and refers to a wide range of behaviors. Thus, prevalence rates vary greatly across countries (DeSouza & Solberg, 2003; Gruber, 2003), ranging from 10–60% for teacher-to-student, 30–86% for student-to-student, and 20–40% for employer- or coworker-to-worker gender harassment and unwanted physical touch. Sexual bribery and coercion is relatively less frequent, being 1–10% by teachers, 2–15% by peers, and 4–10% by employers or coworkers. In Hong Kong, a large territory-wide survey of full-time university students (Tang, 2007a) showed that about 13% of surveyed female students were victims of faculty sexual harassment. Among those who were sexually harassed by their teachers, 11% received unwelcome intimate bodily touch, 9% were subject to gender harassment, and 2.5% were coerced to participate in sexual activities. The prevalence rate of peer sexual harassment was even higher, with 35% of surveyed female students reporting such experiences. In particular, prevalence rates were 26% for peer gender harassment, 22% for peer unwelcome intimate physical touch, and 5% for peer coercive sexuality. When compared to an earlier local study conducted in 1992 (Tang, et al., 1996), the overall prevalence for peer and faculty sexual harassment is similar. While prevalence rates for gender harassment and unwelcome intimate bodily touch have decreased slightly, incidents of sexual coercion perpetrated by peers and teachers are on the rise. In the work setting, a survey conducted in the early 80's showed that about half of surveyed female employees reported personal experiences of sexual harassment at work during the previous three years (Dolescheck, 1984). Another survey on a small sample of female secretaries in the late 1990's revealed that about 30% of these women were subject to sexist remarks and dirty jokes at work, 22% received unwanted physical touch, and 1–4% were bribed or coerced to sexual activities by either their employers, supervisors, or co-workers (Chan et al., 1999). Official statistics on sexual harassment in educational and work settings are not systematically collected. The number of sexual harassment complaints filed to the concerned statutory body, the Equal Opportunities Commission, remains low.

Outcome and Cost of GBV

Victim reactions to GBV are remarkably similar across countries (Briere & Jordan, 2004; Campbell, 2002; WHO, 2002a). In Hong Kong, local case reports and narratives of sexually victimized women do indicate the presence of many aspects of the rape trauma syndrome and adverse impacts on their physical, mental, and interpersonal functioning. For example, Cheung and Ng (2004) found that woman survivors of sexual violence often report severe psychological distress and suicidal ruminations at the time of seeking crisis intervention. Almost half of them have also engaged in self-mutilating behaviors and about 20% have made actual suicide attempts after the sexual assault. Other local studies also document that women who have been sexually victimized or harassed in schools, at work, or in the community typically use indirect and nonassertive coping strategies such as wishing the assault had not occurred, ignoring the incident, avoiding the perpetrator/ harasser, or leaving the situation/setting where the assault or harassment has taken place (Chan et al., 1999; Cheung & Ng, 2004; Tang, 2004, 2005a; Tang et al., 1996). About one-third of women also report lowering of self-esteem as well as feelings of depression, insecurity, and a lack of a sense of belongingness to the institution/organization subsequent to their sexual harassment victimization (Chan et al., 1999; Tang, 2007a; Tang et al., 1996). Victims of sexual harassment also receive less sympathy than victims of other violent behaviors from the general public (Tang 2007a) as well as from public service professionals such as police officers, social workers, and medical officers (Tang, Pun, et al., 2002).

Married women in Hong Kong who had a history of physical or non-physical violence perpetrated by their husbands frequently report high levels of somatic problems, insomnia, depressive moods, or suicidal thoughts (Tang, 1997, 1998). Those who had experienced partner abuse during pregnancy also show symptoms of postnatal depression after delivery (Leung et al., 2002). Consistent with available literature on family violence, children are often intended as well as unintended victims of parental violence. Children witnessing parental violence tend to manifest both internalized and externalized behavioral problems (Chan, 2002; Tang, 1997). Contrary to the common belief that abused wives also batter their children, men who use physically violent acts against their wives are more likely to use physically punitive means to discipline their children (Tang, 1997). Furthermore, many Chinese women still consider that they should be sexually available to their husbands, and see this as an intrinsic part of the role of being a "good" wife, even though this may conflict with their own sexual desires and the need to protect themselves from sexually transmitted disease or AIDS/HIV infection (Choi & Ting, this volunme, Tang et al., 2001). Fear of men's violence also prevents many Chinese women from engaging in safer sex practices, from getting diagnostic tests, and from seeking treatment for the infection. In a large community sample of married women in Hong Kong, 34% of participants never used condoms in the past six months (Tang et al., 2001). Among these surveyed women, 15% felt that satisfying their husbands' sexual needs was more important than adopting safer sex practices, about 7% said their husband insisted condomless sexual intercourse, and 1.5% were afraid their husband might become violent if the latter was asked to wear condom. Indeed, researchers and policy-makers have repeatedly cited that rigid gender norms, widespread of GBV, and fear of men's violence are instrumental in the "feminization" of the AIDS/HIV epidemic (Garcia-Moreno & Watts, 2000; UNPFA, 2005; WHO, 2004b).

Local information on consequences of child sexual abuse can be gleaned from adult survivors' recall of their childhood sexual victimization experiences (Tang, Yan, & Pun, 2004; Tsun, 1999) and from child protection workers' report on sexually victimized children (Rhind et al., 1999). Victimized children manifest many emotional and behavioral symptoms of traumatic sexuality, regardless of their age at which the sexual violence had occurred; and these symptoms frequently persist despite the sexual assault had stopped. Sexually victimized children typically feel shameful, guilty, confused, and powerless. When perpetrators are their fathers or family members, they feel betrayed and yet sometimes find themselves emotionally dependent on them. They become anxious and scared if perpetrators use threat to initiate sexual activities and to prevent the disclosure of their sexual liaison. They are also angry with themselves and other adults in failing to stop the sexual assault. In a case of older brother-younger sister incest (Tsun, 1999), the surviving woman still experienced intense emotional reactions even after the sexual abuse had stopped for almost ten years, and her childhood sexual trauma also negatively affected her current relationship with men. Only 50-60% of child victims tell adults about their victimization experiences, and disclosure is much later in intra-familial than in extra-familial cases (Ho & Mak, 1992; Rhind et al., 1999; Tang, 2002; Tang et al., 2004; Tsun, 1999). Adults, especially mothers, tend to react negatively to the disclosure (Rhind et al., 1999; Tang et al., 2004; Tsun, 1999). They typically refuse to accept sexual abuse had occurred, accuse their daughters of telling lies, and avoid further discussion of the issue. In most cases, disclosure is not followed up or referred to medical doctors, social workers, or police officers.

Given its pervasive and detrimental outcomes, it is not surprising that GBV has become a major health, economic, and development burden for many countries (Yodanis, Godenzi, & Stanko, 2000). In Hong Kong, the extent of the GBV burden may be estimated from its prevalence, reactions of victims and the community, as well as resources necessary to prevent and curb the problem. For example, victimized women's healthy days of life will be shortened by adverse physical, mental, and sexual health impacts of GBV. Children are also adversely affected in incidents of IPV, and if these incidents occur during pregnancy, there will also be detrimental fetal/infant outcomes. All these not only bring about a substantial burden on local health care systems, social costs to the whole community will also be enormous as the development of a significant proportion of women and their children is being compromised. GBV also brings increased costs to legal and criminal justice systems including enforcement and correctional personnel, courts, and detention homes or prisons; to social services including welfare assistance, housing, shelters, child care and protection facilities, and victim/perpetrator treatment and rehabilitation programs; and to organizations through absenteeism, staff turnover, and low productivity. In a community where many traditional patriarchal attitudes and GBV-related myths still persist, substantial financial resources will need to be allocated to launch vigorous and large-scale public education programs on GBV as well as to devise and implement prevention plans to curtail its occurrences. All these point to the heavy costs and immense burden that GBV will bring to Hong Kong.

Current Strategies in Preventing and Eliminating GBV

International attention to GBV only began in the 1980's, despite its detrimental consequences and high prevalence across women's life span. Consequent to international initiatives in the last two decades, there are increasing educational, legislative, administrative, and judicial efforts in addressing GBV by civil society bodies, non-government organizations, and government units at both local and national levels. The WHO (2002a), in reviewing programs around the world aiming at curbing and responding to violence, identifies several important gaps and shortcomings which are of particular relevance to current GBV prevention and intervention efforts. First, very few programs have been rigorously evaluated for their effectiveness. Second, there are insufficient programs aiming at primary prevention, measures to stop violence before it happens, compared with secondary or tertiary prevention such as victim aftercare and rehabilitation programs. Third, there is an imbalance in the focus of programs, with community and societal strategies being under-emphasized as compared with programs addressing individual and relationship factors. Fourth, most violence prevention and intervention programs are devised and tested in developed countries. Thus, there is a pressing need to develop or adapt, implement, and evaluate more prevention and intervention programs in developing countries.

In Hong Kong, GBV was first brought to the public attention by concerted efforts of local community organizations, feminist activist groups, and gender scholars in the 1970's. The War-on-Rape Campaign in 1977 was one of the first attempts to put GBV on the public agenda. As a result of these attempts, there has been increased public awareness toward rape as well as GBV in general. Shortly after, a crisis hotline for rape victims, a shelter for abused wives, and a women's center for promoting women's development in general were established in the 1980's. Similar campaigns such as Campaign Against Sexual Violence in 1990 and Campaign on Violence Against Women in 1997 were also launched in subsequent years, along with diversification of services and upsurge of advocacy groups to address specific forms of GBV. Both local and international feminist groups and scholars have long argued that the most effective way to tackle GBV is not by changing the way women behave, but by challenging gender ideologies and dispelling victim-blaming myths (Cheung, 1987; Gilbert, 2002; Ng & Wong, 2002; Tang, Wong et al., 2002). Furthermore, they argue that merely providing remedial services to victims and enforcing punishment to perpetrators is not enough to eliminate GBV, underlying structures of the society should be reviewed and reformed to eliminate inherent differential power distribution between men and women (Brownmiller, 1975; Dobash & Dobash, 1992; Yodanis, 2004). Thus, strategies to combat GBV must be multi-dimensional and include public education, service provision, advocacy and social actions, legal reforms, and research. In Hong Kong, past and current strategies in addressing GBV have basically followed this multi-dimensional approach.

The majority of local GBV prevention programs and campaigns have a public education component that aims to educate the public and related personnel about the prevalence, etiology and adverse consequences, prevention behaviors, as well as early detection, recognition, and identification of the problem. As most GBV occurs in private and with immense social stigma attached to victims, public education programs are essential to let the public become more supportive of causes and be able to utilize resources more effectively. These programs typically incorporate components on the promotion of gender equality ideologies, enhancement of public awareness of GBV occurrence, clarification of associated myths, and destigmatization of victims. In addition, information about psychological and social consequences faced by victims, positive and negative public attitudes, and resources for victims are also disseminated. Target audiences include the general public, at risks populations, systems that relate to at risks populations, professionals who may be called upon to provide crisis intervention or remedial services, and policy makers.

There is a dearth of information on participation rates and effectiveness of local GBV prevention or public education programs. Recently, Tang & Yan (2004) interviewed 1,600 adults and found that close to 60% demonstrated minimal interest and only 24% indicated definite intention to participate in community prevention programs for child sexual abuse. Student participation in school-based GBV prevention programs is also low. Among surveyed high school students, only 30–37% had attended sexual abuse prevention programs in past school years (Tang, 2004). While 1/3 of surveyed students were aware that their university had held workshops/seminars on sexual harassment, only 4% had actually attended these workshops (Tang, 2007a). However, program evaluation studies have demonstrated that when teenage/adolescent girls did attend public education programs on sexual abuse, they were able to enhance their sexual abuse knowledge and self-protection skills; and these gains were still maintained at three months (Lee & Tang, 1998) and up to eighteen months after participation in these programs (Tang, 2007b). Social workers, nurses, teachers, and police officers, after attending training programs on the understanding and management of GBV, also reported more supportive attitudes toward victims of rape/sexual violence (Cheung & Ng, 2004; Lee & Cheung, 1991) and child sexual abuse (Cheung, 1997).

Local services for GBV typically focus on victims of rape and sexual violence, IPV, and child sexual abuse. They have since inception remained outside of mainstream health/social service provision and planning. Many services are operated as pilot projects with time-limited funding either supported or subsidized by the government; some are branch services from other primary services such as family planning, family services, and youth programs; and a handful is funded by local or overseas charitable organization. Despite inadequate funding and staffing, the nature of these services has in recent years evolved from palliative relief, to rehabilitation, and to prevention of future victimization. Nowadays, services for GBV often include crisis intervention, victim aftercare, and re-training and re-empowerment of survivors. These services have also been extended to perpetrators and social network of victims, as in perpetrator intervention programs, victim support groups, and support groups for caregivers of sexually victimized children. These services are also important sources of information on the number and profile of service recipients. Recently, there are two evaluation studies on local GBV services and both showed very promising results. In a study on the efficacy of group treatment for a small sample of wife batterers, Chan (2003) found that wife batterers, after participating in the group treatment, reported lower levels of physical and psychological aggression when they were assessed shortly after treatment; and about 78% also claimed to have stopped using violence against their wives when they were re-assessed several months after group treatment. In another study on 132 survivors of sexual violence, Cheung and Ng (2004) found that compared to pre-intervention assessment, surveyed women reported less psychological distress and adopted more constructive coping methods after receiving a one-stop crisis intervention service.

Telephone hotline services are present in most services for GBV. Despite being an important gateway to information and crisis intervention, most hotline services are staffed by paraprofessionals of minimal training, with voluntary professionals functioning as trainers and consultants. Major functions of these hotline services are to provide support; give pertinent information on legal, medical, and relevant aspects of GBV incidents; and make appropriate referral to professionals for aftercare services. In addition to these crisis intervention services, victims of GBV can also seek assistance directly from the police for protection and emergency units of hospitals for medical services. Temporary shelters are available for victims, especially victims of IPV and child sexual abuse. There is also a recent proposal for similar shelters or "cooling off places" for perpetrators, especially for wife batterers. Victim aftercare or survivor services are available for various forms of GBV. They are also major sources of information regarding the number of victims seeking assistance, demographic characteristics of victims and perpetrators, situations surrounding GBV incidents, and needs and concerns of victims. Almost all aftercare services also have hotline or crisis intervention services and are mainly staffed by social workers. Depending on target recipients and types of GBV, service organizations often need to maintain close liaison with other agencies, police departments, and child protection services for referral and subsequent intervention.

However, the lack of coordination among various service units has sometimes resulted in frontline personnel being unable to respond in time and tragedies may occur as in the recent incident in Tin Shui Wai. In this family tragedy which happened in April of 2004, a married woman who had sought assistance from family centers, child protection units, a temporary shelter for abused wives, and police departments prior to the tragedy was killed by her violent husband. Her two young children were also killed in this incident and her husband died weeks later. In fact, service providers and recipients have criticized the fragmentation and lack of coordination of local GBV services for a number of years. Parallel to the development of other countries, there is an emerging trend to consolidate GBV-related services to "one-stop centers" to ensure incidents of GBV receive prompt attention and intervention, and victims need not be re-traumatized with repeated telling of their victimization experiences. The first of such one-stop centers in Hong Kong was started in 2000. In addition to hotline services, this center for sexual violence also provides crisis intervention, victim aftercare or survivor services, legal advocacy, and assistance (escorting if necessary) in reporting to the police, in receiving medical examination and treatment, and in collecting forensic evidences. Clients of this one-stop center are generally satisfied with its services and most of them would recommend them to other people in need (Cheung & Ng, 2004).

Similar to other industrialized countries, advocacy for GBV victims in Hong Kong also functions outside of mainstream social and criminal justice systems. It represents joint efforts of feminist activist and women concerned groups, and typically operates on both individual and institutional levels (Pence & Shepard, 1999). At the individual level, advocates help previously victimized women understand their options and negotiate with the legal system, and then later extend to include helping victims access to important resources such as housing, financial assistance, education, and employment. Institutional advocacy entails working to change institutional practices or policies that work against needs of GBV victims and includes such activities as lobbying, working with criminal justice agencies at a local level, and networking with international groups with specific roles and mandates to eliminate GBV. Both individual- and institutional-level advocacy is linked to the idea of re-empowering GBV victims in the society so that they are more equipped with various life skills. Typical local re-empowerment programs include self-help or support groups in which survivors share with and learn from each other their unique life experiences; vocational, assertive, or personal growth training; and community participation in which survivors are encouraged to participate in various activities so that they will become more involved with their community and develop a sense of control for themselves.

In Hong Kong, civil and legal protection of women against GBV relies on both local legislations and international instruments, namely the CEDAW, the International Covenant on Civil and Political Rights, and the Convention Against Torture and Other Cruel, Inhuman or Degrading Treatment or Punishment (Petersen, in this volume). The adoption of these international instruments in Hong Kong necessitates the enactment of new local legislations, such as the Sex Discrimination Ordinance in 1995 and the Family Status Discrimination in 1999, and the establishment of two statutory bodies, namely the Equal Opportunities Commission in 1996 and the Women's Commission in 2001. The latter statutory body, the Women's Commission, is specifically set up to develop a long-term vision and strategies for the advancement of women and to address women's needs and concerns. However, as gleaned from past activities of the Commission, GBV remains a "hidden" or "invisible" agenda in its major public education, research, and networking efforts. Even with its public statement issued shortly after the Tin Shui Wai family tragedy in 2004 and subsequent report on local women's safety in 2006, the Women's Commission fell short of directing public attention to GBV in general but merely focused on violence within the family context (Women's Commission, 2006).

Despite government inertia, local feminists, gender scholars, and women concerned groups have continuously urged for better protection of women against GBV. They have proposed reviewing of existing law and legal procedures to remove discrimination against GBV victims and women in general; to eliminate cumbersome and humiliating procedures in the reporting, investigation, and court hearings of GBV; to provide protection; and to extend eligibility for compensation for GBV victims. With their relentless efforts, specific legal reforms have been made to protect rights of rape and child sexual abuse victims. These reforms provide that rape victims' previous sexual history may not be adduced in evidence at the trial for rape offence, and publications of particulars about the rape and child sexual victims which will reveal their identifies are restricted. Measures have also been taken to reduce victim humiliation, embarrassment, and trauma related to various court procedures. For example, court provisions are made for rape victims' testimony to be heard in camera and video-recording of the testimony of child sexual abuse victims are admissible in courts. Legal steps to protect victims of intimate partner abuse are available in the form of injunction and arrest with which courts can order the abusive partner to stop harassing and hurting the women. There are also changes to legislation to criminalize marital rape and to abolish the corroboration rules in sexual offenses cases.

Subsequent to the family tragedy in Tin Shiu Wai in 2004, an ad hoc government-appointed 3-person panel was set up to review and make recommendations on the provision and service delivery process of family services in the concerned district. In essence, members of this panel recommend that there should be better coordination among various government departments and non-government organizations in welfare planning and service delivery; greater service enhancement and improvement by strengthening professional training on management and outcome research on family and child protection services; and building of community networks to support families (Review Panel on Family Services in Tin Shui Wai, 2004). In addition to these recommendations, there are also demands from concerned groups and the Women's Commission for a review of the two-decade old Domestic Violence Ordinance on the definition of domestic violence and duration of injunction orders (Women's Commission, 2006). There are also proposals to introduce mandatory treatment or counseling for perpetrators of IPV, to legislate against stalking behavior in the context of domestic violence, and to enforce a pro-arrest policy of wife batterers.

Other than the above specific legal reforms, women and feminist activist groups are also actively addressing broader issues related to GBV by enhancing roles and status of women in the society and eliminating various inherent discrimination against women. Their efforts include fighting for women's equal land inheritance rights in the New Territories; attending to the employment difficulties of middle-aged women; eliminating violence in the family; ensuring equal assess to education and women-centered health care facilities; denouncing the promotion of gender stereotypes in education, mass media, and the society; ensuring politicians and policy makers put women's issues and eradication of GBV on their agenda by submitting comments to government consultation papers and producing alternate reports on related issues; and networking with international bodies that have specific mandates to combat GBV.

Directions for Gender Mainstreaming GBV

With its wide-ranging adverse consequences and the complex interplay of associated factors, the prevention and elimination of GBV requires a comprehensive agenda to guide directions for research, action, and policy decisions. The WHO (2002a, 2004a) has recently reaffirmed the public health approach to the prevention and intervention of interpersonal violence. In applying this approach to tackle GBV, the first step is to define its magnitude, scope, characteristics, and consequences through the systematic collection of information. The second step is to identify risk and protective factors that increase or decrease occurrences of GBV. The third step is to determine salient components of prevention and intervention programs, and the final step is to implement these programs in a variety of settings with continuous evaluation of their impact and cost-effectiveness. The United Nations also advocates a gender mainstreaming approach to combat GBV (UNFPA, 2005), and this involves integrating both men's and women's needs and experiences into the design, implementation, monitoring, and evaluation of programs and policies.

The public health and gender mainstreaming approaches to GBV provide directions for current and future related prevention and intervention efforts in Hong Kong. Among the top priority is the collection as well as gender analysis of reliable data on prevalence and pattern of victimization to determine the magnitude and scope of GBV in Hong Kong. While there are increasing calls for using unified measurement tools and protocols to obtain more reliable and comparable estimates of GBV across countries (Kilpatrick, 2004; Saltzman, 2004; WHO, 2002b), cultural and societal variations of GBV cannot be disregarded. In fact, the WHO in its multi-country study on women's health and IPV has also recommended the inclusion of relevant country specific information to reflect local circumstances (WHO, 2002b). Thus, assessment of estimates and patterns of GBV in Hong Kong should attend to both international and locally relevant aspects of the phenomenon. Furthermore, the gender mainstreaming approach entails that women's experiences should be taken priority in determining the scope and impact of GBV, which should be examined in its entirety and across the life span of women. The identification of factors that help to facilitate GBV and support its perpetuation can be guided by the ecological model (WHO, 2002a), which emphasizes the interaction of factors at individual, relationship (family), community, and societal levels.

Given the pervasive nature of GBV, its immediate as well as long term impacts on women in Hong Kong should also be examined to delineate salient components for local victim services and prevention programs. Systematic evaluation of effectiveness of these programs is greatly needed to convince recipients, providers, and policy makers of their value. When designing, implementing, and evaluating GBV programs, special caution should be paid to recent development and controversies in Western countries. For example, post-traumatic stress disorder (PTSD) has in past years received a disproportionate amount of attention relative to other possible outcomes of GBV and various treatment programs have also designed along this focus. More recently, there are increasing arguments that the traditional PTSD framework based on male war veterans is ill fitting for victimized women in the context of serial and escalating forms of GBV, such as stalking and IPV (Brown, 1995; Burstow, 2003; Mechanic, 2004). The construct of PTSD underscores that traumatized individuals who are no longer in danger respond as though the danger still persists. However, for women experiencing IPV and stalking, harassment and continued threats are often perpetrated even after they have exited abusive relationships. Thus, traditional PTSD treatment guidelines that aim to reduce excessive levels of fear and their corresponding hyper-arousal symptoms are clearly contraindicated for women facing potential harm from their current or former abusive intimate partners (Foa, Keane, & Friedman, 2000). Also, intervention models that emphasize individual control may reinforce social blaming that GBV is something with which an individual woman can exercise control, whether through behavior, demeanor, dress, cooking, housekeeping, sexual performance, or fertility. It is important that prevention and intervention programs should be gender-sensitive and highlight GBV as a serious social, health, legal, and human rights problem requiring efforts and changes at individual, interpersonal, family, community, and government levels.

Criminal justice and legal systems as well as advocacy programs in Hong Kong have typically focused on adversarial procedures and retributive punishment for GBV, such as creating new categories of GBV, increasing sentence length, introducing public shaming, and advocating pro-arrests policy. More recently, gender legal theorists in Western countries have suggested that restorative justice should operate alongside with retributive justice in incidents of GBV (Koss, 2000). They propose that more emphasis should be given to restorative justice responses by advocating civil proceedings, victim-offender reparation through mediation, and communitarian approaches. The latter approaches forgo adversarial court procedures and punishment to have family, peers, and advocates design perpetrator rehabilitation, victim restoration, and social reintegration of both victims and perpetrators. Preliminary evaluations of communitarian approaches to GBV show that there are increases in victim satisfaction as well as in social control and support resources (Koss, 2000).

As early as in 1993, the United Nations has called for the development of local, regional, and international community networks in addressing GBV. The Pan American Health Organization (PAHO, 2003), a regional office of the WHO, has devised an integrated model to coordinate and build community networks in the provision of care and support services for GBV and in the promotion of a non-violent community. In this model, each community network plans, implements, and monitors (1) initial detection of GBV survivors and training of providers to screen women during routine health care or social service visits, (2) assessment of the prevalence of GBV and identification of organizations and people that help women, (3) mobilizing community organizations and leaders to form support and service networks, (4) meeting with regional and international networks to plan, implement, and monitor activities that address GBV, and (5) replications of community networks at the regional and national levels. Recently, the WHO (Garcia-Moreno et al., 2005) also reaffirms that the prevention of the commonest form of GBV, intimate partner abuse, requires a combination of social policy, specialized programs, and coordinated community and legal efforts.

Locally, the Women's Commission, as a central statutory body in addressing needs and concerns of women, is in a position to assume a leading and active role in coordinating and building community networks that aim to eradicate GBV in Hong Kong. In a recent report on local women's safety, the Commission has adopted a coordinated community intervention approach in tackling problems related to domestic violence (Women's Commission, 2006). In line with recommendations of the PAHO (2003) and WHO (Garcia-Moreno et al., 2005), the Commission recognizes its mandate to act as a central mechanism in setting up strategic partnership with local stakeholders at all levels in combating domestic violence. These stakeholders include survivor groups, women's groups, government departments, service providers, and gender scholars. It also recommends initiatives to utilize local community resources for training and developing volunteers, to strengthen district networking with government departments, to set up an integrated long term monitoring and evaluation mechanism based on international best practice models, and to facilitate community awareness of gender equality and participation in relevant prevention programs. It also recommends the Government apply a gender mainstreaming approach to all aspects of its work on domestic violence. While the Commission has cogently mapped the direction for ensuring women's safety at home, many of the recommended strategies can in fact be extended to address GBV in general. There is also a need to have further discussions regarding ways to build regional and international networks to plan, implement, and monitor activities that aim to eliminate domestic violence or GBV. Furthermore, local government should also support various recommendations of concerned groups and the Women's Commission by providing adequate funding to related programs and services, by adopting relevant policies, and by ensuring legal frameworks are in compliance with international instruments.

Conclusion

Similar to other countries, GBV happens in many forms and to women of all ages in Hong Kong. It enforces women's subordination, endangers their health, prevents them from exercising their basic rights, and constrains their development. Given GBV is rooted in inherent gender inequality and associated cultural myths, a strong and continued commitment to gender mainstreaming is of vital importance to effectively prevent and eliminate its occurrences. This involves including gender perspectives and ensuring gender equality in local policy development, research, advocacy, legislation, resource allocation as well as planning, implementation, and monitoring of programs and projects. GBV should be understood in light of women's life span, and prevention and combat strategies should tackle this problem in its entirety and complexity. Programs and policies addressing GBV should be "women-centered" so that women's experiences are taken priority. In addition to mobilizing the local community to eradicate GBV, participation in international discussions and actions will also facilitate sharing of information and building of global networks to fight against GBV.

References

Allison, J., & Wrightsman, L. (1993). *Rape: The misunderstood crime.* Newbury Park, CA: Sage.

Astbury, J. (2003). Whose honor, whose shame? Gender-based violence, rights and health. In L. Manderson & L. Bennett (Eds.), *Violence against women in Asian Societies* (pp. 159–171). New York: John Wiley.

Berns, N. (2001). Degendering the problem and gendering the blame: Political discourse on women and violence. *Gender & Society, 15,* 262–281.

Bogard, M. (1988). Feminist perspective on wife abuse: An introduction. In K. Yllo & M. Bogard (Eds.), *Feminist perspectives on wife abuse* (pp. 11–26). Beverly Hills, CA: Sage.

Bohan, J. (1997). Regarding gender: Essentialism, constructionism, and feminist psychology. In S. Davis & M. Gergen (Eds.), *Toward a new psychology of gender* (pp. 31–48). New York: Routledge.

Briere, J., & Jordan, C. (2004). Violence against women: Outcome complexity and implications for assessment and treatment. *Journal of Interpersonal Violence, 19,* 1252–1276.

Brown, L. (1995). Not outside the range. In C. Caruth (Ed.), *Trauma: Explorations in memory* (pp. 100–112). Baltimore: Johns Hopkins University Press.

Brownmiller, S. (1975). *Against our will: Men, women, and rape.* New York: Simon & Schuster.

Burstow, B. (2003). Toward a radical understanding of trauma and trauma work. *Violence Against Women, 9,* 1293–1317.

Burt, M. R. (1980). Cultural myths and supports for rape. *Journal of Personality and Social Psychology, 38,* 217–230.

Campbell, J. (2002). Health consequences of intimate partner violence. *Lancet, 359,* 1331–1336.

Caritas Family Service. (1996). *Study on childhood sexual experiences.* Hong Kong: Author.

Chan, K. L. (2002). *Study of children who witnessed family violence.* Hong Kong: Department of Social Work & Social Administration, The University of Hong Kong.

Chan, K. L. (2003). Group therapy for male batterers: A Chinese experience. *Social Work With Groups, 26,* 79–90.

Chan, K. L. (2004). Correlates of wife assault in Hong Kong Chinese families. *Violence & Victims, 19,* 189–201.

Chan, D., Tang, C., & Chan, W. (1999). Sexual harassment: A preliminary analysis of its effects on Hong Kong Chinese women in the workplace and academia. *Psychology of Women Quarterly, 23,* 661–672.

Cheung, F. (1987). Changing attitudes: The war-on-rape campaign. *Bulletin of the Hong Kong Psychological Society, 19/20,* 41–48.

Cheung, F., & Ng, W. C. (2004). *Rainlily build-in study report.* Hong Kong: The Chinese University of Hong Kong and The Association Concerning Sexual Violence Against Women.

Cheung, M. (1997). Developing the interview protocol for video-recorded child sexual abuse investigations: A training experience with police officers, social workers, and clinical psychologists in Hong Kong. *Child Abuse & Neglect, 21,* 273–284.

Chiu, S., & Ng, W. C. (2001). *Report on sexual violence among secondary school students in Hong Kong.* Hong Kong: The Association Concerning Sexual Violence of Women.

Chou, Y. C. (1995). *Marital violence.* Taiwan, Taipei: Gu-Lyu.

Chow, E., Zhang, N., & Wang, J. (2004). Promising and contested fields: Women's studies and sociology of women/gender in contemporary China. *Gender & Society, 18,* 161–188.

Coleman, D., & Straus, M. (1986). Marital power, conflict, and violence in a nationally representative sample of American couples. *Violence & Victims, 1,* 141–157.

Croll, E. (1995). *Changing identities of Chinese women.* Hong Kong: Hong Kong University Press.

Dekeseredy, W. (2000). Current controversies on defining nonlethal violence against women in intimate heterosexual relationships. *Violence Against Women, 6,* 728–746.

DeSouza, E., & Solberg, J. (2003). Incident and dimensions of sexual harassment. In M. Paludi & C. Paludi (Eds.), *Academic and workplace sexual harassment: A handbook of cultural, social science, management, and legal perspectives* (pp. 3–30). London: Praeger.

Dobash, R., & Dobash, R. (1992). *Women, violence, and social change.* New York: Routledge.

Dolecheck, M. M. (1984). Sexual harassment of women in the workplace — a Hush-Hush topic in Hong Kong. *Hong Kong Manager, 20,* 23–27.

Equal Opportunities Commission. (1997). *A baseline survey of equal opportunities on the basis on gender in Hong Kong.* Hong Kong: Author.

Equal Opportunities Commission. (1999). *Research on family status discrimination.* Hong Kong: Author.

Equal Opportunities Commission. (2000). *Baseline survey of students' attitudes toward gender stereotypes and family roles.* Hong Kong: Author.

Finkelhor, D. (1994). The international epidemiology of child sexual abuse. *Child Abuse & Neglect, 18,* 409–417.

Foa, E., Keane, T., & Friedman, M. (2000). *Effective treatments for PTSD: Practice guidelines from the International Society for Traumatic Stress Studies.* New York: Guilford.

Garcio-Moreno, C. et al. (Eds.). (2005). *WHO multi-country study on women's health and domestic violence against women: Initial results on prevalence, health outcomes and women's response.* Geneva: World Health Organization.

Garcia-Moreno, C., & Watts, C. (2000). Violence against women: Its importance for HIV/AIDS. *AIDS, 14,* S253–265.

Gelles, R. (1993). Through a sociological lens: Social structure and family violence. In R. Gelles & D. Loseke (Eds.), *Current controversies on family violence* (pp. 31–46). London: Sage.

Gilbert, P. (2002). Discourse of female violence and societal gender stereotypes. *Violence Against Women, 8,* 1271–1300.

Gruber, J. (2003). Sexual harassment in the public sector. In M. Paludi & C. Paludi (Eds.), *Academic and workplace sexual harassment: A handbook of cultural, social science, management, and legal perspectives* (pp. 3–30). London: Praeger.

Hanmer, J., & Saunders, S. (1993). *Women, violence, and crime prevention: A West Yorkshire study.* Aldershot: Avebury.

Heise, L., Ellsberg, M., & Gottemoeller, M. (1999). *Ending violence against women: Population reports, No. 27.* Baltimore: Johns Hopkins University.

Heise, L., Pitanguy, J., & Germain, A. (1994). *Violence against women: The hidden health burden.* Washington, DC: Worldbank Discussion Papers, No. 255.

Ho, T., & Mak, F. (1992). Sexual abuse in Chinese children in Hong Kong: A review of 134 cases. *Australian and New Zealand Journal of Psychiatry, 26,* 639–643.

Jaschok, M. (2003). Violation and resistance: Women, region, and Chinese statehood. *Violence Against Women, 9,* 655–675.

Kilpatrick, D. (2004). What is violence against women? Defining and measuring the problem. *Journal of Interpersonal Violence, 19,* 1209–1234.

Kimmel, M. (2002). "Gender symmetry" in domestic violence: A substantive and methodological research review. *Violence Against Women, 8,* 1332–1363.

Koss, M. (2000). Blame, shame, and community: Justice responses to violence against women. *American Psychologist, 55,* 1332–1343.

Koss, M., Goodman, L., & Browne, A. (1994). *No safe haven: Male violence against women at home, at work, and in the community.* Washington, DC: American Psychological Association.

Koss, M., Heise, L., & Russo, N. (1994). The global health burden of rape. *Psychology of Women Quarterly, 18,* 509–537.

Lee, Y., & Tang, C. (1998). An evaluation of a sexual abuse prevention program for female Chinese adolescents with mental retardation. *American Journal on Mental Retardation, 103,* 105–116.

Lee, H.C., & Cheung, F. (1991). The attitude towards rape victim scale: Reliability and validity in a Chinese context. *Sex Roles, 24,* 599–603.

Leung, W., Kung, F., Lam, J., Leung, T., & Ho, P. (2002). Domestic violence and postnatal depression in a Chinese community. *International Journal of Gynecology & Obstetrics, 79,* 159–166.

Leung, W., Leung, T., Lam, Y., & Ho, P. (1998). The prevalence of domestic violence against pregnant women in a Chinese community. *International Journal of Gynaecology & Obstetrics, 66,* 23–30.

Luo, T. (2000). "Marrying my rapists?!" The cultural trauma among Chinese rape survivors. *Gender & Society, 14,* 582–597.

Mechanic, M. (2004). Beyond PTSD: Mental health consequences of violence against women: A response to Briere & Jordan. *Journal of Interpersonal Violence, 19,* 1283–1289.

Milwertz, C. (2003). Activism against domestic violence in the People's Republic of China. *Violence Against Women, 9,* 630–654.

Ng, I., & Wong, M. (2002). *Public opinion on rape and services for rape victims.* Hong Kong: The Hong Kong Polytechnic University and Association Concerning Sexual Violence Against Women.

Okamura, A., Heras, P., & Wong-Kerberg, L. (1995). Asian, Pacific Island, and Filipino Americans and sexual child abuse. In L. Fortes (Ed.), *Sexual abuse in nine North American cultures: Treatment and prevention* (pp. 67–96). Newbury Park, CA: Sage.

Pan American Health Organizations. (2003). *Violence against women: The health sector responds.* Washington, DC: Author.

Pence, E., & Shepard, M. (1999). An introduction: Developing a coordinated community response. In M. Shepard & E. Pence (Eds.), *Coordinating community responses to domestic violence: Lessons from Duluth and beyond* (pp. 3–23). Thousand Oaks, CA: Sage.

Pollard, (1992). Judgments about victims and attackers in depicted rape: A review. *British Journal of Social Psychology, 31,* 307–326.

Rantala, R. (2000). *Effects of NIBRS on crime statistics* (Special Report, NCJ178890). Washington, DC: U.S. Department of Justice.

Review Panel on Family Services in Tin Shiu Wai. (2004). *Report of review panel on family services in Tin Shiu Wai.* Hong Kong: Social Welfare Department.

Rhind, N., Leung, T., & Choi, F. (1999). Child sexual abuse in Hong Kong: Double victimization? *Child Abuse & Neglect, 23,* 511–517.

Saltzman, L. (2004). Definitional and methodological issues related to transnational research on intimate partner violence. *Violence Against Women, 10,* 1235–1243.

Saltzman, L., Fanslow, J., McMahon, P., & Shelley, G. (2002). *Intimate partner violence surveillance: Uniform definitions and recommended data elements* (Version 1.0). Atlanta, GA: Centers for Disease Control and Prevention.

Sanday, W. B. (1981). The socio-cultural context of rape: A cross-cultural study. *Journal of Social Issues, 37*, 5–27.

Stanko, E. (1995). Women, crime, and fear. *Annals of the American Academy of Political and Social Sciences, 539*, 46–58.

Straus, M. (1979). Measuring intrafamily conflict and violence: Conflicts Tactics (CT) Scales. *Journal of Marriage and Family, 41*, 75–88.

Straus, M. (1992). The Conflicts Tactics Scale and its critics: An evaluation and new data on validity and reliability. In M. A. Straus & R. Gelles (Eds.), *Physical violence in American families* (pp. 49–71). New Brunswick, NJ: Transaction Publishers.

Straus, M. (1994). State-to-state differences in social inequality and social bonds in relation to assaults on wives in the United States. *Journal of Comparative Family Studies, 25*, 7–24.

Straus, M., Hamby, S., Boney-McCoy, S., & Sugarman, D. (1996). The revised Conflict Tactics Scales (CTS 2). *Journal of Family Issues, 17*, 283–316.

Tam, S., & Tang, C. (2005). Comparing wife abuse perceptions between Chinese police officers and social workers. *Journal of Family Violence*, in press.

Tang, C. (1994). Prevalence of spouse aggression in Hong Kong. *Journal of Family Violence, 9*, 347–356.

Tang, C. (1997). Psychological impact of wife abuse: Experiences of Chinese women and their children. *Journal of Interpersonal Violence, 12*, 466–478.

Tang, C. (1998). Psychological abuse of Chinese wives. *Journal of Family Violence, 13*, 299–314.

Tang, C. (1999a). Marital power and aggression in a community sample of Hong Kong Chinese families. *Journal of Interpersonal Violence, 14*, 586–602.

Tang, C. (1999b). Wife abuse in Hong Kong Chinese families: A community survey. *Journal of Family Violence, 14*, 173–191.

Tang, C. (2002). Childhood experience of sexual abuse among Hong Kong Chinese college students. *Child Abuse & Neglect, 26*, 23–37.

Tang, C. (2003). Factors influencing responsibility attribution to wife abuse: A study of Chinese police officers. *Criminal Justice and Behavior, 30*, 584–601.

Tang, C. (2004). *A study on adolescent sexuality and peer sexual abuse in Hong Kong*. Hong Kong: The End Child Sexual Abuse Foundation.

Tang, C. (2007a). *Sexual harassment in tertiary institutions in Hong Kong: Revisited after 10 years*. Manuscript in submission.

Tang, C. (2007b). *Training for sexual abuse prevention with Chinese children in Hong Kong*. Hong Kong: The End Child Sexual Abuse Foundation.

Tang, C., & Cheung, F. (1997). Effects of gender and profession type on definitions of violence against women. *Sex Roles: A Journal of Research, 36*, 837–849.

Tang, C., Cheung, F., Chen, R., & Sun, X. (2002). Definition of violence against women: A comparative study in Chinese societies of Hong Kong, Taiwan, and the People's Republic of China. *Journal of Interpersonal Violence, 17,* 671–688.

Tang, C., Critelli, J., & Porter, J. (1995). Sexual aggression and victimization in dating relationships among Chinese college students. *Archives of Sexual Behavior, 24,* 47–53.

Tang, C., & Lee, Y. (1999). Knowledge on sexual abuse and self-protection skills: A study on female Chinese adolescents with mild mental retardation. *Child Abuse & Neglect, 23,* 269–279.

Tang, C., Pun, S., & Cheung, F. (2002). Responsibility attribution for violence against women: A study of Chinese public service professionals. *Psychology of Women Quarterly, 26,* 175–185.

Tang, C., Wong, D., & Cheung, F. (2002). Social construction of women as legitimate victims of violence in Chinese societies. *Violence Against Women, 8,* 968–996.

Tang, C., Wong, D., Cheung, F., & Lee, A. (2000). Exploring how Chinese define violence against women: A focus group study in Hong Kong. *Women's Studies International Forum, 23,* 197–209.

Tang, C., Wong, C., & Lee, A. (2001). Gender-related psychosocial and cultural factors associated with condom use among Chinese married women. *AIDS Education and Prevention, 13,* 329–342.

Tang, C., & Yan, E. (2004). Intention to participate in child sexual abuse prevention programs: A study of Chinese adults in Hong Kong. *Child Abuse & Neglect, 28,* 1187–1197.

Tang, C., Yan, E., & Pun, S. (2004). *A retrospective study on child sexual abuse in Hong Kong.* Hong Kong: The End Child Sexual Abuse Foundation.

Tang, C., Yik, M., Cheung, F., Choi, P., & Au, K. (1995). How do Chinese college students define sexual harassment? *Journal of Interpersonal Violence, 10,* 503–515.

Tang, C., Yik, M., Cheung, F., Choi, P., & Au, K. (1996). Sexual harassment of Chinese college students. *Archives of Sexual Behavior, 25,* 201–215.

Tjaden, P. (2004). What is violence against women? Defining and measuring the problem: A response to Dean Kilpatrick. *Journal of Interpersonal Violence, 19,* 1244–1251.

Tsun, A. (1999). Sibling incest: A Hong Kong experience. *Child Abuse & Neglect, 23,* 71–79.

United Nations Population Fund (UNFPA) (2005). *State of world population 2005.* New York: United Nations.

Whatley, M. (1996). Victim characteristics influencing attributions of responsibility to rape victims: A meta-analysis. *Aggression and Violent Behavior, 1,* 81–95.

Women's Commission. (2001). *Thematic household surveys in the fourth quarter of 2001.* Hong Kong: Author.

Women's Commission. (2006). *Women's safety in Hong Kong: Eliminating domestic violence*. Hong Kong: Author.

Wong, T., Chung, M., Lau, C., Ng, P., Wong, W., & Ngan, J. (1998). Victims of domestic violence presenting to an accident and emergency department. *Hong Kong Practice, 20*, 107–112.

World Health Organization. (2000). *Eliminating sexual violence against women: Toward a global initiative*. Geneva: Author.

World Health Organization. (2002a). *World report on violence and health*. Geneva: Author.

World Health Organization. (2002b). *WHO multi-country study on women's health and domestic violence against women*. Geneva: Author.

World Health Organization. (2004a). *Preventing violence: A guide to implementing the recommendations of the world report on violence and health*. Geneva: Author.

World Health Organization. (2004b). *Women and girls need access to AIDS treatment and protection from violence*. Geneva: Author.

Xu, X., Campbell, J., & Zhu, F. (2001). Intimate partner violence against Chinese women: The past, present, and future. *Trauma, Violence, & Abuse, 2*, 296–315.

Yodanis, C. (2004). Gender inequality, violence against women, and fear: A cross-national test of the feminist theory of violence against women. *Journal of Interpersonal Violence, 19*, 655–675.

Yodanis, C., Godenzi, A., & Stanko, E. (2000). The benefits of studying costs: A review and agenda for studies on the economic costs of violence against women. *Policy Studies, 21*, 263–276.

CHAPTER 11

Our Bodies, Our Stories: Narrating Female Sexuality in Hong Kong

Angela Wai-ching Wong

During the Fifth East Asia Women's Forum held in Hong Kong in December 2005, questions were raised in a session on "Sexuality and Body" on the compatibility between "queer genders" and "mainstream" gender ideology. While "queer genders" was defined as an umbrella term inclusive of women of all kinds of sexual preferences, sexual practices, and sexual identities, the "mainstream" gender ideology is understood as referring to primarily activities and practices of monogamous heterosexuality. The question immediately highlighted the tension between the campaign for gender mainstreaming and the politics of the sexual minorities, between the division of demands for policy changes toward the improvement of women's status within existing social structure, such as that inside marriage, and the demands for female sexual freedom and autonomy, independent of marital status. These different demands are further translated into two completely different streams of discussions that lead to different approaches to the question of gender inequality. There are therefore, on the one hand, defenders of women's rights in the domestic spheres addressing issues such as domestic violence and sexual abuse; and on the other, defenders of sexual right in terms of women's autonomous decision as to when, how, and with whom they may like to enjoy sex.

Among the various points of tensions and division, the best possible point of convergence between gender mainstreaming and the concern for female sexuality is perhaps the defense of sexual right as human/women's right, that sexual freedom and autonomy is taken as part of the changes needed to achieve gender equality. UNESCO defines gender mainstreaming as a process aiming to achieve gender equality and a strategy for making both women and men's concerns an integral dimension of all political, economic and social policies. In this respect, the recognition of sexual rights as an aspect of international human rights is essential to the achievement of women's sexual and reproductive health—one of the primary conditions for gender equality.[1] Indeed, such a principle has been listed on many international human rights documents such as the statement of World Health Organization on sexual right:

> the right of all persons, free of coercion, discrimination and violence, to the highest attainable standard of health in relation to sexuality, including access to sexual and reproductive health care services; seek, receive and impart information in relation to sexuality; sexuality education; respect for bodily integrity; choice of partner; decide to be sexually active or not; consensual sexual relations; consensual marriage; decide whether or not, and when to have children; and pursue a satisfying, safe and pleasurable sexual life.[2]

A MADRE Position Paper on "Sexual Rights are Human Rights" has made the case even more explicit. It defends the significance of sexuality to identity and argues that it is inextricably tied to economic, social and political rights, so much so that "when one [kind of rights] is violated, the others are affected." In the paper, sexual rights are defined as the right to "exercise and express sexuality freely and safely; be protected from sexual violence and discrimination; be in charge of decisions about one's own body; have access to information and services necessary for sexual health; and experience sexual pleasure."[3] These rights are contended to have a firm basis in international law such as the Universal Declaration of Human Rights, the International Covenant on Civil and Political Rights, the International Covenant on Economic, Social and Cultural Rights,[4] and the Convention on the Elimination of All Forms of Discrimination Against Women; they all implicitly protect sexual rights by the provision of rights to personal freedom, health, equal opportunity, and to be free of discrimination and violence.[5] In effect, under the universal campaign to defend women's rights as human rights, women's sexual rights and hence female sexuality as something non-coercive, autonomous and pleasurable found its venue for open articulation with legitimacy for the first time.

Among the international efforts to defend women for their rights to the different aspects and practices of sexuality, issues of sexual exploitation in women have been given the most attention. What I aim to do in this chapter, however, is a narrative engagement of sexuality as experienced by women as agents, away from the conception of women as sexual victims, through oral reports written or narrated by women. Despite its extensive documentation in the respect of exploitation, female sexuality is insufficiently accounted for in the sense of its being an integral part of the life of every man and woman. In other words, female sexuality in this study will be taken seriously with regard to full human development which depends upon the satisfaction of basic human needs such as the desire for contact, intimacy, emotional expression, pleasure, tenderness and love.[6] The articulation of female sexuality in this study is hoped to provide a broadened platform for women to examine, express and enjoy their bodies in an open and inclusive manner, which, according to the international conventions, is a primary condition to women's health and the pursuit of gender equality.

I. Female Sexuality: From Critique to Narration

Not surprisingly, with the rise of feminist consciousness over the last century regarding women's long deprived human and sexual rights in the various traditions and cultures, studies about women's bodies (rather than directly female sexuality) in the twentieth century had largely been concerned with the question of exploitation. From the studies of the Victorian corset, to female circumcision in Africa and footbinding in China, studies have incessantly documented how female body had been monitored, controlled and brutally mutilated. In the movement of anti-pornography started by Catherine McKinnon and Andrea Dworkin in 1983 in the United States, pornography was equated to the exploitation of women's bodies by sexualizing "the subordination of women and which eroticizes violence against women." (Dworkin 1981, 266-267) A similar concern was raised by Lin Fangmei (林芳玫) in her detailed studies on the same subject in Taiwan. She concludes that pornographic materials in the media reinforce men's sexual fantasy of women's bodies and have reduced them into sexual objects for mass consumption. (1999) Unfortunately, such position leads, either consciously or unconsciously, to an assumed equivalence of the female body to male exploitation and eroticism to male sexual desire.[7] Consequently, women are left with no room in the world of eroticism or in the pursuit of sexual pleasure; that eroticism and sexuality are only "male things." In Luce Irigaray's words, a sexualized female is all "senseless, inappropriate, [and] indecent." (1985, 148)

　　If sexual desire is coded as male, then the question for women is if they are really ever sexual? Are women purely sexual victims, or can women be sexual actors at all? The debate on sexuality for women as liberating or oppressive, as domain of pleasure or exploitation, has been at the heart of feminist theorizing since the seventies. For radical feminists such as Adrienne Rich, Dworkin and MacKinnon, sexuality as institutionalized in heterosexual relations is the primary sphere of male power. Male control of female sexuality is perceived as the foundation of patriarchal power; women can only be oppressed and exploited in such a system. Thus MacKinnon warns, so long as there is sexual inequality, attempts to value sexuality as if women possess it, will only confine women to what they are defined as being. (1989, 153) In Rich's phrase, female antiphallic sexuality is only legendary, a form of "ineffectual rebellion" against male power. (1980, 652)

Such feminist stance has shifted gradually during the 1980s, from the insistence of "heterosexual pleasure as anti-woman" to the emphasis of individual choice and sexual pleasure in women. As Carole Vance argues in her chapter, "Pleasure and Danger: Toward a Politics of Sexuality" (1992), sexuality is too complex to be nailed down to either wholly pleasurable or dangerous. It is in fact an ambiguity that needs to be examined carefully; women should feel free to explore their experiences of sexual desire, fantasy, and action. Vance warns, unless women learn about their sexual histories, through daring to speak about them to each other, we could only continue to rely on "myths, prescriptive and over-generalized" about female sexuality. In her observation, questions such as sexual pleasure for women are still minimized and the exploration of women's pleasurable experience remains slight. Even among the feminists, sexuality is taken as trivial, diversionary, or not political. (6) She suggests that in order to release women from the captivity of sexual pleasure taboo, sexuality must be seen as not only a domain of restriction and repression but also one of exploration and agency.

In other words, feminism must be a movement that speaks to sexuality; its politics must not only resist deprivation but also support pleasure. Indeed, sexual pleasure should not be taken as interests of a small and privileged group; it is "a site of struggle — visceral, engaging, and riveting" in women's daily lives. Correspondingly feminism must insist that women's sexual experience is not a blank but women are subjects and agents of sexuality, and that sexual pleasure a fundamental right. (24) Sexual liberation, as Lynne Segal argues, is not about combat against the repression of female sexual essence; it is the struggle to recognize the pleasure of multiple sexualities. In other words, the emphasis on female sexuality and sexual pleasure is to engage a battle at the core of feminist politics on the questions of women's agency and right, and essentialism and multiplicities that takes women's pleasure as its anchoring point. In Segal's words, "Sexual pleasure is far too significant in our lives and culture for women not to be seeking to express our agency through it." (1994, 313–314)

The focus of female sexuality in terms of pleasure is therefore of both strategic and fundamental importance. He Chunrui (何春蕤), one of the most outspoken Chinese feminists on the subject of female sexuality, stresses that understanding female sexuality is the key to the advancement of feminism. In her *Forthright Women: Feminism and Sex Liberation*《豪爽女人：女性主義與性解放》(1994), she advocates for the eradication of all forms of sexual repression for women as the goal of feminism. Being the most powerful repressive discourses of all, "chastity" must be completely forsaken before women can be truly set free. Until women may enjoy fully the pleasure of their bodies instead of being trapped in dull, obligated monogamous sex shall they be transformed. (93–113)

Furthermore, the tie of female sexuality to lesbian and bisexual studies has proved to be an effective analytical tool to feminist studies in the recent years. Teresa de Lauretis is one of the first who identifies female eroticism as the base of women's subjectivity. The crux of the problem for her lies in the system of heterosexual family where female sexuality is suppressed and placed in the control of men. Joining Rich, she contends that lesbianism, which involves purely female eroticism, should be the foundation of a true liberating women's movement. She makes a forceful argument contending lesbianism as not only a form of women's liberation but also the most legitimate place to look for women's subjectivity; this is the only place where a woman is no longer bonded to a man. (de Lauretis 1994) In a similar vein, Monique Wittig upholds lesbian as a category beyond women and men. She contends that lesbians fundamentally challenge the sexual inequalities that have been continuously reinforced by heterosexuality. Being neither totalized unity nor two dichotomous oppositions, they represent for her the possibility for true human diversity. (1992) These sharp criticisms place female eroticism in square opposition to heterosexuality and powerfully subvert the legitimacy of the patriarchal family for women. It questions not only why women have not been encouraged to enjoying sex but also how women have been penalized for it in the social, economic and cultural spheres.

In Hong Kong, female sexuality is a much under-researched topic. Except for the few quantitative general surveys done by Family Planning

Association of Hong Kong (FPAHK),[8] the only more serious analysis of the subject is included in a review of studies of Chinese sex attitudes and the applicability of sex therapy by Ho Wai So and Fanny M. Cheung (2005). Whereas focused survey of female sexuality is yet to be conducted, more systematic interpretative accounts of female sexuality in Hong Kong is completely lacking. Some of the earliest accounts of female sexuality are found scattered in the few popular volumes advocating for the right of homosexuality. But even for two most outspoken advocates for homosexuality, Chou Wah-shan (周華山) and Chiu Man Chung (趙文宗), regrets were made with regard to the general negligence of female sexuality in the homosexual debate in Hong Kong before the 1990s. Such negligence further reinforces a fundamental bias against female sexuality that there can be no sex without men. That is, sex can only take place either between heterosexuals or gays; women are incapable of sexual pleasure if let alone. (Chou and Chiu 1995, 173) Before the debate of homosexuality, the only place for written accounts of female sexuality has been "mailbox columns" on women's magazines and popular newspapers,[9] often disguised as forms of informal sex education and counseling provided for their readers — both male and female. Only until recently, increased interests in female sexuality have been found in literature and films other than those made for pornographic purpose. These include a few documentaries as well as a number of publications that evolved around female sexual experiences.[10]

One of the first such independent documentaries is *Women's Private Parts* (2001) directed by Barbara Wong Chun-chun (黃真真), who interviewed sixty-three women for their "honest" telling of their sexual experiences including orgasm, masturbation, lesbianism, prostitution, marriage, and being mistresses. They include not only the various sexual activities that those women interviewees enjoyed but also their direct expression of sexual wants by hiring male sex workers. This film won the International Film Award in the New York International Independent Film and Video Festival in 2001. Another recent production is *Desire of Egg* 《卵子體慾》, produced by Wong Choi Fung (黃彩鳳). It is a highly exploratory project which video-taped the producer herself naked, as she "talks" to her to-be-aborted fetus, masturbates, and watches a pornographic VCD before the screen. Despite much controversy, the video won the Golden Award of Hong Kong Independent Film Contest of 2003 and was invited for screening in a Gender/Sex Film Festival of Taiwan in 2004.[11]

A stream of literature is produced by the end of the 1990s which includes first of all, the four volumes on female sexuality by Blacksoblack (素黑) which are presented as collection of reports from Su's counseling cases;[12] second, the two oral histories of elderly and young women produced by AAF which include accounts of sexuality as a part of their life; and third, oral reports of female sexuality in lesbians, bisexuals, and sex workers produced by the respective communities themselves. Though fragmented and mostly written in "autobiographical" and semi-biographical form, they provide the first public testimonies of female sexuality in Hong Kong. For the first time, female sexuality is presented outside of pornographic or stereotypical media representation, outside of women being represented as either an angel or a whore, of which neither goes beyond the parameter of sex for male consumption only.

This chapter attempts to outline the problematic of female sexuality and its representation in the recent publications of Hong Kong.[13] Due to its limited availability, except for the two oral histories produced by AAF, the bulk of the sexual stories seem to fall into the category of "unusual" sexuality — accounts of sexuality by lesbians, women bisexuals, and the female sex workers of Hong Kong. For some people, these, especially the last group, may not represent "normal" female sexuality. Their difference lies in some of the most complicated circumstances they are situated in and, most of all, that they are transgressors by the "good woman" standard.[14] Given the last reason, they have been allowed the most "freedom" to express their experience of sexuality outside of the familial/patriarchal control, and are suffering for it at the same time for lack of recognition and legitimacy in the society. Yet most interestingly, they try as much as possible to write as women of "normal" sexuality who desire to love and to be loved, who go through love, hate, anger, and desperation as much as all women, in the midst of the rapid change of Hong Kong society. As such, they are women who aim to convey to the public the experience of their sexual desires and sexual agency as both different and "normal." These testimonies stand out from others that they are consciously produced by women who take their bodily experiences seriously and openly.

For the purpose of this chapter therefore, female sexuality shall include sexual experiences as experienced and told by women. It shall denote any activity of sexual nature, including caress, kissing, and all forms of sexual intimacy performed by or with women. Although this chapter covers many stories of homosexuality, neither the debate nor the history of *Tongzhi* (同 志)[15] movement in Hong Kong is its focus. Rather, narration of bodies and sexualities by women are.

II. Narrating Female Sexuality

"Stories are necessary to weave a web of meaning within which we can live. We all live in story worlds." (Miller Mair)[16]

Except for quantitative reports, all existing accounts of female sexuality in Hong Kong are presented in some forms of biographical stories, self-representation of the individual life, life stories incorporated into the oral histories of women, or narrative reports of counseling cases. This situation is however not unique; it only reflects the growing interests in biographical research and feminist scholarship in the recent decades.

Methodologically, biographical research has become increasingly common in social study over the last century. Robert Park, a leading sociologist in the University of Chicago in the 1920s and 1930s, argues that the use of stories of individuals has illustrated most succinctly the close ties between individual life and its larger, collective, social context. Not only could these individual stories uncover cultural meanings and changes as lived by individuals and groups in their specific social contexts, but also chart the major changes that have taken place in the society through detailed accounts of life experience within their given cultural and structural settings. (Roberts 2002, 5, 34) For these reasons, the "narrative study of lives" has become a major analytical tool in life experience and identity formation, connecting them to social groupings, situations and events. As a result, life writings such as diaries, letters, memoirs, case studies, profiles, journals and etc. have emerged as increasingly significant texts for study. In other words, they are taken not only as writing by the self or about another but the best means to reveal feelings and conceptions of the individual on which the building of one's sense of recognition and uniqueness depends. Such "narrative turn" in the human sciences has marked an important development in social analysis via the stories of the individuals. (115)

In the same vein, feminists find life writings a powerful tool to represent women's knowledge and experience. They believe that women's voices were left out from history because of bias against their lives which were seen as either too trivial or ordinary to be worth recorded. With increased interests to connect the "personal" with the "political," feminists have placed emphasis on women's experience as a vital source in the creation of women's knowledge. And one of the best forms of circulation and transmission of their experience is story-telling. (Skeggs 1995) Summerfield adds, this is where these stories of women take a different shape from that of a male autobiography. Feminist autobiography presents selves as fragmented and relational, comparing to that of the male telling of a unified, transcendent subject, who is so to speak, representative of an epoch. And rather than the emergence of a solitary, powerful subject, women's life writings present their "subjects" interactively and within given location and situations. Through the intentional efforts to focus on eliciting the unspoken stories of the "little" women in the private domain, feminist biographers have often attributed agency and responsibility for actions. (Summerfield 2000)[17]

A combined genre of narrative writing and women's private stories is found in women's sexual stories. Ken Plummer observes a "certainly massive gender skew to sexual story telling." (1995, 30) The genre of personal, story-telling seems to be a tool that are mostly adopted by women and sexual minorities who are struggling with both their sexuality and gender identities. In the words of bell hooks, it is the "oppressed people" who would be drawn mostly to "resist by identifying themselves as subjects, by defining their reality, shaping their new identity, naming their history, telling their story." (1989, 43) One of the most powerful examples is the telling of stories of sexual violence by women. For instance, Plummer finds the stories of rape survivors particularly empowering for women themselves. As they came to tell their stories, the women concerned would gain increased emotional strength which eventually transformed their situation. Further, in practical daily living, the act of their coming together and talking about the events has in some places reformed the practices of police and courts and made the latter aware of the "rape" impacts on women's lives. Therefore the telling of long suppressed stories as such have become important tools to unsettle the dominant sexual morals and values, which have "tormented, terrorized and penalized" women for their sexuality until today. (1995, 27)

More important, sexual stories have come to play a defining moment as much as the sexual minorities are concerned. The examination of "gendered heterosexism" reveals the hierarchy of sexual stories and the way it has been part of the wider discourses and ideologies in society. The telling of stories of being gay, lesbian and bisexuals easily navigates through all different "arenas," interacting among economic, religious, work, home, media and government. They present to the public some of the most difficult experiences they have as sexual minorities, including negative feelings of rejection or some of their long hidden desires — often in terms of intense feelings of loss, sleeplessness, heart bumping, brushings, and excitement etc. The difficulties have actually forced the storytellers to face their own inner desires versus the love and romance as portrayed in the media. As gay and lesbian life story telling increased, new possibilities are opened up for the sexual minorities to claim power over their lives. (27)

In his *Telling Sexual Stories* (1995), Plummer argues that sexual stories are not merely resources to draw upon but interpretations with political consequences. In other words, they are far from providing rays of real truth about sexual lives but stories told for specific purposes.[18] As such, the telling of sexual stories is a political process which negotiates challenges, shifts outcomes, and distributes control and regulations. The genre of story-telling for women and sexual minorities is particular effective in presenting "a different voice" — one that is much less formally rational, linear and abstract than "male voice," more prone to particularities, interconnections and "care." It may be told with less assuredness and boldness, be more qualified and hesitant, initially sound less convincing, and yet no doubt constitute a stream of power for those concerned. It affects hierarchy, patterns of domination, and the distribution of resources; it empowers some lives and marginalizes others. It flows into situations, opening some to become flexible and participatory, and closing up others to become rigid and limiting. In short, sexual stories allow some new possibilities as well as make others impossible. (26–27, 30)

Reflecting on the reading of an oral history on bisexuals, Mak Hoi Shan (麥海珊), an author of *Bisexual Eroticism*《雙性情慾》(2000) finds strength in the stories. To her, the stories are not only powerful and politically forceful; they are also a source of awakening. They help to articulate the "unnamable" experience of heterogeneous sexualities precisely because oral history allows for the existence of contradictions and conflicts. (24) It is therefore no surprise to find in several volumes of sexual stories that their own prefaces openly disavowed the easy categorization of writing sexuality. Rather the editors have stated over and over again that stories included go beyond any one category:

> [T]his volume … truly demonstrates not only one form of "coming out," but from all different background, different "schools," different strategies and they are all magnificent. There are experiences of different classes, genders, and sexual orientations in very different contexts; apparently sex consciousness is not something of one direction, but a pluralistic and continuous flow. If "coming out" means leaving the absolute category of heterosexuality for another fixed category and not advancing further, I could not see how "coming out" would give human development as a whole any progressive or positive meaning. (iv; my translation)

In this sense, the stories of "intimate relations" have become an important ground for the battle of identity politics in the contemporary world. The questions for us are then: how would the stories of female sexuality contribute to women's identity politics in Hong Kong? That is, in what ways are women sexual subjects, agents or actors constituted against the mainstream sex/gender values in Hong Kong? The most significant value of the existing oral reports lies in the affirmation of the existence of female sexuality, in what ways are they subversive to the general allusion of love and loss in the mainstream society? Despite its mere exploratory attempt, it is hoped that the oral histories and reports would add a missing piece to the history of women as well as the history of women's movement — the advancement of gender equality and right — in Hong Kong.

III. Female Sexuality Went Public

"Now I have made the first and most painful step in the dark and miry maze of my confessions. It is the ridiculous and the shameful, not one's criminal actions, that it is hardest to confess. But henceforth I am certain of myself; after what I have just had the courage to say, nothing else will defeat me." (Jean-Jacques Rousseau, *Confessions*, 1782)

When Jean-Jacques Rousseau shocked the world with his diary's revealing of his sadomasochistic desire, it was already four years after his death in 1778. As shown, Rousseau had struggled with his secret obsession in shame and pain through his life. The telling/writing of his deepest desires had become a moment of peace and revelation when he reconciled with himself and regained a sense of certainty of himself — in his words, becoming "undefeatable." This is a powerful testimony to how the telling of sexual stories may indeed empower the narrators, constituting in them a sense of subjecthood. Telling sexual stories in public therefore becomes an effective means to asserting one's identity and freedom. It allows them to be in touch with their repressed desires and dreams and, in turn, challenge the source of repression.

In Hong Kong, telling sexual stories in public outside of the pornographic industry is a relatively recent phenomenon. According to a leading local feminist, Cheung Choi Wan (張彩雲), the attention paid to female sexuality reflects a "shift of focus" in the women's movement in Hong Kong. Before the shift, emphasis was largely placed on the difference between two sexes. Issues such as rape, child molestation, and sexual violence were all about

feminist movement's attention to sex; it was not until the mid 1990s that sexual desire or eroticism gained some importance in its discussion. In Cheung's reflection, the main contributors to such development have been the emergence of lesbian or women *tongzhi* organizations and the effects of the discussion of the "forthright women," initiated by He Chunrui from Taiwan. Both have made strong impact on the younger generation of women. (Cheung 2001, 158–159)

He Chunrui has been one of the most outspoken feminists in Taiwan. Her *Forthright Women* calls for women to free themselves from the myth of chastity. She contends that the deconstruction of the notion of "good woman" is an important strategy to overturn the stereotypical roles of women. Rather than anxiously restraining their sexuality and living up to the name of "chastity," women should go forth and attend to the needs of their bodies. She further argues that liberation of women's bodies and sexuality will strengthen the women's movement by cultivating in women a sense of self-realization. For sexual/erotic practices encourage women's self-imagination and expectation that are essential to one's self-realization. The call of the "unrestrained/forthright women" is therefore an invitation for women to exercise their subjecthood and allow it to transform and change continuously. (3)

In the 1990s, a series of topics evolved around female sexuality emerged in Hong Kong among the younger generation of feminists, who believes that sexuality is an area where a woman may strategically intervene and practically participate in its discussion. The very different practices and resistance of women in sexuality also allow for the understanding of women in their diversities, including their very different background, identities, and experiences. The question is then about how to relate this practice of the individuals to the larger society and eventually transform social inequality. (Cheung 2001, 163–164)

3.1 *"Discovering" Female Sexuality*

From Hon Siu Wan's (韓小雲) review of *Nuliu* of the period, topics of first sex, sexual desires and frustration, female eroticism in pornography, masturbation, falling in love with another woman, and etc. frequent this major feminist magazine in Hong Kong. It is indeed a period of "discovery" of sexuality in women. (2005, 260)

On its February issue of 1988, *Nuliu* reports a discussion taken place in one of the monthly gatherings of AAF. The subject of discussion was sexuality. The gathering was first of its kind for members to share in open their intimate experiences. Inevitably they all began with reflection on the traditional view that tied sex to marriage. Many preliminary questions of sexuality were asked, including: Whether men have stronger sexual appetite than women? Whether women should take a passive role in sex? Or whether wives are obliged to satisfy the sexual needs of their husbands? Or if women possess sexual desires at all and what is "orgasm" in women? (Chan et al. 2005, 272–280) For especially the last question, many writers of *Nuliu* around this period expressed the same doubts on female orgasm and how it is going to be defined without reference to men. In the words of Lee Kam Fung (李金鳳), a mystical point of supposedly optimal sexual excitement has been an ongoing hunch of women. For it has not only been unknown to many of them, but also that it has become a sort of totem or icon for women to secretly desire for and be disappointed. (296) Because of all kinds of social pressure for women to "preserve" chastity, affirmation of women's bodily needs and desires becomes an important first step toward women's affirmation of themselves. (301)

By the turn of the twentieth century, AAF took up two projects that aimed to unsettle the "grand" history of men and re-inscribe women back into history.[19] Two books were published as a result: *Laughing and Crying: An Oral History of Elderly Women*《又喊又笑：阿婆口述歷史》(1998) and *Sixteen Plus: An Oral History of Young Women*《16+：少女口述歷史》(2002). The oral history of elderly women, supported by the Arts Development Council, collects life stories of ten elderly, aged from 63 to 106, who lead their lives through the turbulent twentieth century of Hong Kong. The main focus of these stories is, of course, not female sexuality. Nevertheless, through the twists and turns from war to postwar years, marriage, singlehood, widowhood, rape, incest, abortion, sexual harassment were all natural parts of these women's life stories. Most of these stories told, through disturbing, fragmented episodes, represent female sexuality in a time when women were not approved to enjoy it.

Among the others, elderly So's (阿蘇) experience of sex was practically unending pregnancy and unceasing trials of life-risking contraception and abortion (Tsang and Ng 1998, 190). For elderly Wong (阿黃), intercourse with her husband meant only pain. She was so much haunted by the experience that she decided to take up the job of a live-in domestic servant, working and staying far away from home. (246) Compared with the others, elderly Lam's (阿林) story has been the most positive one which implicates at least a pint of sexual pleasure on the woman's side:

There was not even holding hands though we were courting. Ah Lam was most upright, only talk and talk. A woman would of course expect some kind of experience, but he didn't understand. He's too upright; I made no complaints and just accepted it.... I got married at 20, nobody taught me about sex, seemed like something you would naturally come to know ... I wasn't afraid when I first got married, but I didn't like it that much,... thought it was all for procreation, something natural. It was not until I was about thirty to forty years old I became fond of it.... But when I was getting older in the fifties I gradually lost interests, I felt rather dry and painful, only did it when he wanted. (30, 37–38; my translation)

The positive experience of sex was reported only after years of marriage. Even then it was short-lived. Ignorance of sex was assumed by all including Elderly Lam. Sex for women was seen as an obligation, and sexual needs often came from the men's side. Regardless of whether these elderly women had enjoyed sex or not, their accounts were almost unanimously certain "declaration of sexual innocence." That is, they were all innocently led into sex by men either partially voluntarily or completely involuntarily. Sexual pleasure, or in other words, sexual agency of women was minimal if ever existed.

In 1999, a book representing a bold exploration of female sexuality finally appeared. It was a project initiated by a group of young college women, collectively named themselves *Scream* (尖叫), titled: *Our Spectacles Are Flying*《我們的眼鏡在飛揚》. The cover shows flying bras drew in the shape of spectacles. Such image signifies both freedom and sarcasticism these young women wish to convey regarding their feelings toward their bodies. The book collects exchanges of personal experiences around nine themes, all sex-related, including: menstruation, public toileting facilities, underwear, threats of rape, sexual harassment, cohabitation, pre-marital sex, abortion, and women's subjectivity in sex. As Leung Fuen (梁款) writes in his preface, he only learns of his own ignorance of the daily experience of women's bodies after reading the book. The blood, tears, underwear, face, dignity, fear and resistance written all over the bodies of women simply shock him. (Scream 1999, 8) Choi Po King (蔡寶瓊), another preface writer, reckons that "to scream" is only a beginning — a little first step. Women have yet to discover their bodies and sexuality in laughter, crying, groaning, and even roaring. "To scream" shall therefore be the beginning of a journey toward women's finding their voice and themselves. (6) The book was first of its kind.

"Screaming" is only a start. In 2002, in response to the needs of women from the younger generation, AAF took up another oral history project, focusing this time on young women and produced *Sixteen plus*. It is a book about sixteen women aged from 16 to 26 with a variety of social background and experiences. In contrast to the experience of the elderly women, where the editors wanted to emphasize on life as represented by the older generation of women, the oral history of young women focuses more directly on questions about sex, love, marriage, and work, matters taken as essential to the experience of this generation whether they are married or single. (Hui 1998)

The range of experiences among these young women is amazing. While Yuk (阿玉), aged 21, has very little experience with courting and sex, prefers one love in a life time and only sex within marriage, Kwan (阿君), aged 19, cares less about premarital sex, has already experienced sex with three to four men since form 3, and about 30 to 40 boyfriends since primary 6. While Bonnie, aged 26, has committed to a love relationship for five years, feeling already trapped like a married couple, Jane, aged 24, believes that she could have sex with many persons but not necessarily loving them, the only problem with which is time. Although sex is no longer a myth for most of these young women, what constitutes a loving relationship is still something of a mystery. There has been a mixture of hesitation, uncertainty, shame, guilt, romantic dreams and frustrations in their intimate relationship. What is clear for most of them is that, having experienced isolation, desertedness and loneliness in their upbringing, they are determined to do just what they like and have a say in leading the rest of their life. For this same reason, most of them have no questions with lesbian or premarital relationship but are exercising much more sensitivity toward their own bodies either in terms of care or protection. The criteria of whether they "feel for it" seems to have much heavier weight than the questions of what forms, with whom, with how many or for how long a love relationship should be built. (Ng and Tsang 2002)

In her review essay, Hon makes an interesting comment on the representation of sexuality of young women. She contends that for a long time, the fan culture among young people has served as a venue of their resistance to the dominant culture of sexual repression. There is so much stigmatization of sex that young women have found themselves ever trapped in anxiety, frustration, guilt, and risk bearing. They find no way to share these feelings with their parents, for sexual desires of young people are often seen as something erosive of chastity and morality. The ecstatic obsession with popular stars or the popular fictions in fan culture has therefore served as an outlet for sexual fantasy and imagination especially in young women. Through fan ecstatic behavior, they may at least momentarily flee from all kinds of rules and regulation as exercised by the society. Until there is the space for open discussion and exploration on the various aspects of sexuality, young people could only choose between reproduction of sexual bias or inequality in their relationship and running free and learning about sexuality up a hard, rugged road. Only the breaking of social taboos, more encouragement for the young people to question, share and discuss, and better establishment of the sense of subjectivity, there will be egalitarian and loving sexual practice. (2005, 265)

Some younger generation of AAF has indeed promoted a more open and direct platform for the exploration of female sexuality. Fung Suen Tze (風信子) recalls her experience of learning, imagining, and desiring through masturbation. (Chan et al., 2005, 309). On the other hand, both Kim and Mei (阿美) contend that women should not be the object but subject of pornography, actively reading and responding to it. (300, 305) Mei describes how much she was attracted to both the desirable men's bodies and women's direct expression of their needs in the pornographic films. For her there is not only male gaze in pornography. (304–305) Seventeen (十七) believes that the affirmation of female sexual desire not only improves the relationship between two sexes but also the liberation of women's sexual burden. (310) Such position also leads the feminist movement to ally with lesbians because the latter clearly challenges the traditional sexual framework that feminists used to carry with them. For some, subjectivity of the body and the respect for different sexual orientation must go together. (Hon 2005, 264) What the younger generation of feminists is saying is clear: women are no longer the oppressed but subjects full of power; women's liberation is not only about the transformation of sociopolitical structures, but also the subject of erotic desire and body politics. (253)

3.2 Beyond Heterosexuality: Resistance to Sexual Categorization

Besides the heterosexual stories by women collected above, the series of publications on stories of homosexuality has undeniably constituted the main body of literature on sexuality in Hong Kong from 1990s to early 2000s. Of many volumes on homosexuality, Chou Wah-shan has been the chief contributor through various capacities as an editor, a co-editor, an author or a co-author.[20] According to Chou, his inspiration to study homosexuality owed much to the emergence of feminist scholarship and the women's movement, therefore he has always made sure that there would be women's voices in his studies. Because of this intentional effort, his works have provided some of the earliest voices to women's formulation of their experience and representation of sexuality, despite their confinement to experience of the sexual minorities.

Many of these earliest accounts of female sexuality are collected in two twin volumes published in 1995 and 1996 by Hong Kong Society for the Study of *Tongzhi* (香港同志研究社). The first was edited by Chou Wah-shan, together with Mak Hoi Shan (麥海珊), and Kong Kin Pong (江建邦), titled *Hong Kong Tongzhi Coming Out* (TCO), the second authored by Chou, titled *Stories of Hong Kong Tongzhi* (ST). The first one collects 26 personal stories of gay, bisexuals, lesbians, Buddhist and Christian homosexuals, straight *tongzhi*, and those beyond categories.[21] Since this volume is designed to collect stories of "coming out," one of the main characteristics of them is their struggle to come to terms with their sexual desires. (Chou, Mak and Kong 1995, i–iv) The second one is Chou's personal reflection on the stories he collected in the same project. Oral reports of female sexuality are found in several sessions of TCO and ST namely: bisexuals, lesbians and "beyond categories." According to Chou, the duo publications of TCO and ST were generated from sixty interviews and three hundred questionnaires, with the help of Ten Percent Club, Horizons, the Society of Wellness and Freedom for All (同健與自在社). Among the sixty interviewees, one-third was women.

Three books on lesbian and bisexuals alone were published in the beginning of the twentieth first century. They are: *Bisexual Eroticism*《雙性情慾》(2000), *Seduction of the Moon — Stories of First Love between Women-them: Narrating Our Stories*《月亮的騷動⋯⋯我們的自述》(SMS, 2001), and *Their Women's Love-prints*《她們的女情印記》(2005). They are the first platforms initiated by women for the narration of their minority sexual experiences. Two of them: *Bisexual Eroticism* and *Their Women's Love-prints* were sponsored by Home Affairs Bureau, in response to the government's promotion of greater cultural diversity. Although the books go by the titles of "bisexual" or "lesbian," the labels may not be the best classification for the women who wrote there. For many of them have already grown tired of fighting against different kinds of labels imposed on them and would prefer not to carry any new ones.

Why different sexual categories? This is a question asked again and again in the different episodes of "women in love with women."[22] In ST, Chou presents a story about a woman who learns about her sexuality, so to speak, naturally. She has not been in resistance to her feelings toward women and is living just like any busily engaged professionals who have no time to develop a love relationship. In her quoted words: "what does it matter if [one] is a homosexual or otherwise? [One] has to eat, sleep, and earn a living any way. [Similarly,] who does not possess "seven emotions and six desires, or love, hate, complaint and anger"? There's no big deal about it, why make a fuss?" (Chou 1996, 25) Another woman, Ling (凌), plainly states:

> Loving a woman is such a natural thing; it's like eating when you feel hungry: no need to struggle, no need to fear, no need to feel frustrated, no need to feel anxious. Because I deeply believe that one falls in love with not the lover's body, but her soul. Others find it frightening because they do not understand what love is; and yet, I knew it early. (Kam 2001, 77; my translation)

If the question of "names" and identity is already a battle for lesbian, the question is even more problematic for bisexuals. One of the main advocates for the space for bisexuality, Mak Hoi Shan, find it extremely disappointing with the categories adopted by gay and lesbian themselves. Bisexuals not only do not belong to either but also are double-marginalized because of both groups' exclusion of them. But what is "sameness" (同), what is "different" (異) and what does it mean to be "bi" (雙)? There is simply no space to even talk about them. (2000, 5) Connie Lam, a chief leader of the lesbian movement in Hong Kong, also refuses to be categorized under any "names." She contends that when one is in love, what attracts him or her is not the sex or gender of the lover but his or her quality and personality. According to her, this has been her attitude toward love since she was fourteen. (Chou, Mak and Kong 1995, 164) Resisting any dramatization of "coming out," Chiu Ka Mei (趙嘉薇) expresses her "natural" coming to terms with her sexuality through an intense gratification of a sense of self. She just behaves the way she likes to be:

> Walking amidst the crowd in the MTR station, I kept thinking: consensus is only an accident; I am fundamentally an individual, why does my sexual orientation matter to anyone? Others gave me an unfair label, and then I kept drawing lines between the identities of *tongzhi* or not, alienating and dividing human relationship. To come out in the crowd … is only to openly affirm one's freedom, and to embrace my own sexual orientation. (86; my translation)

For Mary Ann Pui Wai King (金佩瑋), also a leader of lesbian movement, affirms that the claiming of identity in lesbians is not about personal naming but a strategy to drawing strength and power. She argues that for a lesbian feminist, no identity can be a fixed one. She is all at once a feminist, a lesbian and a human right fighter. Indeed, the different identities are not only interrelated but also mutually critical. For the cause of social equality, a lesbian feminist may criticize both feminists and human right-advocates who care only about heterosexual relations; on the reverse, feminists or human right-advocates may challenge lesbians who care only about their own liberation. Liberation of lesbians is fundamentally a movement to fight discrimination of any human beings on the basis of their sexuality, whether one is heterosexual, homosexual or else. (Lo 1998, 90–91)

Both King and Mak agree that multiplicity of sexualities and identities should be the goal of sex liberation. They have no question with one being a lesbian, a S/M-er, and a transsexual at once. They believe that equality among people of different sexualities is important; the various "names" given to them are not. The names are only foreign import. (Lo 1998, 102) Through deliberate efforts to break away from stereotypes, Poon Lai Yee (潘勵宜) finds herself continue to open up to further possibilities including S/M and queer:

> Once again I realize that the autonomous space of one's body can be extended boundless, that desires can be set free from one's own conscious or unconscious repression or denials. Because of this, I've identified myself as a S/Mer so that I may have deeper reflection on myself, re-read my personal growth, and realize more diverse possibility.... For life is flowing unceasingly in the present continuous tense. (Chou, Mak and Kong 1995, 82–83; my translation)

The resistance to sexual categorization is particularly strong with non-heterosexual women. As they contend, love and sex defines their identities as persons but not the sex and gender of their lovers.

3.3 Exploring Female Eroticism

From the discussion of insufficient public meeting places for lesbians in Hong Kong, a woman raises the issue of limited venues for the exploration of female sexuality. She laments on the general repression on women regarding sexuality: that women were not expected to go out at night, they are not expected to actively pursue her own love and desires, or that they only need love not sex. From young, women have been "educated" to care only for deep, dedicated, sacrificial love, not to question the unequal power between men and women or sexual exploitation. Women who openly talk about their sex and love would be seen as lascivious. As a result, any woman who would try to break away from the image of "good woman" is penalized with a heavy guilty conscience. These conscious and unconscious restraints imposed on them would sometimes result in women's narrow social life, even if some honest exchange of love feelings (not sex) is the aim. (Chou 1996: 57–58, 63)

Is there a way to understanding female sexuality then? SMS starts exploring the question by collecting stories of women's "first love," despite its limitation to women's first love with another woman. According to Kam Yip Lo Lucetta (金曄路), the editor, the usual understanding of "first" is usually sex-related. But what she finds in the stories of women's "first love" includes a broader understanding of sexuality: the first close physical contact, the first experience of her desire, or the first frustrating experience over denial of sexual satisfaction. The "first" is really a time when women are ready to express their desire for sex and love, to explore it with no obligation attached and without anxiety over the control and manipulation of another body. Unfortunately, these significant moments of women's awakening to their sexual needs are strictly controlled in our society. (2001) The telling of their stories through the book project provides the rare space for their release.

At other times, a woman's "real" sexual desire is learnt through comparison. A woman didn't realize that she could fall in for women if not for the lament of her roommate over disappointing relationships with men. Joining her roommate, this woman says to herself: "If only I could meet a suitable woman, with whom I fall in love incessantly, I wouldn't fall in for another man again." (Chou 1996, 81) In her experience, she needs someone who could share with her both intellectually and emotionally but it is difficult to find such a man. (79–80) She goes on to draw an interesting comparison between her different sexual experiences with men and women. She has had enjoyable sex with men. But that's only rare. For her, men always want to go instantly, not caring for women's will, and the process is mostly formulaic: erection, finish and sleep. In the case of women, however, they could enjoy kisses and caress, and even with only that, women could be excited and aroused "a hundred percent"! (82)

Eunice, the Executive Secretary of Queer Sisters, prefaces in SMS that the writing of stories of women in love with women is filling an important gap in female eroticism. All the years, she laments, she has to read herself into the place of the male protagonist of heterosexual love stories. There is a serious lack of narration of gentle love sharing between women. The writing project of SMS is therefore not about stories of the individuals but an important reminder to all that nobody should be left alone. The collective space thus created is both a precious experience for one to opening up oneself and an invaluable time for each to enjoy the love of the other women. (Kam 2001, 8–9) It is perhaps no surprise then to find one of the most erotic love scenes in SMS:

> I wanted to roll her into a ball, and unfold it part by part. Only this could I fill my heart with her. ……The venue is my bed: we were like two divided pieces of magnets, not resisting each other and yet always miss by an inch. I said: I want you. Positions could never be matched and all our energies were exhausted. We felt like rolled up tight by plastic wrappings, transparent and yet crooked, with eyes inside useless, hands lost in direction. My mouth was grapping everything coming my way. Technique? Long threw under the bed. (109–110; my translation)

The space created by women loving women has revealed the complex texture of sex and love. Under the multiple layers of desire for intimacy and ecstatic pleasure, there is the pursuit of sincere exchange for growing together both intellectually and spiritually. (Kam 2001, 23–24) In the words of Trash, love demands response of the same level; nothing less. (36–37) It is about physical intimacy, desire and feelings of warmth as much as spiritual depth and mental exchange. (88) It's not about promise of eternity, but about aspiration for ever changing and keeping pace with one another. (104) In its fulfillment, it is an experience of transformation of one's world beyond established "frame of operation" into unforeseeable possibilities. (174) In its best sense, the richness of women's love and sexual gratification together is a life miracle. (179)

For some, falling in love with another woman is confusing as much as highly exploratory. The playing of different sexual role, the direct confrontation with one's own sexual desire and needs, and the responses of seduction and madness are all highly demanding. (124) This is the rare space where a woman may feel free to discover perspiring passion, desiring for a most un-regrettable excitement, tempting, seducing and wanting of certain un-retractable relationship of love. (183) It opens up uncontrollable desire and love and lets out of the "eruption." (185) Because of the instability of the relationships, love becomes wilder. Yet it sets the intellect free. The tragic and the biggest irony of love between women is they undergo a forbidden love at the time as they crossover unthinkable boundaries. For them, it was so rich an experience that without it, life would be at a loss. (186)

Nevertheless, sex and love can be such stress and pain at the same time. Two dearly loving women were confronted by strong objection from their families. The process is filled with fights with parents, lots of tears, and violent separation. One woman protests, "Both of us are quite clear about our sexual orientation since we were born. We do not have a choice, and it's not even easy to make a choice, why couldn't those so-called 'normal' people stand in our shoes and think carefully?" (29–30) Rejection is a common experience simply because love between two women is seen as perversion. Despite months of close friendship, when one reveals her love to another woman, rejection may be as simple as: "I couldn't accept lesbian." (46) And even if a love relation gets started, it could end without clear reasons. It's such a pain when love does not have a future. (66)

> When I first fell in love with another woman, I decided to leave the church. I felt shameful and guilty of "polluting" the temple of God. Many nights I was in tears, confession after confession, with my state of mind bordered on the verge of breaking down. God for me is love. But because of love, I betrayed God. And since then, I lost myself. (23–24; my translation)

Frustration sometimes leads to self-destruction. Pain and hurt remain there for a long time. Life feels like a curse, the spirit and the body completely beaten up. The fate of lesbian love is unending battle with traditional values of family, customs and religion. And the most likely ending is un-fulfillment. (117)

> A deepest split exploded between my faith and love. Why would the most generous God of love not tolerate the passion of an ordinary human being like me? If love is the reason to loving a person, why is it a sin? The struggle was tormenting. Worse, family added their harsh denouncements. After much struggle, heart breaking, and yet coming to realize that it's impossible to change. (179; my translation)

The writing of the diverse and daily experience of minorities, and in this case the sexual minorities, is a project for the building of a healthy culture, in which different communities of different generations may learn to appreciate one another. Mak, one of the chief editors, wishes that the stories could arouse the interests of the public, so that these different experiences and sex consciousness of women and their related minority communities could stimulate a positive discussion in the development of history and culture. (10–11) It is through these stories of "deviation," so to speak, that intimate relations of erotic experiences and painful attraction, tightly tied to female sexuality are representing themselves for their first times.

3.4 Sex for Pay

If "women in love with women" is perverse sexuality for religions and families, sexuality that demands payment seems to offend the general public evermore. One exceptional volume on female sexuality is *Sex is Butter and Bread* 《性是牛油和麵包》 (1999), in which female sex workers talk about their experiences of sex from a very different perspective. How different? In 2005, Zi Teng (紫藤, Acorus Calamus), a non-governmental organization working for the benefits of sex workers, completed a round of photograph exhibitions wherein sex workers displayed their photographs taken from their daily life. One of the workers, Fung (阿鳳) wrote on the exhibition board which was subsequently included in an album: "I hope this exhibition will build a bridge between [us and] the various sectors of society, to communicate to them our real life: nothing special, nothing negative, living not underground, but "upright" like any other people who strive to earn a living, that what we earn is not "immoral" money, but just like them, earning money with 'sweat and blood.'" (Chan 2005, 41) Fung's claim is clear. She wants to be treated just like any other kinds of workers, only that she is earning her living through sex work.

Except for the "different" occasions where they have sex with men as customers but not only lovers or husbands, sex workers go through all kinds of ups and downs of a "normal" life. The "real" difference may only be that sex is a routine of their daily work life. Their economic well-being depends on the frequency of their sex performances each day. While sex becomes dangerous some times, it is quite enjoyable at others. Fong (阿芳) recalls her excitement with foreign customers: "I grew more optimistic recently, it's related to how the others treated me and also to my sex life. There is a big difference between sex with Chinese and foreigners. Foreigners do foreplay and after play, Chinese do nothing. Foreign men play seductively and make one happy." (Chan, Chan and Lai 1999, 87) Other than these, life is at its "ordinary" course — married, divorced, re-married, divorced again, single parenting, cohabitation, and being loved and betrayed. In Oi Sze's (愛詩) simple words, "life is very complicated" and that's all. (28)

Ngai Ka Chun (倪家珍) of Taiwan believes that the women's movement has talked about subjectivity in the context of oppression only. They are not interested in the exploration of women's erotic desires, sex or the body. Her question: what really does a woman need and what not? In her experience, she finds "what is there that a woman needs sexually" is a question that the women's movement in Taiwan is unable to face to date. (Lo 1998, 88) So can we accept the exercise of sexual agency in sex workers? Is not the demand for paid sex a strong statement on the subjectivity of women's bodies?

Referring to the debate on "good woman" versus "bad woman," He Chunrui states that sex is a very tricky question for the women's movement. When the earliest feminists tried to break away from the confines of home and stepped into the public sectors demanding for employment and social participation, they promised themselves to do the best in both domestic and public sectors, and that they would be more chaste, moral and normal than others, in order to be "socially" accepted. And yet these trapped them into following the rules and norms set up by the society and they soon found themselves landed in a situation worse than before. Therefore, what is needed for the women's movement is to challenge the division between good and bad women, especially by refusing to draw the line around women's choice in marriage, love and sexuality. (1994, 96–97) She pleads, "Do not let those who look more normal, more distinguished to set the standard of acceptance; on the contrary, help those who are the most 'abnormal,' the queerest to live most freely. Only this will truly change social discrimination." (97) Only when sexuality is included as one of the central issues of discussion for an open society will the life of women and practice of female sexuality be whole. (100)

IV. Conclusion

"We tell ourselves stories in order to live." (Joan Didion)[23]

During an international Chinese conference on sexuality in 1998, a women caucus was initiated spontaneously by the participants at one of the evenings. The caucus, drew together increasing number of women over its course, was soon turned into an exciting exchange of personal sexual stories.

A woman from San Francisco started by an introduction of sex tools … It soon attracted more than a dozen women, getting together in a circle. Everything was about sex and body: masturbation, body figure, first sex, first love, breast, bra, butch/femme, muscle, positions of making love, orgasm, funny stories about sex, number of sex partners, love and loss, personal experiences, ideal love, outlook, and performance in sex, etc. Everyone was participating, there were nonstop talking, seducing, boasting; there drawing sometimes identification, sometimes shocks; feeling sometimes real, sometimes dreaming; sometimes talking softly and laughing loudly. It was hilarious. (Lo 1998, 276; my translation)

The night exchange was extended into the early morning. According to the report, every woman who took part in it exclaimed how rarely they had such a chance: one that they could fully appreciate female sexuality; that they could learn about the board range of forms of sexual enjoyment and pleasure; and that everyone could be sexual, passionate, and unique. (278)

As Doris Summer warns, these testimonies cannot be seen as just another replaying of woman's "life script" or as merely a reconstruction of the self within an endlessly repeated psycho-biological story. Here the self is to be used to provoke connections and produce new articulations. (1988, 119) As self-narration is agreed to be essential to the constitution of the subject, the narrating of sexuality by women could be the beginning of the construction of a sexual subject and agent for women. The articulation of a long repressed and yet intimately lived experience of women shall return to them the power to speak and hence the basis for political action. (Steedman 2000, 28) Similarly, Liz Stanley argues that self-life-writing both shapes and helps construct selfhood and enact identities. Through telling and writing of their own stories, women recover their fragmented "inner" selves and move toward "women's made-selves." (2000, 43, 48).

The telling and writing of women's stories is thus a critical practice that does not only develop and foster self-consciousness in the narrator but also its readers. At its most radical, it enhances writing and reading as a means of emancipation for various subject-locations. (Kadar 1992, 12) By way of narration, women engage in the process of interpreting themselves. It is then up to the reader to decode, recognize, recontextualize, or abstract the narratives in the interests of reaching a new interpretation of the experience before us. (Josselson and Lieblich 1995, ix)

From a complete silence of women's sexual experience to the telling and writing of stories about their bodies, their feelings of love and loss, eroticism and troublesome sexuality, gender politics are placed on a different horizon from that of demanding socio-political structural changes. It is a battle most intimate, challenging and radical in the sense of women's personal participation and reflection, one that involves not only ideological identification but also physical and most private sense of being women themselves. Indeed, this is a battle could not be fought on a purely empirical analytical ground but nothing less than oral reports and narrative accounts by women.

However, just as Teresa de Lauretis warns about feminist writings, the result could be a deepened "opposition between theoreticism and empiricism, where accusations of jargon, bad writing, or elitism from one camp are met with counteraccusations of essentialism and unsophisticated thinking by the other." (1986, 7) Despite the narrators' desire to provide their sexual stories for the strategic intervention into local gender and sexual politics, their stories are opened to interpretation from an entirely opposite direction. Rather than finding voice for multiple female sexualities, these self-narration and oral reports of women's sexual experiences could be turned into nasty tools of attack by the moral conservatives. This exposes the difficulties of the storytelling methodologies: stories are told for a political purpose and therefore could be turned either way for or against the narrators.

For example, an oral report was quoted negatively by Poon Kwok Sum (潘國森) from *Next Magazine* (壹周刊), issue no. 455 (1998). In contrast to the women's intention to share her struggle as a lesbian, Poon reads her story as one of an unhappy lesbian with a pathetic childhood — discriminated against as girl and thereby neglected by her parents, lacking of room in making decision, feeling lonely all the time, trying to be protective of other girls in order to play the strong and active role, and etc. The narrator of the report says she was quite sure that her homosexual orientation came not from environmental influence. And yet, Poon blames it on her, speculates that she must have had no male admirer, "look abominable and sound terrible," a victim of family negligence, sex discrimination, of being a laughing stalk of family and friends. (2001, 135–136) He goes on to conclude that TBs[24] are those who want to be like man and often dress and behave as one. They are usually victims of broken families, family sex discrimination, having conflicts with their parents, growing up with the absence of fathers, having great difficulties with their mothers, having mothers with failed marriages, trying to avoid becoming like their mothers, feeling repulsive toward female identity, and there, they land on competing with men for women. (137–138)[25] Poon's insistence in finding faults in lesbian relations question the political effectiveness of story-telling for the unsympathetic readers.

For the sympathetic ones, however, many of the stories are pleas for help. Whether they are stories of elderly or young, heterosexual, bisexual, or lesbian, "good" women or "bad" women such as the sex-workers, many are not easily said — they appear with a struggle, often painfully and confusing. The telling of these stories involves the complex social processes that form their background as well as inform the tellers. Most meaningfully, it provides a platform for the tellers to capture their own intimate life through their telling stories about it. Such stories are not simply "languages" or "texts" or even "discourses." They are socially produced in social contexts by embodied concrete people experiencing the thoughts and feelings of everyday life. These personal sexual stories are making a difference to our lives, our communities, our cultures, and our politics. (Plummer 1995, 15–16) In short, stories of sexuality are not simply texts awaiting analysis but social actions embedded in social worlds. Today, women have begun to find female sexuality an essential cause for the advancement of feminism. It has served in the past as a patriarchal tool to control and regulate women; it has become now the ground for women's critical examination of their intimate feelings and hence the challenge to free their bodies for further explorations of their selves and subjectivity.

In this sense, sexual rights expressed in the freedom in women's telling and writing of their bodies and sexualities pertains to gender mainstreaming in the UNESCO's understanding of the term. Carole Vance once says that social movements, feminism included, must move toward a vision. It is not enough to move women away from sexual danger and oppression; it is necessary to move toward something: toward pleasure, agency, and hence self-definition. Feminism would remain vital and vigorous if it is to tap this wellspring of human experiences. Without it, they become dogmatic, dry, compulsive, and ineffective. To persist amid frustrations and obstacles, feminism must reach deeply into women's pleasure and draw on this energy. (1992, 24) Perhaps, we may borrow Plummer's phrase of "intimate citizenship" (1995, 17) to further our vision. In sum, the telling of women's sexual stories is neither a personal nor private matter; it is the envisioning of a "new social order" where women are free to choose what to do with our bodies, our feelings, our identities, our relationships, our genders, our eroticisms and our representations. After all, our bodies are our stories and they are far too significant in women's lives and culture to be taken lightly.

Notes

1. Taken from "Baseline Definition of Key Concepts and Terms," Agreed Conclusions of United Nations Economic and Social Council, 1997/2. Access at http://www.un.org/documents/ecosoc/docs/1997/e1997-66.htm, date: 12/12/2006.

2. Gender and Reproductive Rights Glossary. Geneva: World Health Organization, 2002. Access at http://www.who.int/reproductive-health/gender/glossary.html, date: 12/12/2006.

3. MADRE is an international women's human rights organization that works with community-based women's organization addressing issues of health, reproductive rights, economic development, education and other human rights. Details can be found at http://www.madre.org/

4. The Committee on Economic, Social and Cultural Rights has elaborated on sexual rights in its General Comment No. 14. It confirms that the rights to sexual health, sexual freedom, and sexual education are protected by Article 12 of the International Covenant on Economic, Social and Cultural Rights. The Committee also made it clear that threats of health and discrimination on the basis of sexual orientation is a violation of rights. In fact, a ruling of the same was reiterated by the International Covenant on Political and Civil Rights by the UN Human Rights Committee in 1994, and was once again confirmed by the UN Special Rapporteur on the Right to Health specifying sexual rights as human rights in 2004. E/CN.4.2004/49 paragraph 54. Quoted from MADRE Position Paper, accessed at http://www.madre.org/, date: 30/1/2007.

5. Despite intense opposition from several countries—including the US—which has prevented the inclusion of a resolution addressing directly sexual rights into these international instruments, sexual rights are nonetheless increasingly accepted by the international community as a component of international human rights.

6. The first clause of "Sexual Rights Are Fundamental and Universal Human Rights," adopted in Hong Kong at the 14th World Congress of Sexology, August 26, 1999. The Congress was organized by World Association for Sexual Health (originally dubbed as WAS) as its biannual activity since 1978 at Rome.

7. In the earliest issues of *Nuliu* 《女流》, a major feminist magazine run by Hong Kong Association for the Advancement of Feminism (AAF, 香港新婦女協進會) from the 1980s, men's erotic desires of women's bodies were seriously criticized. TV ads, commercial films, beauty pageant, and sexualized fashion, pornography, all were criticized as serving only the sexual appetite of men by displaying and objectifying women's bodies. At the time, lesbians were unfamiliar to *Nuliu* and they were seen at best, an alternative to even distribution of power within a couple (Hon 2005, 254–257).

8. Several sex-related surveys were published by FPAHK, *Report on Youth Sexual Study (Out-of-school Survey), 1991* (1995), *Knowledge, Attitude and Practice Study on Family Planning* (1997), *Report on Youth Sexual Study (Out-of-school Survey), 1996* (2000a) and *Report on Youth Sexual Study (Form 3-7 Student Survey), 1996* (2000b). They will serve as background to my interpretative study in this paper.

9. The most prominent of such magazines is *Sisters* 《姊妹》 which has served as the main source of sex education for women since the sixties. Cf. Leung Meeping (梁美萍) (2004).

10. Yau Ching's (游靜) independent film titled *Ho Yuk* 《好郁》 has received wide acclaim for its provocative presentation of female sexuality. However, since this paper will focus on the narrative representation of female sexuality, only direct accounts of female sexuality will be taken into consideration. Other forms of media representation such as pornography, popular literature and film will not be dealt with due to their very different forms and nature of production.

11. It was developed into a MPhil thesis by Wong in 2005. Copy of which can be found at the University Library of The Chinese University of Hong Kong.

12. Blacksoblack (素黑), a young woman who initiated herself to be a sex counselor for women and published some of the cases she came across in her books, including: *You Are Not a Person* 《妳不是一個人》 (2002), *Files of History of Women's Sexuality* 《女人性史檔案》 (2003), *Women Loving Sex: Interview Records of History of Sexuality* 《好性女子：性史訪問錄》 (2002), and W*omen's Private Files* 《女人私密檔案》 (2005). Together she exposes stories of repression and liberation of sex in the life experience of women. Nevertheless, since Blacksoblack's books are presented in the format of questions and answers of counseling sessions, it will be very difficult to include them for our discussion here.

13. For the reason stated in n. 6, the two documentaries abovementioned will not be included in this study.

14. The "good woman" versus "bad woman" debate has been a prominent part of feminist criticisms where the power to define and speak for women is at stake.

15. The pinyin of *Tongzhi* is commonly used for "同志." This is a name for gays and lesbians coined by the local community. It also has the connotation of comrades which have been commonly used in mainland China.

16. Quoted by Ken Plummer (1995, 1).

17. For some early feminists, autobiography is masculine writing. It's taken as a major form of constituting the male subject. Writers such as Sidonie Smith believes that women's life are made a "nonstory," a "silent place" and a "gap" in patriarchal culture, and the "self-effacing" rather than "self-promoting" of women denies them of autobiographical writings. (1987, 50) Smith further theorizes the different style and meaning of women's autobiography in her *Subjectivity, Identity, and the Body* (1993).

18. Wong Wai Ching (黃慧貞) contends that women oral histories serve the feminist cause in terms of mutual conscientization, building community and discursive intervention of the male biased history. (2005)

19. Cf. http://www.aaf.org.hk/big5/article.adp?article_id=105, retrieved date: 1/2/2006

20. Chou Wah-shan (2000), *Tongzhi: Politics of Same-sex Eroticism in Chinese Societies*, Binghamton, NY: Haworth Press; Chou Wah-shan (1993), *Heterosexual Hegemony*《異性戀霸權》, Hong Kong: Joint Publishing; and Chou Wah-shan (1994), *Theorizing Tongzhi*《同志論》, Chou Wah-shan, Mak Hoi Shan, Kong Kin Bong (1995), *Hong Kong Tongzhi Coming Out*《香港同志站出來》, Chou Wah-shan (1996), *Stories of Tongzhi in Hong Kong*《香港同志故事》, Chou Wah-shan (1997), *Postcolonial Tongzi*《後殖民同志》, all published by the Hong Kong Society for the Study of *Tongzhi*.

21. This last group reflects the will of those who refuse to be categorized.

22. Adopted from the title of the oral history project initiated by lesbian and bisexual organizations.

23. Both quoted by Ken Plummer (1995, 1).

24. TB is an acronym for lesbians who choose to perform "masculinity" by way of dressing or playing particular sex roles.

25. Another oral report quoted by Poon from ST was a woman who had many male admirers but found her current woman lover one who could understand her best and cared for her in the most detail way. Poon's comment was that her too early love relations (around 13–15 years of age) spoiled her, so much so that she had been tired of unworthy men and immature relationships. Again the problem came from poor family education. Borrowing the testimonies of two lesbian writers of *Lesbian Couples*, D. M. Clunis and G. D. Green, Poon once again concludes that a majority of lesbians turned so because of their previously failed relationship with men. (2001, 151–152)

References

An Oral History Project on Hong Kong Women Who May Fall for Women. (HKWW, 香港會愛上女人的女人口述歷史計劃) (Ed.). (2005). *Their Women's Love-prints — An Oral History on Hong Kong Women Who May Fall for Women: 1950–2004*《她們的女情印記——香港會愛上女人的女人口述歷史：一九五零至二零零四》. Hong Kong: HKWW Executive Committee.

Blacksoblack (素黑). (2002). *You Are Not a Person: Women's Love Files*《妳不是一個人：女子情感檔案》. Hong Kong: Huaqianshu Publishing Ltd.

Blacksoblack. (2005). *Women's Private Files*《女人私密檔案》. Hong Kong: Cosmos Books Ltd.

Blacksoblack. (2002). *Women Loving Sex: Interview Records of History of Sexuality*《好性女子：性史訪問錄》. Hong Kong: Sisters Culture Publishing Ltd.

Blacksoblack. (2003). *Files of History of Women's Sexuality*《女人性史檔案》. Hong Kong: Cosmos Books Ltd.

Chan, K. W. (陳錦華) et al. (Ed.). (2001). *Difference and Equal — New Challenges to Hong Kong Feminist Movement*《差異與平等惺輕鍼袖k運動的新挑戰》. Hong

Kong: AAF and Social Policy Study Center, Department of Applied Social Science of Hong Kong Polytechnic University.

Chan, P. K., Chan, W. F., & Lai, P. Y. (陳寶瓊、陳惠芬、及黎佩兒) (Eds.) (1999). *Sex is Butter and Bread*《性是牛油和麵包》. Hong Kong: Zi Teng.

Chan, Wai Fong (陳惠芳), ed. 2005. *My Life: Photographs by Sex Workers*《我的性生活：性工作者攝影集》. Hong Kong: Zi Teng.

Cheung, Choi Wan (張彩雲). 2001. "Creating Female Erotic Space (continued) — Reflection on Hong Kong Feminist Movement" (創造女性情慾空間——對香港婦女運動的意識反思). In *Difference and Equal — New Challenges to Hong Kong Feminist Movement*《差異與平等——香港婦女運動的新挑戰》, Chan Kam Wah et al.; 157–166. Hong Kong: AAF and Social Policy Study Center, Department of Applied Social Science of Hong Kong Polytechnic University.

Chou, Wah-shan (周華山). 1993. *Hegemony of Heterosexuality*《異性戀霸權》. Hong Kong: Joint Publishing.

Chou, Wah-shan and Chiu, Man Chung (周華山、趙文宗). 1995. *History of "Closet" Sexuality: Tongzhi Movement of Hong Kong, Britain and America*《衣櫃性史：香港及英美同志運動》. Hong Kong: Hong Kong Society for the Study of Tongzhi.

Chou, Wah-shan, Mak Hoi Shan, and Kong Kin Pong (周華山、麥海珊、江建邦), eds. 1995. *Hong Kong Tongzhi Coming out*《香港同志站出來》. Hong Kong: Hong Kong Society for the Study of Tongzhi.

Chou, Wah-shan. 1994. *Theorizing Tongzhi*《同志論》. Hong Kong: Hong Kong Society for the Study of Tongzhi.

Chou, Wah-shan. 1996. *Stories of Hong Kong Tongzhi*《香港同志故事》. Hong Kong: Hong Kong Society for the Study of Tongzhi .

Chou, Wah-shan. 1997. *Postcolonial Tongzhi*《後殖民同志》. Hong Kong: Hong Kong Society for the Study of Tongzhi.

Cosslett, Tess, Celia Lury, and Penny Summerfield, eds. 2000. *Feminism and Autobiography: Texts, Theories, Methods*. London: Routledge.

De Lauretis, Teresa, ed. 1986. "Feminist Studies/Critical Studies: Issues, Terms, and Contexts." In *Feminist Studies/Critical Studies*; 1–19. Basingstoke : Macmillan Press.

De Lauretis, Teresa. 1994. *The Practice of Love: Lesbian Sexuality and Perverse Desire*. Bloomington: Indiana University Press.

Dowrkin, Andrea. 1981. *Pornography: Men Possessing Women*. London: The Women's Press.

Family Planning Association of Hong Kong (FPAHK). 1995. *Report on Youth Sexual Study (Out-of-school Survey), 1991*. Hong Kong: FPAHK.

FPAHK. 1997. *Knowledge, Attitude and Practice Study on Family Planning*. Hong Kong: FPAHK.

FPAHK. 2000a. *Report on Youth Sexual Study (Out-of-school Survey), 1996*. Hong Kong: FPAHK.

FPAHK. 2000b. *Report on Youth Sexual Study (Form 3–7 Student Survey), 1996.* Hong Kong: FPAHK.

He, Chunrui (何春蕤). 1994. *Forthright Women: Feminism and Sex Liberation*《豪爽女人：女性主義與性解放》. Taipei: Crown Literature Publishing Co. Ltd.

Hon, Siu Wan (韓小雲). 2005. "Fighting for a Space for Sex Issues" (打拼性議題的空間). In *Re-reading Nuliu II*《再讀『女流』——下集》, Chan Po King et al.; 253–271. Hong Kong: Hong Kong Association for the Advancement of Feminism (AAF).

hooks, bell. 1989. *Talking Back: Thinking Feminist, Thinking Black.* Boston: South End Press.

Hui, Long Yeung (許朗養). 1998. "History of Elderly Women, Made in Hong Kong" (阿婆歷史，香港製造). *Nuliu*《女流》, 27: 22–23. In *Re-reading Nuliu II*, Chan Po King et al.; 479–482. Hong Kong: AAF, 2005.

Irigaray, Luce. 1985. Trans. Catherine Porter. *This Sex Which Is Not One.* Ithaca, NY: Cornell University Press.

Josselson, R. and A. Lieblich, eds. 1999. *The Narrative Study of Lives, Making Meaning of Narratives.* London: Sage.

Kadar, Marlene, ed. 1992. *Essays on Life Writing: From Genre to Critical Practice.* Toronto: University of Toronto Press.

Kam, Yip Lo (金曄路), ed. 2001. *Seduction of the Moon — Stories of First Love between Women-them: Our Narratives*《月亮的騷動——她她的初戀故事：我們的自述》. Hong Kong: Cultural Act Up.

Leung, Mee Ping (梁美萍). 2004. *The Extension of Female Erotic Space from "Zimei" to "Sisters"*《從『姊妹』到『Sisters』——女性情慾空間的展佈》, PhD Colloquium paper, unpublished.

Lin, Fangmei (林芳玫). 1999. *Studies of Pornography: From Freedom of Speech to Signifieds*《色情研究：從言論自由到符號擬象》. Taipei: Fembooks Co. Ltd.

Lo, Kim Hung (盧劍雄), ed. 1998. *New Reader on Chinese Tongzhi: 1998 Chinese Tongzhi Conference Proceedings*《華人同志新讀本：1998華人同志交流大會文集》. Hong Kong: Huasheng Bookstore.

MacKinnon, Catharine. 1989. *Towards a Feminist Theory of the State.* Cambridge, Mass.: Harvard University Press.

Mak, Hoi Shan and Mary Ann Pui Wai King (麥海珊、金佩瑋). 2000. *Bisexual Erotics*《雙性情慾》. Hong Kong: Hong Kong Women Christian Council.

Ng, Chun Hung and Tsang Ka Yin (吳俊雄、曾嘉燕), eds. 2002. *Sixteen Plus: Young Women's Oral History*《16+少女口述歷史》. Hong Kong: AAF.

Plummer, Ken. 1995. *Telling Sexual Stories: Power, Change and Social Worlds.* London: Routledge.

Poon, Kwok Sum (潘國森). 2001. *Penetrating Homosexuality: Studies of Perverse Behavior*《透視同性戀：異常性行為研究》. Hong Kong: Subculture Co. Ltd.

Probyn, Elspeth. 1993. *Sexing the Self: Gendered Positions in Cultural Studies.* London: Routledge.

Rich, Adrienne. 1980. "Compulsory Heterosexuality and Lesbian Existence." *Signs* 5 (4): 631–660.

Roberts, Brian. 2002. *Biographical Research*. Buckingham, PA: Open University Press.

Scream (尖叫). 1999. *Our Spectacls Are Flying*《我們的眼鏡在飛揚》. Hong Kong: Stepforward Multimedia Co. Ltd.

Segal, Lynne. 1994. *Straight Sex: The Politics of Pleasure*. London: Virago Press.

Skeggs, B. 1995. *Feminist Cultural Theory: Process and Production*. Manchester and New York: Manchester University Press.

Smith, Sidonie. 1987. *A Poetics of Women's Autobiography: Marginality and the Fictions of Self-Representation*. Bloomington: Indiana University Press.

Smith, Sidonie. 1993. *Subjectivity, Identity, and the Body: Women's Autobiographical Practices in the Twentieth Century*. Bloomington: Indiana University Press.

So, Ho-wai and Fanny M. Cheung. 2005. "Review of Chinese Sex Attitudes & Applicability of Sex Therapy for Chinese Couples with Sexual Dysfunction." *The Journal of Sex Research*, 42 (2): 93–101.

Sommer, Doris. 1988. "'Not Just a Personal Story': Women's *Testimonios* and the Plural Self." In *Life/Lines: Theorizing Women's Autobiography*, ed. Bella Brodzki and Cleste Schenck. Ithaca, NY: Cornell University Press.

Stanley, Liz. 2000. "From 'Self-made Women' to 'Women's Made-selves'? Audit Selves, Simulation and Surveillance in the Rise of Public Woman." In *Feminism and Autobiography: Texts, Theories, Methods*, ed. Tess Cosslett, Celia Lury and Penny Summerfield; 40-60. London: Routledge.

Steedman, Carolyn. 2000. "Enforced Narratives: Stories of Another Self." In *Feminism and Autobiography: Texts, Theories, Methods*, ed. Tess Cosslett, Celia Lury and Penny Summerfield; 25–39. London: Routledge.

Summerfield, Penny. 2000. "Dis/composing the Subject: Intersubjectivities in Oral History." In *Feminism and Autobiography: Texts, Theories, Methods*, ed. Tess Cosslett, Celia Lury and Penny Summerfield; 91–106. London: Routledge.

Tsang, Ka Yin and Ng Chun Hung (曾嘉燕、吳俊雄), eds. 1998. *Crying and Laughing: Oral History of Elderly Women*《又喊又笑：阿婆口述歷史》. Hong Kong: AAF.

Vance, Carole S. 1992. "Pleasure and Danger: Toward a Politics of Sexuality." In *Pleasure and Danger: Exploring Female Sexuality*, ed. Carole S. Vance; 1–24. London: Pandora. Originally published London: Routledge, 1984.

Wittig, Monique. 1992. *The Straight Mind and Other Essays*. Boston: Beacon Press.

Wong, Choi Fung (黃彩鳳). 2005. *The Multiple "I": Reading of Two Texts — From "The Desire of Eggs" to Sex/Gender Movement*《我／我／我／我／我／我：從『卵子體慾』看性／別運動》. MPhil Thesis, The Chinese University of Hong Kong.

Wong, Wai Ching (黃慧貞). 2005. *Making Strange Voices in the Gaps and the Silences*《在空白和靜寂中述說異音》. *Envisage: A Journal Book of Chinese Media Studies*, 3 (April): 84–103.

CHAPTER 12

Media Ideologies of Gender in Hong Kong

Micky Lee and Anthony Fung

During and after the women's movements of the 1960s and the 1970s, feminists in Australia, Canada, Europe and the U.S. began to examine gendered images and the participation of women in the media. There has been a healthy and rapid growth in feminist scholarship in the area of media studies and communication in the past two decades (1980–2000). Not only do major communication journals publish essays deconstructing media ideologies of gender informed by a feminist approach, major communications associations (such as the International Communication Association, the National Communication Association, the Association for Education in Journalism and Mass Communication, and the International Association for Mass Communication Research) now also have caucuses and/or divisions devoted to media and gender studies and feminist scholarship. Most importantly, women and the media is one of the twelve critical areas of concern in the United Nations' Beijing's Platform for Action. This reflects the view that the media can serve women in the areas for peace-keeping and development.

Against the background of ferment in feminist scholarship around the world, this chapter provides an updated picture of media ideologies of gender in Hong Kong. From a critical and interpretivist perspective, we examine how the media construct gender ideologies. We believe that a critical perspective complements an empirical investigation of gender equality phenomenon as discussed in some chapters of this volume. A critical perspective allows us to examine social structures that are constructed and maintained by unbalanced power relations — gender relations being one of them. In addition, we believe that government and public policy, and feminist research are all avenues for intervening gender mainstreaming in society. While other papers in this volume have effectively demonstrated how research informs public policy, we would like to suggest how research itself can transform social change if scholars see research as social responsibilities (Fine, Weis, Weseen, & Wong, 2003).

We begin with a review of the existing studies of media and gender in Hong Kong, with details of gender stereotyping in the media. Gender stereotyping is one of the most common tactics used by the media in order to generalize female and male characteristics, personalities and attributes. Stereotyping helps the audience to construct their world views and thus shapes their knowledge of gender relations. It will be followed up with a discussion about the ubiquitous slimming advertisements and messages in Hong Kong, which we believe have serious implications for the self-conception, identity and social values of women; as well as for the construction and maintenance of gender relations and ideologies in Hong Kong. The media serve as a site from which the culture of slimming flourishes; the audience also helps build gender ideologies by consuming the mediated culture and by producing discourses of the slimming culture. Hence, gender stereotypes and gender ideologies can only be maintained with the involvement of the audience. The paper concludes by suggesting how feminist scholars bear the responsibilities to share their findings with the subjects that are studied.

The strong economic focus of Hong Kong, as well as the commonly held belief that Hong Kong women enjoy a high political, economic and social status in Asia may conceal Hong Kong's gender inequality. Consequently, Hong Kong society discourages a meaningful deconstruction of media ideologies and a feminist discussion of gender. It is indisputable that Hong Kong women are politically, economically and socially more empowered than women in most Asian countries. One illustration of this is that, in 2002, the United Nations Development Programme (UNDP) ranked Hong Kong twenty-third in terms of gender-related development.[1] Among all Asian countries, only Japan was ranked higher than Hong Kong, at twelfth. The two economic dragons of Asia, Singapore and South Korea, were ranked at twenty-eighth and twenty-ninth, respectively. China was ranked at seventy-first. Another piece of evidence is that, in terms of access to the Internet by women, Hong Kong has one of the highest rates in the entire world: the International Telecommunication Union (ITU) has established that 49% of Internet users in Hong Kong are females; only females in the U.S. and China account for a larger percentage among all Internet users in a country.[2] The state plays an active role in promoting the use of new technologies by Hong Kong women. For example, the Home Affairs Department of the Hong Kong government carried out an active campaign in local community centres to encourage women to use new information and communication technologies. Moreover, some women's organizations (such as the Hong Kong Federation of Women's Centres) have organized programmes for women to learn new technologies.

National governments are not the only agent of change of women's status. The Beijing Conference has acutely pointed out that NGOs and the civil society also play a paramount role in gender mainstreaming. National governments often regard media as a peripheral area of concern. Gallagher (2005) found that Platform for Action's Section J "Women and the media" is the second least included section in national plans at the time when Beijing +10 took place in 2005. Lee (2006) found that the two strategic objectives under section J "increase the participation and access of women to expression and decision-making in and through the media and new technologies of communication" (J.1) and "promote a balanced and non-stereotyped portrayal of women in the media" (J.2) received uneven attention from national governments. Most national governments vowed to adjust gender stereotyping in the media, sometimes to the extent of violating freedom of speech. Gender-mainstreaming in new information and communication technologies in contrast received scant attention. Although the first three world conferences on women have urged national governments to improve gender stereotypes in the media, national governments prioritise areas such as women and economy, employment, and health over the media. In addition, the conceptualization of women and the media in Section J is not without problem. As pointed out in Lee (2004), the media are often seen as neutral channels through which positive gender messages can be delivered. For example, the Women's Commission suggests that the media can be used to publicize how to prevent domestic violence. What should not be neglected is that the media are actively constructing gendered images that position women in a weaker and more powerless position. Hence, scrutinizing media messages from a critical perspective is essential to understand how gender is far from being mainstreamed in the media.

A few international studies on the media (e.g. Haavio-Mannila, Dahlerup, Eduards, Gudmundsdóttir, Halsaa, Hernes, Hänninen-Salmesin, Sigmundsdóttir, Sinkkonen & Skard, 1985, Rommes, 2002, van Zoonen, 1994) have found that an improvement in the status of women in society has misled us into believing that women have "made" it and that it is no longer necessary to talk about feminism and feminist ideals. This may be happening in Hong Kong too. In addition, the historical absence of women's/ feminist movements in Hong Kong and the general political apathy of the public may account for the media's silence with respect to feminist issues, and for its silencing of discussions on such issues.

In a five-year review conference on the Beijing Platform for Action, the Gender Research Centre of the Hong Kong Institute of Asia-Pacific Studies found that although some actions have been taken to combat gender stereotype in the media and to promote more positive images of women, gender inequality in and through the Hong Kong media is still a prominent phenomenon. It is not at all difficult to name a few examples: many soft and entertainment news items in newspapers are written by female journalists, while male journalists are assigned to cover hard and financial news; tabloid and entertainment magazines use the female body as a selling-point; and there is a lack of gays' and lesbians' representations in the mainstream media. In addition, the mass media often abuse the freedom of expression to defend their gender-biased stereotypes. It is essential to deconstruct these gendered ideologies and arrive at a feminist understanding of the media. Here, we distinguish a feminist knowledge of the media from a knowledge of "women and the media"; the former is the lens that we use in this paper to evaluate media's portrayal of women and gender. Such a lens helps us to add to knowledge about feminist issues beyond measuring the number of women involved in or represented by the media. It is contended that an overemphasis on quantitative measurements (for example, comparing the number of female students versus male students majoring in communications, the number of female versus male media practitioners, etc.) may limit our understanding of gender and the media. Unlike liberal feminists, we do not believe that gender equality in the Hong Kong media can be assessed merely by counting the number of women and men involved in the media. In determining the ties between women and the media, we embrace a notion of gender that is fluid, inclusive and situational (Olesen, 2003). Gender ideology in the media has to be examined in an historical, political and socioeconomic context.

The social construction of gender is a discursive process (Van Zoonen, 1994) in which one has to experience gender in and through, among other things, the media. The concept of gender challenges the biological determinism of the women/men category and the fixed female/male identities. In other words, whilst it is valuable to study "women and the media" (such as comparing how women and men use the media), conceptualizing women as a static group neglects the complexities and diversities of what is meant by, categorised and labelled as "women." On the other hand, "gender and the media" implies that one has to experience gender in a local situation and that the gendered identity has to be constantly contested and negotiated with other participants and the material world. For example, an educated female university student's understanding of a television programme could be different from that of a recent female immigrant from mainland China with a different national ideology; more, our understanding of gender representations in magazines depends on the contexts in which we consume the mediated gender: whether we read them with friends or family members or on our own; whether we read them at home, at school, or in a mass transit railway compartment.

Given the above, we advocate that feminist scholars of media studies decentralize and demystify the concept of Hong Kong *woman* as a complex and unstable social construct that is constantly being negotiated and contested in and through the media. In addition, we should include and embrace all women and their life experiences. The notion of inclusiveness calls for attention to be paid to marginalised (but not necessarily powerless) groups: single mothers, elderly women, newly-arrived girls and women, foreign domestic helpers, women and men of different sexual orientations, and girls and women in poverty.

Research on Media and Gender in Hong Kong

The late arrival of women's / gender studies in higher education in Hong Kong may explain the lack of scholarship on feminism and the media. Public fora, seminars and conferences on media and gender began to be held in the early 1990s. The early concern came from religious organizations and academic institutions. For example, in December 1990 the Hong Kong Christian Service Communications Centre organized "Mass Media Awareness Seminar: Mass Media and Women in the 90's"; the Gender Research Centre of the Hong Kong Institute of Asia-Pacific Studies in collaboration with the School of Journalism and Communication (both of the Chinese University of Hong Kong) held a seminar in 1996 called "Workshop on Gender and the Media." Studies presented in the seminar suggested that women are not aware that the media construct reality rather than merely reflect it. Many studies were imbued with the subtle goal of helping ordinary women. For example, it was revealed grassroots women felt pressured and helpless because they are particularly vulnerable to ideal images constructed by the mass media. Lastly, in 2001, the Gender Research Centre of the Chinese University of Hong Kong organized a workshop entitled "Women and Information and Communication Technologies."

In the mid-1990s, academic discussion on women and the media became a focus of study for many feminist groups and pressure groups. For example, the Association for the Advancement of Feminism began studying media images from a critical perspective. They found that half of all Hong Kong commercials contained sexist imagery or content that promoted gender inequality and sexual stereotypes (Wu, 1995). All these developments led to the first baseline gender study coordinated by the Equal Opportunities Commission (1997). With the Equal Opportunities Commission data, Fung and Ma (2000) found that Hong Kong people have internalized stereotypes about both male and female. The data suggested that one of the possible reasons is the audience's exposure to mass information. In particular, the entertainment media strengthened the audience's cultural perceptions of females and their sex roles in society.

In the past ten years, studies on gender in the media look at different kinds of media such as television, magazines and popular culture. In the field of television studies, Furnham, Mak, and Tanidjojo (2000), Siu (1996), and Young and Chan (2002) focused on comparing how men and women are portrayed in television advertisements in Hong Kong and other Asian countries. Specifically, Furnham, Mak and Tanidjojo (2000) found that gender portrayals are similar in both Hong Kong and Indonesian television advertisements: while women assume fewer authoritative roles than men, they are more often represented as product users and are frequently associated with body-related products. In a comparison of Hong Kong and Singaporean television advertisements, Siu (1996) found that men are portrayed as figures of authority in both societies and that women in general assume a subordinate role. Young and Chan (2002) found that despite Hofstede's taxonomy classifying Hong Kong as a masculine culture and South Korea as a feminine one, the differences in gender portrayals in children's television advertisements between the two societies are equally biased, and biased in a similar way. In Hong Kong television advertisements, females are commonly found to be less likely than men to be central figures, more likely to be product users (especially body-related and personal products), more dependent, more likely to be in a household setting, more likely to be younger in outlook than the male characters, more likely to be with other females and children than to be in a mixed group, less likely to be voice-overs and narrators, more likely to be parents, and less likely to be professionals. In sum, the female roles are more family oriented and belong to the private than the public realm.

Some scholars adopted a qualitative and interpretive approach and attended to the cultural production of meanings. For example, Lai (2004) conducted an ethnographic study of how three working-class married women understand the television series *True Love*. She found that in contrast to a popular belief that the audience "receives" media messages passively, two of the three interviewed women utilized their cultural capital to read popular texts in a largely oppositional manner. One of them even took up the role of a researcher to gather the opinions of her friends about the shows and acted as an opinion leader.

Studies have long focused on the print media as a site for the formation of gender identity. Fung (2002) found that a female identity is specifically connected not only with the consumption of women's magazines, but also with the capitalist consumption practiced by a community of readers and promoted by the magazines. In another study, Leung (2004) found that local editors of the Hong Kong edition of *Cosmopolitan* are reluctant to publish articles about sex and sexuality like the U.S. original. The translators often tone down words and delete details that are deemed obscene by Hong Kong standards. Therefore, the local editors create a cultural space in Hong Kong in which Hong Kong edition of *Cosmopolitan* is packaged as a high-class magazine for professional women. The femininity of the Hong Kong edition is different from the one sold in the US market. The latter targets a mass audience and can be easily found on supermarket check-out rack. Lee (2004) used the method critical discourse analysis (cf. Norman Fairclough) to examine newspapers coverage of high-ranking female government officials in Hong Kong. He found that, over a long period of time, the discourses used by the newspapers fixed and unfixed the meanings of femininity of Hong Kong high-ranking officials. The representations of female officials shift along the work/family, public/private, and masculinity/femininity dichotomies in different contexts. A good example to illustrate this is the discourses of the former Chief Secretary Anson Chan. During her tenure in both the colonial Hong Kong and Hong Kong Special Administrative Region (SAR) administrations, her image as the "iron lady" was made prominent in the media. Her leadership style and achievement as a Chinese woman in both administrations were highlighted. After her resignation from the SAR government, the media shifted its focus to Anson Chan as a mother, a grandmother and a wife who "respects" her husband.

Erni (2005) argued that Hong Kong popular music (known as Cantopop) reflects gender politics. First, the music industry is patriarchal in nature, and it is rare to find female musicians and lyricists; women have to break the fraternal and paternal glass ceiling in order to succeed. Second, as most lyricists are male, they have to imagine the female and feminine voices. As a result, a lot of Cantopop lyrics are gender-neutral and ambivalent. Hence, a song sung by a female singer can be re-imagined to represent a male point of view. Lastly, the lyrics of political song also reflect a male rather than a female of point of view.

Studies of film and gender have also been conducted on the same lines of femininity and masculinity. Examining movie stars from the 1960s to the 1980s, Choi (2004) showed that femininity and masculinity are not fixed over time. A movie star's femininity / masculinity is co-constructed by both on-screen and off-screen images. The on-screen images help the audience to construct the off-screen images; the vice versa is also true. In the discussion of Siu Fong-Fong and Chan Po-chu, Choi suggested that the femininity that both popular female actresses represent is different because femininity is defined in conjunction with modernity, sexuality, filial piety, westernness, and so forth. Siu Fong-fong's on-screen images are those of a westernized, independent, glamourous, fashionable and competent woman. Her femininity is defined by her modernity. Siu Fong-fong's off-screen image re-informs her movie images of modernity: she has studied abroad, married twice, emigrated abroad and returned to Hong Kong to make "arty," award-winning films. On the contrary, Chan Po-chu's on-screen and off-screen images are more traditional. Chan Po-chu was not active in making movies after her marriage. Hence, her femininity is more confined to a time frame and she does not constantly re-invent herself. Choi further argued that the Hong Kong-born Hollywood star Chow Yut-fat's masculinity is made up of his off-screen image of being a good son, a good husband, as well as his tendency towards homophobia.

As for new media studies, Nip (2004) examined the website of the Queer Sisters and found that the online community could strengthen the offline community only if both share the same goals. Her study suggested that the online participants are more interested in sharing personal thoughts and engaging in self-expression than in activist and political work. In the same study, she found that the queer communities (i.e., excluding lesbian) are not content that the online community is only lesbian-friendly. This implies that queer identities are not homogeneous.

In sum, media play a particularly important role in the highly capitalistic city of Hong Kong. The existing body of literature on women/gender and the media in Hong Kong is not extensive, but is far from insignificant. Difficult as it is to appraise the merits and to critique the shortcomings of the studies as a whole, what is commendable, apart from the large-scale survey of media's impact on values of various femininities, is the inclusion of different marginalised groupings and voices (such as Lai, 2004, Nip, 2004).

Consuming the Slimming Culture

In this section, we describe and discuss the pervasive cultural phenomenon of the past few years in Hong Kong of body slimming. Leung, Wang, and Yang (2004) suggested that eating disorders have become more severe among Chinese adolescent girls. The desire to be thin may be a result of westernization (Leung, Lam and Sze, 2001). Illustrating this phenomenon can deepen and enhance a dialectical understanding among gender, popular culture and media in Hong Kong. Here, we would like to emphasize that the culture of weight loss is not unique to Hong Kong nor is it a wholly contemporary phenomenon. For instance, the South Beach Diet and the Atkins Diet, which both stress the daily intake of specific food groups rather than exercising and taking medication, have created a craze in North America and in the UK for losing weight. Bulimia and anorexia are common among female teenagers and young adults in the US (Kilbourne, 1999). Leung, Wang, and Tang (2004) found that both Chinese and Western adolescent girls share a high level of dissatisfaction with their bodies.

Historically, thinness and fragility were two standards for judging female beauty in ancient China (Leung, Lam, and Sze, 2001). Thinness was a class-related value: upper-class women were thinner than peasant women.

However, the body slimming culture in Hong Kong is unique in two ways: first, Hong Kong women generally suffer from under-weight than over-weight. In 2002, studies showed that 30 per cent of Hong Kong women are under-weight and that close to 50 per cent of women aged 15–24 are under-weight (*Wen Wei Po*, 26 September 2002). Thus, slimming in Hong Kong is a cultural and ideological problem rather than a solution to a physical problem. Even though most of the body slimming advertisements do mention health as a reason for slimming down, the ultimate aim of body slimming is not said to be the achievement of personal gratification, individual happiness, or demonstration of one's sexuality. Rather, it is suggested that becoming slim will help individuals regain their confidence, and build up their self-esteem, because slim body is attractive to the opposite sex and is appreciated by members of the same sex. Body slimming is sold as a strategy for women to compete as sexual beings and gendered aesthetic objects in a patriarchal order.

As a cultural phenomenon, slimming is closely linked to capitalist consumption in Hong Kong: the popular media (popular magazines, mainstream movies, etc.), the beauty industry (beauty salons, fashion companies, health products, etc.), and the society as a whole co-construct a consumption-mediated culture. Reports have shown that advertisements of slimming products and services in *Sudden Weekly* (along with the supplement *Eat and and Travel Weekly*), and *Oriental Sunday* (along with the supplement *Sense*) constituted 47 and 53 percent respectively of all advertisements in 2003.[3] Furthermore, surveys have also revealed that in just the first five months in 2001, beauty salons and services had poured HK$537 million into slimming advertisements. Forty-three per cent of the revenues went to the five television stations and 37 per cent to the print media (*Hong Kong Economic Times*, 19 June 2002). The slimming culture is obviously infused with the cultures of advertising and capitalism. It is also highly institutionalized and well-planned, so that the behaviour and images of women (to a lesser extent, men) in the media are heavily regulated, constantly surveyed, and scrutinized. Consumers who do not conform are severely punished. It is the media that has changed the discourse on women's beauty and ideologies of gender in society.

A Change in the Discourse on Slimming

Prior to the late 1990s, weight loss was mainly an activity for women (and sometimes men) who were considered fat or obese by health standards; losing weight was more about an individual activity and was similar to curing a medical condition that was temporary and clinical. In the late 1990, however, Hong Kong society witnessed a dramatic change in the discourse of weight loss; the term "weight loss" became a passé, replacing it was the term "body slimming." By placing stress on the body over the weight, and on slimming rather than losing, body slimming has successfully been created as a lifestyle pursuit rather than as a one-off attempt to lose weight. The shifting from a discourse on a clinical condition that has more in common with other health problems to a new discourse on body slimming reflects the fact that the image has taken a prominent place in the new currency of weight loss. As in many postmodern works (Kellner, 1995), the discourse on body slimming puts emphases on the presentation of the self and on the superficial image; one's identity is constructed by what one consumes. Moreover, the media arbitrarily associate skinny with virtues such as beauty, diligence, persistence and determination.

We may suggest that a consumption of the body slimming discourse gives consumers a false sense of self. The consumers believe they achieve beauty, diligence, and other fine qualities simply by consuming some empty signs. For example, some body slimming products play with the word "sau" (literally meaning thin) in "sau sun" (to slim the body) by substituting it with another Chinese word with the same pronunciation "sau" but with a connotation of grace and nice-looking. The play on words shows that empty signs have come to displace the action of weight loss.

As a lifestyle, body slimming is more than the action of losing weight, it is more about the selling of a "wholesome" lifestyle. Consumers have to buy more than one type of services or products in order to engage thoroughly in the culture. The types of products and services range from exercising to dieting, purchasing special underwear to medication; in extreme cases, it also involves minor surgery. The culture of body slimming has become so pervasive in Hong Kong society that the advertising discourses of other products and services have to conform to those of body slimming in order to succeed. For example, dairy products cannot be merely promoted as doing good for the health, they have to be promoted as being low in fat so that they do not "harm" the slim body. Hence, it is the body image, not health, that is being highlighted. Traditionally, it was the healthy body that was desirable. The body slimming culture now dictates that it is·the slim body that is desirable.

The Omnipresence of Gendered Media

The current slimming culture in Hong Kong, as we suggested, is largely attributed to the omnipresence of the media in Hong Kong. Van Zoonen (1994) has argued that media are "(social) technologies of gender, accommodating, modifying, reconstructing and producing disciplining and contradictory cultural outlooks…." (p. 41). The media are not only powerful in conveying advertisements produced by beauty salons, but are also able to construct media ideologies and discourses in television dramas, movies, and fiction that collectively promote a culture of body slimming.

For example, entertainment news about the successes and failures of the weight loss efforts of artists; movies and television programmes that include themes and references to body slimming; and advertisements and campaigns that use body slimming as selling points. Prime-time television carries commercials that feature successful cases of women slimming down in the form of reality show. The "real" cases demonstrated on television show how slimming can restore a woman's confidence, enhance her careers, help her make friends, and appeal to the opposite sex.

Furthermore, in recent years, beauty salons have been spending enormous amounts of money to commission popular singers, actresses, models and other socialites to be "spokespersons." To be a spokesperson of a beauty salon means more than advertising their services; the spokesperson replaces the brand and becomes a synonym of the brand. The spokespersons bring in their images forged in other domains (such as those from movies) and their social histories to sell the body slimming culture. The spokepersons are rarely overweight; in fact, some are underweight to the extent that they can be mistaken as anorexic. An example is Sammi Cheng, who is said to have been paid an enormous sum to be the spokesperson of a beauty salon. The image of Cheng that is sold is a hybrid of her image as a successful, popular singer, and as an actress in the comedy *Love on a diet*. The plot revolved around how Mini (played by Cheng) risked losing her beloved because of her inability to control her body size, and how slimming served as a solution for women to acquire love and happiness in life. In general, the persona of Sammi is an icon of slimness, which she exemplifies in reality and in fictional characters. This new tactic of selling both the symbolic (fictional) and the real (body) seems to send a message that even the skinny, the successful, and the rich have to commit to body slimming and disciplining, hence there is no excuse for the ordinary not to conform. While the old tactic was only to display changes in appearances or body shape of ordinary women after their participation in weight loss programmes, the new tactic of the early 1990s combined both the physical fitness and symbolic meaning, reflecting the fact that body slimming of today is more about the selling of an image or a lifestyle than of one-off services.

Famous slimming stars who all enjoy high visibility in Hong Kong media make the culture ubiquitous. Because of the high remuneration to the artists (for instance, some reports suggested that most artists receive over one million Hong Kong dollars for their endorsements), press conferences about their participation in the slimming programmes are high-profile media events and always become the cover stories in entertainment news in Hong Kong. Unsurprisingly, all of these artists are carefully selected. They range from mainland artists for the China market; artists who have given birth;

those with a household image; to those representing the typical Hong Kong young lady. To sum up, body slimming is not only a lifestyle pursued by the unmarried, the unhealthy, and the obese, but also of the married, the healthy, and the skinny.

It seems that the slimming trend also spread to men, when the advertisers began to use male actors to sell slimming products in China in August 2004. Many male slimming participants in reality shows explained that one major aim of joining the slimming programme is to attract the opposite sex. Messages like these could be easily mistaken as signs of gender equality, i.e. that both women and men share equal passion for body slimming. However, few media commentaries have offered alternative views or have suggested that male participation in the slimming culture further perpetuates the gendered culture of our society by placing the symbolic in the position of the primacy.

Women's Participation in the Discourse of Slimming

The success of the slimming culture relies on the shared meanings among the consumers. The predominance of the slimming culture cannot be solely explained by the mere imposition of media images and the advertising of the beauty industry. At least, it is not difficult for us to find instances of friends and family members recounting in casual conversations their successes and failures in trying to slim down. Body slimming, unlike losing weight, is not perceived as shameful, but normal. Those who do not try to slim down are pressured to feel that their current lifestyle is abnormal. The discourse on body slimming is not limited to how salespersons of the products and services interact with customers in beauty salons and beauty shops. It has become more legitimate for friends and family members to talk about body slimming in their daily interactions and conversations. Gradually, the daily discourse perform a regulatory function: friends and family members work with the media to persuade those who do not live the lifestyle of body slimming to conform. Such surveillance is multi-dimensional and multi-directional; it is more powerful than media superimposition. Those who do not conform to the discourse are often being surveyed (such as through comments about body size), monitored (by having others control their diet), and regulated (being reminded of the delinquency and abnormality of not living the lifestyle) (Foucault, 1979). Foucault's notions (1980) of capillary power and delinquency are particularly useful for understanding the culture of body slimming. He suggested that the exercising of power is not unidirectional and top-down, but is exercised through different agencies in an institution. In the case of slimming culture, it is not just the media and capitalists who are imposing this culture on women; rather, all women and men participate in making this a dominant culture in Hong Kong.

To pitch in with the narratives about women consumers, many slimming product brands such as Fancl also publish magazines which are freely distributed to customers to generate "talks" for and among women. Some magazines (e.g. *DHC Hong Kong*) have bulletin boards to crystallize a community of women who can interact, exchange news and share with each others the joys of slimming! From a poststructural perspective, body slimming is a mediated discourse that women as social actors produce and consume for the construction of their gendered identities. Coupled with the web of discourses of the media and daily interactions, body slimming in society becomes a "moment of truth." This is what Foucault's sense of the subject refers to (Hall, 1997): the discourse produces the subjects; at the same time, the subjects are subjugated to the discourses. The subjects only exist discursively.

Ironically, the participation of women in the construction of such discourses constructs and reinforces gender and social relations, perpetuates stereotypes and impedes the improvement of women's status. Through participating in the slimming culture discourse, consumers construct identities that are manufactured and maintained by an industry for which the principal purpose is to make profits. The sense of independence, autonomy, and success that is sold to the consumers does not give them real power. The empowerment of women is commonly believed to be about sharing more power in the economic and political realms; engaging in the slimming culture discourse definitely does not bring women any gains in real power. The body slimming industry is admittedly a profit-making one. In Hong Kong, it is estimated that in a single year a single beauty salon can make up to US$20 million. Here we do not hold the view that maximizing profit is not legitimate. Rather, we would say that, as a business, the industry's primary purpose is not to help society to arrive at gender equality or to empower women. Thus, it is necessary for other social institutions to carry out this task.

In narrating and recounting of personal stories and life experiences, social actors draw on their cultural understanding of body slimming and gender relations and values such as beauty, success, femininity, and sexuality; second, they actively account for their experiences of gender vis-à-vis others and through consumption in the material world. Examining the historical discourse on women in the media and daily life, Sin (2005) documented cases in which women recounted stories about their husbands or boyfriends making jokes with the media persona "fat see-lai." The study points to the fact that to understand the term "see-lai," one has to look into the genealogy of gender relations in Chinese/Hong Kong culture: what do husbands and boyfriends mean to women in the culture (e.g., are they companions or as bread-winners?) under different social situations? Why may a "fat see-lai" not be desirable to husbands and boyfriends? Lastly, we need to deconstruct the connection between "fat see-lai" and body slimming: What do the advertisements of slimming services and products mean to "desperate married women" and how do they understand their identities in relation to the mediated images? An account of the deconstruction of these processes by charting the contour of the political economy of our gendered culture would not only be critical of the dominant discourses but would also encourage (woman) readers to take a position in relation to the discourses.

Although not all audiences are empowered and active, such an analysis could help women articulate the vocabulary, stance and coherent discourse that make negotiated and oppositional meanings of media discourses possible. A critical reading of media discourses is valuable to the targeted groups, women who have enough money to spend on consumer goods and services. Such a deconstruction is also useful for a resource-poor audience: women who may not be able to afford to immerse themselves in a culture of slimming, but who may relate to the body slimming culture in different ways.

Toward a Feminist Approach to Media Studies

To conclude this paper, we would like to remark that feminist scholars of the media in Hong Kong are attempting to explore two dimensions of gender and media analysis. In the first dimension, the scholars aim to incorporate and include diverse narratives that validate female subjectivities and identities at both the macro- and the micro-levels. Anthony Giddens uses the term "structuration" to describe the importance of the dual levels: daily interactions, social structures and their dialectics. While social actions contribute to or disrupt social structures, social structures can also constrain how women and men of diverse backgrounds come to understand the body slimming culture and gender ideologies. The body slimming culture has to be situated in a post-capitalist, consumer culture of Hong Kong and our gender relations in a patriarchal, capitalist system that constrains the experiences of social actors.

In the second dimension, there is an attempt in Hong Kong studies, especially some of those that focus on local developments, to simultaneously contemplate both knowledge and praxis. The aim of such is not just to describe the phenomenon of inequality or to describe stereotypes; they should also probe (however implicit the process is) for social and political changes. Women's concerns in society should be shown as being not segregated from general political issues, but as interconnected. After all, feminism started as a political movement. Fine, et al. (2003) discussed the social responsibilities of researchers: "The purpose of social inquiry in the 1990s is not only to generate new knowledge but to reform 'common sense' and inform critically public policies, existent social movements, and daily community life" (p. 196). The pressure of getting employed, tenure, and promotion in the academia makes it difficult for researchers to share their time with the people whom they are researching. It is as if the participants were only objects to study, not the prime purpose and the endpoint of the studies. If raising consciousness is the first and foremost task for the oppressed to shake off gender and social oppression, then feminist media scholars (regardless of which schools of thought they subscribe to) should have no excuse not to share their research findings with the communities. At present, there are a few fora that provide the opportunities for exchanges. The Gender Research Centre at The Chinese University of Hong Kong organizes an annual gender role workshop that facilitates dialogues among academics, policy makers, service recipients and providers, as well as grassroots women groups. In addition, in 2003, the Women's Commission of the Hong Kong government held a forum "A close-up on the media through gender perspectives" to achieve a similar kind of exchange.[5]

All these efforts that try to raise gender consciousness of grassroots women are not without difficulties: The Association for the Advancement of Feminism reckoned that grassroots women are usually absent in the intellectual discussion of feminisms. This is certainly unsurprising given the lack of free time that grassroots women have and the discrepancies of cultural competency between researchers and grassroots women.[6] The organization also found that grassroots women are indifferent to gender stereotyping in advertising even though they are well aware of their helplessness and their limitations in dealing with matters of everyday life. On a brighter note, recently, women groups in Hong Kong have recently started to realize the significance of explaining the body slimming culture and the ideologies of beauty to the public. There are also self-organized websites that protest against the ubiquitous nature of sliming advertisements and the dominance of the slimming business.[7] Undoubtedly, efforts like these could encourage the emergence of more critical discussions of the media and could empower the audiences to be more self-reflexive.

To this end, how can the sharing of our tale and analysis of body slimming empower women, in particular the ones who feel powerless? Feminist scholars in media studies may not always help grassroots women with their daily necessities and needs, but the empowerment of women can also come through discursively, such as through efforts to help women attain a level of media literacy on the body slimming culture. This may liberate women to free themselves from one form of gendered, social and cultural oppression.

Notes

1. The UNDP measured gender development by taking into account inequalities between men and women in health care, education, and living standard. The index can be found at http://hdr.undp.org/statistics/data/indic/indic_218_2_1.htm. (last access: 7th June 2006).
2. See the Participant's Manual of the "ITU workshops on sustainability in telecommunication through gender and social equality. International Telecommunication Union. Module 7 "Strategic change management." URL: http://www.itu.int/ITU-D/gender/Training_Resources/index.html. Last access: 5th December 2004.
3. Source: http://www.gutsywomen.org.hk/antislim_passage.htm (last access: 1 March 2005).
4. "See-lai" is a local, colloquial Cantonese term that refers to married women. In the old days, "see-lai" mostly refers to those who stayed home. Nowadays, as a large number of Hong Kong married women are in the workforce, the term "see-lai" refers to both married women who work outside home and those who stay home.
5. More information can be found at: http://www.women.gov.hk/eng/activity/activity_2003.html. (last access: 1 March 2005).
6. The researchers are not assumed to have more cultural competency than the grassroots women. They may share different scopes of the competencies.
7. Same to Note 3.

References

Erni, J. (2005, May). *Gender and everyday evasions in Hong Kong.* Paper presented at the meeting of the International Communication Association, New York, NY.

Fine, M., Weis, L., Weseen, S., & Wong, L. (2003). For whom? Qualitative research, representations, and social responsibilities. In N. Denzin, & Y. S. Lincoln (Eds.), *The landscape of qualitative research: Theories and issues* (pp. 167–207) (2nd ed.). Thousand Oaks, CA: Sage.

Foucault, M. (1979). *Discipline and punish: The birth of the prison.* New York: Vintage.

Foucault, M. (1980). *Power/knowledge: Selected interviews and other writings, 1972–1977* (C. Gordon, trans.). New York: Pantheon.

Fung, A. (2002). Women's magazines: Construction of identities and cultural consumption in Hong Kong. *Consumption, Markets and Culture, 5* (4), 321–336.

Fung, A, & Ma, E. (2000). Formal vs. informal use of television and sex role stereotyping in Hong Kong. *Sex Roles, 42* (1/2), 57–81.

Furnham, A., Mak, T., & Tanidjojo, L. (2000). An Asian perspective on the portrayal of men and women in television advertisements: Studies from Hong Kong and Indonesian television. *Journal of Applied Social Psychology, 30* (11), 2341–64.

Gallagher, M. (2005). Beijing's legacy for gender and media. *Media and Development*, (3). Online access: http://www.wacc.org.uk/wacc/publications/media_development.

Haavio-Mannila, E., Dahlerup, D., Maud, E., Gudmundsdóttir, E., Halsaa, B., Hernes, H. M., Hänninen-Salmesin, E., Sigmundsdóttir, B., Sinkkonen, S., & S. Torild. (1985). (Eds.), *Unfinished democracy: Women in Nordic politics.* (Christine Badcock, trans.). Oxford: Pergamon Press.

Hall, S. (Ed.) (1997). *Representation: Cultural representations and signifying practices.* London: Sage.

The Hong Kong Opportunities Commission. (1997). *A baseline survey on equal opportunities on the basis of gender 1996–97.* Hong Kong: The Hong Kong Opportunities Commission.

Kellner, D. (1995). *Media culture: Cultural studies, identity and politics between the modern and the postmodern.* London: Routledge.

Kilbourne, J. (1999). *Can't buy my love: How advertising changes the way we think and feel.* New York: Touchstone.

Lee, F. (2004). Constructing perfect women: The portrayal of female officials in Hong Kong newspapers. *Media, Culture and Society, 26* (2), 207–225.

Lee, M. (2004). UNESCO's conceptualization of women and telecommunications 1970–2000. *Gazette: The International Journal for Communication Studies, 66* (6), 533–552.

Lee, M. (2006, July). A critical assessment of national efforts on gender mainstreaming ICT policies from Beijing to Tunis. Paper presented at IAMCR 25th Conference and General Assembly, Cairo, Egypt.

Leung, F., Lam, S., & Sze, S. (2001). Cultural expectations of thinness in Chinese women. *Eating Disorders, 9*, 339–350.

Leung F., Wang, J. P., & Tang, C. W. Y. (2004). Psychometric properties and normative data of the Eating Disorder Inventory among 12 to 18 year old Chinese girls in Hong Kong. *Journal of Psychosomatic Research, 57*, 59–66.

Leung, L. (2004). Fashioning (western) sexuality for sale: The case of sex and fashion articles in Cosmopolitan Hong Kong. In Anita Chan, & W. Wong (Eds.), *Gendering Hong Kong* (pp. 420–441). Hong Kong: Oxford University Press.

Nip, J. (2004). The relationship between online and offline communities: The case of queer sisters. *Media, Culture and Society, 20* (3), 409–428.

Olesen, V. L. (2003). Feminisms and qualitative research at and into the millennium. In Norman Denzin, and Yvonna S. Lincoln (Eds.), *The landscape of qualitative research: Theories and issues* (pp. 332–387) (2nd ed.). Thousand Oaks, CA: Sage.

Rommes, E. (2002). Creating places for women on the Internet: The design of a 'women's square' in a digital city. *The European Journal of Women's Studies, 9* (4), 400–429.

Sin, W. K. (2005). *(In)visibility of women's discourse in TV and everyday.* Unpublished Master Thesis, School of Journalism and Communication, The Chinese University of Hong Kong.

Siu, W. S. (1996). Gender portrayal in Hong Kong and Singapore television advertisements. *Journal of Asian Business, 12* (3), 47–63.

van Zoonen, L. (1994). *Feminist media studies.* London: Sage.

Wu, R. (1995). Women. In Stephen Y. L. Cheung and Stephen M. H. Sze (Eds.), *The other Hong Kong report 1995* (pp. 121–156). Hong Kong: The Chinese University Press.

Young, S. M., & Chan, K. (2002). Gender portrayal in Hong Kong and Korean children's TV commercials: A cross-cultural comparison. *Asian Journal of Communication, 12* (2), 100–119.

Literature in Chinese

黎肖嫻 (2004) 從長篇電視劇《真情》出發的日常生活網路探索──三個本地主婦的「文化資本」應用. Retrieved from: Cyberculture Express, Gendering Hong Kong, http://www.hku.hk/hkcsp/ccex/text/studyguide/hkgender/31.html.

蔡穎儀 (2004) 傳媒與現象──電影, Retrieved from: Cyberculture Express, Gendering Hong Kong, http://www.hku.hk/hkcsp/ccex/text/studyguide/hkgender/25.html.

CHAPTER 13

Working Women in Hong Kong: *Neuih Keuhng Yahn* or Oppressed Class?

Anne Marie Francesco and Margaret A. Shaffer

Images of working women in Hong Kong offer a great contrast. We read about the phenomenal successes of the *neuih keuhng yahn*[1] (女強人), the superwomen who hold positions of power in government and industry. Yet, of the 60 Legislative Council members taking their seats in September 2004, only 11 of them were women (Ng, 2004). We also see the everyday reality of women working in relatively less desirable jobs earning significantly less than men and struggling to cope with the competing demands of both work and family.

It seems that there are some important differences in the experiences of working women compared to working men. According to a recent report on family-friendly employment policies and practices (FFEPs) in Hong Kong (Siu & Phillips, 2006), men put in more hours at work (50.67 hours per week versus 44.96 hours per week for women), but women spend more time taking care of children and doing housework (16.58 hours per week for women and 13.01 hours for men). Are there barriers that exist in Hong Kong that prevent the equal participation of women in the workforce? How does woman's special role in the Chinese family interface with her working life? In this chapter, we will attempt to find answers to these questions. We will first consider the general conditions of working women in Hong Kong and then look at perceptions of working women and inequality. We then address work and family conflict — one potentially important outcome for Hong Kong women who are often torn between traditional familial expectations and demands and more modern professional/occupational roles and requirements.

General Conditions of Working Women

Women's place in the world of work is largely influenced by cultural and economic context. The traditional Confucian culture relegates women to a secondary role yet also requires family members to make an economic contribution to the family (Westwood, Leung, & Chiu, 1999). In addition to a subordinate role in relation to husbands, females were also expected to take care of home and children while the males went out to work and provided for the family (Lui, 1999). A study commissioned by the Hong Kong Equal Opportunities Commission in 1997 concluded that gender stereotypes derived from traditional Chinese culture were the source of most sex discriminatory practices and misconceptions (Equal Opportunities Commission, 1998). Further, those who held traditional stereotypes of men and women were also more likely to have occupational sex stereotypes.

Relative to other cultures, Hong Kong people score high on work centrality, indicating that they see work as more important and central in life, and their view of work is highly instrumental in that it provides the means to achieve material outcomes that can be used to contribute to the family (Westwood et al., 1999).

Hong Kong has been greatly influenced by decades of economic growth and prosperity that came to an unexpected halt in late 1997/early 1998 as a result of the Asian financial crisis. The decades of rapid growth provided greater job opportunity for everyone, but when the economic slowdown occurred, there was belt tightening all around.

Earlier chapters by Ngo and Pun and Lee, Li, and Zhang present a detailed picture of the general situation for women over time. There has been a slight increase in female labor force participation attributed to declining fertility rates, increasing numbers of women seeking higher education, and greater opportunities in the service sector (Ng & Chiu, 1999). However, women still continued to be paid significantly less than men. Women's work is segregated both horizontally into traditional "pink collar" work and vertically into lower-level, non-managerial type work (Ng & Chiu, 1999). It is also interesting that a much higher percentage of working women (39.1 percent) compared to working men (30.7) has never married with an especially large gap between females and males working as managers and administrators (27.6 percent for females versus 13.9 percent for males) (Ng & Chakrabarty, 2005).

Although women in Hong Kong are legally protected from discriminatory employment practices, these laws have only been in effect since

1996. Consequently, strong case precedents have not yet been established, and Hong Kong organizations have not created a strong "equal employment" culture.

Perceptions of Working Women and Gender Inequality

Over the past few years, several studies have been done that examine perceptions of working women and gender inequality. These include studies of both university students and working people. Taken as a group, these studies show a fairly consistent pattern with women of different backgrounds stating somewhat similar views that on the whole show some differences from those expressed by men.

A study commissioned by the Hong Kong Equal Employment Opportunities Commission in 1996 considered the views of over 2,000 Hong Kong citizens over the age of 16. A large majority of respondents believed that gender discrimination at work, including incidents such as inequality in pay and job opportunities, was common in Hong Kong with women generally more aware of such inequity. However, among this same group of people, only four percent reported any personal experience of discrimination (Equal Opportunities Commission, 1997).

A more recent study commissioned by the Equal Opportunities Commission focused on primary and secondary students' attitudes toward gender stereotypes and family roles (Equal Opportunities Commission, 2001). In this study of over 3,000 students, both males and females perceived a clear differentiation in jobs that were considered suitable for men versus women, and the students generally only considered gender-appropriate career choices for themselves. For example, nursing and teaching were thought to be suitable careers for women. Although both boys and girls were in favor of women having a career, they also thought the man should be the major breadwinner in the family and that the woman was more suitable for taking care of young children.

A study of first year male and female undergraduate students describes their personal experiences of differential treatment based on gender (Ng, 2001). The majority of these experiences involved sex discrimination against women. The nature of the discrimination varied and included experiences at home, at school, and at work. Female students encountered four categories of discrimination during their casual, summer, or part-time jobs: gender stereotyping of jobs, sexual harassment, assignment of job duties and responsibilities on the basis of gender, and tokenism. Ng (2001) concludes that Hong Kong Chinese girls and women "face blatant and subtle sexist attitudes and discrimination in the spheres of family, school/university, and work" (p. 6). Interestingly, both male and female students mentioned several experiences of reverse discrimination towards men, particularly at work. For example, men might be overlooked for certain job positions that were considered as traditionally feminine, or male employees might be asked to do thing like loading or carrying goods. Overall, 85% of the female students in this study had personal experience of sex discrimination indicating that this is a pervasive situation that is already apparent to people at a fairly early age.

Ng and associates also studied working women's experiences of sex discrimination at work (Ng, Ng, & Tse, 1998). The subjects in this study ranged in age from 15 to 50 and worked in a variety of occupations. Unlike the students, the majority of them did not suffer from sex discrimination. Only 11.5% had experienced discrimination during job recruitment, over half felt their salaries were similar to male colleagues in the same position, and 71.8% felt they enjoyed the same promotion opportunities as males doing similar work. Many women thought that male colleagues enjoyed higher pay and better promotion prospects because these men were more educated or capable. In other words, they felt that dissimilar treatment of males and females at work may be justified.

Another study of perceived gender inequality was conducted with male and female church workers who were pastors or preachers at local churches (Ngo, Foley, Wong, & Loi, 2003). This sample is interesting as gender inequality is an important concern among local church workers. However, in spite of concern over the issue, both men and women perceived inequality in the workplace with female subjects perceiving greater inequality than did male subjects. Further, more gender inequality was perceived in organizations with certain characteristics: lower or higher proportions of women employees, a male person in charge, and greater job segregation by gender. Thus, although gender inequality was perceived to exist by both men and women in all types of church organizations, the level of perceived inequality varied considerably based on the gender of the perceiver and the type of organization where he or she worked.

Another study of middle-class educated single women in their 20s found a range of views regarding perceptions of inequalities (Lam, 2004). Respondents fell into three categories, endorsers, opponents, and accommodating respondents. Endorsers generally could not recall personal experiences of gender inequality. However, further exploration revealed that in fact they had been involved in situations where males and females were treated differently. When asked to explain this, the majority of the endorsers felt that such differential treatment was justified. They tended to see each situation as due to specifics rather than as reflective of societal behavior overall. The opponents on the other hand, were very conscious of gender inequality and actively fought against it. Finally, the majority of the women in this study fell into the category of accommodating respondents. They had complex responses that reflected ambivalent emotions and evaluations. They generally were pragmatic in their views and saw males and females to be similar in some situations but different in others. Thus, this study suggests that perceptions of sexual inequality may not be so straightforward.

Two studies focused on the perceptions of entrepreneurs, one concerned with those in the clothing industry (Chu, 2004) and the other with women lawyers (Lee, 2003). Since a higher percentage of female entrepreneurs can be found in Hong Kong's clothing industry than in any other manufacturing industry (Chu, 2004), this was an interesting group to study. The female entrepreneurs in the sample perceived gender inequality at work and also had negative feelings about it. For many of them, the motivation for them to start a business was family-oriented, reflecting a need to fulfill family obligations rather than for personal reasons such as to gain job satisfaction. One common complaint was that they often faced problems with their marriages or with finding a spouse if they were single due to their business commitments. Being an entrepreneur also created more of an impact on home life than it did for male entrepreneurs.

In the other study, female lawyers who ran their own law firms either as sole practitioners or in partnership with others reported various forms of discrimination including being moved into jobs that were less prestigious and that paid less (before they opened their own firms), problems in getting clients, having to work harder (than male lawyers) to get and maintain business, and having to take major responsibility for home and family matters. In spite of these problems though, the vast majority felt happy with women's status in the legal profession and the general status of women in Hong Kong. Summing up this apparent contradiction between experiences and perceptions of discrimination, Lee concludes that, "… the Hong Kong superwoman has to be successful in both career and family. However, she does not associate this with oppression, inequality, or exploitation. On the contrary, she believes she has acquired a sense of freedom and agency in choosing her own life course" (Lee, 2003, p. 95).

Three other studies look specifically at Hong Kong women managers (Ng & Pine, 2003; Venter, 2002; Westwood & Leung, 1999). The first study compared male and female hotel managers' perceptions of gender and career development issues (Ng & Pine, 2003). Men and women had similar perceptions of both success factors and obstacles. Among those who had a preference (and many respondents did not,) both males and females were more comfortable working for a male supervisor or supervising a male employee. When asked to identify problems or obstacles to women managers in the hospitality industry, females most often mentioned gender stereotypes and men's discriminatory attitudes towards women. "Irregular work hours/ work-family conflict" and "old boys' network" were also seen as problems. In dealing with these and other issues, the women hotel managers felt they needed to work hard to prove themselves, rather than expecting or asking for any accommodation such as family-friendly policies. Interestingly, this study also reported that compared to the females, a higher percentage of male hotel managers are married with children.

In the second study, based on interviews with 50 female managers, Westwood and Leung (1999) explore women's experiences of stereotypes, discrimination, and sexism; their perceptions of gender differences in the job of manager; how they manage gender identity; and how they cope and succeed as female managers. Similar to women in the studies mentioned previously, the majority did not report experiences of overt discrimination. However, many of the subjects did experience some forms of discrimination, for example women were systematically underrepresented in management ranks or certain departments which restricted their career opportunities. Some women felt that their organizations were dominated by men and that sex stereotypes limited opportunity. For example, the traditional view that the family depends on the male as the primary breadwinner was linked to the idea that men were in greater need of promotion. The female managers in the Westwood and Leung (1999) study reported more incidences of sexist attitudes and behaviors than discrimination, and a few of the women reported that they were sexually harassed. Another concern that was raised was the existence of informal groups of men which excluded women. Particularly in Hong Kong, where relationships are so important for success, not being able to participate in such groups could impede women's career progression.

On the topic of perceived gender differences in working as a manager, there was a strong view that men and women did manage differently. These differences were believed to result from socialization and learning, rather than to be inborn. Although some of the female attributes could be seen as positive, often they constituted a "double-edged sword" and in fact, women suffered as a result of these views. One theme that was mentioned here was that women leaders were perceived as masculine, but failure to include this masculine element was seen as ineffective. Another popular belief among the women managers was that women needed to work harder than men in order to be successful. Further, they thought that women were more competent in handling detail and in getting a job done. However, men were seen as more strategic as they could see the bigger picture.

Women managers were also considered to be more relationship-oriented, again a seemingly positive trait that could be reinterpreted as women managers being "too soft." Two other differences that were mentioned were first, that men were more concerned with issues of "face," such that there was an expectation that women should give and protect the face of men, and second, that women were seen as better communicators and better at managing relationships. The final theme on gender differences was advantages and disadvantages of being female and a manager. Some women felt that they were protected and that their mistakes were more easily accepted and forgiven. Women managers were also seen as more likely to get what they wanted from men as the men were not willing to create conflict with them. However, this could also be a disadvantage. With such a relationship-oriented style, the women might be less assertive. Women were also seen as less decisive than men in decision making and in some cases were considered to be "bitchy," emotional, and lacking drive and commitment.

In terms of managing gender identity, there were mixed views. Some women managers agreed that successful managers are defined in terms that are more masculine and further that they themselves may have consciously tried to adopt such a style or in some cases, their natural style was already more aggressive or masculine.

The final topic in the interviews was how to cope and succeed as a female manager. The majority of respondents said that to be successful they had to give up something. More than half the women in the sample were not married, and some were divorced or separated. Women also reported sacrificing hobbies, leisure, and social time. Most notable was the regret and guilt expressed by women who did not have enough time to spend with their children. Westwood and Leung (1999) conclude that Chinese women managers in Hong Kong face many of the same problems experienced by women managers in other countries. However, within a strong cultural tradition of patriarchy, there is a feeling of pragmatism in business that provides women in Hong Kong opportunities to move ahead.

The other study of managers contrasted female managers in Britain and Hong Kong by interviewing both men and women managers in each location (Venter, 2002). Here we will only discuss those findings related to the Hong Kong group. First, family and family relations were found to be important for Hong Kong women managers. Often the women's access to jobs and organizations was due to family connections. Due to the strong influence of collectivist culture, women in Hong Kong were expected to take up more responsibility for the family. In spite of this, a good support network exists for most Hong Kong women that allows them to focus on their managerial careers. Due to the availability of cheap labor in surrounding countries, women managers can also afford to hire domestic helpers who provide further assistance with home and family. As a result, few women managers quit their jobs if they marry or have children.

The women managers in this study took responsibility for their own career successes and failures and generally believed that hard work could lead to success while bad choices and mistakes were responsible for failure. Although they acknowledged that the labor market was male-oriented, they did not use that as an excuse for not doing well. In fact, women were seen as having to work harder to achieve senior positions; it was more difficult for them because of traditional gender-role attitudes. Further, these women took an opportunistic approach to career. They looked for any opportunities to move ahead, rather than planning specific career moves. Their main concern was with financial success, having a job and moving in an upward direction.

At the office, women reported a code of social behavior with fairly formalized relationships where women are treated as ladies. Sexist behavior was seen as acceptable, and in fact the view was that women should not be treated in the same way as men. More than half the managers interviewed felt that it was difficult for men to take senior women seriously. Overall, the managers interviewed don't perceive much discrimination; over 80% of males and females see female and male managers as being treated equally. "The Hong Kong women generally feel that they have been treated well, that there have been few problems associated with being women, and that they are respected and valued by their organizations and their colleagues. This is not a view stemming from ignorance or lack of awareness as, despite this perception, the women simultaneously believe that women have to be better than their male counterparts to progress and that when all things are equal, it will be men who are promoted" (Venter, 2002, p. 70).

The experience of inequality by women within the working world of Hong Kong is somewhat complex. Although many women have experienced differential treatment, not all of them view it as unfair or unjustified. For example, perhaps women and men are differentially motivated for managerial positions. Two studies, one of students and the other of managers, explore this possibility. In the first (Ebrahimi, 1999), there were no differences found between undergraduate female and male business and MBA students on motivation to manage. Ebrahimi concluded that, "… in terms of their managerial motivation, Hong Kong female business students are capable of being as effective as their male counterparts" (1999, p. 49). Extending the study to working male and female managers, Ebrahimi, Young, and Luk (2001) also did not find any gender differences in motivation to manage, assertiveness, or competitiveness. They conclude that lack of managerial motivation can not explain the under representation and underutilization of women as managers in Hong Kong.

Another aspect of the situation that can be considered is possible gender differences in perceived leadership effectiveness. According to the results of Project GLOBE, a 61-country study of culture and leadership, Hong Kong is the most gender egalitarian country of those in the sample (House et al., 1999). Within Hong Kong organizations, there is also a moderately favorable culture towards women leaders (Chow, 2005). Further, there are few significant differences between male and female subordinates in perceptions of leadership attributes (Chow, 2005).

So what then may be some other reasons for the less favorable position of working women in Hong Kong? Could it be that women are less educated than men? In fact, the opposite seems to be true. From 1991 to 2001, a slightly higher proportion of females aged three to 18 was attending school compared to males (Hong Kong Government, Census and Statistics Department, 2001 Population Census). At the tertiary level, 54% of students studying in government-funded universities are women, and 65 % of those studying at sub-degree level are women (Ng, 2004). Hong Kong parents are also reported to spend equal amounts of money educating sons and daughters (Equal Opportunities Commission, 1997).

But, perhaps these students perceive some types of "glass hurdles" if they wish to pursue a career in management or the professions. Glass hurdles reflect perceptions of greater difficulty faced by females compared to males in achieving career success (Yim & Bond, 2002). A study of male and female first year business students found significant differences in how the two groups viewed themselves compared to a successful middle manager. The women students' profile of themselves was much further from the profile of the successful middle manager than was the male students' (Sze, 1998).

A later study asked the question of whether this perceptual difference would change after two years of higher education (Yim & Bond, 2002). In spite of two years' of university business education, gender stereotypes regarding the successful middle manager persisted. Both males and females saw the successful middle manager as more like the typical male than the typical female. At the personal level, the self-perceptions of all the students moved closer to the profile of the successful middle manager after two years. However, women students perceived themselves as less assertive than male students. This could be a barrier for women since assertiveness is one of the key personality characteristics of successful managers.

Media portrayals of working women might also influence popular perceptions. One analysis of media coverage of top government officials in Hong Kong suggests that they are depicted as "perfect women" (Lee, 2004). In 2000, the number of female top officials in Hong Kong was perhaps the highest in the world, and these women were presented as possessing "... both rationality and passion, who excel both at work and in the family" (Lee, 2004, p. 211). The relatively high number of females in senior government positions was considered as evidence that Hong Kong had a fair amount of gender equality.

Despite the positive media portrayal of gender equality in Hong Kong, our review of the perceptions and experiences of female students, managers and professionals suggests that Hong Kong men and women are not equal. Gender discrimination, sexist attitudes, and gender role stereotypes are pervasive and propitious in creating stress, especially for women, in both work and family domains. As the superwomen of Hong Kong strive to achieve success in both domains, however, they must also manage the incompatible demands and responsibilities emanating from work and family and the ensuing work-family conflict. To better understand the challenges of balancing work and family that Hong Kong women face, we review the work-family conflict literature in the next section. We first report the scope of the problem by comparing levels of work-family conflict for employees in Hong Kong, Mainland China, and the United States. Next, we review the antecedents and outcomes of work-family conflict, highlighting those that are especially relevant to Hong Kong.

Work-Family Conflict in Hong Kong

The juxtaposition of socio-economic trends and the prevailing culture in Hong Kong have resulted in a stressful environment for women in particular as they struggle to balance the competing demands of work and family. As described at the beginning of this chapter and in other chapters of this book, there have been several socio-economic trends relevant to the experiences of women in Hong Kong including increased labor force participation, increased educational attainment by women, the passing of equal employment opportunity legislation, etc.

Corresponding shifts in culture and gender role expectations have not kept pace with these socio-economic changes. Hong Kong society is influenced by the philosophical traditions of Confucianism (King & Bond, 1985), which emphasize a conflict-free system of social relationships (i.e., harmony), consciousness of personal position in the social system (i.e., hierarchy), and rejection of personal enhancement as a threat to established group hierarchies (i.e., collectivism). These philosophical underpinnings have resulted in what Trompenaars and Hampton-Turner (1998) refer to as a diffuse culture in which life roles such as work and family are integrated rather than separated. Consequently, Hong Kong people view work as more important than leisure and as contributing to family welfare instead of competing with it (Redding, 1993; Redding & Wong, 1986). Because the most important function of the individual is in the maintenance and preservation of the household, people in Hong Kong also tend to assign lower importance to sufficient time for personal and family life than do Westerners (Redding, 1993). As a masculine society (Hofstede, 1980), Hong Kong people maintain very strong gender role stereotypes; they believe males have the responsibility to work and to improve the family welfare while females are primarily responsible for caring for family members (Kao, 1987).

The competing socio-economic and cultural forces facing Hong Kong women have created a climate conducive to stress, and one manifestation of this is work-family conflict. Defined as a form of interrole conflict that occurs when responsibilities from the work and family domains are incompatible (Greenhaus & Beutell, 1985), work-family conflict has been conceptualized in terms of two forms: work interference with family (WIF) and family interference with work (FIW) (e.g., Adams, King, & King, 1996). Although research in this area has been dominated by Western studies, the universality of work-family conflict has been recognized (e.g., Aryee, 1992), and several recent studies in non-Western countries support this (e.g., Aryee, Fields, & Luk, 1999; Lee & Choo, 2001; Ng, Fosh & Naylor, 2002; Yang, Chen, Choi, & Zou, 2000).

The universality of work-family conflict, however, does not preclude the possibility that the process, or *how* work-family conflict occurs, differs across cultures. In considering these differences, we address two important issues with respect to the experience of work-family conflict in Hong Kong. One issue has to do with the extent to which work-family conflict occurs in Hong Kong compared with other cultures. To examine this, we collected and analyzed data from employees in Hong Kong, Mainland China, and the United States (Joplin, Shaffer, Lau, & Francesco, 2003). The other issue has to do with the determinants and consequences of work-family conflict. Does the process parallel that of individuals in Western societies, or are there unique inputs or outcomes for Hong Kong people? To assess this, we review the growing body of literature that investigates work-family conflict in Hong Kong and compare and contrast the findings with those from Western studies. Although most of these studies include both men and women, evidence suggests that the experience of work-family conflict is especially poignant for females (Luk & Shaffer, 2005).

Levels of Work-Family Conflict

Based on the discordance between the shifts in socio-economic conditions and cultural values in Hong Kong, we expect stress, in the form of work-family conflict, to be especially intense (Burke, 1996; Thoits, 1991). To assess the extent to which Hong Kong employees experience work-family conflict, we compared self-report ratings of work-family conflict reported by employees in Hong Kong, the United States, and Mainland China. We also looked at the average number of hours worked per week as an indicator of stress. The data for this comparison comes from a larger cross-cultural study on life balance that we are conducting. We chose the United States and Mainland China as comparison groups because, relative to Hong Kong, the United States has a distinctive culture and similar socio-economic milieu and Mainland China has a distinctive socio-economic environment and analogous cultural values.

For both forms of work-family conflict and average work hours, Hong Kong employees reported much higher levels than their counterparts in the United States and Mainland China (see Table 1). Interestingly, there were no significant differences between respondents in the United States and Mainland China. For all three groups, however, levels of work interference with family (WIF) were much higher than those of family interference with work (FIW). This suggests a more universal tendency for employees to "take work home" and to keep family out of the workplace. This is consistent with the strong value that Chinese place on work as a means of contributing

Table 1: Comparison of Stress Indicators

Variables	Hong Kong		United States		Mainland China	
	Males	Females	Males	Females	Males	Females
WIF Conflict	4.91	4.65	4.18	4.45	4.09	4.02
FIW Conflict	3.43[a]	2.85[a]	2.71	2.39	2.84	2.51
Average Work Hours (per week)	50.62	50.26	45.09[a]	38.79[a]	42.41	43.18

WIF = Work Interference with Family
FIW = Family Interference with Work
Superscripts ([a]) denotes significant mean difference between males and females.
N = 112 for Hong Kong, 110 for Mainland China, and 68 for the United States

to family welfare. Interestingly, Hong Kong men reported higher levels of FIW conflict, perhaps because women were better able to demarcate the boundaries between work and home. Although there were no significant differences between Hong Kong men and women's experience of WIF conflict, other studies have reported that women in Hong Kong do experience more work-family conflict than men (Aryee, Luk, Leung, & Lo, 1999; Luk & Shaffer, 2005). This is indicative of the masculine cultural values that are predominant in this Chinese city.

Determinants and Consequences of Work-Family Conflict

Attempts to understand employees' efforts to effectively integrate the work and family domains have mainly construed work-family conflict from a stressor-stress-strain perspective (Edwards & Rothbard, 2000). Stressors predicting work-family conflict generally represent increased demands and decreased resources from both the work and family domains (e.g., Grandey & Cropanzano, 1998). Strains associated with work-family conflict include negative affect such as work and family dissatisfaction, depression, and life stress (e.g., Frone, Russell, & Cooper, 1992; Kossek & Ozeki, 1998) and dysfunctional behaviors such as turnover (e.g., Good, Page, & Young, 1996). Such outcomes are detrimental to the well-being of individuals and organizations. In the next sections, we review the major stressors and strains associated with work-family conflict and highlight those that are especially relevant to Hong Kong.

Antecedents of work-family conflict. Existing literature supports the effect of domain-specific stressors on the corresponding forms of work-family conflict (e.g., work stressors affect WIF conflict and family stressors influence FIW conflict). Demands in terms of role overload, hours worked and organizational/family expectations are all conducive to work-family conflict (e.g., Aryee, 1992; Boles & Babin, 1996; Higgins, Duxbury & Irving, 1992). Organizational and family characteristics such as hierarchical position and family structure have also been associated with work-family conflict (Kinnunen & Mauno, 1998; Voydanoff, 1988). Oftentimes, managers in higher-level positions have increased time and role demands placed on them, and these may result in higher levels of conflict. With respect to family structures, most research has focused on dual-career families (Burley, 1994) and married employees (e.g., Aryee et al., 1999b). Organizational and family support have been linked with work-family conflict (Adams et al., 1996; Thomas & Ganster, 1995), and a wide range of support resources, including both social (e.g., supervisor and spouse support) and instrumental (e.g., organizational family-friendly policies and domestic helpers) forms of support have been identified.

Demands and resources that span domains have received less attention in the literature. One domain-spanning variable that has been found to be relevant is personal aspirations, especially career and financial goals that individuals have. Duxbury and Higgins (1991) reported an important influence of spousal career pursuits on work-family conflict. Other domain-spanning inputs to work-family conflict include a variety of individual differences. Recent investigations of personal traits such as hardiness, extraversion and self-esteem have supported their influence on both forms of work-family conflict (Bernas & Major, 2000; Grandey & Cropanzano, 1999; Grzywacz & Marks, 2000).

With a few exceptions, studies conducted in Hong Kong generally support the findings from Western countries (see Table 2). Among work antecedents, job conflict (Aryee et al., 1999a), work hours (Fu & Shaffer, 2001; Luk & Shaffer, 2005), role conflict and role overload (Aryee et al., 1999b; Fu & Shaffer, 2001), organizational practices such as work schedule flexibility (Lo, 2003; Lo, Stone, & Ng, 2003), and supervisor support (Fu & Shaffer, 2001) were predictive of work interference with family conflict. Also consistent with the literature were several influences on family interference with work, including family conflict (Aryee et al., 1999a), family hours (Fu & Shaffer, 2001), and spouse support (Aryee et al., 1999b).

Recognizing the more permeable boundaries between work and family for Hong Kong Chinese, Luk and Shaffer (2005) tested and found support for domain-spanning work and family variables. In particular, they

Table 2: Antecedents and Outcomes of Work-Family Conflict for
Hong Kong Employees

	WIF	FIW	OVERALL WFC
Work Antecedents			
Job Conflict	Aryee, Fields & Luk (1999)		Chiu (1998)
Work Hours	Fu & Shaffer (2001) Luk & Shaffer (2005)		Lo, Stone & Ng (2003)
Inflexible Work Schedule			Lo, Stone & Ng (2003)
Work Restructuring			Lo, Stone & Ng (2003)
Flexible Hours			Lo (2003)
Control over Work Schedule			Lo (2003)
Parental Leave			Lo (2003)
Role Conflict	Fu & Shaffer (2001)		
Role Overload	Fu & Shaffer (2001) Aryee, Luk, Leung & Lo (1999)	Aryee, Luk, Leung & Lo (1999)	
Supervisor Social Support	Fu & Shaffer (2001)		
Work Role Expectation	Luk & Shaffer (2005)	Luk & Shaffer (2005)	
Family Friendly Policies		Luk & Shaffer (2005)	
Family Antecedents			
Family Conflict		Aryee, Fields & Luk (1999)	Chiu (1998)
Family Hours		Fu & Shaffer (2001)	Lo, Stone & Ng (2003)
Children's Homework			Lo, Stone & Ng (2003)
Spouse Support	Aryee, Luk, Leung & Lo (1999)		Lo, Stone & Ng (2003)
Domestic Help		Fu & Shaffer (2001)	Lo, Stone & Ng (2003)
Tutor for Children			Lo, Stone & Ng (2003)
Parental Demands	Luk & Shaffer (2005)	Luk & Shaffer (2005) Aryee, Luk, Leung & Lo (1999)	
Family Role Expectation	Luk & Shaffer (2005)		
General Antecedents			
Exhaustion			Lo, Stone & Ng (2003)
Multiple Roles			Lo, Stone & Ng (2003)
'Superwoman' Mentality			Lo, Stone & Ng (2003)
Gender		Fu & Shaffer (2001)	Aryee, Luk, Leung & Lo (1999)
Work Outcomes			
Job Satisfaction		Aryee, Fields & Luk (1999) Aryee, Luk, Leung & Lo (1999)	
Career Progression			Ng, Fosh, & Naylor (2002)
Family Outcomes			
Family Satisfaction	Aryee, Fields & Luk (1999)		
General Outcomes			
Life Satisfaction	Aryee, Fields & Luk (1999)	Aryee, Luk, Leung & Lo (1999)	

found that work role expectations and parental demands influenced both forms of work-family conflict. In contrast with the literature, however, other family domain variables (i.e., family time commitment and family role expectation) did not have a significant effect on FIW conflict. A possible explanation is that an overwhelming majority of respondents (83.3%) in this sample was male. Past research indicates that men balance work and family identity without trading-off one for the other (Dibenedetto & Tittle, 1990). Also, Hong Kong Chinese assign greater importance to family roles (Aryee et al., 1999), so it is likely that respondents in this study perceived that family is the main part of their life. Time committed to their families, therefore, was absolutely necessary. At the same time, Hong Kong Chinese maintain very strong gender role stereotypes; thus family time commitment and family role expectation had no impact on FIW.

Other distinctions between studies in Hong Kong and the West have to do with the role of family-friendly policies in alleviating work-family conflict. Given the relative paucity of family-friendly policies in Hong Kong (see Chiu & Ng, 1999 and Siu & Phillips, 2006, for a review of these policies), researchers have not been able to substantiate the potentially important influence of such practices. Qualitative studies (e.g., Lo, 2003) suggest that such practices are important in reducing the amount of work-family conflict experienced by employees, but a quantitative test of their influence showed null effects (Luk & Shaffer, 2005). A recent report commissioned by the Equal Opportunities Commission and Women's Commission of Hong Kong (Siu & Phillips, 2006), however, indicates that Hong Kong employees support more family-friendly policies and practices. Furthermore, those who worked with a firm that had family-friendly practices reported less work stress and greater work-family balance.

Familial conditions may also contribute to work-family conflict. Lo et al. (2003) highlighted the potential influence of children's education on work-family conflict. Western researchers (e.g., Bedeian, Burke, & Moffett, 1988) contend that because younger (pre-school) children are more dependent on their parents than are older children, they will generate more work-family conflict. However, in Hong Kong, the stress associated with children stems more from educational demands rather than parental time and energy needed for care of younger children. The relative lack of young children as a source of stress in Hong Kong may be due to the availability of domestic helpers in Hong Kong. With domestic help, working mothers in Hong Kong need to perform less housework, which results in more time to concentrate on families. More research in this area is needed, however, as Fu and Shaffer

(2001) reported that, contrary to expectations, domestic helpers contributed to work-family conflict. For some, a domestic helper represented another source of stress.

Outcomes of work-family conflict. Extensive research examining the consequences of the work interference with family and family interference with work conflict suggests that domain-specific affective and behavioral outcomes as well as individual health outcomes are associated with each form (see Frone, 2003, for a review). Work interference with family conflict has been associated with family dissatisfaction (e.g., Carlson & Kacmar, 2000; Frone, Yardley, & Markel, 1997) and family-related absenteeism, tardiness and poor performance (e.g., Frone et al., 1997; MacEwen & Barling, 1994). Corresponding results have been reported for the effects of family interference with work conflict on job dissatisfaction, (e.g., Carlson & Kacmar, 2000; Frone et al., 1997) and work-related behaviors such as absenteeism, tardiness, and poor performance (Frone et al., 1992). Both forms of work-family conflict have been predictive of various individual psychological and physiological health outcomes (e.g., Frone, Russell, & Barnes, 1996; Frone, 2000).

In Hong Kong, limited research has been devoted to understanding the consequences of work-family conflict. Consistent with Western studies, job dissatisfaction occurred as a result of family interference with work (Aryee et al., 1999a and 1999b) and work interference with family was predictive of family dissatisfaction (Aryee et al., 1999a). Conclusions regarding the effects of work-family conflict on life satisfaction are more tenuous. Although Western studies support the influence of family interference with work conflict on life satisfaction, Hong Kong studies indicate that both forms of conflict affect life satisfaction (Aryee et al., 1999a and 1999b). The only other outcome addressed by Hong Kong researchers is career progression. Ng et al. (2002) and Ng and Fosh (2004) reported evidence supporting the contention that work-family conflict is more likely to adversely affect the progression of women in Hong Kong. That is, Hong Kong women may intentionally put their careers on hold or set less ambitious goals for themselves as a means of reducing or avoiding conflicts between the work and family domains.

Conclusion

The images of Hong Kong's working women do reflect the reality: a complex economic and socio-cultural milieu in which women have the opportunity to become very successful in the careers of their choice. Yet, this success may be harder to achieve than it would be for a man. To answer the question of our chapter title, the evidence seems to indicate that working women in Hong Kong can become *neuih keuhng yahn* in spite of being part of an oppressed class. There are many examples of successful women in various sectors. Yet, it seems that success can only come to women who work harder than and show themselves to be more competent than men. Since accommodation to women in the form of family-friendly benefits is so limited (Chiu & Ng, 1999; Siu & Phillips, 2006) successful women often must sacrifice some aspect of family, personal, or social life to achieve career success. Indeed, even in firms offering family-friendly benefits, Hong Kong women were less likely than their male counterparts to use them (Siu & Phillips, 2006).

Hong Kong women are practical, and they look for career success in terms of financial security that can be a help to their families. For them, their two most important life roles of work and family are integrated such that work is more important because of the contribution it can make to the family. As we have noted, Hong Kong women do experience work-family conflict, perhaps even more than their male counterparts. However, based on our own observations and recent trends in the work-family literature in general, we know that this is only part of the story. In fact, many women (and men) are enriched through the interface of work and family activities (see Greenhaus & Powell, 2006 for a review.) Moving away from what has been a dominant focus on work-family conflict, researchers have begun to consider positive outcomes of the work-family interface. Greenhaus and Powell (2006) refer to this as "enrichment", which they define as "the extent to which experiences in one role improve the quality of life in the other role" (p. 73). Given the permeability of work and family within the Hong Kong context, enrichment may be a more common occurrence than conflict. Tang and coauthors (2002) found that working women in Hong Kong reported less psychological distress than nonworking women. Thus, for the superwomen of Hong Kong, multiple roles in the work, family, and community domains, may be a source of enrichment. We encourage future researchers to examine the lives of these superwomen so we can learn from their successes as wives and mothers, as employees and as citizens of Hong Kong. And, we encourage the Hong Kong Government and Hong Kong firms to create work climates conducive to the effective interface between work and family.

References

Adams, G. A., King, L. A., & King, D. W. (1996). Relationships of job and family involvement, family social support, and work-family conflict with job and life satisfaction. *Journal of Applied Psychology, 18* (4), 411–420.

Aryee, S. (1992). Antecedents and outcomes of work-family conflict among married professional women: Evidence from Singapore. *Human Relations, 45,* 813–837.

Aryee, S., Fields, D., & Luk, V. (1999a). A cross-cultural test of a model of the work-family interface. *Journal of Management, 25(4),* 491–511.

Aryee, S., Luk, V., Leung, A., & Lo, S. (1999b). Role stressors, interrole conflict, and well-being: The moderating influence of spousal support and coping behaviors among employed parents in Hong Kong. *Journal of Vocational Behavior, 54(2),* 259–278.

Bedeian, A. G., Burke, B. G., & Moffett, R. G. (1988). Outcomes of work family conflict among married male and female professionals. *Academy of Management Journal, 14,* 476–491.

Bernas, K. H., & Major, D. A. (2000). Contributors to stress resistance: Testing a model of women's work-family conflict. *Psychology of Women Quarterly, 24,* 170–178.

Boles, J. S., & Babin, B. J. (1996). On the front lines: Stress, conflict, and the customer service provider. *Journal of Business Research, 37,* 41–50.

Burke, P.J. (1996) Social identities and psychosocial stress, In H. B. Kaplan (Ed.), *Psychosocial stress: Perspectives on structure, theory, life-course, and methods* (pp. 141–174). San Diego, CA: Acadmic Press.

Carlson, D. S., & Kacmar, K. M. (2000). Work-family conflict in the organization: Do life role values make a difference? *Journal of Management, 26,* 1031–1054.

Chiu, W.C.K., & Ng, C.W. (1999). Women-friendly HRM and organizational commitment: A study among women and men of organizations in Hong Kong. *Journal of Occupational and Organizational Psychology, 72,* 485–502.

Chow, I.H.S. (2005). Gender differences in perceived leadership effectiveness in Hong Kong. *Women in Management Review, 20(4),* 216.233.

Chu, P.P.H. (2004). *The making of women entrepreneurs in Hong Kong.* Hong Kong: Hong Kong University Press.

Dibenedetto, B., & Tittle, C. K. (1990). Gender and adult roles: Role commitment of women and men in a job-family trade-off context. *Journal of Counselling Psychology, 37,* 41–48.

Duxbury, L. E., & Higgins, C. A. (1991). Gender differences in work-family conflict. *Journal of Applied Psychology, 76(1),* 60–74.

Ebrahimi, B.P. (1999). Managerial motivation and gender roles: A study of females and males in Hong Kong. *Women in Management Review, 14(2),* 44–53.

Ebrahimi, B.P., Young, S.A., & Luk, V.W.M. (2002). Motivation to manage in

China and Hong Kong: A gender comparison of managers. *Sex Roles*, *45(5/6)*, 433–453.

Edwards, J. R., & Rothbard, N. P. (2000). Mechanisms linking work and family: Clarifying the relationship between work and family constructs. *Academy of Management Review*, *25*, 178–199.

Equal Opportunities Commission (2001). A research report of a baseline survey of students' attitudes toward gender stereotypes and family roles. Department of Social Work & Social Administration, The University of Hong Kong. [accessed January 17, 2006] available from http://www.eoc.org.hk/CE/research/index.htm

Equal Opportunities Commission (1998). Survey on public attitudes towards sex as a genuine occupational qualification. [accessed January 17, 2006] available from http://www.eoc.org.hk/CE/research/index.htm

Equal Opportunities Commission (1997). A baseline survey on equal opportunities on the basis of gender 1996-97. [accessed January 17, 2006] available from http://www.eoc.org.hk/CE/research/index.htm

Frone, M. R. (2000). Work-family conflict and employee psychiatric disorders: The national comorbidity survey. *Journal of Applied Psychology*, *85*, 888–895.

Frone, M. R. (2003). Work-family balance. In J. C. Quick & L. E. Tetrick, (Eds.) *Handbook of Occupational Health Psychology*, (pp 143–162). Washington, DC: American Psychological Association.

Frone, M. R., Russell, M., & Barnes, G. M. (1996). Work-family conflict, gender, and health-related outcomes: A study of employed parents in two community samples. *Journal of Occupational Health Psychology*, *1*, 57–69.

Frone, M. R., Russell, M., & Cooper, M. L. (1992). Antecedents and outcomes of work-family conflict: Testing a model of the work-family interface. *Journal of Applied Psychology*, *77*, 65–78.

Frone, M. R., Yardley, J. K., & Markel, K. S. (1997). Developing and testing an integrative model of the work-family interface. *Journal of Vocational Behavior*, *50*, 145–167.

Fu, C.K., & Shaffer, M. A. (2001). The tug of work and family: Direct and indirect domain-specific determinants of work-family conflict. *Personnel Review*, *30(5)*, 502-522.

Good, L., K., Page, Jr., T. J., & Young, C. E. (1996) Assessing hierarchical differences in job-related attitudes and turnover among retail managers, *Journal of the Academy of Marketing Science*, *24*, 148–156.

Grandey, A. A., & Cropanzano, R. (1999). The conservation of resources model applied to work-family conflict and strain. *Journal of Vocational Behavior*, *54*, 350–370.

Greenhaus, J. H., & Beutell, N. J. (1985). Sources of conflict between work and family roles. *Journal of Management Review*, *10(1)*, 76–88.

Greenhaus, J. H., & Powell, G. N. (2006). When work and family are allies: A theory of work-family enrichment. *Academy of Management Review, 31*, 72–92.

Grzywacz, J. G., & Marks, N. F. (2000). Reconceptualizing the work-family interface: An ecological perspective on the correlates of positive and negative spillover between work and family. *Journal of Occupational Health Psychology, 5*, 111–126.

Higgins, C. A., Duxbury, L. E., & Irving, R. H. (1992). Work-family conflict in the dual-career family. *Organizational Behavior and Human Decision Processes, 51*, 51–75.

Hofstede, G. (1980). *Culture's consequences: International differences in work related values*. Thousand Oaks, CA: Sage.

Hong Kong Government, Census and Statistics Department, 2001 Population Census, Thematic Report — Women and Men, "Key Statistics of Women and Men in Hong Kong," [accessed November 3, 2004], available from www.info.gov.hk/censtatd/eng/news/01c/women&men.pdf

House, R. J. et al. (1999). Cultural influences on leadership and organizations: Project GLOBE. In W.M. Mobley (Ed.) *Advances in Global Leadership*, Vol. 1 (pp. 171–233). Greenwich, CT: JAI Press.

Joplin, J. R., Shaffer, M. A., Lau, T., & Francesco, A. M. Life balance: Developing and validating a cross-cultural measure. Presented at the Academy of Management Meetings, Seattle, August 2003.

Kao, R. S. (1987). Status of women in Hong Kong. *International Journal of Sociology of the Family, 17*, 25–40.

King, A. Y. C., & Bond, M. H. (1985). The Confucian paradigm of man: A sociological view. In W. S. Tseng and D. Y. H. Wu (Eds) *Chinese Culture and Mental Health* (pp. 29–45). Orlando, FL: Academic Press.

Kinnunen, U., & Mauno, S. (1998). Antecedents and outcomes of work-family conflict among employed women and men in Finland. *Human Relations, 51*, 157–177.

Kossek, E. E., & Ozeki, C. (1998). Work-family conflict, policies, and the job-life satisfaction relationship: A review and directions for organizational behavior – human resources research. *Journal of Applied Psychology, 83*, 139–149.

Lam, M. (2004). The perception of inequalities: A gender case study, *Sociology, 38(1)*, 5–23.

Lee, E. W. Y. (2003). Individualism and patriarchy: The identity of entrepreneurial women lawyers in Hong Kong. In E. W. Y. Lee (Ed.), *Gender and change in Hong Kong: Globalization, postcolonialism, and Chinese patriarchy* (pp. 78–96). Vancouver: UBC Press.

Lee, F. L. F. (2004). Constructing perfect women: The portrayal of female officials in Hong Kong newspapers. *Media, Culture & Society, 26 (2)*, 207–225.

Lee, S. K. F., & Choo, S. L. (2001). Work-family conflict of women entrepreneurs in Singapore. *Women in Management Review, 16 (5)*, 204–221.

Lo, S. (2003). Perceptions of work-family conflict among married female professionals in Hong Kong. *Personnel Review, 32 (3)*, 376–390.

Lo, S., Stone, R., & Ng, C.W. (2003). Work-family conflict and coping strategies adopted by female married professionals in Hong Kong. *Women in Management Review, 18(3/4)*, 182–190.

Lui, H. K. (1999). Women workers in Hong Kong: Narrowing the gender gap. In P. Fosh, A. W. Chan, W. W. S. Chew, E. Snape, & R. Westwood, R. (Eds.), *Hong Kong management and labour: Change and continuity* (pp. 94–106). London: Routledge.

Luk, D. M., & Shaffer, M. A. (2005). Work and family domain stressors and support: Direct and indirect influences on work-family conflict. *Journal of Occupational and Organizational Psychology, 78*, 489–508.

MacEwen, K. E., & Barling, J. (1994). Daily consequences of work interference with family and family interference with work. *Work and Stress, 8*, 244–254.

Ng, C. (2004, September 15). Under-represented and undervalued. *South China Morning Post*, 15.

Ng, C. W. (2001). Locations of sex discrimination and reverse discrimination: Hong Kong university students' experiences and perceptions. *Equal Opportunities International, 20 (3)*, 1–11.

Ng, C. W., & Chakrabarty, A. S. (2005). Women managers in Hong Kong: Personal and political agendas. *Asia Pacific Business Review, 11 (2)*, 163–178.

Ng, C. W., & Chiu, W. C. K. (1999). Women-friendly human resource management in Hong Kong: Concept and practice. In P. Fosh, A. W. Chan, W. W. S. Chew, E. Snape & R. Westwood (Eds.), *Hong Kong management and labour: Change and continuity* (pp. 185–198). London: Routledge.

Ng, C. W., & Chiu, W. C. K. (2001). Managing equal opportunities for women: Sorting the friends from the foes. *Human Resource Management Journal, 11 (1)*, 75–98.

Ng, C. W., & Fosh, P. (2004). The effect of career ambition and satisfaction on attitudes towards equal opportunities and family-friendly policies for women: A case study in Hong Kong. *Community, Work & Family, 7 (1)*, 43–70.

Ng, C. W., Fosh, P., & Naylor D. (2002). Work-family conflict for employees in an east Asian airline: Impact on career and relationship to gender. *Economic and Industrial Democracy, 23 (1)*, 67–106.

Ng, C. W., Ng, M. P. Y., & Tse, S. C. K. (1998). Supposed beneficiaries' opinions of anti-discrimination legislation in Hong Kong-Women's and the physically handicapped's viewpoints. *Equal Opportunities International, 17 (6)*, 13–24.

Ng, C. W., & Pine, R. (2003). Women and men in hotel management in Hong Kong: Perceptions of gender and career development issues. *Hospitality Management, 22*, 85–102.

Ngo, H., Foley, S., Wong A., & Loi R. (2003). Who gets more of the pie? Predictors of perceived gender inequity at work. *Journal of Business Ethics, 45 (3)*, 227–241.

Redding, S. G. (1993). *The spirit of Chinese capitalism.* New York: de Gruyter.

Redding, S G., & Wong, G. Y. Y. (1986). The psychology of Chinese organizational behaviour. In M. H. Bond (Ed.), *The Psychology of Chinese People* (pp. 267–295). New York: Oxford University Press.

Tang, C. S., Lee, A. M., Tang, T., Cheung, F. M., & Chan, C. (2002). Role occupancy, role quality, and psychological distress in Chinese women. *Women & Health, 36*, 49–66.

Siu, O. L., & Phillips, D. R. (2006). A Consultancy Study on Family-friendly Employment Policies and Practices (FEPPs) in Hong Kong. Hong Kong: Equal Opportunities Commission and Women's Commission.

Sze, W. W. (1998). The sex stereotype of managers and the self-concept of business students in Hong Kong, unpublished BSSc thesis, The Chinese University of Hong Kong cited in P. C. Y. Yim, & M. H. Bond (2002), Gender stereotyping of managers and the self-concept of business students across their undergraduate education. *Women in Management Review, 17(7/8)*, 364–372.

Thoits, P. A. (1991). On merging identity theory and stress research. *Social Psychology Quarterly, 54*, 101–112.

Thomas, L. T., & Ganster, D. C. (1995). Impact of family-supportive work variables on work-family conflict and strain: A control perspective. *Journal of Applied Psychology, 80(1)*, 6–15.

Trompenaars, R., & Hampton-Turner, C. (1998). *Riding the waves of culture.* New York: McGraw-Hill.

Venter, K. (2002). *Common careers, different experiences.* Hong Kong: Hong Kong University Press.

Voydanoff, P. (1988). Work role characteristics, family structure demands, and work/family conflict. *Journal of Marriage and the Family, 50*, 749–761.

Westwood, R., & Leung, A.S.M. (1999). Women in management in Hong Kong and Beijing: Between pragmatism and patriarchy. In P. Fosh, A. W. Chan, W. W. S. Chew, E. Snape, & R. Westwood (Eds.), *Hong Kong management and labour: Change and continuity* (pp. 199–219). London: Routledge.

Westwood, R., Leung, A. S. M., & Chiu, R. K. (1999). The meaning of work: The reconfiguration of work and working in Hong Kong and Beijing. In P. Fosh, A. W. Chan, W.W.S. Chew, E. Snape, & R. Westwood, (Eds.), *Hong Kong management and labour: Change and continuity* (pp. 127–150). London: Routledge.

Yang, N., Chen, C. C., Choi, J. and Zou, Y. (2000). Sources of work-family conflict: A Sino-U.S. comparison of the effects of work and family demands, *Academy of Management Journal, 43*, 113–123.

Yim, P. C. Y., & Bond, M. H. (2002). Gender stereotyping of managers and the self-concept of business students across their undergraduate education. *Women in Management Review, 17 (7/8)*, 364–372.

Note

1. The term *neuih keuhng yahn* literally means "female strong person" in the local Cantonese dialect. It usually refers to strong successful women working in business or the professions.

CHAPTER 14

Re-gendering Hong Kong Man in Social, Physical and Discursive Space

Siumi Maria Tam, Anthony Fung, Lucetta Kam, and Mario Liong

Introduction

The cosmopolitan outlook of Hong Kong has often led to misconceptions that gender relations in this society are equal and that people are open-minded about changing gender roles and identities. The authors believe, however, that behind this façade is a patriarchal social structure that forms the basis of Hong Kong culture. This structure has naturalized male domination in most of public and private life, including areas that have traditionally been understood as "female spheres", such as the family and the beauty industry. Because of this naturalization and fetishization of the genders, this paradoxical situation is often left outside of public discussion. Most importantly, it has rendered invisible the role of the standard setters and the diversity among the practitioners — men as a social class and as individuals. This chapter sets out to partly fill this void, by providing ethnographic data on aspects of maleness that have escaped public attention. Against the backdrop of a recent men's movement, the chapter also points out the urgency to incorporate gender concerns in the formulation of public policy.

The emergence of women's studies over the past two decades has accumulated a considerable amount of knowledge on the changes in women's status and roles in local history, and of how women have variously suffered, resisted, and taken part in the construction and reproduction of a patriarchal system (see for example Jaschok & Miers 1994). Various studies have shown that despite economic development, legislative reforms and generally a more receptive social environment in relation to equal opportunity between the sexes, today, in 2008, Hong Kong men's and women's access to political, economic, social and cultural resources are still far from being equal. Compared to their male counterparts, women are expected to take up triple burdens as they juggle salaried work, domestic responsibilities, and community building. In the workplace female employees still receive less pay for work and suffer more sexual harassment. As the supplementary labor force on the market, women are the first to lose jobs in an economic downturn. In the family, their primary role as mother-wives render them carers and supporters, which is still the principle cultural institution that restricts women's development as individuals. In popular culture, women are targets of commodification and captive in a beauty myth that usurps their control over their own body.

What are men's roles in these various aspects of women's subjugation? To what extent are they beneficiaries of a gender-biased labor market and a male-centered family system? Do men get better treatment in media representation? Are they free to practice their choices or are they, like their female counterparts, products of socialization and enculturation; and willingly or unwillingly, take part in the production of gender stereotypes? How do class and ethnic background affect their opportunities? Can men be victims of a patriarchal system? These are some of the questions we believe must be asked, in order to realistically understand the gender culture in Hong Kong. Thus a logical question is: What is the nature of masculinity and men's agency in Hong Kong society? To answer this, we need to learn more about men as individuals in their various subject positions, or, to re-gender the social identity called "Male".

Much as women's common predicaments are often generalized as "female" and results of femininity, in popular discourse as well as scholarly works, individual men have often been abstractized into the "male", equating them with the privileges they enjoy especially in the economic and political system (Kimmel, 1993, Messner, 1997). Thus, men are categorized into a faceless, sometimes even demonic, social existence. We suggest that studies of men must emphasize the complexity of interactions of various social and cultural factors, and contextualize men's action and agency in specific time-spaces. In a fast-paced society like Hong Kong, constant tensions occur between change and continuity. Individuals as gendered beings must make choices among uncertainties, while gender relations and identities are inevitably contested and re-negotiated. We must pay attention to men's subject positions as individual members of society, to their subjective interpretations of what it means to be male, as well as to their action in operationalizing masculinity.

The following discussion examines male identities in three specific areas in contemporary Hong Kong society. Firstly we look at the family, a social institution in which men have traditionally learned and played the role of a responsible father and husband. Secondly, we examine the beauty industry as a space in which men take part to re-produce concepts of the body and in literally changing their male looks. Finally, we turn our attention to how the media constitutes socio-cultural space in which popular views of gender are constantly redefined. By looking at gender perceptions in these three areas, we seek to understand male behavior which sometimes abides by social norms but other times deviates from them; we describe how men as individuals practice their own versions of masculinity, as well as how their identities are defined by others. By juxtaposing what constitutes the "male" in these three areas, we hope to shed light on the variability and fluidity of masculinity, as men exchange and create information on gender role, appearance, and sexual orientation.

Our analysis focuses specifically on 1) the social normalization of men who keep mistresses in mainland China; 2) the physical departmentalization of men who purchase facial treatment in beauty salons; and 3) the media's heterosexualization of metrosexuals. On the surface, these three types of males may be considered socially deviant, and are often stigmatized to different degrees. Taken together, however, they show how non-legitimate behavior interplays with, and in fact reinforces, the mainstream male-centered ideology and patriarchal system that is the basis of gender relations in Hong Kong society. We further argue that these cases show how masculinity has a material base, that it is at the same time social-relational and discursive, and how men themselves are actively creating new forms of manhood through the adoption of conventional and unconventional roles and identities.

The Invisible Hong Kong Man

How much do "Hong Kong men" catch the popular imagination in Hong Kong? Not much. In the process of writing this paper, we conducted a literature search on Hong Kong men and literally faced a dearth of knowledge on the topic. A search on the keywords "Hong Kong men" in the Chinese University of Hong Kong Library catalogue, for example, yielded a total of four items, which includes three 20-minute features produced by Radio Television Hong Kong (RTHK) and one postgraduate thesis. The MPhil thesis by Li Wai-ki (2002) is a study on the phenomenon of Hong Kong men looking for potential wives on Mainland China. It coincides with one of the three RTHK documentaries, which features a private detective who gathers evidence on the extra-marital affairs of Hong Kong men on the Mainland. In these two studies Hong Kong men's alleged interest in Mainland women highlights the gender inequality on the Mainland, as much as in Hong Kong society itself. The phenomenon epitomizes how women are often commoditized in marriage or para-marriage relationships. The second RTHK video follows a gay couple who went from Hong Kong to Canada to get married, and challenges the audience to ask questions about the nature and social implications of marriage. The third documentary explores Hong Kong men's the health or the lack of it, and concludes that "[i]n Hong Kong, men have shorter life-spans ... The more we expect men to be tough, the more likely they are to die earlier."

While these publications deal with topics as diverse as health, gayness and cross-border marriage, Hong Kong men in general do seem to be invisible from the public gaze, except when they deviate from conventional understanding, are exoticized, or even stigmatized. Thus while society is getting to understand more about women and their situation in Hong Kong, we have no idea what men as individuals are doing, nor the range of their moral values, the change in their status, and the nature of problems that men in different social classes face. We know even less about men in the family, as fathers and spouses — how they rear children, and how they perceive their marital relations and so on. There is no Men's Studies in Hong Kong vis-à-vis Women's Studies as an academic discipline, although there is a growing literature on studies of gay men (see for example Zhou, 1997 and Tang, 2004).

A review of current studies outside of Hong Kong shows that research on representations of men's bodies have received significantly less attention from scholars than topics such as sexuality, violence, work, family, education and health (McKay, Mikosza and Hutchins, 2005). Comparing men and women, Kimmel (1993) argues that the very processes that confer privilege to one group and not to another are often invisible to those upon whom that privilege is conferred. This means that in a patriarchal Chinese society like Hong Kong, we would actually find that the dominated women are even more visible than the dominating men in public arenas. The hegemonic men have been conspicuous as athletics, politicians, and scientists, but their status as men in these positions is largely indiscernible and invisible (Kimmel, 1993). To explicate the invisibility of men, Witz (2000) suggests that academics and even our society have constructed men as inherently social and women as essentially corporeal, and that theoretically men's bodies have always inhabited a liminal space. In other words, in a real space in which men and women could possibly be co-present, men's bodies are usually hidden and subtle, so as to highlight the social status, representations and identities of their counterpart women. As women are brought to the forefront, they become the others that are viewed and studied, and are measured against the male standards that have become the social standards. Gender is thus so embedded in social structure that it has become invisible.

In Hong Kong, this male invisibility is obvious in academic research. In a recently compiled bibliography on gender studies in Hong Kong (Tam and Leahy, 2005), the majority of titles are about adult women, and a smaller number on children and adolescents, and a still smaller number of titles involving a comparison of genders. As to studies on men, there is a glaring lack. In some sections, such as Education Section and Migration Section, there are no entries specifically on men. The section on Health and Medicine fares better. Out of 136 entries, 4 are specifically studies on men, 15 are studies of both sexes (including minors), and the rest all have women as the target of research. It thus appears that men have no medical, educational or migration adjustment problems! In fact, of course, as feminist scholars readily point out, this phenomenon reflects the "gender-blind" situation in which men are so much the standard or the norm, that history means men's history, and economics means men's economics, and so on. In other words, men are taken as the "general population" or "society" — the norm. When women are studied, they are treated separately, as abnormal, problematic, and thus literally the "other". Yet, while we think we know men, we actually only know the social systems that they have created, and not men as social beings.

Hong Kong society, however, has its own version of men's movement, which started in the early 1990s, although it was already 20 years later than that in the West. Men's studies in the form of social and medical research has begun in academia, and issues concerning "deviant" men like unemployed men, house-husbands, and male victims of domestic violence, have caught the attention of the media. Since the beginning of the 21st century, men's issues have been put on the political agenda, among many other movements such as cultural heritage preservation and universal suffrage. It was as if there was a cultural movement brewing in the society, and a rethinking of men's gender status was a peripheral part of it. Below we describe some of the more salient points in the local men's movement.

The earliest social action concerning men's cultural role started as something similar to the Promise Keepers in the USA (Chan, 2001). Breakthrough, a Protestant organization, organized seminars and workshops, and published widely on the so-called "new men's roles" and "new fatherhood" in the 1990s (Chan, 2001). The central idea of their work was to urge Hong Kong men to face their changing roles, and to learn from role models in the Bible (see Ou & Zeng, 2001; Cai & Ou, 1998; Ou, 2003). Although since the late 1990s Breakthrough gradually faded out from the promotion of a Christianity-based masculinity, another non-government social service agency, Caritas Personal Growth Centre for Men, has picked up the work. Established in 1998, this Catholic organization encourages men to liberate themselves from traditional male roles and urged them to assume their family roles as good husbands and fathers. Since 2001, the Centre has organized an annual "Men's Festival" on April 10, to promote the notion of the "new good man" (新好男人). Through such activities as public forums and carnivals, the Festival has carried out public education on how to become good fathers and good husbands.

This approach in the men's movement recognizes that men can no longer hold on to one single interpretation of masculinity. As the argument goes, it is bad for them as individuals because it places undue stress on men's mental and physical health, and it is not conducive to a harmonious society because it leads to negative relationships in the family and society in general. Those who promoted this approach argued for gradual changes among men and opted for men's liberation. Yet many traditional or even patriarchal gender values remain untouched. On one hand, this men's movement encouraged men to accept their new roles — to face their emotions and to be caring to their wives and children; on the other hand men were taught to retain their traditional roles — to be the leader of the household and to be successful in both career and marriage. In addition, a strong message in this movement is that masculinity can only be acquired and learned from male figures.

Apart from this more prominent organization and its activities, there were other men's groups which took very different approaches towards men's contemporary situation. Groups that concerned themselves with promoting "men's rights" believed that men have been suffering from discrimination and oppression; these include unemployed men and victims of both physical and mental domestic violence. These groups lobbied the government for legal reforms; in particular they believed that while women had a Women's Commission to take care of women's problems, so the government should set up a Men's Commission to oversee men's needs in government policies. They blamed women for "enjoying too many benefits and resources" provided for by taxes. The underlying logic is of course that the pursuit of women's rights or feminist goals is antagonistic to men's rights and benefits. This war-of-the-sexes argument pitched women against men instead of seeing systemic factors in creating an unjust society.

This "men's right" approach of the men's movement in Hong Kong may be seen as a backfire to the changes in gender relations since World War II. With legal reforms in most public arenas, such as in the education system and job market, men could no longer monopolize resources in social life. Even in the area of family, men were regarded to be giving in to women's demands — men could not marry concubines from 1971 onwards, instead monogamy required that they shared equal status and rights with their wives. As government policies incorporated women's needs (Lai, Au & Cheung, 1997), men were increasingly stripped off the title of sole head of household, symbolically and practically; for example in the taxation system as women and men were assessed separately for salary tax and not as husbands and wives (Pegg, 1986; Kwok, Chow, Lee, & Wu, 1997). Men thus found that they had to co-operate (and compete) not only with other men but also women in their work and study. At the same time, traditional masculinities were challenged by feminist claims. Men were urged to express their emotions, to seek help, to be more caring, to share childcare, housework, and decision-making power with their wives, and not to focus on work only.

The contradictory goals of different men's groups or indeed their schizophrenic requirements, manifest the fluidity of maleness and the contestedness of its interpretations. As such in the early 21st century, we see that while some men choose to learn to liberate themselves from traditional gender constraints, others opt to maintain the status quo. More men, however, operate on the micro-level to follow or resist the changes in gender concepts and relations. It is an understatement to say that masculinity in Hong Kong manifests itself as an array of diverse streams that go in different directions, but nonetheless it is clear that patriarchy is still the common, underlying current.

In the following discussion, we will explore men's behavior and their identities in three specific social arenas, and re-visualize them as they negotiate, perform, maintain, and transform masculinity in Hong Kong society. The first arena is the family as social space in which men as mistress-keepers portrayed themselves as responsible husband-fathers; the second is the beauty parlor as physical space where male customers are rendered non-existent; and lastly, the discursive space within which homosexual men are re-categorized as heterosexual in the discussion of metrosexuals.

The Transparent Polygamous Man

This section[1] examines the phenomenon dubbed *bao er nai*[2] (literally "keep second wife") across the Hongkong-China border, and seeks to re-visualize the men as mistress-keepers in the social space of the family. While Hong Kong has a monogamous system, these married men had found a grey area where keeping mistresses was not punishable by Hong Kong law — in China.[3] The People's Republic of China also has a monogamous system, but because it would be very difficult for the Hong Kong wives to pursue their marriage rights in China, these Hong Kong husbands were able to take advantage of a liminal social space. Tam has argued earlier (Tam, 1996) that the Hong Kong social-moral economy has created a cultural context in which mistress-keepers were in effect forgiven and we may even say encouraged for their behavior. This paradoxical situation is constructed as various levels of social life, including legislature, the media, social service providers, and wives together make use of a discourse based on the needs of the patrilineal family system. This discourse focused on the economic restructure, the role of the wife and mistress, and even the jurisdiction of the police — but side-stepped the central figure, the men who were the actual agents bringing about the phenomenon. In the process, these explanations normalized men's behavior in a supposedly inevitable situation and explained (away) the responsibility of the men. This resulted in an essentialization of Chinese masculinity and making the polygamous men socially transparent — we know they are there, but we cannot scrutinize them. They are physically outside the home and morally out of the social gaze for acceptable behavior. In the same vein, the men in this present study were able to shed off the blame that they were irresponsible men who deserted their wives and children. In fact many of these men maintained their relationship with their wife and continued to play the father and breadwinner role. We argue that despite the fact that the mistress-keeping behavior was ideologically frowned upon, in practice it had become transparent, as the men's infidelity was not punished (or punishable) by the law, was taken-for-granted culturally, and to a large extent tolerated morally.

Most of the mistress keepers were Hong Kong men who worked as cross-border truck drivers, or as cooks, technicians, engineers, and factory executives in Shenzhen and/or the Pearl River Delta. This took place as Hong Kong's economy becomes increasingly enmeshed in South China's post-1978 economic growth, and as Hong Kong's own economic downturn necessitated a structural transformation in which manufacture-related low to mid level skilled work was no longer of value. The re-organization of work across the border interfaced with the gender asymmetry in which men were considered superior and women inferior, and with the identity politics in which Hongkongese presumed a financial-cultural sophistication over mainland Chinese. Simultaneously, amidst these rapid socio-cultural changes, traditional Chinese gender concepts and relations still held sway. Men taking up cross-border work as a survival strategy saw themselves as breadwinners shouldering the familial responsibilities expected of good fathers and husbands. These same traditional values paradoxically provided a hotbed on which extra-marital relationships were justified. It is within this complex social and cultural milieu that we examine the ideology and practice of masculinity among these polygamous men.

According to government statistics, in the year 2004, over 240,000 Hong Kong people[4] crossed the Hongkong-China border to find a livelihood, and several times more Hongkongers "went north"[5] regularly for entertainment and to purchase consumer goods. It is important to note that this mobility is highly gendered. Particularly in Shenzhen Special Economic Zone, Hong Kong's next-door neighbor, a convergence of the male mobility from Hong Kong and a female mobility from other parts of China was obvious. From Hong Kong, men arrived following their employment and investment needs.[6] From different parts of China, women came to seek new job and marriage opportunities. Class is an important factor in the interaction of these two groups. While Hong Kong men in general held professional or skilled jobs such as engineers, managers, cooks and truck drivers, most Chinese women found themselves typically confined to semi- and unskilled work, and having access to only dead-end jobs such as factory workers, restaurant waiters, salespersons, hair-washers in hair salons, and beauticians and masseurs. At the same time these jobs were also markers of low social status and were highly stereotyped and stigmatized. To many Chinese women, the way out of their working class fate was to find a good husband. For the truck drivers from Hong Kong, even though their job was defined as working class, the money they made (over HK$20,000 before 1997) would categorize them as middle class. And, even as their income was drastically reduced with the economic downturn since 1997 (averaging HK$10,000 in 2004), the economic discrepancy between Hong Kong and China still allowed working class Hong Kong males to enjoy a middleclass lifestyle in the heavily consumerist society of Shenzhen. To many Hong Kong men, the epitome of their consumerist power lied in the ability to purchase and monopolize female service through keeping a Chinese mistress.

In 2004 Tam and Wong conducted a survey of truck drivers (all male) who regularly crossed the border to transport goods between Hong Kong and China.[7] Out of 1200 questionnaires distributed at petrol stations, 193 were returned on a voluntary and anonymous basis. Twenty-five percent of the respondents reported to "have had a second wife (*er nai*)" and 40% said they "have had a girlfriend (*nu peng you*)" in China. Since both having a "second wife" and "girlfriend" were defined by the men as having a stable relationship with a woman and providing material benefits in exchange for domestic rights, both having *er nai* and having *nu peng you* were understood as "mistress keeping". The very high incidence of the men's admitting to extra-marital affairs may be a result of self-selection and/or of occupational bias. Tam also carried out in-depth interviews between 2002 and 2004. Those interviewed included Hong Kong men who regularly crossed the Hongkong-Chinese border for work and/or leisure, including six men who admitted having had or were having Chinese mistresses at the time of interview. Also interviewed were 15 Hong Kong wives whose husbands had *bao er nai*, as well as 15 Chinese women who had been mistresses to Hong Kong men. These data sets constitute the basis of the following discussion.

Zooming-in on the Mistress Keeper

Data from Tam and Wong's survey shows that the typical man who had had a "second wife/girlfriend" exhibited the following characteristics. He was on the average 42 years old, had been married for 14 years, and was a father of two. He had finished junior high school, had worked as a cross-border driver for seven years, and earned over HK$10,000 a month. In a typical month, he spent about 10 days in China, and was on the road over 10 hours a day. He had less than an hour of rest per working day (besides sleep), and considered his work as a driver in China "stressful". For security reasons, he often spent the night in his truck. When the trip was long, he stayed overnight in a motel or a massage parlor. He usually spent his leisure time with fellow drivers, as they had meals, went to karaoke bars and visited massage parlors together. Although the occupations of the men interviewed by Tam differed, these characteristics in their experience were strikingly similar. The commonailties were most obvious in the physical separation from home due to a cross-border work structure, the relative affluence and sense of superiority, the clear distinction of gender roles, and the patricentric position they enjoyed both in and outside of home.

Based on the above survey and the individual interviews, we will reconstruct a typical case whom we call Chow Heung Wah,[8] a Hong Kong man in his early 40s who worked in a Shenzhen factory. He stayed in Shenzhen from Monday to Saturday, living in an apartment provided to him by his employer. He returned weekly to his Hong Kong home where his wife and two adolescent children lived, and spent the weekend in Hong Kong. During his work week, he would spend his leisure time mainly with co-workers from Hong Kong. They visited the same massage parlor and over time had become regular clients of a group of masseurs from poorer county seats in the inland. Chow's favorite masseur was Li Xiaoqing who came from Sichuan. Chow found Li attractive, younger and prettier than his wife, and he felt young again when he was with her. He believed that Li adored him because he was a Hongkongese. And as he could speak English, he enjoyed feeling like a hero in front of her. After a few months he decided to "keep" her as a mistress, and paid her RMB 4,000 a month. Although he did not rent an apartment for her to live in, the *bao er nai* relationship was recognized by both Li's and Chow's acquaintances. According to Chow, he kept a mistress because he was lonely, needed a home in China where he stayed for a week at a time, and that all men had sexual needs. He also justified his infidel behavior by saying that most of his Hong Kong friends in China had a mistress, and that it was cheap to keep a Chinese mistress. He also claimed that it was even more common for mainland Chinese men to have a second wife, so he felt he should also have one too. Thus he considered it "just natural" for him to *bao er nai*.

Stages of the Extra-marital Relationship

From the description obtained in individual interviews with wives, mistresses and husbands, we found that mistress-keeping went through three stages: an incubating period, a honeymoon period, and a dilemma period. The incubating period consisted of the long period of enculturation which inculcated a male-superior, female-inferior mentality. It was built into conventional wisdom that men and women were born different, and reinforced day-to-day by mass media, justifying men's supposedly inborn superiority and a corresponding social elevation. Men's rightful place was not only the public, but also the domestic in which his needs as head of household and center of attention were part of the natural order of things. In return, his responsibilities as breadwinner were defined as primary — a man's ability to provide for his wife and children was a central part of the measure of his achievement. We note, however, that these responsibilities were often taken at face value, that is, a responsible man is one who makes money which he gives to his wife to maintain his children. Period. Once he has provided the money, he considers his duty done. The rest of the needs of a family is the job of his wife, and he comes home to enjoy its fruition. The Chinese family, based on patrilineality and operationalized through patrilocal residence and patronomy, is a highly patricentric form of social organization. The cross-border work structure served as a catalyst, in which Hong Kong men enjoyed even more privileges in Shenzhen where their gendered consumer power was elevated to a disproportionately high status. The mass media had also helped to construct Shenzhen as the backyard of Hong Kong, where the consumer was king, and Hong Kong men took part in the collective imagination that, like other commodities, female services and bodies (indeed individual women) could be bought.

The second stage, or the honeymoon period, began when Chow, our typical case, began his mistress-keeping. He visited Li whenever he felt like it, as he believed that he had exclusive rights to her body and services. Li would take leave from work whenever he visited, and Chow enjoyed being pampered by a submissive and soft-speaking woman. He also extracted excitement from the fact that he was cheating on his wife. On the other hand, he needed reassurance that Li would not ask for a formal marriage relationship. He believed that since she had no means to travel to Hong Kong, she would not be able to cause any trouble for him. On his part, he bought her gifts including clothes, mobile phones, and watches. When her family had a financial need, he was often giving a hand. These regular exchanges of rights and responsibilities established the husband-mistress relationship. Now that he had a second wife, Chow felt he was able to prove to his peers that he had financial ability as well as sexual potency. To show off his new exploit, he often took Li to good restaurants and karaoke bars, where they would be considered a couple. In addition, he felt he could "take care of two households"[9] as he continued to financially support his wife and children in Hong Kong. He believed he had established himself as a resourceful man and therefore gained face among his peers. Chow felt that he had achieved the status of this ideal manhood, *qi ren*, and the costs were low.

The honeymoon period lasted the next three or four months, after which Chow gradually found it financially difficult to support two households. Li had also begun to complain about his absence and to ask him not to return to his Hong Kong home. And then came the ultimate demand — she wanted him to divorce his wife and marry her. On the other side of the border, the wife was in a state of helplessness. We shall reconstruct a typical wife's response below. Mrs Chow was extremely upset after she found out about her husband's infidelity. Like other wives who suspected that their husband was seeing another woman in China, she had been observing him for two years, but she hesitated to confront him because she feared that confrontation would only lead to his departure. She believed that a divorced woman was a failed woman, and she was very worried about her children being discriminated against when people knew that they "did not have a father". She felt that it was her duty to keep the family together, and so she chose to wait and see, hoping that he would repent. In the mean time, family relationships deteriorated, and the two adolescent children had begun to develop problems in their school work, and in their social relations and emotional stability — all of which Mrs Chow defined as originated in her own failure to make the marriage work.

Mr Chow was facing a dilemma. He believed that as a responsible husband and father, he should maintain his family. But also as a successful man he did not want to give up his mistress. His masculinity was all of a sudden challenged. He began to show physical symptoms such as disorders of the digestive system, psychological stress, and even depression. He was experiencing loss of libido, and was worried that he would be infected with HIV/AIDS. In the survey we found that one of the responses of men to this psychological stress was to take out life insurance and accident insurance. Nonetheless, these were passive measures that did not help to solve the problem, but may be a safe way to please himself that he had actually done something about his fault. In fact, adulterous men refrained from seeking help from social workers and medical professionals. They believed that they could tackle the problem themselves, and tried to hold on to a strong man image for as long as possible. In the process, the mistress-keepers have resisted the problematicization of men as a gender, and refused to be visualized by social scrutiny — and reinforced the transparency and naturalized power asymmetry in a patriarchal society.

The Non-existent Male Customers in the Beauty Industry

The following analysis focuses on how the beauty salons in Hong Kong attempted to accommodate men as consumers under the capitalist logic, though yet they were managed in a careful way to avoid culturally trespassing the traditional gender taboo. As in other highly capitalized cities, Hong Kong's beauty industry is an expansive amalgamation of a few image-oriented industries (most notably beauty salons, cosmetic products, and advertising), which survives by creating low esteems for women and then giving hope to them. However, having firmly established its markets among women and facing a relatively saturated market, the beauty industry finds it necessary to turn its attention to men. Male consumers traditionally have focused mainly on grooming products such as fragrances, deodorants, hair color treatment, and exercise equipment in health clubs. Eager to take advantage of this new market, the beauty industry has modified its strategy for women customers, by telling men how ugly they look with their big tummy, pimpled face, and a bald head, and how its newest technology will rebuild their stomach muscle, tone their chest, smoothen their face, and restore their hair, etc. Literature (for example Dotson, 1999) documenting the hype of male beauty in the media and advertisements shows that the mystification and romanticization of the male sexy and muscular body in fiction and adventure stories, is actually happening side-by-side with the pejorative images of the rotting, aging, and impotent body, in order to propel men into turning to the beauty industry for help.

Thus the search for beauty by men has been camouflaged by health needs. The beauty salon's success formula traditionally focuses on remedying hair loss, with advertising and media coverage often constructed as "expert knowledge". Today, this para/pseudo-medical tradition is continued (see for example People.com.cn, 2001). Under this tradition men's cosmetics are represented as functionally related to three domains, namely, curing the problems of oily skins (such as acnes and other inflammation), after-shave skin needs, and anti-oxidant agents to procrastinate aging. However, we are able to see a change in the conception on what is socially acceptable for men. Society seems to be more receptive of certain types of men, perhaps those pejoratively labeled as "feminized" and "gay" men, and more tolerant for men in general to pay more attention to their appearance.

Nevertheless, as society becomes more open, various parties including consumers, owners of beauty salons, and cosmetics salespersons, are more likely to admit that they are involved in activities related to men's beauty. Whereas before no beauty salons would advertise that they welcome men customers, now salons aggressively compete for the men's facial care market. Health clubs clamor to help men to reshape their body (usually becoming slimmer, not more muscular). Internationally renowned cosmetics brands such as Shisedo, Clinque, Clarins, Biotherm and Lancome have all developed their men's beauty lines. All these companies share the same goal: to extend their business arm to the male market when the women's market has become over-saturated. This new market has proved to be a great success. In 2000, male's beauty products have already reached 5 percent of the industry's global sales, amounting to US$5.15 billon (BJBusiness 2004). Although no official figure is released for the market in Hong Kong, 2003 figures reveal that the Mainland Chinese market was expanding with an annual rate of 30 percent, compared to the 8 percent of the women's market (Deng 2005). Besides, according to the international research company Mintel, the value of the male beauty products market in China in 2003 (42 million pounds) was six times its size in 1998 (7 million pounds) (BJBusiness, 2004).

Advertising Men's Beauty

With a strong market force, huge advertising campaigns of beauty products and services can be seen targeting men. Mass media have to frame that men's uses of beauty services and their connection to beauty are healthy, modern and trendy. In September 2004, the volume of men's beauty products advertisement was increasing quickly in China. According to the National Cosmetics Print Media Advertising Chart, two men's beauty lines took the 38th and 89th places among the 102 advertised brands (Deng 2005).

In the Asian mass media, it is now common to see male celebrities serving as spokespersons for male cosmetics. A good example is popular Japanese TV artist Nakamuka. In Hong Kong, movie star Ekin Cheng and singer Aaron Kwok were spokespersons of the Japanese cosmetics brand Shisedo and French brand Clarins in 2001 and 2005 respectively. Sometimes male celebrities are even hired to advertise women's cosmetics. Jay Chou, the popular singer/actor from Taiwan starred in the advertising campaign for the Japanese brand DHC in both its Chinese and Hong Kong markets. Aside from facial products manufacturers, body slimming companies are also expanding into the male market. In Hong Kong, the company Sau Sun Tong was diversifying its business to men. In the company's TV advertisements, men testified how the treatment programs had not only restored their bodies but had also been instrumental in their career development and a bright future. There is also a tendency that advertising of beauty products has shifted from women's magazines to magazines targeting at men professionals (Deng 2005). It is obvious that all these advertising campaigns not only persuade men to use those products, but also attempt to legitimize the use of beauty products and services by men.

Marginalizing Men in a Women's Market

However, the fact that the lion's share of the beauty products market is still a women's market has made it imperative that women's needs are prioritized over men's, especially when the two come into conflict. This conflict is keenly observed in beauty salons and cosmetics sales counters where women feel vulnerable and would resist the transgression of their space by men. Beauty salon owners cannot afford to expand their male market at the expense of the female market. In the discussion below, we provide information on how the shop-owner's dilemma was temporarily resolved with spatial re-arrangements, thereby rendering men's bodies invisible in a female-dominated space.

In Hong Kong society, heterosexual men project a threat to women, as they are considered potentially dangerous due to their "predatory sexuality" and use of prostitution (Fung, 1995). Cosmetics, traditionally classified as women's domain, can be considered as female space. Yet, when men try to purchase beauty products, they have to intrude into the space designated as female. In Fung's observations in a famous cosmetics brand counter in a department store, men's products were put on a shelf in the middle of the consignment area. This means that men had to physically penetrate into the heartland of women's space, posing a threat towards women who were trying on different kinds of makeup. Likewise, in beauty salons or spas where women may be naked or wearing pajamas, they feel particularly "fragile". Indeed salon owners have been discrete and careful about "protecting" their female customers by shielding off spa sections from the public areas, precisely to prevent them from being exposed to men's view. The phenomenon of the invisibility of men's body is documented by the researcher's ethnography study. Over a period of two and a half years in 2002–2004, Fung did participant observation in two different shops: a large chain-store spa and a small-size beauty salon. He purchased various kinds of "face and body improvement work", and in the process observed and indeed experienced first-hand how men were made invisible. He also interviewed some customers, salon owners, and sales agents of beauty products to understand how these beauty spaces and products construct men's bodies.

Gender Spatialization

The delineation of social space for specific genders has been a common instrument to ease away conflicts and contractions arising out of perceived sex differences. Usually when the sanctity and gender superiority of men have to be maintained, females have to be excluded or expelled, formally or informally, from certain social spaces. Gender segregation in occupation, schooling, and religion are well known examples of social spheres by which male dominance is reinforced. However, this seems to be turned around in Hong Kong today, as power has been shifted from the sphere of production to that of consumption. While production is still regarded as the onus of men, consumption is closely tied to the fulfillment of various female desires, particularly in fashion and cosmetics. Thus, many sites of consumption are designed to attract women customers, literally at the expense of men. This does not mean that men's needs are not catered for. Quite the contrary, they are the real winners because they control the benefits that flow out of women's consumption behavior and the representations constructed for these consumption. For example, the owner of a beauty salon and one of the agents of a French beauty product whom Fung interviewed were men who stayed in the backstage — while in public the customers only saw the women business partners. This reflected a supposedly female definition of certain social spaces as female. Fung interviewed a female customer in the spa, for example, and she reported that she would not even go shopping with her husband because it would be too embarrassing for both of them. Likewise, the modern shopping center or department store tended to departmentalize shopping space for males and females so that they would not physically and spatially interfere with each other. Often these spaces were catered to the habits of women customers who were targeted as the primary group of consumers. The mannequins used in the store windows were mostly female, for example, and all the easily accessible floors in department stores and shopping malls tended to house the "female departments". Departments that sold men's goods were usually upstairs or even squeezed in some remote parts of the store.

This case study of a spa shows that spatialization is a result of departmentalizing women and men. This arises from the fact that the spa was originally designed for females only, but because of the need to expand the male market, the owner had to find a way to accommodate the increasing number of men seeking beauty service. This resulted in the need to physically partition the shop space to make men's bodies invisible. There were two typical ways to spatialize. Observations in small beauty salons showed that the shops either had a separate shop for male customers, or they designated an enclosed corner in the salon to "hide" the men. In essence, except the lobby or common area of the shop which allowed the co-presence of both sexes, other spaces were designed to make men's bodies invisible to female customers.

The spatialization process was particularly interesting in the larger spa house where participant observation was carried out. Like most spas, the shop was located in the upper floor of an up-market commercial building. In-keeping with a policy to protect its women customers, it had "conduits" (long corridors) built to run through the entire shop, which were connected to the various cubicles where customers received their treatments individually. On the surface these conduits were used for human traffic and for transporting equipment for facial and body care. However, they were designed in such a way that people moving from a rear room to the lift lobby would not be seen by other clients. A customer could be taken to a cubicle at one end of the conduit, and he or she would in effect be "locked up" there. This design made it possible for male customers to be taken directly from the lobby to his cubicle, and thus be accommodated unnoticed in a beauty parlor catered for female customers.

Of course, male customers could break the rules by leaving the room where they were supposed to stay. The way to prevent this from happening was close surveillance. Beauticians (all female) would accompany the male customers every step of the way. They were instructed to take all female customers down one particular corridor in order to avoid running into the male "intruders", and to make sure that the men stay in their cubicles properly. If a male customer needed to use the bathroom, the beauticians and security staff would coordinate via walkie-talkies to ensure that the corridor was "clear" (of women).

Simultaneously, the male customers knew very well that they were being closely watched, and felt the panoptic pressure (a la Foucault, 1979). They understood clearly that should they trespass the female space, their privileges to use facial care or body care services might be terminated. In fact, they were told by the staff at the outset when they paid for their treatment programs, before they received the services, that the shop was providing the service to them at the shop's discretion, and that they must abide by the rules in this normally female space. There was no dissatisfaction on the side of the men customers though they were taking up a docile position which was very different from the normally dominant position that men had in mainstream society. Thus both the surveillance of the female staff and the compliance of the male customers contributed to this cultural "disappearance" of males' bodies in the beauty salons, resulting in a "powerless" state of the males — a temporary reversal of gender power relations.

Heterosexualized Metrosexuals

> They're in the lift carefully adjusting their hair in the mirror. They're standing in the food line ordering a salad with Diet Coke. They're in the bar drinking Bacardi Breezers. They smell fresh and fragrant with the latest scent from Hugo Boss. *Gay in attitude but straight at heart*, they seem to be everywhere these days ... especially when they casually reach down to, don't laugh, open their man-bags. They're Metrosexuals, a breed that's growing faster than bad government.
>
> (*HK Magazine*, January 28, 2005, emphasis added.)

It would be an exaggeration to say that metrosexuals (also known as metromen) are everywhere in Hong Kong, but we could imagine their appearance when we think of soccer player David Beckham, Japanese SMAP band member/actor/model Kimura Takuya, or the gay experts in the Bravo production — a reality television series called *Queer Eye for the Straight Guy*. It is very true that the term "metrosexual" is a relatively recent (media) phenomenon and an overused word. But to say it is a new male style is to ignore the fact that the image has been in existence, at least in the gay world, for years. Carefully trimmed and beautifully dressed male bodies, and men with a keen interest in body building and skincare are widely acknowledged images of gay men. The invisibility of this gay-inspired male image in local mainstream media over the years can be explained in large part by our society's deep-rooted prejudice against male homosexuality and male femininity. Yet the recent media celebration of metrosexuality does not necessarily imply a relaxation of such prejudices. The emergence of metrosexuality in the media tells more of a discursive shift of the ideal urban masculinity than the development of a new male identification for men in real life or the liberation of gender roles and sexuality.

In this section, we will discuss how media representation on metrosexuals contributes to the construction of a new discourse on masculinity in Hong Kong, in particular, the heterosexualization of the metrosexual in mainstream media. "Gay in attitude but straight at heart", as defined in the above quotation, tells the very kind of masculinity that is represented and promoted by mainstream media through the imported concept of metrosexuality. We will discuss the ways metrosexuality became heterosexualized in mainstream media and how this mainstreaming of gayness affects the dominant discourse of masculinity, sexuality and gender in Hong Kong society. In addition, we attempt to draw upon this discussion to examine mainstream cultural assumptions of normative masculinity. The discussion is based on the media representations of metrosexuality in Hong Kong between 2003 to early 2005, during which the term was introduced and increased in popularity.

Metrosexual: Where It all Began

The word metrosexual was first coined in 1994 by Mark Simpson, a British journalist and popular culture commentator. He wrote,

> The promotion of metrosexuality was left to the men's style press, magazines such as *The Face, GQ, Esquire, Arena and FHM*, the new media which took off in the Eighties and is still growing (*GQ* gains 10,000 new readers every month). They filled their magazines with images of narcissistic young men sporting fashionable clothes and accessories. And they persuaded other young men to study them with a mixture of envy and desire. (Simpson, "Here come the mirror men," *The Independent*, November 15, 1994)

Simpson wrote a more elaborated definition of the term in 2002 for an online magazine, and since then the word "metrosexual" has become a widely cited word in trendy lifestyle magazines and other popular media, in both Britain and North America. In 2003, the word was voted Word of the Year by the American Dialect Society. Simpson's (2002) more elaborate definition is as follows:

> The typical metrosexual is a young man with money to spend, living in or within easy reach of a metropolis — because that's where all the best shops, clubs, gyms and hairdressers are. He might be officially gay, straight or bisexual, but this is utterly immaterial because he has clearly taken himself as his own love object and pleasure as his sexual preference. Particular professions, such as modelling, waiting tables, media, pop music and, nowadays, sport, seem to attract them but, truth be told, like male vanity products and herpes, they're pretty much everywhere.

The definition provided by its creator does not stress the sexual orientation of the metrosexual. However, later elaborations in the media have increasingly stressed the centrality of his heterosexuality. The soccer star Beckham has been widely cited worldwide as an international icon of metrosexuality. The identity of being a husband and father is part of the metrosexuality package, and at the same time it protects his heterosexuality. Elsewhere, icons of metrosexuality are predominately heterosexual men (at least as their image are projected publicly). Examples include the all-men singer group F4 from Taiwan, Hong Kong actor Fang Zhongxin who was the cover metroman of the September 2004 issue of *T.O.M.*[10] and PRC Olympic medallist Tian Liang who was the cover metroman of the December 2004 issue of *Men's Uno Hong Kong Edition*[11]. The heterosexualisation of the metrosexual man has almost become a media consensus when the much cited book *The Metrosexual Guide to Style: A Handbook for the Modern Man*, defines him as a "straight, urban man with heightened aesthetic sense" (Flocker 2003). The most obvious attempt of mainstream society to "straighten" or to de-gay the metrosexual is the recent inclusion of the term by the influential guide to the English language, *The Concise Oxford English Dictionary* published by the Oxford University Press (Eleventh Edition, 2004). The term is now clearly defined, in black and white.

metrosexual

n. (informal) a *heterosexual* urban man who enjoys shopping, fashion, and similar interests traditionally associated with women or homosexual men. — origin 1990s: blend of metropolitan and heterosexual. (Emphasis added)

The sexual identity of the metrosexual is granted an official clarification. The process of heterosexualization of the metrosexual has come to a definitive, final end.

Metrosexuals in Hong Kong

Since 2003, the term has been well circulated in the popular media of both Hong Kong and Mainland China. This phenomenon is especially prevalent in the print media, such as in men's lifestyle magazines. The metrosexual, with his polished urban masculinity and spending power, becomes an obvious choice to construct as a role model for the aspiring cosmopolitan young middle class who is eager to turn their economic capital into visible style status markers. To lifestyle magazine editors and advertisers, the meterosexual represents a shared identity for style-conscious, young male professionals. It seems to be a perfect means of channeling these affluent urban men into docile consumers.

In Hong Kong, metrosexuality as the new model of masculinity emerged in mainstream media predominately in the second half of 2003, with the broadcasting of *Queer Eye for the Straight Guy* by TVB Pearl, the major free English TV channel in town. The original definition of the term as outlined by its creator Mark Simpson, especially the part concerning the metrosexual's sexual preference, has been increasingly ignored by mainstream media. The most prominent appropriation of Simpson's definition of "metrosexual" is, ironically, its heterosexualization and its connotations. Below are some examples of the popular interpretations of metrosexuals by Hong Kong's mainstream print media.

(1) Our society adores fashionable and steadfastly straight-identified men. The wild, hot and crazy, player-type is passé, signifying a reconfiguration of the traditional man. The male homo sapiens has become a newly discovered target for marketing and narcissism is no longer a gay man's privilege. The heterosexual male has risen to become the new icon for narcissism and the all-powerful cosmopolitan consumer. (*Men's Uno Hong Kong*, December 2004, Issue 21, p. 235. Original text in Chinese.)

(2) The metrosexual, straight-identified urban male is absolutely confident and devastatingly beautiful. His careless and generous spending habits, expensive and trendy tastes, have indulged entrepreneurs and women alike. Needless to mention, it has sparked off an unprecedented, new era for the male species. (*Men's Uno Hong Kong*, December 2004 Issue 21, p. 41. Original text in Chinese.)

(3) Metrosexuals have occupied a position in society as the irreplaceable and devoted. Their diverse images and styles signify a taste for high fashion, a wealth of knowledge, a passion for busy and entertaining lifestyles, all a part of their narcissistic nature. They are hoarders of fashion houses, always craving for adventures and flaunting their feminine traits. Being sexy, intellectual, romantic and energetic is very much a part of their daily repertoire. The notion of living as a metrosexual is synonymous with being the hot item for this year's Autumn and Winter collection. (*T.O.M.*, September 2004, Issue 29, p. 76. Original text in Chinese.)

Three ways of appropriation can be generalized from the media representation of metrosexuals: a) heterosexualization, b) commercialization, and c) politicization of the term in the language of men's liberation. Usually the three work together in media representations. The heterosexualization of the metrosexual can be witnessed almost everywhere in mainstream media. The dominant local interpretation of metrosexual guys is as follows: he is a style-conscious heterosexual male who shares the gay men's aesthetic taste. He does not have to be macho. As long as "he loves women", he can have his nails polished, eyebrows plucked, and skin well treated with specialized creams. Metrosexuals in Hong Kong media, as elsewhere in the world, must be unquestionably straight. They can be queer in every visible way, but for the invisible part, their heart, it must be undoubtedly straight. "Gay in attitude but straight at heart" is the ultimate guideline of being a metrosexual. It is important to note that gay censorship is everywhere in popular culture, regardless of whether it is applied to a real person or on an abstract image.

Commercial interests play a great part in the straightening of metromen. The heterosexualization of the metrosexual can be seen as a marketing strategy to make him more appealing to a supposedly heterosexual majority in society. The commercial potential of the metrosexual as a new model of masculinity, shows that it may only be a packaged form of commercial masculinity. This has already begun since Mark Simpson coined this term in 1994. In the 1990s, particularly during the later half of the decade, there was a visible growth of men's grooming and fashion industries. The sale of men's cosmetics and skincare products expanded at an unprecedented rate. The role of the media was significant. The success of queer TV shows such as the British and American series of *Queer as Folk* and *Queer Eye for the Straight Guy* has helped to attract entrepreneurs to cash in on the growing market of men's grooming products.[12] Together with the established discourse of gay aestheticism and the rising popularity of the softer man, the metrosexual is the dream man for advertisers to promote market-driven urban masculinity. In line with the heterosexual hegemony, the re-defined notion of metrosexuality is strategically severed from its ultimate threat — of being gay. In this new converged discourse, being narcissist is what a modern man ought to be, and it is not exclusive to homosexuals. It thus adds an aesthetic twist to the heterosexual mainstream — metrosexuals are romantic; they love women; they make women happy. The most important fact is, of course, they make market executives very happy. Metrosexuality today is a mediated commercial or consumerist masculinity, deeply embedded in the logic of commercialism and consumerism.

But the media tell us that metrosexuals are no slaves of consumerism, nor are they victims of gender stereotypes. Most of the time, they are represented through the language of men's liberation. The dominant description of metrosexuals goes like this: fashion is not exclusive to women, and the desire to pay more attention to his softer and feminine side is not the privilege of gay men. The metrosexual is presented as part of gender equality and a form of liberation from homophobia. The media's adoption of a discourse of gender equality and men's liberation is strategically based on the political climate in which inclusion and diversity are the order of the day. Femininity and gay aesthetics are promoted by the media and the fashion industry as positive attributes of contemporary urban masculinity. Metrosexuality thus projects a form of masculinity that can liberate men from rigid gender stereotypes such as the all-work-and-no-play breadwinner, and also from the fear of being labeled as gay. Men are encouraged to join in with their gay counterparts and women to indulge in the experience of self-pampering. It is, simply put, politically correct to embrace gender equality and to renounce traditional masculinity.

Beyond the Queer Guise

How liberating is it for a Hong Kong man to be metrosexual? Can metrosexuality really broaden the current framework of masculinity? What are the implications of mainstreaming metrosexuality for existing norms of gender and sexuality? Will the public accept a more positive reading of gayness as they become more exposed to the concept of metrosexuality? In short, beyond the queer guise and the commercial potential, what is the critical edge of metrosexuals as a more liberated male model? Or, is there a critical edge at all?

Images of metrosexual men on the fashion pages of men's magazines do have an impact of subverting the visual norms of male representation in local media. One good example is the fashion pages modeled by Hu Bing on *Esquire Hong Kong Edition* (September 2004). The pages are titled "You've never looked so beautiful". "Sexy", "beautiful", and "narcissistic" are terms increasingly used by mainstream media as positive adjectives for straight men, though they are previously related exclusively to females. Metrosexuality has indeed opened up cultural space for a new form of masculine expression, even though the space is restricted to the visual sphere. It has brought diversity to the traditional, rigid models of masculine representation, which are built on the exclusion of feminine forms of expressions and on the condemnation of erotic desires among men. In practice it provides an alternative form of imagined identity or visual paradigm for men who are struggling to express their maleness in a more colourful way.

For men, femininity and gayness *in style* are no longer taboos. Metrosexuality has at least dissolved some previously strictly held norms of gender and sexuality. It has incorporated new elements such as femininity and gay aesthetics into the mainstream discourse of masculinity. What are previously deviant gender expressions are now assimilated into the centre. The metrosexual broadens up the public imagination of what is meant to be a man.

However, this liberation is only skin deep. It starts with the fabrics and it also ends there. If we look at the implications of metrosexuality for men's liberation to which it is purposefully associated, we will find that it is more a liberation of the gender expression of the professional class who has a good disposable income, than a true liberation of gender roles and sexuality of men in general. From the popularity of the television series *Queer Eye for the Straight Guy*, we witnessed the mainstreaming of gay aesthetics (although it comes with a reinforcement of gay stereotypes). From the mainstreaming of the metrosexual, we witnessed the assimilation of gay aesthetics by the dominant heterosexual masculinity. Yet, interestingly, the heterosexualization process has almost peeled off the entire layer of gayness from the metrosexual man.

The gay experts are highly acknowledged in *Queer Eye for the Straight Guy*, but for the metromen in local media, their gayness is deliberately suppressed or even brutally denied. Metrosexuals are explicitly heterosexual in local representations. Almost every description of metrosexuals comes together with an emphasis on their straightness. This acutely shows the deep-seated cultural anxiety of male homosexuality. Gay as a masquerade is fun and trendy, but one's gayness must not go deeper than the pink Dolce & Gabana shirt that he wears. Heterosexuality is still the central regulating force for legitimate masculinity. Gayness can only be legitimized as an aesthetic in the dominant discourse of gender expression. Metrosexuals are thus men in queer guise only. They are harmless hedonistic pleasure seekers as long as they do not deviate from the heterosexual norm. When Simpson's metrosexual man meets commercialism, he must bow to market forces. He is immediately "straightened" up to avoid upsetting the homophobic society. Thus the visibility of this gay-inspired male image is built upon the forced invisibility of its original non-heterosexual male prototype. This strategic avoidance of gay associations reminds us of the prevalence of anti-gay sentiment in our society, despite the fact that many will deny that there is any prejudice against gays, in as much the same way as the denial of discrimination against gay masculinity as a form of legitimate masculinity, and gay people as legitimate citizens.

Conclusion

Since 1980 when gender studies research began in Hong Kong's higher education institutions, academic studies on various aspects of women's experience have accumulated to provide a rather comprehensive picture of women's lives. Realizing that more in-depth examinations of women's situation are still very much needed, we also believe that gender identities exist in relation and not in isolation. As in other parts of the world, discourses on masculinity and manhood in Hong Kong are changing, as women's and men's roles have both become increasingly diverse. Kimmel and Kaufman (1995) attribute the rise of anti-feminist discourse to the changing global political and economic relations, feminism, and lesbian and gay movement, which have changed the homogeneity of the public domain. In face of these contradictory discourses, some men find their way out by resurrecting the traditional manhood to achieve a sense of security. Paradoxically, while they try to revive their power, they have to admit that men are powerless and inferior in the present situation. While today some men may be holding on to the power with which their sex has privileged them, there are others who are experimenting with alternative forms of social identities, such as full-time house-husbands or self-proclaimed gays. We therefore should find out about the experience of men both as the gender that exercises the power to define the meaning, content, and standards of gender, and as the individuals who at the same time may be stereotyped and made unequal.

As we hope to have demonstrated in this chapter, there is indeed a variety of practices of manhood and masculine identities. Yet we find it alarming that, what is seemingly suppressive of men (as their bodies are marginalized and made invisible in beauty salons) can in effect reinforce the very gender stereotypes that safeguard men's superiority. By the same token, new identities like metrosexuals can be co-opted by mainstream heterosexual discourse, and old identities such as the polygamous husband have found new life in the cross-border economic restructuring. Faced with the persistence of patriarchy, we challenge scholars to take up the critical study of manhood and the nature of masculinity, and to endeavor in the theorization of gender relations and ideology that is specific to Hong Kong at this historical juncture. The study of the culture of gender must be firmly grounded in ethnographic studies, as social practice cannot and should not be isolated from the political economy of which it is part. Only by scrutinizing the social forces that make up the cultural context of gender relations can we understand how and why the different genders are constantly contested, modified and reproduced. Men and women, and for that matter any other genders, should not be treated as diametrical opposites, but rather as problematics whose very existence, representations, and the politics involved therein, need to be re-examined and not taken for granted.

In this chapter we have discussed some practices and representations of Hong Kong men in the early 21st century, focusing specifically on the mistress-keepers who became culturally transparent; the beauty-seeking men who purchased facial treatments and were made non-existent in beauty salons; and the metrosexuals who were heterosexualized by mainstream media. We explicated how their familial role, bodies, and sexuality may be highlighted, hidden, and distorted; how they are sometimes made visible, and other times invisible, by the capitalist and cultural forces in Hong Kong society. In so doing, we point out, like others before us, that there are multiple masculinities which may not have a common basis but which all involve relations of power (Hooper 2000), and which come into existence at particular times and places (Connell, 1995). Power negotiations may exist between men and women, or among men of different sexual orientations, or among women who take different sides, literally, on either side of the Hongkong-China border. We argue for the need to revisualize the presence of men in various contexts, and thereby provide a more comprehensive and realistic understanding of gender relations in Hong Kong society.

References

Baker, H. (1979). *Chinese family and kinship*. London: Macmillan Press.

Benwell, B. (Ed.) (2003). *Masculinity and men's lifestyle magazines*. Oxford: Blackwell.

BJ Business (北京現代商報) (2004). 男性護膚品市場成'雄市', www.bjbusiness. com.cn, February 12, 2002, retrieved on December 4, 2004.

Cai, Y. Y. and X. J. Ou 蔡元雲，區祥江 (1998). *Nan ren de mian ju* 男人的面具 (The Mask of Men). Hong Kong: Breakthrough.

Census and Statistics Department. (2004). *Census report 2004*. Hong Kong: Hong Kong Special Administrative Region Government.

Chan, K. W. (2001). Gendering men's services in Hong Kong: Backlash or pursuit of gender equality? In Bob Pease and Keith Pringle (Eds.), *A man's world? Changing men's practices in a globalised world*. London and New York: Zed Books.

Chua, B. H. (Ed.) (2000). *Consumption in Asia: Lifestyles and identities*. New York and London: Routledge.

Clatterbaugh, K. (1997). *Contemporary perspectives on masculinities: Men, women, and politics in modern society*. Boulder, CO: Westview Press.

Connell, R. W. (1987). *Gender and power: Society, the person and sexual politics*. Cambridge: Polity Press.

———. (1995). *Masculinities: Knowledge, power and social change*. Berkeley: University of California Press.

Flocker, M. (2003). *The Metrosexual guide to style: A handbook for the modern man*. Cambridge, MA: Da Capo Press.

Deng, M. (2005). 揭開男性護膚品的面紗. *Top marketing*, http://www.cmmo.com. cn/article/2005-04/1406.shtml, April 4, 2005, retrieved on May 1, 2005.

Dotson, E. W. (1999). *Behold the man: The hype and selling of male beauty in media and culture*. New York: Haworth Press.

Ebrey, P. (2003). *Women and the family in Chinese history*. London: Routledge.

Foucault, M. (1979). *Discipline and punishment: The birth of the prison*. New York: Vintage.

Freedman, M. (1957). *Chinese family and marriage in Singapore*. London: Her Majesty's Stationery Office.

———. (1970). *Family and kinship in Chinese society*. Stanford: Stanford University Press.

Fung, R. (1995). Burdens of representation, burden of responsibility (pp. 291–298). In M. Berger, B. Wallis and S. Watson (Eds.), *Constructing masculinity*. New York: Routledge.

Grossman, A. (2000). The rise of homosexuality and the dawn of communism in Hong Kong film: 1993–1998. In Andrew Grossman (Ed.), *Queer Asian cinema: Shadows in the shade*. New York: Harrington Park Press.

Hooper, C. (2000). Masculinities in transition: The case of globalization. In Marianne H. Marchand and Anne Sisson Runyan (Eds.), *Gender and global restructuring: Sightings, sites and resistances*. London and New York: Routledge.

Hurwich, J. (1992). *The Psychological Consequences of Impending National Change: Anxiety, depression and somatization among homosexual and heterosexual men living in Hong Kong*. PhD thesis. California School of Professional Psychology at Berkeley/Almeda.

Jaschok, M., & Miers, S. (Eds.) (1994). *Women and Chinese patriarchy: Submission, servitude and escape*. Hong Kong: Hong Kong University Press.

Kam, L. (2002). *Theorizing Chinese masculinity: Society and gender in China*. Cambridge: Cambridge University Press.

Kam, L., & Low, M. (Eds.) (2003). *Asian masculinities: The meaning and practice of manhood in China and Japan*. New York and London: RoutledgeCurzon.

Kimmel, M. (1993). Invisible masculinity. *Society* (September/October 1993): 28–35.

Kimmel, M. S., & Kaufman, M. (1995). Weekend warriors: The new men's movement. In Michael S. Kimmel (Ed.), *The politics of manhood: Profeminist men respond to the mythopoetic men's movement* (and the mythopoetic leaders answer) (pp. 15–43). Philadelphia: Temple University Press.

Kwok, P. L., Chow, G., Lee, C. K., & Rose Wu. 1997. Women and the state in Hong Kong. In Fanny M. Cheung, ed., *Engendering Hong Kong society* (pp. 237–266). Hong Kong: The Chinese University Press.

Lai, B. L. L., Au, K. C., & Cheung, F. M. (1997). Women's concern groups in Hong Kong. In F. M. Cheung (Ed.), *Engendering Hong Kong society* (pp. 237–266). Hong Kong: The Chinese University Press.

Li, V. W.-K. (2002). *Seeking an ideal wife: Why Hong Kong men pursue mainland Chinese spouses.* MPhil thesis, The Chinese University of Hong Kong.

Lu, S. (2001). *China, transnational visuality, global postmodernity.* Stanford: Stanford University Press.

Mac an Ghaill, M., (Ed.) (1996). *Understanding masculinities.* Buckingham, Philadelphia: Open University Press.

McKay, J., Mikosza J., & Hutchins, B. (2005). Gentlemen, the lunchbox has landed: Representations of masculinities and men's bodies in the popular media. In M. Kimmel, J. Hearn, & R. W. Connell (Eds.), *Handbook of studies on men and masculinities* (pp. 270–288). Thousand Oaks: Sage.

Messner, M. A. (1997). *Politics of masculinities: Men in movements.* Thousand Oaks, London and New Delhi: Sage.

Ou, X. J. 區祥江. (2003). *Nan ren de ming tu: Cong dawei jue ze san si zi shen* 男人的命途：從大衛王的抉擇三思自身 (The Fate of Men: Reflections from King David's Decisions). Hong Kong: Breakthrough.

Ou, X. J, & Zeng, L. H. (2001). *Nan ren de ai shang* 男人的哀傷 (The Sadness of Men). Hong Kong: Breakthrough.

Pegg, L. (1986). *Family law in Hong Kong.* Singapore: Butterworths.

People.com.cn (人民網) 21世紀新好男人要護膚, www.people.com.cn, March 12, 2001, retrieved on April 4, 2005.

Simpson, M. (2002). Meet the metrosexual. www.Salon.com, July 22, 2002.

Tam, S. M. (1996). Normalization of "second wives": Gender contestation in Hong Kong. *Asian Journal of Women Studies 2*: 113–132.

Tam, S. M., & Leahy, P. (2005). *A bibliography of genders studies in Hong Kong 1998–2003.* Hong Kong: Gender Research Centre, HKIAPS, The Chinese University of Hong Kong.

Tamney, J., & Chiang, L. H.-L. (2002). *Modernization, globalization, and confucianism in Chinese societies.* London: Praeger.

Tang, W. M. (2004). Identity negotiation between religion and sexuality: A study of gay Christians in Hong Kong. MPhil thesis, The Chinese University of Hong Kong.

Watson, J. (1982). Chinese kinship reconsidered: Anthropological perspectives on historical research. *China Quarterly 92*: 589–622.

Watson, J., & Watson, R. (2004). *Village life in Hong Kong: Politics, gender, and ritual in the New Territories.* Hong Kong: The Chinese University Press.

West, R., & Lay, F. (Eds.) (2000). *Subverting masculinity: Hegemonic and alternative versions of masculinity in contemporary culture.* Amsterdam: Rodopi.

Wolf, M. (1972). Uterine families and the women's community. In *Women and the family in rural Taiwan.* Stanford: Stanford University Press.

Zhou H. S. 周華山. (199). 後殖民同志. Hong Kong: Xianggang tong zhi yan jiu she.

Notes

1. The study on which this section is based is funded by the Research Grants Council (RGC Ref. No. CUHK4349/01H, anthropology).

2. Chinese terms in this paper are transliterated using the pinyin system. For names of Hong Kong persons, the conventional method of translation adopted by the Hong Kong Government is used.

3. For clarity of writing, "China" in this section refers to mainland China, and "Chinese" refers to those who live on the mainland or originate from there. Women and men from Hong Kong who are mostly of Chinese ancestry, are referred to as "Hong Kong" men and women.

4. According to Census Report 2004, Hong Kong Special Administrative Region Statistics Department.

5. Since mainland China is to the north of Hong Kong, the movement of people from Hong Kong to China is locally dubbed *bei shang*, or literally "going up north".

6. There has been a steady increase in the number of Hong Kong women working in the PRC since the Asian financial crisis, but the number remained less than 10% of the total "going north" population (HKSAR Census Dept 2004). The localities women worked in tended to be close to Hong Kong, ie, mobility was still very much a male phenomenon.

7. This survey forms part of the research project described in footnote 1.

8. To ensure anonymity of the interviewees, all individual interviewees are given pseudonyms. Information of individuals such as occupation or place of work may be changed where they do not affect the cultural context.

9. In Chinese idiom, a man with more than one wife is called a *qi ren*, who according to legend was a man in the Spring and Autumn Period. As he had the ability to make both wives happy, he became an icon of domestic bliss and success for men.

10. *T.O.M.* is a magazine currently distributed on mainland China. It was launched in April 2002 by the Guangzhou-based Modern Media Group. The Group bought

City Magazine (a lifestyle and cultural magazine in Hong Kong established since 1970s, which targets at the middle class professionals in the city) in September 2003. A majority part of its editorial content is provided by *City Magazine*. *T.O.M.* "is a high quality men's magazine targeting at the successful male business executives", as defined by its official website (www. theoutlookmagazine.com).

11. *Men's Uno (Hong Kong)* was launched in 2003. Its parent edition is *Men's Uno (Taiwan)* which was established in 1997, published by the Taiwan-based Chic Publishing Inc. The Hong Kong Edition positions itself as the "Men's Lifestyle Magazine for Chinese over the World" (大中華連線男士生活雜誌, www. mensuno.com.hk).

12. "Also helping the (men's grooming) industry is the popularity of shows on cable networks, including Bravo's *Queer Eye for the Straight Guy*. Men's grooming has become a $7.7 billion industry, according to a 2003 industry study released by MarketResearch.com. The study says men's grooming products and services will reach the $10 billion mark by 2008." (*South Florida Sun-Sentinel*, July 15, 2004)

PART IV

Institutional Mechanisms
and Responses

Central Mechanisms: The Equal Opportunities Commission and The Women's Commission

Fanny M. Cheung and Priscilla Ching Chung

Despite the existence of laws and international conventions, experiences from the women's movement have affirmed the need to establish an institutional mechanism within the government for the advancement of women. The institutional machinery will ensure that the state will take up its responsibility to implement international obligations and its own commitment to protect the interests and promote the status of women. The call for a central mechanism was highlighted in the Beijing Platform for Action adopted at the Fourth World Congress on Women in Beijing in 1995, and has been advocated for the implementation of the Convention for the Elimination of All Forms of Discrimination Against Women. In this chapter, we recount the history of the establishment of institutional mechanisms for the advancement of women in Hong Kong. We, the authors, have been participants in the process and the mechanisms, and our account may be viewed as insiders' perspectives to a certain extent. We aim to recall the facts and discuss the challenges for gender mainstreaming through institutional mechanisms in Hong Kong.

Call for a Central Mechanism for Women

Women's concerns in Hong Kong have traditionally been marginalized as the agenda of women's groups. While the state exerts influences on women's lives, women's voices have largely been left out from government structure and policies (Cheung, Wan, & Wan, 1994; Kwok, Chow, Lee, & Wu, 1997). The international women's community called for the establishment of national machineries for the advancement of women as early as the 1970s. The World Conference on Women in Mexico City in 1975 adopted the recommendation, and the United Nations Commission on the Status of Women highlighted the issue as a priority theme in 1988. In Hong Kong, the call for a central mechanism came after the growth of local women's concern groups in the late 1980s (Lai, Au, & Cheung, 1997).

The first local call was a modest request made in 1989 by several New Territories women's groups when they met with Office of the Members of the Executive and Legislative Council (OMELCO) to urge the government to set up a central committee to look after women's issues. Around the same time, coalitions of other women's concerns groups sprouted to promote a collective voice for women. A joint committee of nine community women's groups was formed to work on a Women's Broadsheet to review the status of women. A coalition of 12 women's groups formed the Women's Joint Political Platform to advocate a comprehensive strategy of advancing women's status. The Platform included urging the government to extend the United Nations Convention on the Elimination of All Forms of Discrimination Against Women (CEDAW) to Hong Kong, as well as the creation of a working group on women's policy in the government to conduct research, formulate policies, and coordinate services for women (Women Voters Development Plan Association, 1991).

With the introduction of direct election to the Legislative Council (LegCo), women's groups began to lobby for the support of elected legislative councillors to voice women's concerns. As the guest of honour at the annual meeting of the Women's Centre in 1990, the Hon. Martin Lee agreed to bring the question on advancement of women's status back to the Legislative Council. In 1991, he and another female legislator, the Hon. Leung Wai-tung, raised a LegCo question, to which Secretary of Home Affairs (SHA) responded that there was no discrimination against women in Hong Kong. Nevertheless, the Legislative Council set up an Ad Hoc group, chaired by the Hon. Emily Lau, to study the need for a Women's Commission. In 1992, the Legislation Council also passed a motion raised by the Hon. Peggy Lam calling for the extension of CEDAW to Hong Kong.

In 1992, 14 women's and community groups campaigned for the establishment of a women's commission by the government and for the application of CEDAW, with a rally on March 8 chaired by Fanny Cheung, an academic who had been active in the women's movement. In the booklet published by the Campaign (Campaign for a Women's Commission and for CEDAW, 1993), the proposed Women's Commission was anticipated to play an advisory role for the Hong Kong government, and conduct research with emphasis on sex discrimination in the workplace, social services, media projection of women's image, sexual violence, and the enactment of legislation protecting women from discrimination. The Campaign suggested the setup of complaints units in the Women's Commission to provide support and advice to women. It was recommended that the Commission be an inter-departmental unit that would hold regular meetings with government departments concerned with issues affecting women's lives.

In response to the call from the community, the government published in 1993 a *Green Paper on Equal Opportunities for Women and Men* (Hong Kong Government 1993, 1994). This was the first time that the Hong Kong government compiled any data focusing on women's status. Basically, the Green Paper denied that there were problems of sex discrimination in Hong Kong. However, at the urging of the Legislative Council, the government commissioned the Gender Research Programme of the Chinese University of Hong Kong to conduct a community survey on equal opportunities for women and men in 1994. Using more sensitive survey approaches, the study recognized there were distinct areas of sex discrimination, especially in relation to employment, New Territories land inheritance, as well as educational opportunities.

In 1994, the debate and subsequent passage of the New Territories Land (Exemption) Ordinance by the Legislative Council, which gave indigenous women residents of the New Territories the intestate inheritance rights, raised public attention to the deep-rooted discriminatory attitudes towards women still prevailing in Hong Kong. It was around this time that the government had to respond to the Hon. Anna Wu's private member's bill in the Legislative Council on equal opportunities, which covered a broad range of grounds including sex discrimination. The Government reacted by introducing its own version of the Sex Discrimination Bill (see Petersen's chapter for a full discussion of the legislative process). The Sex Discrimination Ordinance (SDO) was enacted in 1995. The Equal Opportunities Commission was formed in May 1996 under the SDO. In October of the same year, CEDAW was extended to Hong Kong.

The Equal Opportunities Commission

The Equal Opportunities Commission (EOC) was established under Article 63 of the SDO. Its Chairperson and 16 members of the Commission were appointed by the government. Its principal responsibility initially was to administer the SDO and the Disability Discrimination Ordinance (DDO). The Family Status Discrimination Ordinance (FSDO) was passed in 1997 and its implementation was also allocated to the EOC. This chapter focuses only on the roles and functions of the EOC in relations to sex discrimination and areas of concerns that affect women's status specifically.

The SDO renders as unlawful acts which treat a person less favourably on the ground of the person's sex, marital status, and pregnancy. Sexual harassment was also made unlawful under the ordinances. The fields covered under the laws include employment, education, provision of goods, services, facilities, access to and management and disposal of premises and eligibility to vote for and to be elected or appointed to advisory bodies, and government activities. With the enactment of the FSDO in 1997, discrimination on the ground of having responsibility for the care of a family member, for which women are usually the caretaker, was also made unlawful. The aggrieved person may lodge a complaint with the EOC, which will investigate the matter and endeavour to work with the parties concerned through conciliation to find an acceptable solution. If this fails, then the aggrieved party may apply to the EOC for legal assistance to go to court.

In addition to investigating and conciliating complaints for aggrieved persons, the EOC may apply to the court to enjoin the publication of unlawful discriminatory advertisements, including the use of a job description in an employment advertisement which is sex specific. It also has the power to conduct a formal investigation on unlawful discriminatory acts which are grave or have pervasive implications.

While Hong Kong people value the rule of law, they were not familiar with Western models of human rights and anti-discrimination legislation. So the concepts of equal opportunities (EO) and the role of the EOC were not widely understood by the general public. Many individual complainants, advocates and women's groups confused the protection of rights under civil laws with notions of criminal justice whereby there would be a law enforcement agency to arraign the culprit on behalf of the victim. In the traditional notion of justice, "law was the instrument of the ruler and was therefore primarily public law consisting of penal rules. The ruler used law as commands (or orders) backed by sanction (or threat of sanctions) to control and regulate the behaviour of his subjects..." (Kuan, 1992, p. 162). The understanding of protection of rights under civil laws was new to the general public.

The tension was especially true of the SDO, where many sectors of the society, in general, did not believe that women were discriminated against and did not harbour a sense of urgency about discrimination issues. The general public perceived gender roles through stereotypical lenses. They confused the notion of equal opportunities with absolute equality and argued that women and men could not be the same inherently. On the other hand, advocates for women's rights had expectations of EOC that the Commission could not meet, as the EOC has no power to adjudicate and its powers are limited by what is prescribed in the SDO. Instead, aggrieved persons have to assert their rights by filing a complaint with the EOC or lawsuit in the District Court. Under the belief that EOC served the function of the institutional mechanism that they had expected, women's groups, which had been advocating the formation of the Women's Commission, were initially critical. They found the SDO to be a double-edged sword, since it protects the rights of both women and men, and therefore did not always address the needs of women specifically. Their expectations were fueled by the government's claim that the establishment of the EOC had now fulfilled their demands for a central mechanism for women. Some of the more active women's groups formed a coalition to monitor and critique the EOC's work. In time, the advocates began to gain a better understanding of the roles and the limits of the EOC, lowered their expectations and began to work constructively with the EOC.

Although the whole commission is a body corporate that is responsible for policy decisions, the leadership of the EOC Chairperson has been influential in steering the direction of the commission.

Breaking New Ground: The First Three Years

The first Chairperson was Dr. Fanny Cheung Mui-ching, a professor of Psychology, who had been a leader in the women's movement in Hong Kong for two decades. She was also active in promoting community acceptance of persons with psychiatric disabilities in the 1980s. She got the Commission quickly off the ground and was able to establish the office, hire the staff, and commence the implementation of the non-employment-related provisions of the SDO and DDO within the first three months. The employment-related provisions were brought into effect three months later after two rounds of consultation on the Codes of Practices in Employment for the two ordinances. In addition, discriminatory advertisement on the basis of sex, which constituted one third of employment advertisements in newspapers in 1996, was largely eliminated through education, warning and legal action within six months. The EOC received over 1,200 complaints during the first three years and among the cases that entered into conciliation, the success rate was about 66 percent. Sixteen cases were granted legal assistance and by the end of her term, two cases had been heard in court. In both cases, the EOC won on behalf of the plaintiff.

To address systemic discrimination that affects a large sector of the community, the EOC made use of its other statutory powers to conduct a formal investigation for the first time in 1998. The EOC launched its first formal investigation into the Secondary School Places Allocation ("SSPA") system used by the Education Department since 1978. The EOC recommended that the Education Department reviewed the SSPA system to ensure compliance with the Sex Discrimination Ordinance and to remove the discriminatory elements so that boys and girls were not discriminated on the basis of sex when they were placed in secondary schools. Another approach to address systemic discrimination was through research, such as the large-scale Feasibility Study on Equal Pay for Work of Equal Value that commenced in 1998.

The work of the EOC could be broadly defined within two general areas under the law: to work towards the elimination of discrimination, and to promote equal opportunities. The EOC decided that while discriminatory acts could be addressed by legislation, discriminatory attitudes have to be changed by education. Under Cheung's leadership, the EOC launched a four-pronged public education approach from the start through: 1) Awareness raising in the general public via large scale publicity, using television, radio, newspaper, internet, newsletters and pamphlets; 2) educating specific target groups by offering stakeholders talks, guidelines, Codes of Practice, and leaflets on good management practices, as well as puppet shows for schools; 3) involving community participation by bringing community road-shows to all 18 districts in Hong Kong, and providing financial support to community organizations to organize promotional activities; and 4) training the trainers by producing training modules for human resource practitioners, labour unionists, advocates and teachers.

These promotional activities increased public awareness of the EOC from 35% in September 1996 to 87% in March 1998. Over 70% of the general public indicated that they would seek EOC's help in conciliation if they encountered discrimination. The number of complaints received multiplied steadily with 195% increase in the second year and another 109% increase in the third year. Employers sought EOC's assistance in setting up equal opportunities and sexual harassment policies.

In addition to public education, the EOC also established the groundwork for understanding discrimination through research. The research studies provided important knowledge on issues, monitored public perception and attitudes as well as established benchmarks for future trends. Ten research projects were commissioned during the first three years, including community and students' attitudes toward discrimination, what constituted sex as genuine occupation qualification, stereotypes and biases in school textbooks.

The achievements of the first three years of the EOC laid a solid foundation for a cultural evolution. By 1999, discrimination was regarded as a legitimate concern. The mechanism for redress was in place and individuals were learning to assert their rights. The role of the EOC was acknowledged by the public (Cheung, 1999).

Extending EOC's Impact: The Next Four Years

The second Chairperson, Ms. Anna Wu, was an attorney who had been responsible for initiating the anti-discrimination legislation while serving in the Hong Kong Legislature. Building on the solid foundation of the first three years, the EOC set out to mainstream equal opportunities and to create a fair and inclusive society.

It was during her term that several court cases, initiated during the first three years, came to judgment. These court actions were able to foster fairer access to education and ensure equal opportunities in employment for both the disabled and for pregnant women. Practical experiences were gained from these cases. In one unsuccessful sexual harassment case, the EOC recognized that it was emotionally difficult for the complainant to undergo cross-examination at court, and since there were often no witnesses, it would be difficult to prove that it had occurred. Subsequently, a practice was developed whereby sexual harassment complainants may be recommended to seek counselling from relevant women support groups while their case was being handled. If the case should go to court, the complainant would have a counsellor from relevant support group to help her through the emotional crisis.

During these four years, the EOC also successfully focused on several areas including a study into insurance practices that affect the provision of coverage and premium on the ground of sex and disability, and advocating Information Technology (IT) for all, especially for persons with disabilities.

To strengthen training and research, the EOC established a Training Unit to focus on training employers and employees on the anti-discrimination legislation, and a Policy Support and Research Unit to meet the increasing demand for policy analysis and research support. The EOC continued to foster understanding of equal opportunities principles and to help change preset perceptions and attitudes through research and public education projects.

The most prominent feature of this era was the bringing of high profile court cases against the government, which included the legal assistance given to the plaintiffs in a disability discrimination case related to the recruitment of disciplinary forces personnel on the ground of the mental disability of family members, and the judicial review case brought by the EOC against the Education Department on sex discrimination in the Secondary School Places Allocation (SSPA) system as the Education Department refused to comply with the findings of the Formal Investigation completed in 1999. The High Court of Appeals, ruled in 2001 that the SSPA unlawfully discriminated on the ground of sex. This case is described in greater details in Petersen's chapter on Hong Kong's legal framework for gender equality.

Beyond the Controversy

In the summer of 2003, Judge Wong Kin-chow, a retired judge of the Court of Appeal, was appointed as the third Chairperson of the EOC. Shortly after his appointment, a controversy arose from the termination of a new appointee to the position of Director of Operations, who had been offered appointment right before the outgoing Chairperson left office. The events following the controversy resulted in the resignation of Judge Wong after serving for only three months.

An interim Chairperson — Mrs. Patricia Chu Yeung Pak-yu — was appointed for one year. Mrs. Chu was an experienced civil servant who had retired from the Department of Social Welfare after 34 years of service. She reaffirmed her commitment to neutrality in dealing with complaints and litigation against the government, promising to handle all matters in a fair and open manner and in accordance with the law. To restore the credibility of the EOC, she concentrated on consolidation, capacity building, and communicating with the different stakeholders.

In continuation of the process initiated by the previous chairperson, the EOC looked into the feasibility of an equal opportunities tribunal to handle discrimination cases, offering a less time-consuming and less adversarial alternative to civil proceedings in the district court. In 2004, the EOC completed an organizational review initiated by the previous chairperson in 2003 and a human resource management review on internal policies procedures and practices. The EOC also worked with the Home Affairs Bureau on the possible introduction of the Race Discrimination legislation, which, if enacted, will be implemented by the EOC.[1]

The fifth Chairperson, Mr. Raymond Tang, was appointed in January 2005 for a five-year term together with a completely new cohort of members to give a fresh start for the Commission. A lawyer in background, and the Privacy Commissioner before assuming the present post, Mr. Tang highlighted the regulatory role of the EOC. Initially, EOC remained in the political limelight which distracted the public from substantive issues of equal opportunities. As the new EOC settled into place, a number of long-term projects were initiated to mainstream the concept of equal opportunities in the community, including the Equal Opportunities Club and the EO Diversity Project on radio. The organizational structure of the EOC was finalized with an integrated Operations Division headed by a director promoted from within.

Ten Years Onward

As the EOC passed its 10th anniversary, its jurisdiction was extended to take up a new anti-discrimination ordinance on race discrimination that was later passed in 2008. Without a separate Gender Division, the EOC has consolidated its previous efforts on advocating for gender equality, and has collaborated with the Women's Commission in some of these efforts. These include undertaking a survey on family friendly policies to improve parenting and caring roles for men and women to achieve a better work/life balance, and cooperating with the Curriculum Development Institute of the Education and Manpower Bureau to enhance understanding and acceptance of gender equality in the school curriculum. The EOC also published the full reports of the various studies undertaken to address the controversial issue of equal pay for equal value.

As part of its 10th anniversary celebration, EOC launched the inauguration of the Equal Opportunities Club in 2006 to support a network of employers, human resource practitioners, and workplace trainers in implementing equal opportunities standards in employment. In 2007, it co-organized with the Swedish Consulate-General, Swedish Institute and the Chinese University a public seminar and a youth forum to share the stories of Hong Kong and Sweden on their respective experiences of policies, programmes and best practices in advancing gender equality. At the public forum, the first and the current EOC Chairpersons reviewed the advances in women's status and gender equality in the past decade. In particular, the Hong Kong and the Swedish speakers addressed the importance of abandoning gender stereotypes, transforming traditional gender roles at work and in the family, and engaging men as equal partners and full participants to achieve gender equality.

Powers of the EOC

The powers of the EOC to eliminate discrimination lie in two major functions that serve people who are aggrieved: investigation and conciliation, and legal assistance. While Petersen's chapter in this book elaborates on the legal framework of these functions, we provide an account of the operational statistics in this chapter to illustrate EOC's functions. In addition, we examine the approach the EOC has adopted to address systemic discrimination that affect not just individuals.

Investigation and Conciliation

Since the SDO and DDO were brought into effect in late 1996, the EOC received a steady increase in enquiries and complaints. In 2001, the number of enquiries received rose to over 12,470 and complaints for investigation and conciliation received was at its peak of 1,622 (Table 1). The increase in this year was partly contributed by the large number of individual complaints arising at the conclusion of the court case on the Education Department's Secondary School Places Allocation Scheme. The rise in the year 2003 was partly related to discrimination complaints related to the SARS epidemic.

To ensure the quality of the handling of investigations of complaints, specialists from the Australian Human Rights and Equal Opportunity Commission (HREOC) were contracted to review the mechanisms and processes. The legal framework in the establishment of the EOC has followed closely the Australian model. These consultants found the quality of the work to be equal to, and in some cases superior to, work performed in similar commissions in Australia. The consultants also identified some areas for improvement and the need for restructuring. To enhance the efficiency and effectiveness of complaint handling, the EOC office was reorganized by combining the two previously separate complaint handling divisions for

Table 1. EOC Statistics on Complaints for Investigation and Conciliation
from 1997 to 2006

Period	Ordinance	Complaint for investigation and conciliation			Remarks
		Received	Handled*	Concluded	
Jan to Dec 1997	SDO	70	70	36	
	DDO	93	98	52	
	FSDO	0	0	0	Conciliation rate
	Total	**163**	**168**	**88**	= 73.7%
Jan to Dec 1998	SDO	118	152	95	
	DDO	264	310	195	
	FSDO	11	11	4	Conciliation rate
	Total	**393**	**473**	**294**	= 64.7%
Jan to Dec 1999	SDO	213	271	167	
	DDO	192	307	195	
	FSDO	28	35	22	Conciliation rate
	Total	**433**	**613**	**384**	= 61.8%
Jan to Dec 2000	SDO	323	427	244	
	DDO	339	451	248	
	FSDO	24	37	17	Conciliation rate
	Total	**686**	**915**	**509**	= 60.8%
Jan to Dec 2001	SDO	1165	1348	627	
	DDO	416	619	425	
	FSDO	41	61	23	Conciliation rate
	Total	**1622**	**2028**	**1075**	= 66.8%
Jan to Dec 2002	SDO	390	1111	960	
	DDO	341	535	392	
	FSDO	26	64	56	Conciliation rate
	Total	**757**	**1710**	**1408**	= 61.3%
Jan to Dec 2003	SDO	450	601	457	
	DDO	408	551	421	
	FSDO	57	65	45	Conciliation rate
	Total	**915**	**1217**	**923**	= 53.2%
Jan to Dec 2004	SDO	198	352	274	
	DDO	347	485	345	
	FSDO	21	41	31	Conciliation rate
	Total	**566**	**878**	**650**	= 61%
Jan to Dec 2005	SDO	210	288	221	
	DDO	400	540	408	
	FSDO	23	33	26	Conciliation rate
	Total	**633**	**861**	**655**	= 66%
Jan to Dec 2006	SDO	251	318	234	
	DDO	383	515	380	
	FSDO	24	31	28	Conciliation rate
	Total	**658**	**864**	**642**	= 68%

(Source: Equal Opportunities Commission, received 13 Feb, 2007)

* Handled cases include those received in the current year and those carried over from previous
years.

sex and disability into a single operations division to facilitate greater sharing of expertise and better use of resources.

Legal Assistance

According to the SDO, the EOC may give legal assistance to complainants in cases where questions of principle are raised or if it is unreasonable to expect the applicant to deal with the case unaided. Between 1997 and 2006, it has granted assistance to 160 of the 381 applications, a total of 42.0 percent (Table 2). It should be noted that the figures are based on all cases, not only those related to the SDO and FSDO. Of those granted, 80 cases were settled out of court and 14 of those that went to trial have been concluded. Among those that went to trial, 12 were won and two were lost, giving a success rate of 86%. Since court cases may take more than a year from initiation to conclusion, the outcome of many cases are still not known.

Due to its budgetary constraints, the EOC had not been able to assist all cases meriting legal support to bring their cases to court. The contentious nature of litigation and the restrictive conditions of legal aid from the government have also discouraged some complainants from pursuing their cases in court. While advocates continued to urge the EOC to "prosecute"

Table 2. EOC Statistics on Legal Assistance

| | YEAR | | | | | | | | | | |
	97	98	99	00	01	02	03	04	05	06	Total
No. of applications received	5	19	21	41	33	60	71	51	50	30	381
No. of applications not granted	2	10	11	15	18	42	39	38	25	17	217
No. of applications granted	3	9	10	26	15	12	23	27	19	16	160
Withdrawal before decision	0	0	0	0	0	0	0	1	0	0	1
Withdrawal	0	1	4	4	6	1	11	7	7	4	45
Settled	0	1	2	3	5	13	11	21	14	10	80
Trial concluded	0	0	2	3	4	1	1	0	2	1	14

(Source: Equal Opportunities Commission, received 13 Feb, 2007)

more cases in court (Kershaw & DeGolyer, 2006), the power of the EOC in assisting the complainants to bring their personal case to court instead of being the prosecutor of individual cases of discrimination, given the civil nature of the anti-discrimination laws, has remained unclear to the general public and the advocates (Cheung, 1998).

Fighting Systemic Discrimination

The formal investigation and the subsequent judicial review of the SSPA illustrate some of the powers that the EOC has adopted to address sex discrimination in education that affected a cross-section of the school population. In the field of employment, the EOC embarked on a number of studies to address the systemic discrimination embedded in pay inequity such as "equal pay for work of equal value" (EPEV), which means that men and women doing different jobs should receive the same pay if the work they do is of equal value, as the Hong Kong government is bound by a number of international treaties to implement the principle of EPEV. Without any explicit legislation, the issue of equal value was left to the Code of Practice on Employment under the SDO.

The principle and implementation of EPEV are complex matters. Since 1998, the EOC has conducted a number of studies to examine the issues. A Task Force was appointed in 2001 and an implementation plan, dividing the work into three phases, was developed: the first phase was to address the issue within the public sector; in the second phase, large employers with more than 200 employees; and in the third phase, small and medium enterprises. Consultants were hired for the first phase and these consultants, working with the EOC staff and the Task Force, completed and handed in its study and recommendations in August of 2004. Given the complex nature of EPEV, the findings of the various studies were conflicting, and the views of the consultants and members on the full implementation of EPEV differed. In 2006, the EOC published a report stating that while identifying the prevalence of job segregation, there was no conclusive evidence on systemic discrimination in pay anomaly. Possible sources of salary discrimination against women could be attributed to discriminatory socialization resulting from history and culture, which should be addressed through public education. Instead of proposing new legislation, as recommended by the consultants in 2004, the EOC said that it would use its regulatory role to deal with EPEV complaints and that it would review its Code of Practice on Employment under the SDO to enhance public awareness and to encourage best practices. The full report of the 1998 study by the first group of consultants and the 2004 recommendations made by the second group of consultants were appended to the Report (Equal Opportunities Commission, 2006).

Challenges of the EOC

The EOC faces different kinds of challenges in its fight against discrimination, apart from the controversy in which it was embroiled in 2003. Part of it relates to the legal nature of its work, and part of it is due to the way it is structured and its relationship to government.

To date, the majority of people in Hong Kong are aware of the EOC and that it could be used as a redress mechanism if the aggrieved persons so desire. Yet, under the existing legislation, the EOC is only able to fight unlawful discrimination against an individual defined within the law and through a process described in the law. Therefore, the EOC must, at times, wait until a complaint is filed. It also has to attempt conciliation before considering legal assistance for bringing the case to court. On the one hand, the legal profession and business sector have been concerned about EOC's dual role as the advocate for equal opportunities as well as the impartial conciliator of the complainant and respondent, which may give rise to potential conflict. On the other hand, community groups have been critical of the EOC for sticking too closely to the letter of the law, waiting for complaints and not "pushing the envelope" as is done in many of the countries where anti-discrimination practices are more established. The EOC has asked for legislative review to add the power to seek declaratory and/or injunctive relief in its own name, in respect of unlawful acts and unlawful conduct under the discrimination laws, as well as in respect of discriminatory policies and practices. Until the powers of the EOC are revised in legislation, such tensions will remain.

Despite these criticisms, the EOC has made use of advocacy and consultation, in several instances, to make changes based on enquiries rather than complaints. Two examples are listed below:

- Design Technology and Home Economics classes in schools:
  A survey in 1999 showed that 85% of co-educational schools did not give their students the freedom to choose between Design & Technology (boys) and Home Economics (girls). Schools gradually changed their practices after the EOC organized a conference on best practices, with school principals speaking of the benefits of

not restricting the study of the subject by gender, the Education Department promising resources, and the EOC reminding the schools that restricting study of subjects by sex would violate the SDO. By 2000, a study of the Education Department showed that 95% of government schools no longer restricted the study of these two subjects by gender and that every student was given an equal opportunity to participate in these subjects.

- Interpretation of pregnancy for seafarers
  The EOC learned from a labour union that female seafarers dismissed upon becoming pregnant were afraid to lodge complaints as their spouses often worked for the same company. The EOC met with the company concerned, which claimed that it was forced to do so as another statute, administered by the Marine Department, prohibited them from having pregnant workers aboard their vessels. The EOC then met with the Marine Department and shared with them a court ruling on the subject in the United Kingdom. All parties then agreed that the interpretation of "employment at sea shall not be permitted during the term of pregnancy" did not mean that the persons concerned should be dismissed. Instead, they could be transferred to other duties.

The EOC has also had problems with the way it is organized and by its relationship to the HAB. The EOC in Hong Kong is not structured like its counterparts in other jurisdictions where the board members are persons nominated by the community or are appointed mostly for their commitment to fighting discrimination and so are more willing to "push the envelope". In Hong Kong, the EOC Commission members are appointed to represent the interests of different sectors of society, and not necessarily because of their commitment to fight discrimination. Therefore, the EOC's advocacy role can only move at the pace acceptable to these sectors as there may be, at times, a conflict between the interests of the community.

The emphasis on the independence of the EOC from the government is a double-edged sword. In its role as a watchdog of the government and as a arbitrator between private parties, the EOC must be seen to be independent and not considered as agent of the government. However, the distance from the government also created an awkward status for the EOC in its attempt to join the international equal opportunities organizations. When the Hong Kong government sends a delegation to these international meetings, the EOC is not part of the official delegation; instead, it has to participate as an observer or a non-government organization. The EOC also needs approval from the government to join international organizations but approval is not easily obtained, although joining these international organizations would strengthen the institutional framework of the EOC, develop a proper international standing as well as expose its Commissioners and staff to work of human rights organizations on a regular basis.

The personnel controversy in the fall of 2003 pointed to another problem in the relationship between the government and the EOC, which had grave effects on corporate governance — the appointment of the full-time Chairperson. At the time, the government had not given adequate notice to the outgoing Chairperson of the status of appointment or reappointment. In so doing, the organization remained in an unstable state and staff vacancies could either be held open — thus leaving a workload problem for the staff — or appointments could be made that the incoming Chairperson may not agree with, such as what occurred in the Fall of 2003, which led to threats of lawsuits and the resignation of the then newly appointed Chairperson. With a more adequate succession process, there could be better consultation on handover arrangements in matters regarding management and personnel changes.

Furthermore, as in most other public appointments, the government did not engage in consultation with the community in the appointment of the Chairperson. The stakeholders may not feel that the leadership of the EOC was committed to fighting discrimination. By not doing so, the government again faced criticism in the appointment of the current Chairperson in 2005.

The Independent Panel of Inquiry (February 2005) has recognized these problems and in its report, formally titled "The Report of the Independent Panel of Enquiry on the Incidents Relating to the Equal Opportunities Commission" made a series of recommendations to strengthen the institutional framework of the EOC. Among these recommendations, it emphasized the importance of enhancing the transparency and accountability in the system for the appointment of members to the EOC, and maintaining the independence and pluralism of the Commission. It also stressed that proper handover arrangements for the outgoing and incoming Chairpersons should be formalized.

These important recommendations, if implemented, could address many of the criticisms currently faced by the EOC. For example, the Panel recommended that, like overseas organizations of this type, the government should invite nominations from organizations representing community groups for appointment and those appointed should be supportive of the principles of equal opportunities, similar to the practice in overseas organizations of this nature.

In the appointment of the Chairperson, the Panel emphasized the qualities of the EOC Chairperson, especially his/her "strong commitment to promoting equal opportunities and building an inclusive, barrier-free and harmonious society". To avoid problems in handover, the Panel recommended that the government should announce the appointment or cessation of appointment of the incoming and outgoing Chairperson respectively two months before the commencement of the new term.

The Panel also emphasized the importance for the EOC to maintain its independence from the government and recommended that the government should distance itself from the operations of the EOC — but at the same time giving favourable consideration and assistance to the EOC's request to join international organizations that are concerned with the elimination of discrimination.

In a hearing at LegCo on 21 March 2005, the EOC has said that it accepted all of the recommendations regarding its operation except one that required further consideration as that particular recommendation asked that EOC consider accepting conciliation rate as a performance indicator. The EOC informed LegCo that the success of conciliation depended on the willingness of the parties concerned and the EOC staff should not have a personal interest in the outcome[1].

At the same LegCo meeting, HAB said that 10 of the 70 recommendations made by the Panel had to be further considered or would require changing the law. Although several LegCo members were not satisfied with the Panel's findings on the personnel controversy as they thought it lacked fairness and transparency, LegCo decided to settle the matter and let EOC move on.

Looking Ahead

The EOC has been in existence for over 10 years. During this period, it has raised public consciousness on the importance of equal opportunities; it has established the legal mechanism to handle individual complaints and systemic discrimination; it has also taken the lead in conducting research to inform policies on equal opportunities. Yet, much remains to be done in the area of gender mainstreaming and addressing the roots of sex discrimination. This is not surprising since organizations fighting discrimination in other countries have not yet succeeded in eliminating the gender gap in many domains in life. Gender disparity is rooted in much more fundamental structures at the individual, family, organizational and cultural levels that may not be fully addressed through a rights-based legal framework on anti-discrimination alone. The need for a central mechanism to address women's policies and concerns is clearly demonstrated.

The Women's Commission

In the initial phase of the EOC, women's groups had expected the EOC to be the central mechanism addressing all aspects of women's concerns, some of which were beyond the immediate terms of reference of the statutory body. As the first body set up to address gender equality, the first Chairperson had extended the activities of the EOC to cover issues that may be broadly regarded as infringement of women's rights, such as raising awareness on violence against women through an educational forum. However, the actions of the EOC was limited by legislation and the expectations of the women's groups to address their wide-ranging concerns on policies and services related to education, employment, violence against women, health, welfare, housing, and security could not fall within the confines of the SDO. While the independence of the EOC as a statutory body is an important principle to ensure non-intervention from the government, it also means that the EOC is not considered part of the government and so apart from the scope of its statutory functions, the EOC could not serve the function of coordinating or reviewing government policies and services with respect to women.

The ambivalent relationship between the EOC and the government was clearly highlighted in the NGO status of the EOC when the government submitted its initial report on the implementation of CEDAW to the United Nation in 1998. Although the work of the EOC was reported as part of the government's efforts in the implementation of CEDAW, the EOC was not party to the report or the government delegation to the UN hearing. Instead, EOC had to submit its own report on CEDAW to the UN as an NGO (Equal Opportunities Commission, 1998).

In 1998, in preparation for its report on CEDAW, the EOC invited all the women's NGOs to a series of meetings to discuss possible input into the EOC's report to the UN and all present at these meetings agreed that the need for a central mechanism was a priority to be addressed by all women's NGOs in their own reports to the UN. At a preparatory conference on

CEDAW, the then EOC Chairperson clarified the distinction between the roles of the EOC and a women's commission (Cheung, November 1998). She pointed out that in the absence of a focal point within government to address matters of concern to women, women's groups had tried to seek such a focus within the EOC even though it could not serve all the functions of a central mechanism and that their call for a central mechanism for women had not yet been fulfilled. She also rejected the government's claim in their Initial Report on CEDAW that Policy Groups chaired by the Chief Secretary for Administration already served that purpose (Hong Kong SAR Government, 1998, Part II, section 19). She noted that, in jurisdictions where independent commissions on equal opportunities have been established, there were also separate government ministries on women's affairs. The EOC, as well as many of the NGOs, then submitted reports to the UN reiterating their call for a women's commission. In particular, the then EOC Chairperson actively lobbied the CEDAW Committee members during the 1999 UN hearing on Hong Kong's first CEDAW Report, and explained the distinctive but complementary roles of the EOC and a women's commission.

The UN CEDAW Expert Committee recognized the gap and actively urged the HKSAR government to set up a "national machinery" for women in their Concluding Report on Hong Kong's submission (Committee on the Elimination of Discrimination Against Women, 1999). Initially, the government was still insistent that such a mechanism was unnecessary. At the Legislative Council panel hearing on the UN Report in 1999, Secretary for Home Affairs continued to refute the need for a women's commission, reiterating the existence of an inter-departmental policy mechanism under the Chief Secretary that could address all major issues spanning across departments.

The call for the women's commission persisted. After her term as the first Chairperson of the EOC, Fanny Cheung returned to her academic position, and organized a forum on Beijing Plus Five in February 2000 through the Gender Research Centre at the Chinese University of Hong Kong. The underlying agenda was to coordinate the focus of NGOs and to remind the government of the need for a central mechanism under the Beijing Platform for Action. The pressure on the government was kept up. In May 2000, in her keynote address at a conference organized by the EOC on Beijing Plus Five, the then Chief Secretary, Anson Chan, announced the government's intention to set up a women's commission (Petersen, 2003). The plan was included in the HKSAR report submitted to the UN Beijing

Plus Five meeting in New York in July that year. By October, the formation of the women's commission was listed as a policy objective of Health and Welfare Bureau, and the Women's Commission came into being in 2001. Promoting the well-being and interests of women was highlighted for the first time in the 2001 government policy address (Hong Kong SAR Government, 2001).

Despite the call for a high level status as a central body to advise the Government on all policies related to the development and advancement of women, preferably under the Chief Executive's office or the Chief Secretary for Administration, the Women's Commission (WoC) was set up under the then Health and Welfare Bureau. The government believed that most women's issues would be related to policies under this Bureau, reflecting both an ideological gap between the government and women's groups, and the government's perspective of women's affairs having to deal mainly with health and welfare issues. The Health and Welfare Bureau was also intended to be the liaison and coordinating unit within the government on all matters relating to women. However, women's groups were concerned that the placement of the WoC under this Bureau would be biased toward the traditional notions of women's services being subsumed under health and welfare, and also reinforced the stereotype that women's affairs are family-based. They also worried that the WoC would not have the clout as a central mechanism to address a broader integration of women's issues in the mainstream.

The first WoC chairperson was a legislator, the Hon. Sophie Leung, while the Secretary for Health and Welfare was the Vice-Chairperson. Its membership consisted of three ex-officio members (Director of Social Welfare, representative of the Home Affairs Bureau, and representative of the Education and Manpower Bureau) and 17 non-official members, including several men, who were appointed in their personal capacity. Although women's groups have criticized the WoC membership for being conservative or unfamiliar with women's issues, among its members were a few women who have been actively engaged in different aspects of the women's movement since the 1970s.

The stated mission of the WoC is "to enable women to fully realize their due status, rights, and opportunities in all aspects of life in Hong Kong". Its terms of reference include "advising the Government on the development of a long term vision and strategies related to the development and advancement of women; advising the Government on the integration of policies and initiatives which are of concern to women, which fall under the purview of different policy bureaus; keeping under review, in the light of women's needs, services delivered within and outside the Government and to identify priority areas for action, and monitor the development of new or improved services; initiating and undertaking independent surveys and research studies on women's issues and organizing educational and promotional activities; and developing and maintaining contact with local and international women's groups and service agencies with a view to sharing experience and improving communication and understanding"[2].

With this general framework and the diverse background of its members, the WoC set out to identify its strategic objectives and clarify the basic principles on gender equity. Through a series of brainstorming sessions, members identified and concentrated on three strategic objectives and priority areas in its first three years: gender mainstreaming, empowerment, and public education.

Gender Mainstreaming

The WoC considered gender mainstreaming to be a long-term and fundamental strategy to incorporate women's needs and gender perspectives in the design, implementation, monitoring and review of legislation, policies and services in government. Gender-sensitive decision-making processes ensure that women and men have equitable access to, and benefit from, society's resources and opportunities. Although the concept of gender mainstreaming has been introduced in many Western governments and United Nations organizations, it is an abstract and foreign notion in the local scene. It involves an approach that is based on gender awareness, which is often lacking in administrators and policy makers.

Making reference to international experiences, the WoC drafted an analytic tool in the form of a gender-mainstreaming checklist to facilitate the process (Women's Commission, 2006a). The checklist was tried out with three government bureaus on several policy areas in 2002 before it was refined and revised: the District Council Review, Family Education Programme, Health Care Reform, Enhanced Home and Community Care Services for the Elderly, and Secondary School Places Allocation System. By 2005, 13 policy areas or programmes have adopted the checklist. In conjunction with the analytic tool, gender sensitivity training was offered to civil servants, with an initial focus on bureaus and departments that would have more direct impact on women's policies and services, including social workers, police, Information Officers, Administrative Officers, officers from the Education Department and from the Leisure and Recreational Services Department. Through the coordination of the Women's Division of the Health and Welfare Bureau, which serves as the secretariat to the WoC, officials in 70 bureaus and departments were designated as gender focal points to help to promote and mainstream gender perspectives in their respective units. WoC published a booklet in 2006 (Women's Commission, 2006a) outlining the strategy and sharing the experience of 12 cases of implementing gender mainstreaming in the government.

Empowerment

Adopting an empowerment approach to women's development, the WoC aimed to engage women as agents of change and build up their capacity on the one hand, and create enabling environments that facilitate women's advancement and eliminate barriers to women's full participation on the other hand.

Again, the concept of women's empowerment is abstract and poses a challenge to public dissemination. It is ridden with misconception and rhetoric. To raise public awareness on the concept, WoC involved the community to share their initiatives on the empowerment of women and published the good practices selected from governmental, nongovernmental and business organizations.

One of the goals of women's empowerment is to enhance their role in decision-making that affects their livelihood. Recognizing the low level of women's participation in government-appointed statutory and advisory bodies, the WoC urged the Government to take proactive measures to address the problems and set a minimum of 25% for women's appointment as the initial target. Bureaus and departments were urged to reach out, identify and cultivate women to contribute to the public decision-making process. The WoC also initiated an active exercise to increase the pool of women candidates in the central database within the government from which candidates for appointment are often drawn.

To empower women to face life's challenges and to deal with adverse circumstances at the personal level, WoC considered women's needs and desire for self-improvement. An essential aspect of capacity building among women is the provision of adequate and relevant training programmes. Women have criticized existing programmes that offered vocational related training or retraining for being insensitive to the needs or interests of women, in terms of location, schedule, pre-requisite academic requirements, and choice of subjects. In this connection, WoC initiated a new mode of learning for women in the form of a Capacity Building Mileage Programme (CBMP). CBMP utilized flexible modules on relevant topics that could build up towards milestone goals, radio broadcasting as the forum of instruction, and a network of community-based centres for face-to-face tutorials. Acting as a catalyst, a partnership was forged with the Open University of Hong Kong (OUHK) and Commercial Radio (CR) to launch this programme. In 2004, the year that it was launched, the enrolment was close to 3,500, with many more who listened to the radio programmes without enrolment. By March 2006, over 9,400 persons have enrolled in the programme, and 450 graduates received their certificates recognizing their cumulative mileage points starting from 25 points. By 2008, 16 graduates were awarded Level 5 Certificates (150 mileage points) and 5 graduates were awarded Level 6 Certificates (200 mileage points).

Public Education

Advancing women's status involves a fundamental shift in the cultural gender paradigm. Gender myths and stereotypes perpetuate prejudice and discrimination. To engage the community in a paradigm shift in gender sensitivity, the WoC undertook an ongoing program of public education to raise general awareness and understanding about women-related issues in the form of television drama series, radio programmes, essay competitions, and school activities. Recognizing the pervasive influence of the mass media, WoC engaged media practitioners to discuss how gender-sensitive portrayal of women could be balanced with freedom of the press. In 2008, WoC launched a roving exhibition across different districts to showcase women's contribution and development in the past century and to enhance gender awareness.

Focus on Priority Areas

The strategic objectives that WoC established in the first term were fundamental to women's advancement. The efforts were intended to build up a sustainable foundation for long-term changes. However, they may not appear to respond to the immediate and specific concerns that many women groups have been voicing. Activist groups also criticized the WoC for being unresponsive to women's urgent needs. In its second term, the WoC realigned its structure to address some of these pressing concerns while maintaining its original strategic objectives.

Violence against women has been one of the key concerns of women in the community. In particular, tragic cases of domestic violence revealed inadequacies in the existing legislation and gaps in the coordination of policies and services. The increasing trend of cross-border marriages between Hong Kong men and Mainland Chinese women after the reunification in 1997 has exaggerated the power imbalance in the family system. Despite the existence of an inter-departmental working group within the government to combat domestic violence, the WoC took upon its function as a central mechanism to mobilize the government and the community to work together to adopt a zero tolerance stand. It successfully lobbied the Chief Executive to include zero tolerance on domestic violence in his 2005 policy address. It also set up a platform of consultation with stakeholders in the government and non-governmental organizations to formulate a comprehensive strategy to address domestic violence in a coordinated approach. Before finishing their second term, the Chairperson and the founding members issued their comprehensive policy paper outlining the framework for eliminating domestic violence in Hong Kong (Women's Commission, 2006b).

While continuing with its efforts on the CBMP, a new programme on quality parenting education was launched in the second term in collaboration with a social service organization to promote the concept of a nurturing family. Women's roles as parents have posed increasing strain, and women have expressed a desire for self-development in the area of enhancing competence in parenting. The involvement of fathers in parenting and a harmonious family relationship were also promoted in the training programme.

The second term's public education efforts highlighted school-based education as a priority area, aiming to mainstream gender-sensitive perspectives in the school curriculum and teaching materials. Gender stereotypes prevailed in textbooks and teaching materials in primary and secondary schools (Equal Opportunities Commission, 2001). In this regard, the WoC and the EOC joined hands in collaborating with the Education Department to take on the issue in its curriculum plans and reforms.

A second Chairperson, Ms. Sophia Kao, was appointed in 2006. An active member of the WoC since its inception, Ms. Kao continued the long-term strategies of gender mainstreaming and women's empowerment. In support of the government's policies of building harmonious community and families, the WoC focused on nurturing caring families and quality parenting, studying the core values for the younger generation, and promoting work-family balance, and advocating family-friendly employment policies and practices.

Catalyst and Collaboration

With much less secretarial and administrative support than the EOC, the WoC quickly realized that practically as well as strategically, it could not achieve and sustain its mission on its own. Examining the various roles that could facilitate its function as the focal point for the advancement of women, the WoC identified the importance of being a champion for women's causes, an inspirer of change and initiatives, and a mobilizer of community resources. It also developed a framework for collaboration with community organizations to promote partnership on activities and programmes that aligned with its strategic objectives. For example, it has invited the participation of non-governmental organizations to showcase their best practices in women's empowerment in a competition in 2004 and in the 2007 International Women's Day exhibition. It maintains a database of organizations interested in women's issues and ongoing contacts with local and overseas organizations. These roles would help the WoC to mainstream gender perspectives across society in a more sustainable fashion.

Through the mobilization of the WoC, some major changes in the government could be witnessed. Since 2001, the Census and Statistics Department published an annual report on *Women and Men in Hong Kong: Key Statistics* that provides sex-disaggregated data on key social indicators. Based on the Census and Statistics Department reports, WoC (2007) compiled and published a booklet on *Hong Kong Women in Figures 2007* as a reference on women's development in the first decade following the establishment of the Hong Kong Special Administration Region. To address the lack of funding for women's services and programmes, the WoC facilitated women's organizations' access to the Community Inclusion and Investment Fund administered by the Health, Welfare and Food Bureau, which could provide financial support to their projects that fit in with the objectives of community participation and mutual assistance. The Home Affairs Bureau has also committed to set a target of 25% gender representation in its appointments to advisory and statutory bodies, and has announced that it achieved this target in 2006. In the formulation of its comprehensive paper on domestic violence, the WoC consulted and worked closely with the stakeholders, including government departments, women's groups, social service organizations and academics to identify problems and come up with feasible solutions.

Challenges of the WoC

With a broad vision and a pluralistic membership that rotates every few years, the WoC needs to establish a core set of principles for its operation. During its first term, members spent a long time deriving the strategic objectives, which could be considered fundamental strategies, but may not be regarded by the activists to be responsive to the immediate needs of special target groups and to the pluralistic voices of the women's community. The lack of transparency in the appointment system of members has been criticized in the same way as that of the EOC. The government places more emphasis on pluralism in appointing members from different sectors of society, paying less attention to their experience and familiarity with the substantive aspects of the work of the WoC. Given the complex and abstract concepts of gender analysis and mainstreaming, there is a constant need to align the gender sensitivity of WoC members as well as the staff of the secretariat to what they are preaching.

Other than the substance of its work, the structure of the fledging commission also needs adjustment. The WoC membership, including the Chairperson, consists mainly of unofficial members who participate in their personal capacity and on a voluntary basis. Originally set up as the government's central mechanism on women's issues, the WoC should be focusing on its advisory and policy role, while the executive functions are reliant on the Women's Division within the Health, Welfare and Food Bureau[3]. With the reshuffle of the government structure in 2007, WoC is now housed in the Labour and Welfare Bureau.

In addition to serving as the secretariat of the WoC, the Women's Division also acts as the focal point for women's issues within government, oversees CEDAW, maintains links with international bodies like the UN and APEC, and organizes promotional/educational activities. To the public, there is little distinction between the WoC and the Women's Division. However, with only a small professional staff structure, the driving force of the WoC's work has fallen on the shoulders of a few enthusiastic and dedicated members. With the continuous turnover and rotation of staff in the civil service, and the restricted tenure of appointed members, the sustainability of the WoC's energy and direction as well as the commitment of the government are matters of concern. In particular, the Chief Executive's

2006 policy address indicated the Government's intention of setting up an integrated Family Council to interface the work of various commissions, including the Women's Commission, Youth Commission, and Elderly Commission. Many women's groups were worried that women's interests would again be subsumed under the hegemony of the family and that women's voices and autonomy would be undermined.

Relationship between the EOC and the Women's Commission

When the WoC was set up in 2001, the EOC Chairperson was originally appointed as an ex-officio member. The then chairperson, Anna Wu, later resigned from the WoC citing potential conflict of interest between the work of the EOC and the WoC as the reason, thereby relinquishing the structural link between the two organizations. However, a number of members overlap in their membership on the two bodies.

Notwithstanding the divergent functions of the EOC and the WoC, both are key institutional mechanisms that can impact on the rights and status of women in Hong Kong. Although the establishment of the WoC as a central mechanism for women affairs has shifted the focal point on policy issues affecting women from the EOC to a clearly designated body, the two bodies can complement each other in addressing women's needs and concerns.

As an independent statutory body, the EOC can take action on violations of women's rights under the anti-discrimination ordinances on behalf of complainants against individuals, organizations, as well as the government. By implementing laws on discrimination, the EOC represents a legal framework that safeguards women's rights.

The WoC, on the hand, can directly address issues that are roots of discrimination but may not be defined as unlawful under the SDO, such as sexism, prejudice, and stereotypes. It can take a proactive approach to attend to the needs of women and enhance women's development. As a central mechanism, it works within the government system to advise, review, or coordinate services, policies and legislation concerning women's well being. Without the need to be an impartial conciliator like the EOC, the WoC can speak from a woman's perspective to enlighten the gender blind spots in policy makers and service providers.

There are areas where the EOC and WoC overlap in their activities. Both the EOC and the WoC conduct research related to women's status and concerns, promote public awareness on women's rights and barriers to gender equality, and provide gender-related training. Through the complaints received, the EOC can identify systemic discrimination that is rooted in policies that the WoC could facilitate in reviewing. Close collaboration between the two bodies would strengthen the institutional mechanism on the advancement of women's status.

In 2004, the EOC has re-established a partnership with the WoC whom it regards as a strategic partner in the promotion of gender equality in Hong Kong.[4] The two bodies have collaborated on public education projects and development of training materials to raise gender sensitivity in schools and the civil service. They jointly conducted a survey on family-friendly employment policies and practices. With the merging of EOC's original Gender Division and Disability Division into an Operations Division to handle all complaints related to the discrimination ordinances, there is concern that the liaison with women's groups as one of its stakeholders may be weakened. Its partnership with the WoC will be particularly important for EOC to maintain its function in promoting equal opportunities for women and men.

Central Mechanism and Mainstreaming Gender

The establishment of the EOC in the 1996 and the WoC in 2001 mark two major milestones in the advancement of women's status in Hong Kong. Women's voices are no longer murmurs on the fringe of society by a handful of women's groups. Women's affairs have become a legitimate political agenda and are incorporated into the permanent state structure. Direct input from the WoC was included in the Chief Executive's annual policy address since 2004. Women who suffer from discrimination have recourse for action through the EOC and the courts.

As institutional mechanisms, both the EOC and WoC face the tension from the resistance and stagnancy of the establishment at one end, and the pressure and criticisms from the diverse advocates who have high expectations at the other end. For example, Ng and Ng (2002) critiqued the EOC as lacking in feminist agency in its mandate to address discrimination of women and men alike, although they recognized its statutory function under a legal framework. Feminist activists queried the legitimacy of the power elites who are appointed as members of the EOC and WoC. On the other hand, there are continuous challenges from the general public, especially men, on why there is a need for a women's commission, and not a men's commission. There is a constant need for the WoC to explain the concepts of gender equality and gender sensitivity, which may appear to be contradictory on the surface. In the early stage of development of the concepts of gender equality in Hong Kong, there is a tendency to mistake gender blindness as gender neutrality. Without raising gender sensitivity, there is also the risk of losing the attention on women's special needs in promoting gender mainstreaming.

The establishment of the EOC and WoC in Hong Kong illustrate similar tensions encountered by other central mechanisms on women's issues in other parts of the world. Being a part of as well as outside the establishment requires a sensitive balance in approach and in the choice of priorities. Worldwide, few governments adopt a conscious state feminist agenda. In the UN General Assembly's (16 November, 2000) review of the implementation of the Beijing Platform for Action, the insufficient understanding of gender equality and gender mainstreaming within the government structures, as well as gender stereotypes, discriminatory attitudes and competing government priorities, in addition to inadequate financial and human resources, were identified as major obstacles confronting national machineries. The pluralistic voices of women in the community highlight the need to stay tuned to a diverse spectrum of needs while heeding the calls of the advocates who make the headlines. The community participation strategy in the EOC's public education approach and the collaboration framework of the WoC reflect the recognition of the importance of involving the wider community in mainstreaming gender.

The history of the establishment of the EOC and the WoC highlights the influence of individuals as the driving force behind the movement. While the collective power of the grassroots has built up the context for change, the efforts of individuals in what could be considered privileged elite positions have made inroads into the system to bring forth changes. Their passion and familiarity with the system have enhanced their effectiveness. Many of the members of the EOC and the WoC in the early phases of their formation were dedicated to the cause and contributed actively to the direction and operations of these bodies beyond what was usually found in government committees.

The long-term sustainability of the driving force is a concern that leads us back to the fundamental need for integrating gender perspectives into the system. With the transitory membership in these commissions, the staff of the EOC and the WoC would be the pillars in these institutional mechanisms to push forward their mission. Other than recruiting dedicated and experienced members, building up a staff committed to the cause and sensitive to the gender perspectives and equipped with expert knowledge would provide the foundation for gender mainstreaming that will permeate across the system.

References

Campaign for a Women's Commission and for CEDAW (1993). *A Women's Commission for Hong Kong*. Hong Kong: Author.

Cheung, F. M. (1998). Promoting equal opportunities for women and the disabled in Hong Kong. In S. MacPherson, & H.K. Wong (Eds.), *Social development and societies in transition* (pp. 55–64). Aldershot, UK: Ashgate.

Cheung, F. M. (November 1998). *Implementing the CEDAW Convention: Need for a central mechanism in Hong Kong*. Paper presented at the Conference on CEDAW: Its Implementation in the SAR, organised by the Centre for Comparative and Public Law and the Women's Studies Research Centre, University of Hong Kong, November 28, 1998. Internet edition available from http://www.hku.hk/ccpl/research_projects_issues/cedaw/fannycheungpaper.html

Cheung, F. M. (1999) *Breaking new ground: Promoting equal opportunities in Hong Kong*. Hong Kong: Equal Opportunities Commission.

Cheung, F. M., Wan, P. S., & Wan, O. C. (1994). The underdeveloped political potential of women in Hong Kong. In B. Nelson, & N. Chowdhury (Eds.), *Women and politics worldwide* (pp. 326–346). New Haven, Conn.: Yale University Press.

Committee on the Elimination of Discrimination Against Women (1999). *Concluding remarks of the Committee on the Elimination of Discrimination Against Women on the Initial Report on the HKSAR under the Convention on the Elimination of All Forms of Discrimination Against Women*. Extracted from the Report of the Committee on the 20th session (19 January to 5 February 1999). Internet edition available from http://www.women.gov.hk/eng/document/inter/inter.html

Equal Opportunities Commission (1998). *NGO report on the Convention on the Elimination of All Forms of Discrimination Against Women* (CEDAW). Hong Kong: Equal Opportunities Commission.

Equal Opportunities Commission (2001). *Research on Content Analysis of Textbooks and Teaching Materials in Respect of Stereotypes* (Executive Summary). Hong Kong: Equal Opportunities Commission. Internet edition available from http://www.eoc.org.hk/CE/research/index.htm

Equal Opportunities Commission (2006). *Study on Equal Pay for Work of Equal Value*. Hong Kong: Equal Opportunities Commission. Internet edition available from http://www.eoc.org.hk/eoc/graphicsfolder/inforcenter/research/content.aspx?itemid=7037

Hong Kong Government (1993). *Green Paper on Equal Opportunities for Women and Men.* Hong Kong: Hong Kong Government Printer.

Hong Kong Government (1994). *Green Paper on Equal Opportunities for Women and Men: Compendium of Submissions.* Hong Kong: Hong Kong Government Printer.

Hong Kong SAR Government (1998). *Initial Report on the Hong Kong Special Administrative Region under Article 18 of the Convention on the Elimination of All forms of Discrimination Against Women.* Hong Kong: Printing Department of the HKSAR Government. Internet edition available from http://www.women. gov.hk/eng/document/govern/gov.html

Hong Kong SAR Government (2000). *The Report of the Hong Kong Special Administrative Region Government on the Implementation of the Beijing Platform for Action.* Hong Kong: Printing Department of the HKSAR Government. Internet edition available from http://www.women.gov.hk/eng/ document/govern/gov.html

Hong Kong SAR Government (2001). *Promote the Well-being and Interests of Women: Policy Objectives and Key Result Areas.* Hong Kong: Printing Department of the HKSAR Government. Internet edition available from http:// www.women.gov.hk/eng/document/govern/gov.html

Independent Panel of Inquiry on the Incidents Relating to the Equal Opportunities Commission (February 2005). *Report of the Independent Panel of Inquiry on the Incidents Relating to the Equal Opportunities Commission.* Hong Kong: Government Logistics Department of the HKSAR Government.

Kuan, H. C. (1992). Legal culture: The challenge of modernization. In S. K. Lau, M. K. Lee, P. S. Wan, & S. L. Wong (Eds.), *Indicators of social development: Hong Kong 1990* (pp. 159–172). Hong Kong: Hong Kong Institute of Asia-Pacific Studies, The Chinese University of Hong Kong.

Kwok, P. L., Chow, G., Lee, c. K., & Wu, R. (1997). Women and the state in Hong Kong. In F. M. Cheung (Ed.). *Engendering Hong Kong society: A gender perspective of women's status* (pp. 237–266). Hong Kong: Chinese University Press.

Lai, B. L. L., Au, K. C., & Cheung, F. M. (1997). Women's concern groups in Hong Kong. In F. M. Cheung (Ed.). *Engendering Hong Kong society: A gender perspective of women's status* (pp. 267–305). Hong Kong: Chinese University Press.

Ng, C., & Ng, E. (2002). The concept of state feminism and the case for Hong Kong. *Asian Journal of Women's Studies, 8,* 7–37.

Petersen, C. J. (2003). Engendering a legal system: The unique challenge of postcolonial Hong Kong. In E. W. Y. Lee (Ed.). *Gender and change in Hong Kong: Globalization, postcolonialim, and Chinese patriarchy* (pp. 23–48). Vancouver: UBC Press.

United Nations General Assembly (16 November 2000). *Resolution adopted by the*

General Assembly, S23/3. Further action and initiatives to implement the Beijing Declaration and Platform for Action. http://www.un.org/womenwatch/daw/followup/ress233e.pdf

Women's Commission. (2006a) *Gender mainstreaming: Hong Kong experience.* Hong Kong: Author. Internet edition available from http://www.women.gov.hk/download/gender-mainstreaming-en.pdf

Women's Commission. (2006b). *Women's safety in Hong Kong: Eliminating domestic violence.* Hong Kong: Author. Internet edition available from http://www.women.gov.hk/download/report-full-version-10-jan-06.pdf

Women's Commission (2007). *Hong Kong Women in Figures 2007.* Hong Kong: Author. Internet edition available from http://www.women.gov.hk/download/english-version-2.pdf

Women Voters Development Plan Association. (1991). *Women's joint political platform.* Hong Kong: Author.

Notes

1. Message from the Chairperson, *EOC Newsletter, #*28, pp 2–3.
1. Legislative Council Paper No. CB(2)1083/04-05(08) http://www.legco.gov.hk/yr04-05/english/panels/ha/papers/ha0321cb2-1083-8e.pdf
2. From the website of the Women's Commission, http://www.women.gov.hk
3. The Health and Welfare Bureau was restructured and became the Health, Welfare and Food Bureau in 2003. In the 2007 government reshuffle, WoC was housed under the Labour and Welfare Bureau.
4. Information received from the EOC, Nov. 9, 2004.

CHAPTER 16

Stuck on Formalities? A Critique of Hong Kong's Legal Framework for Gender Equality

Carole J. Petersen

I. Introduction

The value of equality has long been a focus of the global human rights movement and virtually every important international human rights treaty embraces it. There is, however, substantial debate on the meaning of that value, especially when applied to gender. Traditional conceptions of gender equality required only that women receive identical treatment with men. It is now widely acknowledged that this formal approach to equality can perpetuate women's subordination and scholars, policy makers, and activists have increasingly advocated more progressive approaches. Sandra Fredman views these approaches as different stages in the development of the equality movement. For example, the principle of "equality of opportunity" seeks to remove barriers that appear facially neutral but in fact perpetuate inequality. The next development was the principle of "equality of results" (or substantive equality), which maintains that equality is not achieved until women have an equal distribution of jobs, economic resources, and political power. An even more advanced conception is "equality as transformation".

* Interim Director, Matsunga Institute for Peace and Visiting Professor, William S. Richardson School of Law, University of Hawaii at Manoa. This chapter was written in 2004, when the author was an Associate Professor in the Faculty of Law at the University of Hong Kong. Research for this chapter was supported by a grant from the Hong Kong Research Grants Council entitled *Enforcing Equal Opportunities in Hong Kong: A Study of Investigation, Conciliation, and Other Enforcement Mechanisms*.

This view seeks not only a re-distribution of power and resources but also a dismantling of the public-private divide and a restructuring of society so that "child-care and parenting are seen as valued common responsibilities of both parents and the community" (Fredman 2003). Fedman argues that this concept best fits the most important treaty regarding women's rights, the International Convention on the Elimination of All Forms of Discrimination Against Women (CEDAW).[1] Although this treaty was drafted and adopted when formal equality still dominated the discourse on women's rights, a close examination of its provisions reveals a deep-seated commitment to substantive equality and also to transforming society and the traditional roles of women and men.

In Hong Kong the concept of a right to equality is very much in its infancy. As recently as 1990, Hong Kong had virtually no legal framework for gender equality. Fortunately, during the transition period leading to China's resumption of sovereignty (1984–1997), Hong Kong experienced a remarkable period of law reform. The first human rights legislation was enacted and the legislature became slightly more democratic and responsive to women's concerns, eventually compelling the government to abandon its outright opposition to anti-discrimination law. As a result, by the end of 1996, the Sex Discrimination Ordinance (SDO) had come into force, an Equal Opportunities Commission (EOC) had been established, and CEDAW was finally applied to Hong Kong. In 2000, the Hong Kong government also agreed to establish a Women's Commission, which is supposed to serve as the primary enforcement body for CEDAW in Hong Kong. Thus, at the start of the new millennium it appeared that Hong Kong was building a promising legal framework for gender equality.

However, as I will demonstrate in this chapter, the legal framework is still lacking in several respects and there is mounting evidence that it will not progress beyond this stage for many years. This is partly because the Hong Kong government refuses to move beyond the principle of formal equality (with a few nods in the direction of the equal opportunities principle). The government is strongly committed to low-taxes and laissez-faire economic policies. Any suggestion that Hong Kong should embrace the concept of substantive equality is viewed as a threat to those policies and condemned. There also is a general reluctance to admit that there are any structural barriers to women's equality in the existing economic and legal systems. To do so would contradict the government's vision of Hong Kong as "a free and vibrant society that offers ample opportunities to women". (Hong Kong Government 2003a). As a result, calls by women's organizations to take a more "gendered perspective" to such issues as domestic violence, stalking, or social welfare tend to fall upon deaf ears. Moreover, even the concept of formal equality is difficult to enforce because Hong Kong's enforcement model discourages litigation and compels most complaints of sex discrimination to be resolved by the EOC through a confidential process of investigation and conciliation. Those who insist upon publicly litigating to enforce their rights are likely to be viewed as disrupting the normal balance of society.

In Part II of this chapter I provide an overview of Hong Kong's domestic legal framework, noting how the right to equality was first developed, as well as gaps in the legislative framework and certain barriers to additional law reform. In Parts III and IV, I analyse the SDO in greater detail, as it is the most important law promoting gender equality in Hong Kong. In addition to the substantive provisions, I discuss the significant judicial decisions applying and interpreting the SDO and the outcomes of a sample of complaints that have been resolved through the EOC's complaints process. I also draw upon interviews with EOC officers, past complainants, and representatives of organisations that regularly assist women with the EOC's complaints process.

Part V of the chapter considers the extent to which international human rights treaties that apply to Hong Kong can supplement its domestic legal framework. While CEDAW is the most important treaty, other human rights treaties that apply to Hong Kong are also relevant. The international bodies that monitor the implementation of these treaties cannot compel the government to change its policies but there is evidence to suggest that the government does care about the "report card" that it receives from these bodies. I thus argue that Hong Kong women should continue to participate in the enforcement process for these treaties, by writing shadow reports, attending the public hearings, and publicising the concluding comments on Hong Kong. This is a particularly important strategy given that Hong Kong still does not have an elected government or a fully elected legislature, rendering policy makers less responsive to women's demands for law reform.

II. An Overview of Hong Kong's Domestic Legal Framework for Gender Equality

The establishment of a right to equality

The concept of equality was recognised as early as the time of Aristotle and embraced in the constitutional documents of the American and French revolutions. However, it was not until the second half of the 20th century that an enforceable right to equality became prominent in domestic and international law. Numerous countries have now adopted constitutional provisions or domestic legislation (or both) prohibiting discrimination and guaranteeing equal treatment before the law. In the field of international law, all of the primary instruments in the United Nations system of human rights treaties include a right to equality. There are also a number of specialist treaties, such as CEDAW, that address particular forms of discrimination. The State Parties are obligated to implement the treaties in their jurisdictions, which normally entails enacting domestic legislation. State Parties are also required to report periodically on the implementation of the treaties in their jurisdictions. While the international committees that monitor the enforcement of these treaties are not like courts and cannot impose real sanctions, they do review the periodic reports carefully and try to persuade governments to address problems before the next periodic report. The effectiveness of this "soft" enforcement process depends upon the extent to which a government wishes to be viewed as an active participant in the United Nations system and to receive positive comments from the relevant treaty monitoring bodies. (O'Flaherty 1996). It also depends upon the participation of non-governmental organisations (NGOs), which write "shadow reports" critiquing the government reports. These reports are essential to the process because governments often give overly positive reports on their jurisdictions. NGO shadow reports help to keep the governments honest and also give the treaty monitoring bodies the information they need to truly critique government reports. This is one reason why the ratification of international human rights treaties has less impact in countries like China, where NGOs do not enjoy freedom of expression and cannot communicate freely with treaty bodies.

The challenge of establishing an enforceable right to equality in Hong Kong has been complicated by its colonial history. Although the United Kingdom is often referred to as a relatively "benign" ruler, the colonial system was inherently undemocratic and institutionalised inequality. Hong Kong's history books are full of examples of official discrimination against the local Chinese population (Klein 1995) and women (Petersen 1996). The United Kingdom did ratify a number of international human rights treaties during the 1960s and 1970s, and it extended most of these treaties to its dependent territories, including Hong Kong.[2] However, international treaties are not directly enforceable in the local courts in the British and Hong Kong legal systems, and they therefore needed to be implemented through domestic legislation. Yet during the true colonial period, neither the British nor the Hong Kong governments took any steps to incorporate these treaties into Hong Kong's domestic law. There was no constitutional right to equal treatment and no anti-discrimination laws (Byrnes 1992, Samuels 1993). The British government had the responsibility of reporting to the international monitoring bodies and since the Hong Kong community was largely unaware of the reporting process, local NGOs did not initially submit shadow reports critiquing the British reports.

CEDAW was ratified by the United Kingdom in 1985. Interestingly, the British government departed from its normal practice of applying treaties to its dependent territories and decided not to apply CEDAW to Hong Kong at that time. The local colonial government had asked to be left out of the ratification because it had no intention of enacting legislation similar to the UK's Sex Discrimination Act 1975 and opposed the kind of law reform that CEDAW requires. (Byrnes and Chan, 1993). The colonial government justified its position on the ground that it did not wish to interfere with traditional Chinese customs or to "over-regulate" private sector employers. In fact, the government itself maintained discriminatory laws and policies, including ordinances prohibiting women from inheriting much of the land in the New Territories. These colonial ordinances did not just perpetuate the traditional ban on female inheritance found in Chinese customary law. Rather, the ordinances widened the application of Chinese customary law by making it unlawful to probate a will that left New Territories Land to a woman and by extending the ban to include land had been purchased by a woman or by someone who was not a member of the indigenous community (unless the land had been expressly exempted by the Governor) (Jones 1995, Petersen 1996). The government also maintained a system of allocating students to secondary schools that generally required girls to obtain higher scores than boys in order to be admitted to elite co-educational schools (Petersen 2002).

The first opportunities for law reform came during the transition period leading to 1997. Once the Sino-British Joint Declaration was ratified in 1985, public awareness of human rights issues dramatically increased. In 1989, following the massacre in Beijing's Tiananmen Square, more than one million people marched in the streets of Hong Kong and public confidence sunk to an all time low. The colonial government felt an urgent need to boost public confidence and proposed to enact a domestic Bill of Rights Ordinance. The International Covenant on Civil and Political Rights (the ICCPR) was chosen as the model for the Bill of Rights because the Chinese national government had already agreed (both in the Joint Declaration and in the drafts of the Basic Law) that the ICCPR would continue to apply to Hong Kong after 1997. Although the Bill of Rights Ordinance is an ordinary law, the British government simultaneously amended the colonial constitution, the Letters Patent, by adding a clause precluding the Legislative Council from enacting any new laws that violated the ICCPR as it applied to Hong Kong (Ghai 1999). This was the first time in Hong Kong's history that the government and the legislature were obligated under domestic law to protect human rights.

The ICCPR contains three provisions relating to equality. Article 2, paragraph 1, requires state parties to ensure equal enjoyment of the rights recognised in the ICCPR and Article 3 specifically prohibits discrimination on the ground of sex in the enjoyment of those rights. More importantly, Article 26 requires state parties to protect against discrimination, stating, that "the law shall prohibit any discrimination and guarantee to all persons equal and effective protection against discrimination on any ground such as race, colour, sex, language, religion, political or other opinion, national or social origin, property, birth or other status." All three of these provisions were copied into the Hong Kong Bill of Rights. During the consultation period, the Heung Yee Kuk, a conservative male-dominated body, argued that an exemption should be inserted for the "lawful traditional rights" of the New Territories indigenous residents, including the ban on female inheritance of land (discussed above). The women's movement argued strongly against such an exemption and the legislature ultimately decided not to include one. In the end, however, the ban on female inheritance was dealt with legislatively. In 1994, the Hong Kong government introduced the New Territories Land (Exemption) Bill to exempt urban land from the ban and legislator Christine Loh successfully amended the Bill so as to exempt both urban and rural land (Jones 1995, Petersen 1996).

The Chinese government opposed the enactment of the Bill of Rights and threatened to repeal it in 1997. Ultimately, however, Beijing decided only to remove a few introductory provisions and this has had no practical impact upon the enforcement of the Bill of Rights Ordinance (Wesley-Smith 1977). Although the Letters Patent ceased to apply on 1 July 1997, Article 39 of the Basic Law has now taken over the job of incorporating the ICCPR into Hong Kong's constitution. Article 39 provides that the provisions of the ICCPR, ICESCR, and international labour conventions that applied to Hong Kong before 1997 "shall remain in force and shall be implemented through the laws" of the Hong Kong SAR. In *HKSAR v. Ng Kung Siu* [1999] 3 HKLRD 907, the Court of Final Appeal held that this language incorporates the ICCPR into the Basic Law. Thus the equality provisions contained in the ICCPR (and in the Bill of Rights) are now incorporated into the Basic Law, Hong Kong's highest law and constitutional instrument. This is important because the rest of the Basic Law is strangely silent on the right to equality, despite the fact that it has extensive, and extremely detailed, provisions protecting human rights (Ghai 1999). Article 25 of the Basic Law is the only other provision that expressly protects equality and it is very brief, stating only that "all Hong Kong residents shall be equal before the law."

The initial draft of the Bill of Rights would have bound everyone but the business community successfully argued that it was too general and expansive a law to be applied in the private sector and should only bind the government and public authorities. The government and the Legislative Council agreed to this request at the time of enactment. This greatly disappointed the women's movement, which had hoped to use the Bill of Rights as a weapon against sex discrimination in the private sector. However, women's organizations used the debate on this issue as an opportunity to educate legislators about the extent of sex discrimination and thereby gained several supporters. A number of legislators promised that they would support a specific bill to prohibit sex discrimination if it were introduced (Petersen 1996.)

In the Hong Kong legal system, the government drafts and proposes most new legislation. Individual legislators normally only study, propose amendments, and vote on the government bills. However, in this case, the initiative had to come from an individual legislator because the government was still strongly opposed to anti-discrimination laws. Thus, in September 1993, legislator Anna Wu began drafting the Equal Opportunities Bill (EOB). She based her bill upon Western Australian legislation which prohibits discrimination on a wide range of grounds (including sex, race, age, disability, family status, and sexuality) in both the public and private sectors. The EOB was considered radical by the government but received support from the Democratic Party and a number of independent legislators. Fearing that the EOB might be enacted, the government reluctantly abandoned its opposition to the concept of anti-discrimination legislation and introduced two, more conservative, competing bills — the Sex Discrimination Bill and the Disability Discrimination Bill. Wu then agreed to withdraw the sex and disability provisions of her EOB in favour of the government bills, largely because the government had the constitutional power to create a publicly funded commission to assist with enforcement. (Wu had also drafted a companion bill to establish a human rights and equal opportunities commission but she was required to obtain the Governor's permission to introduce it, since it required public money to implement, and this was not granted.) Wu did, however, successfully propose several amendments to the government's bills, strengthening certain aspects of the law (Petersen 1996).

The SDO was enacted in 1995 and came fully into force by the end of 1996. It prohibits discrimination, on the grounds of sex, marital status, and pregnancy, and also sexual harassment. It applies to a wide range of fields, including employment, education, housing, the provision of goods and services, rural elections, and the administration of laws and government programmes. Although only a small number of cases have been litigated (which are discussed in Part III of this chapter) the law has led many institutions and employers to adopt policies prohibiting sex discrimination and sexual harassment. There are very few exemptions for the private sector but some controversial exemptions for government policies and practices. One example is the exemption for the Small House Policy, a government program that benefits only male indigenous residents of the New Territories. This is also the subject of a reservation in the application of CEDAW to Hong Kong (Petersen 1996).

Gaps in the legal framework and barriers to additional law reform

The remaining provisions of Wu's EOB (which would have prohibited age, race, sexuality, and family status discrimination) were put to a vote in 1995 but were defeated. Women's organisations continued to lobby for broader legislation and a Family Status Discrimination Ordinance (FSDO) was enacted in 1997. The FSDO prohibits discrimination on the ground of having responsibility for the care of a family member. However, private member's bills that would have prohibited race, age, and sexuality discrimination were strongly opposed by the government and defeated in 1997 (Petersen 1999a).

On 1 July 1997 China resumed sovereignty and the Basic Law came into force. Unfortunately, the Basic Law severely restricts the law-making powers of individual legislators, far more so than the colonial constitution. Article 74 now prohibits legislators from introducing bills relating to public expenditure, political structure, or the operation of government and requires a legislator to obtain the Chief Executive's permission before introducing any bill relating to "government policies". Thus, under the current constitutional regime, it is almost impossible for an individual legislator to push the government to legislate in an area in which it does not want to legislate (as Anna Wu did with her EOB). This means that the only way to significantly expand Hong Kong's legal framework for gender equality is to persuade the government to introduce a bill, which is extremely difficult since the government itself is not elected by the general public.

The government and the business community are strongly opposed to legislation prohibiting age discrimination and unlikely to change their position on that issue. Age discrimination continues to be a major issue for Hong Kong women but it is only addressed by a voluntary code of practice (Hong Kong Government 1997, Petersen 1999a). This is also true of sexuality discrimination, despite a growing movement for the rights of sexual diversities in Hong Kong (Petersen 1997). Thus far, the only area in which the Hong Kong government has indicated a willingness to expand the framework for equality is with respect to racial discrimination. The government has been severely criticized for having no legislation prohibiting race discrimination in the private sector and has recently agreed to introduce a bill by 2005. In September 2004 the government issued a Consultation Paper on the contents of this legislation (Hong Kong Government 2004b). The Consultation Paper indicates that the new law will prohibit discrimination, harassment, and vilification on the grounds of race, colour, descent, and national or ethnic origin (the grounds stated in the International Convention on the Elimination of All Forms of Discrimination). In other respects it will largely copy the basic format of the SDO and will apply to employment, education, housing, and the provision of goods and services. The bill will be welcomed by Hong Kong's ethnic minority communities. Some of these communities (for example, the Filipino and Indonesian communities) are predominantly female as Hong Kong employs a large number of foreign domestic helpers from these countries.[3]

One of the controversial issues in the public consultation on the race discrimination bill will be whether and how to address discrimination suffered by new immigrants from Mainland China, a large percentage of which are women who move to Hong Kong to join their husbands. The government acknowledges that this discrimination occurs but has taken the position that does not fall within the intended scope of a racial discrimination bill. The Consultation Paper points out that most of the new immigrants from Mainland China are Han Chinese and therefore "of the same ethnic stock" as local Hong Kong Chinese (Hong Kong Government, 2004b). This is a somewhat confusing statement and may have inadvertently created the impression that the government thinks that racial discrimination is only possible between members of different racial groups, which is not the case. Assume, for example, that a Chinese headmaster refuses to hire a Chinese person to teach English because the headmaster thinks that only Caucasian English teachers look "authentic" to students and their parents. That would be an example of a Chinese person discriminating on the grounds of race against another Chinese person and would certainly be prohibited under the government's proposed bill. Moreover, a Chinese person who has recently immigrated to Hong Kong from the Mainland would be protected from that type of discrimination in the same way that a Chinese person born in Hong Kong would be protected.

The issue, therefore, is not whether immigrants from China will be covered by the bill but rather what "grounds" of discrimination will be included in the bill and whether the discrimination that Mainland immigrants most commonly suffer will fit within one of those grounds. The government's position is that it will not fit because the discrimination that Mainland immigrants suffer is a form of "social discrimination" rather than a form of racial discrimination. However that is not entirely clear. As noted above, the government has acknowledged that the bill should prohibit discrimination on the ground of "national origin". The term "national origin" generally refers to the country from which a person (or her ancestors) immigrated and one of the purposes of prohibiting discrimination on this ground is to ensure that immigrant communities have equal opportunities in employment, education, and other fields. Of course, in most jurisdictions immigrants come from outside the country. In contrast, since there is a border between Hong Kong and Mainland China, we have immigrants who come from within the same country. It is therefore arguable that the concept of "national origin" needs to be adapted to the special circumstances of Hong Kong. It could be defined in the bill so as to include "origin from any territory outside the Hong Kong SAR". In this way, a new immigrant from Mainland China would enjoy the same protection from discrimination that a new immigrant from Nepal or some other country would enjoy. Alternatively, the bill could expressly prohibit discrimination on the ground that a person is "an immigrant to the Hong Kong SAR", an approach that has been adopted in some jurisdictions. Whether this is done will depend to a large extent on the ability of the NGOs who work with new immigrants to lobby the government and legislators on their behalf.

Another area that requires law reform is the Domestic Violence Ordinance (Cap 189 of the laws of Hong Kong). Most experts agree that its scope is too narrow and that it needs to be amended to apply to wider forms of abuse and to relationships other than just husband and wife (South China Morning Post 2004b). The threshold for obtaining an order from the court is also considered too high and stalking needs to be made a criminal offence. The Law Reform Commission issued its report on stalking (which included recommended amendments to the Domestic Violence Ordinance) more than four years ago but no legislation has been enacted (Law Reform Commission 2000). The police also appear to need far more training in the field. (Tang 2003, Tang, Pun and Cheung 2003). In April 2004 a mother and her two daughters were killed in their public housing flat just hours after she had left a government-run shelter and sought help from the police. An independent inquiry into the murders cited a lack of co-ordination between the government and social service organisations (South China Morning Post 2004c).

The government's Second Report to the CEDAW Committee acknowledges that domestic violence is an acute social problem, and describes its efforts to increase training for police and the services (e.g. shelters) that are available (Hong Kong Government 2003a). The government has also proposed certain legislative changes that have been enacted, including amendments to the Crimes Ordinance to clarify that marital rape is a crime (Emerton 2001) and legislation to compel spouses to give evidence in certain proceedings (Hong Kong Government 2003a). The government also deserves credit for having taking the initiative to repeal the corroboration rule which formerly required judges to give juries a special warning on the "dangers of convicting on the complainant's evidence alone" in rape and other sexual offences (Hong Kong Government 1999). Ironically, the government faced strong opposition from the Hong Kong Bar Association, which is normally supportive of equality rights but in this case seemed to genuinely believe that women have a tendency to lie when it comes to sex. Fortunately, the Evidence Ordinance was successfully amended in spite of the Bar's opposition and the requirement for a corroboration warning in rape and other sexual offences is no longer required (Evidence Ord., section 4B, added by Ord. 43 of 2000).

The government could do more, however, not only by reforming the Domestic Violence Ordinance but also by providing women who flee violence a legal right to housing and social welfare. In theory, Hong Kong people enjoy a right to social welfare, pursuant to Article 36 of the Basic

Law. Similarly, Article 9 of International Covenant on Economic Social and Cultural Rights (ICESCR) recognises the "right of everyone to social security and social insurance" and Article 39 of the Basic Law provides that the ICESCR shall be implemented though the laws of Hong Kong. This seems to imply that there should be an ordinance governing entitlement to social security. In fact, the government regulates this field almost entirely as a matter of executive policy. Moreover, the government's approach is constrained by its commitment to low-taxes, laissez-faire economic policies, and the philosophy of self-reliance. Hong Kong does not have a graduated income tax and the low tax policy is expressly enshrined in Article 108 of the Basic Law. This makes it almost impossible to argue for a justiciable right to social security and during the recent recession there have been significant reductions in social welfare benefits. Although the government has argued that the reductions are only deflationary adjustments and do not reduce real spending power, they have generated significant criticism from NGOs and international monitoring bodies. Since women are significantly more likely than men to be single parents and to live in poverty, they are disproportionately affected by the cuts.

Another controversial development is a new residency requirement for social welfare. Prior to 2004, a person could apply for social welfare after being a resident of Hong Kong for one year. The government wanted to send a clear message to potential immigrants that they should plan carefully and ensure that they have sufficient means to support themselves in Hong Kong. Thus, with effect from January 2004, an adult is generally only eligible for benefits if s/he has been considered a resident of Hong Kong for at least seven years and has resided in Hong Kong continuously for at least one year immediately before applying for assistance (with no more than 56 days away from Hong Kong in that one year) (Hong Kong Government 2003b). The new policy will create hardship for women who are recent arrivals from the Mainland, many of whom are already living in difficult circumstances. The seven-year residence requirement also applies to public housing, which is in high demand. The government's Second Report to the CEDAW Committee emphasises that this residential requirement can be relaxed to help newly arrived women who have housing problems because of "unexpected family changes" and that battered women with "genuine" housing needs can always apply for public housing on compassionate grounds (Hong Kong Government 2003a). In practice, however, social workers tend to interpret the criteria narrowly when determining whether a genuine need exists (Chan and Chan 2003). A woman who cannot obtain safe and suitable housing for her children will naturally feel that she has no option but to stay with her husband, even if he is abusive.

The provision of social security in old age is another area in which the government has shown a lack of gender perspective. In 1995 the Hong Kong government enacted the first Mandatory Provident Fund Scheme Ordinance which requires employers and employees to contribute to private trust schemes. The employee will then receive benefits upon retirement, corresponding to the contributions made. Although women's organisations have lobbied the government to expand the coverage of the law it still makes no provision for homemakers and others who do not participate in the paid workforce. These are but a few examples of areas in which a more advanced concept of equality (one that includes the concepts of substantive equality and equality as transformation) could contribute to law reform in Hong Kong. In theory, the recent promise by the government to adopt "gender mainstreaming" in policy making (a major project of the Women's Commission) should bring more of a gender perspective into law and policy making. Thus far, however, I am not aware of any actual changes to policies or laws that have come about as a result of gender mainstreaming. In practice, the government's commitment to formal equality, a low-tax regime, and the philosophy of self-reliance is likely to inhibit this process.

Finally, the most serious violation of the right to equality lies in Hong Kong's election laws. Prior to the enactment of the SDO in 1995, a significant percentage of villages either prohibited women from standing for election or applied the "head of household" rule to prevent most women from voting (Petersen 1996). Fortunately, Section 35 of the SDO now prohibits sex discrimination in rural elections and this provision has been applied in the case of *Secretary for Justice v. Chan Wah* [2000] 4 HKC 429 (although this case primarily addressed discrimination against non-indigenous residents of the village). Yet Hong Kong's general election system still discriminates against women, albeit in a more indirect manner. The Chief Executive is selected by a small Election Committee of 800 people and then appointed by the Central Government, guaranteeing that the government will be led by a conservative person who embraces the economic policies of the current government. Moreover, only one-half of Hong Kong's legislators are directly elected, with the remaining half being chosen by elitist "functional constituencies". Some of these functional constituencies are professional groups (e.g. lawyers, social workers, or accountants), in which individuals vote. Other constituencies are by industry (e.g. the banking industry) and actually have corporate voting, which is particularly undemocratic (Young and Law 2004). Women are seriously underrepresented as voters in this system. Moreover, while a few functional constituency representatives have liberal views (such as Margaret Ng, who has represented the legal functional constituency since before 1997), most tend to be conservative, pro-business, and pro-government in their views. This is not surprising and indeed it is the goal of the system and the reason why Beijing is reluctant to allow reforms (Chaney 2004).

In the last colonial election, Governor Patten made the system somewhat more democratic. Thus the 1995 election law dramatically expanded the size of certain functional constituencies, so as to give every working person a vote in a functional constituency. This significantly increased the number of women voting for this type of legislator (Ghai 1999). Yet that law was also discriminatory, not only because the size of the constituencies varied so greatly but also because homemakers were not represented in any functional constituency. The system was challenged on that basis in the case of *Lee Miu Ling and Law Oui v. Attorney General* (1995) 5 HKPLR 23. The challenge was unsuccessful, largely because the British Government had amended the Letters Pattent (the colonial constitution) to expressly provide for the system. Since 1997 the election law has been even more discriminatory because far fewer people can vote in a functional constituency, corporate voting has been reinstated, and women are excluded to a greater degree. However, since the functional constituency system is expressly provided for in the Basic Law it would be difficult to challenge it in the courts.

Although the democracy movement has gained significant public support in Hong Kong in recent years, Beijing has ruled out any universal suffrage for the selection of the Chief Executive in 2007 and for the 2008 legislative elections. In its April 2004 Interpretation, the Standing Committee of the National People's Congress (NPCSC) set stringent procedures for proposing any amendments to the method of selecting the Chief Executive and the Legislative Council. This was followed by a "Decision" of the NPCSC that rules out any reduction in the percentage of seats held by the functional constituencies for the 2008 legislative elections. Denial of the right to equal participation in the political system is one of the most serious violations of the right to equality, not only because it is so fundamental but also because it affects law and policy-making in so many other spheres. A government and a legislature that is not fully elected by the people and gives undue representation to the wealthy business classes cannot be expected to advance the cause of equality in any significant way. For these reasons, it is highly unlikely that Hong Kong will significantly expand, in the near future, to its current legal framework for gender equality. Therefore, the next two sections of the chapter examine the most important law in that framework, the SDO.

III. The Sex Discrimination Ordinance and Judicial Application

General approach and scope of the SDO

The SDO prohibits discrimination (against both women and men) on the grounds of sex, pregnancy, and marital status and applies to many fields, including employment, education, housing, the provision of goods and services, and the administration of laws and government programmes. Most of the complaints arise in the field of employment and the law has broad application here, protecting not only employees but also job applicants, contract workers, and commission agents (Petersen 2001). The SDO prohibits discrimination in the terms of employment and clearly requires equal pay for equal work. In my view the SDO also requires employers to implement the principal of equal pay for work of equal value, although some uncertainty on this point has been created due to unclear language in the EOC's Sex Discrimination Ordinance Code of Practice on Employment (Petersen 2000).

The SDO provides, at section 46, that an employer will normally be held vicariously liable for an unlawful act of an employee in the course of employment, regardless of whether the act was done with the employer's consent or knowledge. Thus, if a manager discriminates against women when he makes hiring decisions, the company will normally be liable for his actions. An employer can, however, avoid vicarious liability by demonstrating that it took such steps as were "reasonably practicable" to prevent the employee from committing the unlawful act. This is intended to encourage employers to adopt policies promoting equal opportunities in hiring, promotion, and training. The EOC maintains a training unit for employers and other institutions who wish to develop such policies. Hong Kong's six universities have now adopted policies prohibiting sex discrimination and sexual harassment, which was not the case before the law was enacted.

The SDO also prohibits, at section 9, "victimisation", which is discrimination against a person on the ground that the person has made allegations of unlawful discrimination or harassment, has given evidence, or has taken steps to enforce one of the anti-discrimination ordinances. This provision is intended to protect employees from retaliation if they make a complaint of discrimination or sexual harassment or if they agree to serve as a witness for another person's compliant.

The definition of discrimination

The SDO defines unlawful discrimination with the classic concepts of direct and indirect discrimination. Direct discrimination is defined, in section 5, as unfavourable treatment on the ground of sex, marital status, or pregnancy. Hong Kong courts have generally applied UK case law, including the "but for" test, to determine whether there has been direct discrimination. This means that the plaintiff must prove to the court that the defendant would have treated her more favourably "but for" her sex, pregnancy, or marital status. Normally this requires the plaintiff to identify a real or hypothetical "comparator" and to demonstrate that the comparator either received or would have received better treatment than she received from the defendant.

Often a case turns on how that comparator is defined. For example, in the case of *Helen Tsang v. Cathay Pacific Airways Ltd (No. 2)* [2001] 4 HKC 585, the plaintiff was a former flight attendant of Cathay Pacific. She successfully sued on the ground that she had been required to retire at a younger age than male flight attendants who were hired at the same time. Interestingly, in 1993 (before the SDO was enacted), Cathay Pacific changed its policy and made the retirement age for all newly appointed staff 45. However, men who had been appointed under the old policy were given the option of keeping the original male retirement age of 55 while women who were hired under the old policy were only permitted to keep their original female retirement age of 40 or switch to the new general retirement age of 45. The court agreed with the plaintiff that the relevant "comparator" in her case was not a recent male hire but rather a male who had been hired when Tsang was originally hired. That male attendant would have been allowed to work until the age of 55. Thus, but for her sex, Tsang would also have been allowed to work until the age of 55. This was a particularly important case because it established that employers can be sued for discriminatory acts that commenced before the SDO came into force, as long as the act continues to have a discriminatory effect upon the plaintiff after the law came into force. The case is also noteworthy in that it was one of the few cases in which a plaintiff litigated a claim under the SDO on her own, without assistance from the EOC.

When seeking to prove a case of direct discrimination the plaintiff can rely upon section 4 of the SDO. This section provides that if an act is done for two or more reasons and one of the reasons is the sex, pregnancy, or marital status of the plaintiff then it shall, for the purposes of the SDO, be taken to have been done for that reason. The District Court applied this section in *Chang Ying Kwan v Wyeth (HK) Ltd* [2001] 2 HKC 129, a successful case alleging pregnancy discrimination supported by the EOC legal division. The plaintiff, a former marketing manager of Wyeth, gave notice that she was pregnant. Soon after, she was given an ultimatum to either resign or accept a demotion to marketing assistant. The plaintiff refused and made a complaint to the EOC. She continued to work but claimed that she suffered detrimental treatment (including harassment by staff) and she ultimately resigned and claimed constructive dismissal. The court did not find that the company treated pregnant employees badly in general. Rather, the Judge concluded that certain employees did not like the plaintiff and used her pregnancy as a reason to give her the ultimatum, hoping that she would resign. Nonetheless, the pregnancy was a factor in the co-workers' decision to treat her badly. Applying section 4 of the SDO, if an act is done for two or more reasons and one of the reasons is the pregnancy of the plaintiff then it shall, for the purposes of the SDO, be taken to have been done for that reason.

The Wyeth case is also significant because the plaintiff's claim for victimization, under section 9 of the SDO, was upheld by the court. The plaintiff was treated with great hostility after she contacted the EOC for advice. For example, she was given many threatening "warning letters" for trivial matters. Our study of complaints filed with the EOC indicates that the facts of the Wyeth case are all too typical (Petersen 2001, Petersen, Wong and Rush, 2003). It is very common for a woman to be fired after she announces her pregnancy or soon after she returns from maternity leave. Many employers are aware that this is unlawful and they therefore try to persuade a woman to resign (arguing that this will look better on her record and that she can then receive a favourable reference letter). If she refuses or threatens to go to the EOC, as the plaintiff did in the Wyeth case, the employer may attempt to manufacture a paper record to justify dismissing her. Thus a previously satisfactory employee will suddenly receive a stream of warning letters from her supervisor, claiming that her attitude needs improvement, that she returned a few minutes late from lunch, or that her performance has "slipped". No doubt the people who are issuing these warnings think that they are building a defense to an action for discrimination. However, the

Wyeth case indicates that judges can see through such ploys if the plaintiff has the means and the determination to litigate.

Indirect discrimination is a more complex concept than direct discrimination and thus far the Hong Kong courts have not had much opportunity to consider it. Under section 5 of the SDO, indirect discrimination occurs if the plaintiff cannot comply with a "requirement or condition" which has been applied uniformly by the defendant but which has a disproportionate and detrimental impact upon the group that is protected from discrimination and which cannot be justified under the circumstances. The classic example of indirect sex discrimination is a height requirement with which fewer women than men will be able to comply. Such a requirement is unlawful unless the employer can demonstrate that it is justified by the circumstances of that job. It should be noted that the United Kingdom has since adopted a broader definition of indirect discrimination. Legislators Anna Wu and Christine Loh attempted to persuade the Hong Kong government to also adopt a broader definition but were unsuccessful (Petersen 1999).

Exemption for voluntary special measures

In general, the SDO embraces "formal" rather than substantive equality and it does not obligate the government or anyone else to practice affirmative action. The government has always been hostile to suggestions that affirmative action or quotas should be used to assist women to overcome the historical effects of sex discrimination, arguing that this would be inconsistent with Hong Kong's commitment to meritocracy and to a free economy. In its second report to the CEDAW Committee the government could not cite even one example of a "special measure" adopted to advance women's equality. In its original draft of the Sex Discrimination Bill, there also was no exemption for temporary special measures and thus the law might have rendered unlawful even voluntary affirmative action. Fortunately, during the Bills Committee's deliberation of the bill, in the 1994-1995 legislative year, the government agreed to add an exemption for voluntary special measures. This now appears in section 48 of the SDO. Suppose, for example, that an engineering firm that has never hired a female engineer wishes to show preference for female applicants for a period of time to redress the imbalance. This should be perfectly lawful under section 48 as it would constitute a special measure "reasonably intended" to ensure that women have equal opportunities, in a field which has been traditionally male-dominated.

There is, however, no indication that any employer or institution in Hong Kong intends to use special measures on behalf of women. Indeed, the only time section 48 has been raised was in the case of *EOC v. Director of Education* [2001] 2 HKLRD 777, a case in which the government attempted to defend its policy of giving boys preferential treatment when applying to secondary schools, which is discussed below.

Discrimination in education: the case of EOC v. Director of Education

Hong Kong's system of secondary schools is highly segregated. Students are assessed at the end of primary school, divided into different ability bands, and then allocated to schools in order of ability band. A student who is placed in a "band one" school is almost certain to go on to university and to enjoy a bright future. In contrast, the lower band schools are considered dead ends and graduates are far less likely to enter university. In 1998, the EOC received complaints from female students who alleged that they had been rejected from elite secondary schools while boys with lower results on the assessments had been admitted. The EOC conducted a formal investigation and determined that the entire allocation system violated the SDO. Female students performed, on average, better than male students but the Education Department had been secretly scaling those results, boosting the results of the top 30% of the boys. It also banded male and female students separately so that band one did not consist of the top 20% of students but rather the top 20% of female students and the top 20% of male students. Thus a girl could be assigned to band two although she had higher results (even after gender scaling) than a boy assigned to band one. The government also allowed elite co-educational schools to set gender quotas. Although in some school nets individual boys suffered from the process, far more girls than boys were adversely affected and the government admitted that a primary purpose of the mechanisms was to ensure that girls did not obtain a majority of the places in the elite secondary schools (EOC 1999).

When the government refused to change the system, the EOC applied for judicial review. In its defense the government argued that the gender-based adjustments fell within the exemption for special measures provided in section 48 of the SDO. This position was, of course, completely inconsistent with the government's professed opposition to affirmative action and hugely ironic since it flatly refuses to introduce special measures for women, although they are still earning far less than men in the market place and far more likely to be living in poverty. The Judge might have rejected the defense on the simple ground that CEDAW only permits special measures on behalf of women, the purpose being to redress the historical effects of discrimination (Byrnes 1999a). Instead, the Judge rejected the defense on the ground that special measures are only permitted under CEDAW if applied on a temporary basis. The Director of Education had been secretly applying the gender-based adjustments for almost 20 years and had no intention of abandoning them. Moreover, the Judge concluded that none of the mechanisms were intended to assist boys to overcome whatever caused them to perform at a lower standard than girls. Rather, the government had simply developed a system that would manufacture a permanent advantage in favour of boys, at the expense of individual girls (Petersen 2002).

In one sense the litigation was a major victory for the EOC. Unlike many court cases, which only have immediate effect upon one or a few plaintiffs, this case had a truly systemic impact. The government was compelled to abandon the gender adjustments and, as expected, a larger percentage of girls earned places in the higher-ranked schools (*South China Morning Post* 2002). Since the vast majority of Hong Kong women pass through the public school system and the reputation of one's secondary school plays a significant role in future opportunities here, this is a tangible benefit for women. In other respects, however, the victory was a hollow one. First, the case did not address the broader issue of whether it is fair to categorize children at such a young age and to give some children, whether male or female, a better educational environment than others. (The EOC had no jurisdiction to challenge that general issue, only to ensure that the allocation did not discriminate on the ground of sex.) Moreover, the case brought the EOC into direct conflict with powerful government officials. Following the litigation, the government decided not to renew the contract of the chairperson of the EOC, Ms. Anna Wu and there has been widespread speculation that this was intended to send a signal to the EOC, particularly as it was not the first time that the government had declined to reappoint a chairperson of a public body (Human Rights Monitor 2002). Such actions would violate the Paris Principles on national human rights institutions, which require that bodies enforcing human rights be given absolute independence and that the appointment procedures be open and transparent (United Nations 1993, Petersen 2003).

Sexual harassment

The SDO expressly defines and prohibits sexual harassment and complaints alleging sexual harassment make up the second largest category of cases filed under the SDO. Thus the plaintiff need not prove that the harassment was discriminatory (which is the case under US law and was the case under British law when the Sex Discrimination Act was originally enacted). Both quid pro quo and hostile work environment are included in Hong Kong's statutory definition of sexual harassment (which was borrowed from Australian legislation) although the definition is not really organized into those two categories (Samuels 2000).

In essence, section 2(5)(a) of the SDO defines sexual harassment as including an unwelcome sexual advance or conduct that is sexual in nature in relation to the victim in circumstances in which "a reasonable person, having regard to the circumstances, would have anticipated that [s/he] would be offended, humiliated, or intimidated." This is a partly subjective and partly objective test and it includes not only quid pro quo but also much of what we think of as hostile environment harassment, so long as the conduct was "in relation" to the plaintiff. The second, alternative, definition of sexual harassment (in section 2(5)(b)) includes "conduct of a sexual nature which creates a sexually hostile or intimidating work environment". This definition does not require the plaintiff to show that that conduct was in relation to her. At present, this alternative definition only applies to the employment field but the government has agreed to introduce a similar category for the educational field (based upon the concept of "hostile learning environment"). Moreover, the limited case law indicates that Hong Kong courts will apply a reasonably flexible interpretation of "in relation to". In *Ratcliff v the Secretary for the Civil Service* [1999] 4 HKC 237 (a case interpreting an internal police headquarters order that defined sexual harassment in similar terms) the Court of Appeal held that "in relation to" should not be interpreted too narrowly and could include, for example, unwelcome sexual stories told to a woman even if the stories were not about her. Thus the scope of section 2(5)(a) is fairly wide.

The first case of sexual harassment litigated in Hong Kong was the case of *Yuen Sha Sha v. Tse Chi Pan* [1999] 1 HKC 731. The plaintiff, a female student at Chinese University, had been secretly videotaped by her roommate's boyfriend, who had hidden a camcorder in her dormitory room and aimed it directly at her dressing area over a period of several months. This is one of the few reported judgements in which liability for sexual harassment has been based entirely upon an invasion of the victim's privacy and the case therefore established an important precedent (Petersen 1999b). The judgement also greatly increased public awareness of sexual harassment and virtually every tertiary institution in Hong Kong now has some sort of policy prohibiting sexual harassment and procedures for filing complaints. Yet the case also demonstrated the inherent difficulties in enforcing gender equality through litigation. Although, the plaintiff discovered the camera in her room in early 1997, her complaint did not go to trial until early 1999. In addition to the stress of testifying, she endured embarrassing press coverage and continued harassment by the defendant and his friends, who pressured her to abandon the case. The court awarded exemplary damages as a result of the defendant's behaviour, but the total damages awarded (HK$80,000, which is approximately US$10,000) could not possibly have compensated her for the time and emotional stress that the incident and the litigation cost her (Petersen 1999b).

The stress and the slowness of litigation has led many experts to conclude that alternative dispute resolution is a better method for resolving complaints of discrimination and harassment, although it is acknowledged to have many disadvantages (Chapman 2000). In any event, in Hong Kong the EOC complaints resolution process is clearly where the great majority of complaints involving gender discrimination are being resolved. Thus, it is important to consider a sample of those complaints and the remedies that are being obtained.

IV. The Legal Framework for Gender-Related Complaints at the EOC

The origins of the conciliation-based enforcement model

When proposals for anti-discrimination legislation were first debated in Hong Kong some commentators suggested that it should follow the example of Japan, where the employment discrimination legislation initially relied chiefly upon persuasion. One labour expert argued that the Japanese model had successfully signaled the "moral importance" of the rights of women "while remaining prudent enough to recognize traditionally enshrined customs and practices" (Ng 1994). However, women's organizations were aware of the limited impact of the Japanese law and had already expressed their opposition to a similar proposal made by the government in its 1993 *Green Paper on Equal Opportunities for Men and Women* (Hong Kong Government 1993, 1994). By this time, the government also knew that it had to propose a bill that would serve as a viable alternative to Anna Wu's EOB. It therefore agreed that the SDO would create legal duties and that its enforcement would be supported by an EOC with the power to conciliate complaints. However, the government rejected Anna Wu's proposal to create an inexpensive equal opportunities tribunal to resolve complaints that could not be conciliated (Petersen 1996). Thus, if conciliation fails there is no inexpensive tribunal to resolve the complaint.

It is not surprising that the government and the business community would prefer a model in which most complaints are settled through an internal process at the EOC. Employers and government departments are potential respondents to these complaints and conciliation is faster, less expensive, and far less public than litigation. The more interesting question is whether a conciliation-based model is also better for complainants. It is also often argued that Chinese communities have a traditional preference for mediation over adversarial procedures. (Wong 2000). Moreover, in any cultural context it is likely that a significant percentage of complainants, particularly victims of sexual harassment, would prefer to resolve their complaints in a private environment, away from the glare of the media. On the other hand, during the debate on the legislative model, it was clear that some women's organizations were suspicious of the proposal. In particular, they were concerned that power imbalances would be perpetuated in conciliation and that the confidential nature of the process would limit the social impact of the law. They insisted upon the right to litigate, without any obligation to engage in prior conciliation.

The result was a compromise model but one that clearly discourages litigation. A victim of discrimination or sexual harassment has the right to file her complaint directly in the District Court and need not use the EOC at all. However, most complainants go to the EOC, if only because they cannot afford a lawyer. Hong Kong has high legal fees and does not permit lawyers to work on a contingency fee basis (in which the lawyer charges no fee if the claim is unsuccessful). Once a complainant decides to use the EOC, she is effectively obligated to attempt conciliation if the respondent is willing to do so. This is because the EOC has a statutory obligation to attempt to conciliate a complaint before granting assistance. Thus, if the complainant refuses to conciliate or rejects what the EOC considers to be a reasonable offer then it is highly unlikely that it will grant her further assistance.

In order to gain a better understanding of the complaints process and how it affects female complainants, my research assistant and I reviewed a random sample of 197 complaints that were processed by the EOC in a nine-month period in 2000–2001. We also interviewed EOC officers, past complainants, and representatives of women's organizations who regularly assist women with the EOC's process of investigation and conciliation. We examined 188 complaints filed under the SDO and an additional 9 filed under the FSDO. Of the 188 SDO complaints in our sample, 73 alleged pregnancy discrimination, 55 alleged sexual harassment, 43 alleged sex discrimination, and seven alleged marital status discrimination. An additional 10 alleged victimization. The vast majority of the complaints we examined (about 85%) were in the field of employment. We obtained a range of information from each complaint, including the extent to which the parties had legal representation, the requested remedies, and the outcome. While the study also included complaints of disability discrimination (the data for which can be found in Petersen, Fong, and Rush 2003), the remainder of this chapter highlights the findings most relevant to gender equality.

The EOC's complaints process

When the EOC receives a complaint it conducts an initial screening. Some complaints will be discontinued at the screening point (e.g. if it is outside the EOC's jurisdiction) and others will be discontinued at some later stage in the investigation. The discontinuation rate in our sample was quite high, representing 45% of our sample. The EOC has the power, and indeed the obligation, to discontinue the complaint if it does not allege an unlawful act or if the EOC concludes that it is frivolous or lacking in substance, despite efforts to obtain evidence from the complainant. In our sample, however, the EOC discontinued only 28 complaints on one of these grounds. An additional 47 complaints were discontinued because the complainant herself decided not to pursue the complaint. It generally was not possible, from the file, to ascertain why so many complainants chose to withdraw their complaints and we had no opportunity to ask them (as our data base does not include the names of any of the parties). However our interviews and focus groups with a selection of women who have either been complainants themselves or assisted complainants (discussed later in this section) indicate that many women simply grow tired of the process and decide that the final remedy is unlikely to justify the effort involved. A small number of complaints were discontinued for a range of additional reasons. For example, the complaint may have been settled outside the EOC process, or as part of the settlement in a related complaint.

In its early years of operation, the EOC completed a full investigation of the complaint before determining whether it should proceed to conciliation. However, during the period of our study the EOC began a trial programme of "early conciliation", which it later adopted generally. Under this approach, the EOC officer will invite the complainant and respondent to attempt conciliation before the EOC completes its investigation. The EOC has found that the two parties are often more willing to reach an agreement early in the process, before they have invested a great deal of time in the investigation and become "hardened" in their respective positions. The EOC also recognised that the parties on both sides of the complaint grow weary if the investigation phase drags on too long. If early conciliation fails, the complaint can still proceed to a full investigation and then on to post-investigation conciliation. If, however, the parties are unable to reach an agreement at that stage then the complaint will be categorised as "unsuccessfully conciliated". At that stage the complainant's only options are to: (1) apply for EOC legal assistance; (2) litigate at her own expense, which rarely occurs; or (3) abandon her complaint.

Remedies obtained in the conciliated complaints

A little more than one-half of the complaints in our sample proceeded to some form of conciliation by the EOC. Of these, 25 were categorised as unsuccessfully conciliated while 81 were categorised as "conciliated". This means that an agreement was reached in more than 80% of the cases that proceeded to conciliation (generating an overall conciliation rate of about 42% of the SDO/FSDO complaints in our original sample). While this is compares favourably with other jurisdictions (Hunter and Leonard 1995), one must also examine the remedies that were obtained in order to assess the impact of the process. The two remedies that were most commonly sought in complaints that proceeded to the conciliation stage were monetary compensation and an apology. Interestingly, a significant number of complainants who sought monetary compensation and went through the conciliation process either reached no agreement (in which case their complaint was categorised as unsuccessfully conciliated) or had to give up on monetary compensation in order to reach agreement. Of the complaints that were successfully conciliated, monetary compensation was sought in 35 but received in only 24 cases. The average amount of monetary compensation for an SDO/FSDO complaint was HK$82,904 (about US $10,628) but this average is somewhat skewed by a few very large settlements. The median settlement, which is a better indication, was HK$30,000 (about $US3,846). The highest amount obtained in any one SDO complaint was HK$624,000 and the smallest award was HK$751.

Of course, many women do not seek monetary compensation or do not feel that strongly about obtaining it. Indeed, in focus groups and interviews, many past complainants and representatives of women's organisations expressed the view that an apology or a promise by the company to change its policies was worth more to them. Some women, who had alleged sexual harassment, even found the suggestion of monetary compensation offensive. They felt that it would be equivalent to telling the respondent that he had permission to touch or otherwise harass women, as long as he paid for it. For these women, an apology would have more meaning. Apologies were requested in 34 and received in 21 of the conciliated SDO/FSDO complaints in our sample. The settlement terms also frequently included a new reference letter or a promise by the respondent to institute training or a policy against sexual harassment in the workplace, which would be viewed positively by many complainants so long as the promise is kept. (The EOC does not keep track of whether these promises are implemented, although it will take note if a similar complaint is later made against the same company.)

Women's experiences in the process of investigation and conciliation

In most of the employment cases the complainant alleged that she had lost her job (or had been compelled to resign) due to pregnancy discrimination, sex discrimination, or sexual harassment. Typically she had been employed in a clerical or sales-related job, on a salary of HK$10,000–15,000 per month. Complainants generally do not have legal representation during the EOC complaints process. In our sample of 188 complaints, none of the complainants were represented by a lawyer, although some had assistance from a women's concern group or from a friend or relative. We found that respondents are also unlikely to retain an outside lawyer for the EOC complaints process. This does not, however, mean that respondents are necessarily on an equal footing with complainants. First, most respondents are not individuals but rather are companies, government departments, or other institutions. This automatically gives the respondent an advantage because it can choose a skilled and knowledgeable employee to deal with the complaint during the investigation. That person may be an in-house lawyer, a personal manager, or someone with training in the field. The respondent will almost certainly appoint an employee with more education and greater socio-economic power than the complainant.

Our interviews indicate that many women who file complaints with the EOC find that the process of investigation is exhausting, stressful and surprisingly adversarial. The past complainants who we interviewed are not necessarily representative of complainants generally as they were not located randomly but rather through contacts with women's concern groups. However, their comments were consistent with the opinions expressed by representatives of women's groups, who regularly assist complainants at the EOC. These comments indicate that the idealistic view of the EOC process as a non-adversarial process is just that — an idealistic view. Once a complaint is filed with the EOC and the respondent is notified of it, a legal contest begins. The respondent (or its lawyer) will naturally fight hard to persuade the EOC that the complaint has no merit and should be discontinued. For example, if a complainant alleges that she was fired because of her pregnancy the employer will insist that she was fired because she was incompetent. The complainant must then produce evidence to support her version of the facts. If she does not do so she risks having her complaint discontinued by the EOC. While this process is not necessarily as stressful as a public hearing, it does compel a woman to defend her own record against the respondent's attacks.

Our interviews also reveal that there is a significant gap between the expectations that complainants have of the EOC officer and the role that the officer plays during the investigation. Lay people often assume that the EOC officer is like a police officer investigating a criminal complaint. They expect the EOC officer to leave the office, look for witnesses, and search for evidence of the unlawful act. In fact, the EOC officer largely depends upon the complainant to provide the evidence. Interviewees also expressed surprise that the officers do not give them more help in refuting the arguments put forth by respondents. One of our interviewees, a former complainant, described her distress when she received a letter drafted by the respondent's lawyer, consisting of 20 pages and several appendices. The EOC officer sent the lawyer's letter to the complainant with a cover letter asking for the complainant's response. When she asked the EOC for assistance in responding the officer refused, saying that she must remain "neutral towards the complaint." The complainant felt that this was unfair, since the respondent could afford legal representation and she could not. Ultimately, the complainant received help from a women's group but she was still bitter about the experience.

When we interviewed EOC officers they confirmed that complainants often feel overwhelmed by the investigation process and seek help from the officer. The EOC officers feel they cannot give more advice, in view of their duty to remain objective. This reveals the problems with the "formal" approach to equality. The complainant and respondent are treated equally by the EOC officer during the investigation but since the respondent is less likely to need assistance (having a lawyer or a human resource manager to advise it) the effect is to perpetuate the sense of powerlessness that the complainant had in the first place. The conciliation conference (whether it is conducted before or after an investigation) is also a stressful time for the complainant. Complainants find it very difficult to face the person who fired them or sexually harassed them and often feel intimidated. Some complainants simply refuse to meet with the other party, which means that the EOC officer practices "shuttle diplomacy", moving from room to room or passing messages back and forth over the telephone. Some complainants are shocked to find that they have to negotiate with the respondent. They often assume that the EOC will issue some kind of "judgement" after it investigates the complaint and are disappointed to find that it has no power to do so. The complainant also often expects the EOC officer to advise her during the conciliation and even advocate for her. In fact the officers are careful not to do so and told me that respondents frequently complain if they detect that the officer is giving any assistance to the complainant during the negotiations.

Adding to the power imbalance is the fact that complainants do not know, when they participate in conciliation, whether they will receive legal assistance if conciliation fails. They are not permitted to apply for EOC legal assistance until after the complaint is designated as "unsuccessfully conciliated". Complainants are reminded (by the EOC literature and by the officers) that there is no guarantee that a request for legal assistance will be granted, even if the complaint has merit. This is understandable because the EOC has a limited budget and will look for cases that raise important issues or are likely to establish a precedent in the field. The result, however, is that the respondent holds most of the bargaining power during the conference. The respondent can offer a very meagre remedy and sit back to see if the complainant accepts it. The respondent knows that she may be tempted to accept the low offer rather than risk walking away from the process with no remedy. In contrast, the respondent has little risk. In the unlikely event that the complainant does reject the offer and obtains legal assistance from the EOC, the respondent can almost certainly still settle the complaint out of court with a more reasonable offer.

The confidential nature of conciliation

Remedies obtained in conciliated cases are generally kept confidential and therefore do little to raise awareness in society or to change systemic patterns of discrimination. Although the EOC has attempted to address this problem by creating a data base of conciliated cases on its website (with the parties' identities concealed), this does not have the same impact as a public hearing and a judgment. Many of the activists we interviewed would like to see an equal opportunities tribunal established. Although there are many different models of tribunals, the goal would be to give complainants the opportunity to receive a hearing and a judgment, in a reasonably informal and inexpensive venue. Of course, a large percentage of complainants would still attempt confidential conciliation. Most SDO complaints are filed by individual women against former employers and a woman who has either just started a new job or is still seeking one will not want to be branded as a trouble-maker. However, the knowledge that they have the option of filing a complaint in an inexpensive tribunal may increase their bargaining power with the respondent. Moreover, our interviews with past complainants, women's support groups, and also EOC officers indicate that a certain percentage of complainants are inherently dissatisfied with the notion of a conciliated outcome and would be willing to risk the publicity in order to obtain a more satisfying and more systemic remedy.

V. Using International Treaties to Supplement Hong Kong's Legal Framework

CEDAW is the most important treaty relating to women's equality and is often referred to as the "international bill of rights" for women. It was adopted by the General Assembly in 1979, largely the result of lobbying by women activists, who argued that existing human rights instruments failed adequately to address women's issues. Unlike the ICCPR, it has not been directly incorporated into Hong Kong's domestic law. Thus, CEDAW cannot be the sole basis of a legal action or a complaint to the EOC. However, in an action based upon the SDO the court can look to CEDAW for guidance in interpreting any vague provisions of that Ordinance. As noted earlier in this chapter, the court relied upon CEDAW, in the case of *EOC v. Director of Education*, to interpret section 48 of the SDO. The court held that it was appropriate to look to CEDAW for guidance because the legislative history clearly demonstrated that the SDO had been enacted to comply with Hong Kong's obligations under CEDAW. If a provision of the SDO clearly contradicts CEDAW, the court must enforce the SDO because it is domestic law, whereas CEDAW is not part of Hong Kong's domestic law. However, as long as a provision of the SDO can be interpreted in a way that is consistent with CEDAW then the courts should give it such an interpretation (Petersen and Samuels 2002, Petersen 2000).

Moreover, this is not the only way that CEDAW can be used by Hong Kong women. Article 18 of CEDAW requires Hong Kong to report every four years on the implementation of the treaty. The report is submitted to and reviewed by the United Nations Committee on the Elimination of Discrimination Against Women (the "CEDAW Committee"), consisting of twenty-three experts elected by state parties. Although Hong Kong officially submits its report as part of China's report, the Hong Kong report is a distinct document prepared by our local government, which then sends officials to attend the hearings. The report should describe the legislative, judicial and administrative measures that have been adopted in Hong Kong to implement CEDAW and should also identify problem areas. While the Hong Kong government has a tendency (like most governments) to present an overly positive assessment, the women's movement can monitor and correct this. The Hong Kong government normally produces an outline of its report for public consultation, giving women's organizations an opportunity to ask that other topics be included. NGOs may also produce their own "shadow reports" commenting upon the government's report and monitor the extent to which the government honours any promises made to the CEDAW Committee. A recent study comparing the involvement of UK and Hong Kong women's organizations in the CEDAW enforcement process demonstrates that Hong Kong women are actively participating in the process and making better use of CEDAW in their lobbying than British women, despite the fact that CEDAW has applied longer in the UK (Petersen and Samuels 2002).

The impact of the NGO reports and briefings could be seen in the questions asked by the CEDAW Committee in its review of Hong Kong's first report under CEDAW (Erickson and Byrnes 1999). Members asked the Hong Kong government representatives several difficult questions and pursued the key issues in its concluding comments. For example, the Committee recommended amendments to the Domestic Violence Ordinance (so as to expand its coverage and provide for treatment and counseling of offenders). It also recommended that the government enhance services for victims of domestic violence and take steps to protect commercial sex workers and women migrant workers from abuse. It also recommended, in very strong terms, that the Hong Kong government establish a "national machinery" to better implement CEDAW. This was an issue that Hong Kong women's organizations and also the EOC had stressed in their shadow reports. (EOC 1998, Coalition of Women's and Human Rights Organizations 1999). While the Hong Kong government did not agree to adopt all of the CEDAW Committee's Concluding Comments it has responded to some of them. For example, it made statutory amendments so as to clarify that marital rape is a crime. It also agreed to create the Women's Commission, although it had long insisted that this was not necessary.

The recent adoption of the Optional Protocol to the Women's Convention is one of the most important reforms designed to enhance enforcement of the treaty (Byrnes and Connors 1996). The Optional Protocol provides two important mechanisms. The communications procedure allows individuals or groups of individuals who claim to be victims to assert that there has been a violation of any of the rights in the Convention (provided that they have first exhausted local remedies). The inquiry procedure allows the Committee itself to investigate grave or systematic violations of the rights in the Convention by a state party. Thus far there are 76 signatories to the Optional Protocol and 67 state parties (Division for the Advancement of Women 2004). Unfortunately Hong Kong is not a party. As Hong Kong is now a Special Administrative Region of China, any decision to ratify the Protocol would have to be approved by the Chinese national government, which is highly unlikely at this time.

Two other important treaties for Hong Kong women are the ICCPR and the ICESCR. As noted earlier in this chapter, both of these treaties (as well as applicable ILO conventions) are referred to in Article 39 of the Basic Law. Women's groups did make use of the ICCPR reporting process before CEDAW applied to Hong Kong and should continue to do so, if only because concluding comments by the United Nations Human Rights Committee tend to receive significant attention in the press. Moreover, the ICCPR is fully incorporated into Hong Kong's domestic laws and the three equality provisions therefore bind all government departments and public authorities. Thus, the process of writing shadow reports on breaches of the equality provisions in the ICCPR may identify practices and policies that could be litigated against in court under the Bill of Rights and Article 39 of the Basic Law. It appears that Hong Kong's equality movement is not making full use of these provisions in the Bill of Rights. For example, the discriminatory elements of the secondary school allocation system became unlawful in 1991, when the Bill of Rights was enacted. Yet the action for judicial review did not commence until 2000, after the SDO was in force. One reason for this is that the government did a good job of keeping the practices secret.

Another is that there is no human rights commission to investigate or litigate violations of the Bill of Rights and the EOC is restricted to enforcing the specific anti-discrimination ordinances.

Although the ICESCR is also referred to in Article 39 and lawyers have attempted to rely upon it in court, thus far the courts have not been particularly receptive, holding that the treaty is "aspirational" and "promotional" in nature. (See, for example, *Chan To Foon v. Director of Immigration* [2001] 3 HKLRD 109.) The Committee on Economic Social and Cultural Rights has since urged the government not to argue in court proceedings that the Covenant is merely 'promotional' or aspirational in nature". The government responded, in its most recent report to the Committee that it accepts that it "creates binding obligations at the international level" (Hong Kong Government 2003b). The use of the words "at the international level" may indicate that the government does not consider the Covenant to be part of domestic law, despite the reference in Article 39. The government has also declined to enact a single ordinance incorporating the ICESCR into domestic law. Nonetheless, Hong Kong women can participate in the "soft" enforcement process, by writing shadow reports, attending the hearings, and publicizing the concluding comments of the Committee. The ICESCR contains many specific rights that are not otherwise stated in the Basic Law. For example, apart from Article 33, which provides for freedom of choice of occupation, the Basic Law is largely silent with respect to workers' rights. In contrast, the ICESCR contains many specific provisions on workers' rights. Shortly before the handover, the Legislative Council enacted laws that would have expanded workers' right to collective bargaining and protected workers from summary dismissal for union activity. These laws were, however, repealed by the Provisional Legislative Council in 1997 and the Committee on Economic, Social and Cultural Rights has criticized the government for the lack of protection for workers and has urged it to fully implement the principle of equal pay for work of equal value (Committee on Economic, Social and Cultural Rights 2001). When the hearings are held on Hong Kong's Second Report (Hong Kong Government 2003b), the Committee will likely chastise the government for its failure to develop anti-poverty strategies, for the recent cuts to social welfare, and for the attacks on the independence of the EOC. All of these issues are significant to gender equality in Hong Kong.

While the government is not legally obligated to implement the recommendations of these international monitoring bodies, experience shows that it will try to show at least some progress when the time comes for the next report. For example, the recent decision to draft a bill prohibiting race discrimination in the private sector appears to have been made at least in part because so many international monitoring bodies had criticized the government for failing to legislate. The government does like to promote Hong Kong's image as a territory that adheres to human rights standards and takes the international reporting process seriously. Unlike some Asian governments, the Hong Kong government has openly embraced international standards and universalist theories of human rights. Although government officials occasionally make appeals to traditional Chinese values, this is fairly rare in the government's human rights discourse and officials are loathe to justify their actions with relativist theories of human rights. This is partly because the international community has paid extra attention to Hong Kong's human rights record since 1997 and the government is anxious to demonstrate that it has not deteriorated. The government also knows that it lacks legitimacy because it is not an elected government and a positive human rights record is one way that it can enhance its legitimacy.

It should be noted, however, that Hong Kong's reports to international monitoring bodies are submitted with China's reports in the case of treaties that have also been ratified by China, such as CEDAW and the ICESCR. Thus far, these bodies have continued to set aside time to consider the separate Hong Kong report and to question Hong Kong officials. The monitoring bodies also issue separate concluding comments on Hong Kong. It is, however, inevitable that the report of Mainland China, a much larger territory with more severe problems, will capture more attention from members of the relevant committee. Thus the key, for the women's movement, is to identify a few significant issues that a large coalition of Hong Kong NGOs can agree to emphasize in their shadow reports and then to follow up at the local level once the concluding comments are issued. The Legislative Council has shown that it is willing to assist with this process by requesting regular reports from the government on any actions taken to respond to the concluding comments (Hong Kong Government 2000). In this manner, the women's movement can continue to use international treaties to supplement the domestic legal framework and to encourage Hong Kong to gradually embrace more progressive concepts of gender equality.

References

Byrnes, A. (1992). Equality and non-discrimination. In R. Wacks (Ed.), *Human rights in Hong Kong* Hong Kong: Oxford University Press.

Byrnes, A. (1999a). The Committee on the Elimination of Discrimination Against Women. In P. Alston (Ed.), *The United Nations and human rights: A critical appraisal* (2nd Edition). Oxford: Oxford Clarendon Press.

Byrnes, A. (1999b). Affirmative action, Hong Kong law, and the SSPA, paper presented at *Equal opportunities in education: boys and girls in the 21st century* (conference organized by the Equal Opportunities Commission, 8 November 1999). Hong Kong: Equal Opportunities Commission.

Byrnes, A., & Chan, J. (1993). *Public law and human rights: A Hong Kong sourcebook*. Singapore: Butterworths.

Byrnes, A., & Connors, J. (1996). Enforcing the human rights of women: A complaints procedure for the women's convention. *Brooklyn Journal of International Law 21*: 679.

Chan W. C., & Chan, F. Y. (2003). Inclusion or exclusion? housing battered women in Hong Kong, *Critical Social Policy 23* (4): 526.

Chaney, C. (2004). "The Hong Kong Executive Authorities' Monopoly on Legislative Power: Analysis of the Legislative Council's Second term Voting Records", Centre for Comparative and Public Law Occasional Paper No. 13, University of Hong Kong (available at ww.hku.hk/ccpl/).

Chapman, A. (2000). Discrimination complaint-handling in New South Wales: The paradox of informal dispute resolution, *Sydney Law Review 22*: 321.

Committee on the Elimination of Discrimination Against Women (the "CEDAW Committee"). (1999). *Concluding Comments on the Initial Report on the Hong Kong Special Administrative Region*, UN Doc CEDAW/C/1999/L.1/Add.7.

Committee on Economic, Social and Cultural Rights (2001). Concluding observations on the initial report of the Hong Kong Special Administrative Region, E/C.12/1/Add.58.

Coalition of Women's and Human Rights Organisations (1999). *Submission to the CEDAW Committee on the Initial Report on Hong Kong Under the Convention on the Elimination of All Forms of Discrimination Against Women by Non-Governmental Organisations* (endorsed by 10 women's and human rights organisations and available on the "CEDAW in Hong Kong" webpage maintained by the Centre for Comparative and Public Law, Faculty of Law, University of Hong Kong, www.hku.hk/ccpl/research_projects_issues/cedaw/cedaw4.html).

Division for the Advancement of Women, United Nations (2004). What is an optional protocol? (at http://www.un.org/womenwatch/daw/cedaw/protocol/whatis.htm).

Equal Opportunities Commission (1998). *NGO report on the convention on the elimination of all forms of discrimination against women*. Hong Kong: Equal Opportunities Commission.

Equal Opportunities Commission (1999). *Formal investigation report: Secondary School Places Allocation (SSPA) System*. Hong Kong: Equal Opportunities Commission.

Equal Opportunities Commission (Undated). *What is conciliation?* Hong Kong: Equal Opportunities Commission (brochure distributed to advise complainants and respondents on the nature of the conciliation process).

Emerton, R. (2001). Marital rape and the related sexual offences: a review of the proposed amendments to Part XII of the Crimes Ordinance. *Hong Kong Law Journal 31*: 415.

Erickson, M., & Byrnes, A. (1999). Hong Kong and the convention on the elimination of all forms of discrimination against women. *Hong Kong Law Journal 29*: 350.

Fredman, S. (2003). Beyond the dichotomy of formal and substantive equality: Towards a new definition of equal rights. In Boerefijin, Ineke et al. (Ed.), *Temporary special measures: accelerating de facto equality of women under Article 4(1) UN Convention on the Elimination of All Forms of Discrimination Against Women*. Antwerpen: Intersentia.

Ghai, Y. (1999). *Hong Kong's new constitutional Order: The resumption of Chinese sovereignty and the Basic Law* (2nd ed.). Hong Kong: Hong Kong University Press.

Hong Kong Government, Education and Manpower Branch (1997). *Practical guidelines for employers: Eliminating age discrimination in employment*. Hong Kong: Hong Kong Government Printer.

Hong Kong Government (1993). *Green paper on equal opportunities for women and men*. Hong Kong: Hong Kong Government Printer.

Hong Kong Government (1994). *Green paper on equal opportunities for women and men: Compendium of submissions*. Hong Kong: Hong Kong Government Printer.

Hong Kong Government (1998). *Initial report on the Hong Kong Special Administrative Region under Article 18 of the Convention on the Elimination of All Forms of Discrimination Against Women*. Hong Kong: Hong Kong Government Printer.

Hong Kong Government (1999). Department of Justice, "Legislative Council Brief: Evidence (Amendment) Bill 1999, File Ref.: L/M (1) to LP 5014/19/1/1C V, 22 June 1999. (The Bill was enacted by Ord 43 of 2000).

Hong Kong Government (2000). *Progress Report for the LegCo Panel on Home Affairs: Follow-up on Concluding Comments of the United Nations Committee on the Elimination of Discrimination Against Women on the Initial Report of the HKSAR under the Convention on the Elimination of All Forms of Discrimination Against Women*. (Health and Welfare Bureau).

Hong Kong Government (2003a). *Second report on the Hong Kong Special Administrative Region under Article 18 of the Convention on the Elimination of All Forms of Discrimination Against Women. Hong Kong: Hong Kong Government Printer*. (Released in 2004.)

Hong Kong Government (2003b). *Second report of the Hong Kong Special*

Administrative Region of the People's Republic of China in the light of the international covenant on economic social and cultural rights. Hong Kong: Hong Kong Government Printer. (Released in 2004.)

Hong Kong Government (2003c). Health, Welfare and Food Bureau, "Legislative Council Brief: Residence Requirements for Social Security Benefits", HWF CR/3/4821/99(03), 3 June 2003.

Hong Kong Government (2004a). Health, Welfare and Food Bureau, "Residence Requirements for Comprehensive Social Security Assistance and Social Security Allowance", Paper No. CB(2)734/03-04(01), prepared for discussion before the Legco Panel on Welfare Services, 18 December 2004.

Hong Kong Government (2004b). Home Affairs Bureau, *Legislating against racial discrimination: A consultation paper*, September 2004.

Human Rights Monitor (2002). *EOC appointment and independence of statutory watchdogs*. Press Release and Open Letter to Tung Chee-hwa of 29 July 2002 (available on the website of the Human Rights Monitor at http://hkrm.org.hk).

Hunter, R., & Leonard, A. (1995). *The outcomes of conciliation in sex discrimination cases*. Centre for Employment and Labour Relations Law Working paper No. 8, August 1995.

Jones, C. (1995). The New Territories Inheritance Law: Women colonialization and the elites. In V. Pearson, & B. K. P. Leung, *Women in Hong Kong*. Hong Kong: Oxford University Press.

Klein, R. (1995). Law and racism in an Asian setting: An analysis of the British rule of Hong Kong, *Hastings International & Comparative Law Review 18*: 223.

Law Reform Commission of Hong Kong (2000). *Report: stalking* (available at www. hkreform.gov.hk/reports/index.htm).

Ng, S. K. (1994). Employment and human rights in Hong Kong: Some recent developments, *Hong Kong Law Journal 24*: 108.

O'Flaherty, M. (1996). *Human rights and the UN: Practice before the treaty bodies*.

Petersen, C. J. (1996). Equality as a human right: The development of anti-discrimination law in Hong Kong, *Columbia Journal of Transnational Law 34*: 335.

Petersen, C. J. (1997). Values in transition: The development of the gay and lesbian rights movement in Hong Kong. *Loyola of Los Angeles International & Comparative Law Journal 19*: 337.

Petersen, C. J. (1999a). Equal opportunities: A new field of law for Hong Kong. In R. Wacks (Ed.), *Hong Kong's new legal order*. Hong Kong: Hong Kong University Press.

Petersen, C. J. (1999b). Implementing equality: An analysis of two recent decisions under Hong Kong's anti-discrimination law. *Hong Kong Law Journal 29*: 178.

Petersen, C. J. (2000). Implementing equal pay for work of equal value: A feminist perspective. In Proceedings: *Equal pay for work of equal value*. Hong Kong: Hong Kong Equal Opportunities Commission.

Petersen, C. J. (2001). Investigation and conciliation of employment discrimination claims in the context of Hong Kong, *Employee Rights and Employment Policy Journal 5*: 627.

Petersen, C. J. (2002). The right to equality in the public sector: An assessment of post-colonial Hong Kong, *Hong Kong Law Journal 32*: 103.

Petersen, C. J. (2003). The paris principles and human rights institutions: Is Hong Kong slipping further away from the mark? *Hong Kong Law Journal 33*: 513.

Petersen, C., & Samuels, H. (2002). The convention on the elimination of all forms of discrimination against women: A comparison of its implementation and the role of non-governmental organisations in the United Kingdom and Hong Kong. *Hastings International and Comparative Law Review 26*: 1.

Petersen, C., Fong, J., & Rush, G. (2003). *Enforcing equal opportunities: Investigation and conciliation of discrimination complaints in Hong Kong*. Hong Kong: Centre for Comparative and Public Law.

Samuels, H. (1993). Women and the law in Hong Kong: A feminist analysis. In R. Wacks (Ed.), *Hong Kong, China and 1997: Essays in legal theory*. Hong Kong: Hong Kong University Press.

Samuels, H. (2000). Sexual harassment in employment: Asian values and the law in Hong Kong. *Hong Kong Law Journal 30*: 432.

Tang, C. S. K. (2003). Factors influencing responsibility attribution in wife abuse: a study of Chinese police officers. *Criminal Justice & Behaviour 30*: 584.

Tang, C. S. K., Pun S. H., & Cheung, F. M. (2002). Responsibility attribution for violence against women: A study of chinese public service professionals, *Psychology of Women Quarterly 26*: 175.

United Nations Commission on Human Rights (1993). *Further promotion and encouragement of human rights and fundamental freedoms, including the question of the programme and methods of work of the commission: national institutions for the promotion and protection of human rights*. UN Doc. E/CN. 4/1993/33.

Wesley-Smith, P. (1997). Maintenance of the bill of rights, *Hong Kong Law Journal 27*: 15

Women's Commission (2002). *Gender mainstreaming strategy of women commission*. Paper WoC 15/02, Discussion Papers at the Meeting of the Women's Commission held on 7 May 2002 (available on the Women's Commission website at http://www.women.gov.hk).

Wong. B. K. Y. (2000). Traditional Chinese philosophy and dispute resolution, *Hong Kong Law Journal 30*: 304.

Young, S. N. M. and Law, A. (2004). A critical introduction to Hong Kong's functional constituencies, Centre for Comparative and Public Law Research Report, University of Hong Kong (available on the CCPL website at www.hku.hk/ccpl).

Newspaper Articles
South China Morning Post (2002a). 121 pupils win better places after bias claims. 5 July 2002.
—— (2002b). 121 pupils win better places after bias claims. 5 July 2002.
——. (2002c). Alarm sounds as smart girls push out boys. 5 July 2002.
——. (2003). Anna Wu sued too often: EOC veteran. 18 November 2003.
——. (2004a). Survey on wife beating unfair, police tell researcher. 22 May 2004.
——. (2004b). Domestic violence laws "need reform". 24 July 2004.
——. (2004c). Families in trouble not getting help, says inquiry. 30 October 2004.

Domestic Legislation and Legislative Proposals
Basic Law of the Hong Kong Special Administrative Region of the People's Republic of China, (enacted 1990 by the National People's Congress and brought into force on July 1, 1997).
Domestic Violence Ordinance, Cap. 189, *Laws of Hong Kong*.
Disability Discrimination Ordinance, Cap. 487, *Laws of Hong Kong* (also available on the EOC website at http//eoc.org.hk).
Evidence Ordinance, Cap. 8, *Laws of Hong Kong*.
Family Status Discrimination Ordinance, Cap. 527, *Laws of Hong Kong* (also available on the EOC website at http//eoc.org.hk)
Equal Opportunities Bill 1994, *Hong Kong Government Gazette*, Legal Supplement No. 3, 1 July 1994 pp. C991-C1275 (not enacted).
Hong Kong Bill of Rights Ordinance, Cap. 383, *Laws of Hong Kong*.
Human Rights and Equal Opportunities Commission Bill, draft distributed for public consultation and published in Edwards, George and Byrnes, Andrew, eds, 1995. *Hong Kong's Bill of Rights: 1991–1994 and Beyond*. Hong Kong: University of Hong Kong.
Sex and Disability Discrimination (Miscellaneous Amendments) Ordinance 1997. *Hong Kong Government Gazette*, Legal Sup. No. 1, Part I of II (June 27, 1997).
Sex Discrimination Ordinance, Cap. 480, *Laws of Hong Kong* (also available on the EOC website at http//eoc.org.hk).

International Treaties
International Convention on the Elimination of All Forms of Discrimination Against Women, G.A. Res. 34/180 of 18 December 1979 (entered into force Sept. 1981).
International Convention on the Elimination of All Forms of Racial Discrimination, G.A. Res. 2106A (XX) of 21 December 1965 (entered into force Sept. 1981).
International Covenant on Civil and Political Rights, G.A. Res. 2200A (XXI) of 16 Dec. 1996 (entered into force March 1976).
International Covenant on Economic, Social and Cultural Rights, G.A. Res. 2200A (XXI) of 16 Dec. 1996 (entered into force January 1976).
Joint Declaration of the Government of the United Kingdom of Great Britain and

Northern Ireland and the Government of the People's Republic of China on the Question of Hong Kong, signed in Beijing on December 19, 1984 and ratified on May 27, 1985.

Notes

1. G.A. Res. 180, U.N. GAOR, 34th Sess. Supp. No. 46 at 193, U.N. Doc. A/34/46 (1979) (entered into force Sept. 1981). Strictly speaking, the abbreviation CEDAW only refers to the Committee on the Elimination of All Forms of Discrimination Against Women (the enforcement body for the Convention). However, it has become common to refer to the Convention itself as CEDAW and to refer to the Committee as the "CEDAW Committee", and this is the terminology that I use in this chapter.

2. In particular, the Hong Kong government became bound (by virtue of the United Kingdom's ratification on behalf of Hong Kong) by the International Convention on the Elimination of All Forms of Racial Discrimination (ICCPR) (ratified by the United Kingdom and extended to Hong Kong in 1969); by the International Covenant on Civil and Political Rights, and the International Covenant on Economic, Social and Cultural Rights (both ratified by the United Kingdom and extended to Hong Kong in 1976). These treaties, together with the reservations that apply to Hong Kong and commentary on their application to Hong Kong during the colonial period can be found in Byrnes and Chan 1993. The Chinese government agreed to the continued application of these treaties to Hong Kong after 1997 and information on the current status of reservations and the most recent reports to the treaty monitoring bodies is available on the website of the Hong Kong Government's Home Affairs Bureau: www.hab.gov.hk.

3. After this chapter was completed, the Hong Kong government introduced the Race Discrimination Bill but did not base it on the SDO, as promised in the 2004 Consultation Document. Instead, the government drafted a bill that is much weaker than the SDO. See Carole J. Petersen, "Hong Kong's Race Discrimination Bill: A Critique and Comparison with the Sex and Disability Discrimination Ordinance", published by the Hong Kong Legislative Council's Bills Committee on the Race Discrimination Bill at: http://www.legco.gov.hk/yr06-07/english/bc52/papers/bc52cb2-2232-1-e.pdf.

CHAPTER 17

Gender Research and Women's Studies in Tertiary Education

Siumi Maria Tam and Hon Ming Yip

Since the United Nations' Fourth World Conference on Women in 1995, much has been deliberated on how considerations for gender differences should be systematically integrated into social policies on various levels, that is, on how gender could be "mainstreamed." To scholars and activists alike, gender mainstreaming is generally understood as:

> "the process of assessing the implications for women and men of any planned action, including legislation, policies of programmes, in all areas and at all levels. It is a strategy of making women's as well as men's concerns and experiences an integral dimension of the design, implementation, monitoring and evaluation of policies and programmes in all political, economic and societal spheres so that women and men benefit equally and inequality is not perpetuated. The ultimate goal is to achieve gender equality" (Rai, 2003, p. 16).

While gender mainstreaming may effect changes in the way public policy is carried out, it will not on its own lead to gender equity. Sustained social reform must come from education which brings about change in knowledge and in the way this knowledge itself is constructed. It is evidence-based research and systematic training in gender awareness that form the basis of critical rethinking of the ideology and practice of gender in society, and hence of a possible attitude change. It is thus essential that in the domain of education, gender research and women's studies are integrated into the mainstream curriculum, entailing "a recognition of the need to correct sexist myths and notions at every level of the educational process in different subject areas" (De Dios, 1994, p. 46). In other words, the mainstreaming process has to be accompanied by the institutionalization of gender studies and women's studies as an integral part of academic institutions (Chen, 2004, p. 5).

This chapter reviews the development of gender research and women's studies in Hong Kong's tertiary education sector, and discusses its interaction with the changes of women's status in the larger society. The authors will introduce gender-related courses taught in the local universities, and trace how gender scholars have tackled hurdles as they tried to bring about the institutionalization of gender research and women's studies in their respective universities. They further argue that scholarship and social action must be organically amalgamated to produce a lasting social-cultural impact that contributes to gender equality.

Institutionalization of Gender/Women's Studies

To some scholars, the development of gender studies and women's studies in Hong Kong's tertiary education sector has not arisen from a solid feminist movement, unlike what happened in the West. Among Chinese societies, while the feminist movement in Taiwan has contributed to the emergence and growth of women's studies (Chen, 2004, p. 159), in Hong Kong and mainland China gender/women's studies can be considered a result of rapid social change since the 1980s (Yip, p. 1998, p. 82; Li, 1995, p. 5). Chu & Tang (1997, p. 18) likewise argue that it was mainly a response of the academe to the changing socioeconomic realities and the increased visibility of women in politics, in economic life, and in male-dominated professions. Nevertheless, it can be observed that gender research and women's studies in Hong Kong have developed alongside the local women's movement which can be chronologically divided into three phases (Leung, 2001; see also Wong, 2000; Zhang, 1992). The first phase of the movement started after the Second World War and lasted up until the 1970s, when concern for women's welfare and rights became increasingly vocal. The general target was to improve women's situation through legislative reform. Such efforts included the Hong Kong Council of Women's long war to abolish polygamy, the "equal pay for equal work" movement in the 1960s, as well as the fight to change court procedures for rape cases and to improve women employees' pregnancy benefits in the 1970s.

In the second phase, the 1980s, the emphasis of the movement shifted to women's public participation. The number of associations aiming at promoting feminist awareness increased dramatically, with most founding members coming from the well-educated middle class. NGOs such as the Association for Advancement of Feminism organized study groups and training courses in feminist theories, while smaller grassroots groups were set up under social service agencies. These various organizations had very diverse interests, ranging from reproductive rights, domestic violence, and sexual harassment, to tax reform, childcare, pornography, and gender awareness education. They also represented different political stands and social classes. During this period the Sino-British talks over Hong Kong's sovereignty made it more pressing to review the role and future of the women's movement.

Against this backdrop, feminist scholars in the universities were conducting research or offering courses on gender issues, as well as supervising postgraduate thesis research on gender-related topics. Among these scholars there were members of the above-mentioned feminist organizations and thus their feminist concerns were reflected in the content of the courses they taught. Truly multi-disciplinary in nature, gender scholars however were not organized as they mostly worked separately in their respective departments.

Not until 1985 did the situation change when a group of scholars at The Chinese University of Hong Kong formed the Gender Role Research Programme under the Centre for Hong Kong Studies, which became the first organized unit on gender research in Hong Kong. The Programme was renamed Gender Research Programme in 1990 and then Gender Research Centre (GRC) in 2000. Since its inception, the GRC has tried to encourage interdisciplinary exchange in the academic community through monthly meetings, international conferences and joint research projects, as well as to spread gender awareness in the larger society through training workshops and public seminars. In the early 1990s, GRC members initiated courses with a gender focus, such as "Gender and Culture" (Anthropology Department) and "Women and Literature" (English Department). In 1996 members of this group proposed to the university to set up an academic programme based on the discipline of gender studies. In 1997 the Gender Studies Programme was formally established, housed in the Anthropology Department.

Much of these happenings coincided with changes in the larger society in the third phase of the women's movement. In the 1990s, gender as a cultural concept and gender rights as politics became very much a cause of public debate. The two issues that aroused the most heated discussion were: 1) whether Hong Kong men's mistress-keeping in mainland China should be criminalized, and 2) whether women in the New Territories should enjoy inheritance rights. In 1994 the amendment of the New Territories Ordinance established women's inheritance rights in the New Territories. In the next two years, the Sex Discrimination Ordinance (1995) was passed, and the Equal Opportunities Commission (1996) was established. Together these legal reforms sent out the important message that gender equality is one of the principles of social life. With the establishment of the Women's Commission in 2001, gender mainstreaming was finally given legitimate attention especially in government practice. These reforms of the 1990s provided a suitable climate both in and outside of the academia for the establishment and development of gender studies in the tertiary education sector.

More or less at the same time, at the University of Hong Kong a group of women's studies scholars established the Women's Studies Research Centre which organized regular seminars and later proposed to set up a degree programme in women's studies. While the proposal was not approved by the university, the group was established as a unit under the Centre of Asian Studies, though little tangible resources were allocated. Members of the group continued to offer non-major gender–related courses at their respective departments, such as Women and Politics (Politics and Public Administration Department), or add a gender focus in "extension courses" or general education courses.

In a discussion session organized by the Association for Advancement of Feminism[1] it was found that the two major hurdles in the development of gender studies and women's studies in Hong Kong's tertiary education have been: 1) institutional constraints which defined gender/women's studies as peripheral and not part of the core curriculum, and 2) a market orientation which measured the value of the courses by student enrolment. These problems in fact reflected the lack of understanding of women's studies and gender studies on the part of the universities' administration. In the university community there was also an obvious suspicion for gender studies scholars who were often stereotyped as being aggressive towards men. In response to this, feminist scholars working in the universities had the formidable task of educating their colleagues through research work, and some scholars found it a useful strategy to distinguish between the two terms "women's studies" and "gender studies". In Hong Kong, the former term often conjures up militant feminist images of the 1970s and attracts criticisms of being hostile to men, while the latter is seen as less threatening or even creating a sense of inclusiveness as men studies may be involved. Intellectually gender studies emphasizes the interaction among the genders and their relationship with the larger society, and hence differs from women's studies which has a clear focus on women. Gender studies thus meets with (relatively) less resistance from the administration and from unsympathetic colleagues. It should be pointed out that while gender studies at the Chinese University of Hong Kong has had a history of over 20 years, it is still interpreted by many administrative as well as teaching staff as equivalent to women's studies, and is considered a marginal discipline as demonstrated by their ignorance and indifference of the issues concerned.

At other public universities, feminist scholars have also tried to institutionalize women's studies, and met with different degrees of support and/or resistance from the administration. At the City University of Hong Kong and the Hong Kong Polytechnic University, faculty proposing to offer a course with a gender perspective were often told that such a course would not fit in with the major disciplinary concern, or that the curriculum was very full and students' workload was already very heavy. If the teachers persisted (sometimes for six or seven years), the course may finally be approved as an elective or general education course, which may be cancelled if not enough students enrolled. One example was a course entitled Gender Perspectives in Social Work, an elective for evening part-time students at the City University of Hong Kong. The offering of the course was contingent upon whether student enrolment reached the minimum of 15. At the Hong Kong Polytechnic University, Gender Studies and Social Work was offered as an elective for both part-time and full-time social work undergraduates, while a team-taught course entitled Sex and Sexuality was offered as part of the general education program. For other faculty members, overcoming institutional hurdles often meant resorting to incorporating feminist content in their various courses instead of offering separate gender-specific courses.

At the same discussion session held at the Association for Advancement of Feminism, it was found that because the Hong Kong University of Science and Technology was primarily a university specializing in science, engineering and business, there was no major programme in the social science or humanities. Both Division of Social Science and Division of Humanities offered minor programmes and a wide range of general education subjects, but the university had no plan to develop specific substantive areas such as gender studies. Indeed the Division of Social Science remained dominated by male academics with "mainstream" or traditional male-oriented concerns. Nevertheless, because the academic program had a relatively loose structure, faculty members were able to propose courses of their choice, including gender-related courses. A number of faculty members have built in a gender dimension in their courses, such as Hong Kong Culture in the Social Science Division, while courses with a gender focus such as Women in Chinese Society have only been taught by visiting lecturers.

Institutional Development of Research on Gender and Women[2]

The Gender Research Centre (GRC) at the Chinese University of Hong Kong contributed to the formalization of gender studies as a discipline in Hong Kong. Fanny Cheung, founder and Director of the Centre, together with other members, deliberately chose to adopt "gender" rather than "women" in the Centre's name so as to broaden the perspective of research (Cheung, 1994, p. 71; Cheung, Yip & Kwok 1995, p. xvi). This decision to focus on gender instead of women might invite accusations of giving insufficient prominence to women's issues or of not treating women's problems independently. The merit of gender studies, nevertheless, lies in the dynamic approach which emphasizes the relational character of women's issues. By highlighting how women fare in contrast to men in the patriarchal social structure, it provides important data for the understanding of the patricentric culture and thus contributes to gender equality (Yip, 1998, p. 89).

In its initial years, the GRC encouraged gender research through the compilation of databases on gender issues and bibliographies of publications. As one of the strategic research programs of the Hong Kong Institute of Asia-Pacific Studies, GRC activities expanded to include the organization of community-based annual workshops, publication of a newsletter, exchange with visiting scholars, consultancy, and public advocacy. As both local and global concern for gender issues became more prominent, activities of the Centre have become more diverse, and its impact extended beyond the realm of academia. With members coming from a wide range of academic fields including the humanities, education, social sciences, business administration, and medicine, GRC has become a knowledge hub that has played a role in local and regional policies on women. Through its train-the-trainer programs for civil servants, for example, GRC took part in the re-education of frontline service providers. Its national and international network of academics, practitioners, NGOs and inter-governmental bodies has become a resource which was often consulted by policy makers, the Women's Commission as well as the media. To summarize, the GRC aims to serve four major functions:

1. Research: It organizes research projects, seminars, and conferences grouped under four themes: Gender Equality and Civil Society; Gender, Development and Globalization; Gender, Identity and Culture; and Gender and Health.
2. Training: It offers courses on gender analysis methodology and gender awareness programs for service providers.
3. Advocacy and Consultancy: It provides advice on and input into gender-related policies and practices.
4. Information and Resources: It maintains a special collection of documents, papers, and books at the Hong Kong Institute of Asia-Pacific Studies' Documentation Unit, regularly updates the bibliography on gender studies in Hong Kong, and publishes occasional papers and edited volumes on gender issues.

The GRC has served a special role as the bridge between local, regional and international scholars. This has been carried out through establishing exchange relations with other gender research institutes. By 2007, the GRC has exchange relations with women's studies institutes at Peking University, Monash University and Keimyung University. It has working relations with the All China Women's Federation, the Chinese Women's University, and women's studies centres at the National Taiwan University and Ewha University. In addition, the GRC provides a forum where feminist researchers from different parts of the world, especially mainland China, Taiwan, and Asian countries, share their findings and formulate new research directions. This is done particularly through GRC's widely popular international conferences. Themes of past conferences are as follows:

- Gender Studies in Chinese Societies (1989)
- Gender and Society: The Pacific Rim Experience (1991)
- Comparative Perspectives on Women, the State, and Industrial Restructuring in East Asia (1992, jointly organized with the University of California at Davis)
- Women in Management in Asia (1993)
- Violence against Women: Chinese and American Experiences (1994)
- Gender and Development in Asia (1997)
- Gender Mobilities in Asia (1999, jointly organized with the International Union of Geographers)
- Globalization and Women's Health: Challenges in a Changing Asia (2000)

- Chinese Culture and Women (2002, jointly organized with the Centre for Women's Studies, Peking University)
- Gender and Religion Workshop (2002)
- Globalization and Gender: The Implications of Global Economic Restructuring for Women in China and Southeast Asia (2003)
- Symposium on Gender and Trade Liberalization: Perspectives from Asia (2005, jointly organized with South East Asia Research Centre of the City University of Hong Kong and International Gender and Trade Network)
- Twenty Years of Gender Research in Chinese Societies (2005, jointly organized with the Centre for Women's Studies, Peking University)
- Women and Issues of Education (2006, jointly organized with the Centre for Women's Studies, Peking University)
- Women's Policy in China and Korea: Thinking from Women's Lives (2007, jointly organized with the Centre for Women's Studies, Peking University, and Institute of Women's Studies, Keimyung University)

In promoting dialogue with the public, GRC has organized the Annual Gender Role Workshop that bring together government officials, practitioners, NGOs, service users, the media and academics to discuss women's issues. Topics in the past years include:

1991   Hong Kong Families in the 1990s: Contradictions and Outlook
1992   Sexual Harassment in the Workplace
1993   Community Participation by Women
1994   Little Women, Little Men: Gender Role Stereotype and Conflicts in Development
1995   Women and Health
1996   Gender and the Media
1997   Towards Equal Employment Opportunities: Ideal and Reality
1998   Women and AIDS
1999   Protect Myself and My Children: Say No to Sexual Violence
2000   Beijing Plus Five
2001   Women and Information and Communication Technologies
2002   Life-long Education and Economic Empowerment of Women
2003   The Impact of Split Households on Gender Relations
2004   Women and Political Participation
2005   Beijing Plus 10
2006   Work-Family Interface and Women in Hong Kong
2007   Domestic Violence and Law: Women's Perspectives

Proceedings of the annual workshops and international conferences were published which helped to disseminate the findings. Other ongoing activities include the compilation of databases such as sex-segregated statistics, and the publication of research reports. The GRC has also carried out collaborative or commissioned research projects, on such themes as women's participation in community affairs, youth and elections, violence against women, equal opportunities in Hong Kong, sexual harassment, gender and disability, gender and occupational qualification, child abuse, family status discrimination, and gender and the church in Hong Kong.

Furthermore, gender-related training has now become part of the gender mainstreaming strategy of the Hong Kong Special Administrative Region Government. Since 2001, the Centre has been commissioned by the Government's Health, Welfare and Food Bureau and the Civil Service Training and Development Institute to conduct training workshops for civil servants to enhance their gender awareness and mainstream gender perspective in their work. Through the years, gender-related workshops were held for newly recruited administrative officers in the government, the Women's Commission, the Police Force, Educational Planning and Curriculum Development Department, Leisure and Cultural Services Department, Information Services Department, and Social Welfare Department (Hong Kong Institute of Asia-Pacific Studies 2005:56).

Among the small number of gender research academic units in Hong Kong, the GRC as the most established research-oriented organization has proved to be conducive to the development of gender/women's studies in Hong Kong. Other local research organizations also played a role in promoting women's studies, notably the University of Hong Kong's Women's Studies Research Centre (WSRC) established in 1995. Subsequently courses related to women's studies were offered in various departments in the University of Hong Kong (Chu & Tang, 1997, p. 25). However, the WSRC's proposal to set up a degree programme in women's studies was not approved, and the GRC has been fighting a lonely battle in institutionalizing gender/women's studies in Hong Kong's tertiary education sector. The Gender Studies Programme which GRC helped to launch is the first and still the only academic curriculum locally. Since its establishment in 1997, it has grown from one undergraduate minor programme, to various postgraduate programmes in 2007. The development of the Gender Studies Programme (GRS) and its role in Hong Kong's gender/women's studies deserves a closer look.

Gender Studies Teaching at the Chinese University of Hong Kong

1. The Programme

GRS offers an Undergraduate Minor Programme, a taught MA Programme, two research-based postgraduate programmes — M.Phil. and Ph.D. in Gender Studies, as well as a postgraduate diploma program taught at the Chinese Women's College.

The Undergraduate Minor Programme in Gender Studies is open to students from all faculties on campus. Minor students complete five courses including the required course Gender and Culture, and four elective courses from the following:

> Marriage, Family and Kinship
> Gender in Asia
> Media, Sex and Violence
> Body Politics in Literature and Representational Culture
> Feminisms: East and West
> Queer Theory and Culture
> Feminist Reading & Women's Writing
> Gendering Modernity
> Women, Religion and Chinese Literature
> Religion and Gender Studies
> Family Economics
> Gender and Literature
> Gender and Language
> Women, Men and Culture
> Women, Men and Language
> Gender Issues in Hong Kong
> Philosophy of Love
> Gender and Education
> Gender and Sexuality in contemporary Society
> Sexuality and Culture
> Topic Studies in Traditional Chinese History
> Topic Studies in Comparative History
> Topic Studies in Asian History
> Gender, Law and Politics
> Gender and History
> Psychology of Gender

Marriage and Family
Gender and Society
Theology and Feminism

The taught MA programme began as MA in Women's Studies, and was renamed MA in Gender Studies in 2007. Students complete eight courses to graduate, including two required courses: 1) Gender Studies: Theory, and 2) Contemporary Women's Issues, and six electives from the following:

Gender Studies: Methodology
Advanced Topics in Gender Studies I
Advanced Topics in Gender Studies II
Women and Literature
Media and Gender Representations
Feminism and Civil Society
Genders and Sexualities in Asia
Psychology of Gender
Gender and History
Gender and Culture
Gender in Asia

The M.Phil. Programme in Gender Studies is truly an interdisciplinary arrangement. Students simultaneously enroll in the programme and a home discipline they select, and must fulfill both sets of requirements to graduate. Two core courses covering training in gender theory and methodology are required in the first year, while students also complete the requirements of their home disciplines. In the second year, students complete the required courses Advanced Topics in Gender Studies I and II, where current research are presented in seminars. They also fulfill requirements of their home disciplines, and write a gender-related thesis based on original research. As students need to complete two sets of requirements, they often face greater pressure, but at the same time they form the core of an active gender academic community.

The Ph.D. Programme in Gender Studies was designed to encourage further research of gender issues at an advanced level, with a focus on East and Southeast Asian societies. Students complete a minimum of 21 units, including the required courses Seminar in Gender Studies I & II, Advanced Topics in Gender Studies I & II, and Thesis Research.

As demonstrated by its curricular structure and design, GRS has the following characteristics and problems:

a) It is interdisciplinary. Currently it consists of academics from 21 departments of 6 faculties in the University. These faculty members are full time teaching staff of the University, and contribute their expertise to GRS by teaching minor courses, serving as members of the various administrative and thesis committees, and/or providing advice and supervision to GRS students. All the work related to the GRS, however, is not counted towards the teachers' normal workload.

b) Administratively the GRS is an inter-faculty programme. Although it is housed in the Faculty of Social Science, the Programme carries out most of its administrative responsibilities independently and is a separate cost centre. In its day-to-day operation, the Gender Studies Programme Office is supported by only one full time assistant who carries out decisions of the gender studies committee which the governing body of the GRS, and comprised of representatives from participating departments. Members of the Committee elect the Graduate Panel, as well as the Undergraduate Committee. All these members are concurrent appointments and receive no extra remuneration.

c) The GRS provides a full range of academic programmes, including an undergraduate minor, a taught MA programme, and the research-based MPhil and PhD programmes. In addition, it has offered a Postgraduate Diploma Programme in Beijing, in collaboration with the University of Michigan and the Chinese Women's College. In a normal year undergraduate minor students average around 15, while postgraduate students average around 30. These are carried out however without its own full time faculty until 2004 when a fulltime instructor was hired.

d) The GRS Programme works closely with centres of women's studies and gender studies in Hong Kong and mainland China, and maintains cooperative relations with similar institutions in Taiwan and Australia. Most significantly the GRS has a very close relationship with the Gender Research Centre (GRC) on campus, and a considerable overlap of membership between the two exists.

2. Development of the Programme

GRS began by offering an Undergraduate Minor Programme in gender studies in the year 1997–98, in which existing undergraduate courses are coordinated to form a curriculum that provides basic knowledge and training. These courses are offered by separate departments, and hence the GRS has no control over which courses are offered, as well as the quota offered to GRS minor students.

In the following year, an MPhil Programme in Gender Studies was established and the first cohort of five students was admitted. Students over a two-year period (four years if part time) work on their thesis on a gender-related topic. The student quota is centrally allocated, and the Programme has no power whatsoever in altering the number of students to be admitted. Administratively, this Programme is run on a "home discipline" model, by having students affiliated with an existing department such as anthropology, history, psychology etc. On the one hand students study gender courses, and on the other they study the home discipline's courses and write their thesis using the discipline's specific approach and methods. Under this model, there is no faculty staff hired specifically to teach gender studies. All teachers and administrators of the postgraduate programme are faculty members of existing departments and hence are all volunteers. The monetary resources calculated on the headcount of postgraduate students have to be split with the home departments of the teachers. The financial and administrative implications are obvious — the programme has to struggle to survive on a tiny budget, and is run on the goodwill of gender scholars on campus.

In 2002, GRS initiated three new programmes: MA in Women's Studies, Ph.D. Degree Programme in Gender Studies, and Postgraduate Diploma Programme in Women's Studies. The MA in Women's Studies programme is a one-year taught programme (non-thesis) which caters to professionals whose work requires knowledge in women's studies, such as social workers and policy makers. The Postgraduate Diploma in Women's Studies Programme was offered in Beijing as a short term project funded by the Henry Luce Foundation, and aimed at providing basic training in feminist theory and methodology for mainland Chinese teachers and researchers. As they returned to their own universities, they helped to train further generations of feminist scholars and researchers. These two programmes are particularly appropriate for the dissemination and reinforcement of knowledge on issues and problems faced by women today. In the course "Contemporary Women's Issues" for example, students critically examine concerns such as domestic violence, inequality in the workplace, and learn about the implementation of international instruments such as CEDAW. These academic programmes, together with strategic partnerships with centres and programmes outside of Hong Kong, strengthen the GRS's ability to play an active role in the development of women's studies and gender studies in Hong Kong and mainland China.

As seen from the list of postgraduate thesis titles, student interests are not limited to women's studies. They have studied lesbian and queer relationships, and transsexuality, and are pioneers in this field in Hong Kong. There is also student interest in the study of masculinity, fatherhood, and gay relationships. Today, GRS and GRC work together in expanding the boundary of gender studies in Hong Kong by exploring the development of men's studies. A few male colleagues from different disciplines have shown interest in forming a research group, and it is hoped that this will further reinforce gender studies as an interdisciplinary academic programme.

3. Role in Local Policy

GRS faculty members help to teach in the Gender Research Centre's training courses, as described in the above section. In collaboration with GRC as well, GRS members take an active part in conducting studies on various issues such as gender stereotypes in the education system and textbooks, sexual harassment on campus, and the impact on women due to the increase of cross-border mobility between Hong Kong and the mainland. The results and policy recommendations are published and disseminated through such venues as policy forums and workshops in which government officials, social service users, women's organizations, and the media are brought together to engage in dialogue over the issues.

The GRS also engages in activities that help to communicate with and educate the public on gender issues. These include acting as consultant for the Hong Kong Heritage Museum's 2002–03 exhibition on the History of Hong Kong Women, as well as staging a multi-media exhibition on "Women of Hong Kong: Gender Roles in Flux" in November to December 2003, and on "Women of HK: A Century of Conttribution and Development" in November 2007.

In individual capacities, GRS members take an active part in influencing government decision-making on gender equity as well as non-governmental services for women. For example, Fanny Cheung, member of the GRS Committee, is the founding chair of the Equal Opportunities Commission and a former member of the Women's Commission, and Co-chairperson Maria Tam is a current member of the Women's Commission. Numerous GRS members serve on the University's Committee against Sexual Harassment and its Task Force on Education, while off campus they serve on boards and executive committees of various NGOs that work for women's rights and welfare, such as HIV/AIDS prevention and reproductive rights. Students and graduates of the Programme are active members of NGOs and pressure groups that monitor government policies concerning women, gender equality and human rights. An MPhil graduate contended successfully in the government District Board elections, whose platform included equity for different genders and sexual orientations.

Gender/Women's Studies in Other Tertiary Institutions

At other local universities, there may not be degree programmes in gender/women's studies, but quite a number of gender courses have been offered by various departments. Some examples follow:

1. The University of Hong Kong

Some departments in the Faculties of Arts, Social Sciences, and Education at the University of Hong Kong offer courses on gender/women's studies, such as "An Introduction of Chinese Women's Literature" at the Chinese Department, "Women, Feminism and Writing" and "Language and Gender" at the English Department, and "Women in Japan and Hong Kong" at the Department of Japanese Studies. The Department of Comparative Literature seems to be the teaching unit that offers the largest number of courses of this kind, ranging from theories to specific topics. Some examples follow:

> Introduction to Comparative Literary and Cultural Studies II: Gender
> Studies
> Feminist Cultural Studies
> Literature and "Queer" Theory
> Histories of Sexuality: Freud and Foucault
> The History of Modern Sexual Identity and Discourse
> Gender and Sexuality in Contemporary Chinese Literature and Film
> The Making of Modern Masculinities
> Fashioning Femininities
> Childhood, Feminine Roles and Cultural Myths

While the Faculty of Education offers the course "Gender and Teaching", the Faculty of Social Sciences offers "Gender and Society" and "Sociology and Sexuality" at the Department of Sociology, "Women and Politics" at the Department of Politics and Public Administration, and "Men, Women and Sex" at the Department of Social Work and Social Administration. Besides undergraduate courses, there are a small number of graduate courses such as "Questioning Sex and Difference" (for Master of Arts in Literary and Cultural Studies), "Feminism and Modernism" (for MA in English Studies), and "Women, Crime and Social Control" (M.Soc.Sc.).

In addition to courses on gender issues, some teachers also incorporate gender-related topics in their courses on film, popular culture, Jane Austen, travel writing, and European histories. Besides, the Hong Kong Culture and Society Programme of the Centre of Asian Studies has published an online study guide entitled "Gendering Hong Kong".

2. Hong Kong Baptist University

Gender/women's studies courses are mainly offered by departments of humanities and social sciences at Hong Kong Baptist University. They include "Love and Eros in the World of Chinese Literature" at the Department of Chinese Language and Literature, "Gender and Literature" at the Department of English, "Gender and Translation" at the Department of Translation, "History of Chinese Women to 1911" at the Department of History, "Sexuality and Christian Values" as complementary studies in Religion and Philosophy, "Sex, Gender and Society" and "Women in China" at the Department of Sociology.

3. Lingnan University

As one of the key departments at Lingnan University, the Department of Cultural Studies includes the following courses on gender/women's studies in its curriculum:

Feminism and Cultural Politics
Gender, Sexuality and Cultural Politics
Special Topics in Socio-Political Studies: Queer Studies
Topics in Cinema and Media Studies: Gender and Genre in Cinema

Courses at other departments include "History of Women and Children in China" at the Department of History, "Gender, Language and Translation" at the Department of Translation, "Family, Gender and Society" at the Department of Sociology, and "Women's Health Issues" at the Department of Applied Community Health Studies. Some gender-related topics are also included in courses such as "Mass Communications and Public Opinion",

"Selected Population Dynamics and Their Social Consequences", and "Selected Social Problems in Hong Kong".

4. The Hong Kong University of Science and Technology

Both the Division of Humanities and Division of Social Science at the University of Science and Technology of Hong Kong include courses related to gender/women's studies in their curricula. For example, the Division of Humanities offers the following:

Women's Literature
History of Chinese Women
Palace Women and Court Politics in Imperial China
Kinship and Gender in China
Gender and Chinese Modernity
Gender and Sexuality in the Media
Marriage, Family and Kinship in Cross-Cultural Perspectives
Family and Lineage in South China

The following are courses of the Division of Social Science:

Gender, Economy and Society
Gender, Culture and Society
Gender Relations in Hong Kong
Gender in Contemporary Chinese Societies
Gender in Chinese Society
Marriage and the Family
Gender, Development and Fertility

5. The Hong Kong Polytechnic University

Gender-related courses seem to be concentrated in the area of General Education at the Hong Kong Polytechnic University. The following courses are frequently offered:

Love, Intimacy and Sexuality
Gender and Ethics
Gender Relations in Hong Kong
Sexual Themes in Literature: East and West
The Representation of Gender and Sexuality
The Modern History of Chinese Women
Sex and Sexuality

Besides, the Chinese Studies Department offers "Gender and Sexuality in Chinese Society" in its minor programme, the Department of English offers "Language and Gender" as an elective course, and as mentioned before, "Gender Studies and Social Work" is offered as an elective course by the Department of Social Work.

6. City University of Hong Kong

As mentioned above, "Gender Perspectives in Social Work" is offered as an elective course for evening part time students of the City University of Hong Kong. Another elective course of the Department of Applied Social Science is "Women and Development in Asia". The curriculum of the Department of English and Communication includes courses such as "Gender Discourse", "Sex, Violence, and the Media" or "Images of Gender in Visual Media", and "Images of Gender in Korean TV Dramas". In addition, courses in the fields of law, popular media, sociology are offered. Examples are:

Law and Gender
Camera Eye and Gender
Gender in Popular Media
Sociology of Marriage and Family
Understanding Gender Relations
Human Sexuality
Feminisms and Family Ethics
Love and Sex, Life and Death

Tracing the development of gender studies teaching in Hong Kong's universities, we find that there is a steady increase in the number of gender-related courses. Most of these are discipline-based, indicating that gender has been recognized as a possible analytical perspective by many fields of study, although courses of this kind are still highly concentrated in two areas: social sciences and humanities. However, these courses remain loosely structured without systemic curricular organization. In other words, further institutionalization and mainstreaming of gender teaching in local tertiary education are necessary.

Conclusion

Summing up the situation of gender research and women's studies among tertiary institutions in Hong Kong, it is obvious that scholars in gender/

women's studies are consciously incorporating gender-aware material and orientations into course content and research design, as well as helping to promote gender equality on the political/personal level. They proactively seek to cooperate with male colleagues and to work with available resources of the university administrative structure. In their own research, they help in mainstreaming gender in the studies of local society. In the classroom, they strategize to engender academic disciplines by incorporating the gender perspective into the teaching of their subject areas. As a group, they consciously promote intellectual activism and empower themselves and their students through feminist knowledge production and dissemination.

In institutionalized programmes such as the Gender Studies Programme at the Chinese University of Hong Kong, gender-related courses are mainstreamed into the degree curricula and students will become gender studies graduates. At the Gender Research Centre of the same university, evidence-based investigation projects have contributed to gender mainstreaming on the government level, and commissioned training workshops have helped to facilitate the mainstreaming mechanism in the larger society. As the most institutionalized academic units in Hong Kong, GRC and GRS are governed by volunteer directors, a very small staff set-up and a minimal, though regular, budget; and their faculty members are all fulltime staff of other departments; they work concurrently in both gender studies area and their home disciplines. Being the only degree programme of gender/women's studies in Hong Kong, GRS makes use of cross-listed courses to enrich its undergraduate and postgraduate curricula. Thus in both its research arm (GRC) and teaching arm (GRS), gender studies suffer from a lack of adequate human resources, and it is far fetched to say that there is an independent, interdisciplinary academe that is part of the regular set up of the institution.

Experience in Taiwan and American societies show that if a gender/ women's studies programme becomes further institutionalized, it may attain a departmental status with a larger budget leading to more autonomy and recognition, including the ability to hire its own faculty (Chen, 2004, pp. 5–6; McMartin, 1993; Boxer, 1998; Stromquist, 2001). In comparison, in Hong Kong today, gender/women's studies as an academic field remain at the initial stage of development, despite two decades of evolution. As Abregana argues, the most formidable odds for gender equality in Hong Kong and other Asian societies are the adherence to the status quo, the concept of male supremacy, and the lack of understanding about and appreciation for women's studies in higher education (Abregana, 1995, p. A-25). Among many local gender/women's studies scholars, there is a general feeling of frustration as they have to overcome institutional barriers or work in less-than-friendly environments on a day-to-day basis, for long periods of time, simply because women's studies and gender studies are seen to threaten the patriarchal structure/culture within the institution. In the process, teachers of gender-related subjects and members of gender studies programmes have to work under undue stress, and many of them have subsequently burnt out as they fight an uphill battle — often as volunteers. Universities tend to be oblivious towards gender/women's studies, although when the gender courses are established there is considerable academic freedom for teachers. Often faculty members have to fight harder to just get their courses approved, and after the courses are approved they have to struggle to keep them. Without sustained course offerings on gender/women's studies, there is no continuity in the education of gender equality on campus. Due recognition must be given to faculty staff's effort in organizing and teaching gender studies programmes and courses, rather than having them work as volunteers and supplementary labor.

All in all, gender/women's studies in Hong Kong's universities are still located in the "shadow structure" of their respective institutions. Like strangers in the tower, they are often considered nontraditional, and must struggle to make their presence recognized and to obtain even minimal resources to survive (Lim and Herrera-Sobek, 2000, p. 2). In reality, gender/women's studies are often reduced to mere tokenism in the academy (Dever, 1993, p. 12). The development of the discipline has in most cases been an endeavor of collaborative efforts from the bottom up, the work of individuals lower on the academic hierarchical structure, with little support from the authorities. Still worse is the ever-growing market-driven climate and managerialism that characterize the "corporate" or "consumer" university (Glazer-Raymo, 1999, p. 202), which will further peripheralize gender/women's studies as "academic housework" in the shadow of capital (Bauer, 2002, pp. 245–257). With severely limited resources and rewards, gender/women's studies, along with other non-profit making studies, have to fight an uphill battle.

Gender mainstreaming in tertiary education today is mostly tokenism, and it borders on academic hypocrisy should it continue to be marginalized by the respective institutions. In this regard, Hong Kong is not unlike other regions in the world when gender mainstreaming efforts are bought over by male-stream forces. At times, mainstreaming machineries work as tokens rather than as the substance of reform (True & Mintrom, 2001). Without a strong academic activist solidarity across institutions to challenge the status quo, gender/women's studies practitioners in Hong Kong are fighting alone and making little headway in the uphill battle. More than our counterparts in Taiwan (Chen 2004, pp. 252, 256), Hong Kong gender scholars need to develop effective networking strategies to empower the existing feminist epistemic community, and to further strengthen the field through collective action and critical scholarship.

References

Abregana, B. C. (1995). *Women's studies in UBCHEA-related institutions in Asia: A preliminary report.* A report to the United Board for Christian Higher Education in Asia.

Bauer, D. M. (2002). Academic housework: Women's studies and second shifting. In Robyn Wiegman (Ed.), *Women's studies on its own: A next wave reader in institutional change.* Durham: Duke University.

Boxer, M. J. (1998). *When women ask the questions: Creating women's studies.* Boston: Routledge & Kegan Paul.

Chen, P. Y. (2004). *Acting "otherwise": The institutionalization of women's/gender studies in Taiwan's universities.* New York: Routledge Falmer.

Cheung, F. M. (1994). Promoting women's development. In Committee on Women's Studies in Asia (Ed.), *Changing lives: Life stories of Asian pioneers in women's studies.* New York: Feminist Press.

Chu, S. S. H., & Tang, C. S. K. (1997). *Educating for change: Development of women's/gender studies and its challenges for Hong Kong.* Occasional Paper No. 66, Hong Kong Institute of Asia-Pacific Studies, The Chinese University of Hong Kong. Hong Kong: Hong Kong Institute of Asia-Pacific Studies, the Chinese University of Hong Kong.

De, D., & Javate, A. (1994). Triumphs and travails: Women's studies in the academy. In Committee on Women's Studies in Asia (Ed.), *Changing lives: Life stories of Asian pioneers in women's studies.* New York: The Feminist Press.

Dever, M. (1993). Symposium on "women's studies and the curriculum". *Gender Studies: News and Views, 6.*

Glazer-Raymo, J. (1999). *Shattering the myths: Women in academe.* Baltimore: Johns Hopkins University Press.

Hong Kong Institute of Asia-Pacific Studies, The Chinese University of Hong Kong (2005). *HKIAFS at 15: The fifteenth anniversary commemorative volume of the Hong Kong Institute of Asia-Pacific Studies, 1990–2005.* Hong Kong: Hong Kong Institute of Asia-Pacific Studies, The Chinese University of Hong Kong.

Leung, L. C. (2001). Choices and limitations: A review of the feminist movement in Hong Kong. In *Difference and equality: new challenges for Hong Kong's feminist movement.* Hong Kong: Association for the Advancement of Feminism and the Centre for Social Policy Research, the Hong Kong Polytechnic University.

Li X. J. (1995). Funü yanjiu zai Zhongguo delu de fazhan ji qianjing (The development and prospect of women's studies in mainland China). In Zhang M. Q., et al. (Eds.), *Xingbiexue yu funü yanjiu: Huaren shehui de tansuo* (Gender and women studies in Chinese societies). Hong Kong: The Chinese University Press.

Lim, S. G. L. and Herrera-Sobek, M. (2000). Introduction in Power, race and gender in academe: Strangers in the tower? New York: Modern Language Association.

McMartin, F. P. (1993). The institutionalization of women's centres and women's studies programs at three research universities. Doctoral dissertation, University of California, Berkeley.

Rai, S. M. (2003). Institutional mechanisms for the advancement of women: Mainstreaming gender, democratizing the state? In S. M. Rai (Ed.), *Mainstreaming gender, democratizing the state? Institutional mechanisms for the advancement of women.* Manchester: Manchester University Press.

Stromquist, N. P. (2001). Gender studies: A global perspective of their evolution, contribution, and challenges to comparative higher education. *Higher Education, 41.*

True, J., & Mintrom, M. (2001). Transnational networks and policy diffusion: The case of gender and mainstreaming. *International Studies Quarterly, 45*(1).

Wong, P. W. (2000). Negotiating gender: The women's movement for legal reform in colonial Hong Kong. PhD Thesis, UCLA.

Ye H. M. (2005). Funü, xingbie ji qita: jin nian nian Zhongguo dalu he Xianggang de jindai Zhongguo funüshi yanjiu jiqi fazhan qianjing (Women, gender, and others: Research on modern Chinese women's history in mainland China and Hong Kong during recent twenty years and its prospective development). *Research on Women in Modern Chinese History 13.*

Yip, H. M. (1998). Into the postcolonial era: Women's studies in Hong Kong. In G. Hershatter, et al. (Comps. & Eds.), *Guide to women's studies in China.* Berkeley: Institute of East Asian Studies, University of California.

Zhang, C. Y., et al. (Eds.). (1992). *Ling yiban tiankong: Zhanhou Xianggang funü yundong* (The other half of the sky: Women's movement in postwar Hong Kong). Hong Kong: Association for the Advancement of Feminism.

Notes

1. The Association for Advancement of Feminism convened a discussion session on November 8, 2003, to review the situation of gender studies and women's studies in Hong Kong's tertiary education. Five scholars who were currently teaching in four different universities attended, representing the Chinese

   University of Hong Kong, the City University of Hong Kong, the Hong Kong Polytechnic University, and the University of Hong Kong.

2. This chapter's main concern is the institutional development of research. For a review of major works in research areas covering women and current social, economic and political conditions such as marriage and family, social welfare, deviant and criminal behavior, education, career and employment, sex role and stereotyping, sociopolitical movement, etc., see Yip 1998:82–88. For research in the fields of the history of Chinese women and women in Hong Kong's history, see Ye 2005:124–139.